ENGLISH / JAPANESE

英語／日本語

OXFORD PICTURE DICTIONARY

SECOND EDITION

OPD

Jayme Adelson-Goldstein
Norma Shapiro

198 Madison Avenue
New York, NY 10016 USA

Great Clarendon Street, Oxford OX2 6DP UK

Oxford University Press is a department of the University of Oxford. It furthers the University's objective of excellence in research, scholarship, and education by publishing worldwide in

Oxford New York

Auckland Cape Town Dar es Salaam Hong Kong Karachi Kuala Lumpur Madrid Melbourne Mexico City Nairobi New Delhi Shanghai Taipei Toronto

With offices in

Argentina Austria Brazil Chile Czech Republic France Greece Guatemala Hungary Italy Japan Poland Portugal Singapore South Korea Switzerland Thailand Turkey Ukraine Vietnam

OXFORD and OXFORD ENGLISH are registered trademarks of Oxford University Press.

Library of Congress Cataloging-in-Publication Data

Adelson-Goldstein, Jayme.
The Oxford picture dictionary. Monolingual / Jayme Adelson-Goldstein and Norma Shapiro.– 2nd ed.
p. cm.
Includes index.
ISBN-13: 978-0-19-474015-9

1. Picture dictionaries, English. 2. English language–Textbooks for foreign speakers. I. Shapiro, Norma. II. Title.
PE1629.S52 2008
423'.1–dc22

2007041017

Database right Oxford University Press (maker)

Executive Publishing Manager: Stephanie Karras
Managing Editor: Sharon Sargent
Development Editors: Glenn Mathes II, Bruce Myint, Katie La Storia
Associate Development Editors: Olga Christopoulos, Hannah Ryu, Meredith Stoll
Design Manager: Maj-Britt Hagsted
Project Manager: Allison Harm
Senior Designers: Stacy Merlin, Michael Steinhofer
Designer: Jaclyn Smith
Senior Production Artist: Julie Armstrong
Production Layout Artist: Colleen Ho
Cover Design: Stacy Merlin
Senior Image Editor: Justine Eun
Image Editors: Robin Fadool, Fran Newman, Jenny Vainisi
Manufacturing Manager: Shanta Persaud
Manufacturing Controller: Faye Wang
Translated by: Techno-Graphics & Translations, Inc.

ISBN: 978 0 19 474015 9

Printed in China

10 9 8 7

This book is printed on paper from certified and well-managed sources.

The OPD team thanks the following artists for their storyboarding and sketches: Cecilia Aranovich, Chris Brandt, Giacomo Ghiazza, Gary Goldstein, Gordan Kljucec, Vincent Lucido, and Glenn Urieta

Illustrations by: Lori Anzalone: 13, 70-71, 76-77; Joe "Fearless" Arenella/Will Sumpter: 178; Argosy Publishing: 66-67 (call-outs), 98-99, 108-109, 112-113 (call-outs), 152, 178, 193, 194-195, 196, 197, 205; Barbara Bastian: 4, 15, 17, 20-21, 162 (map), 198, 216-217 (map), 220-221; Philip Batini/AA Reps: 50; Thomas Bayley/Sparks Literary Agency: 158-159; Sally Bensusen: 211, 214; Annie Bissett: 112; Peter Bollinger/Shannon Associates: 14-15; Higgens Bond/Anita Grien: 226; Molly Borman-Pullman: 116, 117; Jim Fanning/Ravenhill Represents: 80-81; Mike Gardner: 10, 12, 17, 22, 132, 114-115, 142-143, 174, 219, 228-229; Garth Glazier/AA Reps: 106, 118-119; Dennis Godfrey/Mike Wepplo: 204; Steve Graham: 124-125, 224; Graphic Map & Chart Co.: 200-201, 202-203; Julia Green/Mendola Art: 225; Glenn Gustafson: 9, 27, 48, 76, 100, 101, 117, 132, 133, 136, 155, 161, 179, 196; Barbara Harmon: 212-213, 215; Ben Hasler/NB Illustration: 94-95, 101, 148-149, 172, 182, 186-187; Betsy Hayes: 134, 138-139; Matthew Holmes: 75; Stewart Holmes/Illustration Ltd.: 192; Janos Jantner/Beehive Illustration: 5, 13, 82-83, 122-123, 130-131, 146-147, 164-165, 184, 185; Ken Joudrey/Munro Campagna: 52, 68-69, 177, 208-209; Bob Kaganich/Deborah Wolfe: 10, 40-41, 121; Steve Karp: 230, 231; Mike Kasun/Munro Campagna: 218; Graham Kennedy: 27; Marcel Laverdet/AA Reps: 23; Jeffrey Lindberg: 33, 42-43, 92-93, 133, 160-161, 170-171, 176; Dennis Lyall/Artworks: 198; Chris Lyons:/Lindgren & Smith: 173, 191; Alan Male/Artworks: 210, 211; Jeff Mangiat/Mendola Art: 53, 54, 55, 56, 57, 58, 59, 66-67; Adrian Mateescu/The Studio: 188-189, 232-233; Karen Minot: 28-29; Paul Mirocha/The Wiley Group: 194, 216-217; Peter Miserendino/P.T. Pie Illustrations: 198; Lee Montgomery/Illustration Ltd.: 4; Roger Motzkus: 229; Laurie O'Keefe: 111, 216-217; Daniel O'Leary/Illustration Ltd.: 8-9, 26, 34-35, 78, 135, 136-137, 238; Vilma Ortiz-Dillon: 16, 20-21, 60, 98-99, 100, 211; Terry Pazcko: 46-47, 144-145, 152, 180, 227; David Preiss/Munro Campagna: 5; Pronk & Associates: 192-193; Tony Randazzo/AA Reps: 156, 234-235; Mike Renwick/Creative Eye: 126-127; Mark Riedy/Scott Hull Associates: 48-49, 79, 140, 153; Jon Rogers/AA Reps: 112; Jeff Sanson/Schumann & Co.: 84-85, 240-241; David Schweitzer/Munro Campagna: 162-163; Ben Shannon/Magnet Reps: 11, 64-65, 90, 91, 96, 97, 166-167, 168-169, 179, 239; Reed Sprunger/Jae Wagoner Artists Rep.: 18-19, 232-233; Studio Liddell/AA Reps: 27; Angelo Tillary: 108-109; Ralph Voltz/Deborah Wolfe: 50-51, 128-129, 141, 154, 175, 236-237; Jeff Wack/Mendola Art: 24, 25, 86-87, 102-103, 134-135, 231; Brad Walker: 104-105, 150-151, 157, 206-207; Wendy Wassink: 110-111; John White/The Neis Group: 199; Eric Wilkerson: 32, 138; Simon Williams/Illustration Ltd.: 2-3, 6-7, 30-31, 36, 38-39, 44-45, 72-73; Lee Woodgate/Eye Candy Illustration: 222-223; Andy Zito: 62-23; Craig Zuckerman: 14, 88-89, 112-113, 120-121, 194-195.

Chapter icons designed by Von Glitschka/Scott Hull Associates

Cover Art by CUBE/Illustration Ltd (hummingbird, branch); Paul Mirocha/The Wiley Group (cherry); Mark Riedy/Scott Hull Associates (stamp); 9 Surf Studios (lettering).

Studio photography for Oxford University Press done by Dennis Kitchen Studio: 37, 61, 72, 73, 74, 75, 95, 96, 100, 180, 181, 183, 226.

Stock Photography: Age FotoStock: 238 (flute; clarinet; bassoon; saxophone; violin; cello; bass; guitar; trombone; trumpet; xylophone; harmonica); Comstock, 61 (window); Morales, 221 (bat); Franco Pizzochero, 98 (cashmere); Thinkstock, 61 (sink); Alamy: Corbis, 61 (table); Gary Crabbe, 220 (park ranger); The Associated Press: 198 (strike; soldiers in trench); Joe Rosenthal, 198 (Iwo Jima); Neil Armstrong, 198 (Buzz Aldrin on Moon); CORBIS: Philip Gould, 198 (Civil War); Photo Library, 220 (Yosemite Falls); Danita Delimont: Greg Johnston, 220 (snorkeling); Jamie & Judy Wild, 220 (El Capitan); Getty Images: 198 (Martin Luther King, Jr.); Amana Images, 61 (soapy plates), The Granger Collection: 198 (Jazz Age); The Image Works: Kelly Spranger, 220 (sea turtle); Inmagine: 238 (oboe; tuba; French horn; piano; drums; tambourine; accordion); istockphoto: 61 (oven), 98 (silk), 99 (suede; lace; velvet); Jupiter Images: 61 (tiles); 98 (wool); 99 (corduroy); Foodpix, 98 (linen); Rob Melnychuk/Brand X Pictures, 61 (glass shower door); Jupiter Unlimited: 220 (seagulls); 238 (electric keyboard); Comstock, 99 (denim); Mary Evans Picture Library: 198 (women in factory); NPS Photo: Peter Jones, 221 (Carlsbad Cavern entrance; tour; cavern; spelunker); OceanwideImages.com: Gary Bell, 220 (coral); Photo Edit, Inc: David Young-Wolff, 220 (trail); Picture History: 198 (Hiram Rhodes); Robertstock: 198 (Great Depression); Punchstock: 98 (t-shirt), Robert Glusic, 31 (Monument Valley); Roland Corporation: 238 (organ); SuperStock: 99 (leather); 198 (Daniel Boone); Shutterstock: Marek Szumlas, 94 (watch); United States Mint: 126; Veer: Brand X Pictures, 220 (deer); Photodisc, 220 (black bear); Yankee Fleet, Inc.: 220 (Fort Jefferson; Yankee Freedom Ferry), Emil von Maltitz/Lime Photo, 37 (baby carrier).

This second edition of the Oxford Picture Dictionary is lovingly dedicated to the memory of Norma Shapiro.

Her ideas, her pictures, and her stories continue to teach, inspire, and delight.

Acknowledgments

The publisher and authors would like to acknowledge the following individuals for their invaluable feedback during the development of this program:

Dr. Macarena Aguilar, Cy-Fair College, Houston, TX

Joseph F. Anselme, Atlantic Technical Center, Coconut Creek, FL

Stacy Antonopoulos, Monterey Trail High School, Elk Grove, CA

Carol Antunano, The English Center, Miami, FL

Irma Arencibia, Thomas A. Edison School, Union City, NJ

Suzi Austin, Alexandria City Public School Adult Program, Alexandria, FL

Patricia S. Bell, Lake Technical Center, Eustis, FL

Jim Brice, San Diego Community College District, San Diego, CA

Phil Cackley, Arlington Education and Employment Program (REEP), Arlington, VA

Frieda Caldwell, Metropolitan Adult Education Program, San Jose, CA

Sandra Cancel, Robert Waters School, Union City, NJ

Anne Marie Caney, Chula Vista Adult School, Chula Vista, CA

Patricia Castro, Harvest English Institute, Newark, NJ

Paohui Lola Chen, Milpitas Adult School, Milpitas, CA

Lori Cisneros, Atlantic Vo-Tech, Ft. Lauderdale, FL

Joyce Clapp, Hayward Adult School, Hayward, CA

Stacy Clark, Arlington Education and Employment Program (REEP), Arlington, VA

Nancy B. Crowell, Southside Programs for Adults in Continuing Education, Prince George, VA

Doroti da Cunha, Hialeah-Miami Lakes Adult Education Center, Miami, FL

Paula Da Silva-Michelin, La Guardia Community College, Long Island City, NY

Cynthia L. Davies, Humble I.S.D., Humble, TX

Christopher Davis, Overfelt Adult Center, San Jose, CA

Beverly De Nicola, Capistrano Unified School District, San Juan Capistrano, CA

Beatriz Diaz, Miami-Dade County Public Schools, Miami, FL

Druci J. Diaz, Hillsborough County Public Schools, Tampa, FL

Marion Donahue, San Dieguito Adult School, Encinitas, CA

Nick Doorn, International Education Services, South Lyon, MI

Mercedes Douglass, Seminole Community College, Sanford, FL

Jenny Elliott, Montgomery College, Rockville, MD

Paige Endo, Mt. Diablo Adult Education, Concord, CA

Megan Ernst, Glendale Community College, Glendale, CA

Elizabeth Escobar, Robert Waters School, Union City, NJ

Joanne Everett, Dave Thomas Education Center, Pompano Beach, FL

Jennifer Fadden, Arlington Education and Employment Program (REEP), Arlington, VA

Judy Farron, Fort Myers Language Center, Fort Myers, FL

Sharyl Ferguson, Montwood High School, El Paso, TX

Dr. Monica Fishkin, University of Central Florida, Orlando, FL

Nancy Frampton, Reedley College, Reedley, CA

Lynn A. Freeland, San Dieguito Union High School District, Encinitas, CA

Cathy Gample, San Leandro Adult School, San Leandro, CA

Hillary Gardner, Center for Immigrant Education and Training, Long Island City, NY

Martha C. Giffen, Alhambra Unified School District, Alhambra, CA

Jill Gluck, Hollywood Community Adult School, Los Angeles, CA

Carolyn Grimaldi, LaGuardia Community College, Long Island City, NY

William Gruenholz, USD Adult School, Concord, CA

Sandra G. Gutierrez, Hialeah-Miami Lakes Adult Education Center, Miami, FL

Conte Gúzman-Hoffman, Triton College, River Grove, IL

Amanda Harllee, Palmetto High School, Palmetto, FL

Mercedes Hearn, Tampa Bay Technical Center, Tampa, FL

Robert Hearst, Truman College, Chicago, IL

Patty Heiser, University of Washington, Seattle, WA

Joyce Hettiger, Metropolitan Education District, San Jose, CA

Karen Hirsimaki, Napa Valley Adult School, Napa, CA

Marvina Hooper, Lake Technical Center, Eustis, FL

Katie Hurter, North Harris College, Houston, TX

Nuchamon James, Miami Dade College, Miami, FL

Linda Jennings, Montgomery College, Rockville, MD

Bonnie Boyd Johnson, Chapman Education Center, Garden Grove, CA

Fayne B. Johnson, Broward County Public Schools, Fort Lauderdale, FL

Stavroula Katseyeanis, Robert Waters School, Union City, NJ

Dale Keith, Broadbase Consulting, Inc. at Kidworks USA, Miami, FL

Blanche Kellawon, Bronx Community College, Bronx, NY

Mary Kernel, Migrant Education Regional Office, Northwest Educational Service District, Anacortes, WA

Karen Kipke, Antioch High School Freshman Academy, Antioch, TN

Jody Kirkwood, ABC Adult School, Cerritos, CA

Matthew Kogan, Evans Community Adult School, Los Angeles, CA

Ineza Kuceba, Renton Technical College, Renton, WA

John Kuntz, California State University, San Bernadino, San Bernadino, CA

Claudia Kupiec, DePaul University, Chicago, IL

E.C. Land, Southside Programs for Adult Continuing Education, Prince George, VA

Betty Lau, Franklin High School, Seattle, WA

Patt Lemonie, Thomas A. Edison School, Union City, NJ

Lia Lerner, Burbank Adult School, Burbank, CA

Krystyna Lett, Metropolitan Education District, San Jose, CA

Renata Lima, TALK International School of Languages, Fort Lauderdale, FL

Luz M. Lopez, Sweetwater Union High School District, Chula Vista, CA

Osmara Lopez, Bronx Community College, Bronx, NY

Heather Lozano, North Lake College, Irving, TX

Betty Lynch, Arlington Education and Employment Program (REEP), Arlington, VA

Meera Madan, REID Park Elementary School, Charlotte, NC

Ivanna Mann Thrower, Charlotte Mecklenburg Schools, Charlotte, NC

Michael R. Mason, Loma Vista Adult Center, Concord, CA

Holley Mayville, Charlotte Mecklenburg Schools, Charlotte, NC

Margaret McCabe, United Methodist Cooperative Ministries, Clearwater, FL

Todd McDonald, Hillsborough Adult Education, Tampa, FL

Nancy A. McKeand, ESL Consultant, St. Benedict, LA

Rebecca L. McLain, Gaston College, Dallas, NC

John M. Mendoza, Redlands Adult School, Redlands, CA

Bet Messmer, Santa Clara Adult Education Center, Santa Clara, CA

Christina Morales, BEGIN Managed Programs, New York, NY

Lisa Munoz, Metropolitan Education District, San Jose, CA

Mary Murphy-Clagett, Sweetwater Union High School District, Chula Vista, CA

Jonetta Myles, Rockdale County High School, Conyers, GA

Marwan Nabi, Troy High School, Fullerton, CA

Dr. Christine L. Nelsen, Salvation Army Community Center, Tampa, FL

Michael W. Newman, Arlington Education and Employment Program (REEP), Arlington, VA

Rehana Nusrat, Huntington Beach Adult School, Huntington Beach, CA

Cindy Oakley-Paulik, Embry-Riddle Aeronautical University, Daytona Beach, FL

Janet Ochi-Fontanott, Sweetwater Union High School District, Chula Vista, CA

Lorraine Pedretti, Metropolitan Education District, San Jose, CA

Isabel Pena, BE/ESL Programs, Garland, TX

Margaret Perry, Everett Public Schools, Everett, WA

Dale Pesmen, PhD, Chicago, IL

Cathleen Petersen, Chapman Education Center, Garden Grove, CA

Allison Pickering, Escondido Adult School, Escondido, CA

Ellen Quish, LaGuardia Community College, Long Island City, NY

Teresa Reen, Independence Adult Center, San Jose, CA

Kathleen Reynolds, Albany Park Community Center, Chicago, IL

Melba I. Rillen, Palmetto High School, Palmetto, FL

Lorraine Romero, Houston Community College, Houston, TX

Eric Rosenbaum, BEGIN Managed Programs, New York, NY

Blair Roy, Chapman Education Center, Garden Grove, CA

Arlene R. Schwartz, Broward Community Schools, Fort Lauderdale, FL

Geraldyne Blake Scott, Truman College, Chicago, IL

Sharada Sekar, Antioch High School Freshman Academy, Antioch, TN

Dr. Cheryl J. Serrano, Lynn University, Boca Raton, FL

Janet Setzekorn, United Methodist Cooperative Ministries, Clearwater, FL

Terry Shearer, EDUCALL Learning Services, Houston, TX

Elisabeth Sklar, Township High School District 113, Highland Park, IL

Robert Stein, BEGIN Managed Programs, New York, NY

Ruth Sutton, Township High School District 113, Highland Park, IL

Alisa Takeuchi, Chapman Education Center, Garden Grove, CA

Grace Tanaka, Santa Ana College School of Continuing Education, Santa Ana, CA

Annalisa Te, Overfelt Adult Center, San Jose, CA

Don Torluemke, South Bay Adult School, Redondo Beach, CA

Maliheh Vafai, Overfelt Adult Center, San Jose, CA

Tara Vasquez, Robert Waters School, Union City, NJ

Nina Velasco, Naples Language Center, Naples, FL

Theresa Warren, East Side Adult Center, San Jose, CA

Lucie Gates Watel, Truman College, Chicago, IL

Wendy Weil, Arnold Middle School, Cypress, TX

Patricia Weist, TALK International School of Languages, Fort Lauderdale, FL

Dr. Carole Lynn Weisz, Lehman College, Bronx, NY

Desiree Wesner, Robert Waters School, Union City, NJ

David Wexler, Napa Valley Adult School, Napa, CA

Cynthia Wiseman, Borough of Manhattan Community College, New York, NY

Debbie Cullinane Wood, Lincoln Education Center, Garden Grove, CA

Banu Yaylali, Miami Dade College, Miami, FL

Hongyan Zheng, Milpitas Adult Education, Milpitas, CA

Arlene Zivitz, ESOL Teacher, Jupiter, FL

The publisher, authors, and editors would like to thank the following people for their expertise in reviewing specific content areas:

Ross Feldberg, Tufts University, Medford, MA

William J. Hall, M.D. FACP/FRSM (UK), Cumberland Foreside, ME

Jill A. Horohoe, Arizona State University, Tempe, AZ

Phoebe B. Rouse, Louisiana State University, Baton Rouge, LA

Dr. Susan Rouse, Southern Wesleyan University, Central, SC

Dr. Ira M. Sheskin, University of Miami, Coral Gables, FL

Maiko Tomizawa, D.D.S., New York, NY

The publisher would like to thank the following for their permission to reproduce copyrighted material:

p. 26: Penny, nickel, dime, quarter-dollar, half-dollar, and dollar coin images from the United States Mint.

pp. 125, 134–135: U.S. Postal Service Priority Mail Logo, Express Mail Logo, Certified Mail, Ready Pack Packaging, Letter Carrier Uniform, Postal Clerk Uniform, Automated Postal Center, Round Top Collection Mailbox, and Lady Liberty Stamp Image are trademarks and copyrighted material of the United States Postal Service and are used with permission.

p. 152: Metrocard is an MTA trademark and is used with permission.

p. 152: Metro token for L.A.'s bus and rail system used with permission.

p. 229: Little League used courtesy of Little League® Baseball and Softball.

p. 231: Frisbee®, a registered trademark of Wham-O, Inc.

Table of Contents 目次

Introduction はじめに . . . ix–xi

1. Everyday Language 日常会話

Meeting and Greeting 人と会ってあいさつする . . . 2–3
Personal Information 自己紹介 . . . 4
School 学校 . . . 5
A Classroom 教室 . . . 6–7
Studying 学習 . . . 8–9
Succeeding in School 学校で良い成績を収める . . . 10
A Day at School 学校での1日 . . . 11
Everyday Conversation 日常会話 . . . 12
Weather 天気 . . . 13
The Telephone 電話 . . . 14–15
Numbers 数字 . . . 16
Measurements 度量衡 . . . 17
Time 時間 . . . 18–19
The Calendar カレンダー . . . 20–21
Calendar Events 年間の行事 . . . 22
Describing Things 物の描写 . . . 23
Colors 色 . . . 24
Prepositions 前置詞 . . . 25
Money 通貨 . . . 26
Shopping 買物 . . . 27
Same and Different 相似と相違 . . . 28–29

2. People 人々

Adults and Children 大人と子供 . . . 30–31
Describing People 人の特徴 . . . 32
Describing Hair 髪型の特徴 . . . 33
Families 家族 . . . 34–35
Childcare and Parenting 保育と育児 . . . 36–37
Daily Routines 日常生活 . . . 38–39
Life Events and Documents 人生の出来事と各種証明書 . . . 40–41
Feelings 感情 . . . 42–43
A Family Reunion 親族会 . . . 44–45

3. Housing 住居

The Home 家屋 . . . 46–47
Finding a Home 家を見つける . . . 48–49
Apartments アパート . . . 50–51
Different Places to Live さまざまな住宅環境 . . . 52
A House and Yard 家と庭 . . . 53
A Kitchen キッチン . . . 54
A Dining Area ダイニング . . . 55
A Living Room リビング . . . 56
A Bathroom 風呂場 . . . 57
A Bedroom 寝室 . . . 58
The Kids' Bedroom 子供部屋 . . . 59
Housework 家事 . . . 60
Cleaning Supplies 掃除・洗濯の用具 . . . 61
Household Problems and Repairs 家の問題と修理 . . . 62–63
The Tenant Meeting 借家人と話し合う . . . 64–65

4. Food 食品

Back from the Market スーパーから戻る . . . 66–67
Fruit 果物 . . . 68
Vegetables 野菜 . . . 69
Meat and Poultry 肉類 . . . 70
Seafood and Deli 魚介類とお惣菜 . . . 71
A Grocery Store スーパーマーケット . . . 72–73
Containers and Packaging 容器とパッケージ . . . 74
Weights and Measurements 重さと計量 . . . 75
Food Preparation and Safety 料理と安全 . . . 76–77
Kitchen Utensils 台所用品 . . . 78
Fast Food Restaurant ファーストフードの店 . . . 79
A Coffee Shop Menu 喫茶店のメニュー . . . 80–81
A Restaurant レストラン . . . 82–83
The Farmers' Market 青物市（ファーマーズマーケット） . . . 84–85

5. Clothing 衣類

Everyday Clothes 普段着 . . . 86–87
Casual, Work, and Formal Clothes カジュアルな服装、仕事着、フォーマルな服装 . . . 88–89
Seasonal Clothing 季節の衣類 . . . 90
Underwear and Sleepwear 下着とスリープウェア . . . 91
Workplace Clothing 作業着 . . . 92–93
Shoes and Accessories 靴とアクセサリー . . . 94–95
Describing Clothes 衣服の説明 . . . 96–97
Making Clothes 服を作る . . . 98–99
Making Alterations サイズ直し . . . 100
Doing the Laundry 洗濯をする . . . 101
A Garage Sale ガレージセール . . . 102–103

6. Health 健康

The Body 体 . . . 104–105
Inside and Outside the Body 体の内側と外側 . . . 106–107
Personal Hygiene みだしなみ . . . 108–109
Symptoms and Injuries 病気の症状とけが . . . 110
Illnesses and Medical Conditions 疾患と症状 . . . 111
A Pharmacy 薬局 . . . 112–113
Taking Care of Your Health 健康に気をつける . . . 114–115
Medical Emergencies 救急の病状 . . . 116
First Aid 応急手当 . . . 117
Medical Care 医療 . . . 118
Dental Care 歯の治療 . . . 119
Hospital 病院 . . . 120–121
A Health Fair ヘルスフェア . . . 122–123

7. Community 地域

Downtown ダウンタウン . . . 124–125
City Streets 街 . . . 126–127
An Intersection 交差点 . . . 128–129
A Mall ショッピングモール . . . 130–131
The Bank 銀行 . . . 132
The Library 図書館 . . . 133
The Post Office 郵便局 . . . 134–135
Department of Motor Vehicles (DMV) 交通局(DMV) . . . 136–137
Government and Military Service 政府と軍隊 . . . 138–139
Civic Rights and Responsibilities 公民権と義務 . . . 140
The Legal System 法律制度 . . . 141
Crime 犯罪 . . . 142
Public Safety 公共の安全 . . . 143
Emergencies and Natural Disasters 緊急事態と自然災害 . . . 144–145
Emergency Procedures 緊急対策 . . . 146–147
Community Cleanup 地域の清掃 . . . 148–149

8. Transportation 交通

Basic Transportation 基本的な交通機関 . . . 150–151
Public Transportation 公共の交通機関 . . . 152
Prepositions of Motion 動作の前置詞 . . . 153
Traffic Signs 交通標識 . . . 154
Directions and Maps 道順と地図 . . . 155
Cars and Trucks 車とトラック . . . 156
Buying and Maintaining a Car 車の購入とメンテナンス . . . 157
Parts of a Car 車の部品 . . . 158–159
An Airport 空港 . . . 160–161
Taking a Trip 旅行する . . . 162–163

9. Work 仕事

The Workplace 職場 . . . 164–165
Jobs and Occupations A-C 仕事と職業 A-C . . . 166
Jobs and Occupations C-H 仕事と職業 C-H . . . 167
Jobs and Occupations H-P 仕事と職業 H-P . . . 168
Jobs and Occupations P-W 仕事と職業 P-W . . . 169
Job Skills 職業技能 . . . 170
Office Skills 事務能力 . . . 171
Career Planning キャリア計画 . . . 172
Job Search 職探し . . . 173
Interview Skills 面接技能 . . . 174
A Factory 工場 . . . 175
Landscaping and Gardening 造園と園芸業 . . . 176
Farming and Ranching 農業と牧畜業 . . . 177
Construction 建設業 . . . 178
Job Safety 職場の安全 . . . 179
Tools and Building Supplies 工具と建設用品 . . . 180–181
An Office オフィス . . . 182–183
A Hotel ホテル . . . 184
Food Service 食品サービス . . . 185
A Bad Day at Work 仕事がうまく行かなかった日 . . . 186–187

Contents 内容

10. Areas of Study 科目

Schools and Subjects 学校と科目 188–189
English Composition 英作文 190–191
Mathematics 数学 192–193
Science 科学 194–195
Computers コンピュータ 196
The Internet インターネット 197
U.S. History アメリカ史 198
World History 世界史 199
North America and Central America 北アメリカと中央アメリカ 200–201
World Map 世界地図 202–203
Geography and Habitats 地理と棲息地 204
The Universe 宇宙 205
A Graduation 卒業 206–207

11. Plants and Animals 植物と動物

Nature Center 自然センター 208–209
Trees and Plants 木と植物 210
Flowers 花 211
Marine Life, Amphibians, and Reptiles 海洋生物、両生類、爬虫類 212–213
Birds, Insects, and Arachnids 鳥、昆虫、蜘蛛類 214
Domestic Animals and Rodents 家畜とげっ歯類 215
Mammals 哺乳類 216–217
Energy and Conservation エネルギーと資源の節約 218–219
U.S. National Parks 米国の国立公園 220–221

12. Recreation レクリエーション

Places to Go 遊びに行く場所 222–223
The Park and Playground 公園と遊び場 224
The Beach 海岸 225
Outdoor Recreation 戸外のレクリエーション 226
Winter and Water Sports ウィンタースポーツとウォータースポーツ 227
Individual Sports 個人競技 228
Team Sports 団体競技 229
Sports Verbs スポーツ関連の動詞 230
Sports Equipment スポーツ用品 231
Hobbies and Games 趣味とゲーム 232–233
Electronics and Photography 電化製品と写真 234–235
Entertainment 娯楽 236–237
Music 音楽 238
Holidays 祝祭日 239
A Birthday Party バースデーパーティ 240–241

Verb Guide 動詞について 242–244
How to Use the Index 索引の使い方 245
English Index 英語索引 246–281
Geographical Index 地理的索引 282–284
Japanese Index 日本語索引 285–304
Research Bibliography リサーチ用参考文献一覧 305

Welcome to the OPD SECOND EDITION

Teaching with the *Oxford Picture Dictionary* Program

The following general guidelines will help you prepare single and multilevel lessons using the OPD program. For step-by-step, topic-specific lesson plans, see *OPD Lesson Plans*.

1. Use Students' Needs to Identify Lesson Objectives

- Create communicative objectives based on your learners' needs assessments (*see OPD 2e Assessment Program*).
- Make sure objectives state what students will be able to do at the end of the lesson. For example: *Students will be able to respond to basic classroom commands and requests for classroom objects.* (pp. 6–7, A Classroom)
- For multilevel classes, identify a low-beginning, high-beginning, and low-intermediate objective for each topic.

2. Preview the Topic

Identify what your students already know about the topic.

- Ask general questions related to the topic.
- Have students list words they know from the topic.
- Ask questions about the picture(s) on the page.

3. Present the New Vocabulary

Research shows that it is best to present no more than 5–7 new words at a time. Here are a few presentation techniques:

- Say each new word and describe it within the context of the picture. Have volunteers act out verbs and verb sequences.
- Use Total Physical Response commands to build vocabulary comprehension.
- For long or unfamiliar word lists, introduce words by categories or select the words your students need most.
- Ask a series of questions to build comprehension and give students an opportunity to say the new words. Begin with *yes/no* questions: *Is #16 chalk?* Progress to *or* questions: *Is #16 chalk or a marker?* Finally, ask *Wh-* questions: *What can I use to write on this paper?*
- Focus on the words that students want to learn. Have them write 3–5 new words from each topic, along with meaning clues such as a drawing, translation, or sentence.

More vocabulary and **Grammar Point** sections provide additional presentation opportunities (see p. 5, School). For multilevel presentation ideas, see *OPD Lesson Plans*.

4. Check Comprehension

Make sure that students understand the target vocabulary. Here are two activities you can try:

- Say vocabulary words, and have students point to the correct items in their books. Walk around the room, checking if students are pointing to the correct pictures.
- Make true/false statements about the target vocabulary. Have students hold up two fingers for true, three for false.

5. Provide Guided and Communicative Practice

The exercise bands at the bottom of the topic pages provide a variety of guided and communicative practice opportunities and engage students' higher-level thinking.

6. Provide More Practice

OPD Second Edition offers a variety of components to facilitate vocabulary acquisition. Each of the print and electronic materials listed below offers suggestions and support for single and multilevel instruction.

OPD Lesson Plans Step-by-step multilevel lesson plans feature 3 CDs with multilevel listening, context-based pronunciation practice, and leveled reading practice. Includes multilevel teaching notes for *The OPD Reading Library.*

OPD Audio CDs or Audio Cassettes Each word in *OPD's* word list is recorded by topic.

Low-Beginning, High-Beginning, and Low-Intermediate Workbooks Guided practice for each page in *OPD* features linked visual contexts, realia, and listening practice.

Classic Classroom Activities A photocopiable resource of interactive multilevel activities, grammar practice, and communicative tasks.

The OPD Reading Library Readers include civics, academic content, and workplace themes.

Overhead Transparencies Vibrant transparencies help to focus students on the lesson.

OPD Presentation Software A multilevel interactive teaching tool using interactive whiteboard and LCD technology. Audio, animation, and video instructional support bring each dictionary topic to life.

The OPD CD-ROM An interactive learning tool featuring four-skill practice based on *OPD* topics.

Bilingual Editions *OPD* is available in numerous bilingual editions including Spanish, Chinese, Vietnamese, Arabic, Korean, and many more.

My hope is that OPD makes it easier for you to take your learners from comprehension to communication. Please share your thoughts with us as you make the book your own.

Jayme Adelson-Goldstein

Jayme Adelson-Goldstein

OPDteam.us@oup.com

Welcome to the OPD SECOND EDITION

The second edition of the *Oxford Picture Dictionary* expands on the best aspects of the 1998 edition with:

- New artwork presenting words within meaningful, real-life contexts
- An updated word list to meet the needs of today's English language learners
- 4,000 English words and phrases, including 285 verbs
- 40 new topics with 12 intro pages and 12 story pages
- Unparalleled support for vocabulary teaching

Subtopics present the words in easy-to-learn "chunks."

Color coding and icons make it easy to navigate through *OPD*.

New art and rich contexts improve vocabulary acquisition.

Revised practice activities help students from low-beginning through low-intermediate levels.

Public Transportation

A Bus Stop

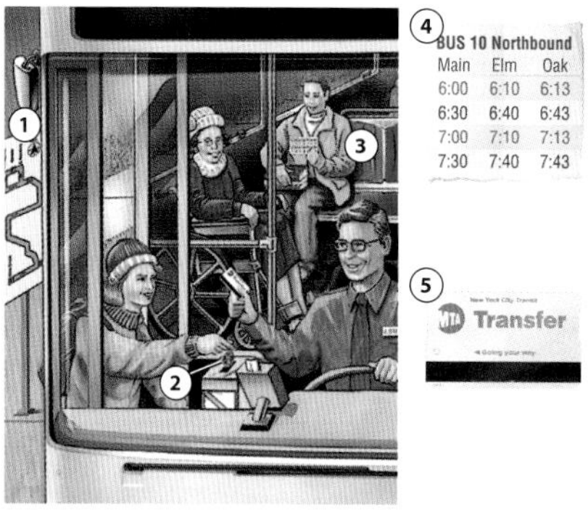

1. bus route
2. fare
3. rider
4. schedule
5. transfer

A Subway Station

6. subway car
7. platform
8. turnstile
9. vending machine
10. token
11. fare card

A Train Station

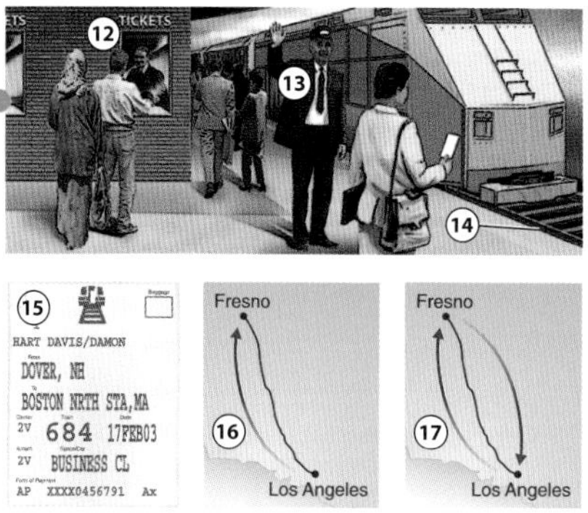

12. ticket window
13. conductor
14. track
15. ticket
16. one-way trip
17. round trip

Airport Transportation

18. taxi stand
19. shuttle
20. town car
21. taxi driver
22. taxi license
23. meter

More vocabulary

hail a taxi: to raise your hand to get a taxi
miss the bus: to get to the bus stop after the bus leaves

Ask your classmates. Share the answers.

1. Is there a subway system in your city?
2. Do you ever take taxis? When?
3. Do you ever take the bus? Where?

152

NEW! Intro pages open each unit with key vocabulary related to the unit theme. Clear, engaging artwork promotes questions, conversations, and writing practice for all levels.

Each intro page teaches key vocabulary items within the unit theme.

Practice activities make it easy to manage multilevel classrooms.

NEW! Story pages close each unit with a lively scene for reviewing vocabulary and teaching additional language. Meanwhile, rich visual contexts recycle words from the unit.

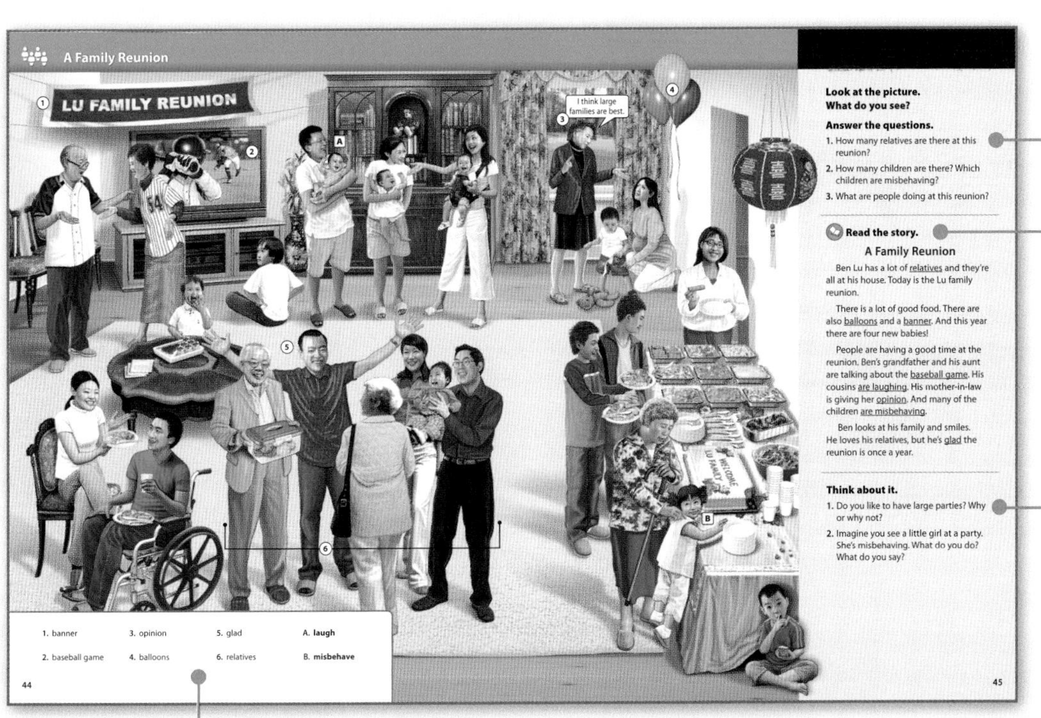

Pre-reading questions build students' previewing and predicting skills.

High-interest readings promote literacy skills.

Post-reading questions and role-play activities support critical thinking and encourage students to use the language they have learned.

The thematic word list previews words that students will encounter in the story.

Meeting and Greeting

人と会ってあいさつする

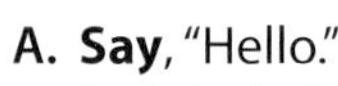

A. **Say**, "Hello."
「こんにちは」と言う

B. **Ask**, "How are you?"
「お元気ですか」と尋ねる

C. **Introduce** yourself.
自己紹介する

D. **Smile**.
笑いかける

E. **Hug**.
抱き合う

F. **Wave**.
手を振る

Tell your partner what to do. Take turns.

1. *Say,* "Hello."
2. *Bow.*
3. *Smile.*
4. *Shake hands.*
5. *Wave.*
6. *Say,* "Goodbye."

Dictate to your partner. Take turns.

A: *Write smile.*
B: *Is it spelled s-m-i-l-e?*
A: *Yes, that's right.*

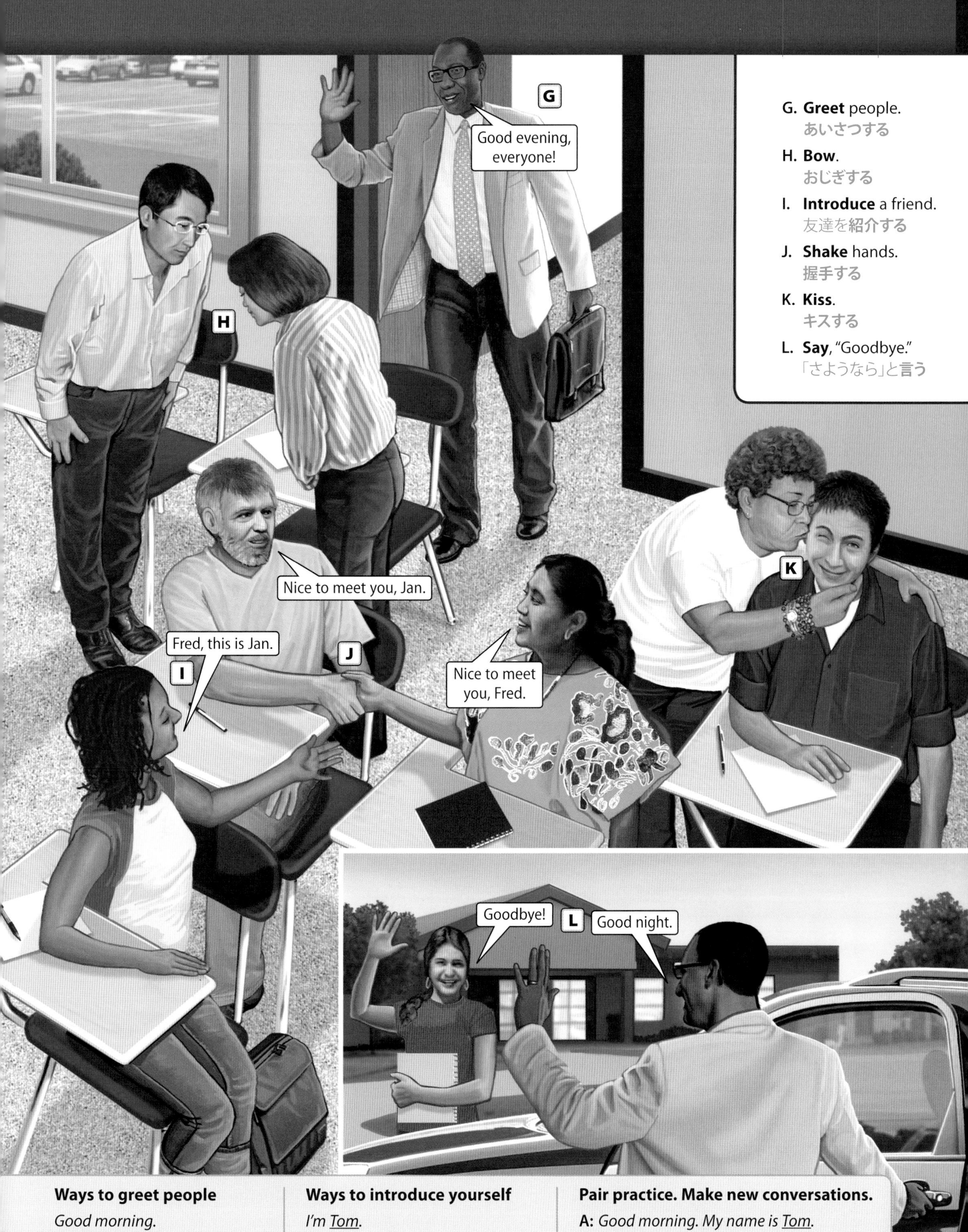

G. **Greet** people.
あいさつする

H. **Bow**.
おじぎする

I. **Introduce** a friend.
友達を紹介する

J. **Shake** hands.
握手する

K. **Kiss**.
キスする

L. **Say**, "Goodbye."
「さようなら」と言う

Ways to greet people

Good morning.
Good afternoon.
Good evening.

Ways to introduce yourself

I'm Tom.
My name is Tom.

Pair practice. Make new conversations.

A: *Good morning. My name is Tom.*
B: *Nice to meet you, Tom. I'm Sara.*
A: *Nice to meet you, Sara.*

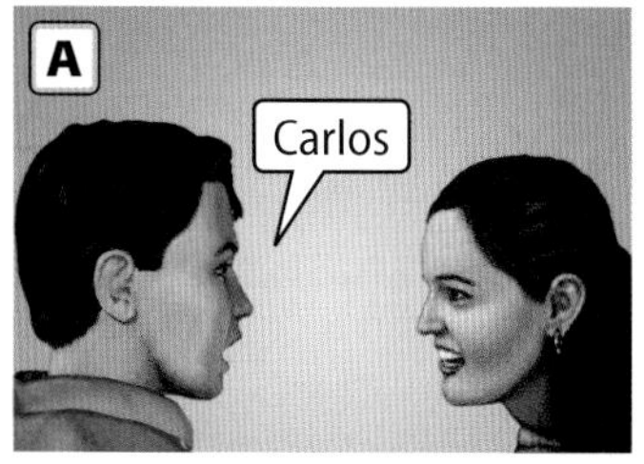

A. Say your name.
名前を言う

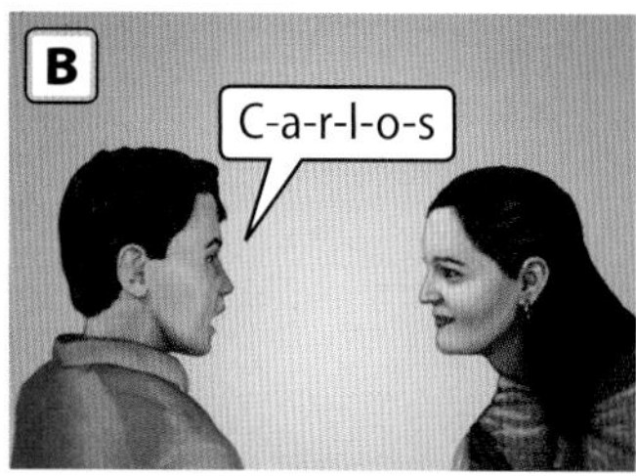

B. Spell your name.
名前をつづる

C. Print your name.
名前を活字体で書く

D. Sign your name.
名前をサインする

Filling Out a Form 用紙の記入

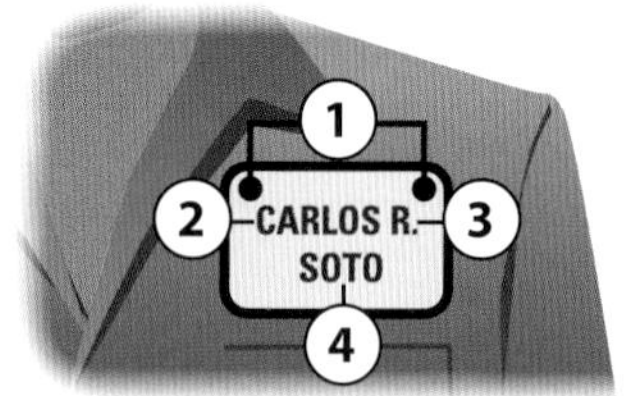

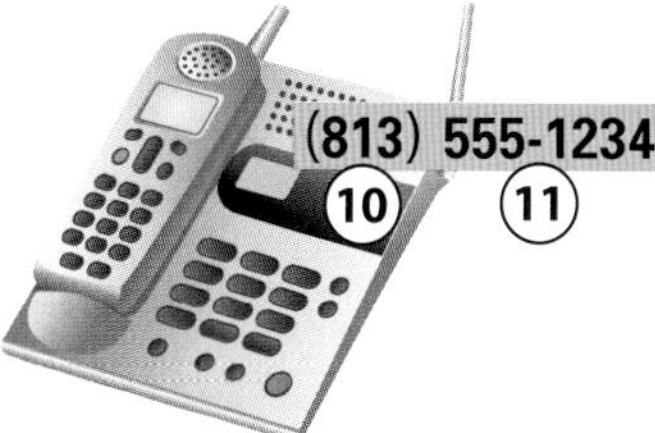

19 *Carlos R. Soto*

School Registration Form 学校登録用の用紙

1. name:
氏名:

2. first name
名

3. middle initial
ミドルネームのイニシャル

4. last name
姓

5. address
住所

6. apartment number
アパート番号

7. city
市

8. state
州

9. ZIP code
郵便番号

( )

10. area code
市外局番

11. phone number
電話番号

( )

12. cell phone number
携帯電話番号

13. date of birth (DOB)
生年月日

14. place of birth
出生地

\- -

15. Social Security number
社会保障番号

16. sex:
性別:

17. male ☐
男

18. female ☐
女

19. signature
署名

Pair practice. Make new conversations.

A: *My first name is Carlos.*
B: *Please spell Carlos for me.*
A: *C-a-r-l-o-s*

Ask your classmates. Share the answers.

1. Do you like your first name?
2. Is your last name from your mother? father? husband?
3. What is your middle name?

Campus キャンパス

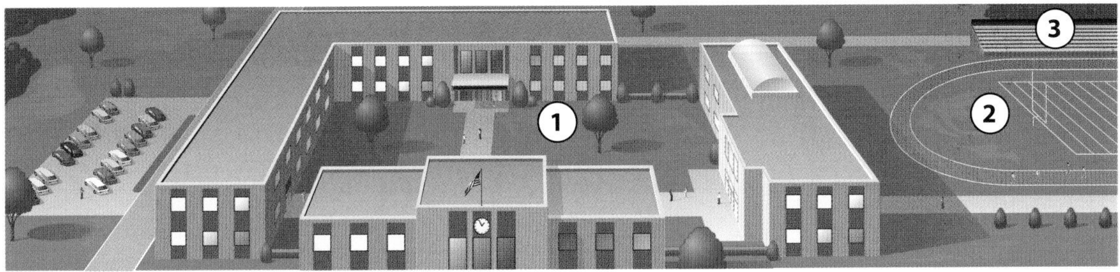

Administrators 管理者

Around Campus キャンパス周辺

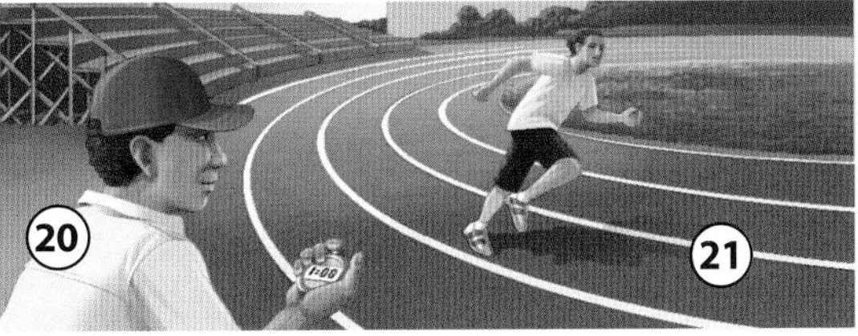

1. quad
   中庭
2. field
   フィールド／競技場
3. bleachers
   観覧席
4. principal
   校長
5. assistant principal
   副校長
6. counselor
   カウンセラー
7. classroom
   教室
8. teacher
   教師
9. restrooms
   トイレ
10. hallway
    廊下
11. locker
    ロッカー
12. main office
    事務室
13. clerk
    職員
14. cafeteria
    食堂／カフェテリア
15. computer lab
    コンピュータ室
16. teacher's aide
    教員助手
17. library
    図書館
18. auditorium
    講堂
19. gym
    体育館
20. coach
    コーチ
21. track
    陸上競技のトラック

More vocabulary

Students do not pay to go to a **public school**.
Students pay to go to a **private school**.
A church, mosque, or temple school is a **parochial school**.

Grammar Point: contractions of the verb *be*

He + is = He's	*He's a teacher.*
She + is = She's	*She's a counselor.*
They + are = They're	*They're students.*

A Classroom

教室

1. chalkboard
黒板
2. screen
スクリーン
3. whiteboard
ホワイトボード
4. teacher / instructor
教師
5. student
学生
6. LCD projector
LCDプロジェクタ
7. desk
机
8. headphones
ヘッドホン

A. **Raise** your hand.
手を**あげる**

B. **Talk** to the teacher.
先生と**話す**

C. **Listen** to a CD.
CDを**聞く**

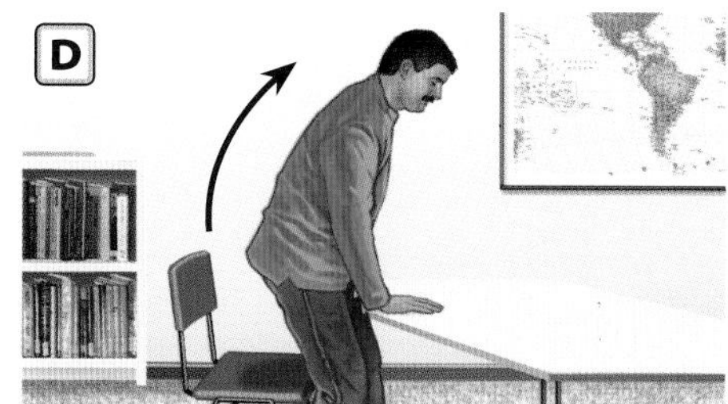

D. **Stand up**.
立つ

E. **Write** on the board.
黒板に**書く**

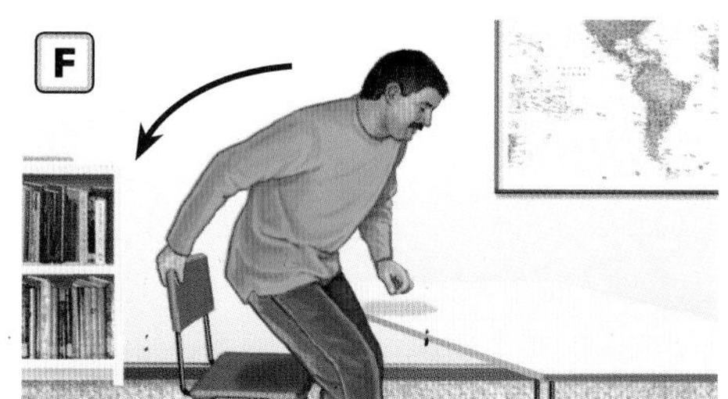

F. **Sit down.** / **Take** a seat.
座る／席に**つく**

G. **Open** your book.
本を**開く**

H. **Close** your book.
本を**閉じる**

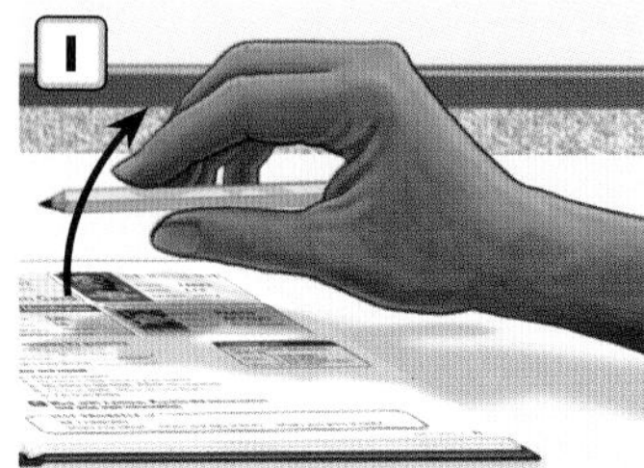

I. **Pick up** the pencil.
鉛筆を**手に取る**

J. **Put down** the pencil.
鉛筆を**置く**

9. clock
時計
10. bookcase
本だな
11. chair
椅子
12. map
地図
13. alphabet
アルファベット
14. bulletin board
掲示板
15. computer
コンピュータ
16. overhead projector
OHP

17. dry erase marker
ホワイトボード用マーカー
18. chalk
チョーク
19. eraser
黒板消し
20. pencil
鉛筆
21. (pencil) eraser
消しゴム
22. pen
ペン
23. pencil sharpener
鉛筆削り
24. marker
マジックペン
25. textbook
教科書
26. workbook
ワークブック
27. 3-ring binder / notebook
3リングバインダー／ノート
28. notebook paper
ルーズリーフ
29. spiral notebook
リングノート
30. dictionary
辞書
31. picture dictionary
絵辞典

Look at the picture.
Describe the classroom.
A: There's a chalkboard.
B: There are fifteen students.

Ask your classmates. Share the answers.
1. Do you like to raise your hand in class?
2. Do you like to listen to CDs in class?
3. Do you ever talk to the teacher?

Learning New Words 新しい単語を学ぶ

A. **Look up** the word.
単語を**調べる**

B. **Read** the definition.
定義を**読む**

C. **Translate** the word.
単語を**訳す**

D. **Check** the pronunciation.
発音を**チェックする**

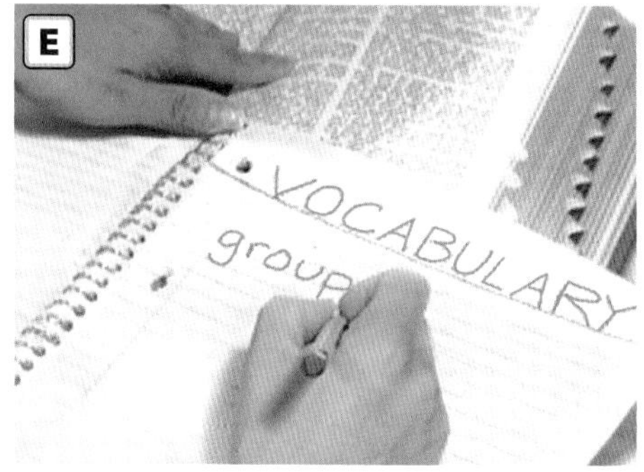

E. **Copy** the word.
単語を**書き写す**

F. **Draw** a picture.
絵を**描く**

Working with Your Classmates クラスメートと学習する

G. **Discuss** a problem.
問題について**話し合う**

H. **Brainstorm** solutions / answers.
解決方法・解答について**アイデアを出し合う**

I. **Work** in a group.
グループで**学習する**

J. **Help** a classmate.
クラスメートを**手伝う**

Working with a Partner 2 人で学習する

K. **Ask** a question.
質問する

L. **Answer** a question.
質問に**答える**

M. **Share** a book.
本を**一緒に使う**

N. **Dictate** a sentence.
文章を**書き取り用に口述する**

Following Directions 指示に従う

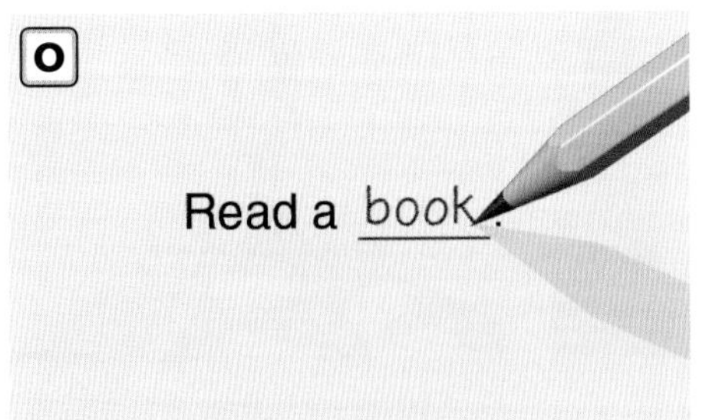

O. **Fill in** the blank.
空欄を**埋める**

P
5. How much is the book?
a. $99.99
b. $9.99
c. $0.99
Study Skills For You
$9.99

P. **Choose** the correct answer.
正しい解答を**選ぶ**

Q
Read the book. pencil.

Q. **Circle** the answer.
答えを**丸で囲む**

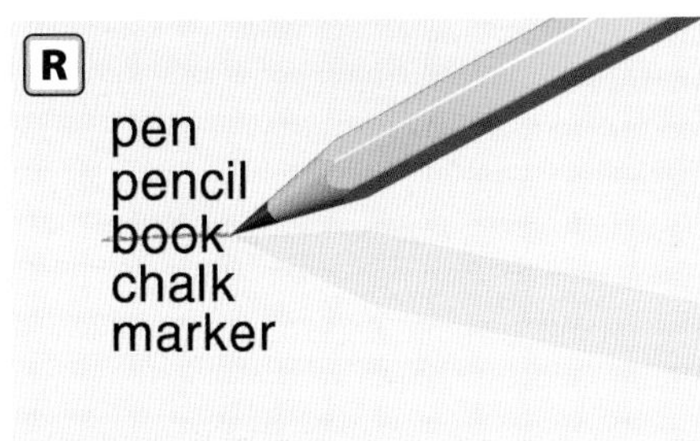

R. **Cross out** the word.
単語を**線で消す**

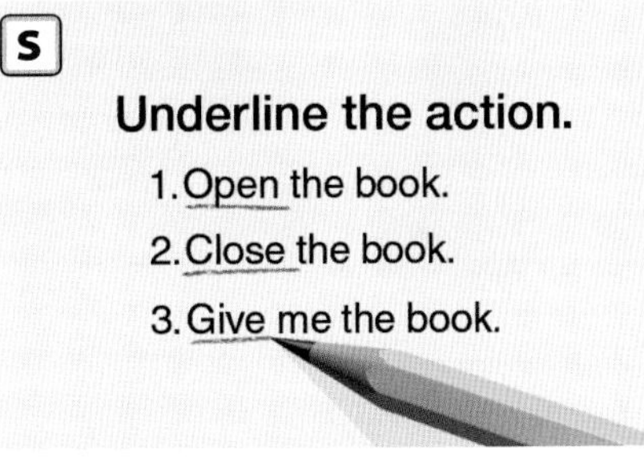

S. **Underline** the word.
単語に**下線を引く**

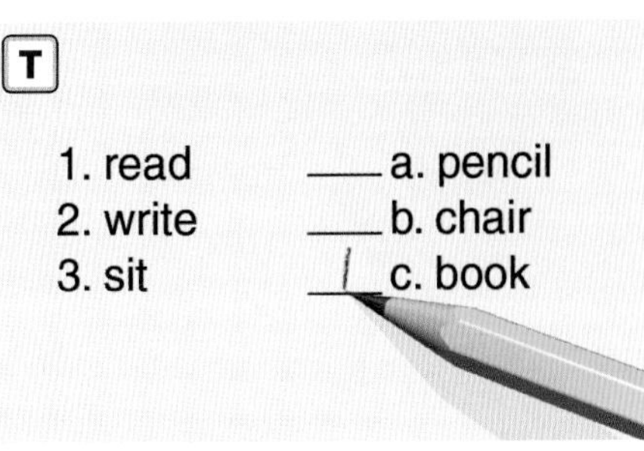

T. **Match** the items.
合う項目を**選ぶ**

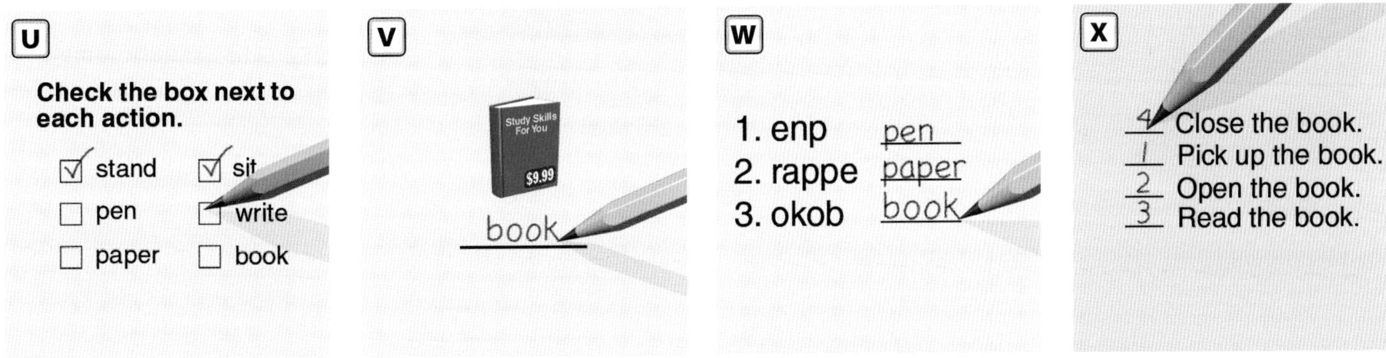

U. **Check** the correct boxes.
正しい欄に**印を付ける**

V. **Label** the picture.
絵に名前を**付ける**

W. **Unscramble** the words.
文字を**並べ替える**

X. **Put** the sentences in order.
文章を正しい順に**並べる**

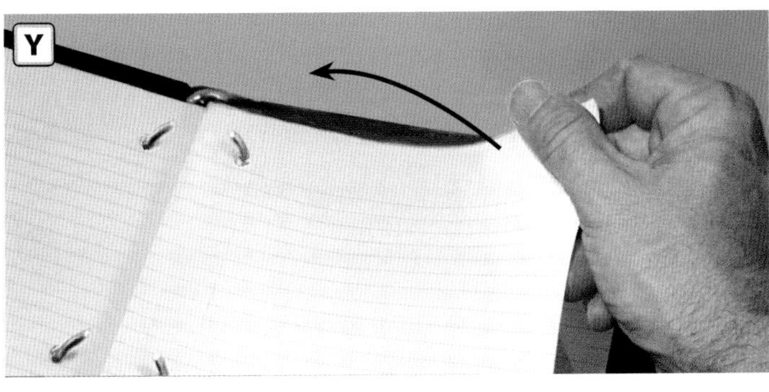

Y. **Take out** a piece of paper.
紙を1枚**取り出す**

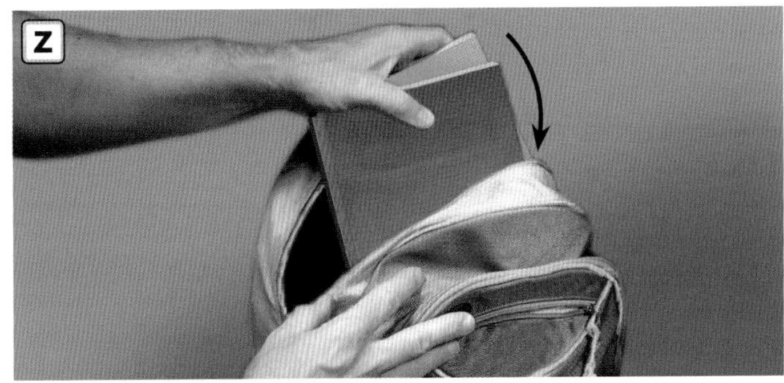

Z. **Put away** your books.
本を**しまう**

Ask your classmates. Share the answers.

1. Do you like to work in a group?
2. Do you ever share a book?
3. Do you like to answer questions?

Think about it. Discuss.

1. How can classmates help each other?
2. Why is it important to ask questions in class?
3. How can students check their pronunciation? Explain.

Succeeding in School 学校で良い成績を収める

Ways to Succeed 良い成績を収める方法

A. **Set** goals.
目標を**立てる**

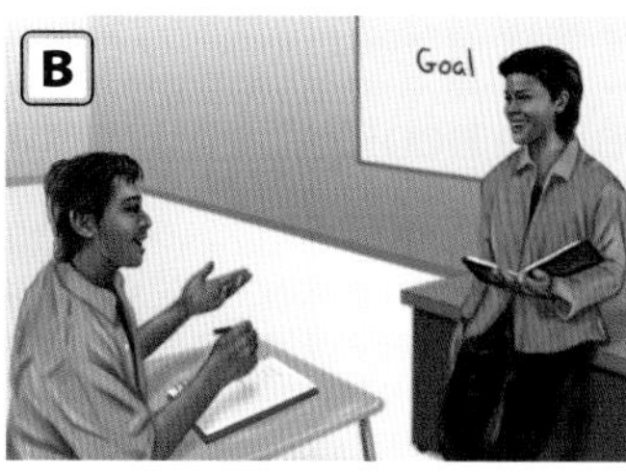

B. **Participate** in class.
授業中のやりとりに**参加する**

C. **Take** notes.
ノートを**取る**

D. **Study** at home.
家で**学習する**

E. **Pass** a test.
テストに**合格する**

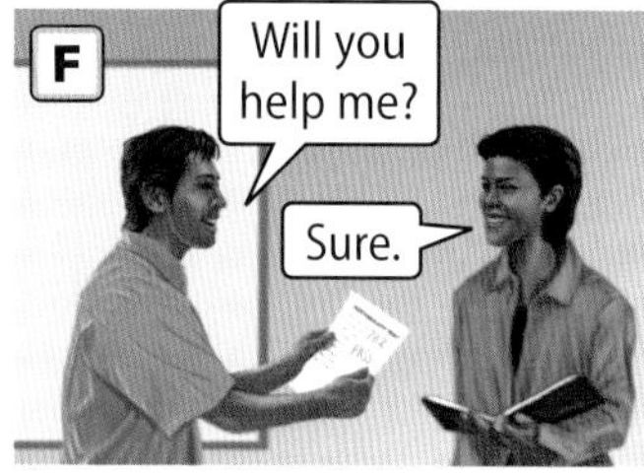

F. **Ask** for help.
援助を**求める**

G. **Make** progress.
進歩する

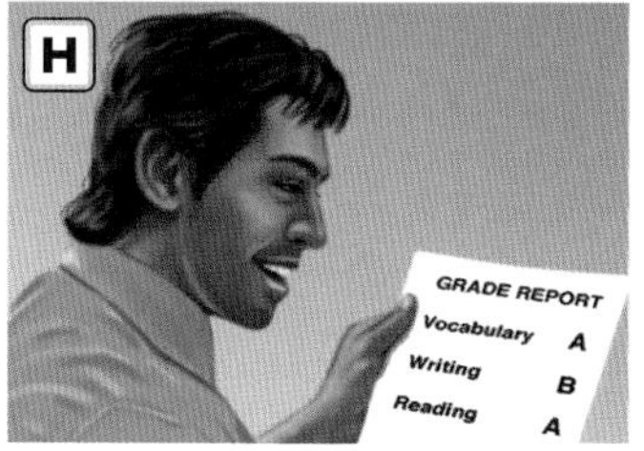

H. **Get** good grades.
良い成績を**取る**

Taking a Test テストを受ける

1. test booklet
テストの問題用紙

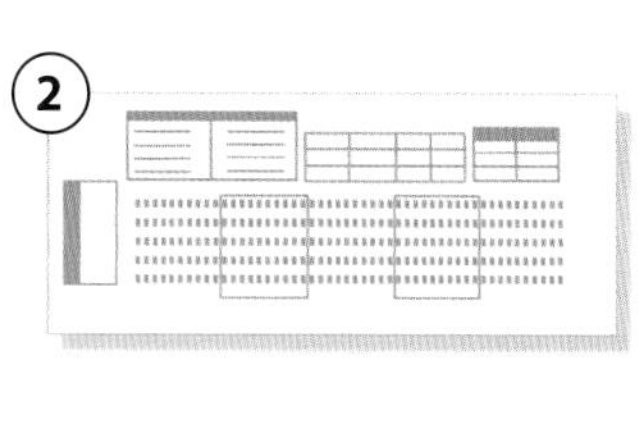

2. answer sheet
解答用紙

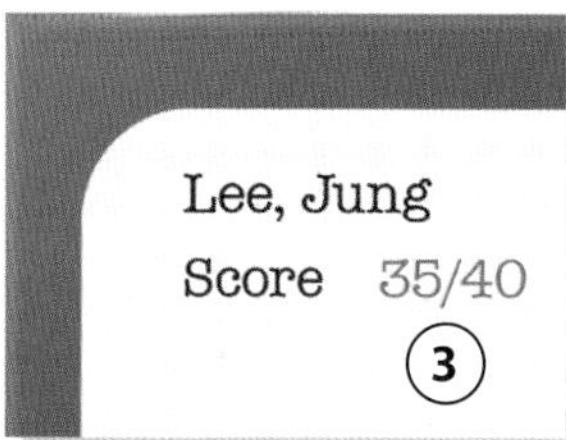

3. score
得点

A	90%-100%	Outstanding
B	80%-89%	Very good
C	70%-79%	Satisfactory
D	60%-69%	Barely passing
F	0%-59%	Fail

4. grades
成績

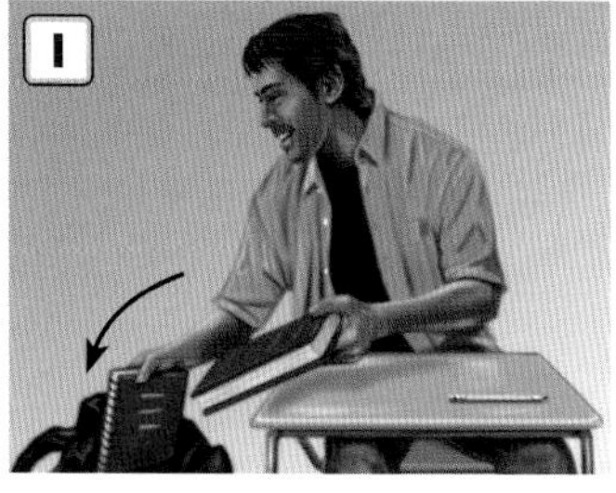

I. **Clear off** your desk.
机の上を**片付ける**

J. **Work** on your own.
自分で**解答する**

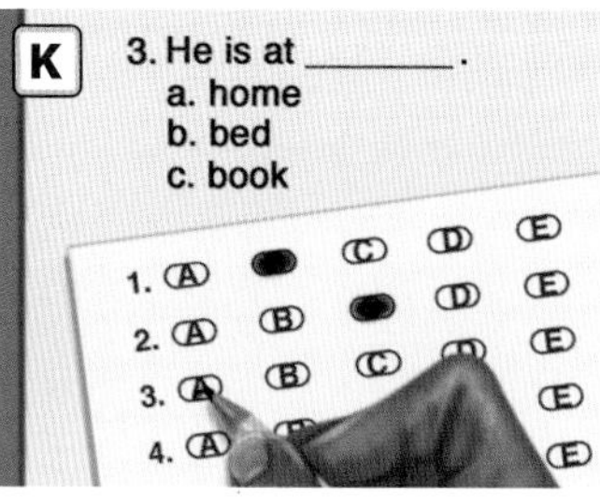

K. **Bubble in** the answer.
解答欄を**塗りつぶす**

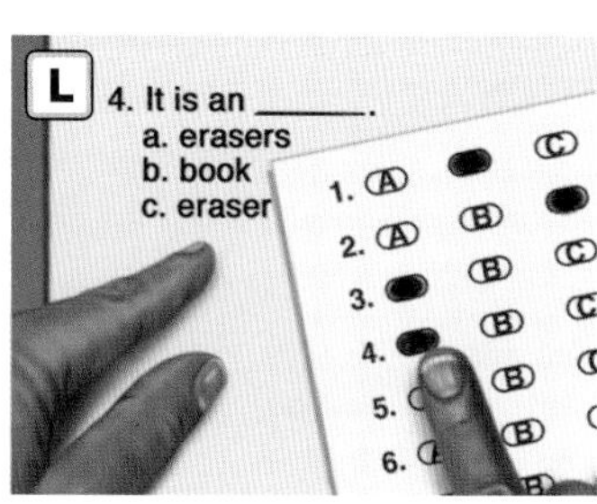

L. **Check** your work.
解答を**確かめる**

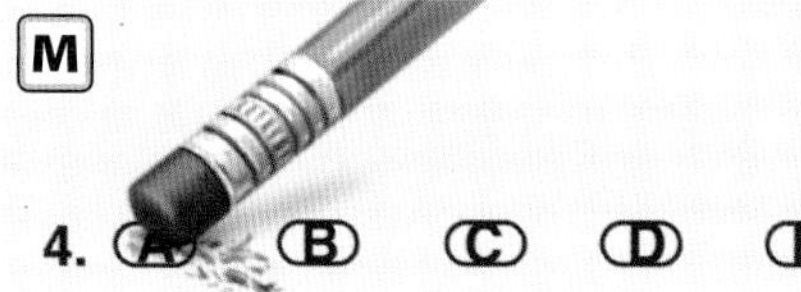

M. **Erase** the mistake.
間違いを**消す**

N. **Correct** the mistake.
間違いを**直す**

O. **Hand in** your test.
テストを**提出する**

学校での1日

A Day at School

A. **Enter** the room.
教室に**入る**

B. **Turn on** the lights.
電気を**つける**

C. **Walk** to class.
教室まで**歩く**

D. **Run** to class.
教室まで**走る**

E. **Lift / Pick up** the books.
本を**持ち上げる**

F. **Carry** the books.
本を**運ぶ**

G. **Deliver** the books.
本を**届ける**

H. **Take** a break.
休憩を**取る**

I. **Eat**.
食べる

J. **Drink**.
飲む

K. **Buy** a snack.
軽食を**買う**

L. **Have** a conversation.
会話を**する**

M. **Go back** to class.
教室に**戻る**

N. **Throw away** trash.
ごみを**捨てる**

O. **Leave** the room.
教室から**出る**

P. **Turn off** the lights.
電気を**消す**

Grammar Point: present continuous

Use **be** + verb + *ing*

*He **is** walk**ing**. They **are** enter**ing**.*

*Note: He is runn**ing**. They are leav**ing**.*

Look at the pictures.

Describe what is happening.

A: *They are <u>entering the room</u>.*

B: *He is <u>walking</u>.*

A. **start** a conversation
会話を始める
B. **make** small talk
雑談する

C. **compliment** someone
誰かをほめる
D. **offer** something
何かを勧める
E. **thank** someone
誰かにお礼を言う

F. **apologize**
あやまる
G. **accept** an apology
謝罪を受け入れる
H. **invite** someone
誰かを招待する
I. **accept** an invitation
招待を受け入れる
J. **decline** an invitation
招待を断る

K. **agree**
同意する
L. **disagree**
反対する
M. **explain** something
説明する
N. **check** your understanding
聞いたことを確認する

More vocabulary

request: to ask for something

accept a compliment: to thank someone for a compliment

Pair practice. Follow the directions.

1. Start a conversation with your partner.
2. Make small talk with your partner.
3. Compliment each other.

Temperature 気温

1. Fahrenheit
華氏
2. Celsius
摂氏
3. hot
暑い
4. warm
暖かい
5. cool
涼しい
6. cold
寒い
7. freezing
凍るように寒い
8. degrees
温度

F C
100° 40°
90° 30°
80°
70° 20°
60°
50° 10°
40°
30° 0°
20° -10°
10°

A Weather Map 天気図

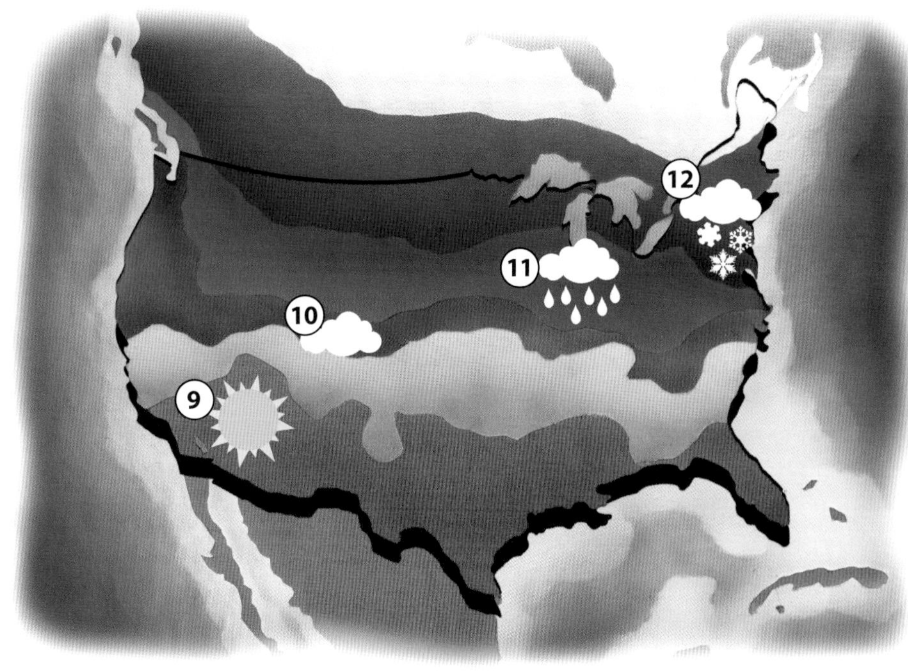

9. sunny / clear
晴れ
10. cloudy
曇り
11. raining
雨
12. snowing
雪

Weather Conditions 気象条件

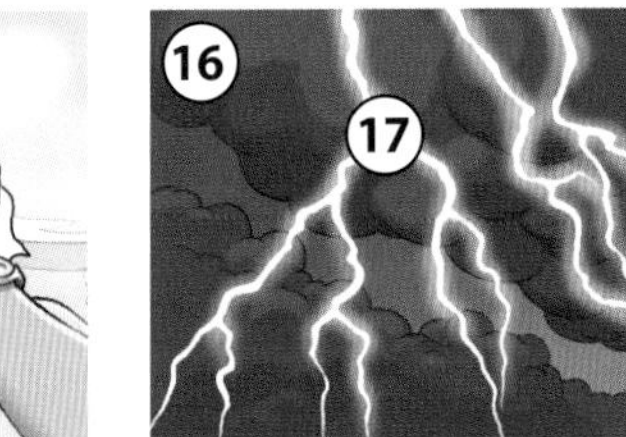

13. heat wave
熱波
14. smoggy
スモッグが出ている
15. humid
湿度が高い
16. thunderstorm
雷雨
17. lightning
稲光り
18. windy
風が強い
19. dust storm
砂塵（さじん）嵐
20. foggy
霧が出ている
21. hailstorm
雹（ひょう）をともなった嵐
22. icy
氷が張っている
23. snowstorm / blizzard
吹雪／猛吹雪

Ways to talk about the weather

It's sunny in Dallas.
What's the temperature?
It's 108. They're having a heat wave.

Pair practice. Make new conversations.

A: *What's the weather like in Chicago?*
B: *It's raining and it's cold. It's 30 degrees.*

PARTS OF A PHONE

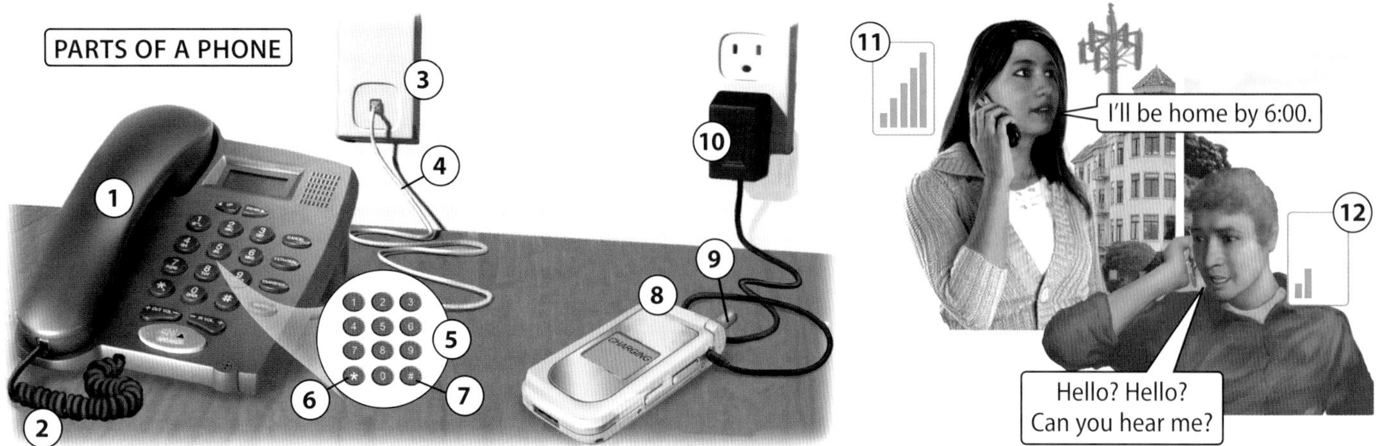

1. receiver / handset
受話器／ハンドセット
2. cord
コード
3. phone jack
電話用ジャック
4. phone line
電話回線コード
5. key pad
キーパッド
6. star key
星印ボタン
7. pound key
シャープボタン
8. cellular phone
携帯電話
9. antenna
アンテナ
10. charger
充電器
11. strong signal
強い信号
12. weak signal
弱い信号

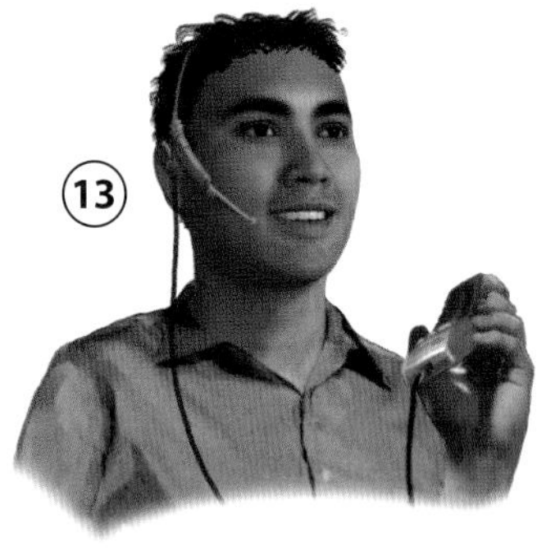

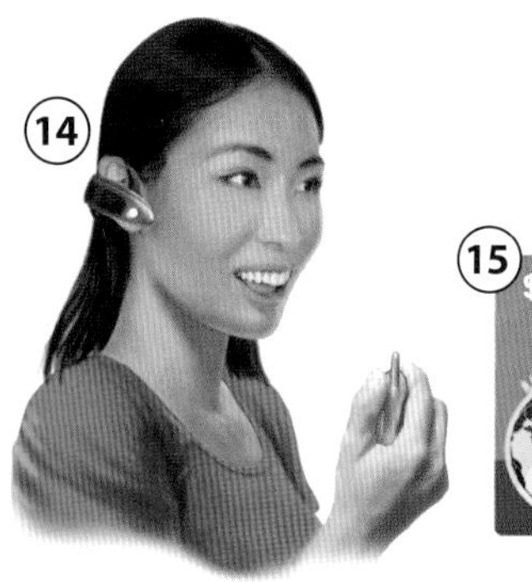

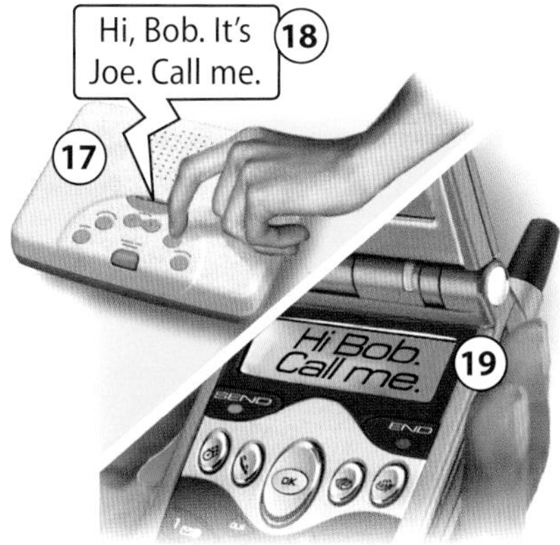

13. headset
ヘッドセット
14. wireless headset
ワイヤレスヘッドセット
15. calling card
テレホンカード
16. access number
アクセス番号
17. answering machine
留守番電話
18. voice message
ボイスメッセージ
19. text message
テキスト（メール）メッセージ

20. Internet phone call
インターネット電話
21. operator
オペレータ
22. directory assistance
番号案内
23. automated phone system
自動電話応答システム

24. cordless phone
コードレス電話

25. pay phone
公衆電話

26. TDD*
聴力障害者用の文字電話

27. smart phone
スマートフォン

Reading a Phone Bill 通話料請求書の読み方

28. phone bill
通話料請求書

29. area code
市外局番

30. phone number
電話番号

31. local call
市内通話

32. long distance call
長距離電話

33. country code
国番号

34. city code
都市コード

35. international call
国際電話

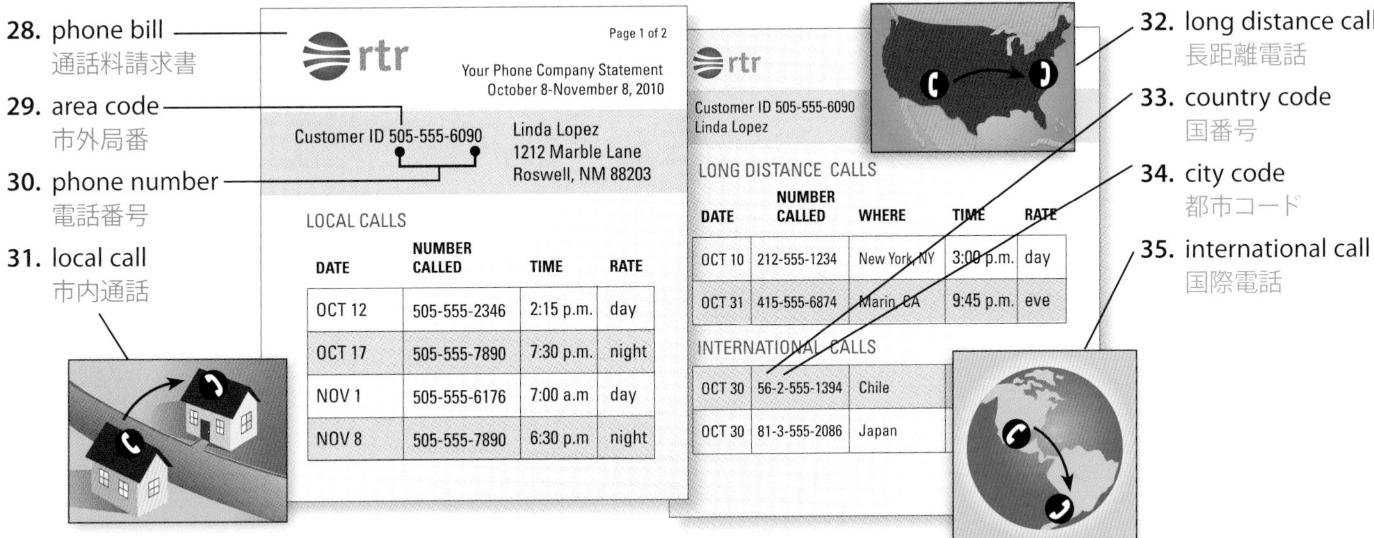

rtr

Page 1 of 2

Your Phone Company Statement
October 8-November 8, 2010

Customer ID 505-555-6090

Linda Lopez
1212 Marble Lane
Roswell, NM 88203

LOCAL CALLS

DATE	NUMBER CALLED	TIME	RATE
OCT 12	505-555-2346	2:15 p.m.	day
OCT 17	505-555-7890	7:30 p.m.	night
NOV 1	505-555-6176	7:00 a.m	day
NOV 8	505-555-7890	6:30 p.m	night

rtr

Customer ID 505-555-6090
Linda Lopez

LONG DISTANCE CALLS

DATE	NUMBER CALLED	WHERE	TIME	RATE
OCT 10	212-555-1234	New York, NY	3:00 p.m.	day
OCT 31	415-555-6874	Marin, CA	9:45 p.m.	eve

INTERNATIONAL CALLS

DATE	NUMBER CALLED	WHERE
OCT 30	56-2-555-1394	Chile
OCT 30	81-3-555-2086	Japan

Making a Phone Call 電話のかけ方

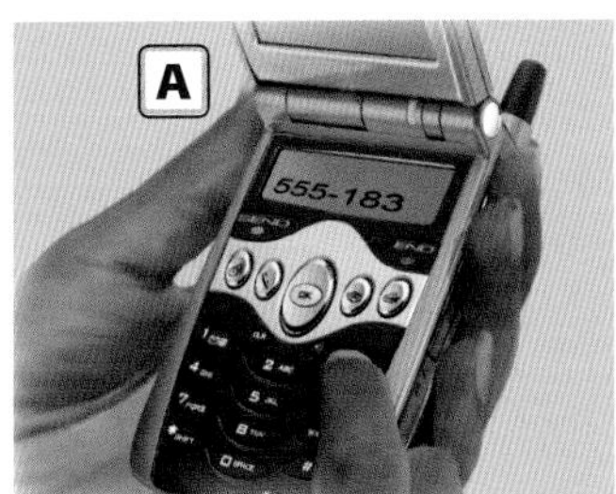

A. **Dial** the phone number.
電話番号を**ダイヤルする**

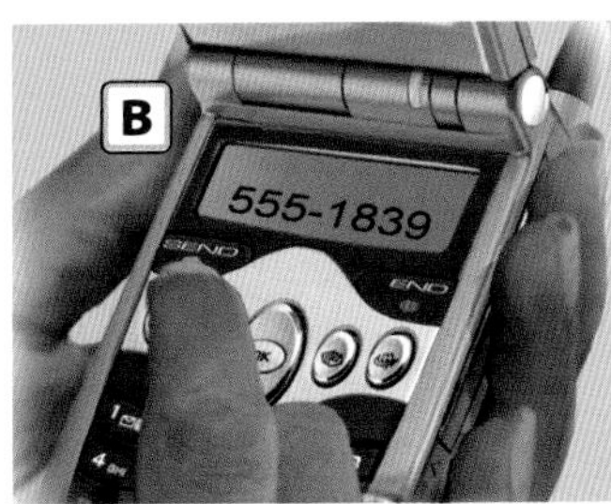

B. **Press** "send".
「通話」を**押す**

C. **Talk** on the phone.
電話で**話す**

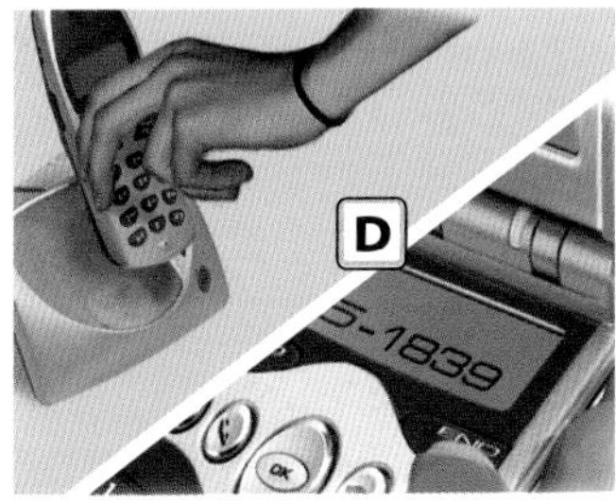

D. **Hang up**. / **Press** "end".
電話を切る／「切」を**押す**

Making an Emergency Call 緊急電話をかける

E. **Dial** 911.
911に**ダイヤルする**

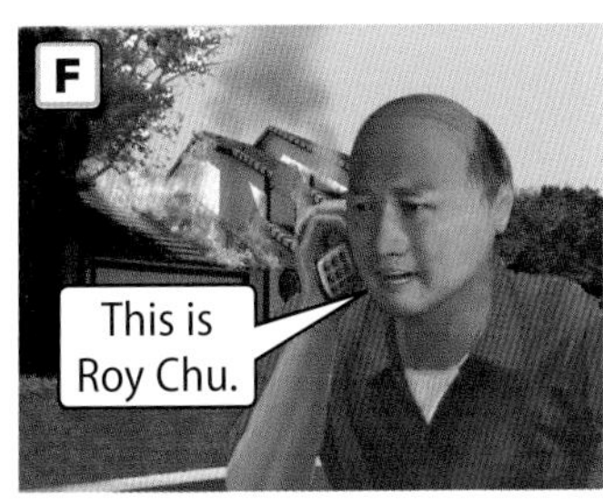

F. **Give** your name.
名前を**名乗る**

G. **State** the emergency.
緊急事態を**説明する**

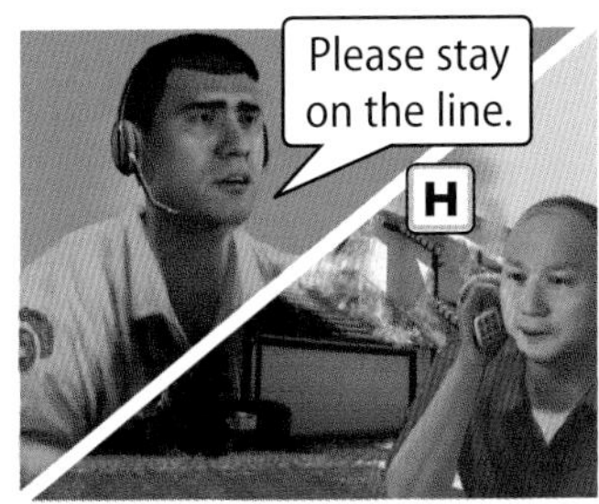

H. **Stay** on the line.
電話を**切らずに待機する**

*telecommunication device for the deaf

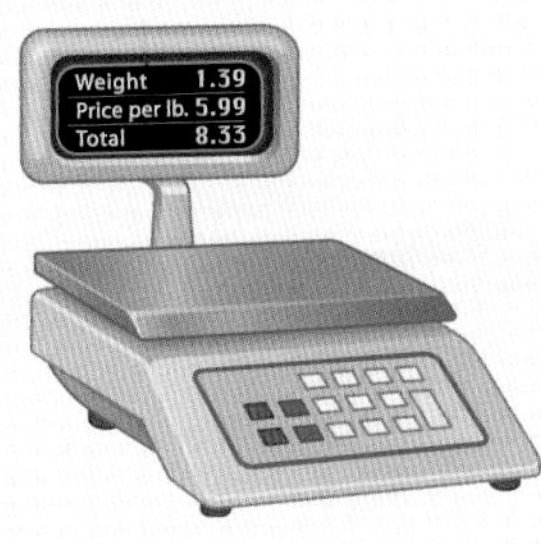

Cardinal Numbers 数字

0	zero ゼロ	20	twenty 二十
1	one 一	21	twenty-one 二十一
2	two 二	22	twenty-two 二十二
3	three 三	23	twenty-three 二十三
4	four 四	24	twenty-four 二十四
5	five 五	25	twenty-five 二十五
6	six 六	30	thirty 三十
7	seven 七	40	forty 四十
8	eight 八	50	fifty 五十
9	nine 九	60	sixty 六十
10	ten 十	70	seventy 七十
11	eleven 十一	80	eighty 八十
12	twelve 十二	90	ninety 九十
13	thirteen 十三	100	one hundred 百
14	fourteen 十四	101	one hundred one 百一
15	fifteen 十五	1,000	one thousand 千
16	sixteen 十六	10,000	ten thousand 一万
17	seventeen 十七	100,000	one hundred thousand 十万
18	eighteen 十八	1,000,000	one million 百万
19	nineteen 十九	1,000,000,000	one billion 十億

Ordinal Numbers 順番

1st	first 一番	16th	sixteenth 十六番
2nd	second 二番	17th	seventeenth 十七番
3rd	third 三番	18th	eighteenth 十八番
4th	fourth 四番	19th	nineteenth 十九番
5th	fifth 五番	20th	twentieth 二十番
6th	sixth 六番	21st	twenty-first 二十一番
7th	seventh 七番	30th	thirtieth 三十番
8th	eighth 八番	40th	fortieth 四十番
9th	ninth 九番	50th	fiftieth 五十番
10th	tenth 十番	60th	sixtieth 六十番
11th	eleventh 十一番	70th	seventieth 七十番
12th	twelfth 十二番	80th	eightieth 八十番
13th	thirteenth 十三番	90th	ninetieth 九十番
14th	fourteenth 十四番	100th	one hundredth 百番
15th	fifteenth 十五番	1,000th	one thousandth 千番

Roman Numerals ローマ数字

I = 1	VII = 7	XXX = 30
II = 2	VIII = 8	XL = 40
III = 3	IX = 9	L = 50
IV = 4	X = 10	C = 100
V = 5	XV = 15	D = 500
VI = 6	XX = 20	M = 1,000

A. **divide**
分割する

B. **calculate**
計算する

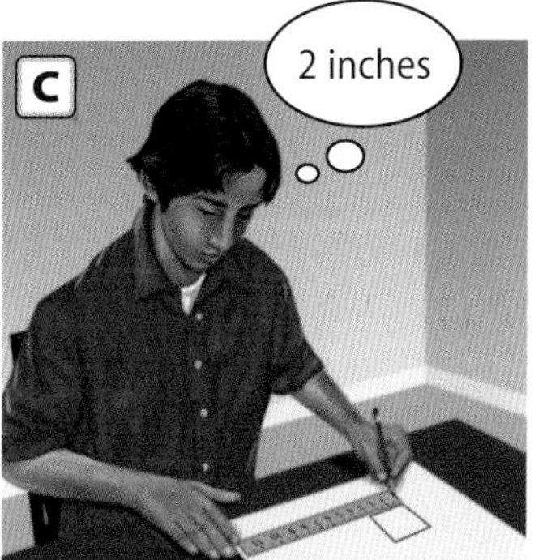

C. **measure**
測定する

D. **convert**
換算する

Fractions and Decimals 分数と小数

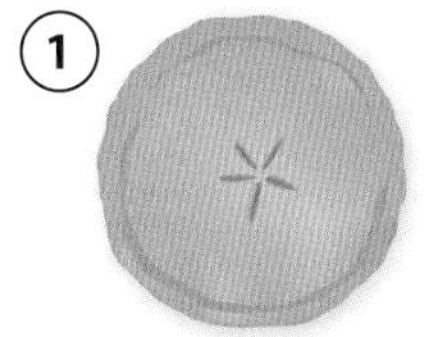

1. one whole
1 = 1.00
全部

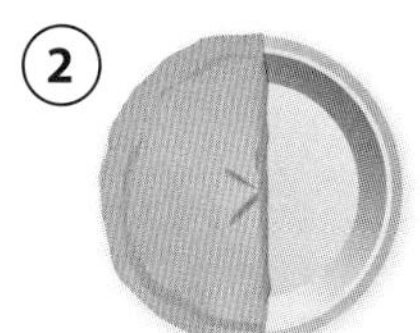

2. one half
1/2 = .5
半分

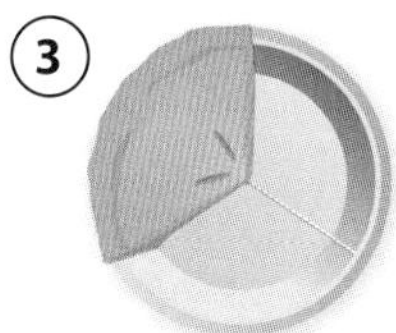

3. one third
1/3 = .333
３分の１

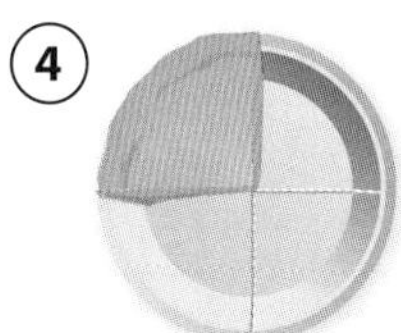

4. one fourth
1/4 = .25
４分の１

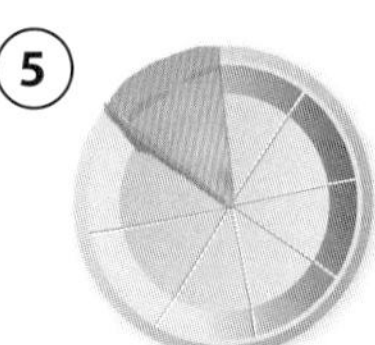

5. one eighth
1/8 = .125
８分の１

Percents パーセント

8	100 percent	100%
9	75 percent	75%
10	50 percent	50%
11	25 percent	25%
12	10 percent	10%

0% 10% 20% 30% 40% 50% 60% 70% 80% 90% 100%

6. calculator
計算機

7. decimal point
小数点

8. 100 percent
100パーセント

9. 75 percent
75パーセント

10. 50 percent
50パーセント

11. 25 percent
25パーセント

12. 10 percent
10パーセント

Measurement 測定

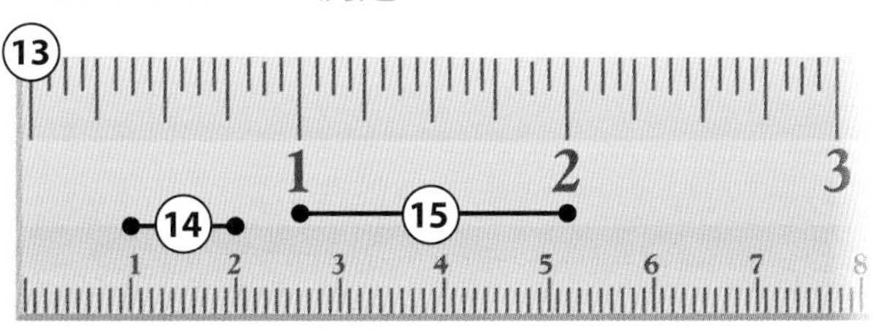

13. ruler
定規

14. centimeter [cm]
センチメートル [cm]

15. inch [in.]
インチ [in.]

Dimensions 寸法

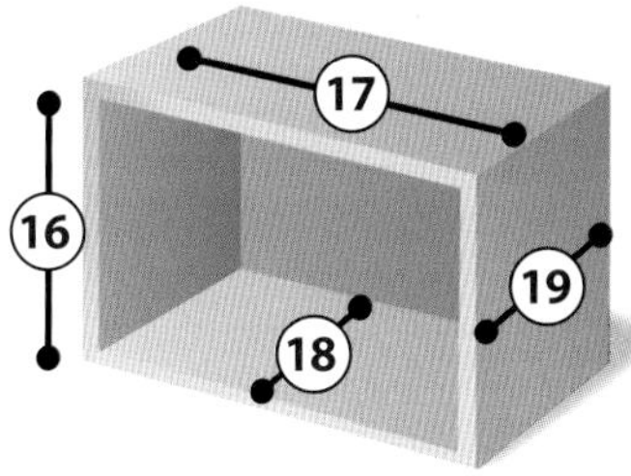

16. height
高さ

17. length
長さ

18. depth
奥行き／深さ

19. width
幅

Equivalencies

12 inches = 1 foot
3 feet = 1 yard
1,760 yards = 1 mile
1 inch = 2.54 centimeters
1 yard = .91 meters
1 mile = 1.6 kilometers

Telling Time 時間を告げる

1. hour 時間

2. minutes 分

3. seconds 秒

4. a.m. 午前

5. p.m. 午後

6. 1:00
one o'clock
1時

7. 1:05
one-oh-five
five after one
1時5分
1時5分すぎ

8. 1:10
one-ten
ten after one
1時10分
1時10分すぎ

9. 1:15
one-fifteen
a quarter after one
1時15分
1時15分すぎ

10. 1:20
one-twenty
twenty after one
1時20分
1時20分すぎ

11. 1:30
one-thirty
half past one
1時30分
1時半

12. 1:40
one-forty
twenty to two
1時40分
2時20分前

13. 1:45
one-forty-five
a quarter to two
1時45分
2時15分前

Times of Day 1日の時間

14. sunrise 日の出

15. morning 朝

16. noon 正午

17. afternoon 午後

18. sunset 日没

19. evening 夕方

20. night 夜

21. midnight 午前零時／真夜中

Ways to talk about time

I wake up at 6:30 a.m.
I wake up at 6:30 in the morning.
I wake up at 6:30.

Pair practice. Make new conversations.

A: *What time do you wake up on weekdays?*
B: *At 6:30 a.m. How about you?*
A: *I wake up at 7:00.*

22. early
早い

23. on time
時間通り

24. late
遅い

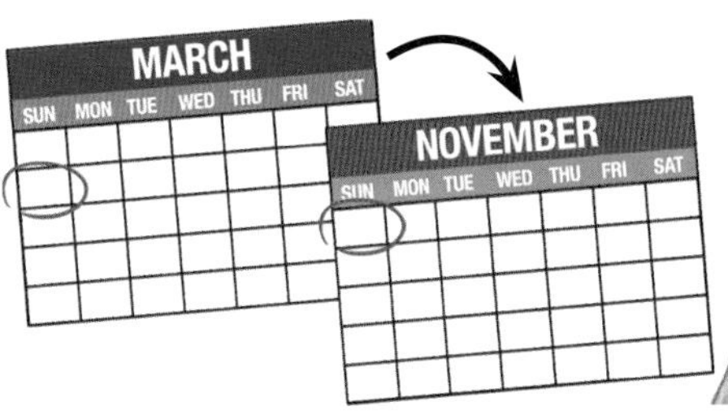

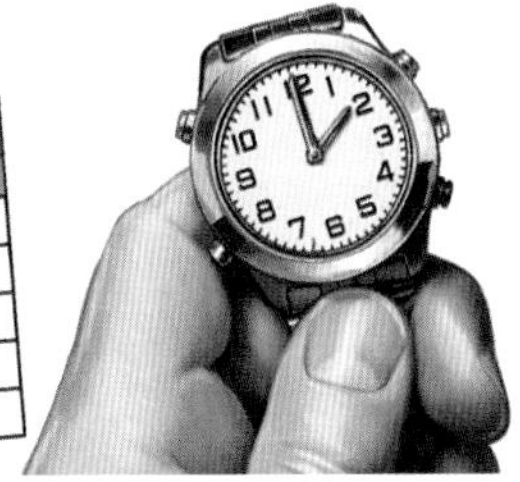

25. daylight saving time
夏時間

26. standard time
標準時

Time Zones タイムゾーン

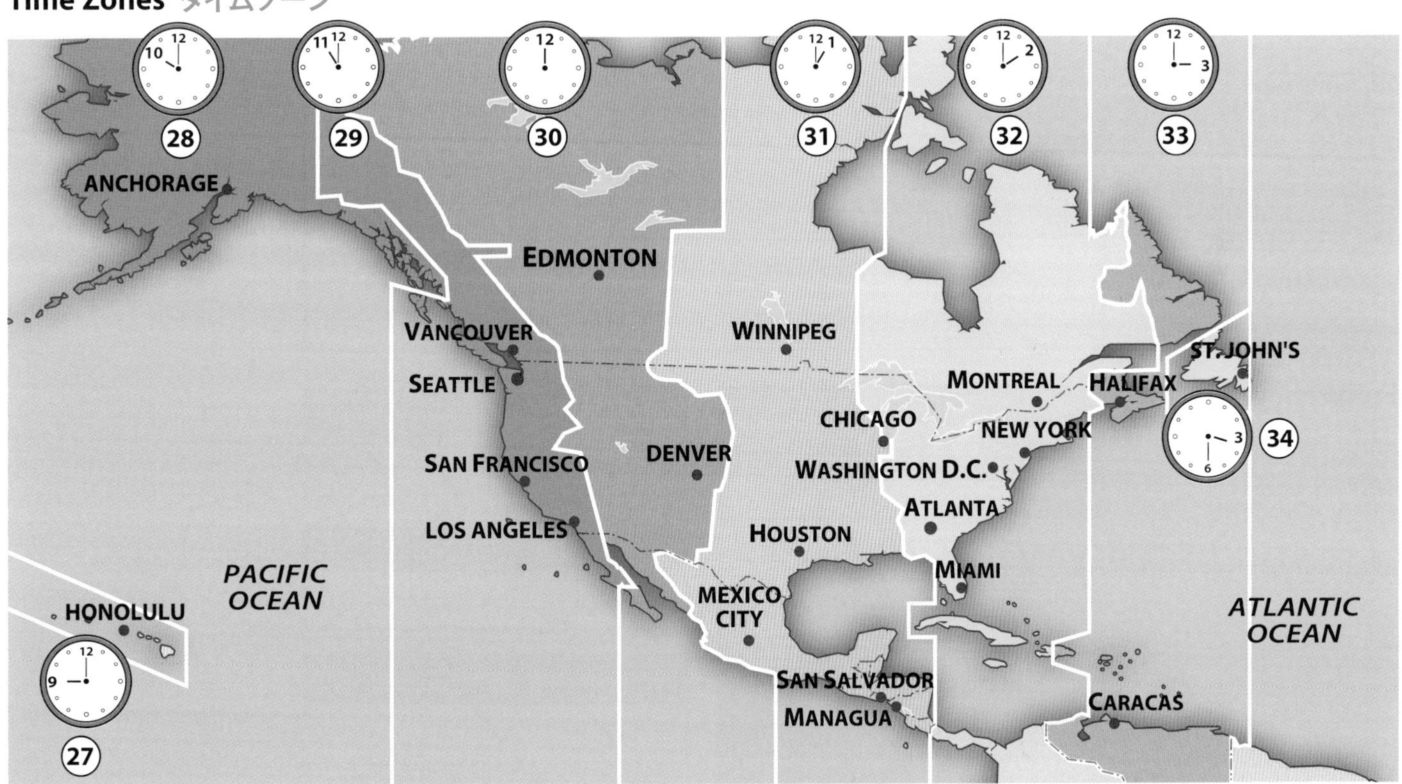

27. Hawaii-Aleutian time
ハワイ・アリューシャン時間

28. Alaska time
アラスカ時間

29. Pacific time
太平洋時間

30. Mountain time
山岳時間

31. Central time
中部時間

32. Eastern time
東部時間

33. Atlantic time
大西洋時間

34. Newfoundland time
ニューファンドランド時間

Ask your classmates. Share the answers.

1. When do you watch television? study? relax?
2. Do you like to stay up after midnight?
3. Do you like to wake up late on weekends?

Think about it. Discuss.

1. What is your favorite time of day? Why?
2. Do you think daylight saving time is a good idea? Why or why not?

1. date
日付
2. day
曜日
3. month
月
4. year
年

5. today
今日
6. tomorrow
明日
7. yesterday
昨日

Days of the Week
曜日

8. Sunday
日曜日
9. Monday
月曜日
10. Tuesday
火曜日
11. Wednesday
水曜日
12. Thursday
木曜日
13. Friday
金曜日
14. Saturday
土曜日

MAY

8 SUN	9 MON	10 TUE	11 WED	12 THU	13 FRI	14 SAT
1	2	3	4 (15)	5	6	7
8	9	10	11 (16)	12	13	14
15	16	17	18	19	20	21 (17)
22	23	24	25	26	27	28
29	30	31				

15. week
週
16. weekdays
平日
17. weekend
週末

Frequency
頻度

18. last week
先週
19. this week
今週
20. next week
来週

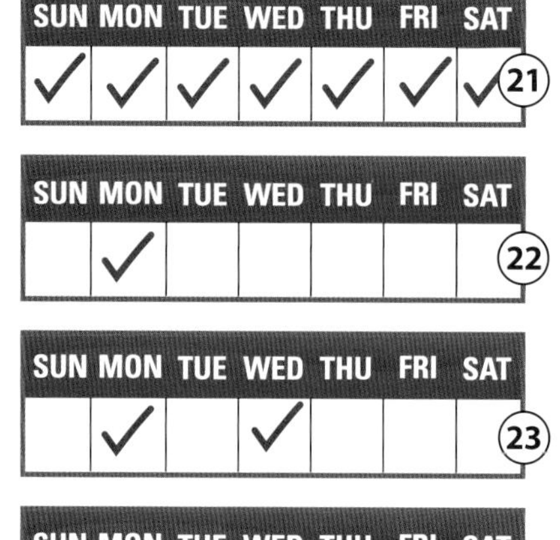

21. every day / daily
毎日
22. once a week
週1度
23. twice a week
週2度
24. three times a week
週3度

Ways to say the date

Today is *May 10th*. *It's the* *tenth*.
Yesterday was *May 9th*.
The party is on *May 21st*.

Pair practice. Make new conversations.

A: *The test is on Friday, June 14th.*
B: *Did you say Friday, the fourteenth?*
A: *Yes, the fourteenth.*

カレンダー

The Calendar

25 JAN

SUN	MON	TUE	WED	THU	FRI	SAT
					1	2
3	4	5	6	7	8	9
10	11	12	13	14	15	16
17	18	19	20	21	22	23
24/31	25	26	27	28	29	30

26 FEB

SUN	MON	TUE	WED	THU	FRI	SAT
	1	2	3	4	5	6
7	8	9	10	11	12	13
14	15	16	17	18	19	20
21	22	23	24	25	26	27
28						

27 MAR

SUN	MON	TUE	WED	THU	FRI	SAT
	1	2	3	4	5	6
7	8	9	10	11	12	13
14	15	16	17	18	19	20
21	22	23	24	25	26	27
28	29	30	31			

28 APR

SUN	MON	TUE	WED	THU	FRI	SAT
				1	2	3
4	5	6	7	8	9	10
11	12	13	14	15	16	17
18	19	20	21	22	23	24
25	26	27	28	29	30	

29 MAY

SUN	MON	TUE	WED	THU	FRI	SAT
						1
2	3	4	5	6	7	8
9	10	11	12	13	14	15
16	17	18	19	20	21	22
23/30	24/31	25	26	27	28	29

30 JUN

SUN	MON	TUE	WED	THU	FRI	SAT
		1	2	3	4	5
6	7	8	9	10	11	12
13	14	15	16	17	18	19
20	21	22	23	24	25	26
27	28	29	30			

31 JUL

SUN	MON	TUE	WED	THU	FRI	SAT
				1	2	3
4	5	6	7	8	9	10
11	12	13	14	15	16	17
18	19	20	21	22	23	24
25	26	27	28	29	30	31

32 AUG

SUN	MON	TUE	WED	THU	FRI	SAT
1	2	3	4	5	6	7
8	9	10	11	12	13	14
15	16	17	18	19	20	21
22	23	24	25	26	27	28
29	30	31				

33 SEP

SUN	MON	TUE	WED	THU	FRI	SAT
			1	2	3	4
5	6	7	8	9	10	11
12	13	14	15	16	17	18
19	20	21	22	23	24	25
26	27	28	29	30		

34 OCT

SUN	MON	TUE	WED	THU	FRI	SAT
					1	2
3	4	5	6	7	8	9
10	11	12	13	14	15	16
17	18	19	20	21	22	23
24/31	25	26	27	28	29	30

35 NOV

SUN	MON	TUE	WED	THU	FRI	SAT
	1	2	3	4	5	6
7	8	9	10	11	12	13
14	15	16	17	18	19	20
21	22	23	24	25	26	27
28	29	30				

36 DEC

SUN	MON	TUE	WED	THU	FRI	SAT
			1	2	3	4
5	6	7	8	9	10	11
12	13	14	15	16	17	18
19	20	21	22	23	24	25
26	27	28	29	30	31	

Months of the Year
月

25. January
1月

26. February
2月

27. March
3月

28. April
4月

29. May
5月

30. June
6月

31. July
7月

32. August
8月

33. September
9月

34. October
10月

35. November
11月

36. December
12月

Seasons
季節

37. spring
春

38. summer
夏

39. fall / autumn
秋

40. winter
冬

Dictate to your partner. Take turns.

A: *Write Monday.*
B: *Is it spelled M-o-n-d-a-y?*
A: *Yes, that's right.*

Ask your classmates. Share the answers.

1. What is your favorite day of the week? Why?
2. What is your busiest day of the week? Why?
3. What is your favorite season of the year? Why?

Calendar Events 年間の行事

1. birthday
誕生日

2. wedding
結婚式

3. anniversary
記念日

4. appointment
（医師などの）予約

5. parent-teacher conference
保護者面談

6. vacation
休暇

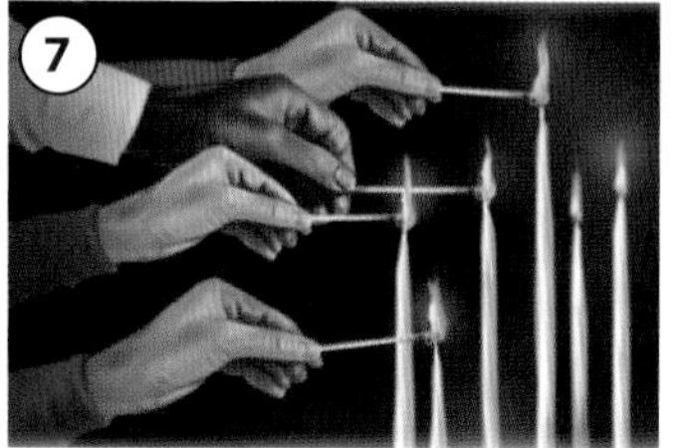

7. religious holiday
宗教上の祭日

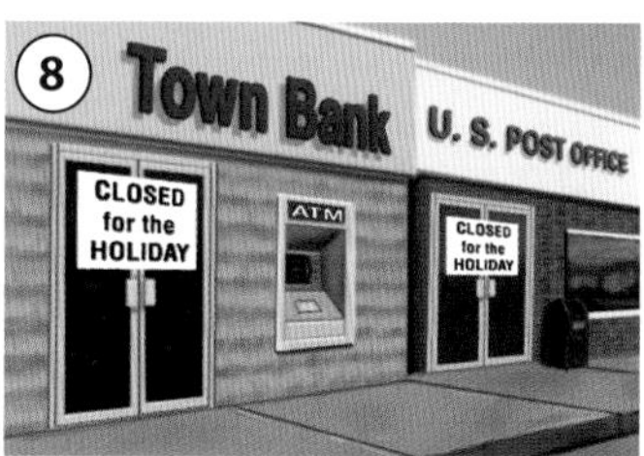

8. legal holiday
法定休日

Legal Holidays 法定休日

9. New Year's Day
元旦
10. Martin Luther King Jr. Day
キング牧師誕生日
11. Presidents' Day
大統領の日
12. Memorial Day
戦没将兵記念日
13. Fourth of July / Independence Day
独立記念日
14. Labor Day
労働者の日
15. Columbus Day
コロンブス記念日
16. Veterans Day
復員軍人の日
17. Thanksgiving
感謝祭
18. Christmas
クリスマス

Pair practice. Make new conversations.

A: *When is your <u>birthday</u>?*
B: *It's on <u>January 31st</u>. How about you?*
A: *It's on <u>December 22nd</u>.*

Ask your classmates. Share the answers.

1. What are the legal holidays in your native country?
2. When is Labor Day in your native country?
3. When do you celebrate the New Year in your native country?

1. **little** hand
   小さい手
2. **big** hand
   大きい手

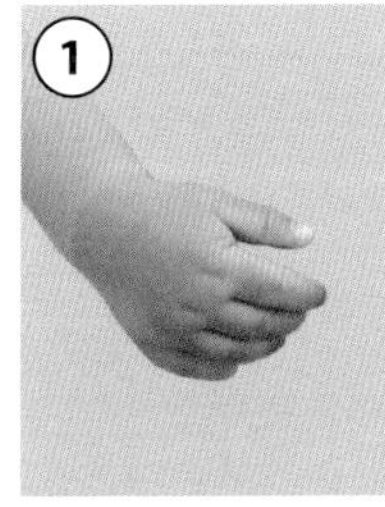
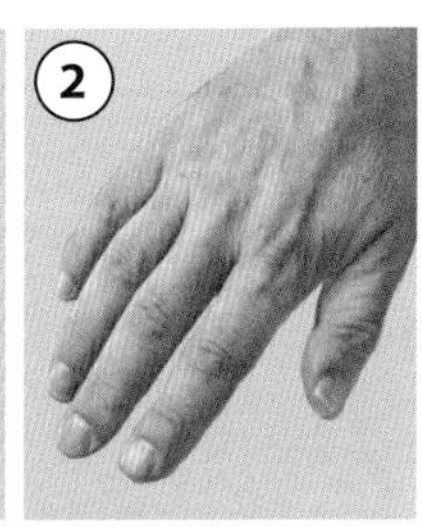
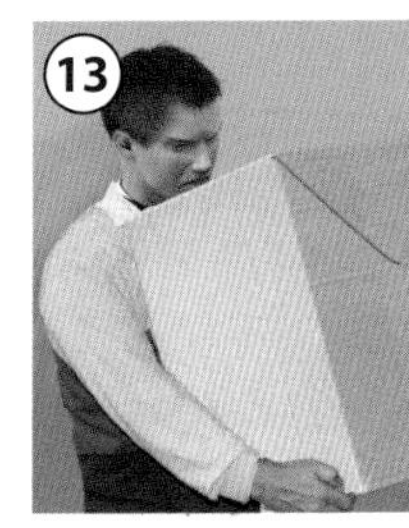

13. **heavy** box
    重い箱
14. **light** box
    軽い箱

3. **fast** driver
   高速で運転する人
4. **slow** driver
   ゆっくり運転する人

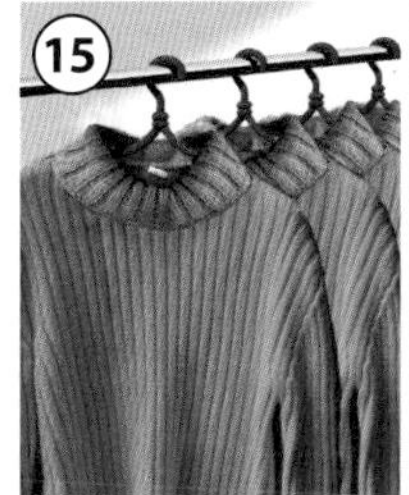

15. **same** color
    同じ色
16. **different** colors
    違う色

5. **hard** chair
   固い椅子
6. **soft** chair
   柔らかい椅子

17. **good** dog
    良い犬
18. **bad** dog
    悪い犬

7. **thick** book
   厚い本
8. **thin** book
   薄い本

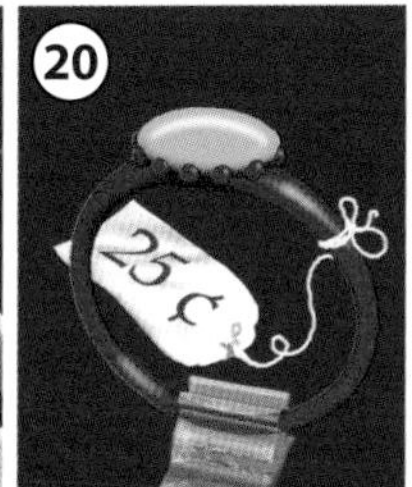

19. **expensive** ring
    高い指輪
20. **cheap** ring
    安い指輪

9. **full** glass
   いっぱいに入ったコップ
10. **empty** glass
    空のコップ

21. **beautiful** view
    美しい眺め
22. **ugly** view
    不快な眺め

11. **noisy** children / **loud** children
    騒がしい子供
12. **quiet** children
    おとなしい子供

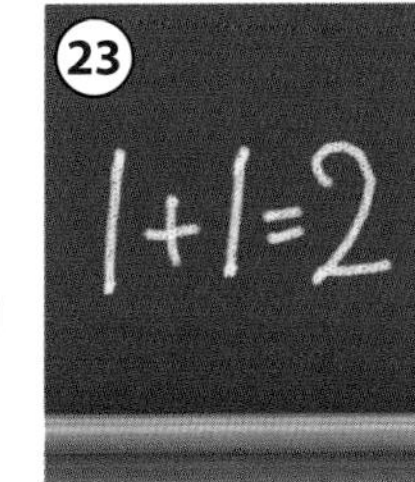

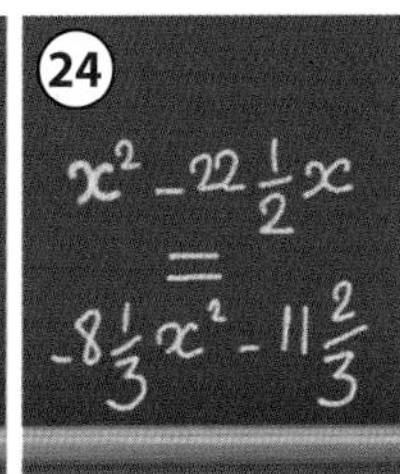

23. **easy** problem
    簡単な問題
24. **difficult** problem / **hard** problem
    難しい問題

Ask your classmates. Share the answers.

1. Are you a slow driver or a fast driver?
2. Do you prefer a hard bed or a soft bed?
3. Do you like loud parties or quiet parties?

Use the new words.

Look at page 150–151. Describe the things you see.

A: *The street* is *hard*.
B: *The truck* is *heavy*.

Colors 

Basic Colors 基本色

1. red
   赤色
2. yellow
   黄色
3. blue
   青色
4. orange
   オレンジ色
5. green
   緑色
6. purple
   紫色
7. pink
   ピンク色
8. violet
   スミレ色
9. turquoise
   青緑色
10. dark blue
    紺色
11. light blue
    水色
12. bright blue
    空色

Neutral Colors 中間色

13. black
    黒色
14. white
    白色
15. gray
    灰色
16. cream / ivory
    クリーム色
17. brown
    茶色
18. beige / tan
    ベージュ色

Ask your classmates. Share the answers.

1. What colors are you wearing today?
2. What colors do you like?
3. Is there a color you don't like? What is it?

Use the new words. Look at pages 86–87.
Take turns naming the colors you see.

A: *His shirt is* *blue*.
B: *Her shoes are* *white*.

Prepositions

1. The yellow sweaters are **on the left**.
   黄色のセーターは**左側**にあります。
2. The purple sweaters are **in the middle**.
   紫色のセーターは**真ん中**にあります。
3. The brown sweaters are **on the right**.
   茶色のセーターは**右側**にあります。
4. The red sweaters are **above** the blue sweaters.
   赤色のセーターは青色のセーターの**上**にあります。
5. The blue sweaters are **below** the red sweaters.
   青色のセーターは赤色のセーターの**下**にあります。
6. The turquoise sweater is **in** the box.
   青緑色のセーターは箱の**中**にあります。
7. The white sweater is **in front of** the black sweater.
   白色のセーターは黒色のセーターの**前**にあります。
8. The black sweater is **behind** the white sweater.
   黒色のセーターは白色のセーターの**後ろ**にあります。
9. The orange sweater is **on** the gray sweater.
   オレンジ色のセーターは灰色のセーターの**上**にあります。
10. The violet sweater is **next to** the gray sweater.
    スミレ色のセーターは灰色のセーターの**隣**にあります。
11. The gray sweater is **under** the orange sweater.
    灰色のセーターはオレンジ色のセーターの**下**にあります。
12. The green sweater is **between** the pink sweaters.
    緑色のセーターはピンク色のセーターの**間**にあります。

More vocabulary

near: in the same area
far from: not near

Role play. Make new conversations.

A: *Excuse me. Where are the red sweaters?*
B: *They're on the left, above the blue sweaters.*
A: *Thanks very much.*

Coins 硬貨

1. $.01 = 1¢
   a penny / 1 cent
   ペニー／1セント
2. $.05 = 5¢
   a nickel / 5 cents
   ニッケル／5セント
3. $.10 = 10¢
   a dime / 10 cents
   ダイム／10セント
4. $.25 = 25¢
   a quarter / 25 cents
   クォーター／25セント
5. $.50 = 50¢
   a half dollar
   50セント
6. $1.00
   a dollar coin
   1ドル硬貨

Bills 紙幣

7. $1.00
   a dollar
   1ドル
8. $5.00
   five dollars
   5ドル
9. $10.00
   ten dollars
   10ドル

10. $20.00
    twenty dollars
    20ドル
11. $50.00
    fifty dollars
    50ドル
12. $100.00
    one hundred dollars
    100ドル

A. **Get** change.
お釣りを**もらう**

B. **Borrow** money.
お金を**借りる**

C. **Lend** money.
お金を**貸す**

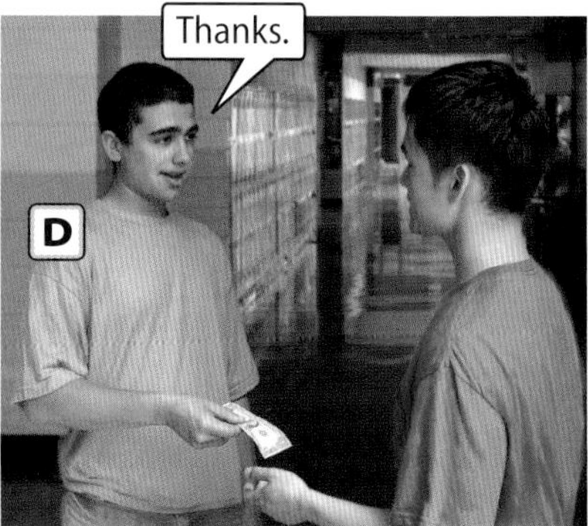

D. **Pay back** the money.
お金を**返す**

Pair practice. Make new conversations.

A: *Do you have change for a dollar?*
B: *Sure. How about two quarters and five dimes?*
A: *Perfect!*

Think about it. Discuss.

1. Is it a good idea to lend money to a friend? Why or why not?
2. Is it better to carry a dollar or four quarters? Why?
3. Do you prefer dollar coins or dollar bills? Why?

Ways to Pay 支払方法

A. **pay** cash
現金で**払う**

B. **use** a credit card
クレジットカードを**使う**

C. **use** a debit card
デビットカードを**使う**

D. **write** a (personal) check
（個人用）小切手を**書く**

E. **use** a gift card
ギフトカードを**使う**

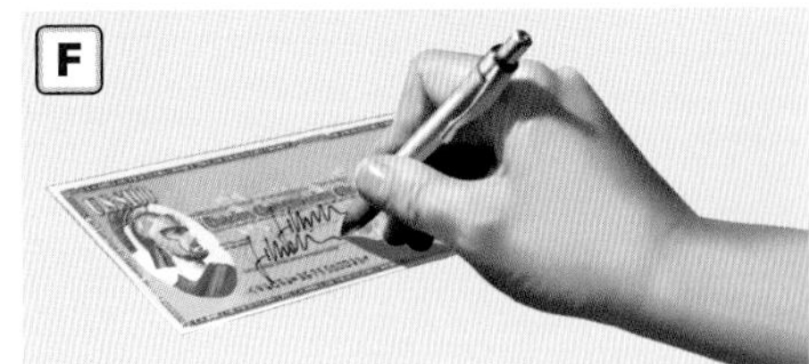

F. **cash** a traveler's check
トラベラーズチェックを**換金する**

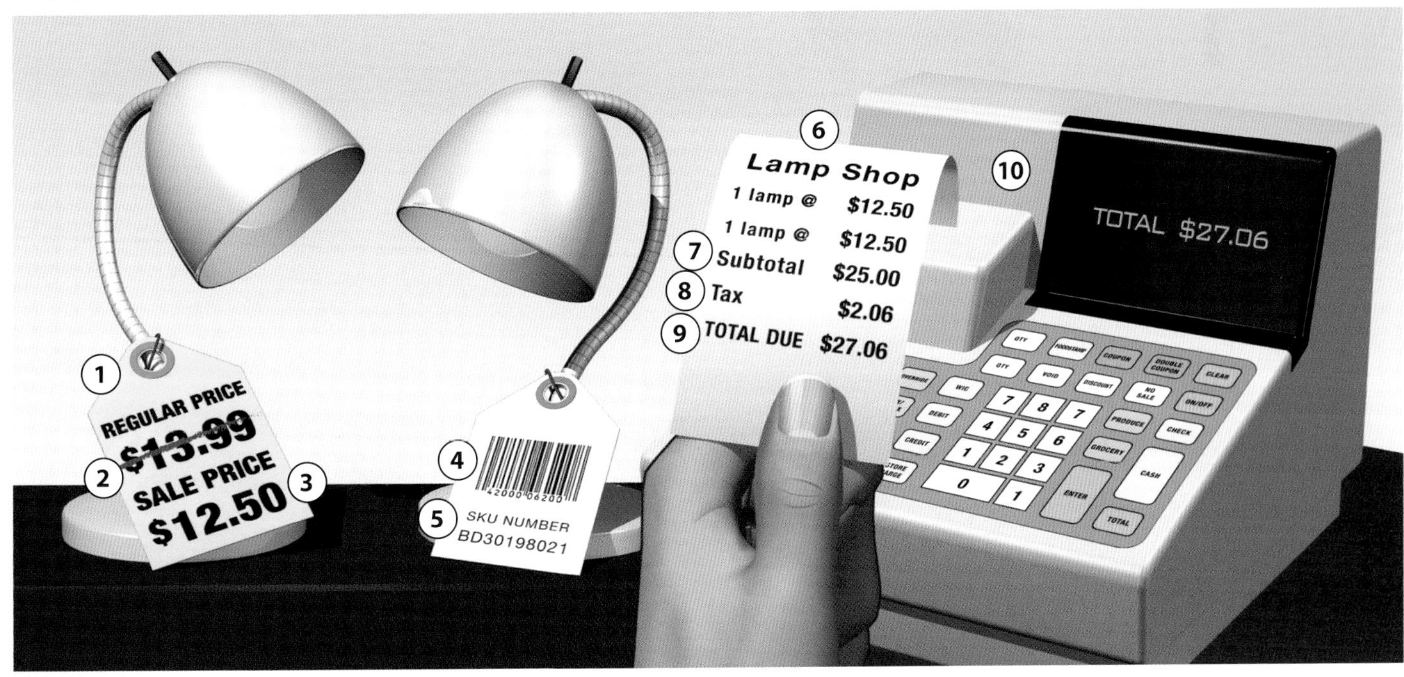

1. price tag
値札
2. regular price
定価
3. sale price
セール価格
4. bar code
バーコード
5. SKU number
SKU（在庫管理）番号
6. receipt
領収書／レシート
7. price / cost
値段／コスト
8. sales tax
売上税
9. total
合計
10. cash register
レジ

G. **buy / pay for**
買う／～の**代金を払う**

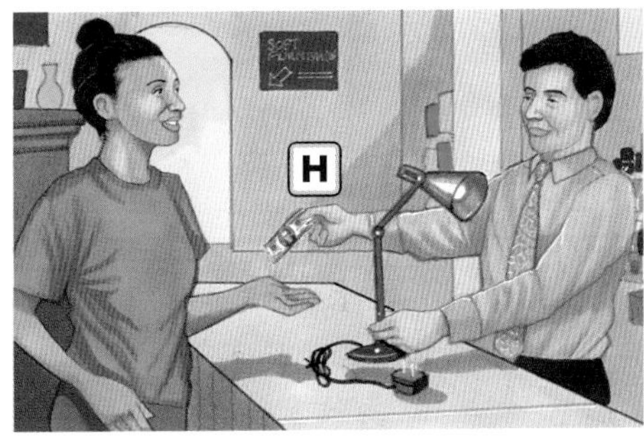

H. **return**
返品する

I. **exchange**
取り替える

Same and Different 相似と相違

1. twins
双子
2. sweater
セーター
3. matching
おそろい
4. disappointed
がっかりする
5. navy blue
紺色
6. happy
幸せな

A. **shop**
買い物をする
B. **keep**
とっておく

Look at the pictures.
What do you see?

Answer the questions.

1. Who is the woman shopping for?
2. Does she buy matching sweaters or different sweaters?
3. How does Anya feel about her green sweater? What does she do?
4. What does Manda do with her sweater?

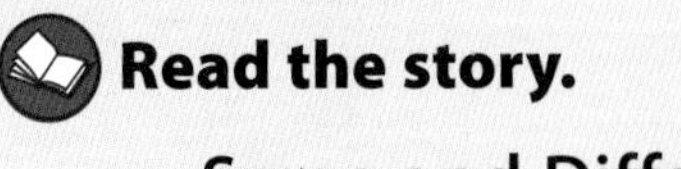

Read the story.

Same and Different

Mrs. Kumar likes to shop for her twins. Today she's looking at sweaters. There are many different colors on sale. Mrs. Kumar chooses two matching green sweaters.

The next day, Manda and Anya open their gifts. Manda likes the green sweater, but Anya is disappointed. Mrs. Kumar understands the problem. Anya wants to be different.

Manda keeps her sweater. But Anya goes to the store. She exchanges her green sweater for a navy blue sweater. It's an easy answer to Anya's problem. Now the twins can be warm, happy, and different.

Think about it.

1. Do you like to shop for other people? Why or why not?
2. Imagine you are Anya. Would you keep the sweater or exchange it? Why?

Adults and Children 大人と子供

1. man
   男性
2. woman
   女性
3. women
   複数の女性
4. men
   複数の男性
5. senior citizen
   高齢者

Listen and point. Take turns.

A: *Point to a* *woman.*
B: *Point to a* *senior citizen.*
A: *Point to an* *infant.*

Dictate to your partner. Take turns.

A: *Write* *woman.*
B: *Is that spelled* *w-o-m-a-n?*
A: *Yes, that's right,* *woman.*

6. infant
乳児
7. baby
赤ちゃん
8. toddler
幼児
9. 6-year-old boy
6歳の少年
10. 10-year-old girl
10歳の少女
11. teenager / teen
ティーンエージャー

Ways to talk about age

1 month – 3 months old = **infant**
18 months – 3 years old = **toddler**
3 years old – 12 years old = **child**
13 – 19 years old = **teenager**
18+ years old = **adult**
62+ years old = **senior citizen**

Pair practice. Make new conversations.

A: *How old is Sandra?*
B: *She's thirteen years old.*
A: *Wow, she's a teenager now!*

Describing People 人の特徴

Age 年齢

1. young
   若い
2. middle-aged
   中年の
3. elderly
   高齢の

Height 身長

4. tall
   背が高い
5. average height
   平均的な身長
6. short
   背が低い

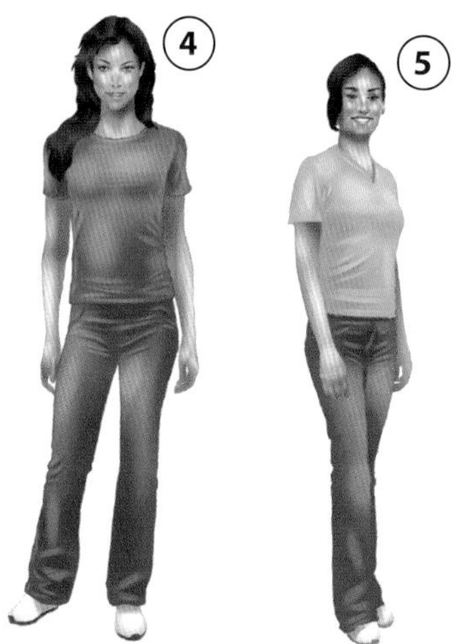

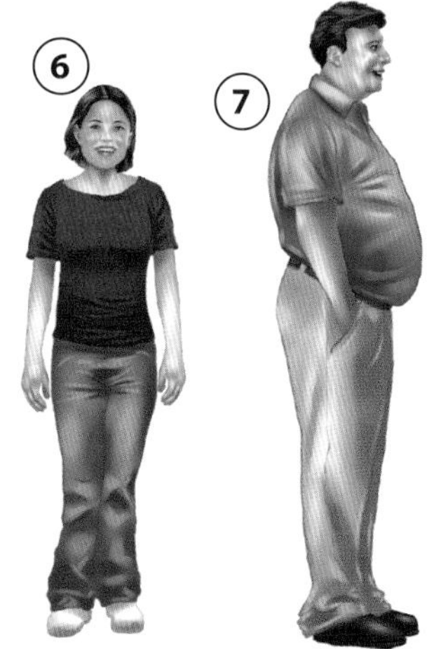

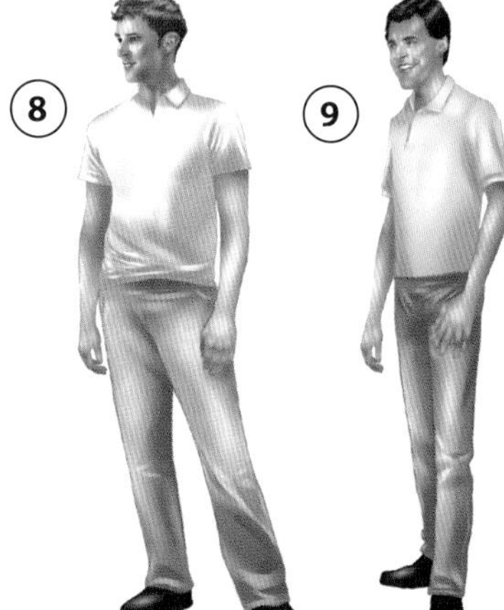

Weight 体重

7. heavy / fat
   太っている
8. average weight
   平均的な体重
9. thin / slender
   やせている

Disabilities 障害

10. physically challenged
    身体障害の
11. sight impaired / blind
    視力障害／目が見えない
12. hearing impaired / deaf
    聴力障害／耳が聞こえない

Appearance 外見

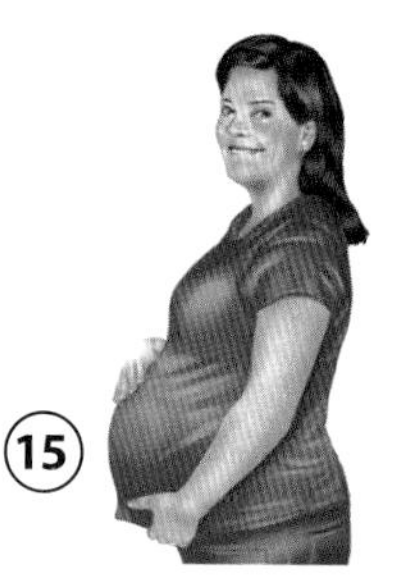

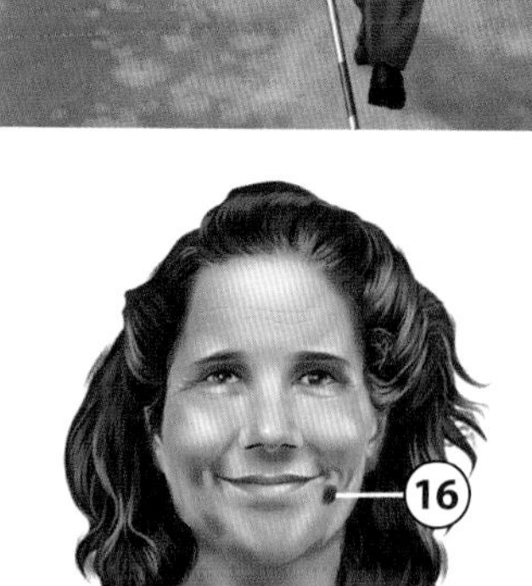

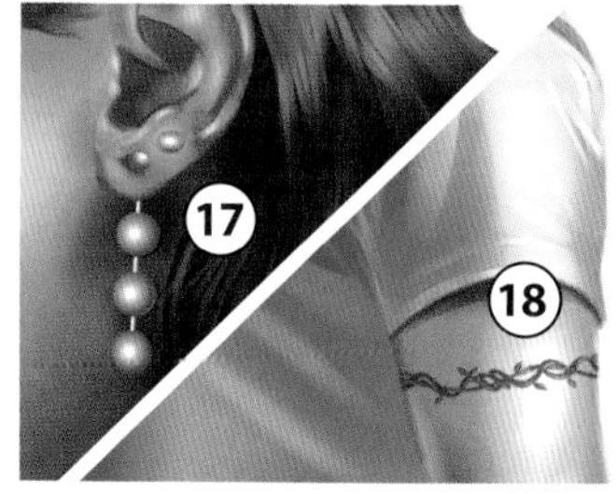

13. attractive
    すてきな
14. cute
    かわいい
15. pregnant
    妊娠している
16. mole
    ほくろ
17. pierced ear
    ピアスをした耳
18. tattoo
    刺青

Ways to describe people

He's a heavy, young man.
She's a pregnant woman with a mole.
He's sight impaired.

Use the new words. Look at pages 2–3.
Describe the people and point. Take turns.

A: *He's a tall, thin, middle-aged man.*
B: *She's a short, average-weight young woman.*

髪型の特徴 Describing Hair

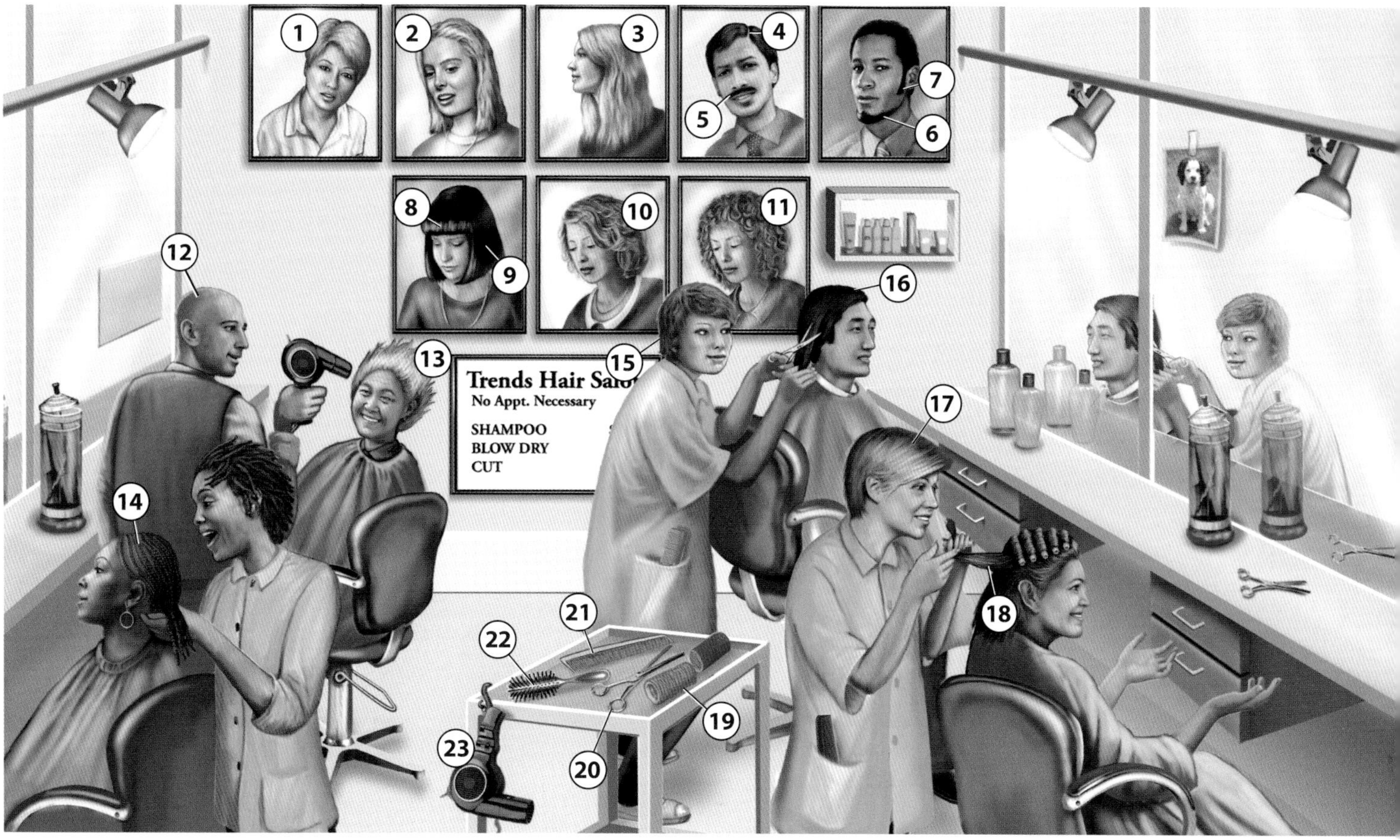

1. short hair
   短髪
2. shoulder-length hair
   肩までの髪
3. long hair
   長髪
4. part
   髪を分ける
5. mustache
   口ひげ
6. beard
   あごひげ
7. sideburns
   もみあげ
8. bangs
   前髪
9. straight hair
   直毛
10. wavy hair
    ウェーブした髪
11. curly hair
    巻毛
12. bald
    はげ
13. gray hair
    白髪
14. corn rows
    コーンロウ（細く編み上げた髪型）
15. red hair
    赤毛
16. black hair
    黒髪
17. blond hair
    金髪
18. brown hair
    茶髪
19. rollers
    カーラー
20. scissors
    はさみ
21. comb
    くし
22. brush
    ブラシ
23. blow dryer
    ヘアドライヤー

Style Hair 髪のスタイリング

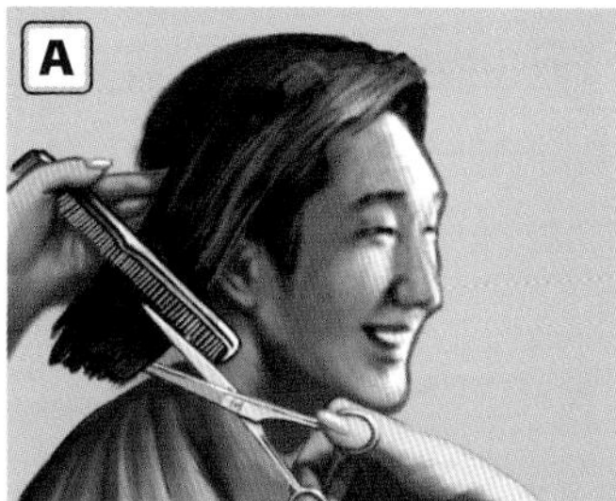

A. **cut** hair
髪を切る

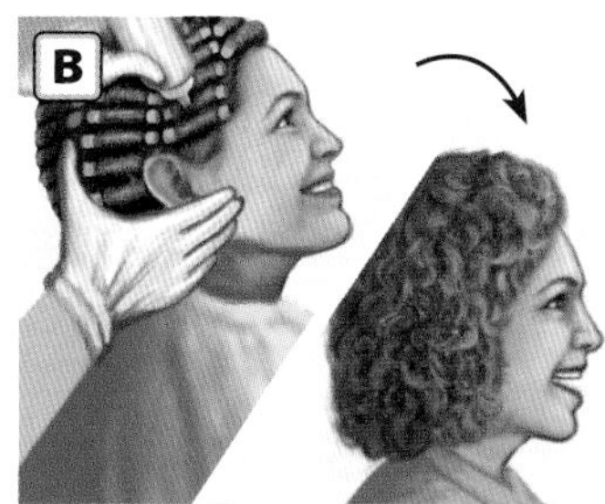

B. **perm** hair
パーマをかける

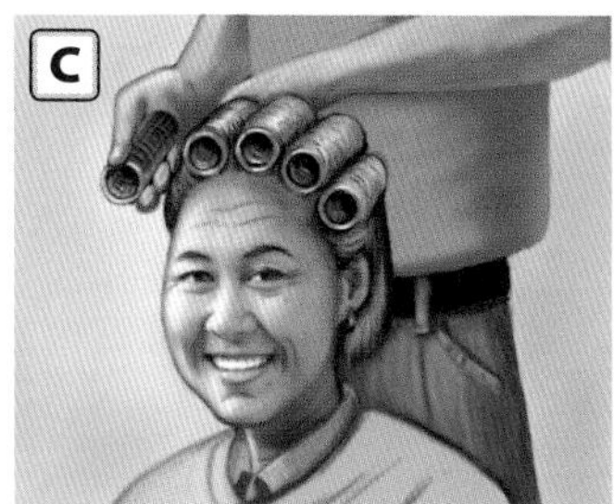

C. **set** hair
髪をセットする

D. **color** hair / **dye** hair
髪を染める

Ways to talk about hair

Describe hair in this order: length, style, and then color.
She has long, straight, brown hair.

Role play. Talk to a stylist.

A: *I need a new hairstyle.*
B: *How about short and straight?*
A: *Great. Do you think I should dye it?*

1. grandmother
祖母
2. grandfather
祖父
3. mother
母親
4. father
父親
5. sister
姉／妹
6. brother
兄／弟
7. aunt
伯母／叔母
8. uncle
伯父／叔父
9. cousin
いとこ

10. mother-in-law
義母
11. father-in-law
義父
12. wife
妻
13. husband
夫
14. daughter
娘
15. son
息子
16. sister-in-law
義理の姉妹
17. brother-in-law
義理の兄弟
18. niece
姪
19. nephew
甥

More vocabulary

Tim is Min and Lu's **grandson**.
Lily and Emily are Min and Lu's **granddaughters**.
Alex is Min's youngest **grandchild**.

Ana is Tito's **wife**.
Ana is Eva and Sam's **daughter-in-law**.
Carlos is Eva and Sam's **son-in-law**.

20. married couple
夫婦
21. divorced couple
離婚した夫婦
22. single mother
シングルマザー
23. single father
シングルファーザー

Lisa Green's Family

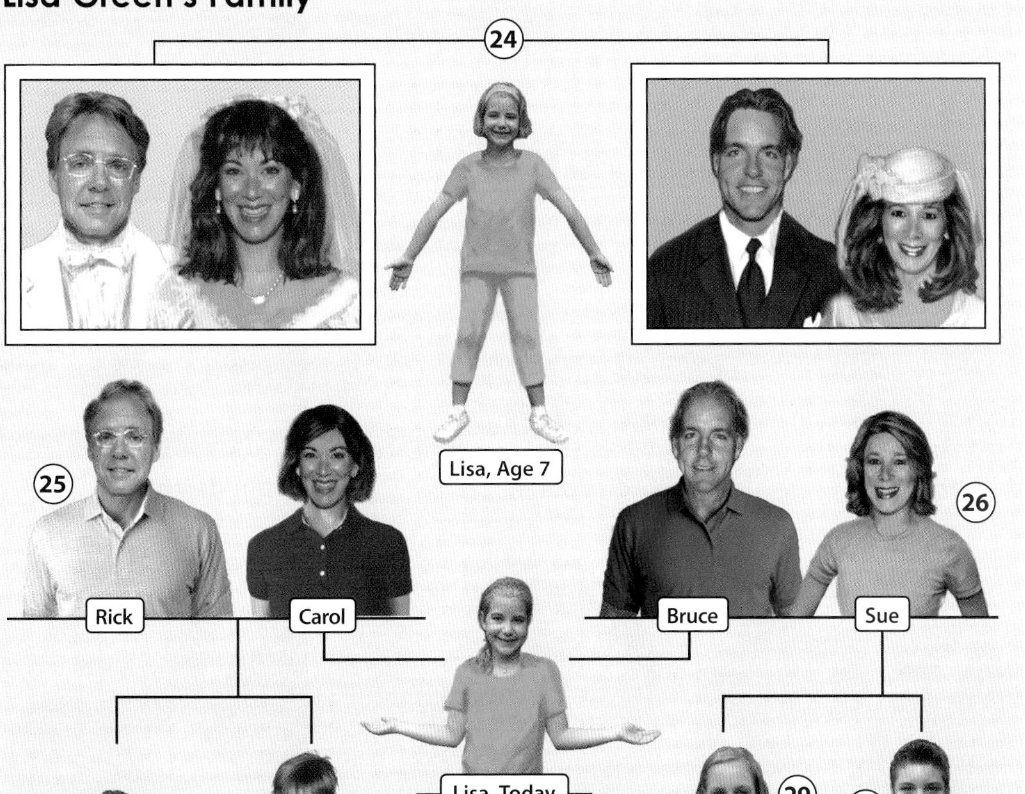

24. remarried
再婚
25. stepfather
継父
26. stepmother
継母
27. half sister
異母(異父)姉妹
28. half brother
異母(異父)兄弟
29. stepsister
継姉妹
30. stepbrother
継兄弟

More vocabulary

Bruce is Carol's **former husband** or **ex-husband**.
Carol is Bruce's **former wife** or **ex-wife**.
Lisa is the **stepdaughter** of both Rick and Sue.

Look at the pictures.

Name the people.

A: *Who is Lisa's half sister?*
B: *Mary is. Who is Lisa's stepsister?*

Childcare and Parenting

保育と育児

A. **hold**
抱く

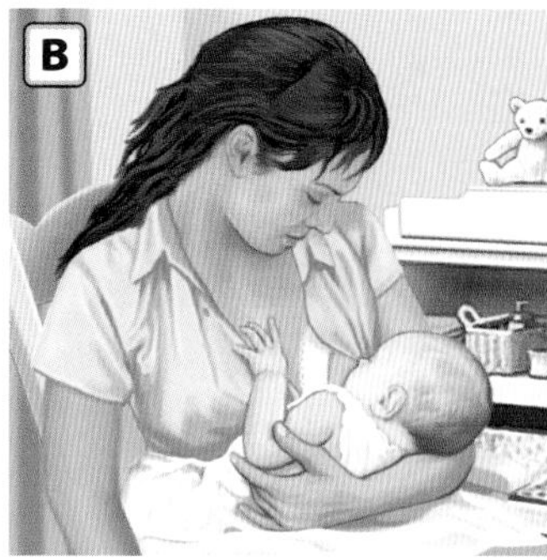

B. **nurse**
授乳する

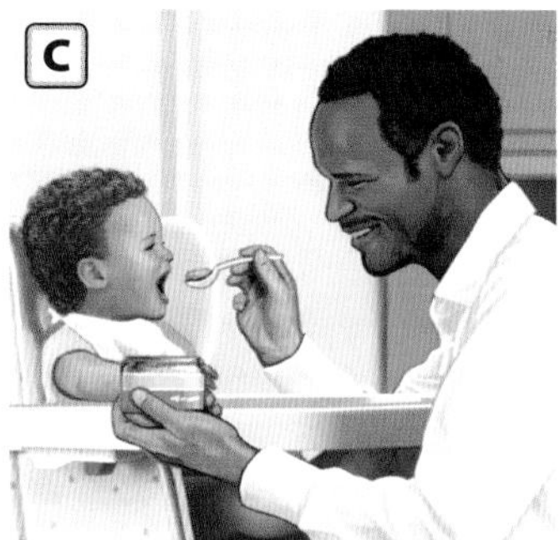

C. **feed**
食事を与える

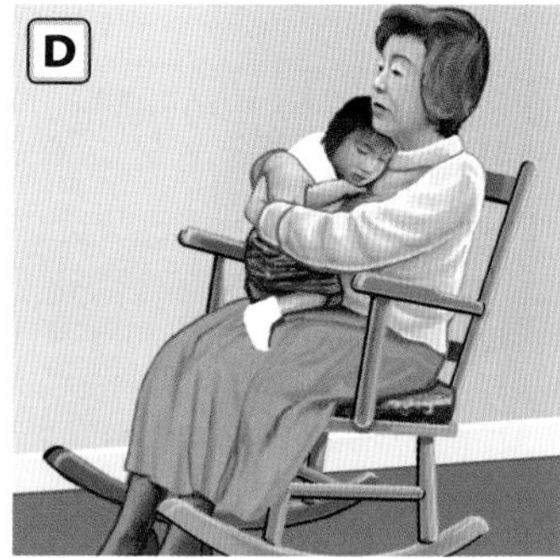

D. **rock**
揺する

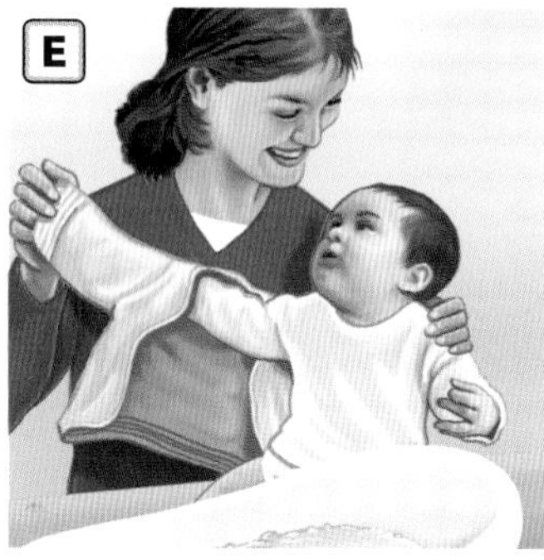

E. **undress**
服を脱がせる

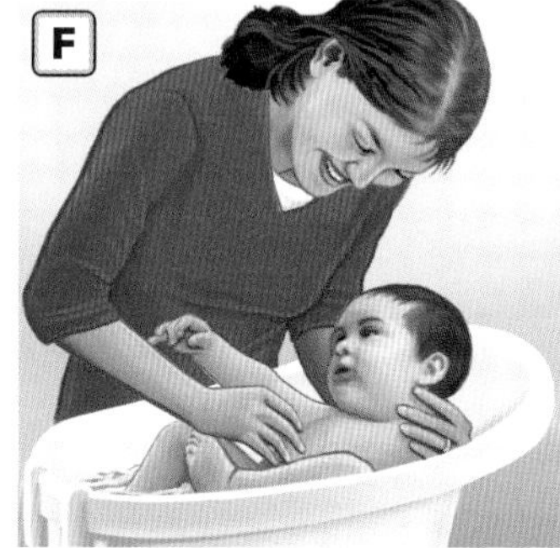

F. **bathe**
入浴させる

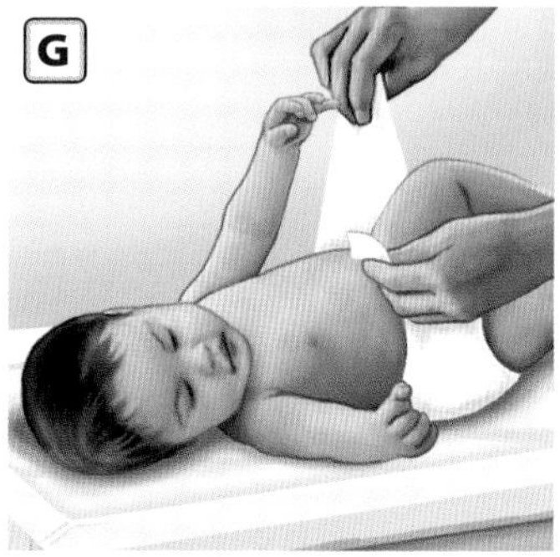

G. **change** a diaper
おむつを替える

H. **dress**
服を着せる

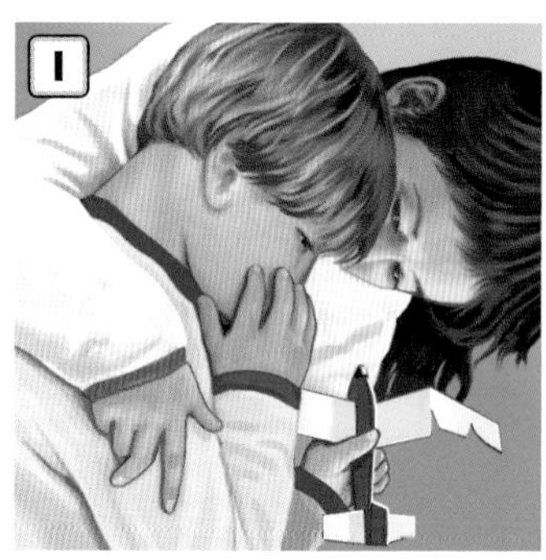

I. **comfort**
なだめる

J. **praise**
ほめる

K. **discipline**
しつける

L. **buckle up**
シートベルトを締める

M. **play** with
一緒に遊ぶ

N. **read** to
本を読み聞かせる

O. **sing** a lullaby
子守唄を歌う

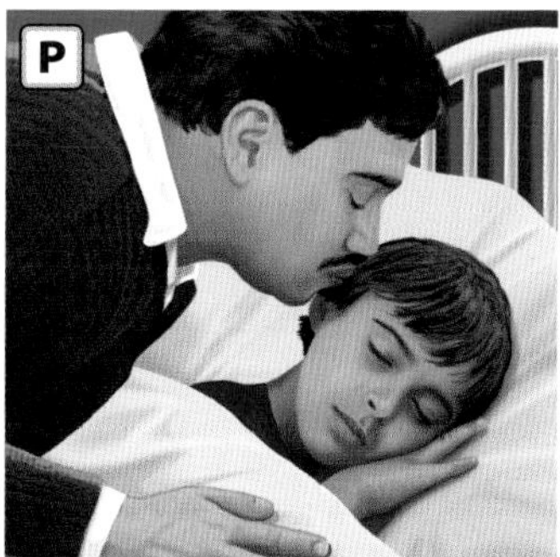

P. **kiss** goodnight
おやすみのキスをする

Look at the pictures.
Describe what is happening.

A: *She's changing her baby's diaper.*
B: *He's kissing his son goodnight.*

Ask your classmates. Share the answers.

1. Do you like to take care of children?
2. Do you prefer to read to children or play with them?
3. Can you sing a lullaby? Which one?

Childcare and Parenting

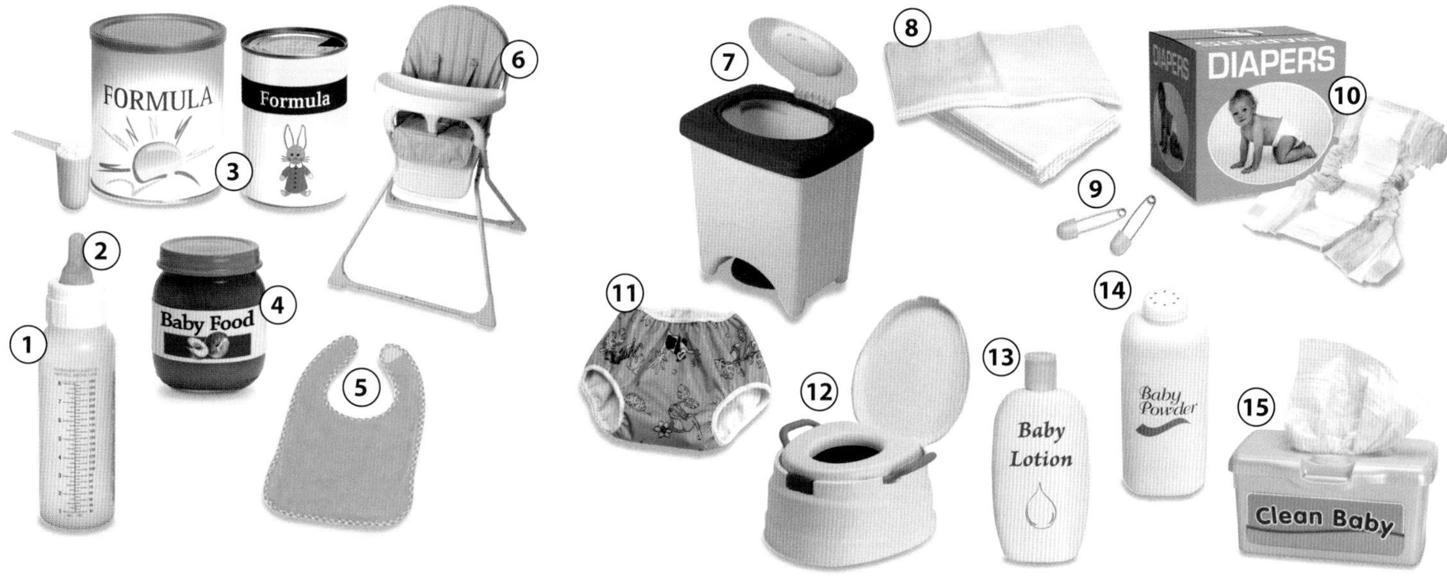

1. bottle
哺乳びん
2. nipple
(哺乳びんの)乳首
3. formula
授乳用ミルク
4. baby food
ベビーフード
5. bib
よだれかけ
6. high chair
ベビーチェア／ハイチェア
7. diaper pail
使用済みおむつ入れ
8. cloth diaper
布おむつ
9. safety pins
安全ピン
10. disposable diaper
紙おむつ
11. training pants
おむつ外しトレーニング用パンツ
12. potty seat
おまる
13. baby lotion
ベビーローション
14. baby powder
ベビーパウダー
15. wipes
おしり拭き

16. baby bag
ベビーバッグ
17. baby carrier
ベビーキャリア
18. stroller
ベビーカー
19. car safety seat
チャイルドシート
20. carriage
乳母車
21. rocking chair
揺り椅子
22. nursery rhymes
童謡
23. teddy bear
テディベア
24. pacifier
おしゃぶり
25. teething ring
歯固めリング
26. rattle
がらがら
27. night light
常夜灯

Dictate to your partner. Take turns.

A: *Write pacifier.*
B: *Was that pacifier, p-a-c-i-f-i-e-r?*
A: *Yes, that's right.*

Think about it. Discuss.

1. How can parents discipline toddlers? teens?
2. What are some things you can say to praise a child?
3. Why are nursery rhymes important for young children?

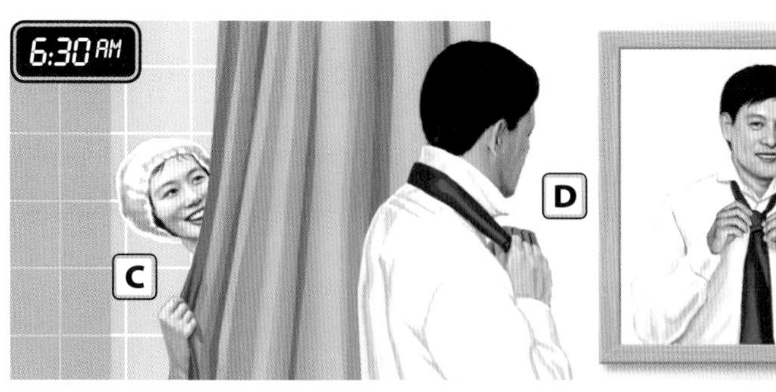

A. **wake up**
目を覚ます

B. **get up**
起きる

C. **take** a shower
シャワーを浴びる

D. **get dressed**
服を着る

E. **eat** breakfast
朝食を食べる

F. **make** lunch
お弁当を作る

G. **take** the children to school / **drop off** the kids
子供を学校に連れていく／学校まで車で連れていく

H. **take** the bus to school
バスに乗って学校に行く

I. **drive** to work / **go** to work
車で通勤する／通勤する

J. **go** to class
授業に行く

K. **work**
働く

L. **go** to the grocery store
スーパーに行く

M. **pick up** the kids
子供を学校に迎えにいく

N. **leave** work
会社を出る

Grammar Point: third person singular

For ***he*** and ***she***, add **-s** or **-es** to the verb:

*He wake**s** up.*	*He watch**es** TV.*
*He get**s** up.*	*She go**es** to the store.*

These verbs are different (irregular):

Be: *She **is** in school at 10:00 a.m.*

Have: *He **has** dinner at 6:30 p.m.*

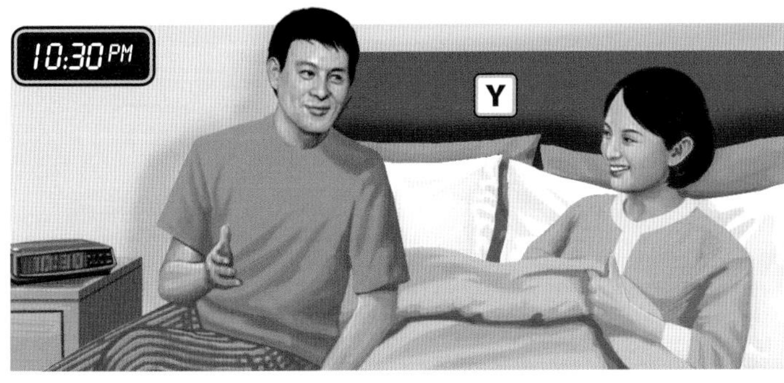

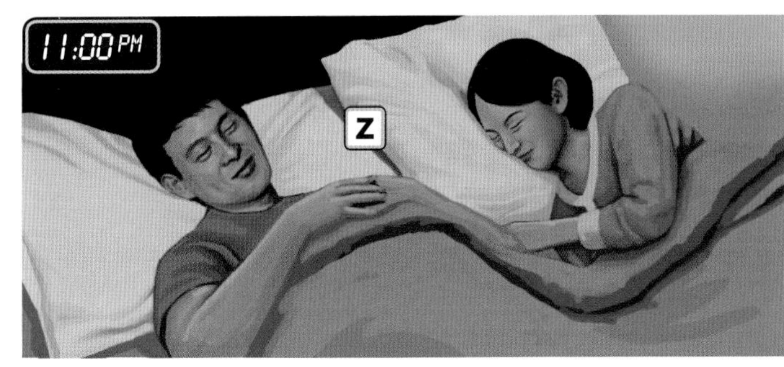

O. **clean** the house
家の掃除をする

P. **exercise**
運動する

Q. **cook** dinner / **make** dinner
夕飯を作る

R. **come** home / **get** home
家に帰る

S. **have** dinner / **eat** dinner
夕食を食べる

T. **do** homework
宿題をする

U. **relax**
くつろぐ

V. **read** the paper
新聞を読む

W. **check** email
メールをチェックする

X. **watch** TV
テレビを見る

Y. **go** to bed
寝る

Z. **go** to sleep
眠る

Pair practice. Make new conversations.

A: *When does he go to work?*
B: *He goes to work at 8:00 a.m. When does she go to class?*
A: *She goes to class at 10:00 a.m.*

Ask your classmates. Share the answers.

1. Who cooks dinner in your family?
2. Who goes to the grocery store?
3. Who goes to work?

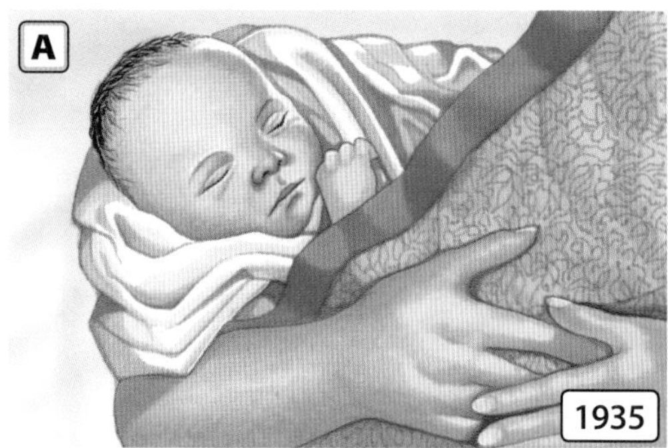

A. **be born**
生まれる

B. **start** school
入学する

C. **immigrate**
移住する

D. **graduate**
卒業する

E. **learn** to drive
車の運転を習う

F. **get** a job
就職する

G. **become** a citizen
米国市民になる

H. **fall in love**
恋をする

1. birth certificate
出生証明書

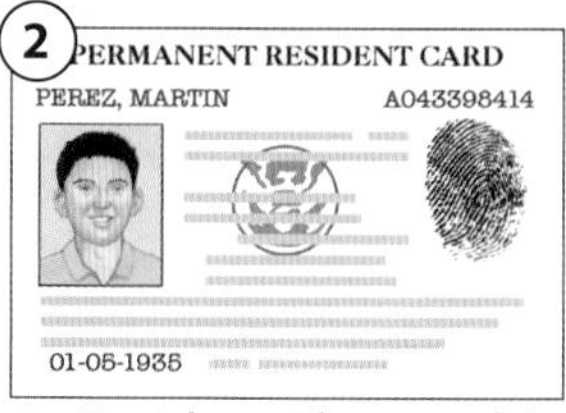

2. Resident Alien card / green card
永住権カード／グリーンカード

3. diploma
卒業証書

4. driver's license
運転免許証

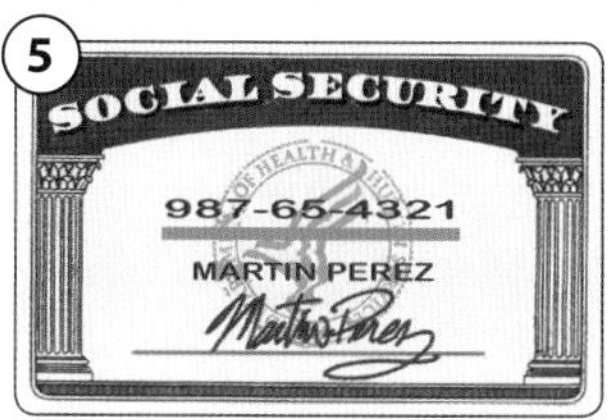

5. Social Security card
社会保障番号証

6. Certificate of Naturalization
市民権獲得証明書

Grammar Point: past tense

start, learn, travel } +ed
immigrate, graduate, retire, die } +d

These verbs are different (irregular):

be – was
get – got
become – became
go – went
have – had
fall – fell
buy – bought

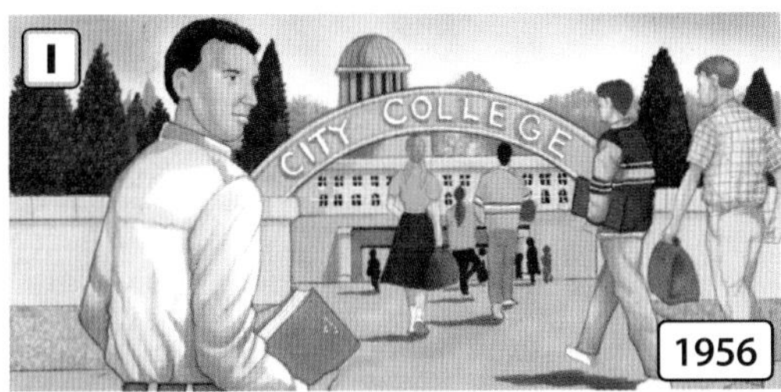

I. **go** to college
大学に進学する

J. **get** engaged
婚約する

7. college degree
大学卒業証書

K. **get** married
結婚する

L. **have** a baby
子どもが生まれる

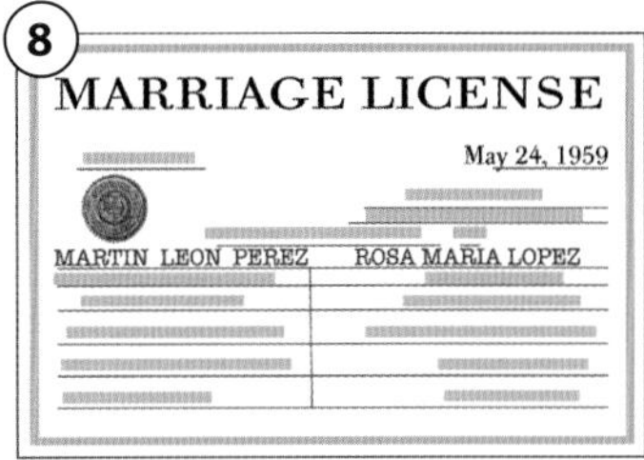

8. marriage license
結婚証明書

M. **buy** a home
家を買う

N. **become** a grandparent
孫が生まれる

9. deed
権利書

O. **retire**
引退する

P. **travel**
旅行する

10. passport
パスポート

Q. **volunteer**
ボランティア活動をする

R. **die**
死ぬ

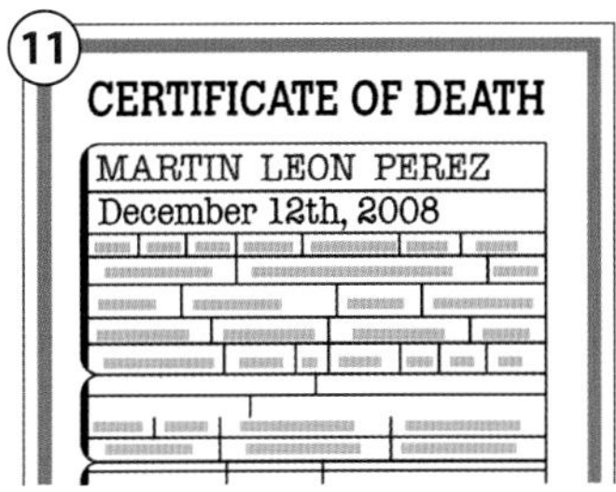

11. death certificate
死亡証明書

More vocabulary

When a husband dies, his wife becomes a **widow**.
When a wife dies, her husband becomes a **widower**.

Ask your classmates. Share the answers.

1. When did you start school?
2. When did you get your first job?
3. Do you want to travel?

Feelings

感情

1. hot
   暑い
2. thirsty
   のどが渇いた
3. sleepy
   眠い
4. cold
   寒い
5. hungry
   お腹がすいた
6. full / satisfied
   お腹がいっぱいの／満腹の

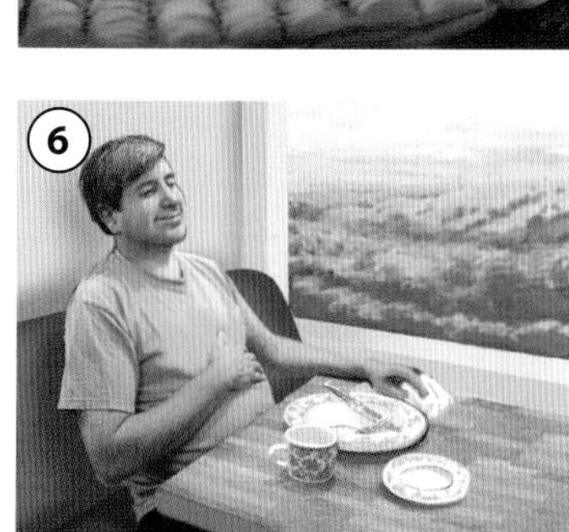

7. disgusted
   いやな
8. calm
   落ち着いた
9. uncomfortable
   不快な
10. nervous
    緊張して

11. in pain
    痛い
12. sick
    気分が悪い
13. worried
    心配して
14. well
    気分が良い
15. relieved
    安心して

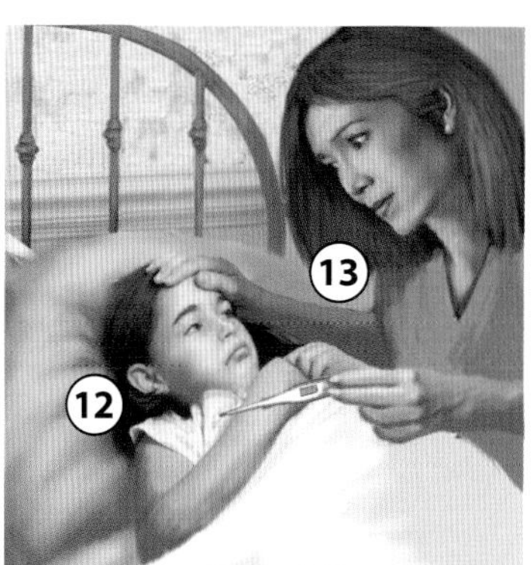

16. hurt
    傷ついた
17. lonely
    寂しい
18. in love
    恋をして

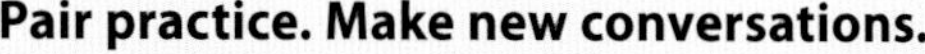

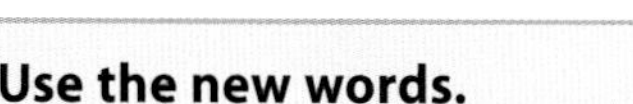

Pair practice. Make new conversations.

A: *How are you doing?*
B: *I'm hungry. How about you?*
A: *I'm hungry and thirsty, too!*

Use the new words.

Look at pages 40–41. Describe what each person is feeling.

A: *Martin is excited.*
B: *Martin's mother is proud.*

19. sad
悲しい
20. homesick
ホームシックにかかった
21. proud
誇りに思って

22. excited
興奮して
23. scared / afraid
おびえて／恐れて
24. embarrassed
恥ずかしい

25. bored
退屈して
26. confused
混乱して
27. frustrated
不満な

28. upset
気が転倒して
29. angry
怒って

30. surprised
驚いて
31. happy
うれしい／幸せな
32. tired
疲れた

Ask your classmates. Share the answers.

1. Do you ever feel homesick?
2. What makes you feel frustrated?
3. Describe a time when you were very happy.

More vocabulary

exhausted: very tired
furious: very angry
humiliated: very embarrassed
overjoyed: very happy
starving: very hungry
terrified: very scared

A Family Reunion 親族会

1. banner
横断幕
2. baseball game
野球の試合
3. opinion
意見
4. balloons
風船
5. glad
うれしい
6. relatives
親戚

A. **laugh**
笑う
B. **misbehave**
無作法にふるまう

Look at the picture.
What do you see?

Answer the questions.

1. How many relatives are there at this reunion?
2. How many children are there? Which children are misbehaving?
3. What are people doing at this reunion?

 **Read the story.**

A Family Reunion

Ben Lu has a lot of relatives and they're all at his house. Today is the Lu family reunion.

There is a lot of good food. There are also balloons and a banner. And this year there are four new babies!

People are having a good time at the reunion. Ben's grandfather and his aunt are talking about the baseball game. His cousins are laughing. His mother-in-law is giving her opinion. And many of the children are misbehaving.

Ben looks at his family and smiles. He loves his relatives, but he's glad the reunion is once a year.

Think about it.

1. Do you like to have large parties? Why or why not?
2. Imagine you see a little girl at a party. She's misbehaving. What do you do? What do you say?

The Home 家屋

1. roof
   屋根
2. bedroom
   寝室
3. door
   ドア
4. bathroom
   バスルーム
5. kitchen
   キッチン
6. floor
   床
7. dining area
   ダイニング

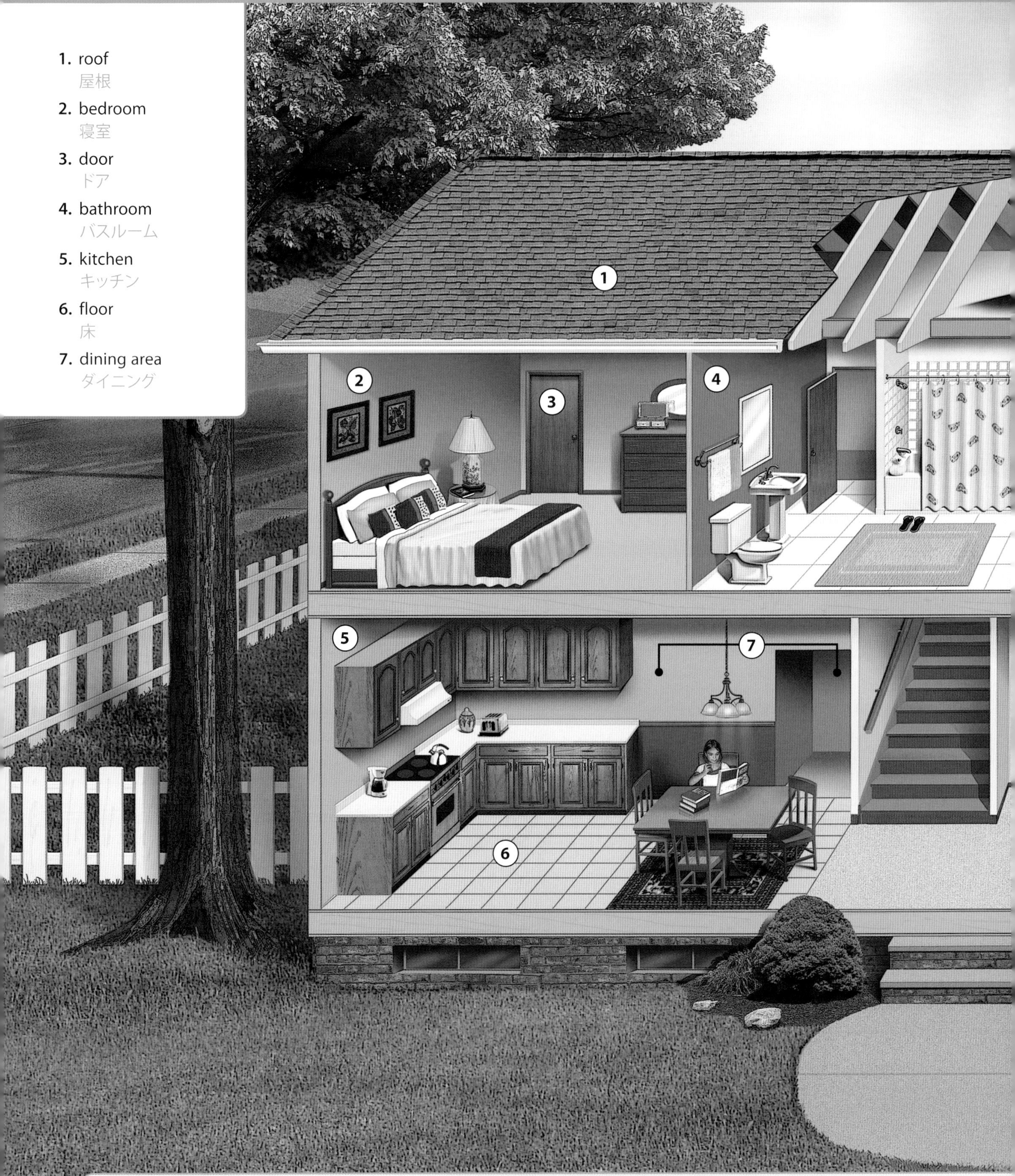

Listen and point. Take turns.

A: *Point to* *the kitchen.*
B: *Point to* *the living room.*
A: *Point to* *the basement.*

Dictate to your partner. Take turns.

A: *Write* *kitchen.*
B: *Was that* *k-i-t-c-h-e-n?*
A: *Yes, that's right,* *kitchen.*

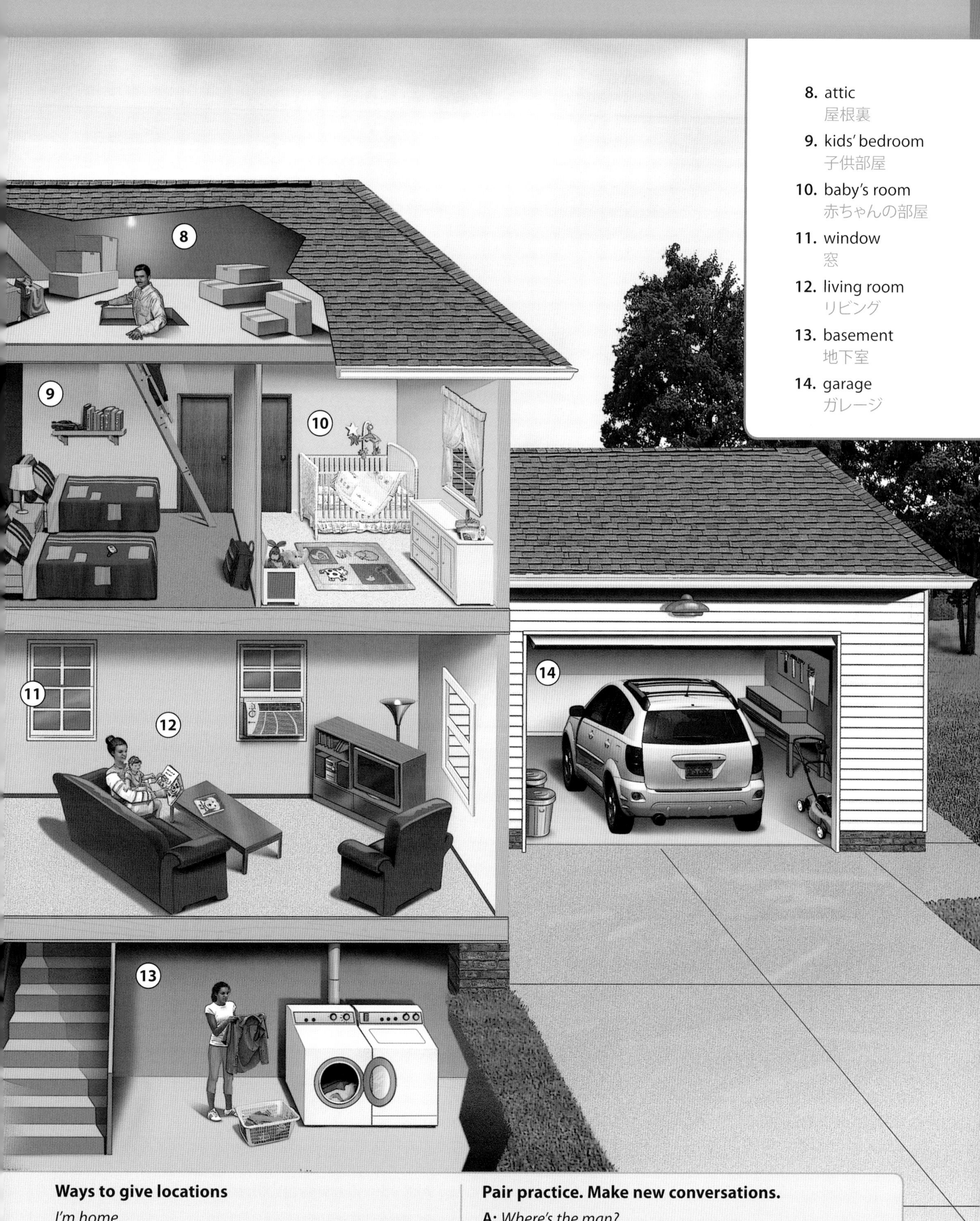

8. attic
屋根裏
9. kids' bedroom
子供部屋
10. baby's room
赤ちゃんの部屋
11. window
窓
12. living room
リビング
13. basement
地下室
14. garage
ガレージ

Ways to give locations

I'm home.
I'm in the kitchen.
I'm on the roof.

Pair practice. Make new conversations.

A: *Where's the man?*
B: *He's in the attic. Where's the teenager?*
A: *She's in the laundry room.*

1. Internet listing
インターネット物件リスト

Apartment For Rent
2 bdrm 2ba city apt
Unfurn Sunny kit
Util incl
$850/mo
Call mgr eves
212-555-2368

2. classified ad
案内広告

Abbreviations

apt = apartment
bdrm = bedroom
ba = bathroom
kit = kitchen
yd = yard
util = utilities
incl = included
mo = month
furn = furnished
unfurn = unfurnished
mgr = manager
eves = evenings

3. furnished apartment
家具付きアパート

4. unfurnished apartment
家具なしのアパート

Gas | Water | Electricity | Phone | Cable | DSL

5. utilities
光熱費

Renting an Apartment アパートを借りる

A. **Call** the manager.
管理人に**電話する**

B. **Ask** about the features.
特徴について**尋ねる**

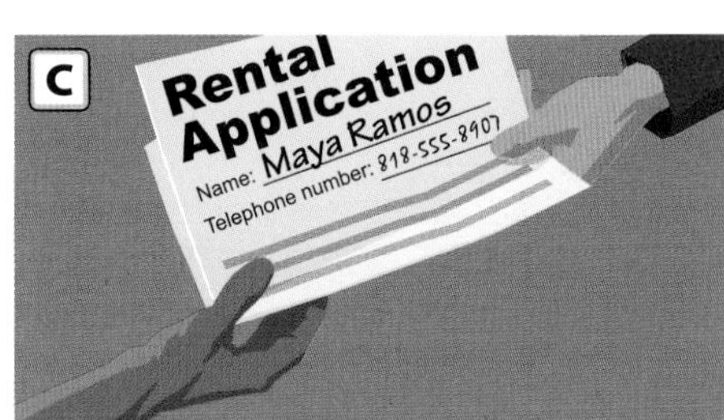

C. **Submit** an application.
申込書を**提出する**

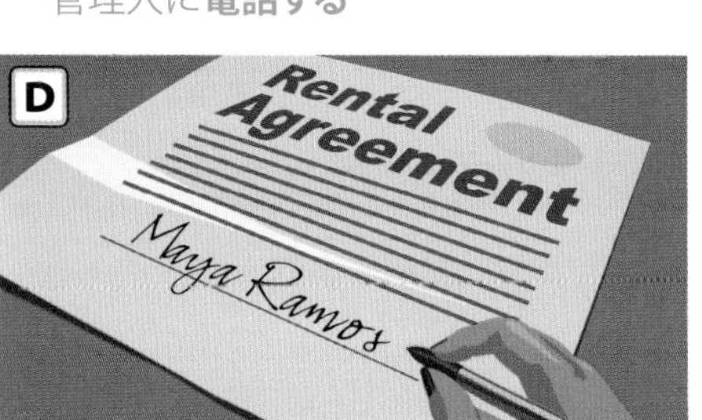

D. **Sign** the rental agreement.
賃貸契約に**署名する**

E. **Pay** the first and last month's rent.
最初の月と最後の月の家賃を**払う**

F. **Move in**.
引っ越す

More vocabulary

lease: a monthly or yearly rental agreement
redecorate: to change the paint and furniture in a home
move out: to pack and leave a home

Ask your classmates. Share the answers.

1. How did you find your home?
2. Do you like to paint or arrange furniture?
3. Does gas or electricity cost more for you?

Buying a House 家を買う

G. **Meet** with a realtor.
不動産業者と**会う**

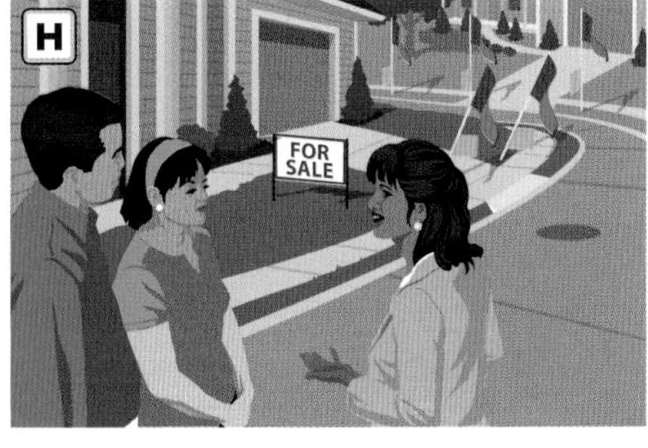

H. **Look** at houses.
家を**見る**

I. **Make** an offer.
買値を**伝える**

J. **Get** a loan.
ローンを**組む**

K. **Take** ownership.
持ち主と**なる**

L. **Make** a mortgage payment.
住宅ローンを**払う**

Moving In 引越し

M. **Pack**.
荷造りする

N. **Unpack**.
荷解きする

O. **Put** the utilities in your name.
電気・水道・ガス会社に連絡し、名義変**更する**

P. **Paint**.
ペンキを**塗る**

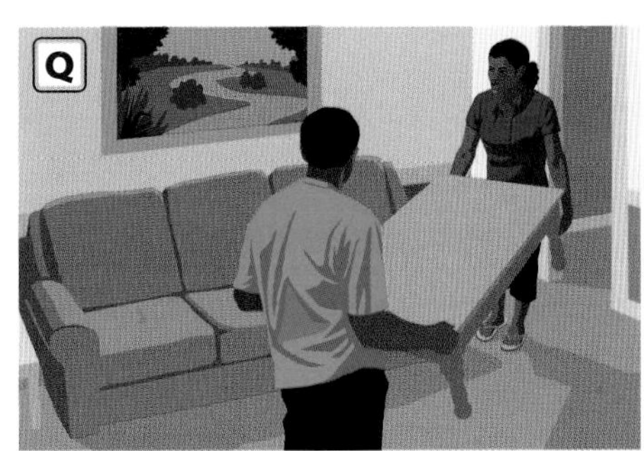

Q. **Arrange** the furniture.
家具を**配置する**

R. **Meet** the neighbors.
近所の人に**あいさつする**

Ways to ask about a home's features

Are utilities included?
Is the kitchen large and sunny?
Are the neighbors quiet?

Role play. Talk to an apartment manager.

A: *Hi. I'm calling about the apartment.*
B: *OK. It's unfurnished and rent is $800 a month.*
A: *Are utilities included?*

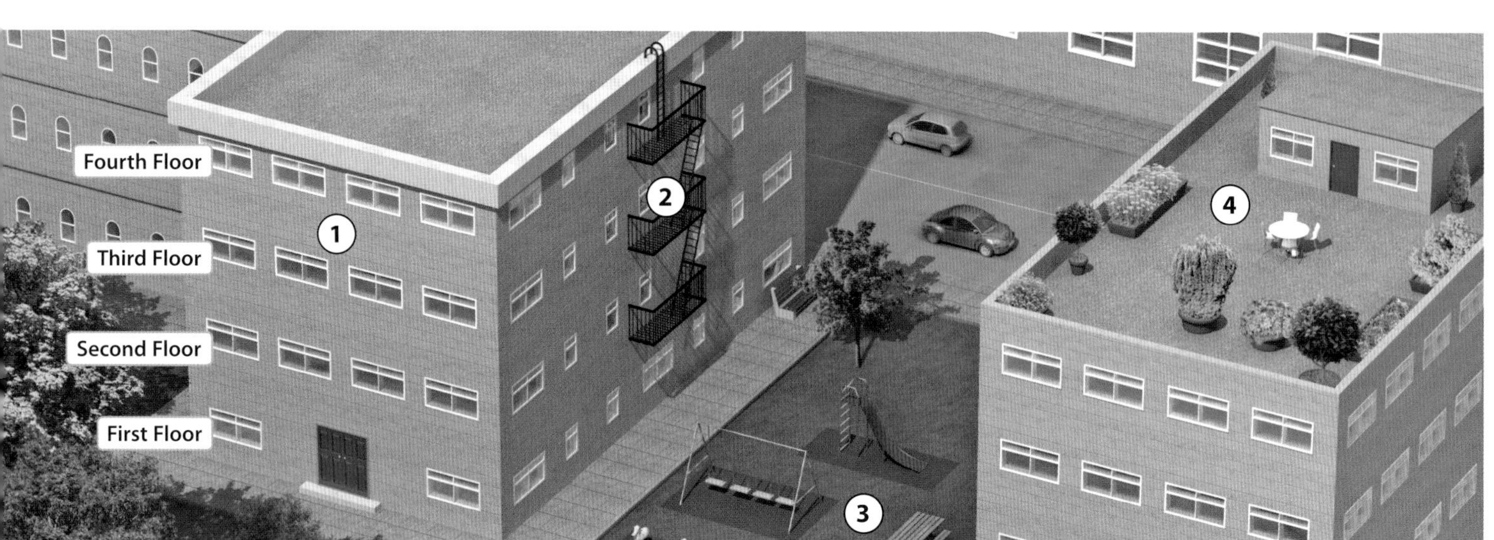

1. apartment building
アパートの建物

2. fire escape
非常口

3. playground
遊び場

4. roof garden
屋上

Entrance 入口

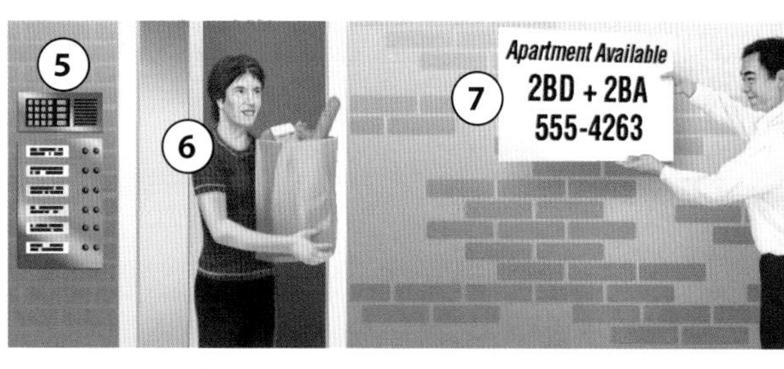

5. intercom / speaker
インターホン

6. tenant
借家人

7. vacancy sign
空部屋の表示

8. manager / superintendent
管理人

Lobby ロビー

9. elevator
エレベーター

10. stairs / stairway
階段

11. mailboxes
郵便受け

Basement 地下室

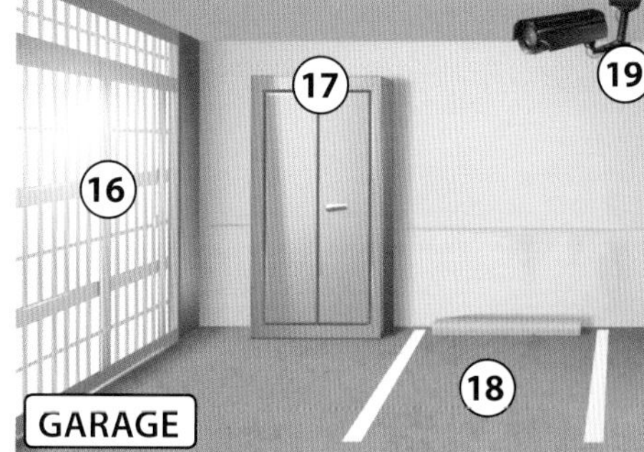

12. washer
洗濯機

13. dryer
乾燥機

14. big-screen TV
大画面テレビ

15. pool table
ビリヤード台

16. security gate
防犯ゲート

17. storage locker
物置

18. parking space
駐車場

19. security camera
防犯カメラ

Grammar Point: *there is / there are*

singular: there is **plural:** there are

There is *a recreation room in the basement.*

There are *mailboxes in the lobby.*

Look at the pictures.

Describe the apartment building.

A: *There's a pool table in the recreation room.*

B: *There are parking spaces in the garage.*

20. balcony
バルコニー

21. courtyard
中庭

22. swimming pool
プール

23. trash bin
ごみ置き場

24. alley
路地

Hallway 廊下

25. emergency exit
非常口

26. trash chute
ダストシュート

Rental Office 管理人室

27. landlord
家主

28. lease / rental agreement
リース・賃貸契約書

An Apartment Entryway アパートの入口

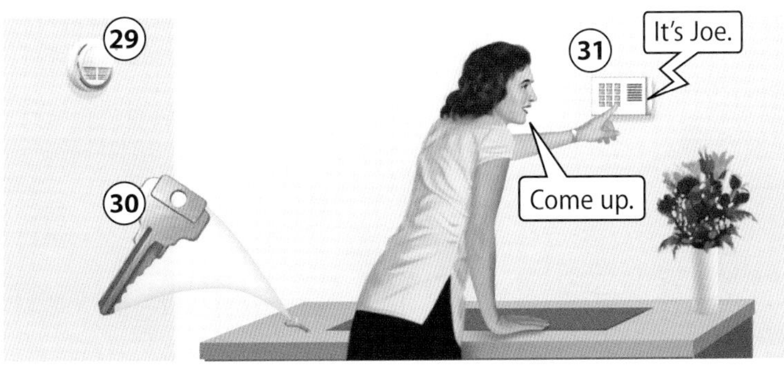

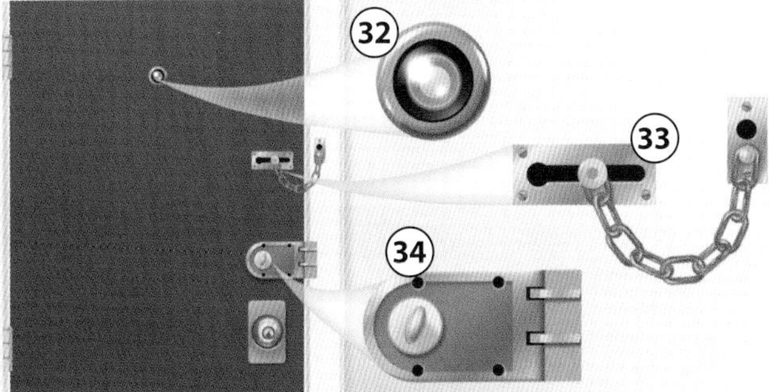

29. smoke detector
煙探知機

30. key
鍵

31. buzzer
ブザー

32. peephole
のぞき穴

33. door chain
ドアのチェーン

34. dead-bolt lock
デッドボルト錠

More vocabulary

upstairs: the floor(s) above you
downstairs: the floor(s) below you
fire exit: another name for emergency exit

Role play. Talk to a landlord.

A: *Is there a swimming pool in this complex?*
B: *Yes, there is. It's near the courtyard.*
A: *Is there…?*

Different Places to Live

さまざまな住宅環境

1. the city / an urban area
都市／都会

2. the suburbs
郊外

3. a small town / a village
小さな町／村

4. the country / a rural area
地方／田園地帯

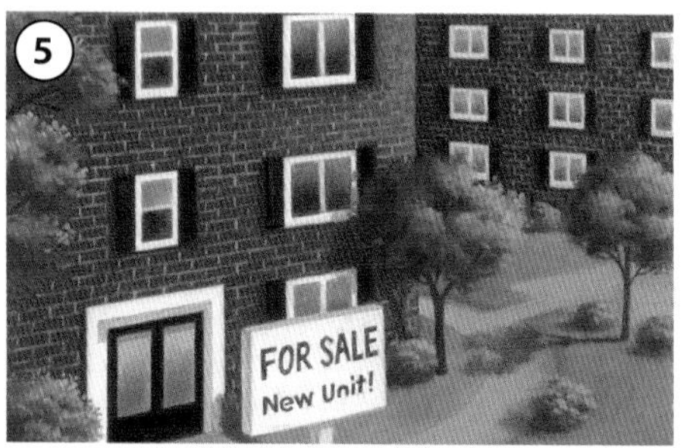

5. condominium / condo
コンドミニアム

6. townhouse
タウンハウス

7. mobile home
トレーラーハウス

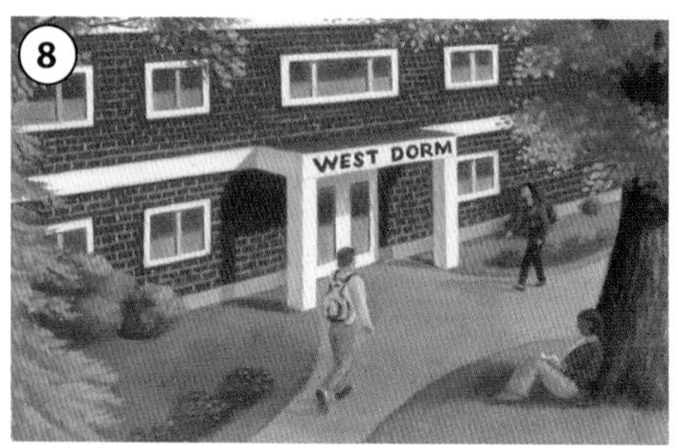

8. college dormitory / dorm
大学の寮／学生寮

9. farm
農家

10. ranch
牧場

11. senior housing
高齢者向け住宅

12. nursing home
老人ホーム

13. shelter
収容施設

More vocabulary

co-op: an apartment building owned by residents
duplex: a house divided into two homes
two-story house: a house with two floors

Think about it. Discuss.

1. What's good and bad about these places to live?
2. How are small towns different from cities?
3. How do shelters help people in need?

Front Yard and House 前庭と家

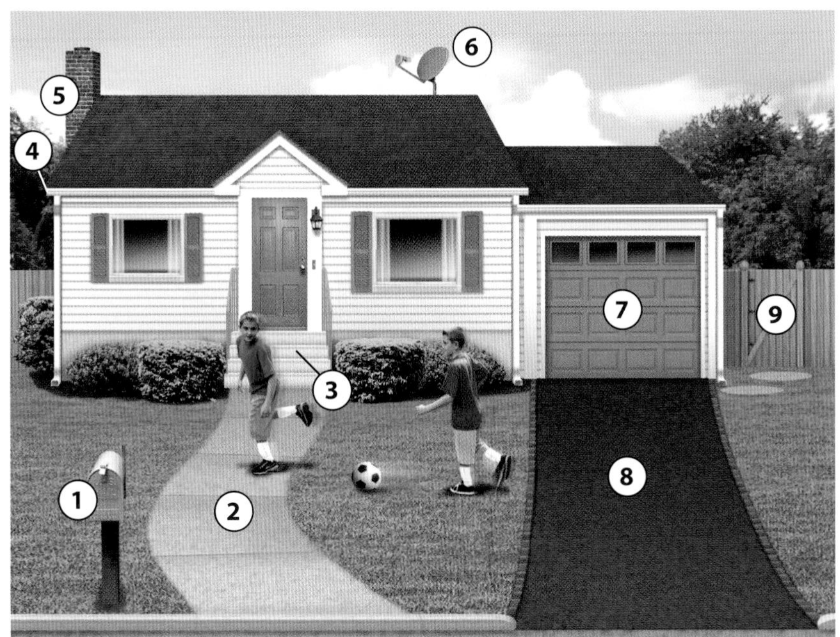

1. mailbox
郵便受け
2. front walk
前道
3. steps
階段
4. gutter
雨どい
5. chimney
煙突
6. satellite dish
衛星放送受信アンテナ
7. garage door
ガレージドア
8. driveway
ドライブウェイ
9. gate
門

Front Porch フロントポーチ

10. storm door
防風ドア
11. front door
玄関のドア
12. doorknob
ドアノブ
13. porch light
ポーチの電灯
14. doorbell
ドアベル
15. screen door
網戸

Backyard 裏庭

16. patio
テラス
17. grill
グリル
18. sliding glass door
ガラスの引き戸
19. patio furniture
テラス用家具
20. flower bed
花壇
21. hose
ホース
22. sprinkler
スプリンクラー
23. hammock
ハンモック
24. garbage can
ごみバケツ
25. compost pile
コンポスト
26. lawn
芝生
27. vegetable garden
家庭菜園

A. **take** a nap
昼寝する
B. **garden**
ガーデニングをする

A Kitchen

キッチン

1. cabinet
   戸だな
2. shelf
   たな
3. paper towels
   ペーパータオル
4. sink
   流し台
5. dish rack
   水切りかご
6. toaster
   トースター
7. garbage disposal
   ディスポーザー
8. dishwasher
   皿洗い機
9. refrigerator
   冷蔵庫
10. freezer
    冷凍庫
11. coffeemaker
    コーヒーメーカー
12. blender
    ミキサー
13. microwave
    電子レンジ
14. electric can opener
    電動缶切り
15. toaster oven
    オーブントースター
16. pot
    鍋
17. teakettle
    やかん
18. stove
    ガスレンジ
19. burner
    コンロ
20. oven
    オーブン
21. broiler
    ブロイラー
22. counter
    調理台
23. drawer
    引き出し
24. pan
    平鍋
25. electric mixer
    電動ミキサー
26. food processor
    フードプロセッサ
27. cutting board
    まな板
28. mixing bowl
    ミキシングボウル

Ways to talk about location using *on* and *in*

Use ***on*** for the counter, shelf, burner, stove, and cutting board. *It's **on** the counter.* Use ***in*** for the dishwasher, oven, sink, and drawer. *Put it **in** the sink.*

Pair practice. Make new conversations.

A: *Please move the blender.*
B: *Sure. Do you want it in the cabinet?*
A: *No, put it on the counter.*

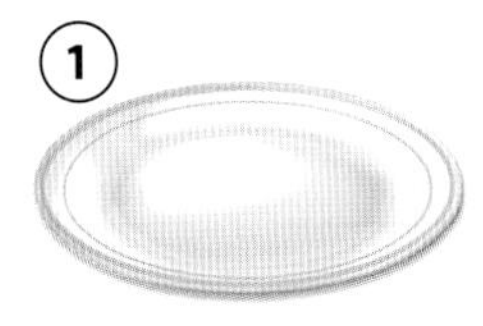

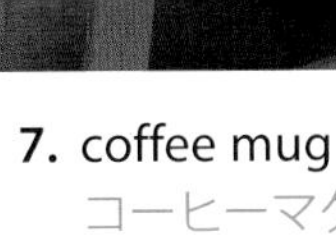

1. dish / plate
   皿
2. bowl
   ボウル
3. fork
   フォーク
4. knife
   ナイフ
5. spoon
   スプーン
6. teacup
   ティーカップ
7. coffee mug
   コーヒーマグ
8. dining room chair
   ダイニングルームの椅子
9. dining room table
   ダイニングテーブル／食卓
10. napkin
    ナプキン
11. placemat
    ランチョンマット
12. tablecloth
    テーブルクロス
13. salt and pepper shakers
    塩入れとコショウ入れ
14. sugar bowl
    砂糖入れ
15. creamer
    クリーム入れ
16. teapot
    ティーポット
17. tray
    お盆
18. light fixture
    照明器具
19. fan
    扇風機
20. platter
    大皿
21. serving bowl
    サービングボウル
22. hutch
    食器だな
23. vase
    花びん
24. buffet
    サイドボード

Ways to make requests at the table

May I have the sugar bowl?
Would you pass the creamer, please?
Could I have a coffee mug?

Role play. Request items at the table.

A: *What do you need?*
B: *Could I have a coffee mug?*
A: *Certainly. And would you...*

1. love seat
ラブシート／2人用ソファー
2. throw pillow
クッション
3. basket
バスケット
4. houseplant
観葉植物
5. entertainment center
テレビ用キャビネット
6. TV (television)
テレビ
7. DVD player
DVD プレーヤー
8. stereo system
ステレオ
9. painting
絵画
10. wall
壁
11. mantle
暖炉だな
12. fire screen
暖炉のついたて
13. fireplace
暖炉
14. end table
サイドテーブル
15. floor lamp
フロアランプ
16. drapes
カーテン
17. window
窓
18. sofa / couch
ソファー
19. coffee table
コーヒーテーブル
20. candle
キャンドル
21. candle holder
キャンドル立て
22. armchair / easy chair
ひじかけ椅子
23. magazine holder
マガジンラック
24. carpet
カーペット

Use the new words.
Look at pages 44–45. Name the things in the room.

A: *There's a TV.*
B: *There's a carpet.*

More vocabulary

light bulb: the light inside a lamp
lampshade: the part of the lamp that covers the light bulb
sofa cushions: the pillows that are part of the sofa

1. hamper
洗濯物かご
2. bathtub
浴槽
3. soap dish
石けん入れ
4. soap
石けん
5. rubber mat
ゴムマット
6. washcloth
体を洗うタオル
7. drain
排水口
8. faucet
蛇口
9. hot water
お湯
10. cold water
水
11. grab bar
手すり
12. tile
タイル
13. showerhead
シャワーヘッド
14. shower curtain
シャワーカーテン
15. towel rack
タオルかけ
16. bath towel
バスタオル
17. hand towel
ハンドタオル
18. mirror
鏡
19. toilet paper
トイレットペーパー
20. toilet brush
トイレブラシ
21. toilet
便器
22. medicine cabinet
戸だな
23. toothbrush
歯ブラシ
24. toothbrush holder
歯ブラシ立て
25. sink
洗面台
26. wastebasket
くずかご
27. scale
体重計
28. bath mat
バスマット

More vocabulary

stall shower: a shower without a bathtub
half bath: a bathroom with no shower or tub
linen closet: a closet for towels and sheets

Ask your classmates. Share the answers.

1. Is your toothbrush on the sink or in the medicine cabinet?
2. Do you have a bathtub or a shower?
3. Do you have a shower curtain or a shower door?

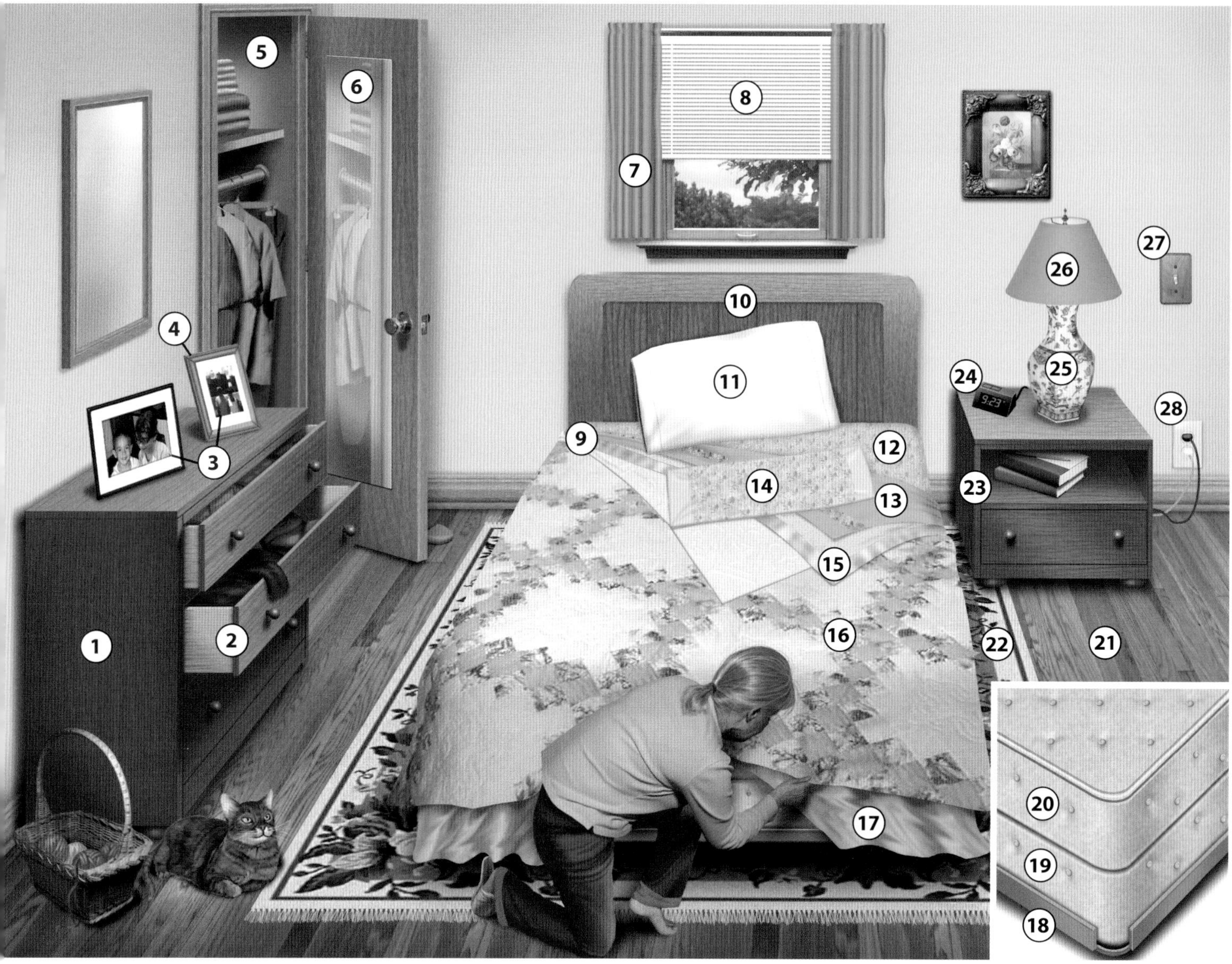

A Bedroom

寝室

1. dresser / bureau
整理だんす
2. drawer
引き出し
3. photos
写真
4. picture frame
写真立て
5. closet
クロゼット
6. full-length mirror
姿見
7. curtains
カーテン
8. mini-blinds
ブラインド
9. bed
ベッド
10. headboard
ヘッドボード
11. pillow
枕
12. fitted sheet
フィットシーツ
13. flat sheet
フラットシーツ
14. pillowcase
枕カバー
15. blanket
毛布
16. quilt
キルト
17. dust ruffle
ベッドスカート
18. bed frame
ベッドフレーム
19. box spring
ボックススプリング
20. mattress
マットレス
21. wood floor
木の床
22. rug
敷物
23. night table / nightstand
ナイトテーブル
24. alarm clock
目覚まし時計
25. lamp
ランプ
26. lampshade
ランプシェード
27. light switch
スイッチ
28. outlet
コンセント

Look at the pictures.
Describe the bedroom.

A: *There's a lamp on the nightstand.*
B: *There's a mirror in the closet.*

Ask your classmates. Share the answers.

1. Do you prefer a hard or a soft mattress?
2. Do you prefer mini-blinds or curtains?
3. How many pillows do you like on your bed?

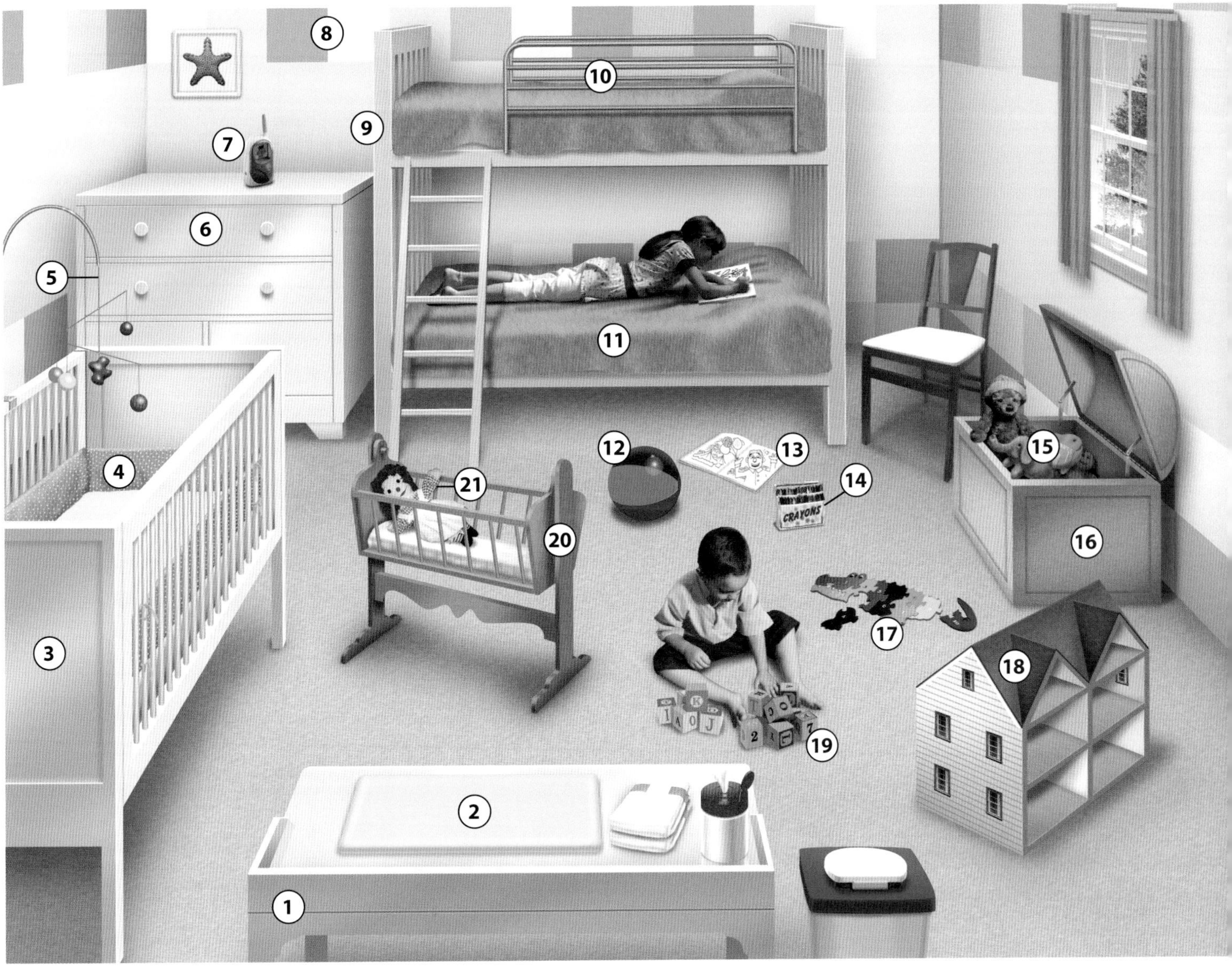

Furniture and Accessories 家具や備品

1. changing table
   おむつ交換台
2. changing pad
   おむつ交換用のパッド
3. crib
   ベビーベッド
4. bumper pad
   安全パッド
5. mobile
   モビール
6. chest of drawers
   たんす
7. baby monitor
   ベビーモニター
8. wallpaper
   壁紙
9. bunk beds
   2段ベッド
10. safety rail
    セーフティレール
11. bedspread
    ベッドカバー

Toys and Games おもちゃやゲーム

12. ball
    ボール
13. coloring book
    ぬりえ
14. crayons
    クレヨン
15. stuffed animals
    ぬいぐるみ
16. toy chest
    おもちゃ箱
17. puzzle
    パズル
18. dollhouse
    人形の家
19. blocks
    積み木
20. cradle
    ゆりかご
21. doll
    人形

Pair practice. Make conversations.

A: *Where's the changing pad?*
B: *It's on the changing table.*

Think about it. Discuss.

1. Which toys help children learn? How?
2. Which toys are good for older and younger children?
3. What safety features does this room need? Why?

A. **dust** the furniture
家具の**ほこりをはらう**

B. **recycle** the newspapers
新聞紙を**リサイクルする**

C. **clean** the oven
オーブンを**掃除する**

D. **mop** the floor
床を**モップで拭く**

E. **polish** the furniture
家具を**みがく**

F. **make** the bed
ベッドを**整える**

G. **put away** the toys
おもちゃを**しまう**

H. **vacuum** the carpet
カーペットに**掃除機をかける**

I. **wash** the windows
窓を**拭く**

J. **sweep** the floor
床を**掃く**

K. **scrub** the sink
流しを**洗う**

L. **empty** the trash
くずかごを**空にする**

M. **wash** the dishes
皿を**洗う**

N. **dry** the dishes
皿を**拭く**

O. **wipe** the counter
調理台を**拭く**

P. **change** the sheets
シーツを**換える**

Q. **take out** the garbage
ごみを**出す**

Pair practice. Make new conversations.

A: *Let's clean this place. First, I'll sweep the floor.*
B: *I'll mop the floor when you finish.*

Ask your classmates. Share the answers.

1. Who does the housework in your home?
2. How often do you wash the windows?
3. When should kids start to do housework?

1

2

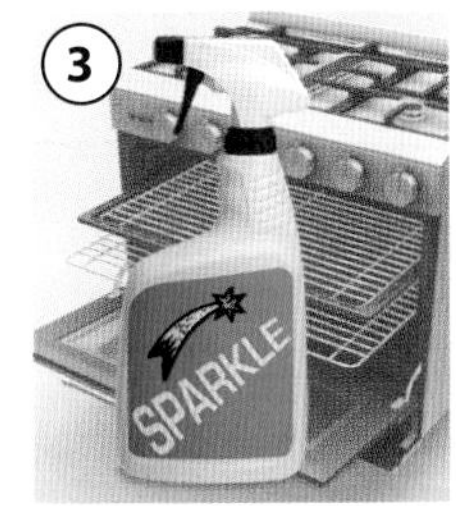
3

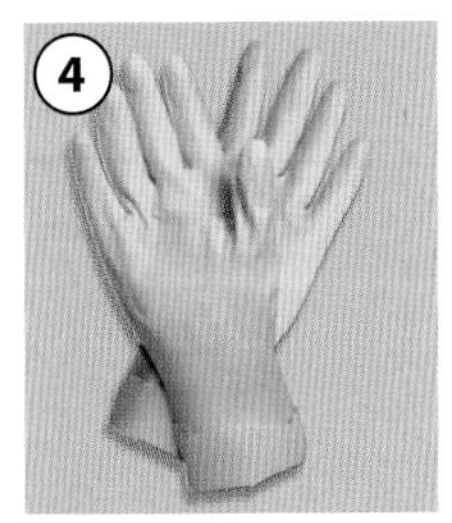
4

5

6

7

8

9

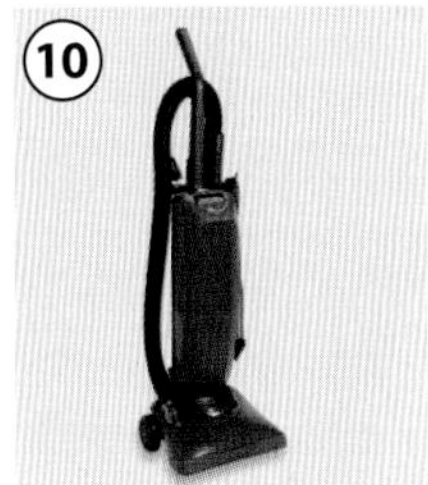
10

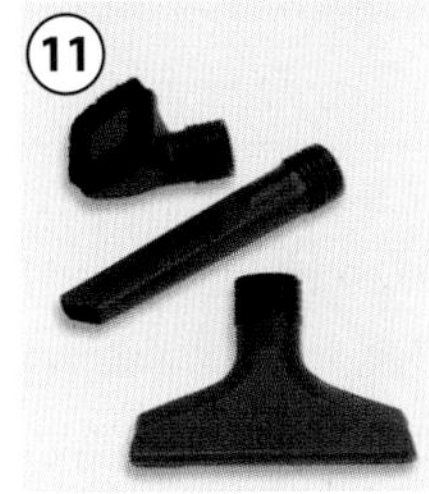
11

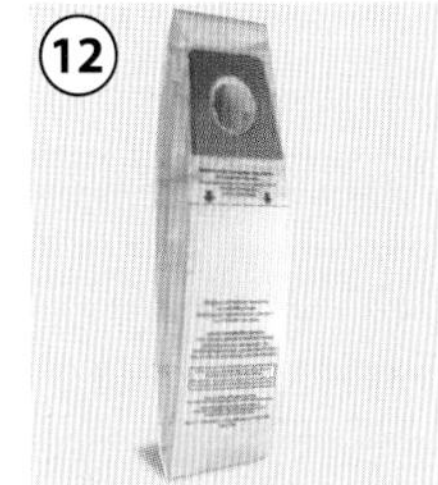
12

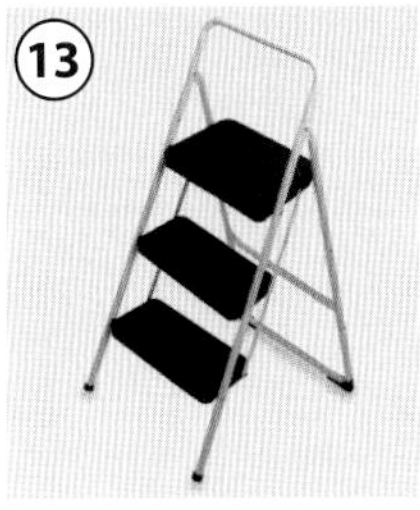
13

14

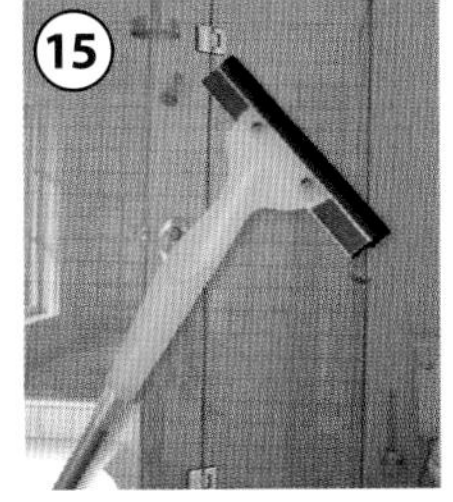
15

16

17

18

19

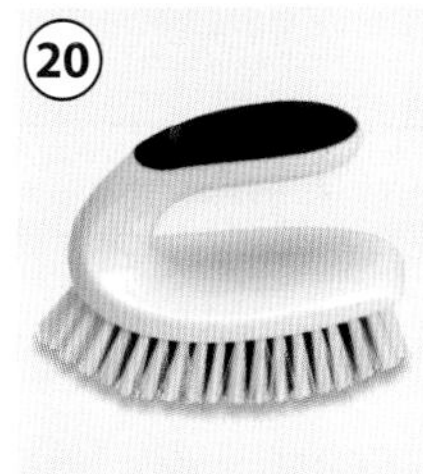
20

21

22

23

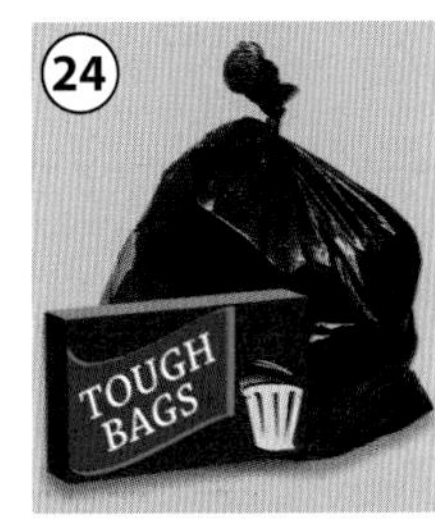
24

1. feather duster
   はたき
2. recycling bin
   リサイクル品入れ
3. oven cleaner
   オーブンクリーナー
4. rubber gloves
   ゴム手袋
5. steel-wool soap pads
   石けん付きスチールウール
6. sponge mop
   スポンジモップ
7. bucket / pail
   バケツ
8. furniture polish
   家具のつやだし
9. rags
   ぞうきん
10. vacuum cleaner
    掃除機
11. vacuum cleaner attachments
    掃除機の付属品
12. vacuum cleaner bag
    掃除機のゴミパック
13. stepladder
    脚立
14. glass cleaner
    ガラスクリーナー
15. squeegee
    ガラスワイパー
16. broom
    ほうき
17. dustpan
    ちりとり
18. cleanser
    クレンザー
19. sponge
    スポンジ
20. scrub brush
    たわし
21. dishwashing liquid
    食器用洗剤
22. dish towel
    ふきん
23. disinfectant wipes
    殺菌ワイプ
24. trash bags
    ごみ袋

Ways to ask for something

Please hand me the squeegee.
Can you get me the broom?
I need the sponge mop.

Pair practice. Make new conversations.

A: *Please hand me the sponge mop.*
B: *Here you go. Do you need the bucket?*
A: *Yes, please. Can you get me the rubber gloves, too?*

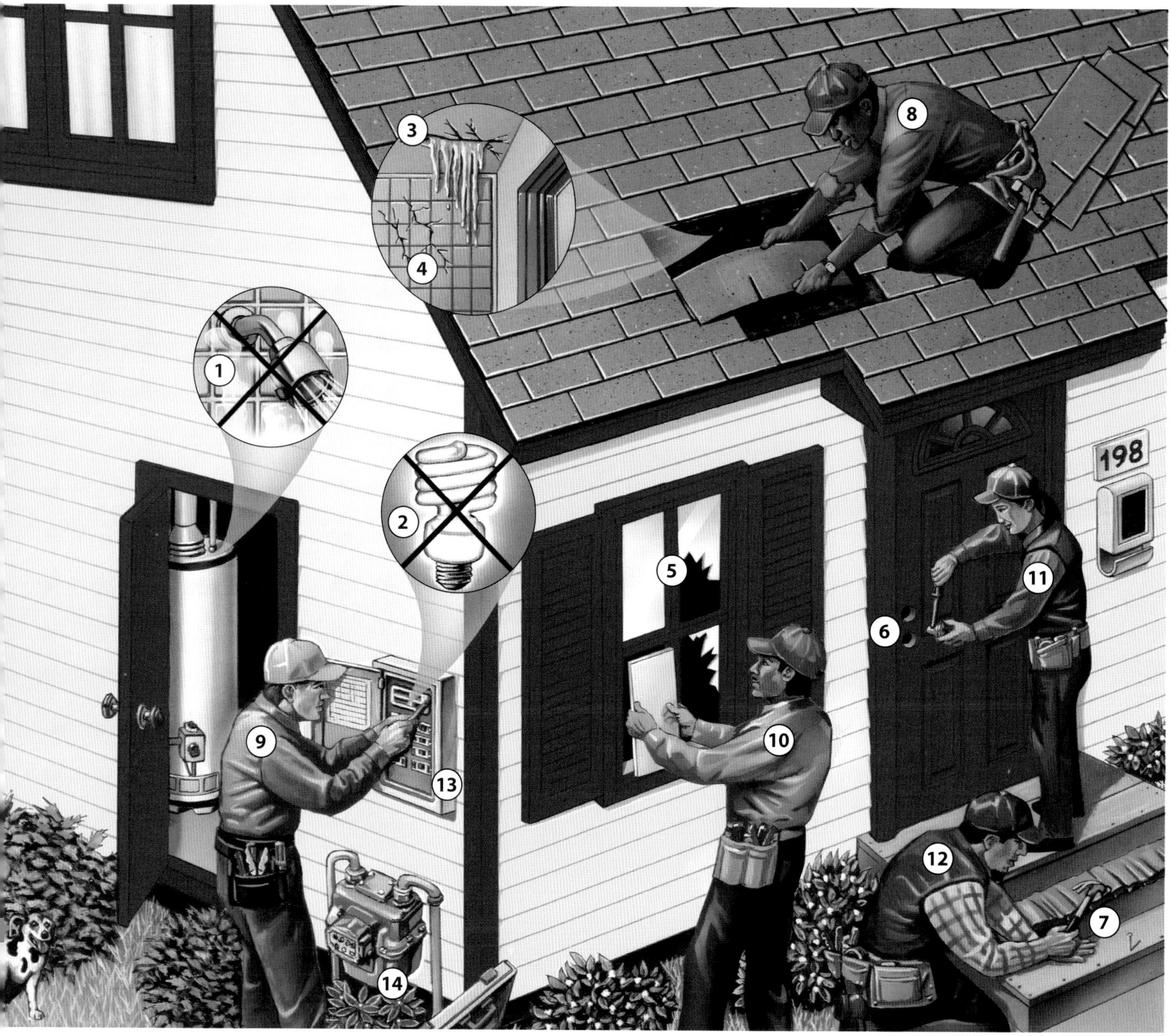

Household Problems and Repairs

家の問題と修理

1. The water heater is **not working**.
   温水器が**故障している**
2. The power is **out**.
   停電している
3. The roof is **leaking**.
   屋根が**雨漏りしている**
4. The tile is **cracked**.
   タイルに**ひびが入っている**
5. The window is **broken**.
   窓が**割れている**
6. The lock is **broken**.
   鍵が**壊れている**
7. The steps are **broken**.
   階段が**壊れている**
8. roofer
   屋根職人
9. electrician
   電気工
10. repair person
    修理人
11. locksmith
    錠前師
12. carpenter
    大工
13. fuse box
    ヒューズボックス
14. gas meter
    ガスメーター

More vocabulary

fix: to repair something that is broken
pests: termites, fleas, rats, etc.
exterminate: to kill household pests

Pair practice. Make new conversations.

A: *The faucet is leaking.*
B: *Let's call the plumber. He can fix it.*

15. The furnace is **broken**.
暖房炉が**故障している**

16. The pipes are **frozen**.
水道管が**凍結している**

17. The faucet is **dripping**.
蛇口が**水漏れする**

18. The sink is **overflowing**.
流しから**水があふれている**

19. The toilet is **stopped up**.
便器が**詰まっている**

20. plumber
配管工

21. exterminator
害虫駆除業者

22. termites
シロアリ

23. ants
アリ

24. bedbugs
南京虫

25. fleas
ノミ

26. cockroaches / roaches
ゴキブリ

27. rats
ネズミ

28. mice*
ハツカネズミ

***Note:** one mouse, two mice

Ways to ask about repairs

How much will this repair cost?
When can you begin?
How long will the repair take?

Role play. Talk to a repair person.

A: *Can you fix the roof?*
B: *Yes, but it will take two weeks.*
A: *How much will the repair cost?*

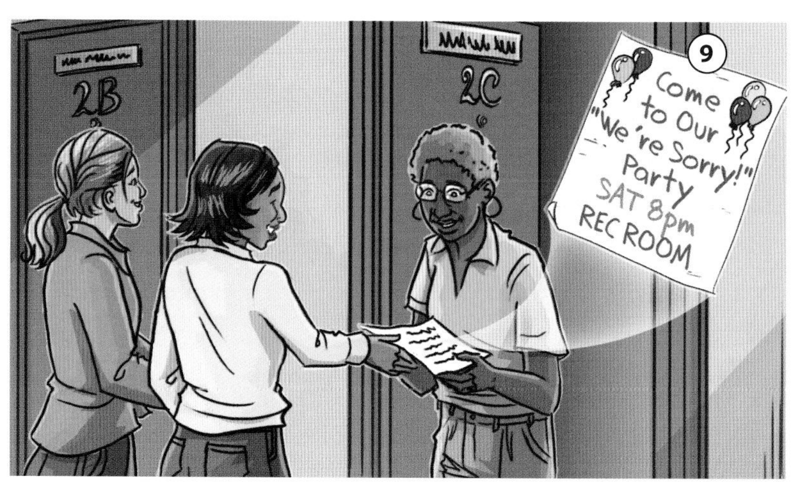

1. roommates ルームメート
2. party パーティ
3. music 音楽
4. DJ DJ
5. noise 騒音
6. irritated イライラする
7. rules 規則
8. mess 散らかし
9. invitation 招待

A. **dance** **踊る**

Look at the pictures. What do you see?

Answer the questions.

1. What happened in apartment 2B? How many people were there?
2. How did the neighbor feel? Why?
3. What rules did they write at the tenant meeting?
4. What did the roommates do after the tenant meeting?

 **Read the story.**

The Tenant Meeting

Sally Lopez and Tina Green are roommates. They live in apartment 2B. One night they had a big party with music and a DJ. There was a mess in the hallway. Their neighbors were very unhappy. Mr. Clark in 2A was very irritated. He hates noise!

The next day there was a tenant meeting. Everyone wanted rules about parties and loud music. The girls were very embarrassed.

After the meeting, the girls cleaned the mess in the hallway. Then they gave each neighbor an invitation to a new party. Everyone had a good time at the rec room party. Now the tenants have two new rules and a new place to dance.

Think about it.

1. What are the most important rules in an apartment building? Why?
2. Imagine you are the neighbor in 2A. What do you say to Tina and Sally?

Back from the Market スーパーから戻る

1. fish
   魚
2. meat
   肉
3. chicken
   鶏肉
4. cheese
   チーズ
5. milk
   牛乳
6. butter
   バター
7. eggs
   卵
8. vegetables
   野菜

Listen and point. Take turns.

A: *Point to the <u>vegetables</u>.*
B: *Point to the <u>bread</u>.*
A: *Point to the <u>fruit</u>.*

Pair Dictation

A: *Write <u>vegetables</u>.*
B: *Please spell <u>vegetables</u> for me.*
A: *V-e-g-e-t-a-b-l-e-s.*

9. fruit
果物
10. rice
米
11. bread
パン
12. pasta
パスタ
13. grocery bag
スーパーの袋
14. shopping list
買い物リスト
15. coupons
割引クーポン

Ways to talk about food.

Do we need eggs?

Do we have any pasta?

We have some vegetables, but we need fruit.

Role play. Talk about your shopping list.

A: *Do we need eggs?*

B: *No, we have some.*

A: *Do we have any...*

Fruit

果物

1. apples
   リンゴ
2. bananas
   バナナ
3. grapes
   ブドウ
4. pears
   洋ナシ
5. oranges
   オレンジ
6. grapefruit
   グレープフルーツ
7. lemons
   レモン
8. limes
   ライム
9. tangerines
   ミカン
10. peaches
    モモ
11. cherries
    サクランボ
12. apricots
    アンズ
13. plums
    プラム
14. strawberries
    イチゴ
15. raspberries
    ラズベリー
16. blueberries
    ブルーベリー
17. blackberries
    ブラックベリー
18. watermelons
    スイカ
19. melons
    メロン
20. papayas
    パパイヤ
21. mangoes
    マンゴー
22. kiwi
    キーウィ
23. pineapples
    パイナップル
24. coconuts
    ココナッツ
25. raisins
    レーズン
26. prunes
    プルーン
27. figs
    イチジク
28. dates
    デーツ
29. a bunch of bananas
    １房のバナナ
30. **ripe** banana
    熟したバナナ
31. **unripe** banana
    熟していないバナナ
32. **rotten** banana
    腐ったバナナ

Pair practice. Make new conversations.

A: *What's your favorite fruit?*
B: *I like apples. Do you?*
A: *I prefer bananas.*

Ask your classmates. Share the answers.

1. Which fruit do you put in a fruit salad?
2. What kinds of fruit are common in your native country?
3. What kinds of fruit are in your kitchen right now?

1. lettuce
   レタス
2. cabbage
   キャベツ
3. carrots
   ニンジン
4. radishes
   ラディッシュ
5. beets
   ビート
6. tomatoes
   トマト
7. bell peppers
   ピーマン
8. string beans
   インゲン
9. celery
   セロリ
10. cucumbers
    キュウリ
11. spinach
    ホウレンソウ
12. corn
    トウモロコシ
13. broccoli
    ブロッコリー
14. cauliflower
    カリフラワー
15. bok choy
    パクチョイ
16. turnips
    カブ
17. potatoes
    ジャガイモ
18. sweet potatoes
    サツマイモ
19. onions
    タマネギ
20. green onions / scallions
    長ネギ／ワケギ
21. peas
    グリンピース
22. artichokes
    アーティチョーク
23. eggplants
    ナス
24. squash
    スクワッシュ
25. zucchini
    ズッキーニ
26. asparagus
    アスパラガス
27. mushrooms
    キノコ類
28. parsley
    パセリ
29. chili peppers
    唐辛子
30. garlic
    ニンニク
31. a **bag of** lettuce
    1袋のレタス
32. a **head of** lettuce
    1個のレタス

Pair practice. Make new conversations.

A: *Do you eat broccoli?*
B: *Yes. I like most vegetables, but not peppers.*
A: *Really? Well, I don't like cauliflower.*

Ask your classmates. Share the answers.

1. Which vegetables do you eat raw? cooked?
2. Which vegetables do you put in a green salad?
3. Which vegetables are in your refrigerator right now?

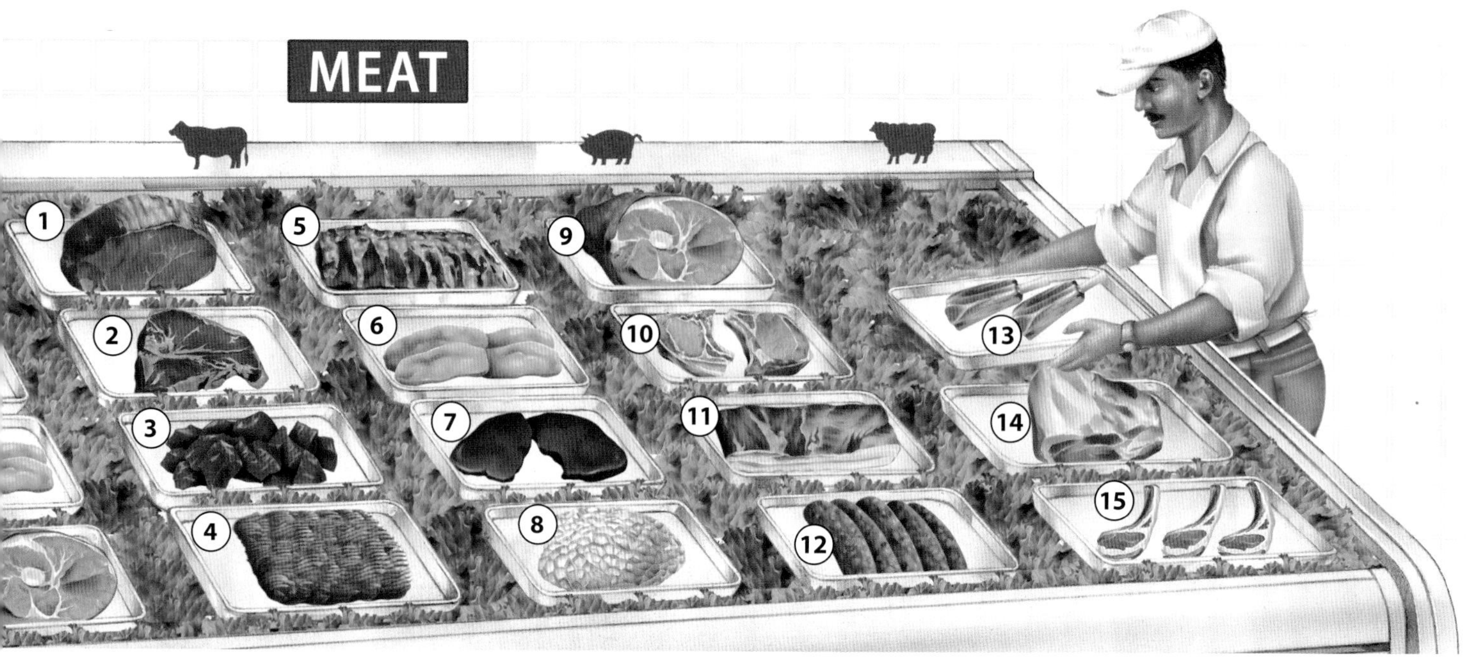

Beef 牛肉

1. roast
   ロース
2. steak
   ステーキ用肉
3. stewing beef
   シチュー用肉
4. ground beef
   ひき肉
5. beef ribs
   骨付きのあばら肉
6. veal cutlets
   カツレツ用子牛肉
7. liver
   レバー
8. tripe
   胃の食用部分

Pork 豚肉

9. ham
   ハム
10. pork chops
    ポークチョップ
11. bacon
    ベーコン
12. sausage
    ソーセージ

Lamb ラム肉

13. lamb shanks
    ラムのすね肉
14. leg of lamb
    ラムレッグ
15. lamb chops
    ラムチョップ

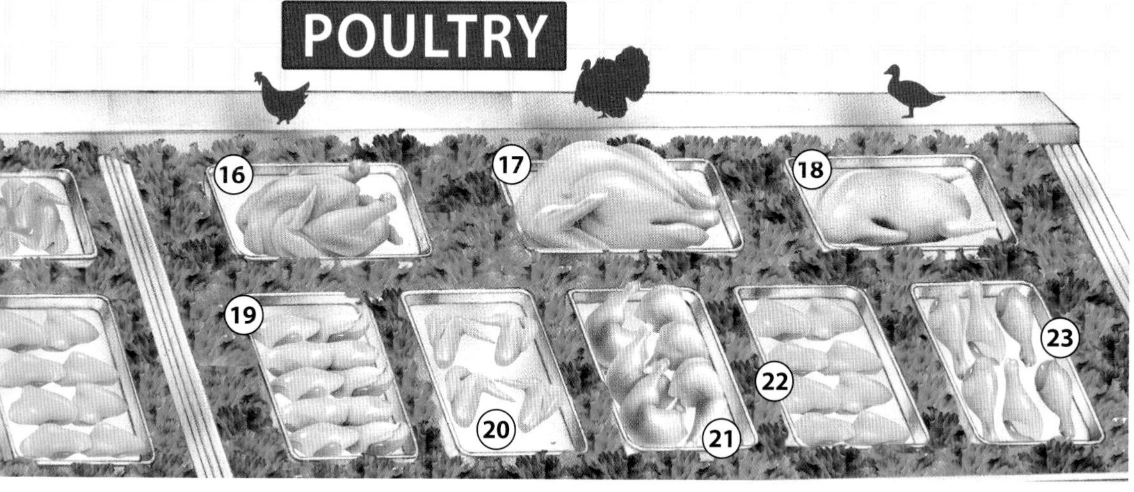

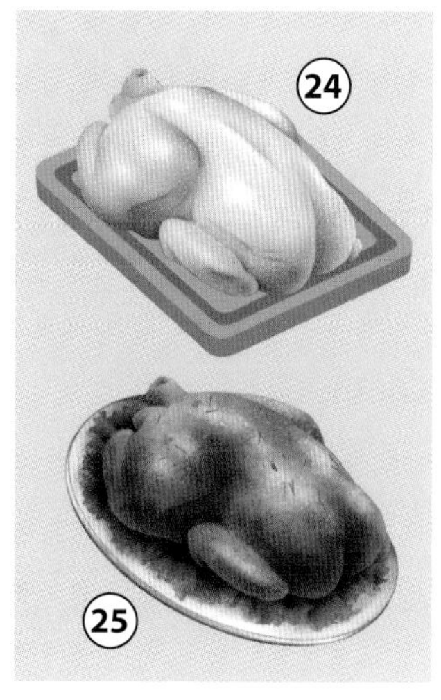

Poultry 家禽

16. chicken
    鶏肉
17. turkey
    七面鳥の肉
18. duck
    カモ肉
19. breasts
    胸肉
20. wings
    手羽
21. legs
    レッグ
22. thighs
    もも肉
23. drumsticks
    ドラムスティック
24. **raw** chicken
    生の鶏肉
25. **cooked** chicken
    調理済みの鶏肉

More vocabulary

vegetarian: a person who doesn't eat meat
boneless: meat and poultry without bones
skinless: poultry without skin

Ask your classmates. Share the answers.

1. What kind of meat do you eat most often?
2. What kind of meat do you use in soups?
3. What part of the chicken do you like the most?

Fish 魚

1. trout
マス
2. catfish
ナマズ
3. whole salmon
サケまるごと１匹
4. salmon steak
サケのステーキカット
5. swordfish
メカジキ
6. halibut steak
オヒョウのステーキ
7. tuna
マグロ
8. cod
タラ

Shellfish 甲殻類

9. crab
カニ
10. lobster
ロブスター
11. shrimp
小エビ
12. scallops
ホタテ貝
13. mussels
ムール貝
14. oysters
カキ
15. clams
ハマグリ
16. **fresh** fish
生の魚
17. **frozen** fish
冷凍の魚

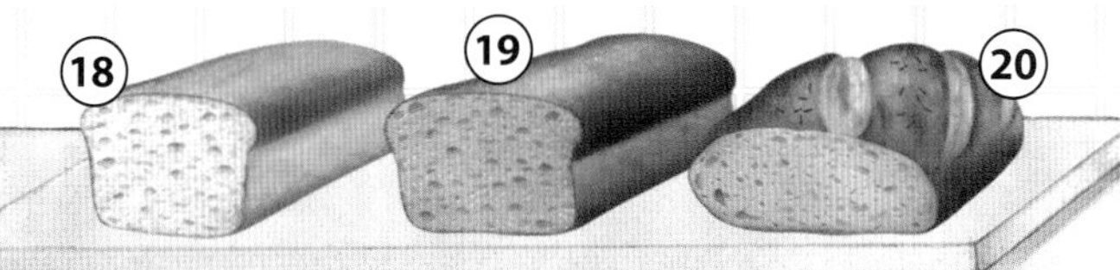

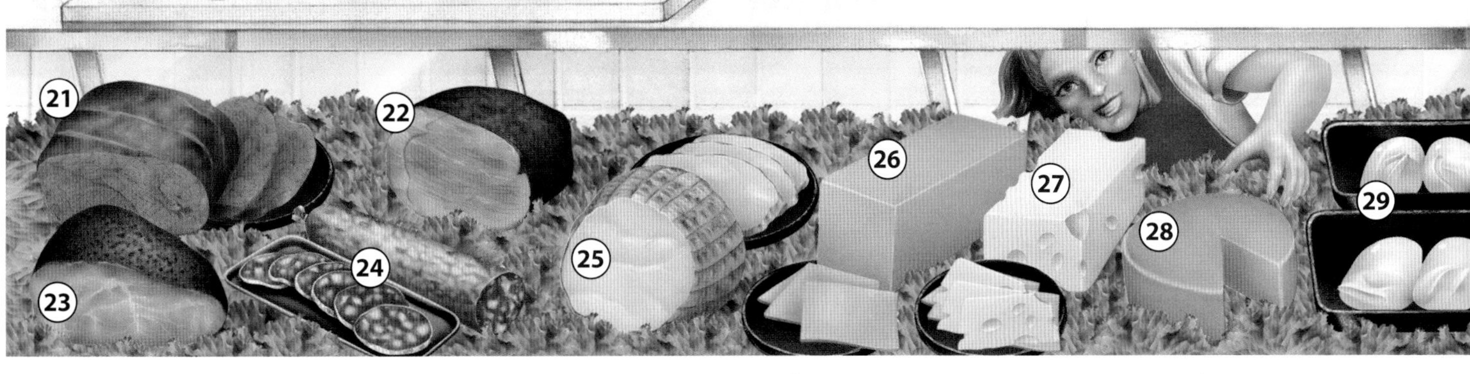

18. white bread
精白パン
19. wheat bread
全粒パン
20. rye bread
ライ麦パン
21. roast beef
ローストビーフ
22. corned beef
コンビーフ
23. pastrami
パストラミ
24. salami
サラミ
25. smoked turkey
スモークターキー
26. American cheese
アメリカンチーズ
27. Swiss cheese
スイスチーズ
28. cheddar cheese
チェダーチーズ
29. mozzarella cheese
モッツァレラチーズ

Ways to order at the counter

I'd like some roast beef.
I'll have a halibut steak and some shrimp.
Could I get some Swiss cheese?

Pair practice. Make new conversations.

A: *What can I get for you?*
B: *I'd like some roast beef. How about a pound?*
A: *A pound of roast beef coming up!*

A Grocery Store

スーパーマーケット

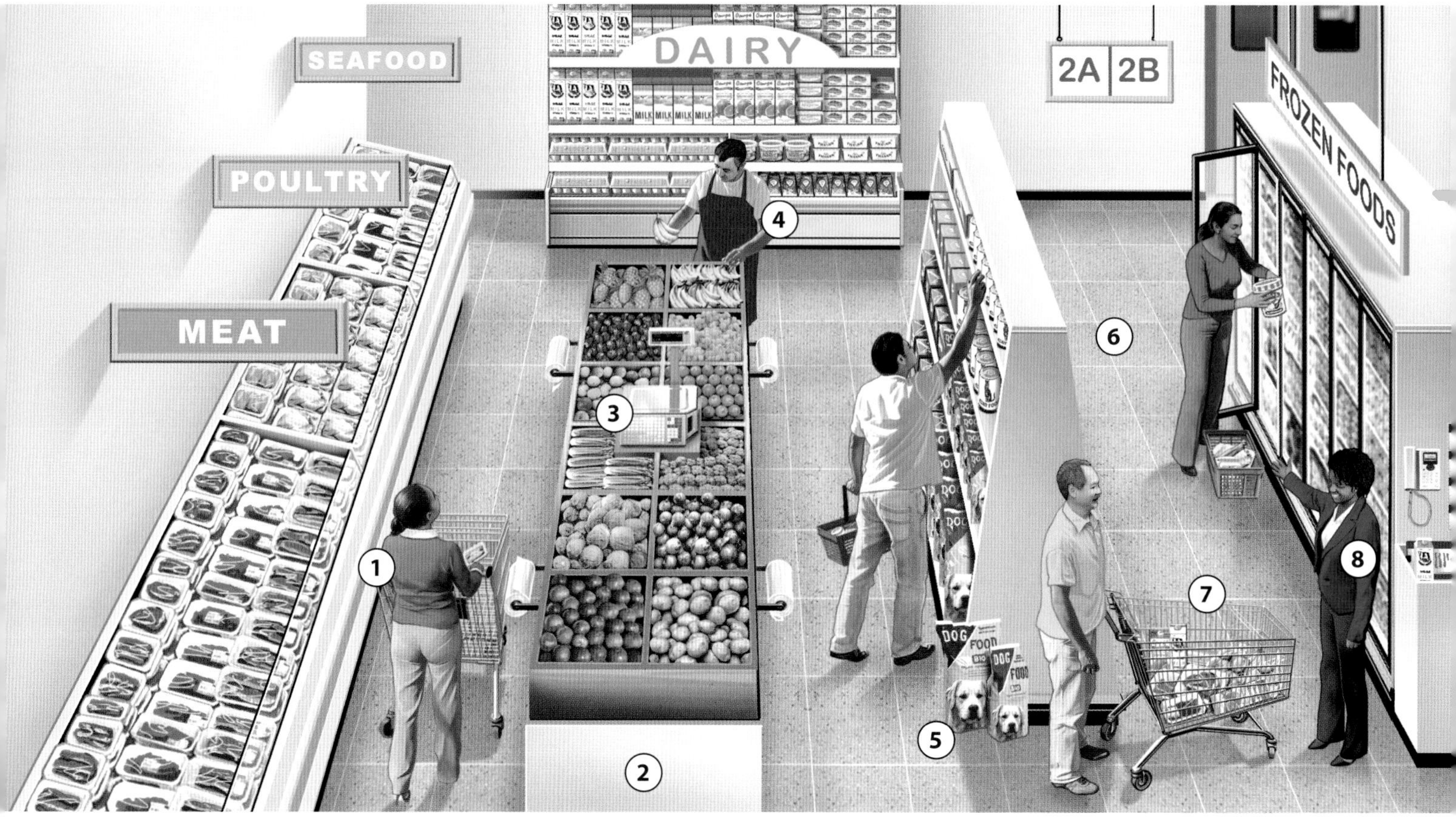

1. customer
顧客
2. produce section
生鮮食品売場
3. scale
はかり
4. grocery clerk
店員
5. pet food
ペットフード
6. aisle
通路

7. cart
ショッピングカート

8. manager
店長

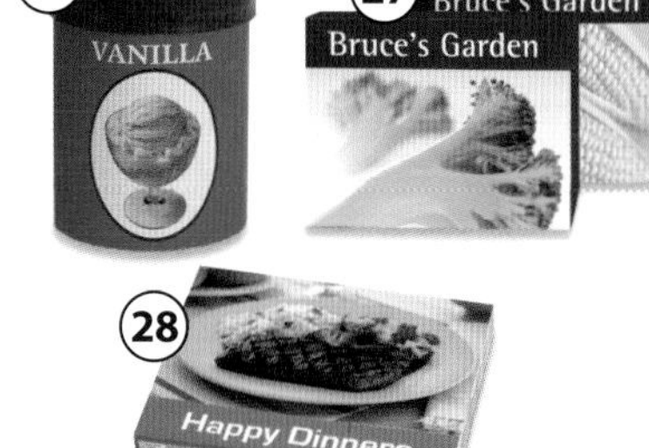

Canned Foods
缶詰

17. beans
豆類
18. soup
スープ
19. tuna
ツナ

Dairy
乳製品

20. margarine
マーガリン
21. sour cream
サワークリーム
22. yogurt
ヨーグルト

Grocery Products
食料雑貨

23. aluminum foil
アルミホイル
24. plastic wrap
食品用ラップ
25. plastic storage bags
食品保存用のビニール袋

Frozen Foods
冷凍食品

26. ice cream
アイスクリーム
27. frozen vegetables
冷凍野菜
28. frozen dinner
冷凍ディナー

Ways to ask for information in a grocery store

Excuse me, where are the carrots?
Can you please tell me where to find the dog food?
Do you have any lamb chops today?

Pair practice. Make conversations.

A: *Can you please tell me where to find the dog food?*
B: *Sure. It's in aisle 1B. Do you need anything else?*
A: *Yes, where are the carrots?*

スーパーマーケット

A Grocery Store

9. shopping basket
買い物かご
10. self-checkout
セルフチェックアウト
11. line
列
12. checkstand
レジ台
13. cashier
レジ係
14. bagger
袋詰め係
15. cash register
レジ
16. bottle return
びんの返却口

Baking Products
ベーキング用製品

29. flour
小麦粉
30. sugar
砂糖
31. oil
油

Beverages
飲み物

32. apple juice
リンゴジュース
33. coffee
コーヒー
34. soda / pop
炭酸飲料

Snack Foods
スナックフード

35. potato chips
ポテトチップ
36. nuts
ナッツ
37. candy bar
板チョコ

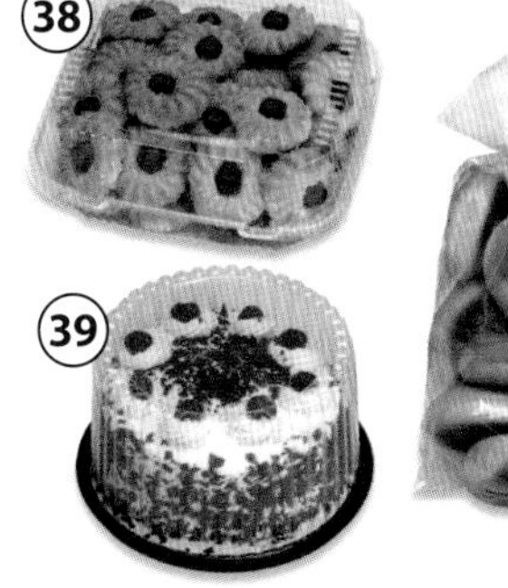

Baked Goods
ベーカリー製品

38. cookies
クッキー
39. cake
ケーキ
40. bagels
ベーグル

Ask your classmates. Share the answers.

1. What is your favorite grocery store?
2. Do you prefer to shop alone or with friends?
3. Which foods from your country are hard to find?

Think about it. Discuss.

1. Is it better to shop every day or once a week? Why?
2. Why do grocery stores put snacks near the checkstands?
3. What's good and what's bad about small grocery stores?

Containers and Packaging

容器とパッケージ

1. bottles
ボトル

2. jars
びん

3. cans
缶

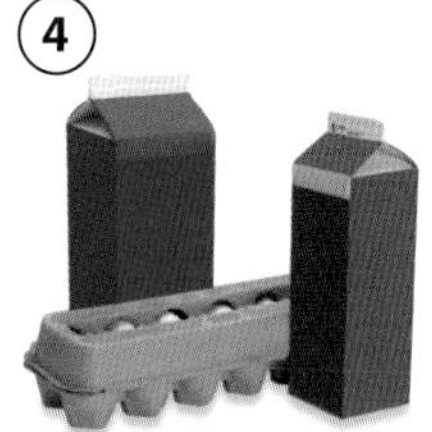

4. cartons
カートン

5. containers
容器

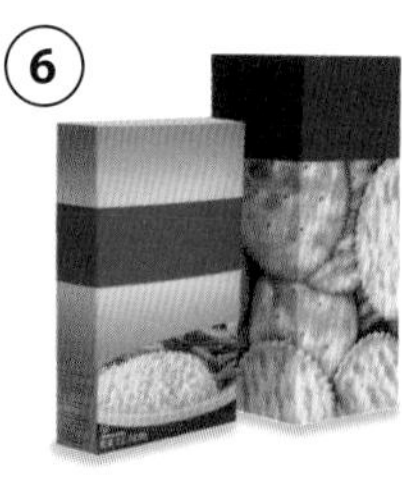

6. boxes
箱

7. bags
袋

8. packages
パッケージ

9. six-packs
6本入りのパック

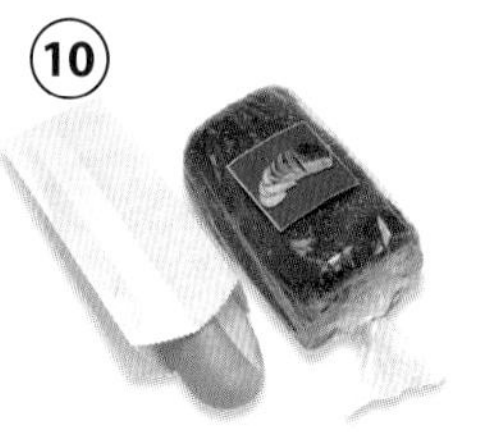

10. loaves
斤／ひとかたまり

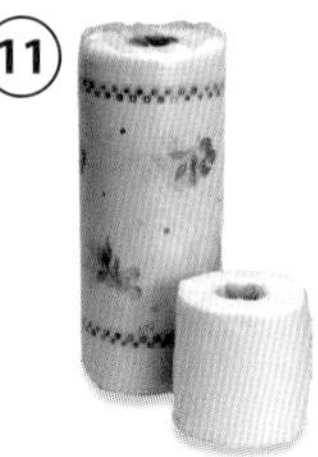

11. rolls
巻

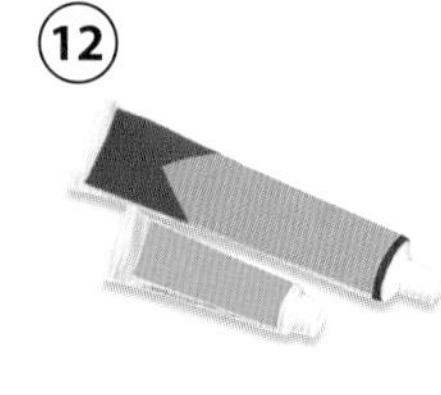

12. tubes
チューブ

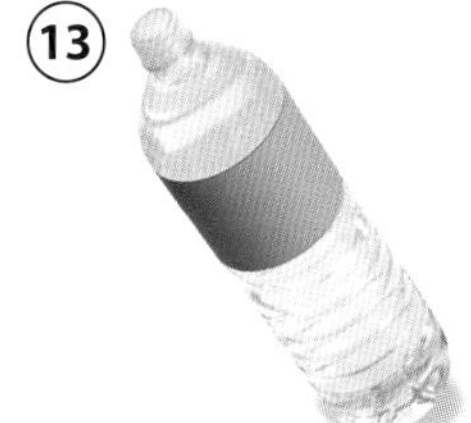

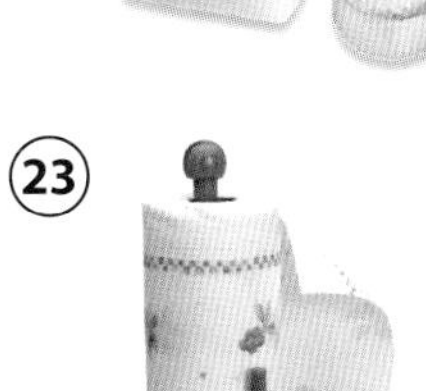

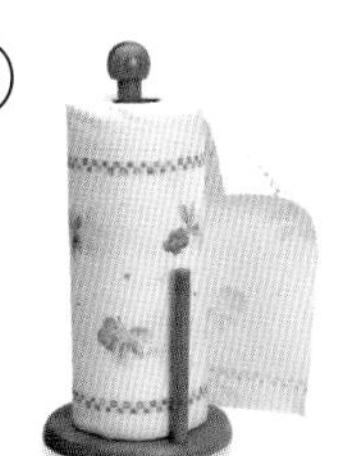

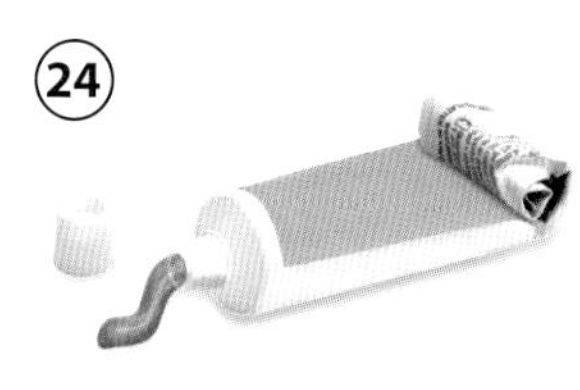

13. a bottle of water
1本の水
14. a jar of jam
1瓶のジャム
15. a can of beans
1缶の豆
16. a carton of eggs
1カートンの卵

17. a container of cottage cheese
1パックのカッテージチーズ
18. a box of cereal
1箱のシリアル
19. a bag of flour
1袋の小麦粉
20. a package of cookies
1箱のクッキー

21. a six-pack of soda (pop)
6本入りのソーダ1パック
22. a loaf of bread
1斤のパン
23. a roll of paper towels
1巻のペーパータオル
24. a tube of toothpaste
1本の練り歯みがき

Grammar Point: count and non-count

Some foods can be counted: *an apple, two apples.*
Some foods can't be counted: *some rice, some water.*
For non-count foods, count containers: *two bags of rice.*

Pair practice. Make conversations.

A: *How many boxes of cereal do we need?*
B: *We need two boxes.*

A. **Measure** the ingredients.
材料を**計る**

B. **Weigh** the food.
食品の**重さを量る**

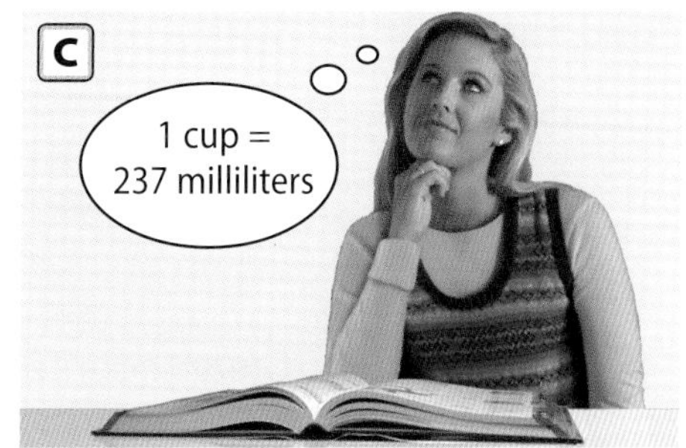

C. **Convert** the measurements.
計量値を**換算する**

Liquid Measures 液体の計量

1 1 fl. oz.

2 1 c.

3 1 pt.

4 1 qt.

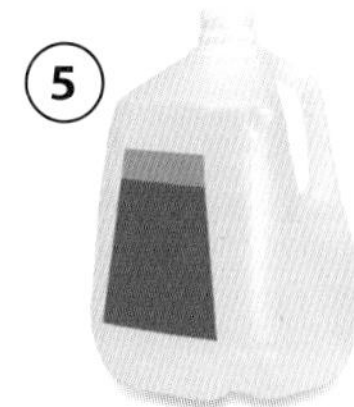

5 1 gal.

Dry Measures 調味料・乾物類の計量

6 1 tsp.

7 1 TBS.

8 1/4 c.

9 1/2 c.

10 1 c.

Weight 重さ

11

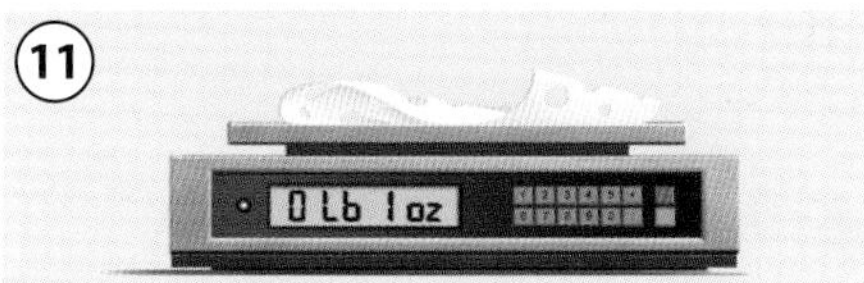

12

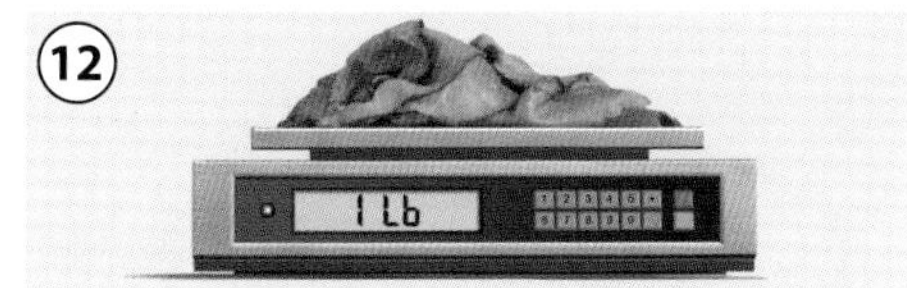

1. a fluid ounce of milk
   牛乳1オンス
2. a cup of oil
   油1カップ
3. a pint of frozen yogurt
   フローズンヨーグルト1パイント
4. a quart of milk
   牛乳1クォート
5. a gallon of water
   水1ガロン
6. a teaspoon of salt
   塩小さじ1杯
7. a tablespoon of sugar
   砂糖大さじ1杯
8. a quarter cup of brown sugar
   三温糖1/4カップ
9. a half cup of raisins
   レーズン1/2カップ
10. a cup of flour
    小麦粉1カップ
11. an ounce of cheese
    チーズ1オンス
12. a pound of roast beef
    ローストビーフ1ポンド

Equivalencies

3 tsp. = 1 TBS.	2 c. = 1 pt.
2 TBS. = 1 fl. oz.	2 pt. = 1 qt.
8 fl. oz. = 1 c.	4 qt. = 1 gal.

Volume

1 fl. oz. = 30 ml
1 c. = 237 ml
1 pt. = .47 L
1 qt. = .95 L
1 gal. = 3.79 L

Weight

1 oz. = 28.35 grams (g)
1 lb. = 453.6 g
2.205 lbs. = 1 kilogram (kg)
1 lb. = 16 oz.

Food Safety 食品の安全

A. **clean**
きれいにする

B. **separate**
分ける

C. **cook**
調理する

D. **chill**
冷やす

Ways to Serve Meat and Poultry 肉類と家禽類の調理方法

1. fried chicken
フライドチキン

2. barbecued / grilled ribs
バーベキュー／グリルしたリブ

3. broiled steak
ブロイルしたステーキ

4. roasted turkey
ローストした七面鳥

5. boiled ham
ゆでたハム

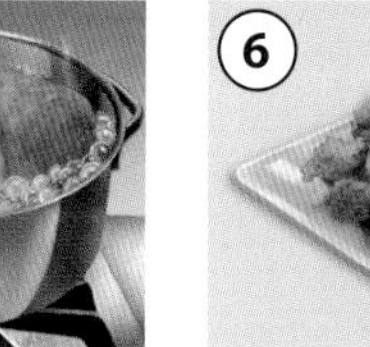

6. stir-fried beef
炒めた牛肉

Ways to Serve Eggs 卵の調理方法

7. scrambled eggs
スクランブルエッグ

8. hardboiled eggs
ゆで卵

9. poached eggs
ポーチドエッグ

10. eggs sunny-side up
目玉焼き

11. eggs over easy
オーバーイージー（両面を焼いた目玉焼きで、黄身は半熟のもの）

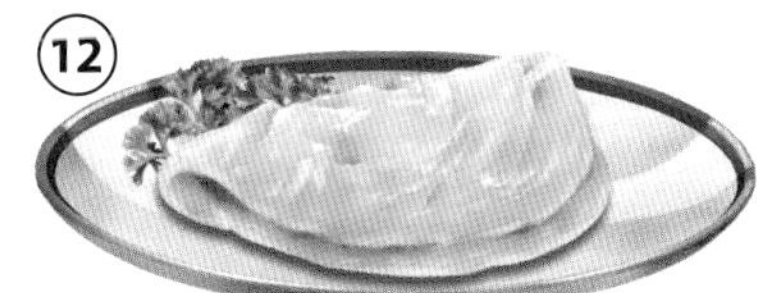

12. omelet
オムレツ

Role play. Make new conversations.

A: *How do you like your eggs?*
B: *I like them <u>scrambled</u>. And you?*
A: *I like them <u>hardboiled</u>.*

Ask your classmates. Share the answers.

1. Do you use separate cutting boards?
2. What is your favorite way to serve meat? poultry?
3. What are healthy ways of preparing meat? poultry?

Cheesy Tofu Vegetable Casserole チーズ入り豆腐と野菜のキャセロール

A. **Preheat** the oven.
オーブンを**予熱する**

B. **Grease** a baking pan.
焼き皿に**油を塗る**

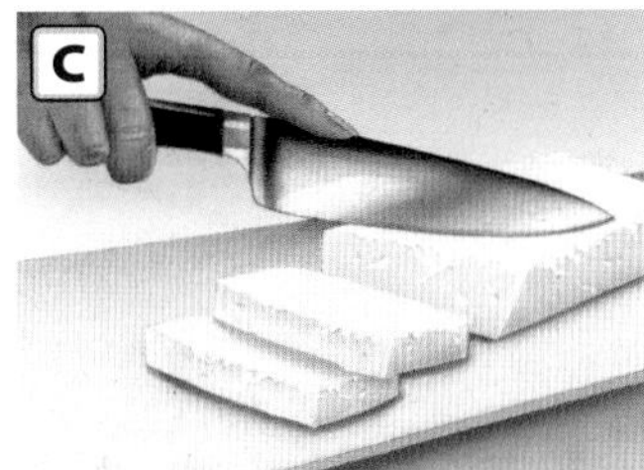

C. **Slice** the tofu.
豆腐を**切る**

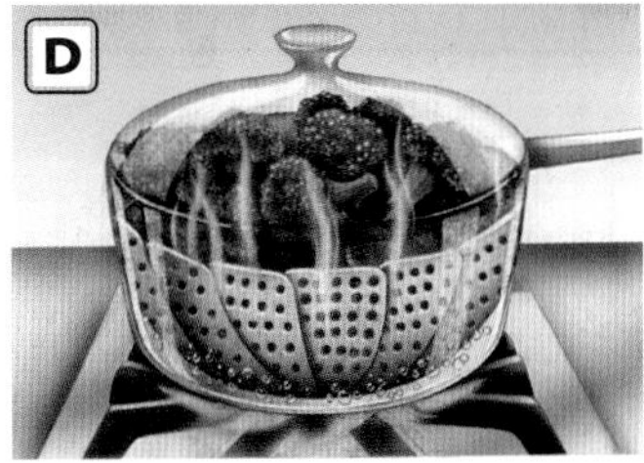

D. **Steam** the broccoli.
ブロッコリーを**蒸す**

E. **Saute** the mushrooms.
マッシュルームを**炒める**

F. **Spoon** sauce on top.
ソースを**スプーンでかける**

G. **Grate** the cheese.
チーズを**おろす**

H. **Bake**.
オーブンで焼く

Easy Chicken Soup 簡単なチキンスープ

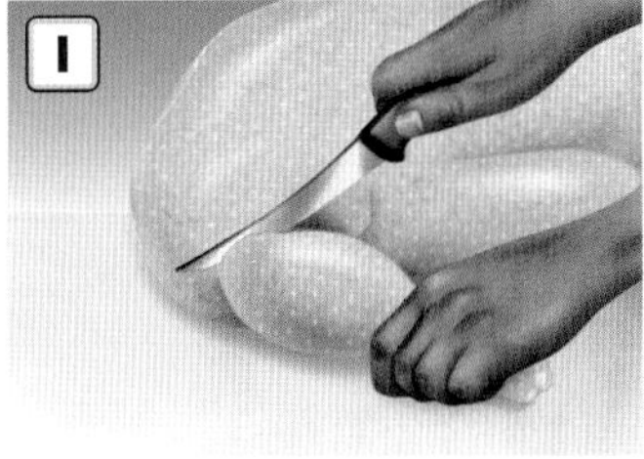

I. **Cut up** the chicken.
鶏肉を**切る**

J. **Dice** the celery.
セロリを**さいの目に切る**

K. **Peel** the carrots.
ニンジンの**皮をむく**

L. **Chop** the onions.
タマネギを**刻む**

M. **Boil** the chicken.
鶏肉を**ゆでる**

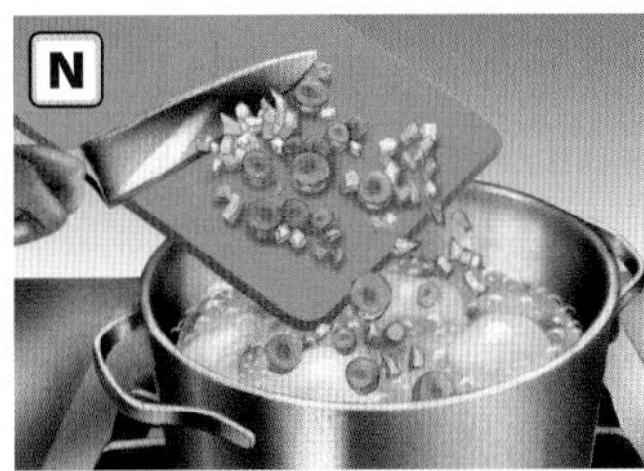

N. **Add** the vegetables.
野菜を**加える**

O. **Stir**.
混ぜる

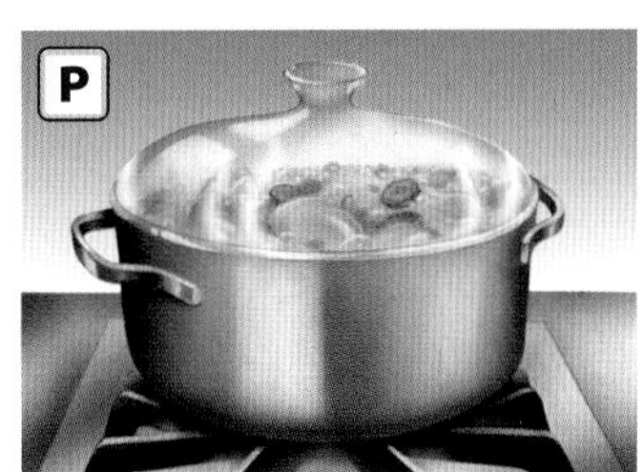

P. **Simmer**.
煮込む

Quick and Easy Cake 素早く簡単にできるケーキ

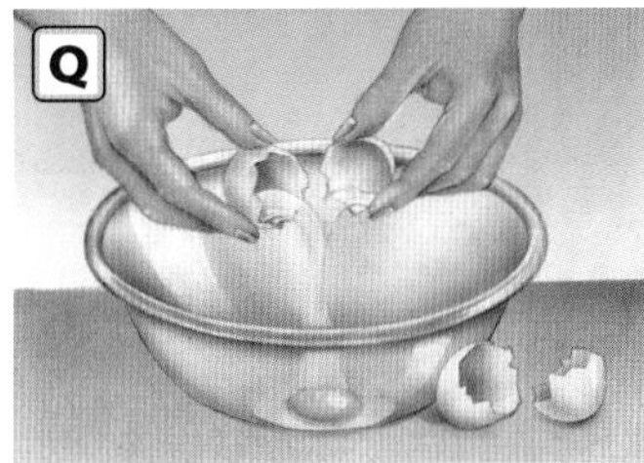

Q. **Break** 2 eggs into a microwave-safe bowl.
卵２個を耐熱ボウルに**割りいれる**

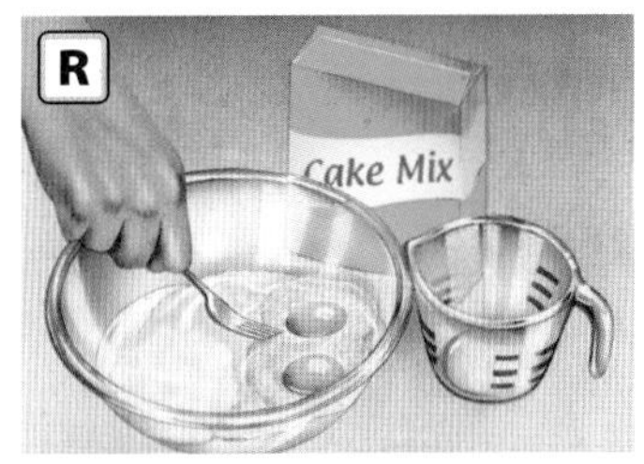

R. **Mix** the ingredients.
材料を**混ぜる**

S. **Beat** the mixture.
混ぜた材料を**泡立てる**

T. **Microwave** for 5 minutes.
5分間**電子レンジで加熱する**

1. can opener 缶切り
2. grater おろしがね
3. steamer 蒸し器
4. plastic storage container プラスチックの保存容器
5. frying pan フライパン
6. pot 鍋
7. ladle おたま
8. double boiler 二重鍋
9. wooden spoon 木のスプーン
10. casserole dish キャセロール皿
11. garlic press ガーリックプレス
12. carving knife 肉切り用ナイフ
13. roasting pan ロースト用天板
14. roasting rack 天板ラック
15. vegetable peeler 野菜の皮むき器
16. paring knife 果物ナイフ
17. colander 水きり器
18. kitchen timer キッチンタイマー
19. spatula 調理用ヘラ
20. eggbeater 卵の泡立て器
21. whisk 泡立て器
22. strainer ざる
23. tongs トング
24. lid ふた
25. saucepan 片手鍋
26. cake pan ケーキ型
27. cookie sheet クッキーシート
28. pie pan パイ皿
29. pot holders 鍋つかみ
30. rolling pin 麺棒
31. mixing bowl ミキシングボウル

Pair practice. Make new conversations.

A: *Please hand me* *the whisk*.
B: *Here's* *the whisk*. *Do you need anything else?*
A: *Yes, pass me* *the casserole dish*.

Use the new words.
Look at page 77. Name the kitchen utensils you see.

A: *Here's* *a grater*.
B: *This is* *a mixing bowl*.

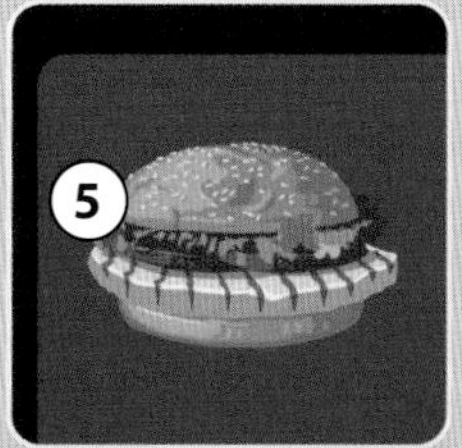

1. hamburger
   ハンバーガー
2. french fries
   フライドポテト
3. cheeseburger
   チーズバーガー
4. onion rings
   オニオンリング
5. chicken sandwich
   チキンバーガー
6. hot dog
   ホットドッグ
7. nachos
   ナチョス
8. taco
   タコス
9. burrito
   ブリトー
10. pizza
    ピザ
11. soda
    炭酸飲料
12. iced tea
    アイスティー
13. ice-cream cone
    アイスクリームコーン
14. milkshake
    ミルクシェイク
15. donut
    ドーナッツ
16. muffin
    マフィン
17. counterperson
    店員
18. straw
    ストロー
19. plastic utensils
    プラスチックのフォークやナイフ
20. sugar substitute
    人工甘味料
21. ketchup
    ケチャップ
22. mustard
    マスタード
23. mayonnaise
    マヨネーズ
24. salad bar
    サラダバー

Grammar Point: yes/no questions *(do)*

***Do** you like hamburgers? Yes, I do.*

***Do** you like nachos? No, I don't.*

Think about it. Discuss.

1. Do you think that fast food is bad for people? Why or why not?
2. What fast foods do you have in your country?
3. Do you have a favorite fast food restaurant? Which one?

1. bacon
   ベーコン
2. sausage
   ソーセージ
3. hash browns
   ハッシュブラウン
4. toast
   トースト
5. English muffin
   イングリッシュマフィン
6. biscuits
   ビスケット
7. pancakes
   ホットケーキ
8. waffles
   ワッフル
9. hot cereal
   温かいシリアル
10. grilled cheese sandwich
    グリルチーズサンドイッチ
11. pickle
    ピクルス
12. club sandwich
    クラブサンドイッチ
13. spinach salad
    ホウレンソウサラダ
14. chef's salad
    シェフサラダ
15. dinner salad
    ディナーサラダ
16. soup
    スープ
17. rolls
    ディナーロール
18. coleslaw
    コールスロー
19. potato salad
    ポテトサラダ
20. pasta salad
    パスタサラダ
21. fruit salad
    フルーツサラダ

Ways to order from a menu

I'd like a grilled cheese sandwich.
I'll have a bowl of tomato soup.
Could I get the chef's salad with ranch dressing?

Pair practice. Make conversations.

A: *I'd like a grilled cheese sandwich, please.*
B: *Anything else for you?*
A: *Yes, I'll have a bowl of tomato soup with that.*

A Coffee Shop Menu

22. roast chicken
ローストチキン
23. mashed potatoes
マッシュポテト
24. steak
ステーキ
25. baked potato
ベークドポテト
26. spaghetti
スパゲッティ
27. meatballs
ミートボール
28. garlic bread
ガーリックブレッド
29. grilled fish
魚のグリル
30. rice
ライス
31. meatloaf
ミートローフ
32. steamed vegetables
蒸した野菜
33. layer cake
レイヤーケーキ
34. cheesecake
チーズケーキ
35. pie
パイ
36. mixed berries
ミックスベリー
37. coffee
コーヒー
38. decaf coffee
カフェインレスコーヒー
39. tea
紅茶
40. herbal tea
ハーブティー
41. cream
クリーム
42. low-fat milk
低脂肪ミルク

Ask your classmates. Share the answers.

1. Do you prefer vegetable soup or chicken soup?
2. Do you prefer tea or coffee?
3. Which desserts on the menu do you like?

Role play. Order a dinner from the menu.

A: *Are you ready to order?*
B: *I think so. I'll have* *<u>the roast chicken</u>*.
A: *Would you also like…?*

1. dining room
ダイニングルーム
2. hostess
案内係
3. high chair
ベビーチェア／ハイチェア
4. booth
ボックス席
5. to-go box
テイクアウトボックス
6. patron / diner
顧客／食事客
7. menu
メニュー
8. server / waiter
給仕人／ウエイター

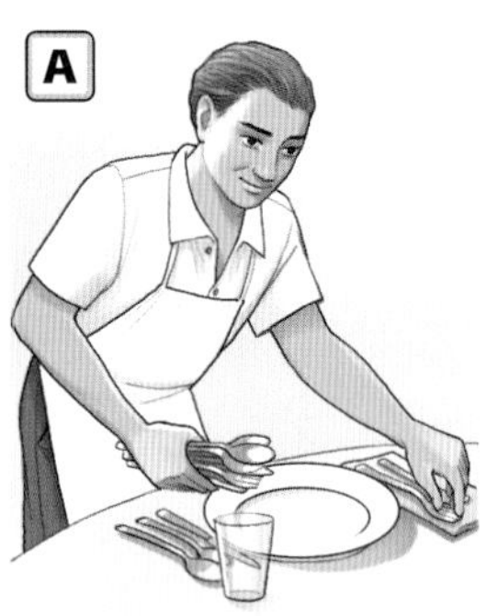

A. **set** the table
テーブルを**整える**
B. **seat** the customer
食事客を**席に案内する**
C. **pour** the water
水を**注ぐ**
D. **order** from the menu
メニューを見て**注文する**
E. **take** the order
注文を**受ける**
F. **serve** the meal
料理を**出す**
G. **clear** / **bus** the dishes
皿を**片付ける**
H. **carry** the tray
お盆を**運ぶ**
I. **pay** the check
勘定を**支払う**
J. **leave** a tip
チップを**置く**

More vocabulary

eat out: to go to a restaurant to eat
take out: to buy food at a restaurant and take it home to eat

Look at the pictures.
Describe what is happening.

A: *She's seating the customer.*
B: *He's taking the order.*

9. server / waitress
給仕人／ウエイトレス
10. dessert tray
デザートトレー
11. bread basket
ブレッドバスケット
12. busser
食後のテーブルを片付ける人
13. dish room
食器用の部屋
14. dishwasher
食器を洗う人
15. kitchen
調理場
16. chef
シェフ

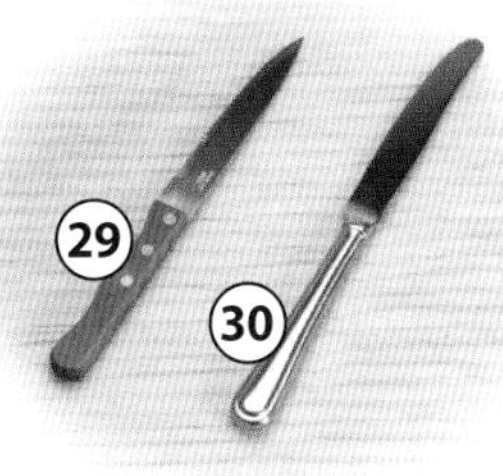

17. place setting
テーブルセッティング
18. dinner plate
ディナー皿
19. bread-and-butter plate
パンとバター用の皿
20. salad plate
サラダ用の皿
21. soup bowl
スープ皿
22. water glass
水を入れるコップ
23. wine glass
ワイングラス
24. cup
コーヒー（紅茶）カップ
25. saucer
受け皿
26. napkin
ナプキン
27. salad fork
サラダフォーク
28. dinner fork
ディナーフォーク
29. steak knife
ステーキナイフ
30. knife
ナイフ
31. teaspoon
ティースプーン
32. soupspoon
スープスプーン

Pair practice. Make new conversations.

A: *Excuse me, this spoon is dirty.*
B: *I'm so sorry. I'll get you a clean spoon right away.*
A: *Thanks.*

Role play. Talk to a new busser.

A: *Do the salad forks go on the left?*
B: *Yes. They go next to the dinner forks.*
A: *What about the…?*

1. live music ライブミュージック	**3.** lemonade レモネード	**5.** samples 試食用サンプル	**7.** vendors 売り子	**9.** herbs ハーブ
2. organic 有機食品	**4.** sour 酸っぱい	**6.** avocados アボカド	**8.** sweets 甘いもの	**A. count** **数える**

Look at the pictures.
What do you see?

Answer the questions.

1. How many vendors are at the market today?
2. Which vegetables are organic?
3. What are the children eating?
4. What is the woman counting? Why?

 **Read the story.**

The Farmers' Market

On Saturdays, the Novaks go to the farmers' market. They like to visit the vendors. Alex Novak always goes to the hot food stand for lunch. His children love to eat the fruit samples. Alex's father usually buys some sweets and lemonade. The lemonade is very sour.

Nina Novak likes to buy organic herbs and vegetables. Today, she is buying avocados. The market worker counts eight avocados. She gives Nina one more for free.

There are other things to do at the market. The Novaks like to listen to the live music. Sometimes they meet friends there. The farmers' market is a great place for families on a Saturday afternoon.

Think about it.

1. What's good or bad about shopping at a farmers' market?
2. Imagine you are at the farmers' market. What will you buy?

Everyday Clothes 普段着

1. shirt
シャツ
2. jeans
ジーンズ
3. dress
ワンピース
4. T-shirt
Tシャツ
5. baseball cap
野球帽
6. socks
ソックス
7. athletic shoes
運動靴
A. **tie**
結ぶ

Listen and point. Take turns.

A: *Point to the dress.*
B: *Point to the T-shirt.*
A: *Point to the baseball cap.*

Dictate to your partner. Take turns.

A: *Write dress.*
B: *Is that spelled d-r-e-s-s?*
A: *Yes. That's right.*

8. blouse
ブラウス
9. handbag
ハンドバッグ
10. skirt
スカート
11. suit
スーツ
12. slacks / pants
スラックス／ズボン
13. shoes
靴
14. sweater
セーター
B. **put on**
着る

Ways to compliment clothes

That's a pretty dress!
Those are great shoes!
I really like your baseball cap!

Role play. Compliment a friend.

A: *That's a pretty dress! Green is a great color on you.*
B: *Thanks! I really like your…*

Casual, Work, and Formal Clothes
カジュアルな服装、仕事着、フォーマルな服装

Casual Clothes カジュアルな服装

1. cap
帽子
2. cardigan sweater
カーディガン
3. pullover sweater
セーター
4. sports shirt
スポーツシャツ
5. maternity dress
妊婦服
6. overalls
オーバーオール
7. knit top
ニットトップ
8. capris
カプリパンツ
9. sandals
サンダル

Work Clothes 仕事着

10. uniform
制服
11. business suit
ビジネススーツ
12. tie
ネクタイ
13. briefcase
ブリーフケース

More vocabulary

three piece suit: matching jacket, vest, and slacks
outfit: clothes that look nice together
in fashion / in style: clothes that are popular now

Describe the people. Take turns.

A: *She's wearing a maternity dress.*
B: *He's wearing a uniform.*

カジュアルな服装、仕事着、
フォーマルな服装

Casual, Work, and Formal Clothes

Formal Clothes フォーマルな服装

14. sports jacket / sports coat
スポーツジャケット／スポーツコート

15. vest
ベスト

16. bow tie
蝶ネクタイ

17. tuxedo
タキシード

18. evening gown
イブニングドレス

19. clutch bag
クラッチバッグ

20. cocktail dress
カクテルドレス

21. high heels
ハイヒール

Exercise Wear スポーツウェア

22. sweatshirt / hoodie
トレーナー／フード付きトレーナー

23. sweatpants
スウェットパンツ

24. tank top
タンクトップ

25. shorts
ショートパンツ

Ask your classmates. Share the answers.

1. What's your favorite outfit?
2. Do you like to wear formal clothes? Why or why not?
3. Do you prefer to exercise in shorts or sweatpants?

Think about it. Discuss.

1. What jobs require formal clothes? Uniforms?
2. What's good and bad about wearing school uniforms?
3. What is your opinion of today's popular clothing?

Seasonal Clothing

季節の衣類

1. hat
   帽子
2. (over)coat
   コート
3. headband
   ヘッドバンド
4. leather jacket
   革のジャケット
5. winter scarf
   マフラー
6. gloves
   手袋
7. headwrap
   ヘッドラップ
8. jacket
   ジャケット
9. parka
   パーカー
10. mittens
    ミトン
11. ski hat
    スキー帽
12. leggings
    スパッツ
13. earmuffs
    防寒用耳あて
14. down vest
    ダウンベスト
15. ski mask
    スキーマスク
16. down jacket
    ダウンジャケット

17. umbrella
    傘
18. raincoat
    レインコート
19. poncho
    ポンチョ
20. rain boots
    雨靴
21. trench coat
    トレンチコート
22. swimming trunks
    海水パンツ
23. straw hat
    麦わら帽子
24. windbreaker
    ウィンドブレーカー
25. cover-up
    ビーチガウン
26. swimsuit / bathing suit
    水着
27. sunglasses
    サングラス

Grammar Point: *should*

*It's raining. You **should** take an umbrella.*
*It's snowing. You **should** wear a scarf.*
*It's sunny. You **should** wear a straw hat.*

Pair practice. Make new conversations.

A: *It's snowing. You should wear a scarf.*
B: *Don't worry. I'm wearing my parka.*
A: *Good, and don't forget your mittens.*

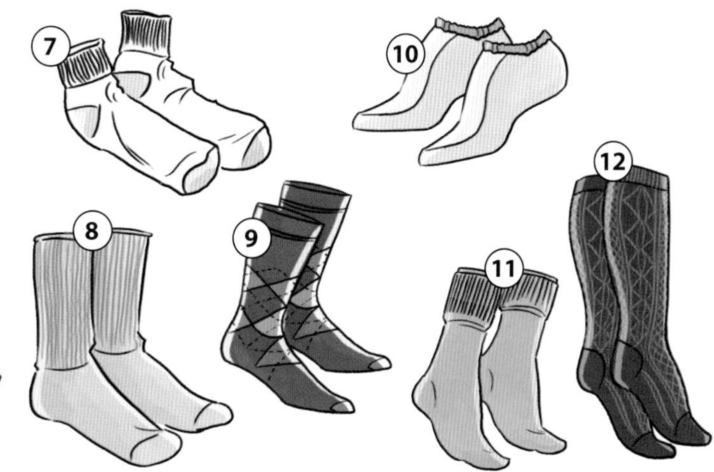

Unisex Underwear
男女兼用の下着

1. undershirt
アンダーシャツ
2. thermal undershirt
サーマルアンダーシャツ
3. long underwear
ズボン下

Men's Underwear
男性用下着

4. boxer shorts
ボクサーショーツ
5. briefs
ブリーフ
6. athletic supporter / jockstrap
男性用スポーツサポーター

Unisex Socks
男女兼用ソックス

7. ankle socks
アンクルソックス
8. crew socks
クルーソックス
9. dress socks
ドレスソックス

Women's Socks
女性用ソックス

10. low-cut socks
ローカットソックス
11. anklets
アンクレットソックス
12. knee highs
ハイソックス

Women's Underwear 女性用下着

13. (bikini) panties
(ビキニ型)
パンティ
14. briefs / underpants
パンツ
15. body shaper / girdle
ボディスーツ／ガードル
16. garter belt
ガーターベルト
17. stockings
ストッキング
18. panty hose
パンティストッキング
19. tights
タイツ
20. bra
ブラジャー
21. camisole
キャミソール
22. full slip
スリップ
23. half slip
ペチコート

Sleepwear スリープウェア

24. pajamas
パジャマ
25. nightgown
ネグリジェ
26. slippers
スリッパ
27. blanket sleeper
カバーオール寝巻き
28. nightshirt
寝巻き
29. robe
ガウン

More vocabulary

lingerie: underwear or sleepwear for women

loungewear: very casual clothing for relaxing around the home

Ask your classmates. Share the answers.

1. What kind of socks are you wearing today?
2. What kind of sleepwear do you prefer?
3. Do you wear slippers at home?

Workplace Clothing

作業着

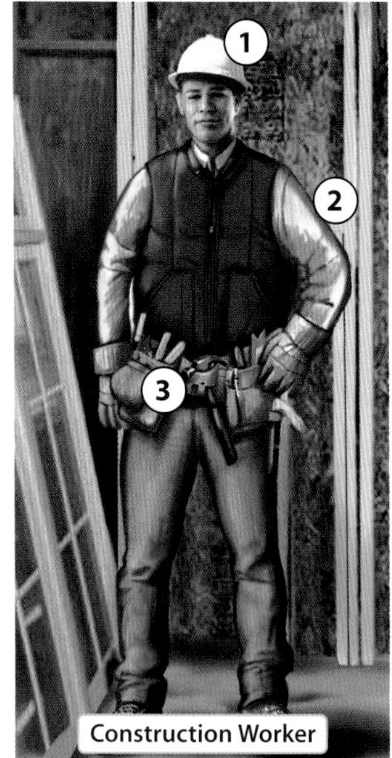

Construction Worker

Road Worker

Automotive Painter

Food Processor

1. hard hat
ヘルメット
2. work shirt
作業用シャツ
3. tool belt
工具ベルト
4. Hi-Visibility safety vest
反射安全ベスト
5. work pants
作業ズボン
6. steel toe boots
つま先がスチールで保護された作業用ブーツ
7. ventilation mask
換気用マスク
8. coveralls
カバーオール
9. bump cap
保護用帽子
10. safety glasses
安全眼鏡
11. apron
エプロン

Manager

Salesperson

Farmworker

Ranch Hand

12. blazer
ブレザー
13. tie
ネクタイ
14. polo shirt
ポロシャツ
15. name tag
名札
16. bandana
バンダナ
17. work gloves
作業用手袋
18. cowboy hat
カウボーイハット
19. jeans
ジーンズ

Pair practice. Make new conversations.

A: *What do <u>construction workers</u> wear to work?*
B: *They wear <u>hard hats</u> and <u>tool belts</u>.*
A: *What do <u>road workers</u> wear to work?*

Use the new words.

Look at pages 166–169. Name the workplace clothing you see.

A: *He's wearing <u>a hard hat</u>.*
B: *She's wearing <u>scrubs</u>.*

Workplace Clothing

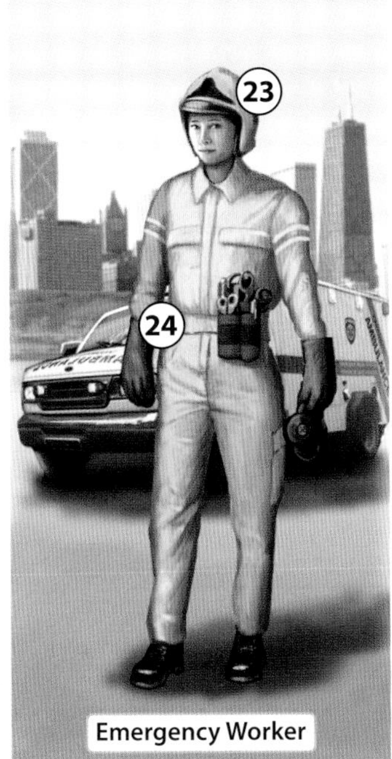

20. security shirt
警備員のシャツ
21. badge
バッジ
22. security pants
警備員のズボン

23. helmet
ヘルメット
24. jumpsuit
ジャンプスーツ

25. hairnet
ヘアネット
26. smock
スモック
27. disposable gloves
使い捨て手袋

28. chef's hat
コック帽
29. chef's jacket
コックコート
30. waist apron
前掛け

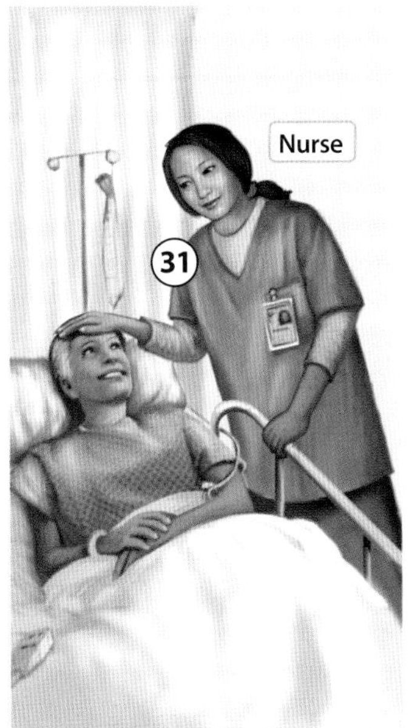

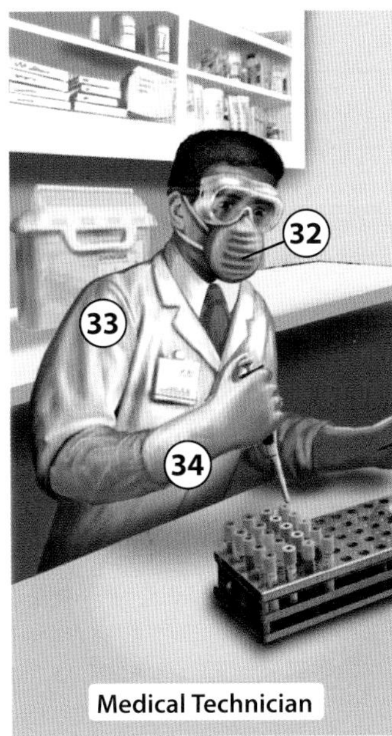

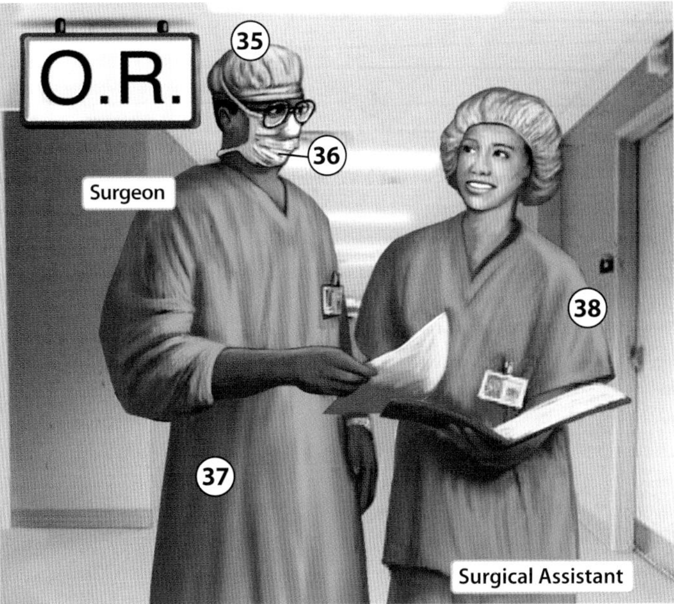

31. scrubs
医療衣
32. face mask
フェースマスク

33. lab coat
白衣
34. latex gloves
ラテックス製手袋

35. surgical scrub cap
手術用帽子
36. surgical mask
手術用マスク

37. surgical gown
手術衣
38. surgical scrubs
手術着

Ask your classmates. Share the answers.

1. Which of these outfits would you like to wear?
2. Which of these items are in your closet?
3. Do you wear safety clothing at work? What kinds?

Think about it. Discuss.

1. What other jobs require helmets? disposable gloves?
2. Is it better to have a uniform or wear your own clothes at work? Why?

Shoes and Accessories

靴とアクセサリー

A. purchase
購入する

B. wait in line
列に並んで**待つ**

1. suspenders
サスペンダー

2. purses / handbags
ハンドバッグ

3. salesclerk
販売員

4. customer
顧客

5. display case
ショーケース

6. belts
ベルト

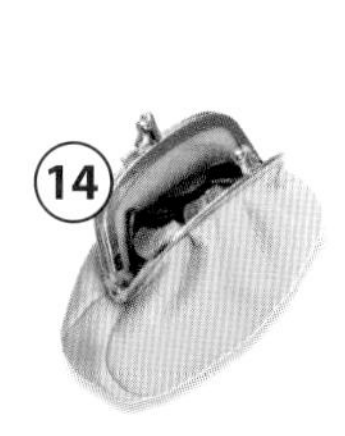

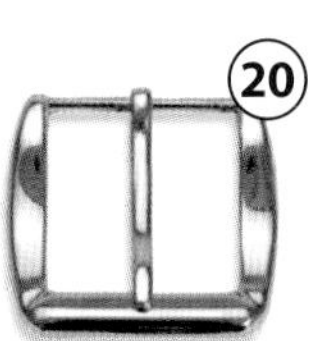

13. wallet
財布

14. change purse / coin purse
小銭入れ

15. cell phone holder
携帯電話ケース

16. (wrist)watch
腕時計

17. shoulder bag
ショルダーバッグ

18. backpack
バックパック

19. tote bag
トートバッグ

20. belt buckle
バックル

21. sole
靴底

22. heel
かかと

23. toe
つま先

24. shoelaces
靴ひも

More vocabulary

gift: something you give or receive from friends or family for a special occasion

present: a gift

Grammar Point: object pronouns

*My **sister** loves jewelry. I'll buy **her** a necklace.*
*My **dad** likes belts. I'll buy **him** a belt buckle.*
*My **friends** love scarves. I'll buy **them** scarves.*

7. shoe department
靴売場
8. jewelry department
宝石売場
9. bracelets
ブレスレット
10. necklaces
ネックレス
11. hats
帽子
12. scarves
スカーフ
C. **try on** shoes
靴を**はいてみる**
D. **assist** a customer
顧客の品選びを**手伝う**

25. high heels
ハイヒール
26. pumps
パンプス
27. flats
フラットシューズ
28. boots
ブーツ
29. oxfords
オックスフォードシューズ
30. loafers
ローファー
31. hiking boots
ハイキングブーツ
32. tennis shoes
テニスシューズ
33. chain
チェーン
34. beads
ビーズ
35. locket
ロケット
36. pierced earrings
ピアス
37. clip-on earrings
クリップイヤリング
38. pin
ブローチ
39. string of pearls
パールのネックレス
40. ring
指輪

Ways to talk about accessories

I need a hat to wear with this scarf.
I'd like earrings to go with the necklace.
Do you have a belt that would go with my shoes?

Role play. Talk to a salesperson.

A: *Do you have boots that would go with this skirt?*
B: *Let me see. How about these brown ones?*
A: *Perfect. I also need…*

Describing Clothes 衣服の説明

Sizes サイズ

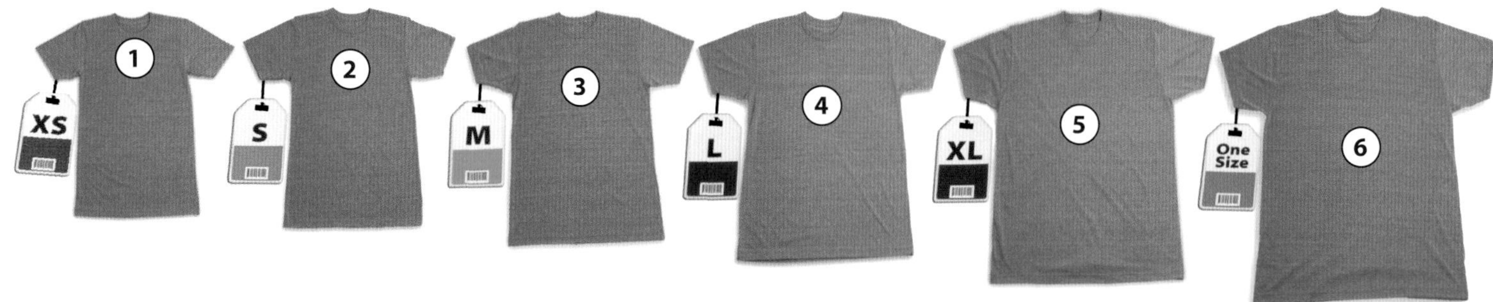

1. extra small
特小
2. small
小
3. medium
中
4. large
大
5. extra large
特大
6. one-size-fits-all
フリーサイズ

Styles スタイル

7. **crewneck** sweater
丸首のセーター
8. **V-neck** sweater
Vネックのセーター
9. **turtleneck** sweater
タートルネックのセーター
10. **scoop neck** sweater
襟ぐりの大きいセーター
11. **sleeveless** shirt
ノースリーブシャツ
12. **short-sleeved** shirt
半袖シャツ
13. **3/4-sleeved** shirt
七分袖シャツ
14. **long-sleeved** shirt
長袖シャツ
15. **mini**-skirt
ミニスカート
16. **short** skirt
ショートスカート
17. **mid-length** / **calf-length** skirt
ミディ丈のスカート
18. **long** skirt
ロングスカート

Patterns 模様

19. solid
無地
20. striped
縞模様
21. polka-dotted
水玉模様
22. plaid
格子柄
23. print
プリント柄
24. checked
チェック柄
25. floral
花柄
26. paisley
ペーズリー柄

Ask your classmates. Share the answers.

1. Do you prefer crewneck or V-neck sweaters?
2. Do you prefer checked or striped shirts?
3. Do you prefer short-sleeved or sleeveless shirts?

Role play. Talk to a salesperson.

A: *Excuse me. I'm looking for this V-neck sweater in large.*
B: *Here's a large. It's on sale for $19.99.*
A: *Wonderful! I'll take it. I'm also looking for…*

Comparing Clothing 衣服の比較

27. **heavy** jacket
厚手のジャケット
28. **light** jacket
薄手のジャケット
29. **tight** pants
きついズボン
30. **loose** / **baggy** pants
ゆるいズボン
31. **low** heels
低いかかと
32. **high** heels
高いかかと
33. **plain** blouse
無地のブラウス
34. **fancy** blouse
装飾の多いブラウス
35. **narrow** tie
細いネクタイ
36. **wide** tie
太いネクタイ

Clothing Problems 衣服の問題

37. It's **too small**.
小さすぎる

38. It's **too big**.
大きすぎる

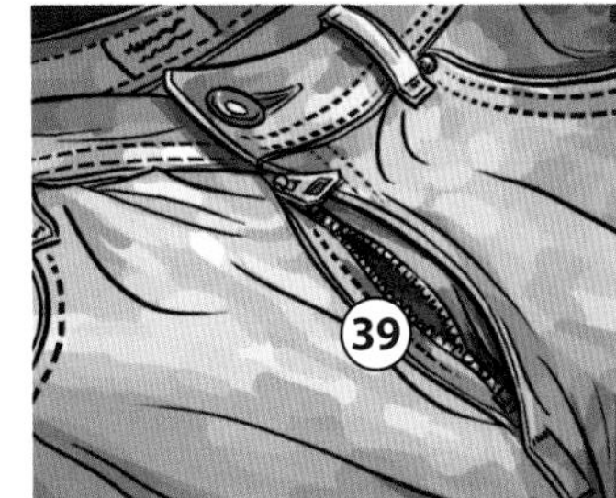

39. The zipper is **broken**.
ファスナーが壊れている

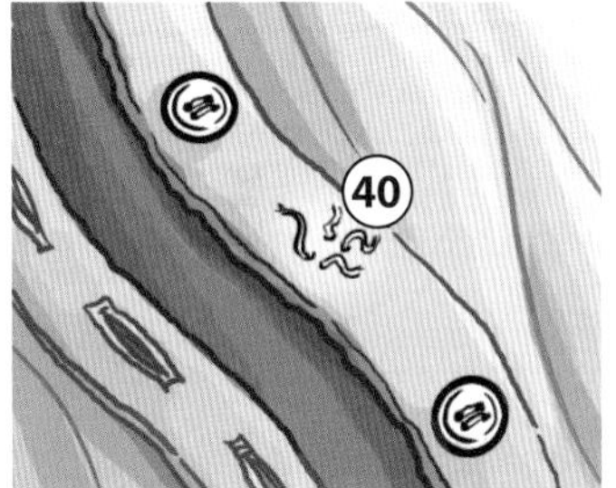

40. A button is **missing**.
ボタンが取れている

41. It's **ripped** / **torn**.
破れている

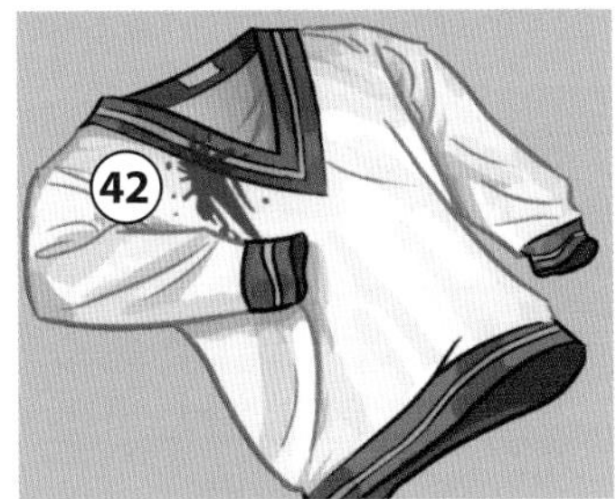

42. It's **stained**.
染みがついている

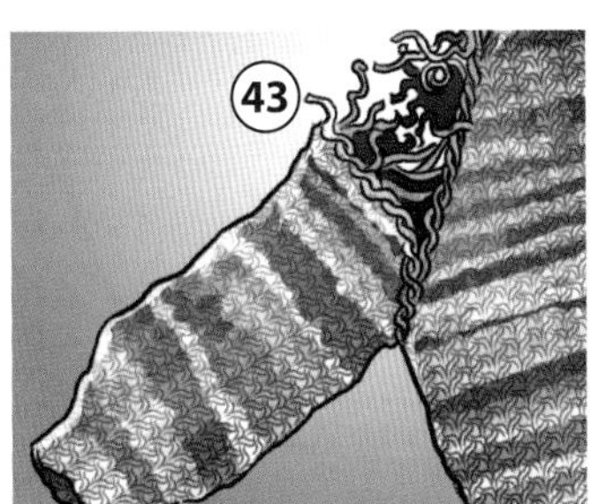

43. It's **unraveling**.
ほつれている

44. It's **too expensive**.
高すぎる

More vocabulary

refund: money you get back when you return an item to the store
complaint: a statement that something is not right
customer service: the place customers go with their complaints

Role play. Return an item to a salesperson.

A: *Welcome to Shopmart. How may I help you?*
B: *This sweater is new, but it's unraveling.*
A: *I'm sorry. Would you like a refund?*

Making Clothes 服を作る

Types of Material 布地の種類

1. cotton
綿

2. linen
麻

3. wool
ウール

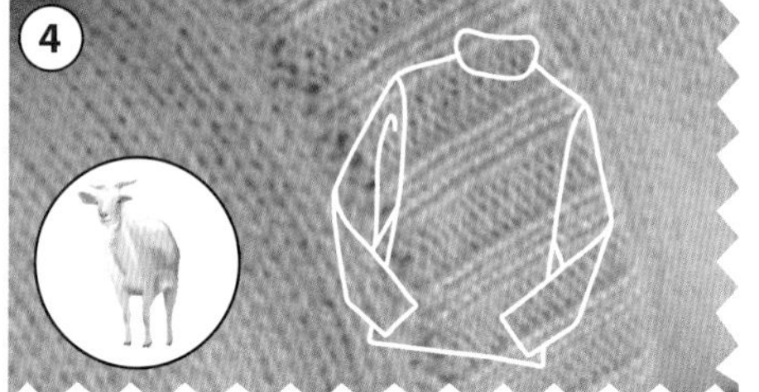

4. cashmere
カシミア

5. silk
シルク

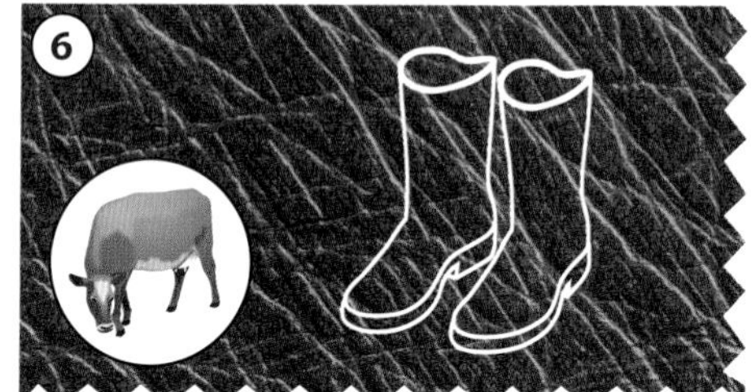

6. leather
革

A Garment Factory 縫製工場

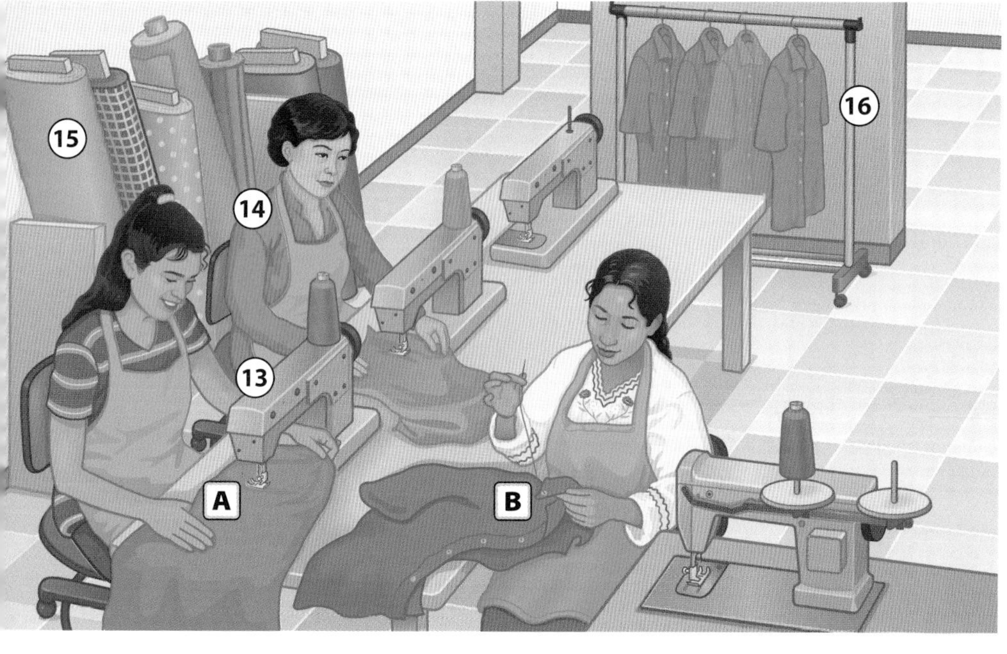

A. **sew** by machine
ミシンで**縫う**

B. **sew** by hand
手で**縫う**

13. sewing machine
ミシン

14. sewing machine operator
ミシンを使う人

15. bolt of fabric
1反の布

16. rack
ラック

Parts of a Sewing Machine ミシンの部品

17. needle
針

18. needle plate
針板

19. presser foot
押さえ金

20. feed dog / feed bar
送り部分

21. bobbin
ボビン

More vocabulary

fashion designer: a person who makes original clothes
natural materials: cloth made from things that grow in nature
synthetic materials: cloth made by people, such as nylon

Use the new words.

Look at pages 86–87. Name the materials you see.

A: *That's denim.*
B: *That's leather.*

Types of Material 布地の種類

7. denim
デニム

8. suede
スエード

9. lace
レース

10. velvet
ベルベット

11. corduroy
コーデュロイ

12. nylon
ナイロン

A Fabric Store 布地屋

Closures ボタン類

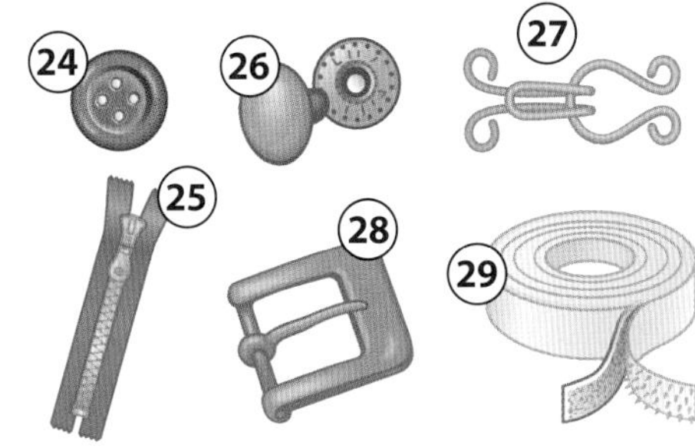

Trim 飾り

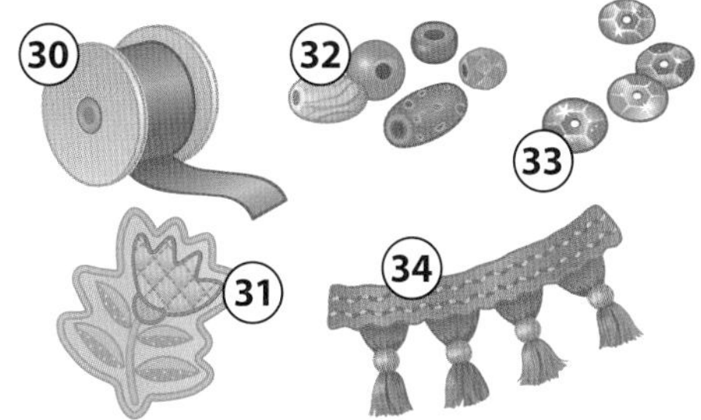

22. pattern
型紙

23. thread
糸

24. button
ボタン

25. zipper
ファスナー

26. snap
スナップボタン

27. hook and eye
カギホック

28. buckle
バックル

29. hook and loop fastener
面ファスナー

30. ribbon
リボン

31. appliqué
アップリケ

32. beads
ビーズ

33. sequins
スパンコール

34. fringe
フリンジ

Ask your classmates. Share the answers.

1. Can you sew?
2. What's your favorite type of material?
3. How many types of material are you wearing today?

Think about it. Discuss.

1. Do most people make or buy clothes in your country?
2. Is it better to make or buy clothes? Why?
3. Which materials are best for formal clothes?

Making Alterations サイズ直し

An Alterations Shop サイズ直しの専門店

1. dressmaker
婦人服の仕立て屋
2. dressmaker's dummy
仕立用のマネキン
3. tailor
仕立て屋
4. collar
襟
5. waistband
ウエストバンド
6. sleeve
袖
7. pocket
ポケット
8. hem
裾
9. cuff
裾の折り返し

Sewing Supplies 裁縫道具

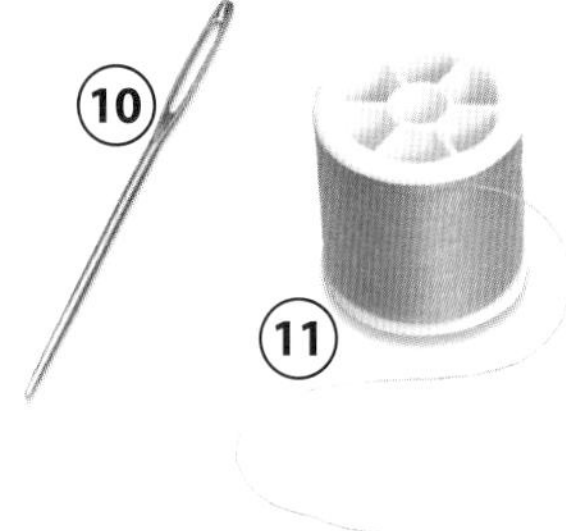

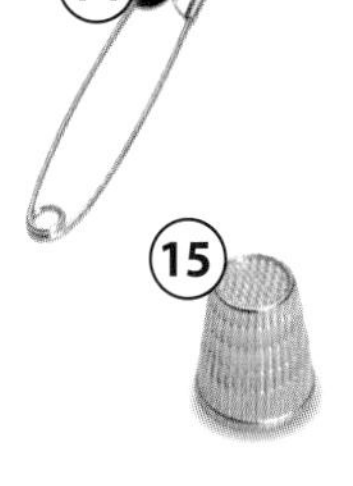

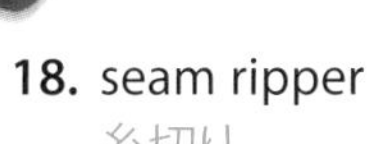

10. needle
針
11. thread
糸
12. (straight) pin
待ち針
13. pin cushion
針刺し
14. safety pin
安全ピン
15. thimble
指ぬき
16. pair of scissors
はさみ
17. tape measure
巻尺
18. seam ripper
糸切り

Alterations サイズ直し

A. **Lengthen** the pants.
ズボンを**長くする**

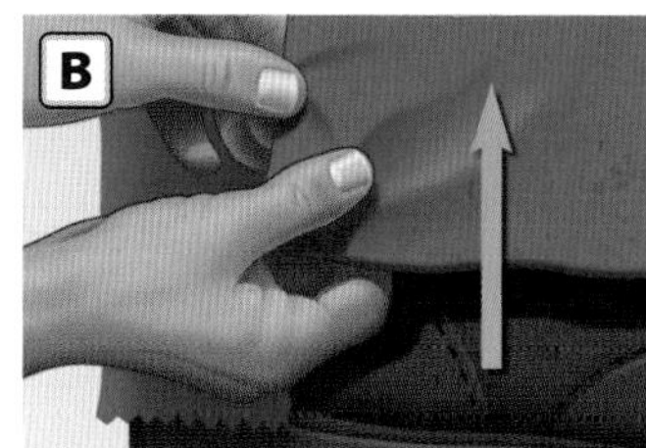

B. **Shorten** the pants.
ズボンを**短くする**

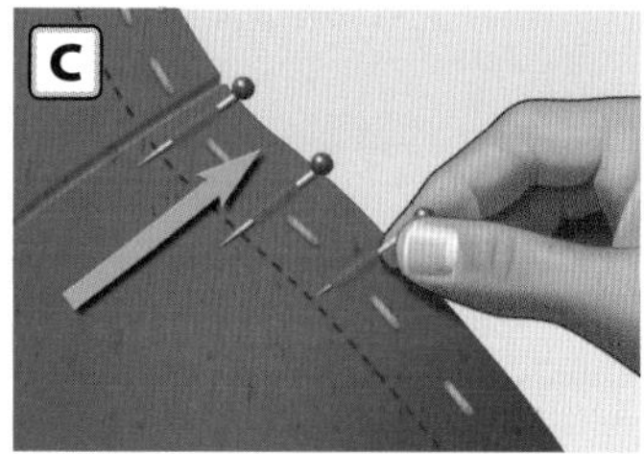

C. **Let out** the pants.
ズボンの**裾を出す**

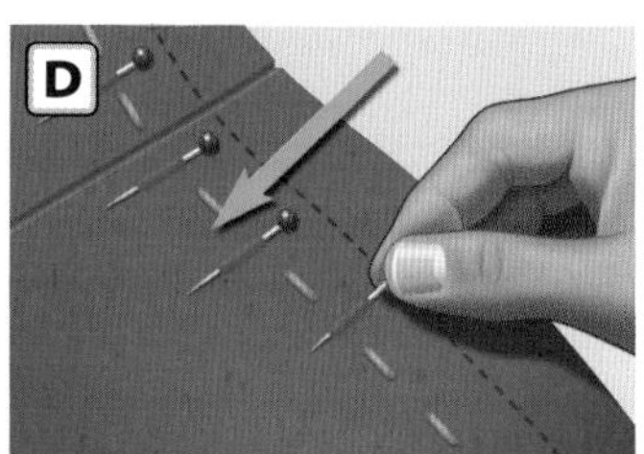

D. **Take in** the pants.
ズボンの**裾を詰める**

Pair practice. Make new conversations.

A: *Would you hand me the thread?*
B: *OK. What are you going to do?*
A: *I'm going to take in these pants.*

Ask your classmates. Share the answers.

1. Is there an alterations shop near your home?
2. Do you ever go to a tailor or a dressmaker?
3. What sewing supplies do you have at home?

洗濯をする

Doing the Laundry 

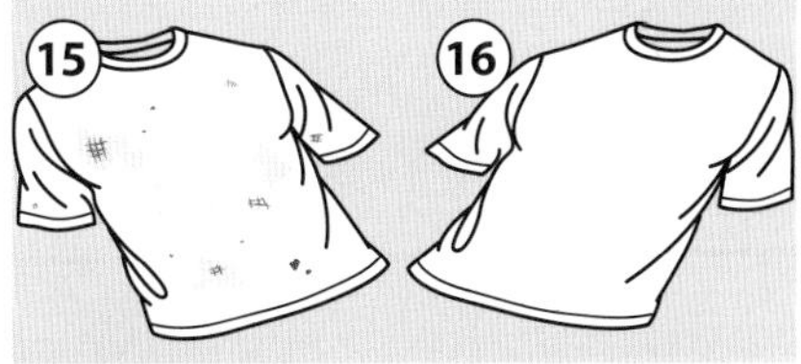

1. laundry
   洗濯物
2. laundry basket
   洗濯かご
3. washer
   洗濯機
4. dryer
   乾燥機
5. dryer sheets
   乾燥機用柔軟剤シート
6. fabric softener
   柔軟仕上げ剤
7. bleach
   漂白剤
8. laundry detergent
   洗濯用洗剤
9. clothesline
   物干しロープ
10. clothespin
    洗濯ばさみ
11. hanger
    ハンガー
12. spray starch
    スプレー糊
13. iron
    アイロン
14. ironing board
    アイロン台
15. **dirty** T-shirt
    汚れたTシャツ
16. **clean** T-shirt
    きれいなTシャツ
17. **wet** shirt
    濡れたシャツ
18. **dry** shirt
    乾いたシャツ
19. **wrinkled** shirt
    しわだらけのシャツ
20. **ironed** shirt
    アイロンのかかったシャツ

A. **Sort** the laundry.
洗濯物を**仕分ける**

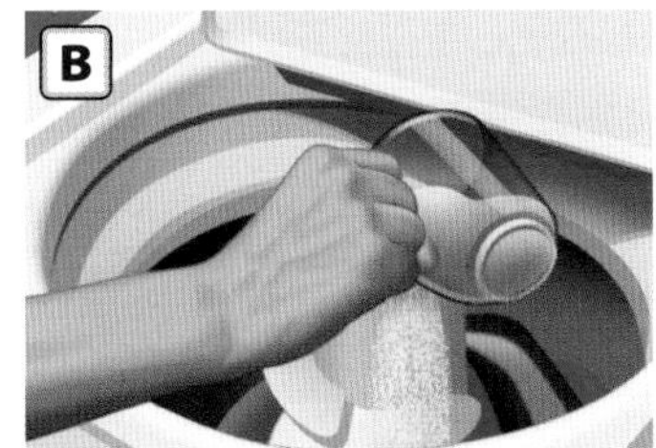

B. **Add** the detergent.
洗剤を**加える**

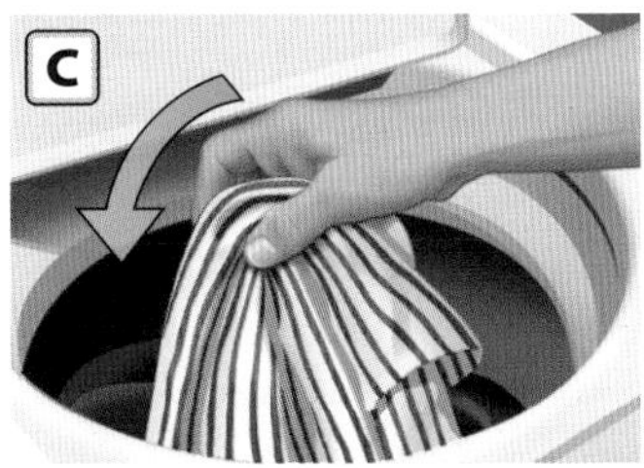

C. **Load** the washer.
洗濯機に**入れる**

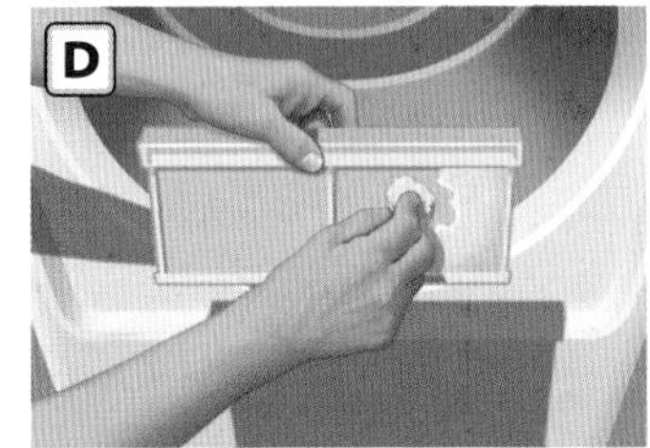

D. **Clean** the lint trap.
糸くずを**取り除く**

E. **Unload** the dryer.
乾燥機から洗濯物を**取り出す**

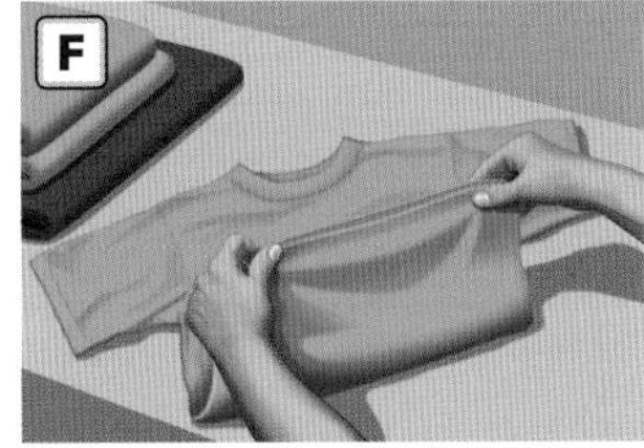

F. **Fold** the laundry.
洗濯物を**たたむ**

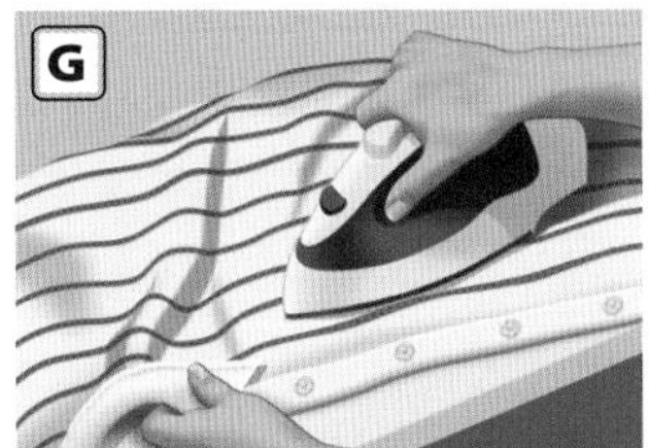

G. **Iron** the clothes.
服に**アイロンをかける**

H. **Hang up** the clothes.
服を**ハンガーにかける**

 wash in cold water

 no bleach

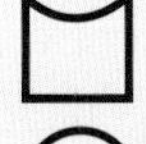 line dry

 dry clean only, do not wash

Pair practice. Make new conversations.

A: *I have to sort the laundry. Can you help?*
B: *Sure. Here's the laundry basket.*
A: *Thanks a lot!*

A Garage Sale ガレージセール

1. flyer 広告
2. used clothing 古着
3. sticker シール
4. folding card table 折りたたみ式テーブル
5. folding chair 折りたたみ椅子
6. clock radio 目覚まし時計付きラジオ
7. VCR VCR／ビデオテープレコーダー

A. **bargain** 値段を交渉する
B. **browse** 見て回る

Look at the pictures.
What do you see?

Answer the questions.

1. What kind of used clothing do you see?
2. What information is on the flyer?
3. Why are the stickers different colors?
4. How much is the clock radio? the VCR?

 **Read the story.**

A Garage Sale

Last Sunday, I had a garage sale. At 5:00 a.m., I put up flyers in my neighborhood. Next, I put price stickers on my used clothing, my VCR, and some other old things. At 7:00 a.m., I opened my folding card table and folding chair. Then I waited.

At 7:05 a.m., my first customer arrived. She asked, "How much is the sweatshirt?"

"Two dollars," I said.

She said, "It's stained. I can give you seventy-five cents." We bargained for a minute and she paid $1.00.

All day people came to browse, bargain, and buy. At 7:00 p.m., I had $85.00.

Now I know two things: Garage sales are hard work and nobody wants to buy an old clock radio!

Think about it.

1. Do you like to buy things at garage sales? Why or why not?
2. Imagine you want the VCR. How will you bargain for it?

The Body 体

1. head
   頭
2. hair
   髪
3. neck
   首
4. chest
   胸
5. back
   背中
6. nose
   鼻
7. mouth
   口
8. foot
   足（くるぶしから下）

Listen and point. Take turns.

A: *Point to the chest.*
B: *Point to the neck.*
A: *Point to the mouth.*

Dictate to your partner. Take turns.

A: *Write hair.*
B: *Did you say hair?*
A: *That's right, h-a-i-r.*

9. leg
脚
10. toe
つま先
11. eye
目
12. ear
耳
13. shoulder
肩
14. arm
腕
15. hand
手
16. finger
指

Grammar Point: imperatives

Please touch *your right foot.*
Put *your hands on your feet.*
Don't *put your hands on your shoulders.*

Pair practice. Take turns giving commands.

A: *Raise your arms.*
B: *Touch your feet.*
A: *Put your hand on your shoulder.*

Inside and Outside the Body

体の内側と外側

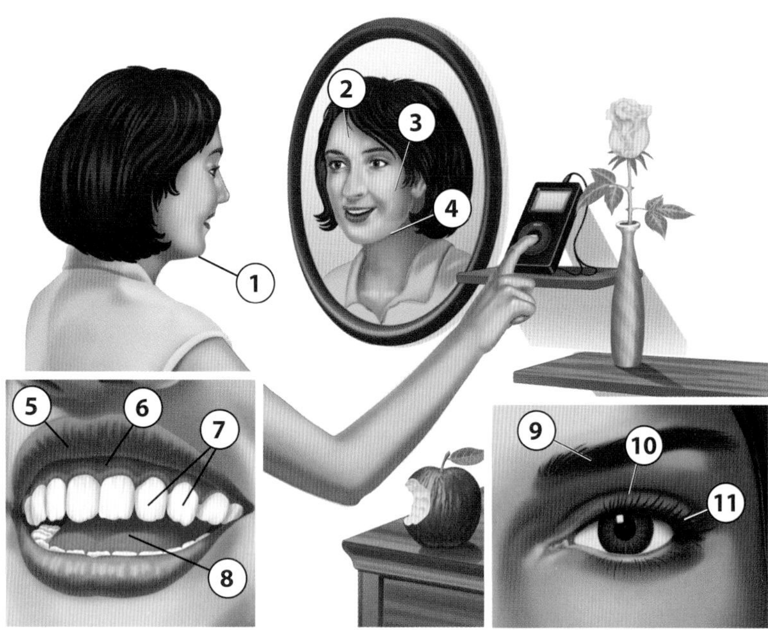

The Face
顔

1. chin
あご
2. forehead
ひたい
3. cheek
頬
4. jaw
下あご

The Mouth
口

5. lip
唇
6. gums
歯茎
7. teeth
歯
8. tongue
舌

The Eye
目

9. eyebrow
眉毛
10. eyelid
まぶた
11. eyelashes
まつげ

The Senses
感覚

A. **see**
見る
B. **hear**
聞く
C. **smell**
匂いを嗅ぐ
D. **taste**
味わう
E. **touch**
触れる

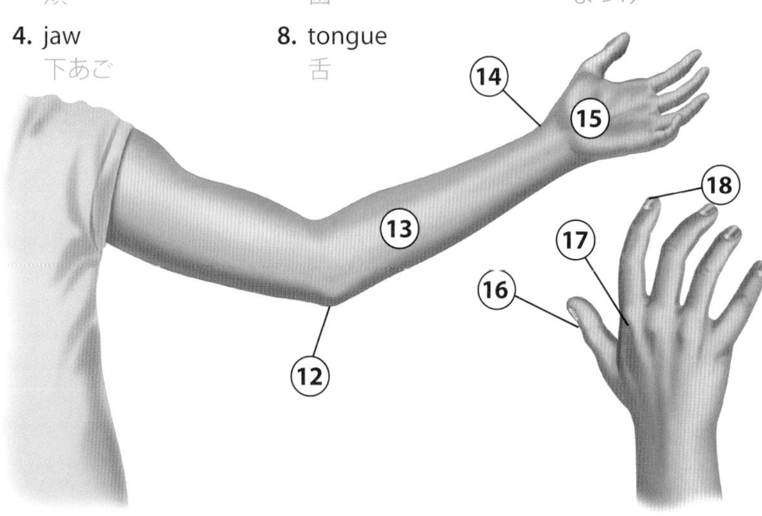

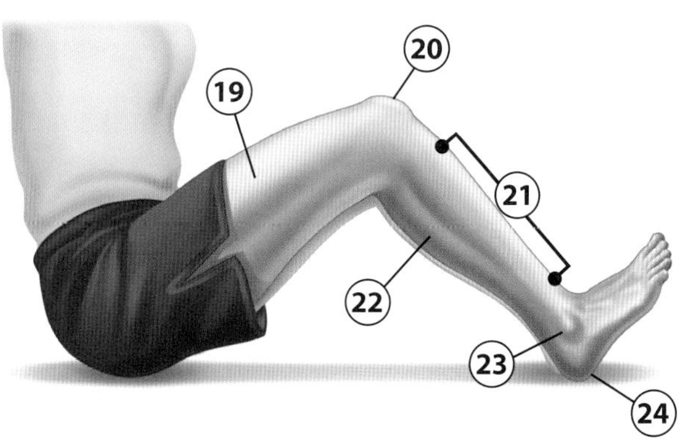

The Arm, Hand, and Fingers 腕、手、指

12. elbow
ひじ
13. forearm
前腕
14. wrist
手首
15. palm
手のひら
16. thumb
親指
17. knuckle
指関節
18. fingernail
爪

The Leg and Foot 脚と足

19. thigh
腿
20. knee
膝
21. shin
すね
22. calf
ふくらはぎ
23. ankle
足首
24. heel
かかと

More vocabulary

torso: the part of the body from the shoulders to the pelvis
limbs: arms and legs
toenail: the nail on your toe

Pair practice. Make new conversations.

A: *Is your arm OK?*
B: *Yes, but now my elbow hurts.*
A: *I'm sorry to hear that.*

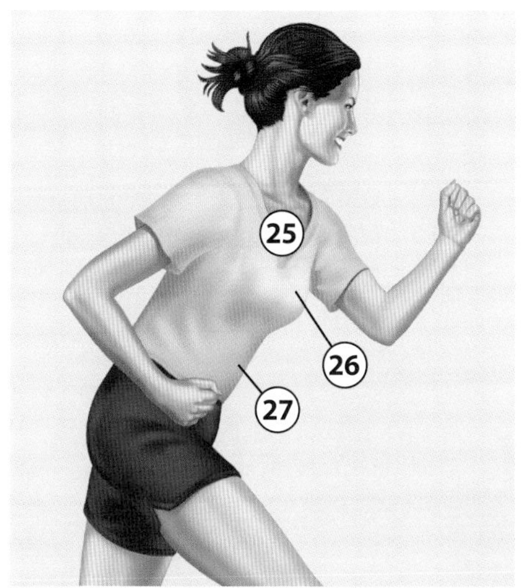

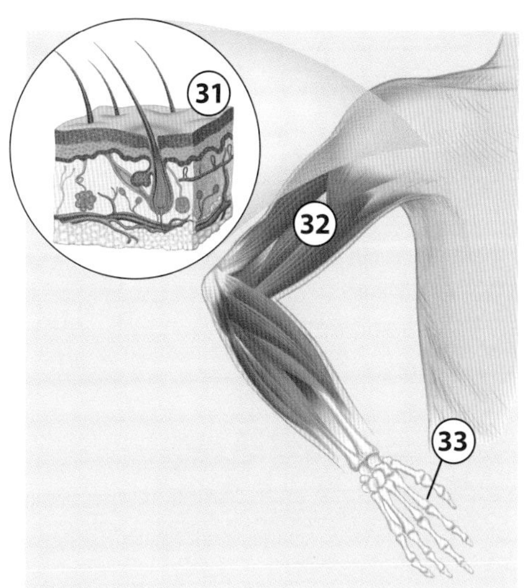

25. chest
胸

26. breast
胸（乳房）

27. abdomen
腹部

28. shoulder blade
肩甲骨

29. lower back
腰

30. buttocks
尻

31. skin
皮膚

32. muscle
筋肉

33. bone
骨

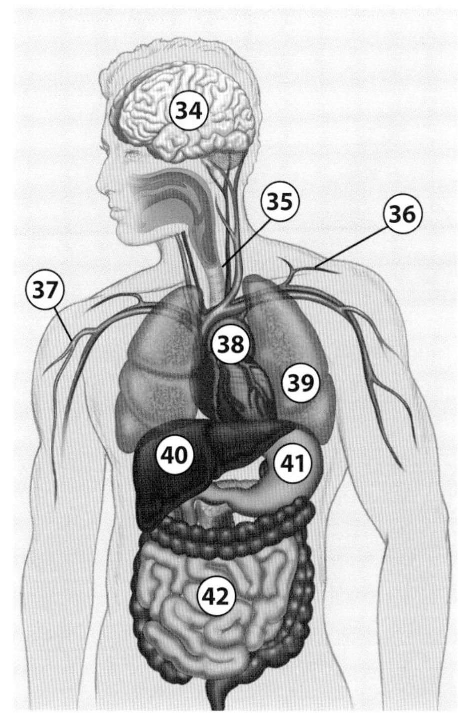

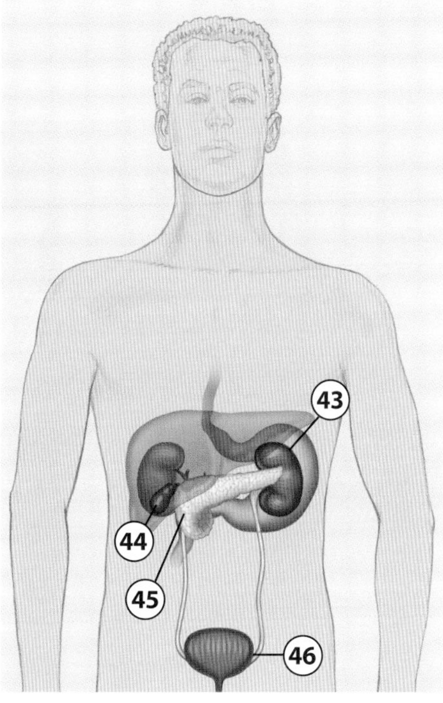

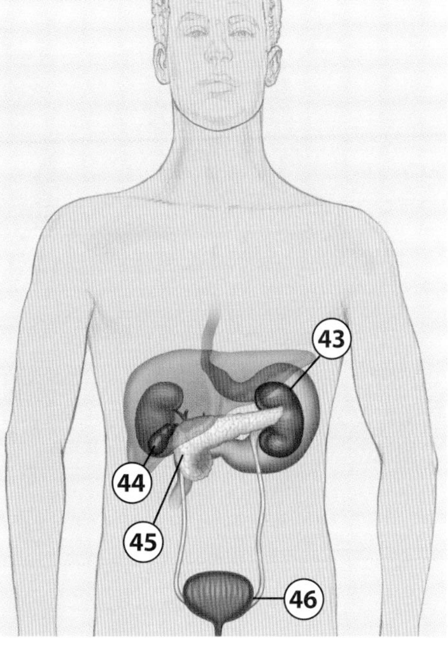

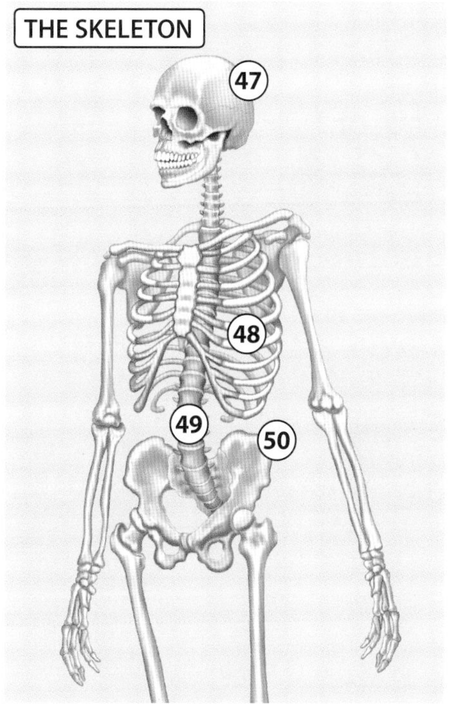

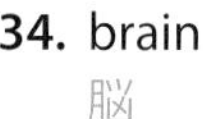

34. brain
脳

35. throat
のど

36. artery
動脈

37. vein
静脈

38. heart
心臓

39. lung
肺

40. liver
肝臓

41. stomach
胃

42. intestines
腸

43. kidney
腎臓

44. gallbladder
胆のう

45. pancreas
すい臓

46. bladder
膀胱

47. skull
頭蓋骨

48. rib cage
肋骨

49. spinal column
脊柱

50. pelvis
骨盤

A. take a shower
シャワーを**浴びる**

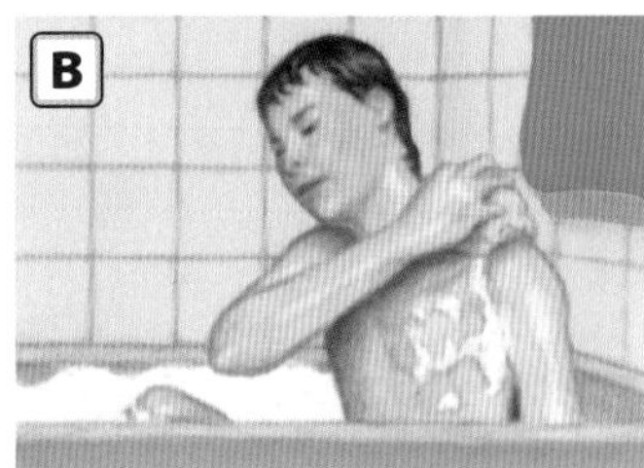

B. take a bath / **bathe**
風呂に**入る**／**入浴する**

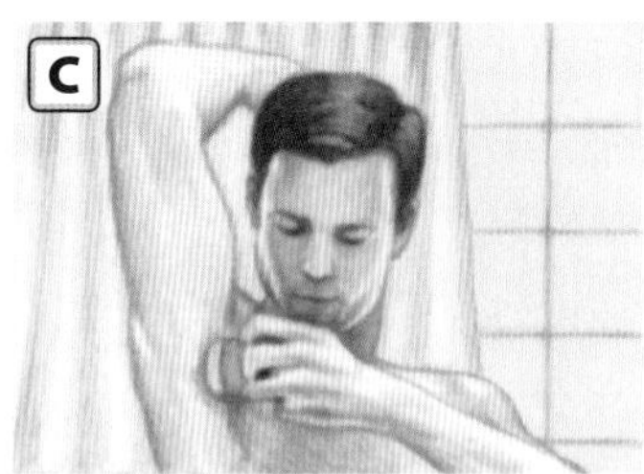

C. use deodorant
デオドラントを**使う**

D. put on sunscreen
サンスクリーンを**塗る**

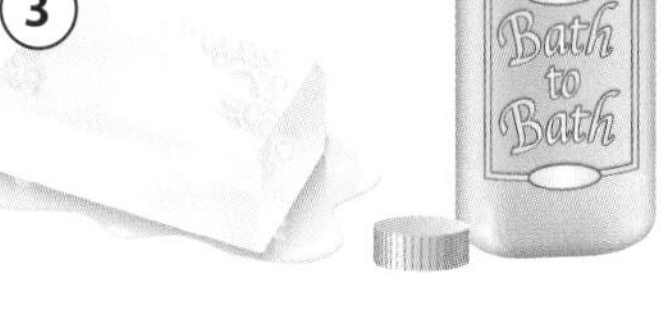

Bath to Bath
Dry & Fresh
Safe Sun SPF 15
Block it SPF 55
Smooth Skin

1. shower cap
シャワーキャップ
2. shower gel
シャワー用ジェル状石けん
3. soap
石けん
4. bath powder
タルカムパウダー
5. deodorant / antiperspirant
デオドラント／制汗剤
6. perfume / cologne
香水／コロン
7. sunscreen
サンスクリーン
8. sunblock
日焼け止め
9. body lotion / moisturizer
ボディローション／
モイスチャライザー

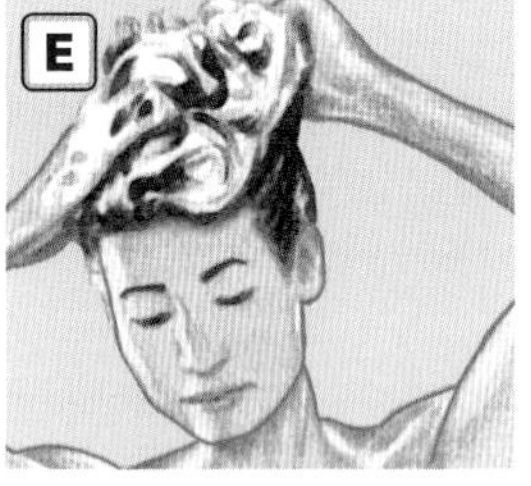

E. wash...hair
髪を**洗う**

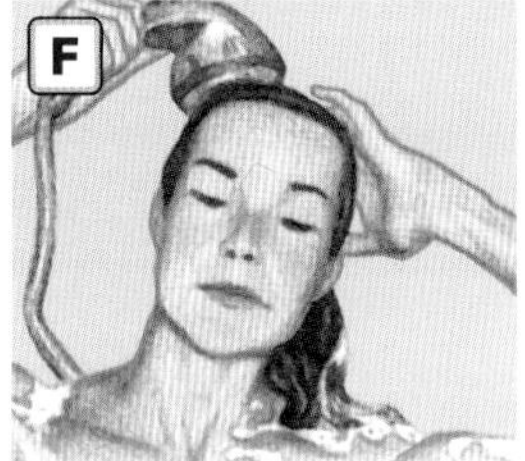

F. rinse...hair
髪を**すすぐ**

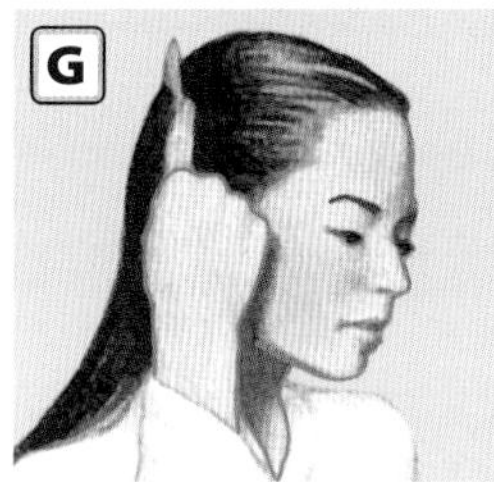

G. comb...hair
髪を**とかす**

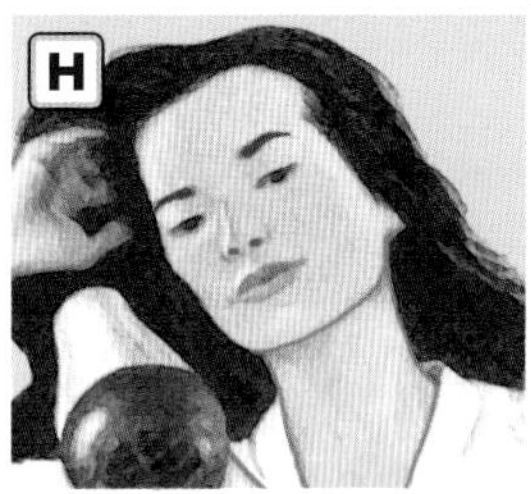

H. dry...hair
髪を**乾かす**

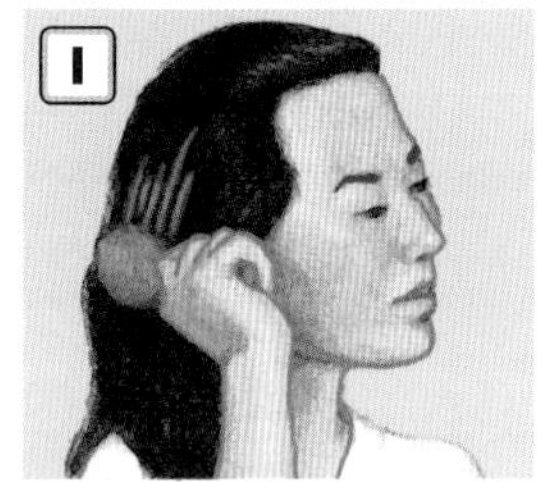

I. brush...hair
髪に**ブラシをかける**

Style it!

10. shampoo
シャンプー
11. conditioner
コンディショナー
12. hair spray
ヘアスプレー
13. comb
クシ
14. brush
ブラシ
15. pick
アフロヘア用コーム
16. hair gel
ヘアジェル
17. curling iron
カーリングアイロン
18. blow dryer
ドライヤー
19. hair clip
ヘアクリップ
20. barrette
バレッタ
21. bobby pins
ヘアピン

More vocabulary

unscented: a product without perfume or scent
hypoallergenic: a product that is better for people with allergies

Think about it. Discuss.

1. Which personal hygiene products should someone use before a job interview?
2. What is the right age to start wearing makeup? Why?

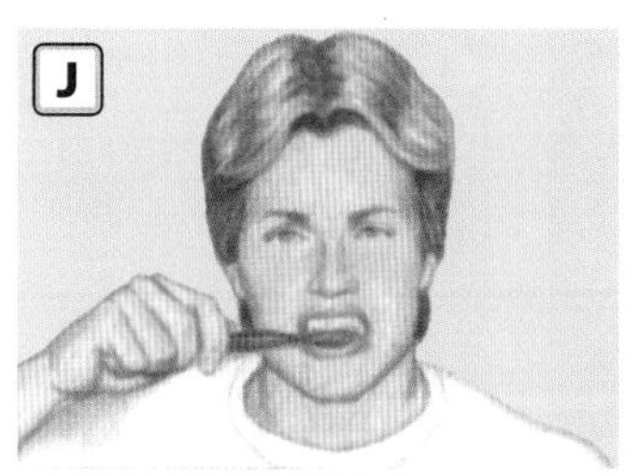

J. brush...teeth
歯を**磨く**

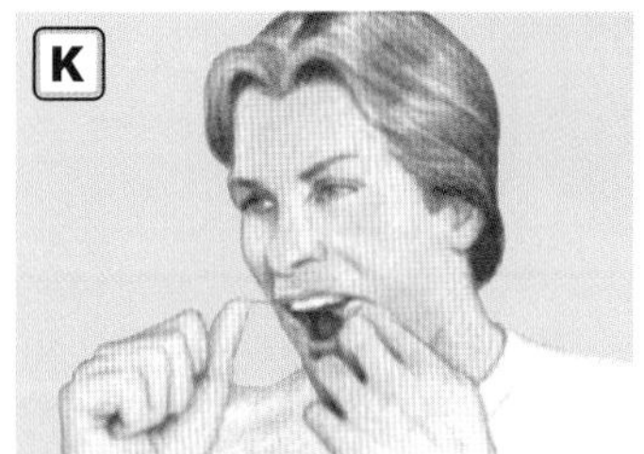

K. floss...teeth
歯に**デンタルフロスをかける**

L. gargle
うがいする

M. shave
ひげを剃る

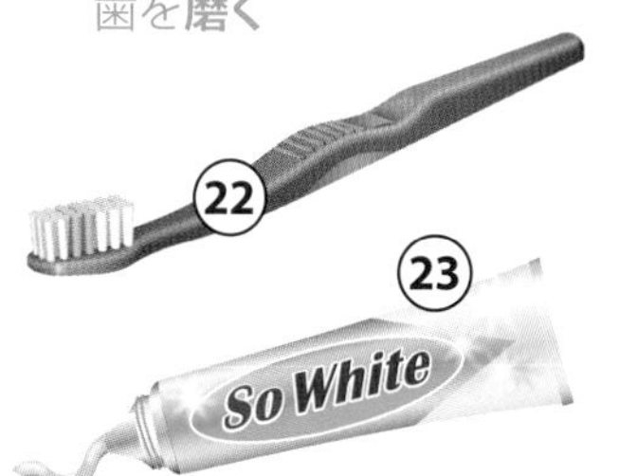

22. toothbrush
歯ブラシ
23. toothpaste
練り歯みがき
24. dental floss
デンタルフロス
25. mouthwash
マウスウォッシュ
26. electric shaver
電気かみそり
27. razor
かみそり
28. razorblade
かみそりの刃
29. shaving cream
シェービングクリーム
30. aftershave
アフターシェーブローション

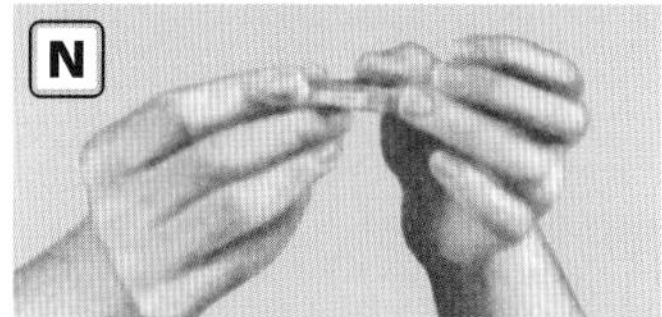

N. cut...nails
爪を**切る**

O. polish...nails
爪に**マニキュアを塗る**

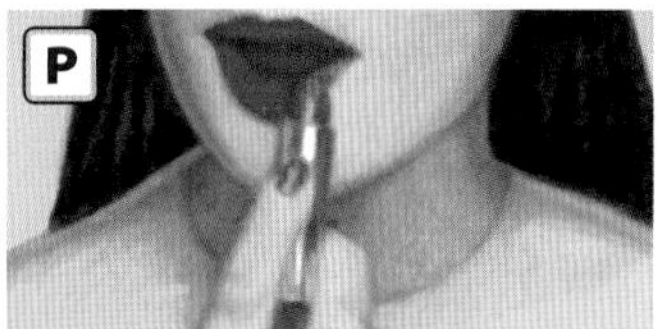

P. put on / apply
つける／塗る

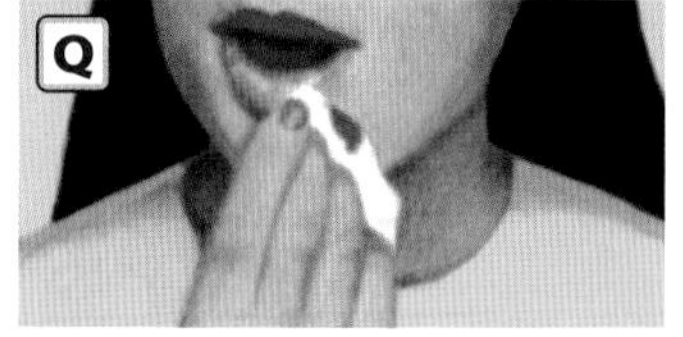

Q. take off / remove
落とす／取る

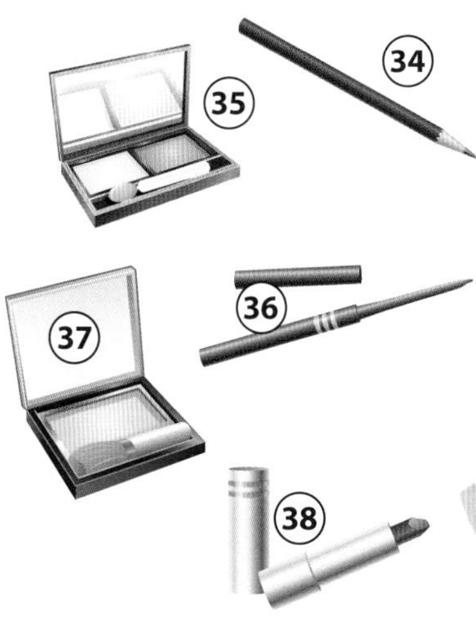

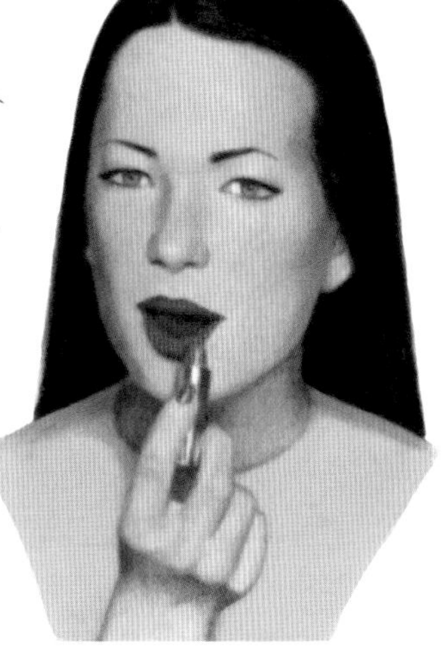

Makeup メークアップ

31. nail clipper
爪きり
32. emery board
爪やすり
33. nail polish
マニキュア液
34. eyebrow pencil
眉墨
35. eye shadow
アイシャドー
36. eyeliner
アイライナー
37. blush
頬紅
38. lipstick
口紅
39. mascara
マスカラ
40. foundation
ファンデーション
41. face powder
おしろい
42. makeup remover
クレンジングクリーム

Symptoms and Injuries

病気の症状とけが

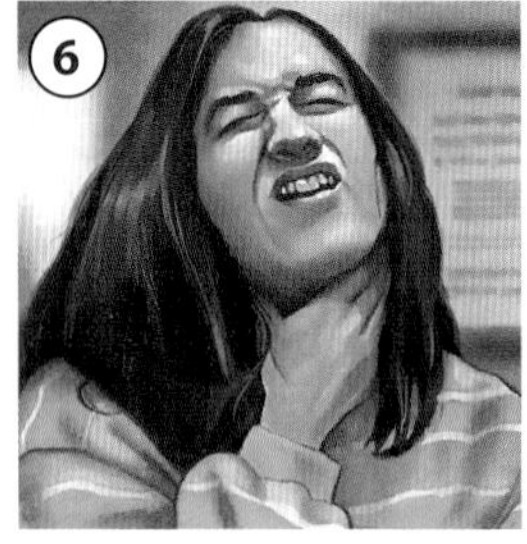
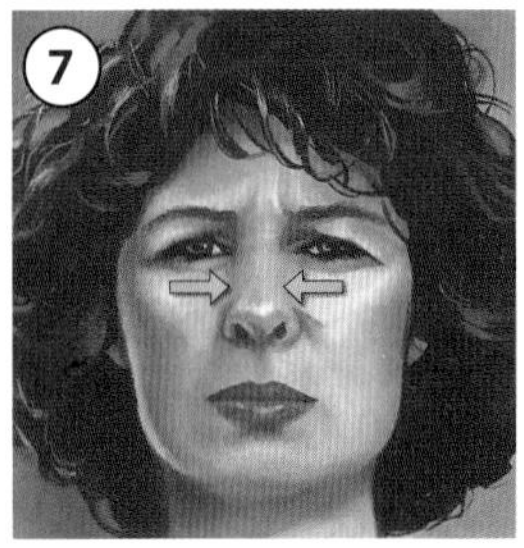
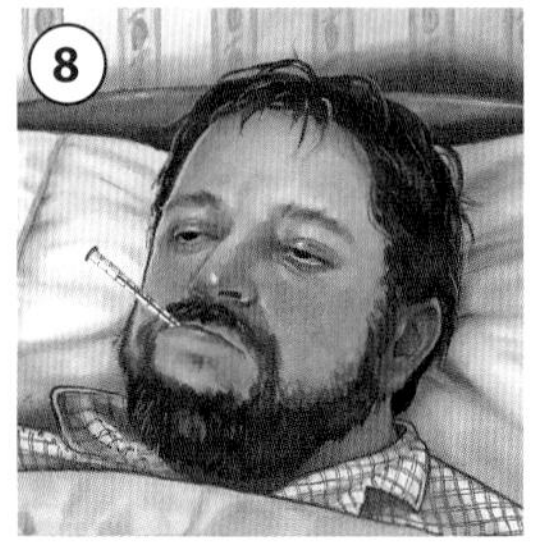

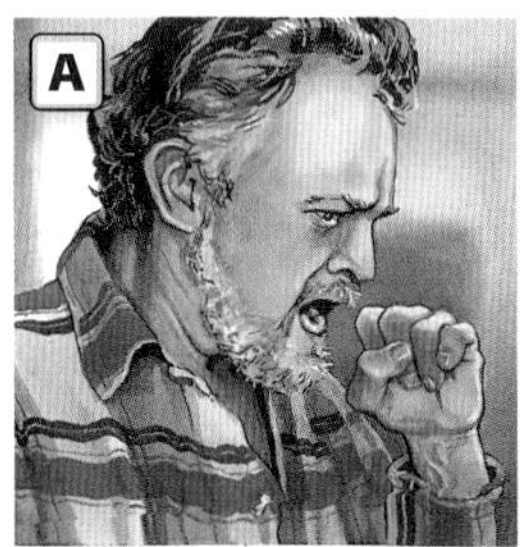
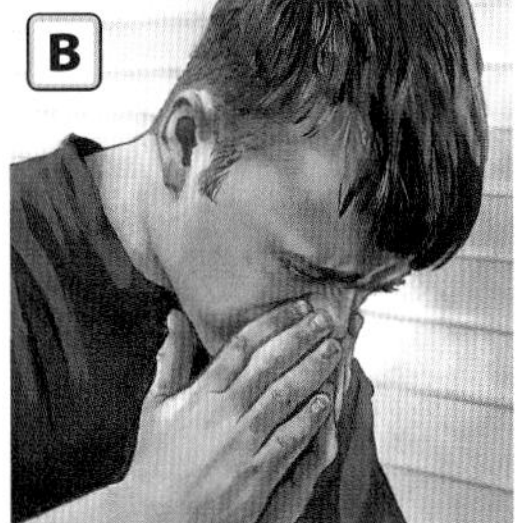

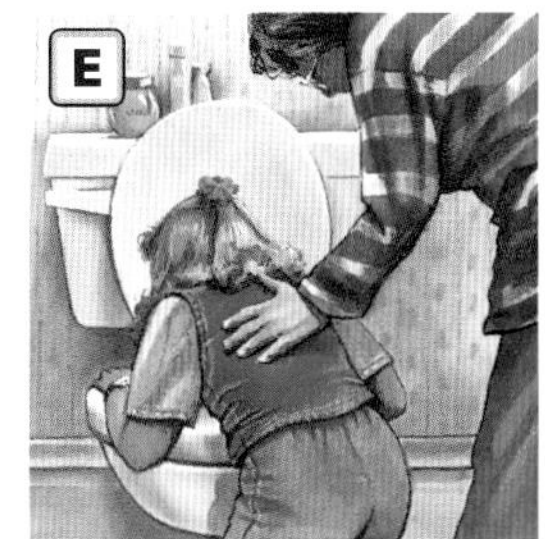

1. headache
   頭痛
2. toothache
   歯痛
3. earache
   耳の痛み
4. stomachache
   胃痛／腹痛
5. backache
   腰痛
6. sore throat
   のどの痛み
7. nasal congestion
   鼻づまり
8. fever / temperature
   熱
9. chills
   寒気
10. rash
    湿疹

A. **cough**
   せきをする

B. **sneeze**
   くしゃみをする

C. **feel** dizzy
   めまいがする

D. **feel** nauseous
   吐き気がする

E. **throw up / vomit**
   吐く

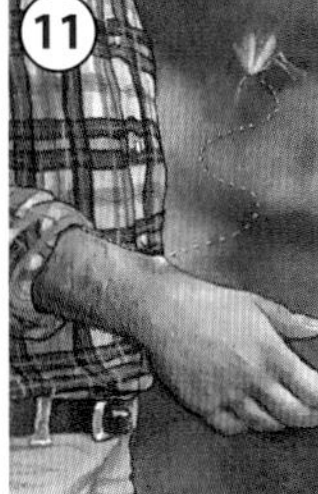
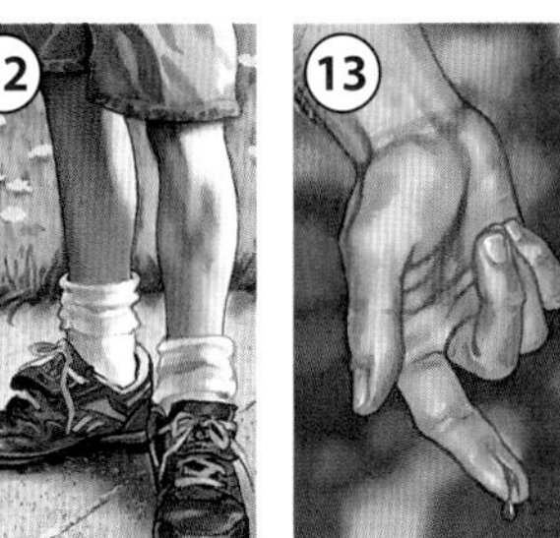
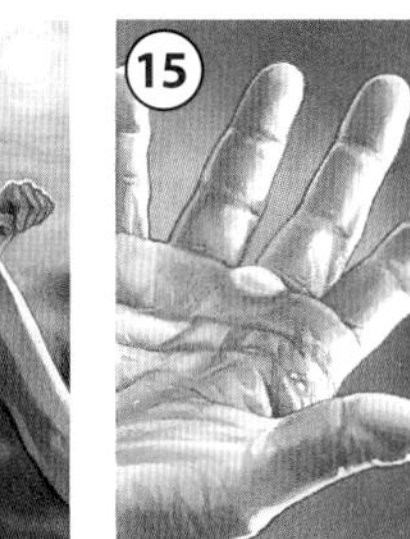
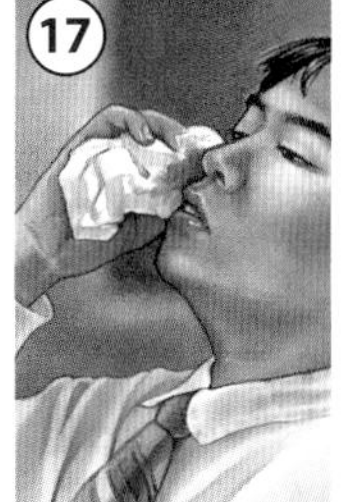

11. insect bite
    虫さされ
12. bruise
    打ち身
13. cut
    切り傷
14. sunburn
    日焼け
15. blister
    水ぶくれ
16. swollen finger
    腫れた指
17. bloody nose
    鼻血
18. sprained ankle
    足首のねんざ

Look at the pictures.
Describe the symptoms and injuries.

A: *He has a backache.*
B: *She has a toothache.*

Think about it. Discuss.

1. What are some common cold symptoms?
2. What do you recommend for a stomachache?
3. What is the best way to stop a bloody nose?

疾患と症状

Illnesses and Medical Conditions

Common Illnesses and Childhood Diseases 一般的な疾患と子供がよくかかる病気

1. cold
風邪

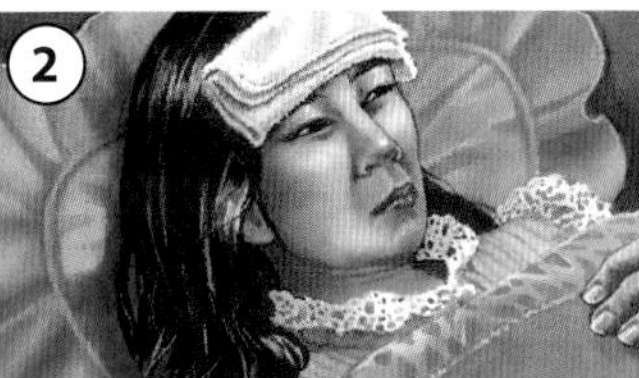

2. flu
インフルエンザ

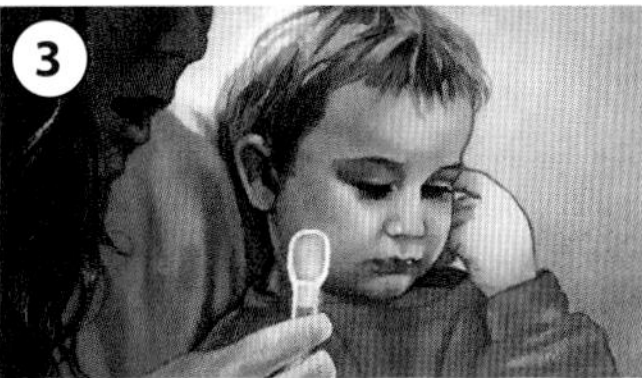

3. ear infection
耳炎

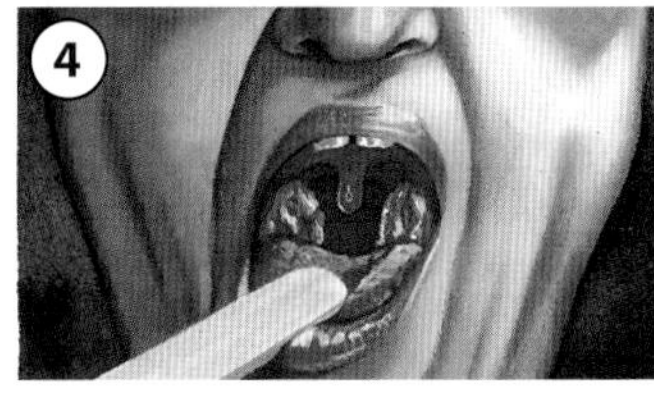

4. strep throat
溶連菌感染による咽頭炎

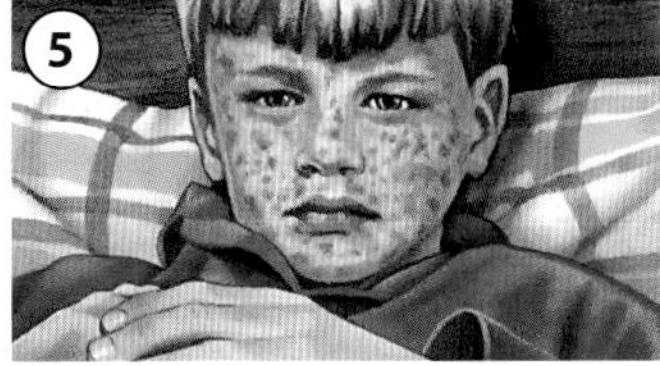

5. measles
はしか

6. chicken pox
水ぼうそう

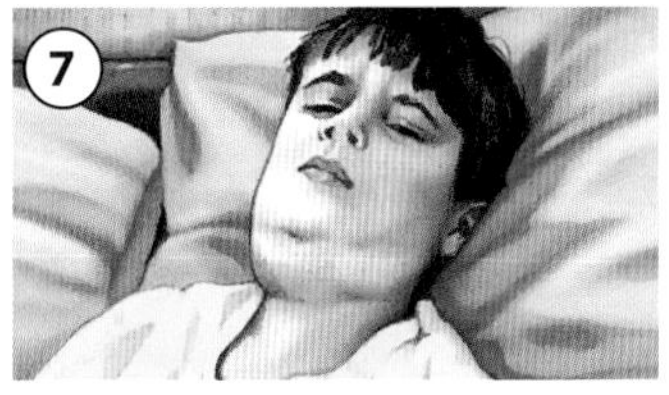

7. mumps
おたふく風邪

8. allergies
アレルギー

Serious Medical Conditions and Diseases 重い症状と病気

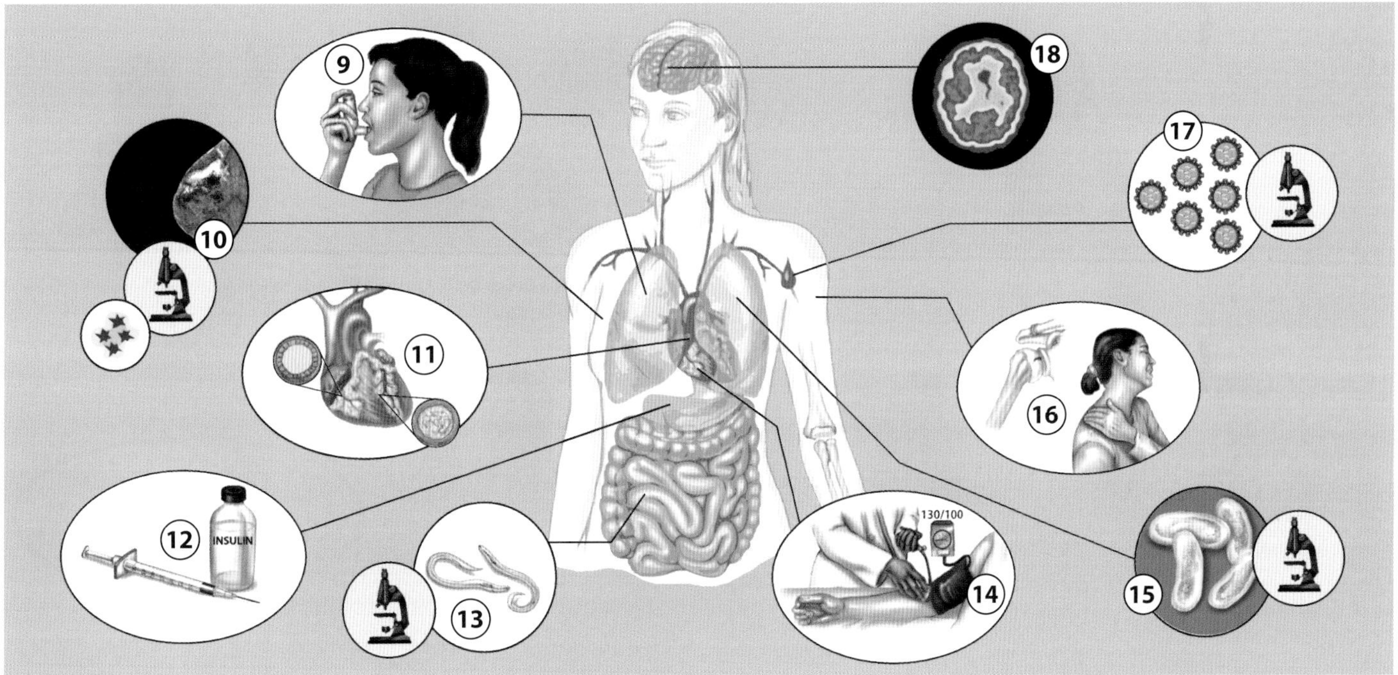

9. asthma
喘息

10. cancer
がん

11. heart disease
心臓病

12. diabetes
糖尿病

13. intestinal parasites
腸の寄生虫

14. high blood pressure / hypertension
高血圧

15. TB (tuberculosis)
結核

16. arthritis
関節炎

17. HIV (human immunodeficiency virus)
HIV (ヒト免疫不全ウイルス)

18. dementia
認知症

More vocabulary

AIDS (acquired immune deficiency syndrome): a medical condition that results from contracting the HIV virus

Alzheimer's disease: a disease that causes dementia

coronary disease: heart disease

infectious disease: a disease that is spread through air or water

influenza: flu

A Pharmacy 薬局

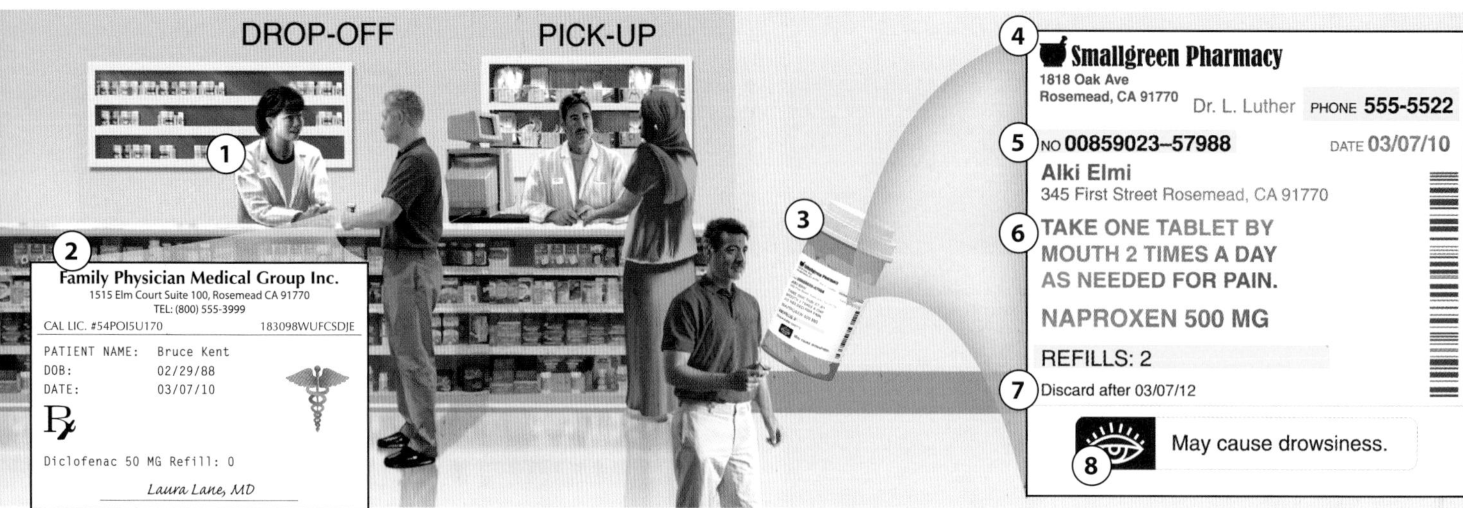

1. pharmacist 薬剤師
2. prescription 処方箋
3. prescription medication 処方薬
4. prescription label 処方ラベル
5. prescription number 処方番号
6. dosage 服用量
7. expiration date 使用期限
8. warning label 警告ラベル

Medical Warnings 服用にあたっての注意

A. **Take** with food or milk.
食物または牛乳とともに**服用してください**。

B. **Take** one hour before eating.
食事の1時間前に**服用してください**。

C. **Finish** all medication.
最後まで服用してください。

D. **Do not take** with dairy products.
乳製品とともに**服用しないでください**。

E. **Do not drive or operate** heavy machinery.
車の**運転**や大型機械の**操作はしないでください**。

F. **Do not drink** alcohol.
アルコール類は**飲まないでください**。.

More vocabulary

prescribe medication: to write a prescription
fill prescriptions: to prepare medication for patients
pick up a prescription: to get prescription medication

Role play. Talk to the pharmacist.

A: *Hi. I need to pick up a prescription for Jones.*
B: *Here's your medication, Mr. Jones. Take these once a day with milk or food.*

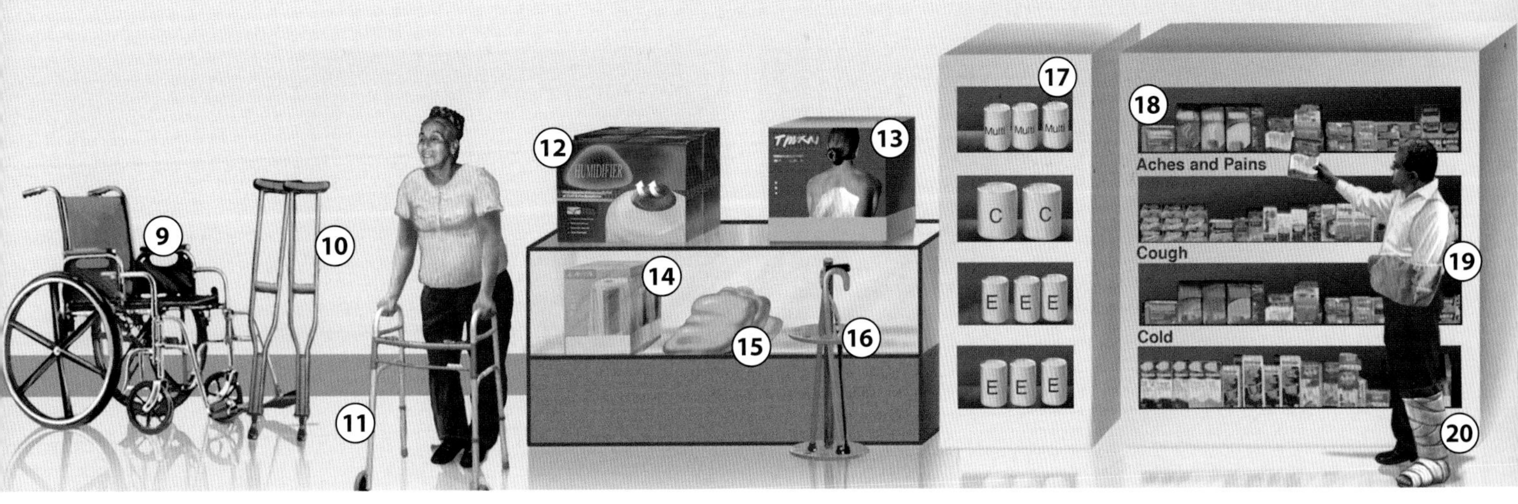

9. wheelchair 車椅子
10. crutches 松葉杖
11. walker 歩行器
12. humidifier 加湿器
13. heating pad ヒーティングパッド
14. air purifier 空気清浄機
15. hot water bottle 湯たんぽ
16. cane つえ
17. vitamins ビタミン
18. over-the-counter medication 市販薬
19. sling つり包帯／三角巾
20. cast ギプス

Types of Medication 薬の種類

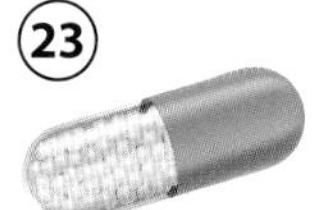

21. pill 丸薬
22. tablet 錠剤
23. capsule カプセル
24. ointment 軟膏
25. cream クリーム

Over-the-Counter Medication 市販薬

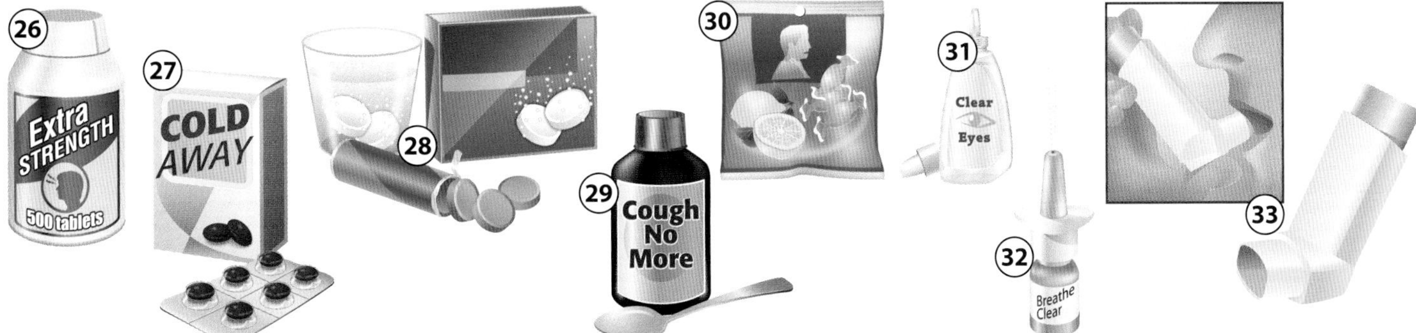

26. pain reliever 鎮痛剤
27. cold tablets 風邪薬
28. antacid 制酸剤
29. cough syrup せき止めシロップ
30. throat lozenges 喉の痛みを和らげる薬用ドロップ
31. eye drops 目薬
32. nasal spray 鼻のスプレー
33. inhaler 喘息用の吸入剤

Ways to talk about medication

Use *take* for pills, tablets, capsules, and cough syrup.
Use *apply* for ointments and creams.
Use *use* for drops, nasal sprays, and inhalers.

Ask your classmates. Share the answers.

1. What pharmacy do you go to?
2. Do you ever ask the pharmacist for advice?
3. Do you take any vitamins? Which ones?

Taking Care of Your Health 健康に気をつける

Ways to Get Well 病気を治す方法

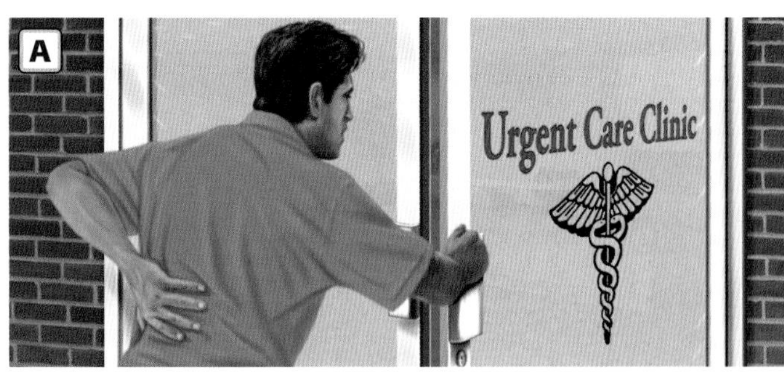

A. **Seek** medical attention.
医師の**診察を受ける**

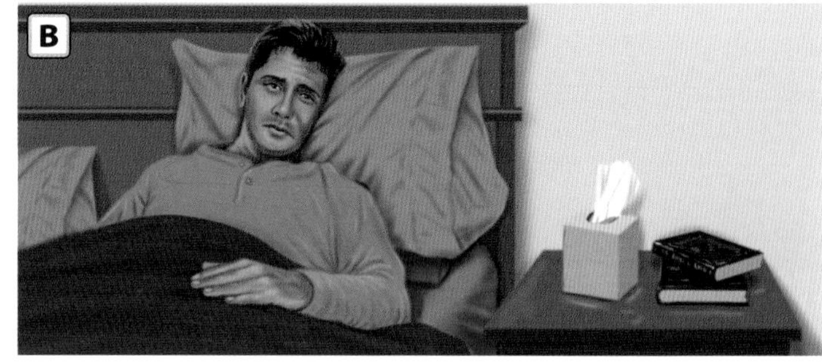

B. **Get** bed rest.
横になって**休む**

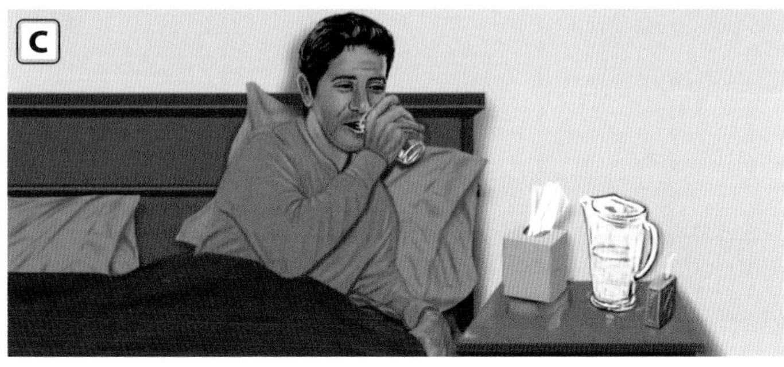

C. **Drink** fluids.
水分を**とる**

D. **Take** medicine.
薬を**飲む**

Ways to Stay Well 健康を維持する方法

E. **Stay** fit.
エクササイズして健康を**維持する**

F. **Eat** a healthy diet.
健康的な食事を**とる**

G. **Don't smoke**.
タバコを吸わない

H. **Have** regular checkups.
定期健診を**受ける**

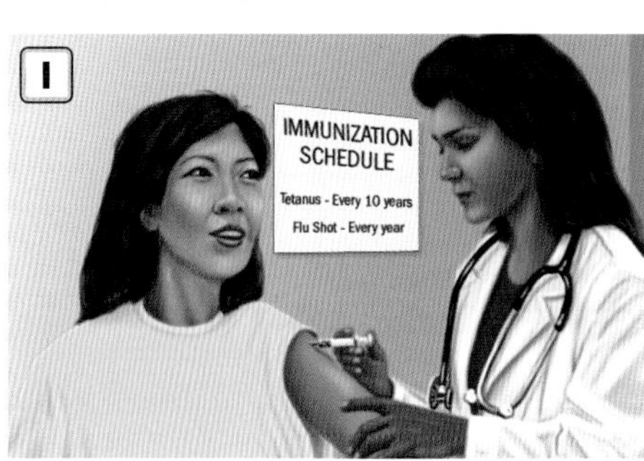

I. **Get** immunized.
予防注射を**受ける**

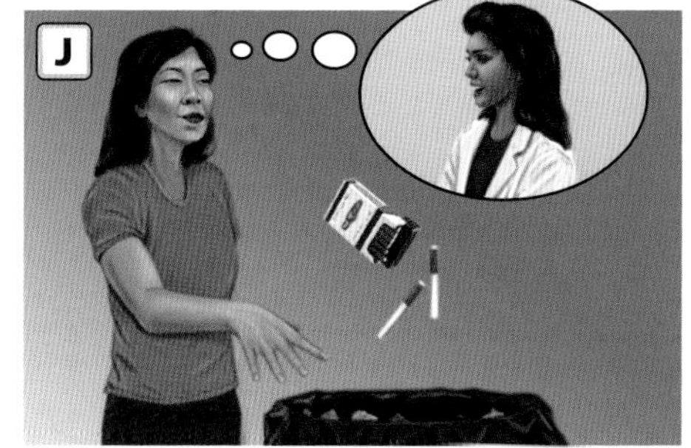

J. **Follow** medical advice.
医師のアドバイスに**従う**

More vocabulary

injection: medicine in a syringe that is put into the body
immunization / vaccination: an injection that stops serious diseases

Ask your classmates. Share the answers.

1. How do you stay fit?
2. What do you do when you're sick?
3. Which two foods are a part of your healthy diet?

Types of Health Problems 健康上のいろいろな問題

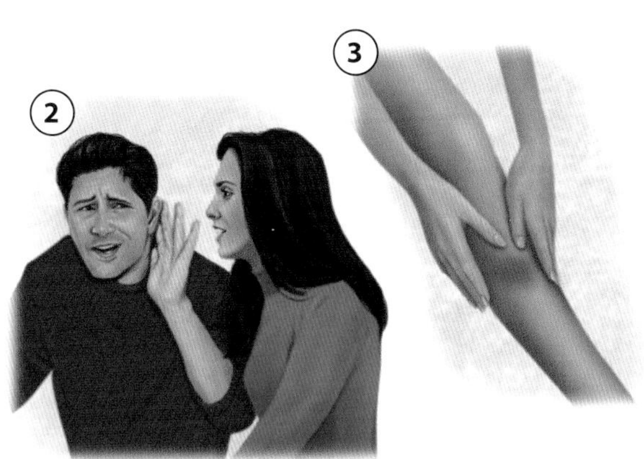

1. vision problems 視力の問題
2. hearing loss 聴力低下
3. pain 痛み
4. stress ストレス
5. depression うつ病

Help with Health Problems 健康問題の改善

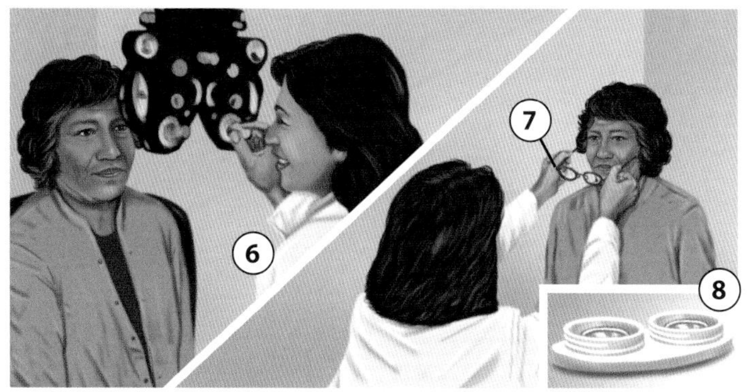

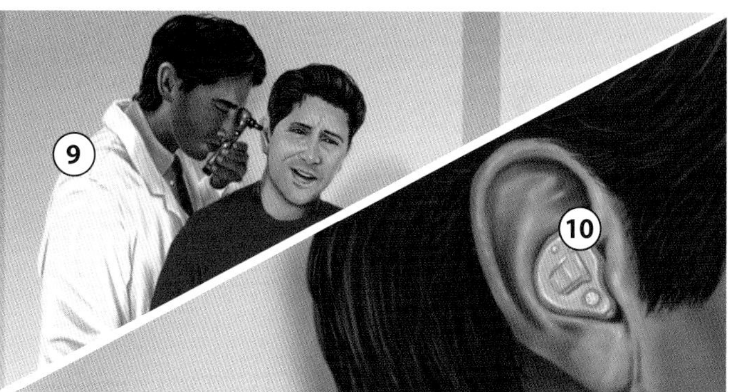

6. optometrist 検眼医
7. glasses 眼鏡
8. contact lenses コンタクトレンズ
9. audiologist 聴覚検査士
10. hearing aid 補聴器

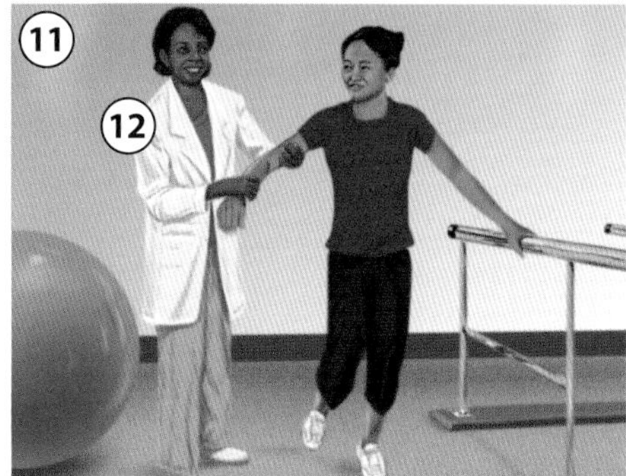

11. physical therapy 理学療法
12. physical therapist 理学療法士
13. talk therapy トークセラピー／話し合い療法
14. therapist 療法士
15. support group サポートグループ

Ways to ask about health problems

Are you in pain?
Are you having vision problems?
Are you experiencing depression?

Pair practice. Make new conversations.

A: *Do you know a good optometrist?*
B: *Why? Are you having vision problems?*
A: *Yes, I might need glasses.*

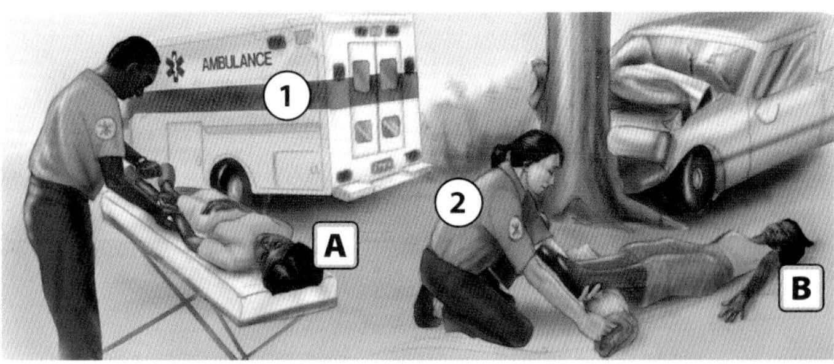

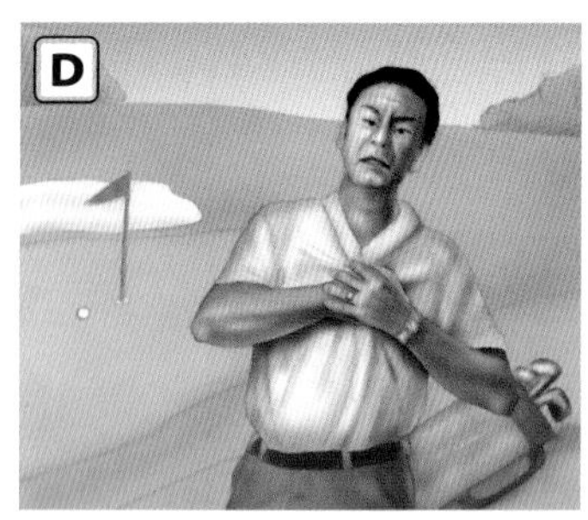

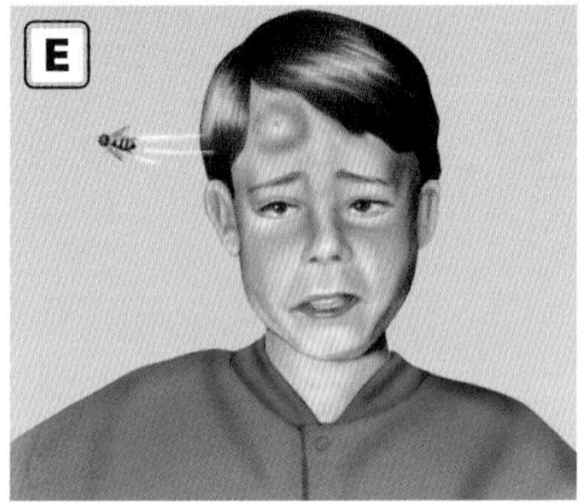

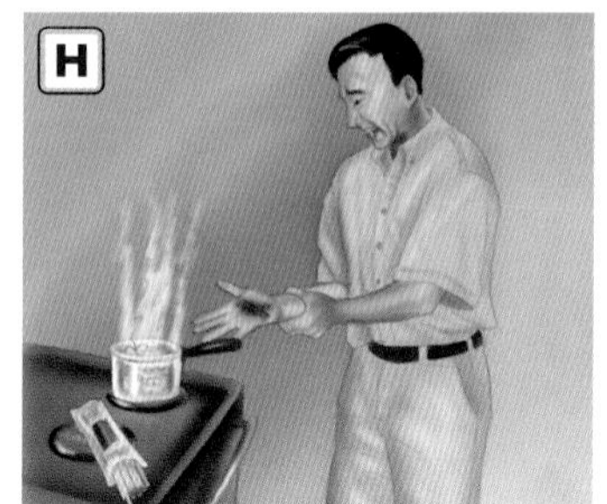

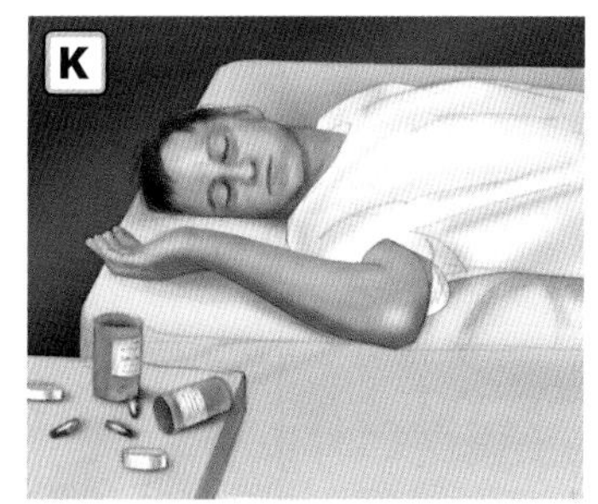

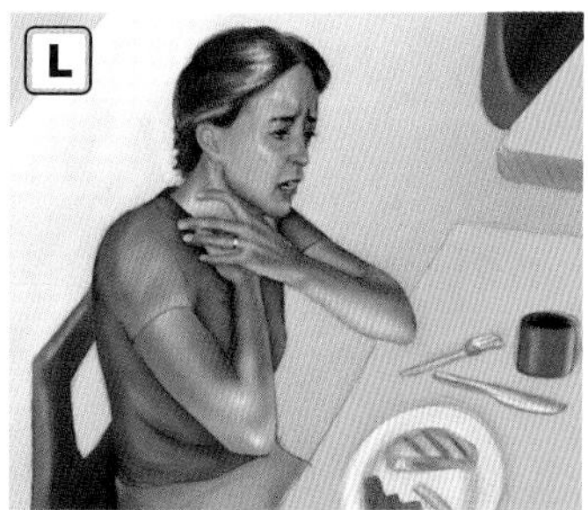

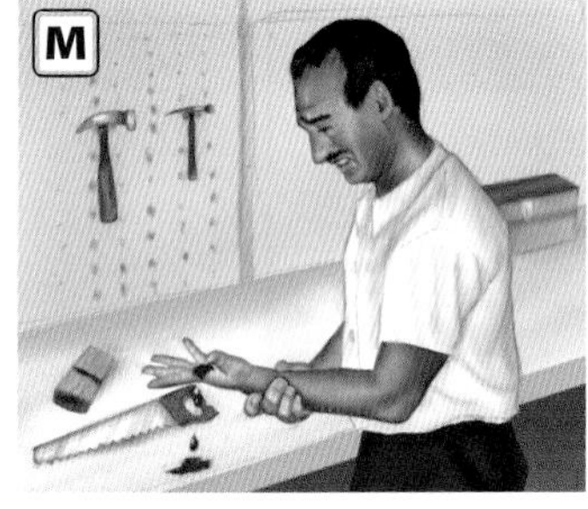

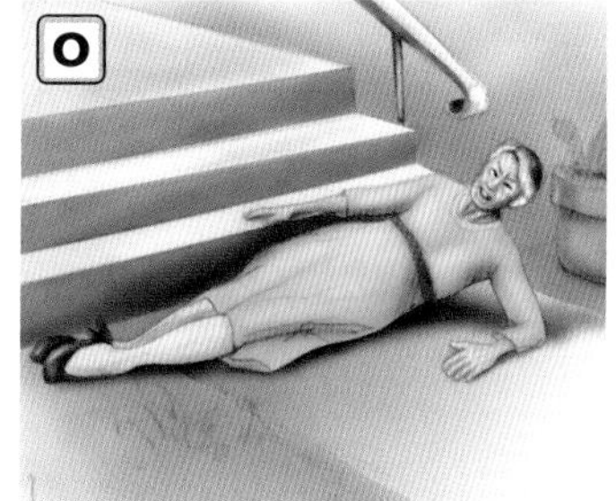

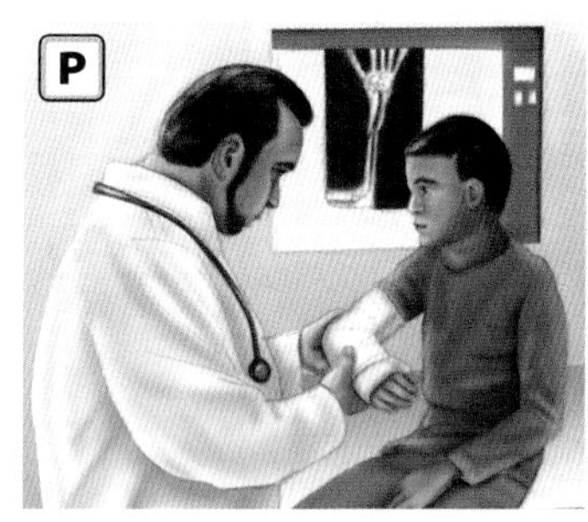

1. ambulance
   救急車
2. paramedic
   救急救命士

A. **be** unconscious
   意識を**失う**
B. **be** in shock
   ショック状態に**なる**
C. **be** injured / **be** hurt
   けがを**する**
D. **have** a heart attack
   心臓発作を**起こす**
E. **have** an allergic reaction
   アレルギー反応を**起こす**
F. **get** an electric shock
   感電**する**
G. **get** frostbite
   凍傷に**なる**
H. **burn** (your)self
   火傷をする
I. **drown**
   溺れる
J. **swallow** poison
   毒物を**飲む**
K. **overdose** on drugs
   薬を**過量にとる**
L. **choke**
   のどがつまる
M. **bleed**
   出血する
N. **can't breathe**
   呼吸できない
O. **fall**
   ころぶ
P. **break** a bone
   骨折する

Grammar Point: past tense

For past tense add –ed:
burned, drowned, swallowed, overdosed, choked

These verbs are different (irregular):

be – was, were
have – had
get – got
bleed – bled
can't – couldn't
break – broke
fall – fell

First Aid 応急手当

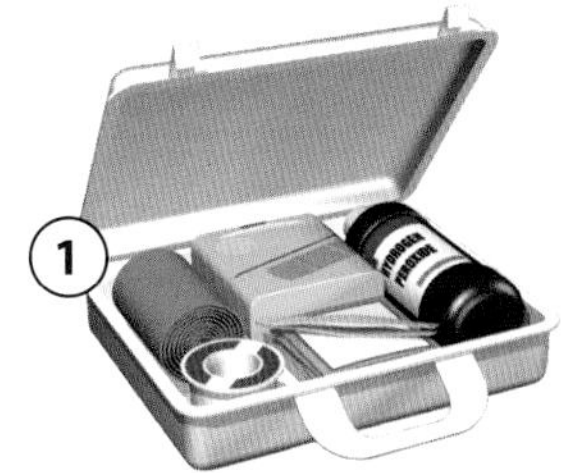

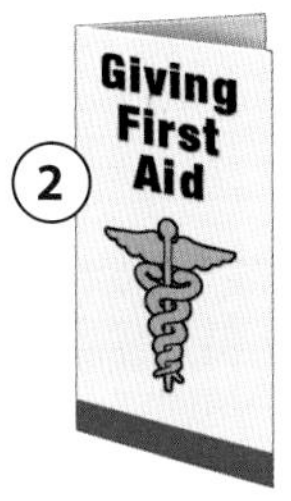

1. first aid kit
救急箱
2. first aid manual
応急処置の手引書
3. medical emergency bracelet
救急用の医療腕輪

Inside the Kit 救急箱の中身

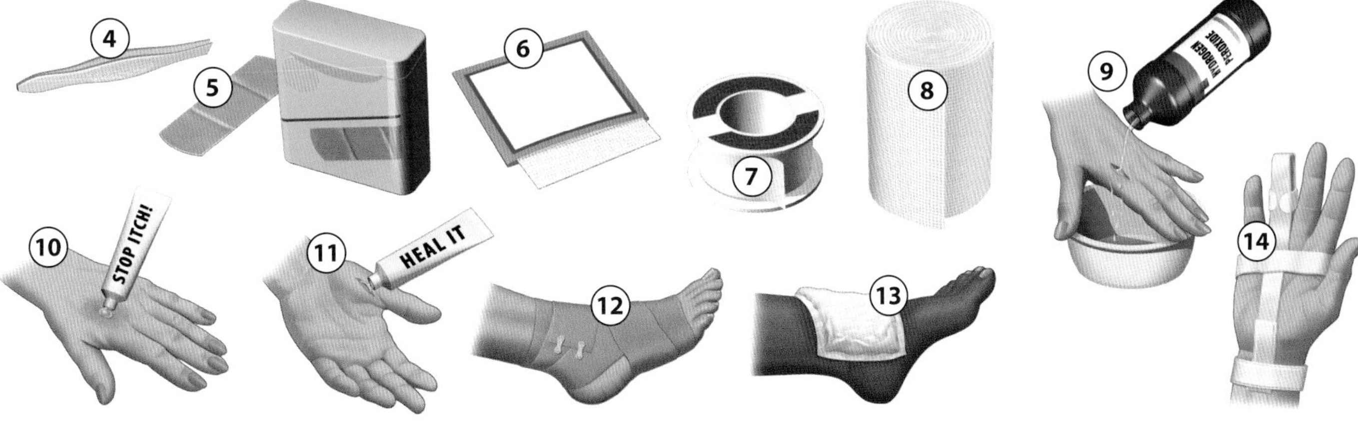

4. tweezers
毛抜き
5. adhesive bandage
ばんそうこう
6. sterile pad
無菌ガーゼ
7. sterile tape
無菌テープ
8. gauze
ガーゼ
9. hydrogen peroxide
オキシドール
10. antihistamine cream
抗ヒスタミンクリーム
11. antibacterial ointment
抗菌性軟膏
12. elastic bandage
伸縮性のある包帯
13. ice pack
氷のう／アイスパック
14. splint
添え木

First Aid Procedures 応急処置

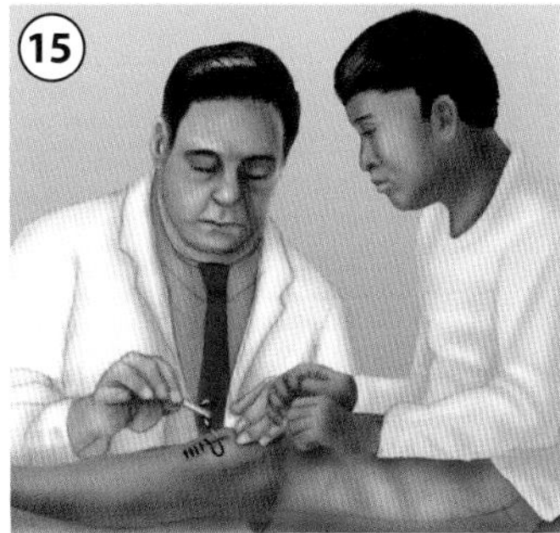

15. stitches
傷口の縫合

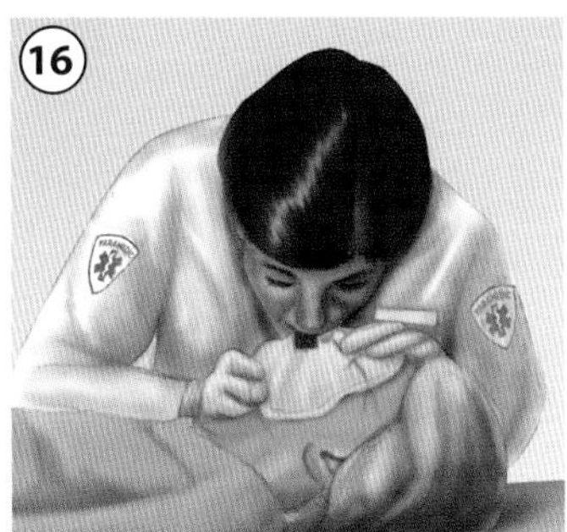

16. rescue breathing
人工呼吸

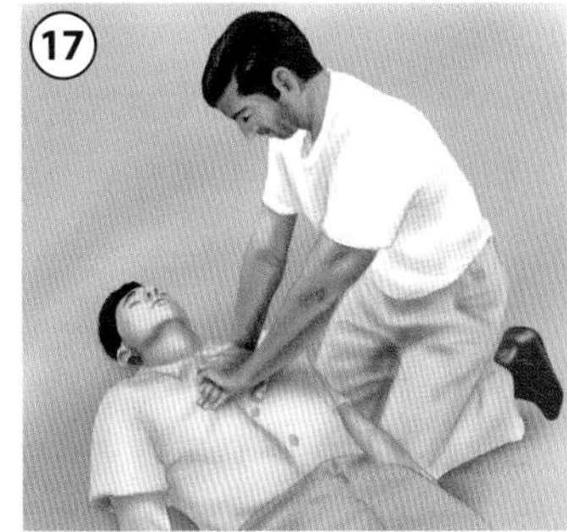

17. CPR (cardiopulmonary resuscitation)
心肺蘇生法

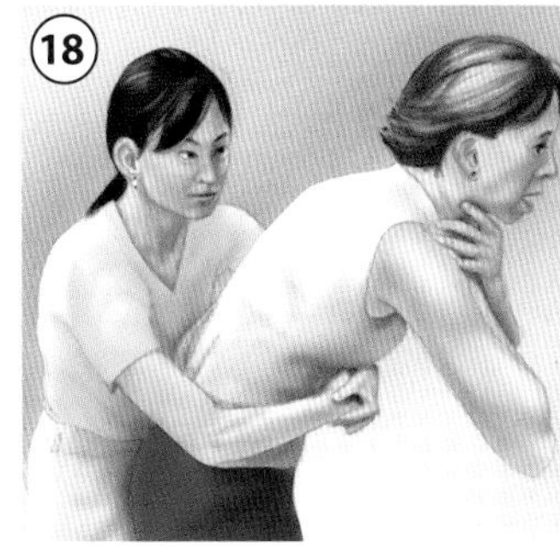

18. Heimlich maneuver
ハイムリック法 (異物を吐き出させる応急処置)

Pair practice. Make new conversations.

A: *What do we need in the first aid kit?*
B: *We need tweezers and gauze.*
A: *I think we need sterile tape, too.*

Think about it. Discuss.

1. What are the three most important first aid items? Why?
2. Which first aid procedures should everyone know? Why?
3. What are some good places to keep a first aid kit?

Medical Care 医療

In the Waiting Room 待合室で

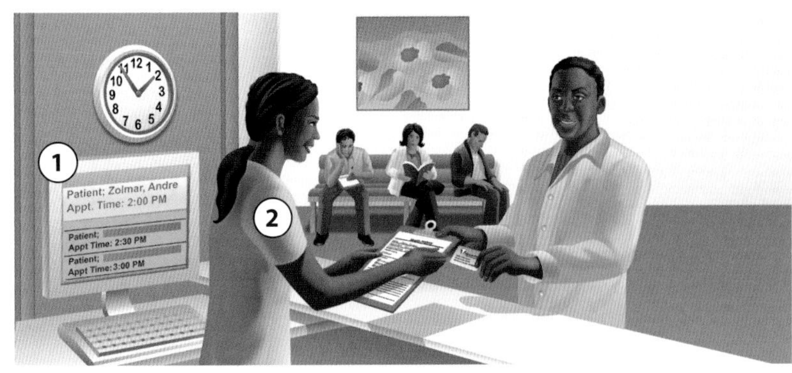

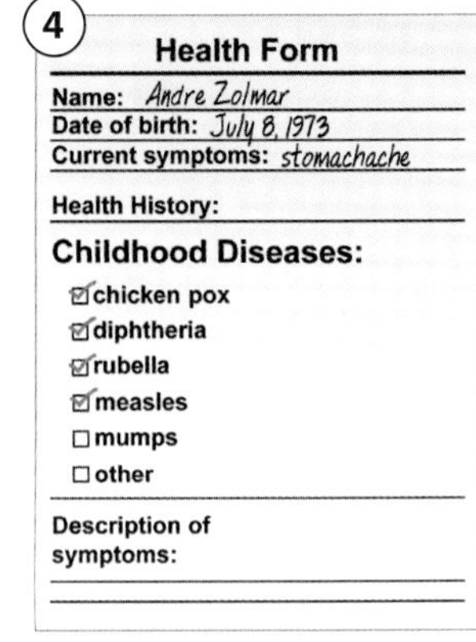

Health Form

Name: *Andre Zolmar*
Date of birth: *July 8, 1973*
Current symptoms: *stomachache*

Health History:

Childhood Diseases:

- ☑ chicken pox
- ☑ diphtheria
- ☑ rubella
- ☑ measles
- ☐ mumps
- ☐ other

Description of symptoms:

HEALTH FIRST
Name: Andre Zolmar
Group Number: 98765
Membership Number: 60756789

1. appointment
（医師や検査の）予約

2. receptionist
受付係

3. health insurance card
健康保険証

4. health history form
問診票

In the Examining Room 診察室で

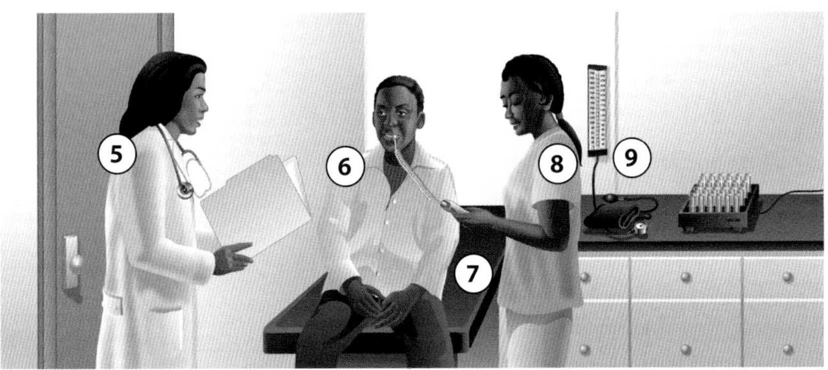

5. doctor
医師

6. patient
患者

7. examination table
診察台

8. nurse
看護師

9. blood pressure gauge
血圧計

10. stethoscope
聴診器

11. thermometer
体温計

12. syringe
注射器

Medical Procedures 治療

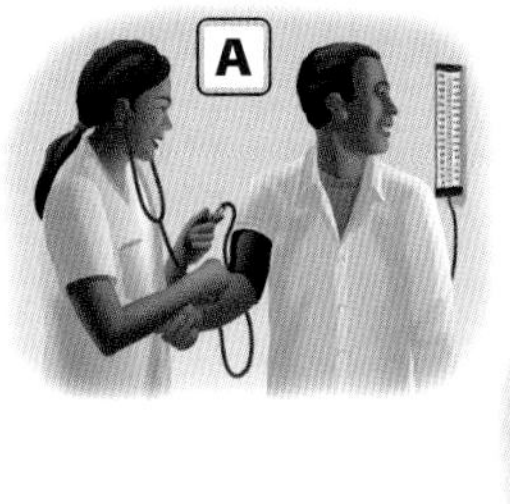

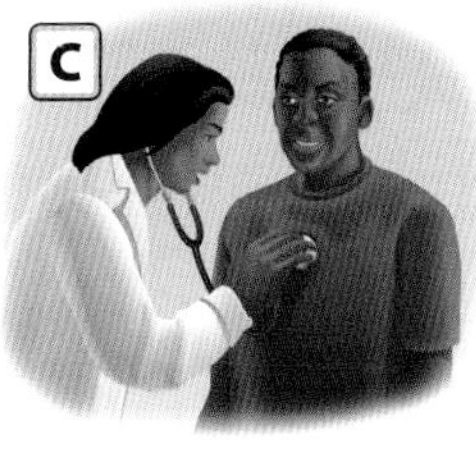

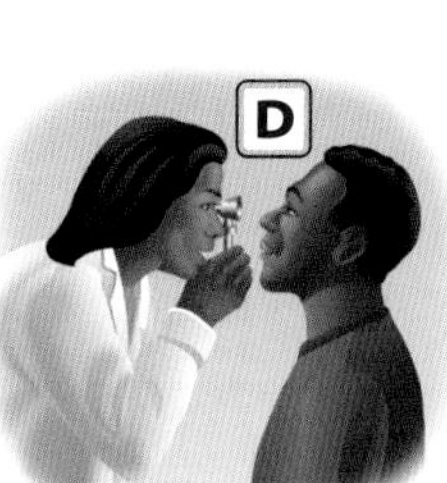

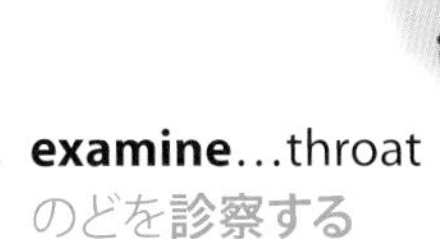

A. **check**…blood pressure
血圧を**測る**

B. **take**…temperature
体温を**測る**

C. **listen** to…heart
心音を**聞く**

D. **examine**…eyes
目を**診察する**

E. **examine**…throat
のどを**診察する**

F. **draw**…blood
血液を**採る**

Grammar Point: future tense with *will* + verb

To show a future action, use ***will*** + verb.
The subject pronoun contraction of ***will*** is ***-'ll.***
She ***will draw*** *your blood. = She'****ll draw*** *your blood.*

Role play. Talk to a medical receptionist.

A: *Will the nurse examine my eyes?*
B: *No, but she'll draw your blood.*
A: *What will the doctor do?*

Dentistry 歯科

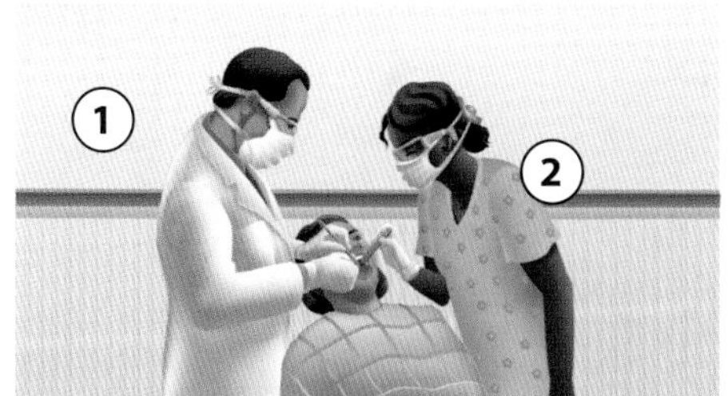

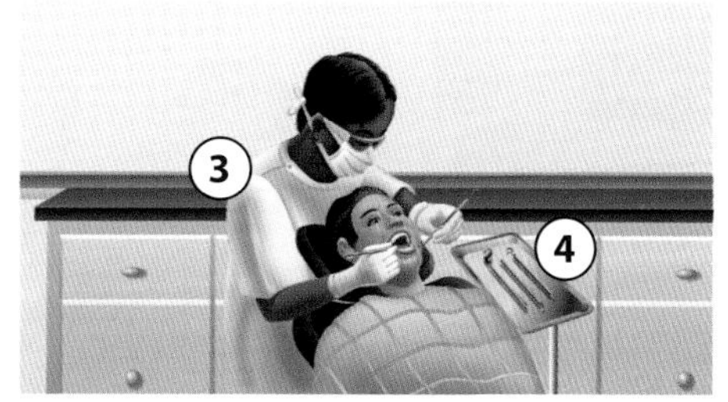

1. dentist
歯科医
2. dental assistant
歯科助手
3. dental hygienist
歯科衛生士
4. dental instruments
歯科器具

Orthodontics 歯科矯正

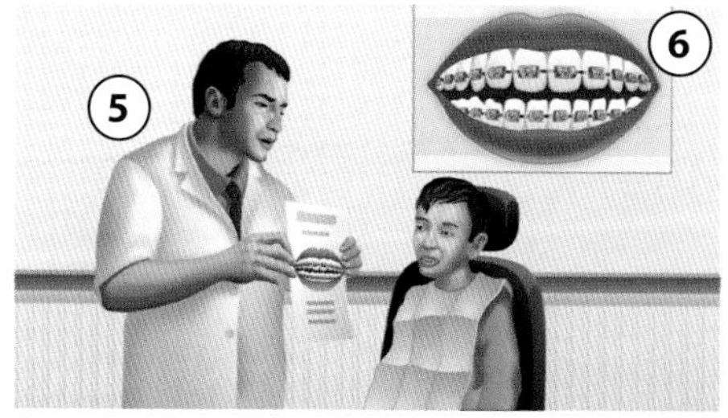

5. orthodontist
歯列矯正医
6. braces
矯正器

Dental Problems 歯の問題

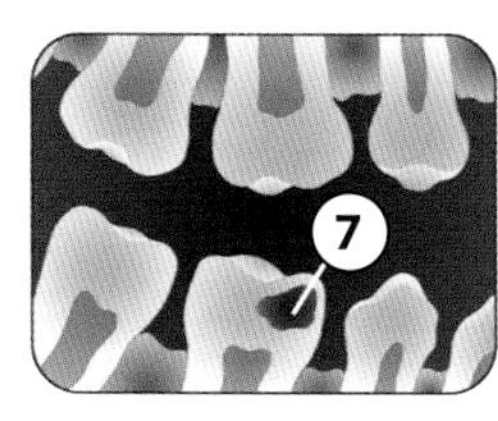

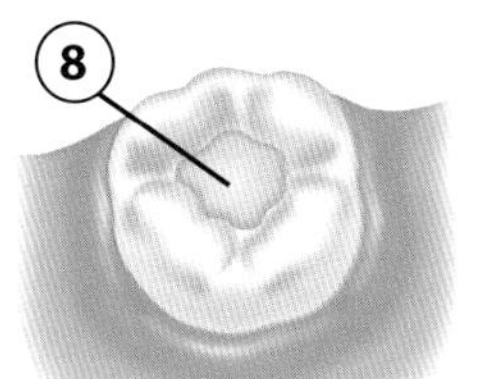

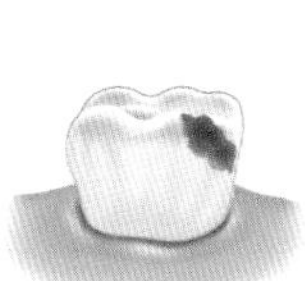

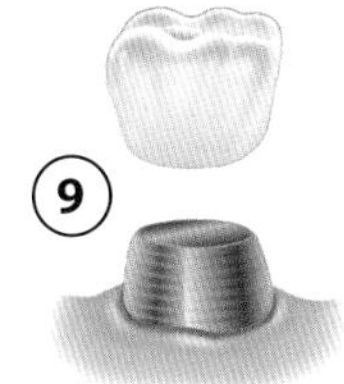

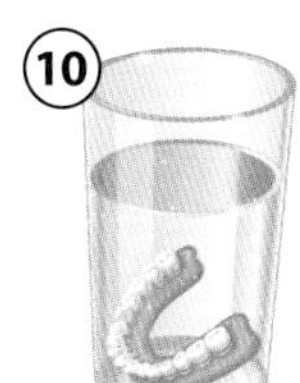

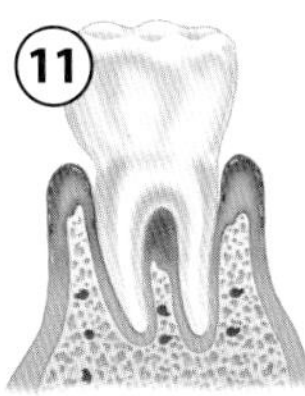

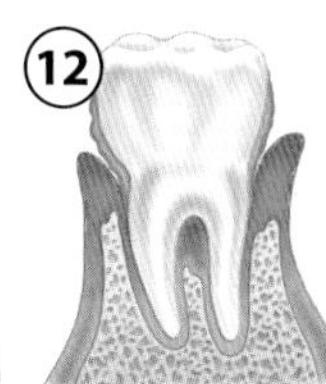

7. cavity / decay
虫歯
8. filling
詰め物／フィリング
9. crown
クラウン
10. dentures
入れ歯
11. gum disease
歯槽膿漏 (のうろう)
12. plaque
歯垢

An Office Visit 歯科医に行く

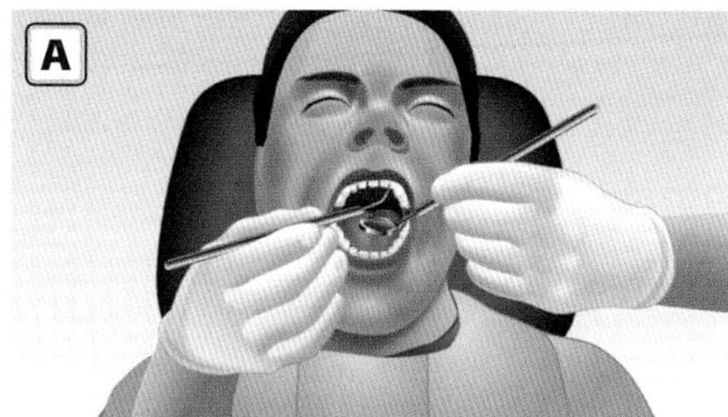

A. **clean**…teeth
歯の**クリーニングを行う**

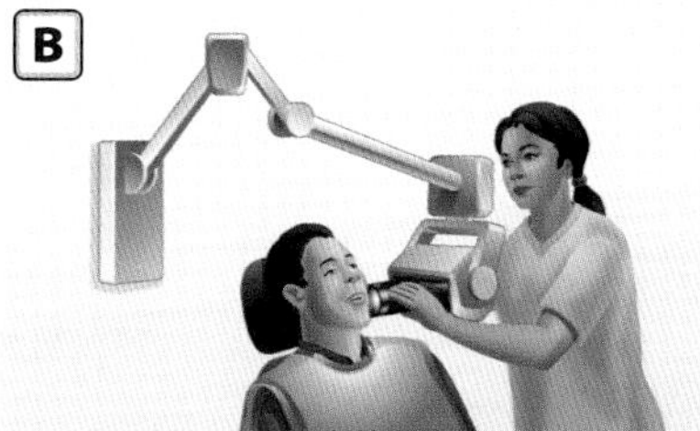

B. **take** x-rays
レントゲンを**撮る**

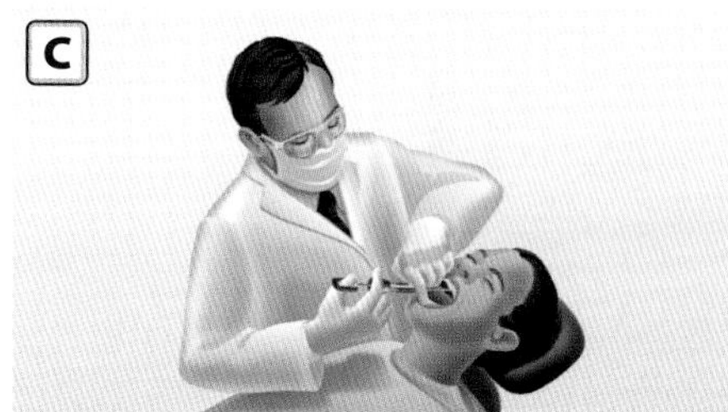

C. **numb** the mouth
口内に**麻酔をかける**

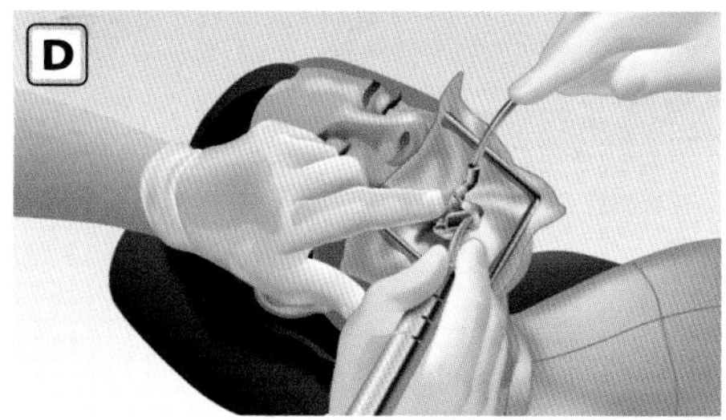

D. **drill** a tooth
歯を**削る**

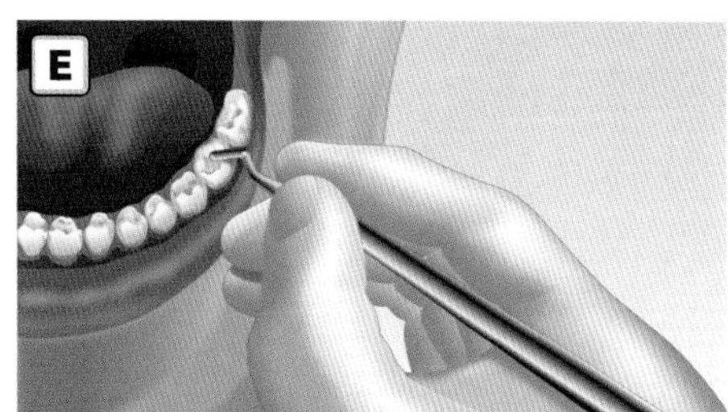

E. **fill** a cavity
虫歯を**埋める**

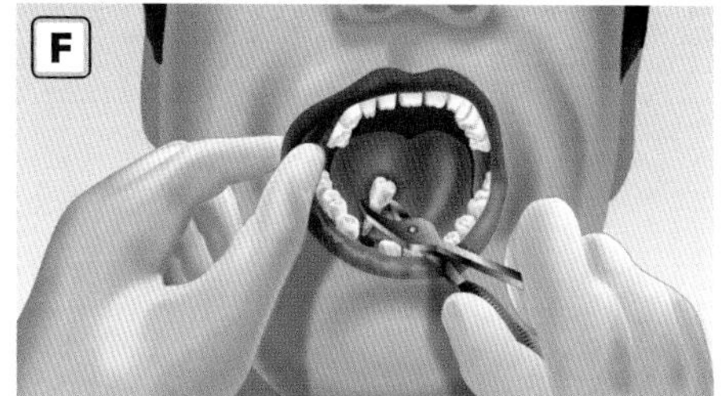

F. **pull** a tooth
歯を**抜く**

Ask your classmates. Share the answers.

1. Do you know someone with braces? Who?
2. Do dentists make you nervous? Why or why not?
3. How often do you go to the dentist?

Role play. Talk to a dentist.

A: *I think I have a cavity.*
B: *Let me take a look.*
A: *Will I need a filling?*

Medical Specialists 専門医

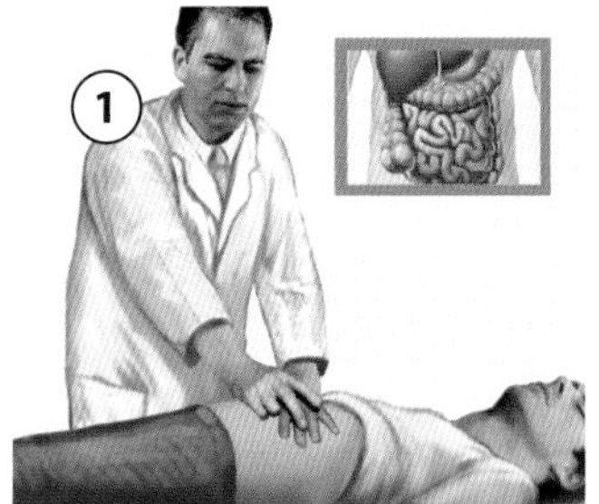
1. internist
内科医

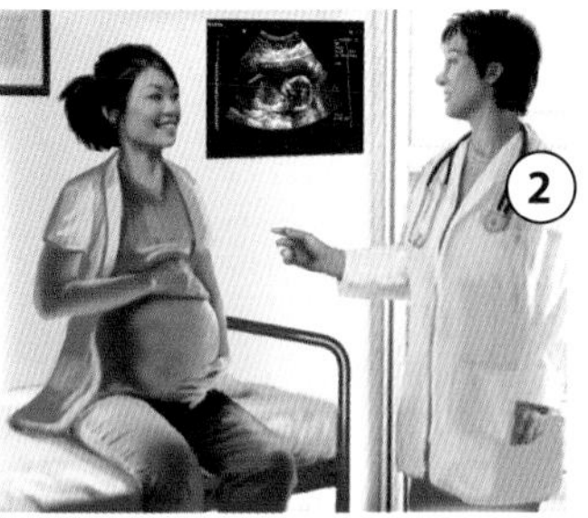
2. obstetrician
産科医

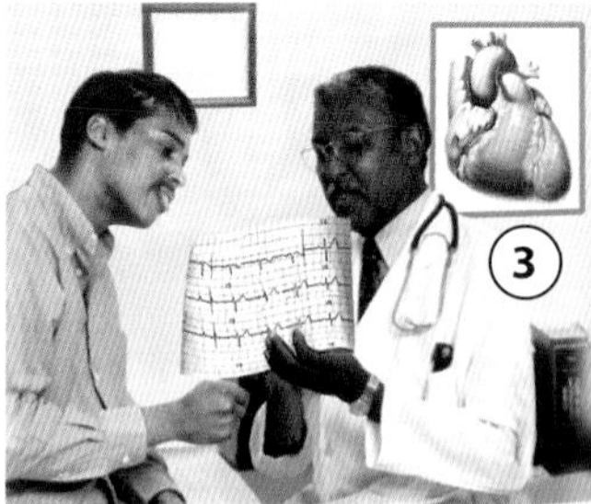
3. cardiologist
心臓専門医

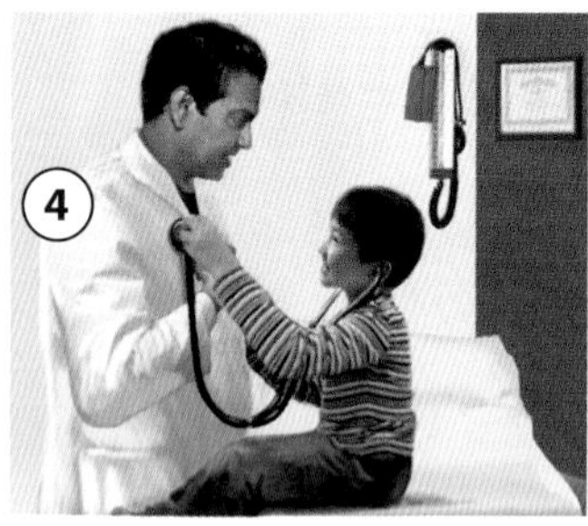
4. pediatrician
小児科医

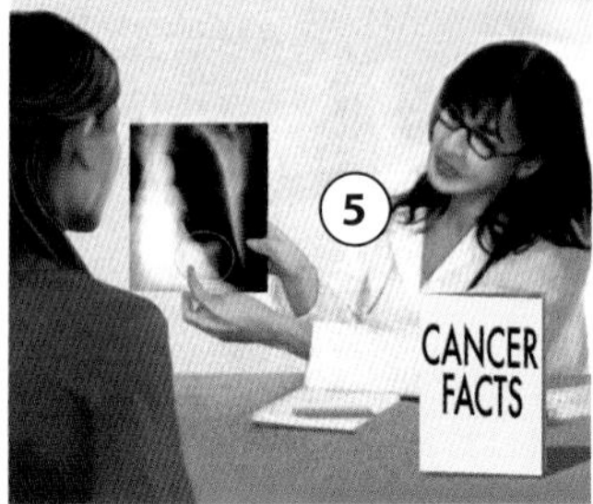

5. oncologist
がん専門医

6. radiologist
放射線医

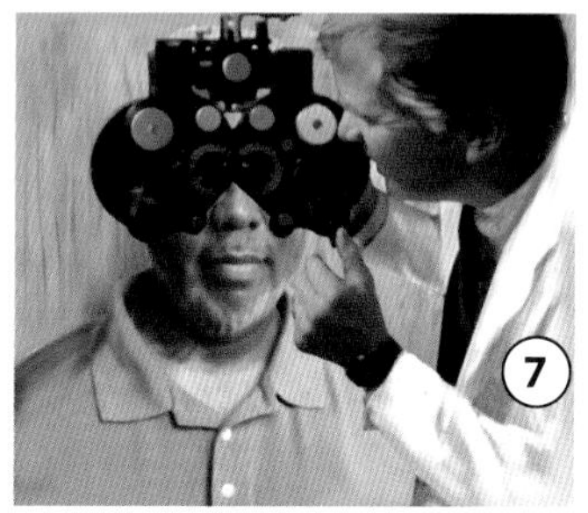
7. ophthalmologist
眼科医

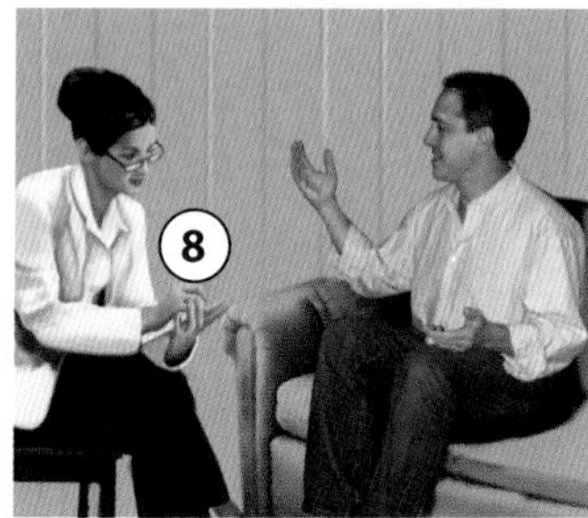
8. psychiatrist
精神科医

Nursing Staff 看護スタッフ

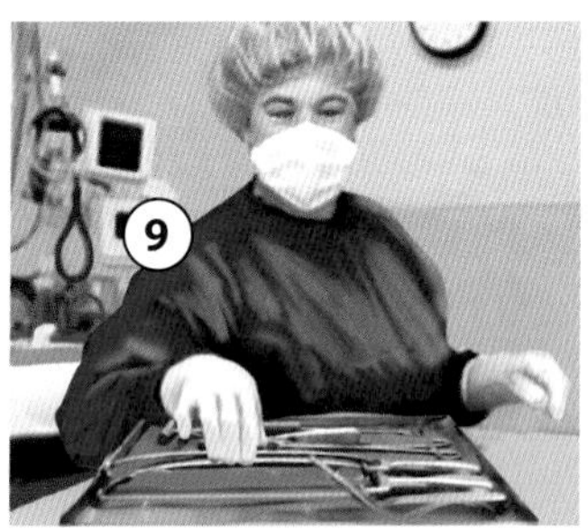
9. surgical nurse
外科専門の看護師

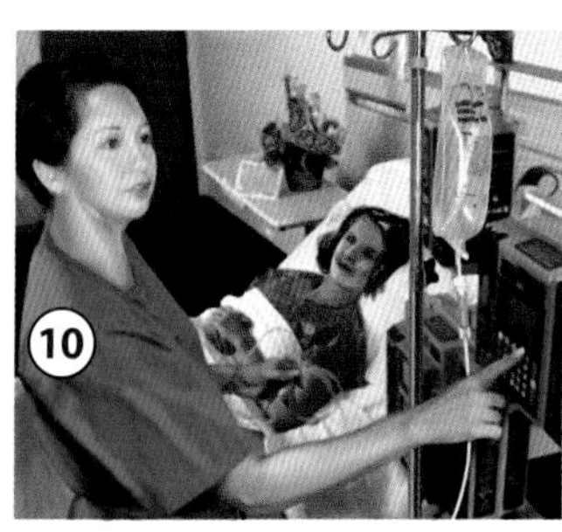
10. registered nurse (RN)
正看護師（RN）

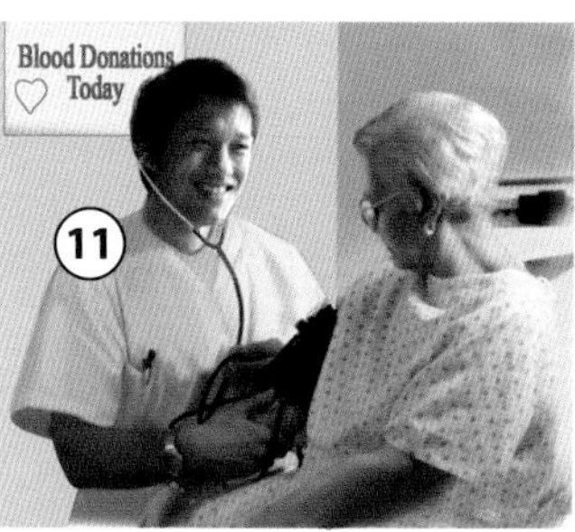

11. licensed practical nurse (LPN)
准看護師（LPN）

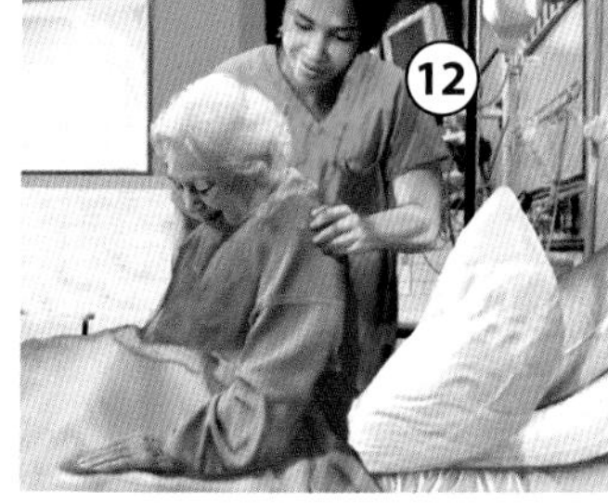
12. certified nursing assistant (CNA)
認定看護助手（CNA）

Hospital Staff 病院の職員

13. administrator
運営管理者

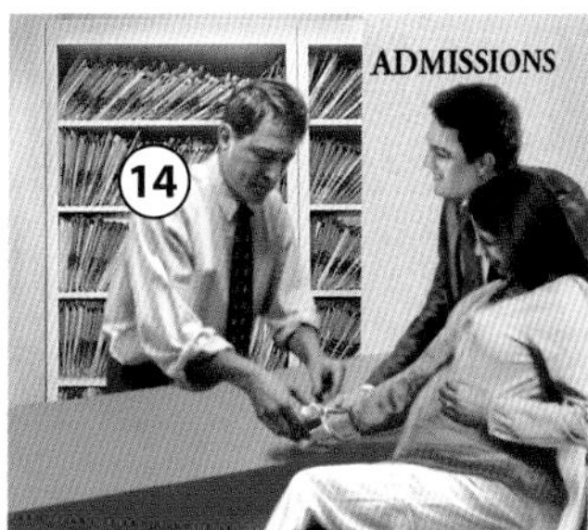

14. admissions clerk
入院受付係

15. dietician
栄養士

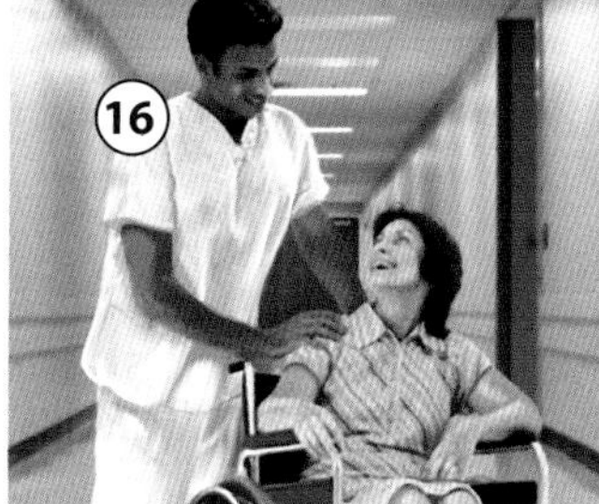
16. orderly
病棟勤務員

More vocabulary

Gynecologists examine and treat women.
Nurse practitioners can give medical exams.
Nurse midwives deliver babies.

Chiropractors move the spine to improve health.
Orthopedists treat bone and joint problems.

A Hospital Room 病室

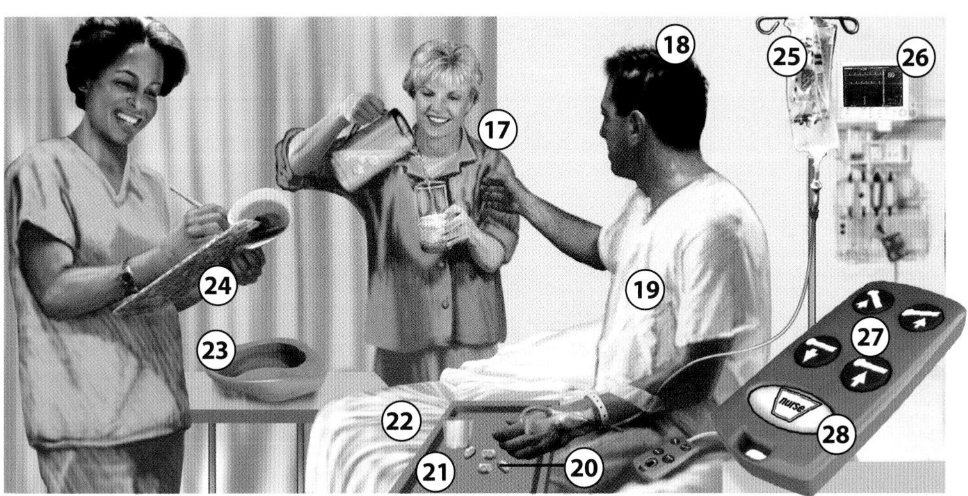

Lab 検査室

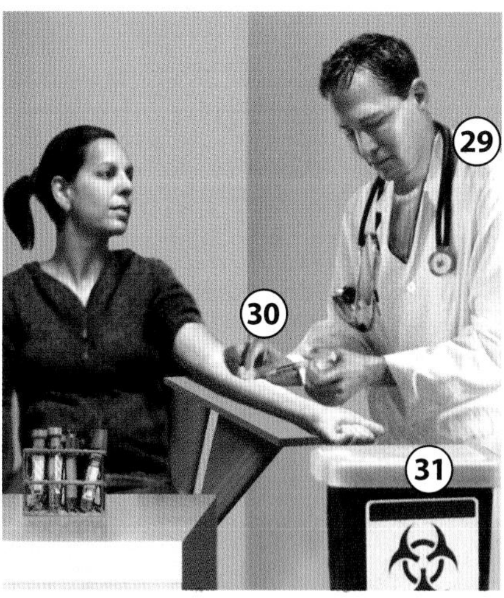

17. volunteer
ボランティア

18. patient
患者

19. hospital gown
診察用ガウン

20. medication
薬

21. bed table
ベッドテーブル

22. hospital bed
病院のベッド

23. bed pan
便器／おまる

24. medical chart
カルテ

25. IV (intravenous drip)
点滴

26. vital signs monitor
呼吸数・脈拍などを示すモニター

27. bed control
ベッド調整

28. call button
呼び出しボタン

29. phlebotomist
採血専門家

30. blood work / blood test
血液検査

31. medical waste disposal
医療廃棄物用ごみ箱

Emergency Room Entrance 救急病院入口

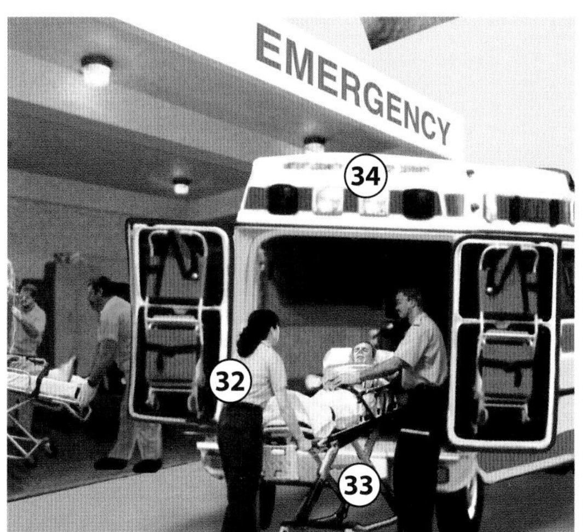

32. emergency medical technician (EMT)
救急医療士

33. stretcher / gurney
車輪つき担架

34. ambulance
救急車

Operating Room 手術室

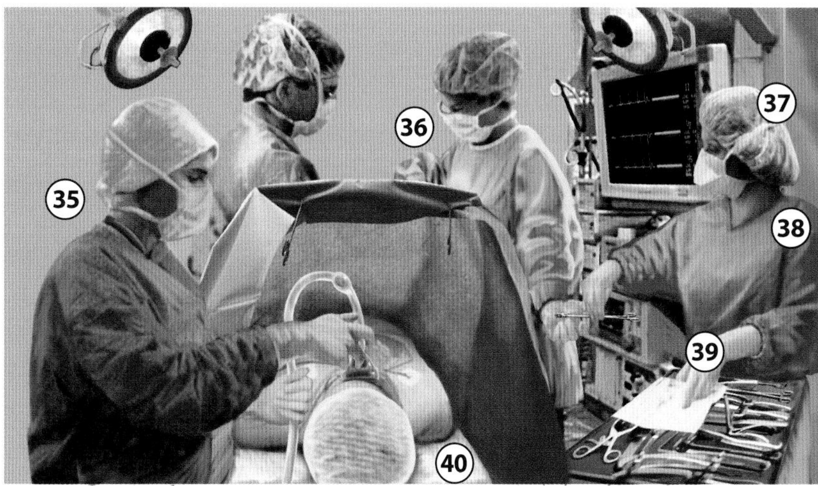

35. anesthesiologist
麻酔医

36. surgeon
外科医

37. surgical cap
手術帽

38. surgical gown
手術衣

39. surgical gloves
手術用手袋

40. operating table
手術台

Dictate to your partner. Take turns.

A: *Write this sentence. She's a volunteer.*
B: *She's a what?*
A: *Volunteer. That's v-o-l-u-n-t-e-e-r.*

Role play. Ask about a doctor.

A: *I need to find a good surgeon.*
B: *Dr. Jones is a great surgeon. You should call him.*
A: *I will! Please give me his number.*

A Health Fair

1. low-cost exam
低料金の健康診断
2. acupuncture
鍼
3. booth
ブース
4. yoga
ヨガ
5. aerobic exercise
エアロビクスエクササイズ
6. demonstration
デモ／実演
7. sugar-free
シュガーレス
8. nutrition label
食品成分ラベル

A. **check** ... pulse
脈を**計る**

B. **give** a lecture
講義**する**

Look at the picture.
What do you see?

Answer the questions.

1. How many different booths are there at the health fair?
2. What kinds of exams and treatments can you get at the fair?
3. What kinds of lectures and demonstrations are there?
4. How much is an acupuncture treatment? a medical screening?

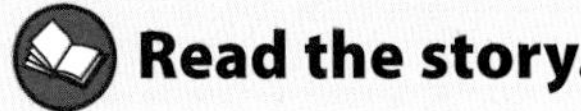

Read the story.

A Health Fair

Once a month the Fadool Health Clinic has a health fair. You can get a low-cost medical exam at one booth. The nurses check your blood pressure and check your pulse. At another booth you can get a free eye exam. And an acupuncture treatment is only $5.00.

You can learn a lot at the fair. This month a doctor is giving a lecture on nutrition labels. There is also a demonstration on sugar-free cooking. You can learn to do aerobic exercise and yoga, too.

Do you want to get healthy and stay healthy? Then come to the Fadool Clinic Health Fair!

Think about it.

1. Which booths at this fair look interesting to you? Why?
2. Do you read nutrition labels? Why or why not?

Downtown ダウンタウン

1. parking garage
   駐車場
2. office building
   オフィスビル
3. hotel
   ホテル
4. Department of Motor Vehicles
   交通局
5. bank
   銀行
6. police station
   警察署
7. bus station
   バス停
8. city hall
   市役所

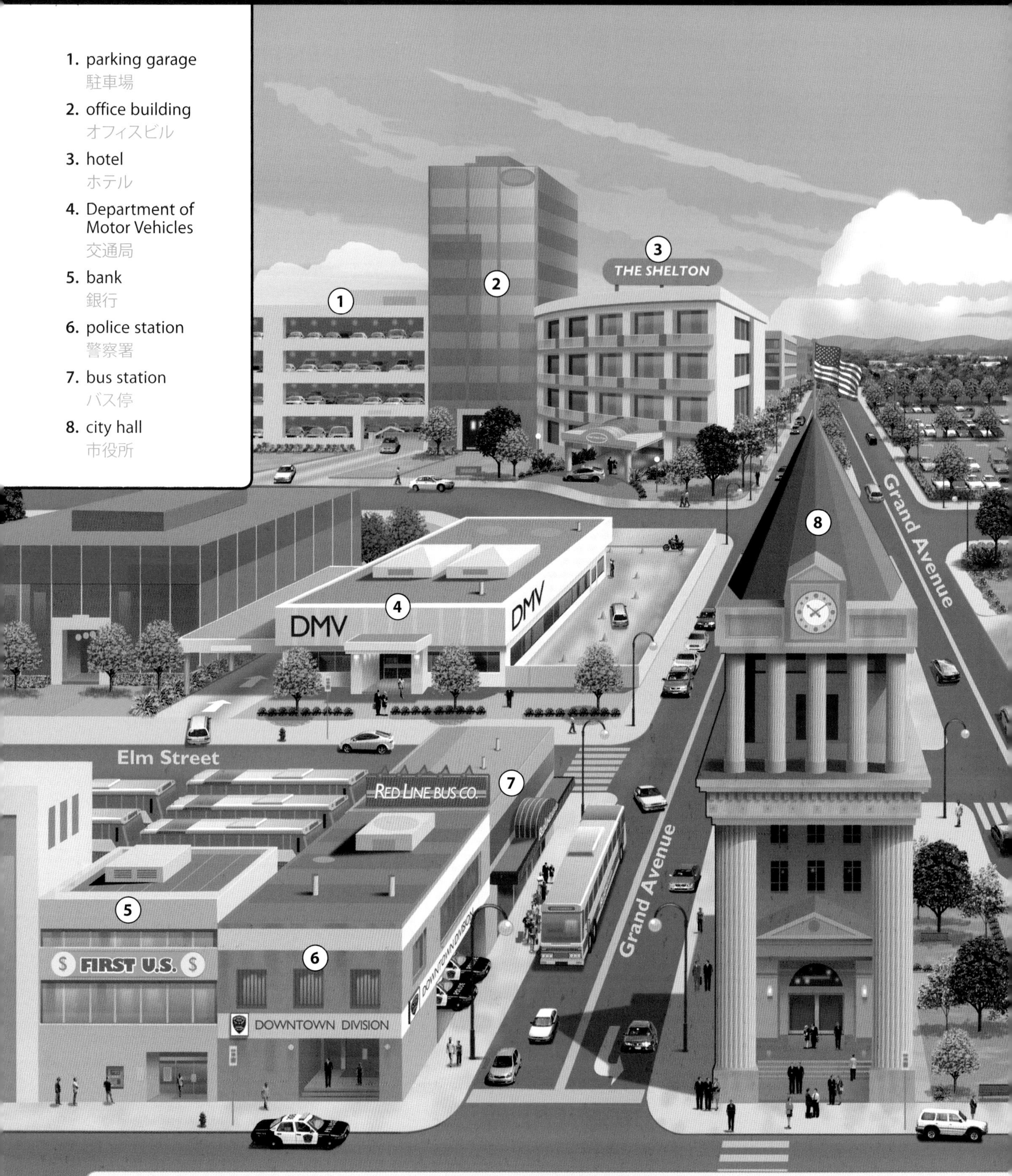

Listen and point. Take turns.

A: *Point to* *__the bank__.*
B: *Point to* *__the hotel__.*
A: *Point to* *__the restaurant__.*

Dictate to your partner. Take turns.

A: *Write* *__bank__.*
B: *Is that spelled* *__b-a-n-k__?*
A: *Yes, that's right.*

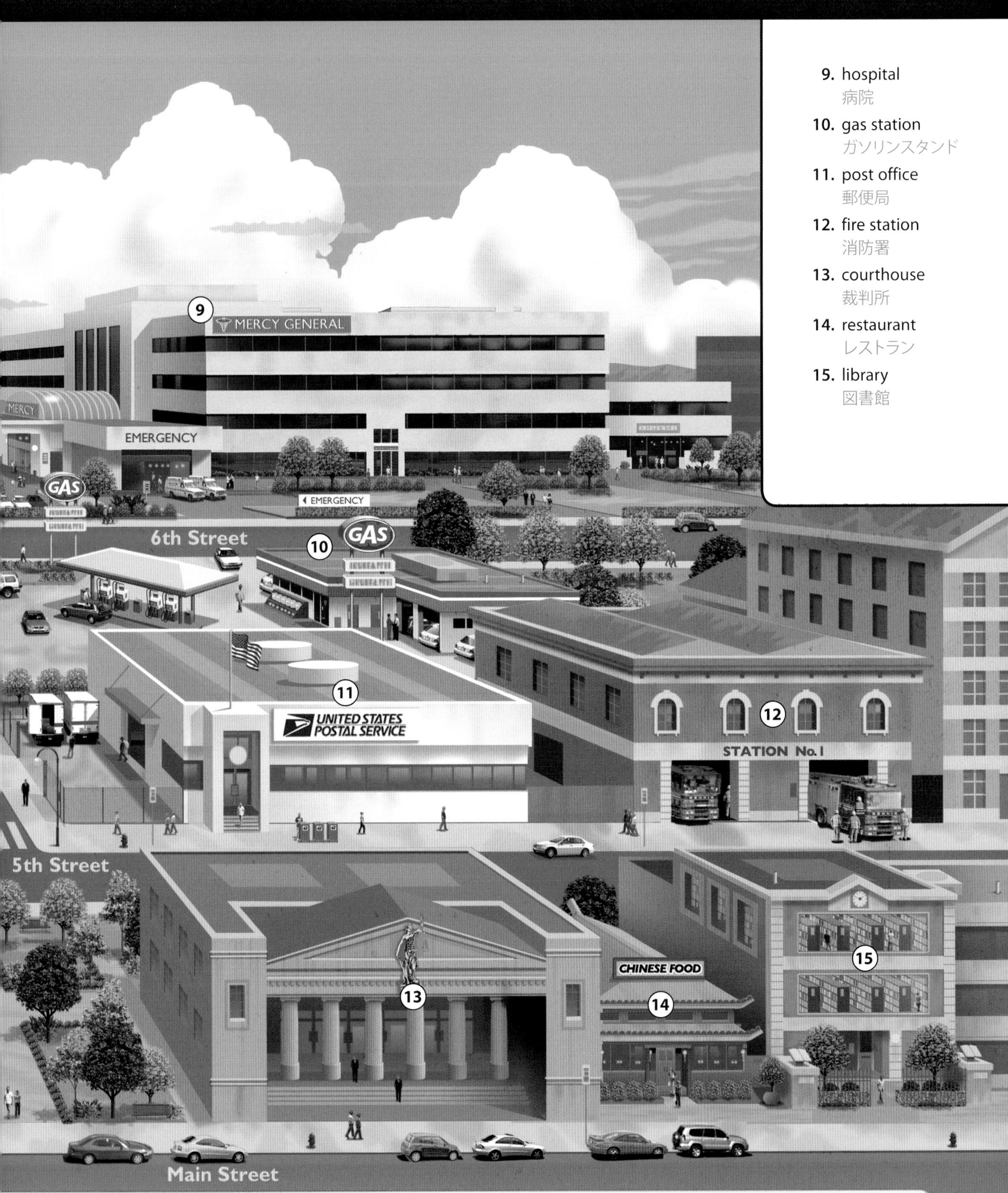

9. hospital
病院
10. gas station
ガソリンスタンド
11. post office
郵便局
12. fire station
消防署
13. courthouse
裁判所
14. restaurant
レストラン
15. library
図書館

Grammar Point: *in* and *at* with locations

Use ***in*** when you are inside the building. *I am **in** (inside) the bank.* Use ***at*** to describe your general location. *I am **at** the bank.*

Pair practice. Make new conversations.

A: *I'm in the bank. Where are you?*

B: *I'm at the bank, too, but I'm outside.*

A: *OK. I'll meet you there.*

1. stadium
   スタジアム
2. construction site
   工事現場
3. factory
   工場
4. car dealership
   自動車販売店
5. mosque
   モスク
6. movie theater
   映画館
7. shopping mall
   ショッピングモール
8. furniture store
   家具屋
9. school
   学校
10. gym
    スポーツジム
11. coffee shop
    喫茶店
12. motel
    モーテル

Ways to state your destination using *to* and *to the*

Use ***to*** for schools, churches, and synagogues.
I'm going ***to*** *school.*
Use ***to the*** for all other locations. *I have to go* ***to the*** *bakery.*

Pair practice. Make new conversations.

A: *Where are you going today?*
B: *I'm going to school. How about you?*
A: *I have to go to the bakery.*

13. skyscraper / high-rise
高層ビル

14. church
教会

15. cemetery
墓地

16. synagogue
ユダヤ教会

17. community college
コミュニティカレッジ

18. supermarket
スーパーマーケット

19. bakery
パン屋

20. home improvement store
ホームセンター

21. office supply store
文房具店

22. garbage truck
ごみ収集車

23. theater
劇場

24. convention center
コンベンションセンター

Ways to give locations

The mall is on 2nd Street.
The mall is on the corner of 2nd and Elm.
The mall is next to the movie theater.

Ask your classmates. Share the answers.

1. Where's your favorite coffee shop?
2. Where's your favorite supermarket?
3. Where's your favorite movie theater?

An Intersection

交差点

1. laundromat
   コインランドリー
2. dry cleaners
   ドライクリーニング店
3. convenience store
   コンビニエンスストア
4. pharmacy
   薬局
5. parking space
   駐車スペース
6. handicapped parking
   身体障害者用駐車スペース
7. corner
   角
8. traffic light
   交通信号
9. bus
   バス
10. fast food restaurant
    ファーストフード店
11. drive-thru window
    ドライブスルー用の窓口
12. newsstand
    新聞雑誌売店
13. mailbox
    郵便ポスト
14. pedestrian
    歩行者
15. crosswalk
    横断歩道

A. **cross** the street
   通りを**渡る**
B. **wait for** the light
   信号が変わるのを**待つ**
C. **jaywalk**
   交通規則を無視して通りを渡る

Pair practice. Make new conversations.

A: *I have a lot of errands to do today.*
B: *Me, too. First, I'm going to the laundromat.*
A: *I'll see you there after I stop at the copy center.*

Think about it. Discuss.

1. Which businesses are good to have in a neighborhood? Why?
2. Would you like to own a small business? If yes, what kind? If no, why not?

16. bus stop
バス停

17. donut shop
ドーナッツ屋

18. copy center
コピーセンター

19. barbershop
床屋

20. video store
ビデオ店

21. curb
縁石

22. bike
自転車

23. pay phone
公衆電話

24. sidewalk
歩道

25. parking meter
パーキングメーター

26. street sign
標識

27. fire hydrant
消火栓

28. cart
カート

29. street vendor
屋台

30. childcare center
保育園

D. **ride** a bike
自転車に**乗る**

E. **park** the car
車を**駐車する**

F. **walk** a dog
犬を**散歩させる**

More vocabulary

neighborhood: the area close to your home

do errands: to make a short trip from your home to buy or pick up things

Ask your classmates. Share the answers.

1. What errands do you do every week?
2. What stores do you go to in your neighborhood?
3. What things can you buy from a street vendor?

A Mall

1. music store
   CD店
2. jewelry store
   宝石店
3. nail salon
   ネイルサロン
4. bookstore
   書店
5. toy store
   おもちゃ屋
6. pet store
   ペットショップ
7. card store
   カードショップ
8. florist
   花屋
9. optician
   眼鏡店
10. shoe store
    靴屋
11. play area
    プレイエリア
12. guest services
    ゲストサービス（案内所）

More vocabulary

beauty shop: hair salon
men's store: men's clothing store
gift shop: a store that sells t-shirts, mugs, and other small gifts

Pair practice. Make new conversations.

A: *Where is the florist?*
B: *It's on the first floor, next to the optician.*

13. department store
デパート

14. travel agency
旅行代理店

15. food court
フードコート

16. ice cream shop
アイスクリーム屋

17. candy store
キャンデーショップ

18. hair salon
ヘアサロン

19. maternity store
マタニティストア

20. electronics store
電気店

21. elevator
エレベーター

22. cell phone kiosk
携帯電話販売所

23. escalator
エスカレーター

24. directory
案内板

Ways to talk about plans

Let's go to the card store.
I have to go to the card store.
I want to go to the card store.

Role play. Talk to a friend at the mall.

A: *Let's go to the card store. I need to buy a card for Maggie's birthday.*
B: *OK, but can we go to the shoe store next?*

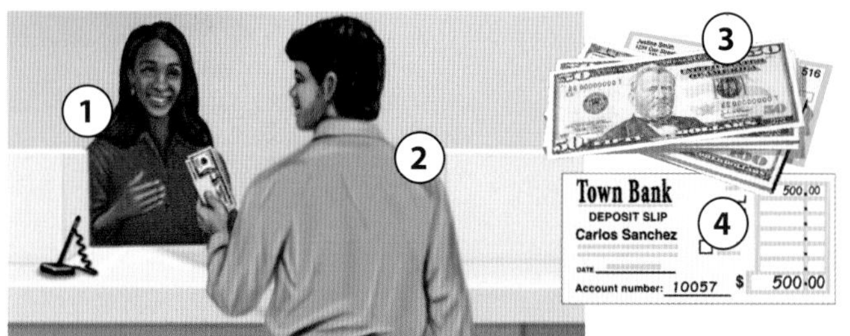

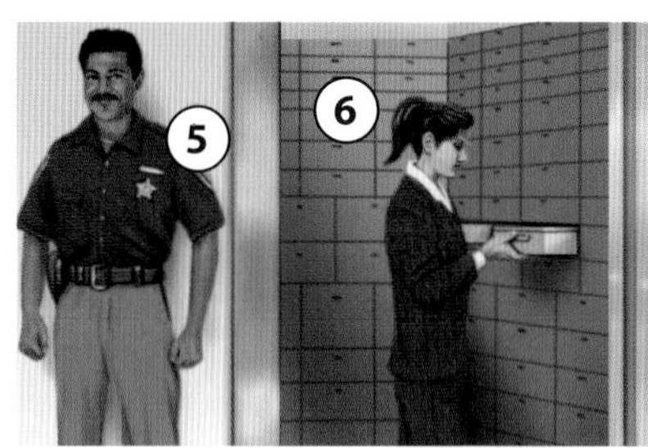

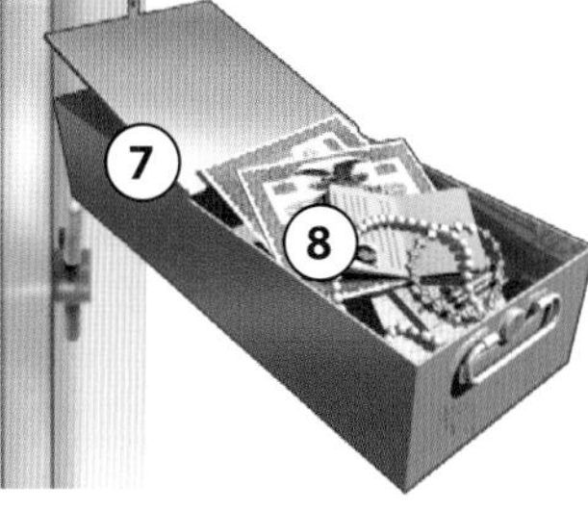

1. teller 銀行の窓口係
2. customer 顧客
3. deposit 預金
4. deposit slip 預金伝票
5. security guard 警備員
6. vault 金庫室
7. safety deposit box 貸金庫
8. valuables 貴重品

Opening an Account 口座を開く

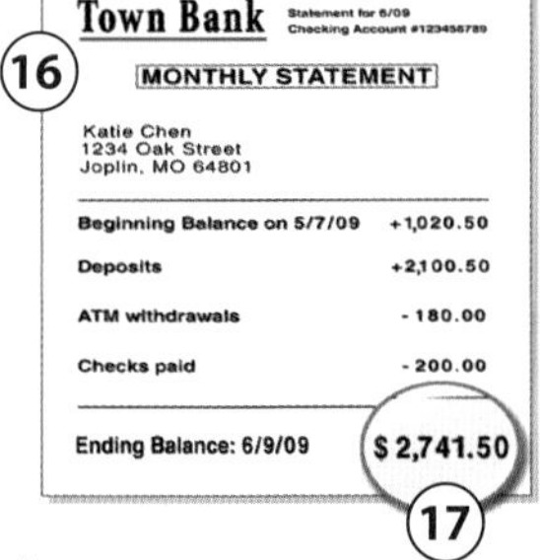

9. account manager 口座担当者
10. passbook 預金通帳
11. savings account number 普通預金口座番号
12. check book 小切手帳
13. check 小切手
14. checking account number 当座預金口座番号
15. ATM card ATMカード
16. bank statement 銀行取引明細書
17. balance 残高

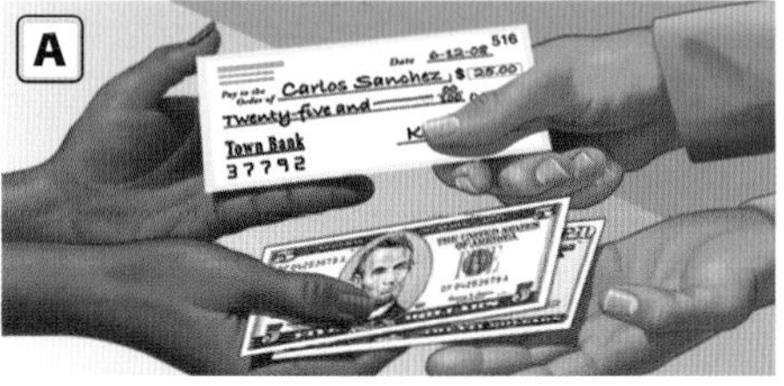

A. **Cash** a check.
小切手を**換金する**

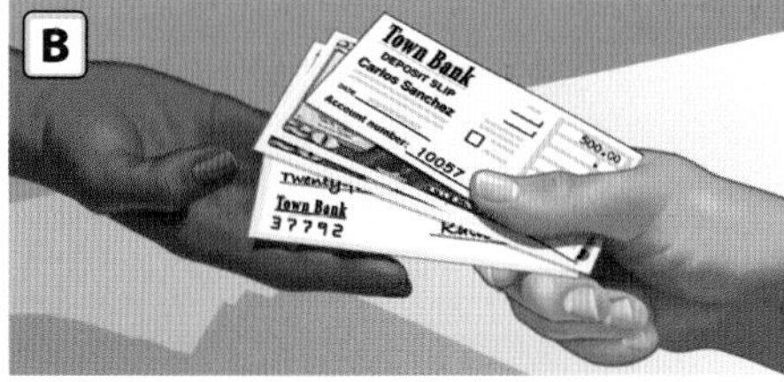

B. **Make** a deposit.
預金**する**

C. **Bank** online.
オンラインで**銀行取引を行う**

The ATM (Automated Teller Machine) ATM（現金自動預入支払機）

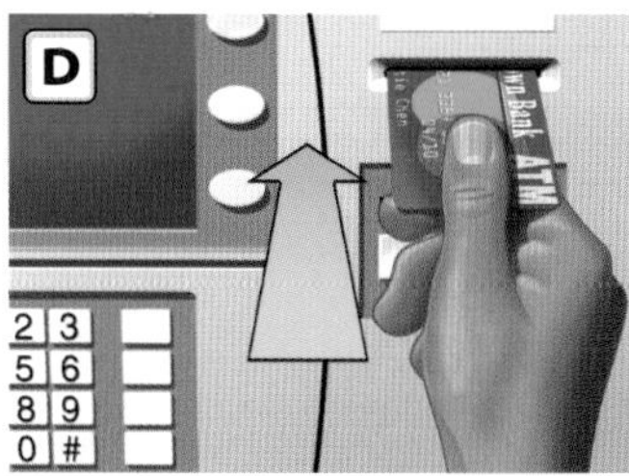

D. **Insert** your ATM card.
ATMカードを**挿入する**

E. **Enter** your PIN.*
暗証番号を**入力する**

F. **Withdraw** cash.
現金を**引き出す**

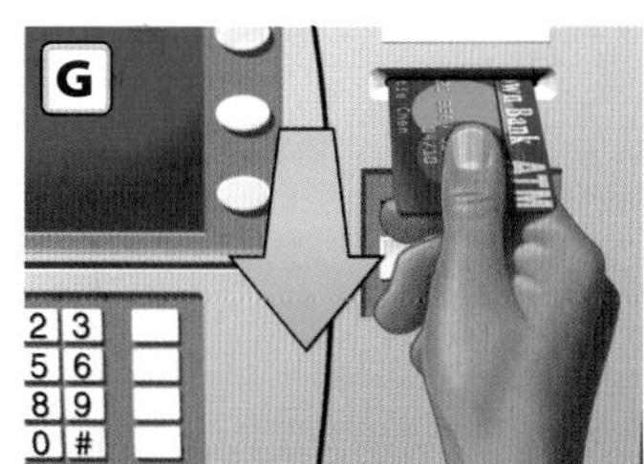

G. **Remove** your card.
カードを**取り出す**

*PIN = personal identification number

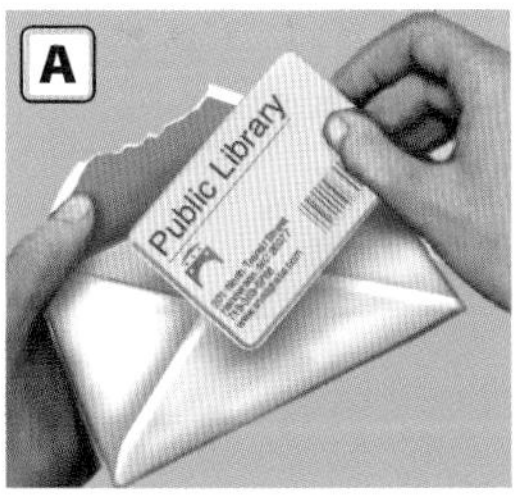

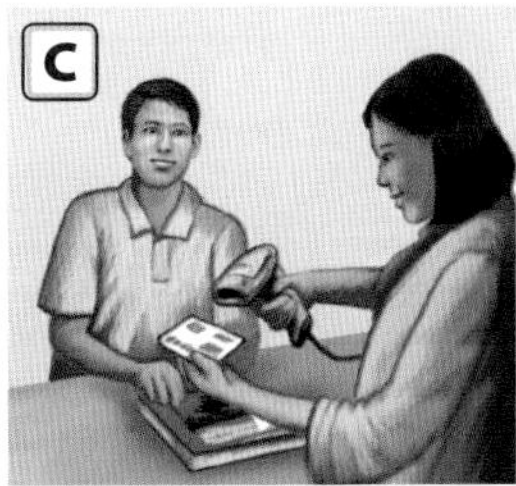

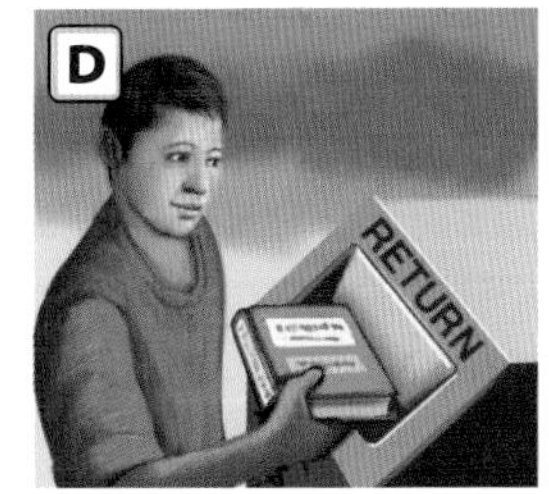

A. **get** a library card
図書館カードを**作る**

B. **look for** a book
本を**探す**

C. **check out** a book
本を**借り出す**

D. **return** a book
本を**返す**

E. **pay** a late fine
延滞料を**支払う**

1. library clerk
図書館員
2. circulation desk
図書館の貸し出し返却受付デスク
3. library patron
図書館利用者
4. periodicals
定期刊行物
5. magazine
雑誌
6. newspaper
新聞
7. headline
見出し
8. atlas
地図帳
9. reference librarian
参考文献担当司書
10. self-checkout
セルフチェックアウト
11. online catalog
オンラインカタログ
12. picture book
絵本

13. biography
伝記
14. title
題名
15. author
著者
16. novel
小説
17. audiobook
オーディオブック
18. videocassette
ビデオカセット
19. DVD
DVD

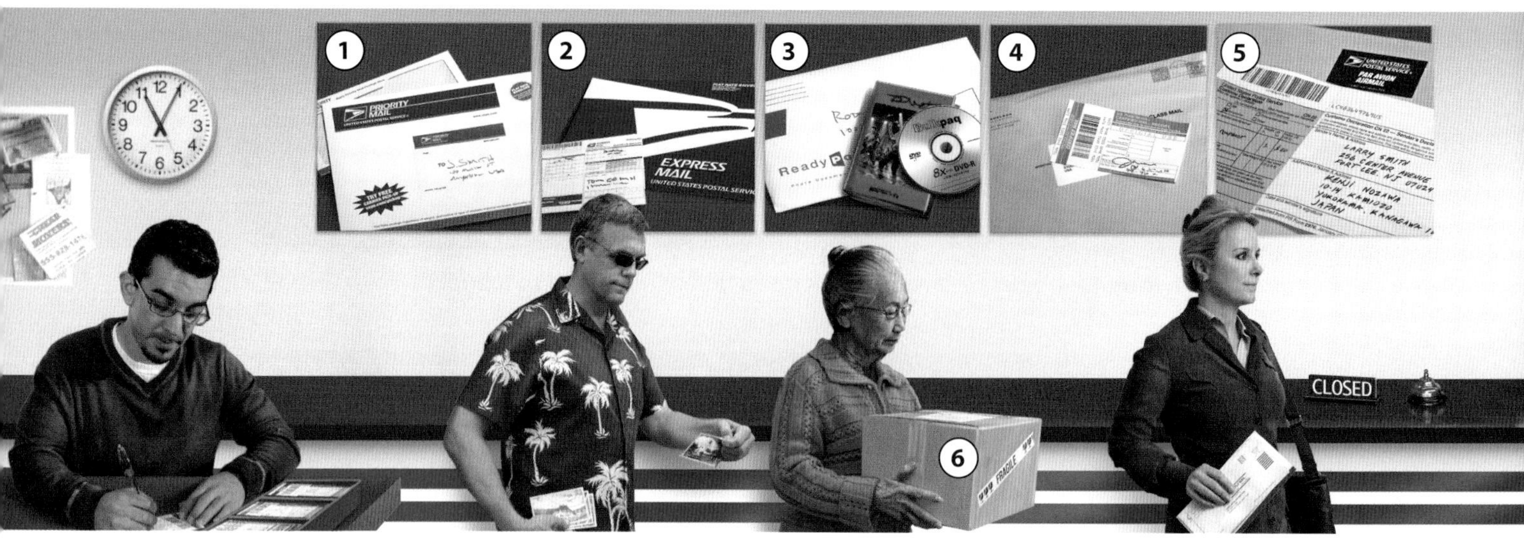

1. Priority Mail®
   プライオリティメール（優先扱い郵便）
2. Express Mail®
   エクスプレスメール（速達）
3. media mail
   メディアメール
4. Certified Mail™
   サーティファイドメール（配達証明付き郵便）
5. airmail
   航空便
6. ground post / parcel post
   小包郵便

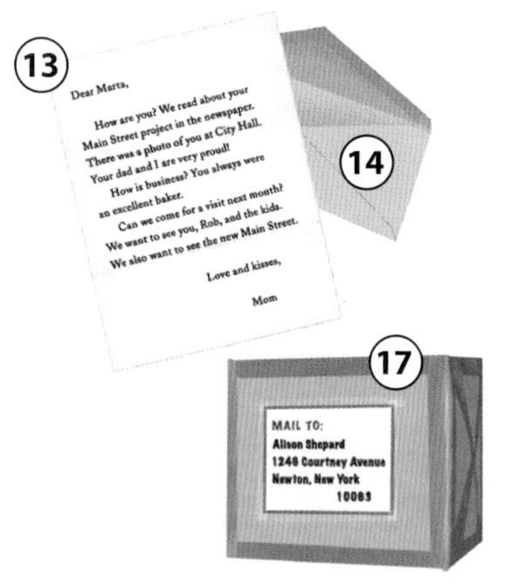

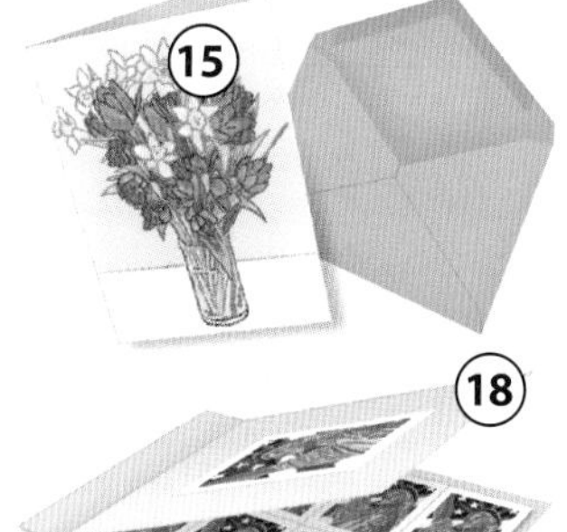

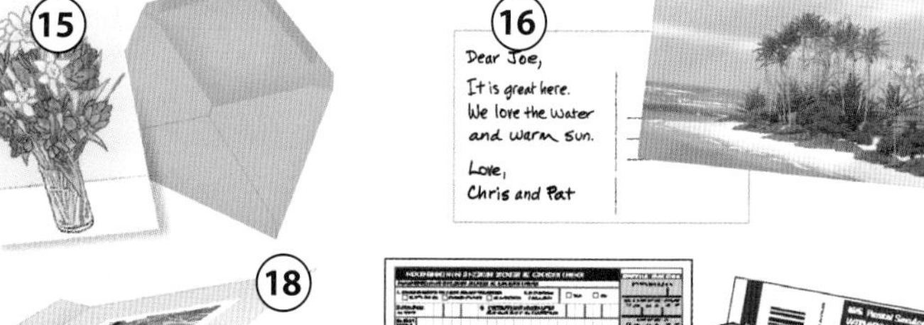

13. letter
    手紙
14. envelope
    封筒
15. greeting card
    グリーティングカード
16. post card
    葉書
17. package
    小包
18. book of stamps
    切手ブックレット
19. postal forms
    郵便関係の書類
20. letter carrier
    郵便集配人

21. return address
    差出人の住所
22. mailing address
    宛先の住所
23. stamp
    切手
24. postmark
    消印

Ways to talk about sending mail

This letter has to get there tomorrow. **(Express Mail®)**
This letter has to arrive in two days. **(Priority Mail®)**
This letter can go in regular mail. **(First Class)**

Pair practice. Make new conversations.

A: *Hi. This letter has to get there tomorrow.*
B: *You can send it by Express Mail®.*
A: *OK. I need a book of stamps, too.*

7. postal clrk
郵便局の係員

8. scale
はかり

9. post office box (PO box)
私書箱

10. automated postal center (APC)
自動郵便業務センター（APC）

11. stamp machine
切手販売機

12. mailbox
郵便ポスト

Sending a Card カードを送る

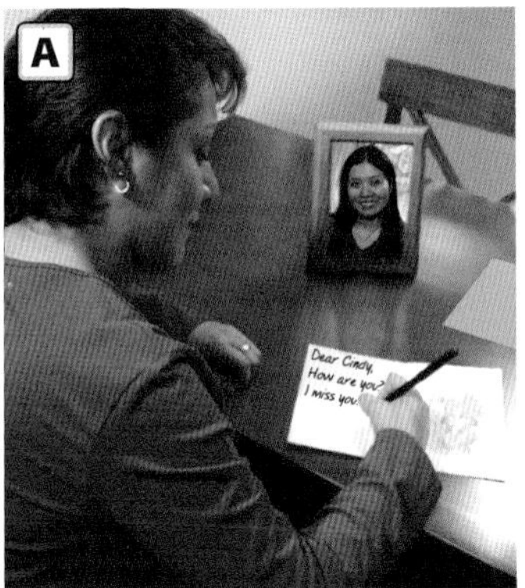

A. **Write** a note in a card.
カードに文章を**書く**

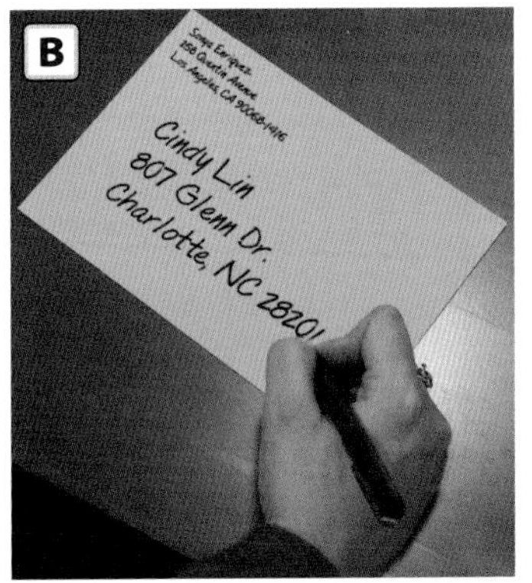

B. **Address** the envelope.
封筒に**住所を書く**

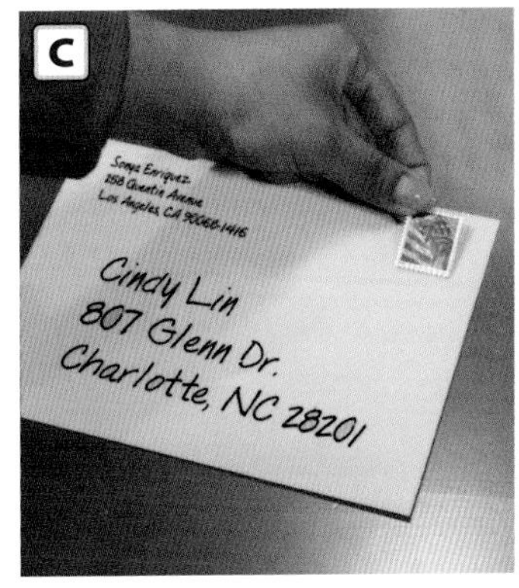

C. **Put on** a stamp.
切手を**貼る**

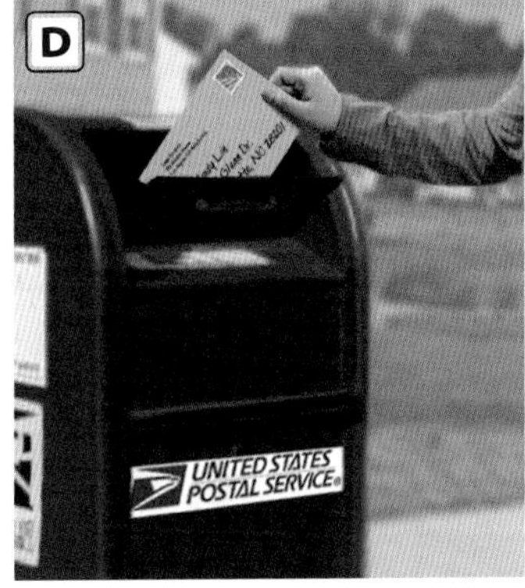

D. **Mail** the card.
カードを**郵送する**

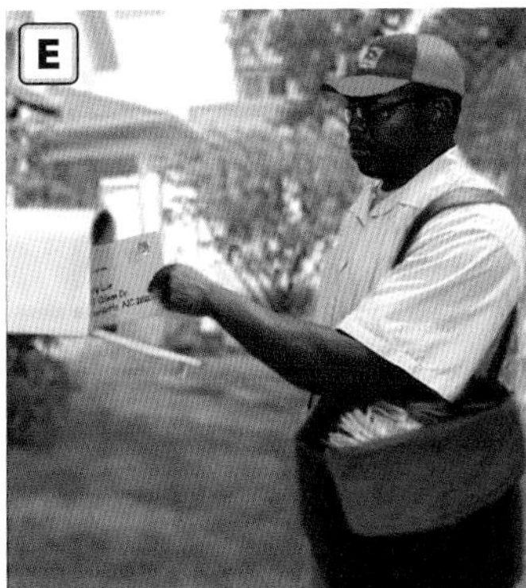

E. **Deliver** the card.
カードを**配達する**

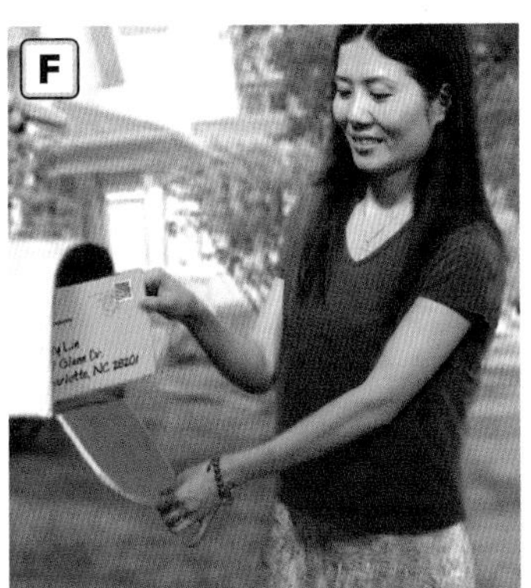

F. **Receive** the card.
カードを**受け取る**

G. **Read** the card.
カードを**読む**

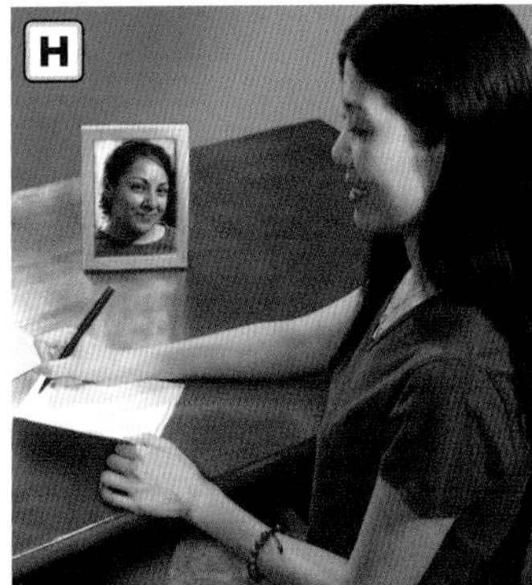

H. **Write** back.
返事を**書く**

More vocabulary

overnight / next day mail: Express Mail®
postage: the cost to send mail
junk mail: mail you don't want

Think about it. Discuss.

1. What kind of mail do you send overnight?
2. Do you want to be a letter carrier? Why or why not?
3. Do you get junk mail? What do you do with it?

Department of Motor Vehicles (DMV)

交通局（DMV）

1. DMV handbook
   DMVハンドブック
2. testing area
   テストエリア
3. DMV clerk
   DMV係員
4. photo
   写真
5. fingerprint
   指紋
6. vision exam
   検眼
7. window
   窓口

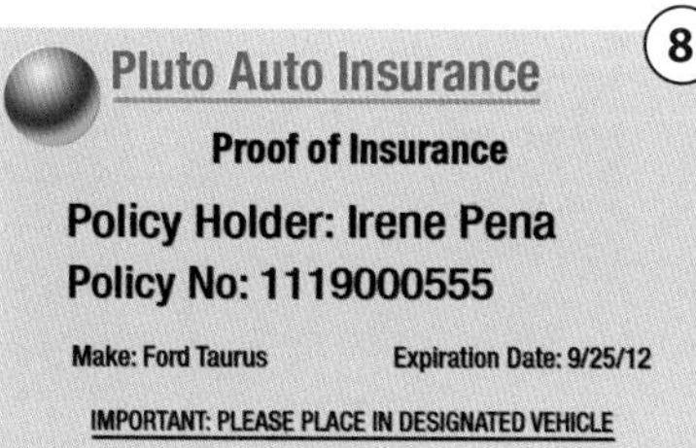

8. proof of insurance
   自動車保険の証明書
9. driver's license
   運転免許証
10. expiration date
    有効期限
11. driver's license number
    運転免許証番号
12. license plate
    ナンバープレート
13. registration sticker / tag
    登録シール

More vocabulary

expire: a license is no good, or **expires**, after the expiration date
renew a license: to apply to keep a license before it expires
vanity plate: a more expensive, personal license plate

Ask your classmates. Share the answers.

1. How far is the DMV from your home?
2. Do you have a driver's license? If yes, when does it expire? If not, do you want one?

交通局（DMV）

Department of Motor Vehicles (DMV)

Getting Your First License 初めて運転免許を取る

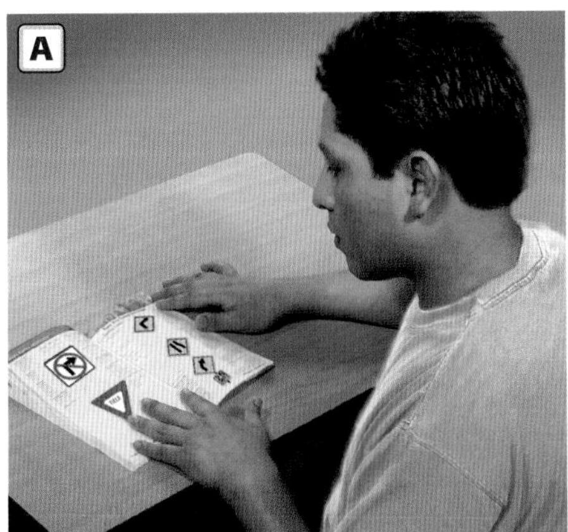

A. **Study** the handbook.
ハンドブックを**学習する**

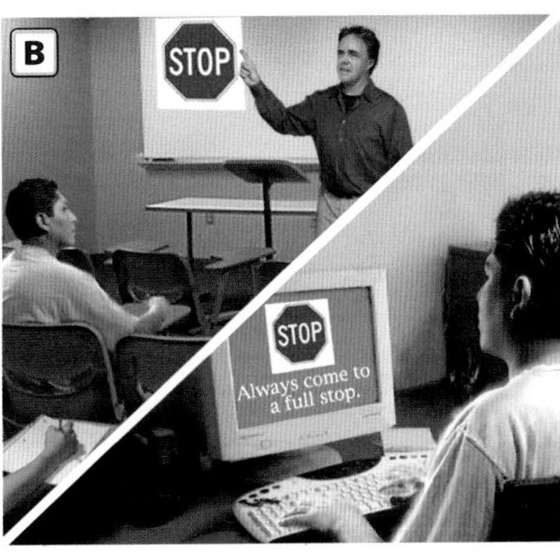

B. **Take** a driver education course.*
教習を**受ける**

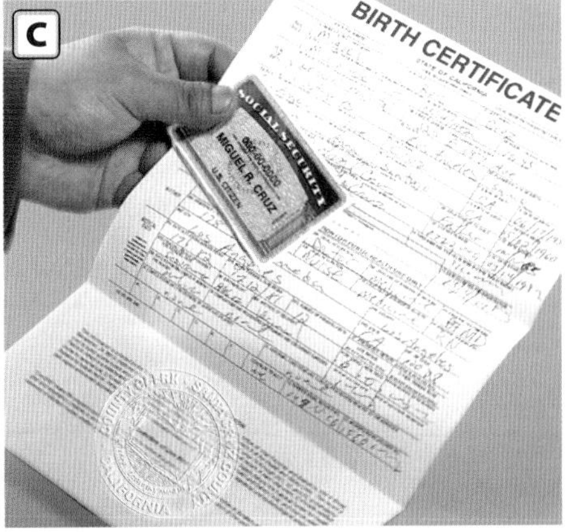

C. **Show** your identification.
身分証明書を**見せる**

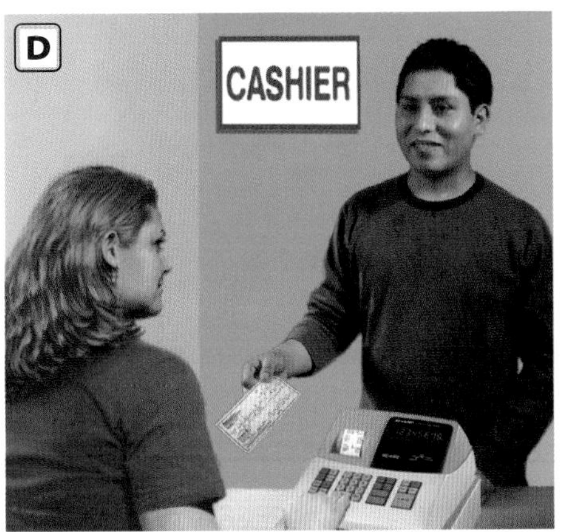

D. **Pay** the application fee.
申請料を**払う**

E. **Take** a written test.
筆記試験を**受ける**

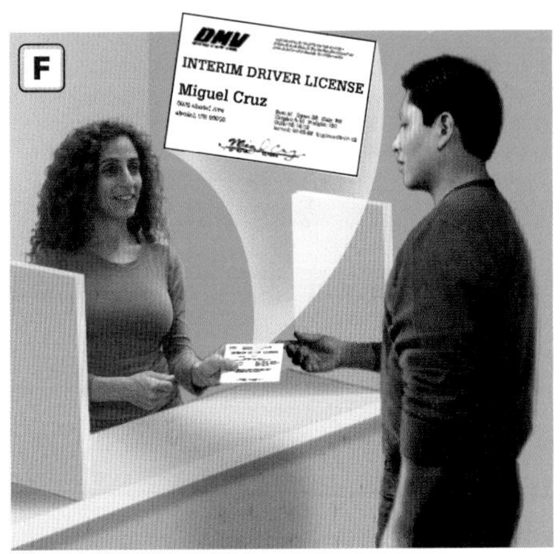

F. **Get** a learner's permit.
仮免許を**取る**

G. **Take** a driver's training course.*
運転教習を**受ける**

H. **Pass** a driving test.
運転試験に**合格する**

I. **Get** your license.
免許を**取る**

***Note:** This is not required for drivers 18 and older.

Ways to request more information

What do I do next?
What's the next step?
Where do I go from here?

Role play. Talk to a DMV clerk.

A: *I want to apply for a driver's license.*
B: *Did you study the handbook?*
A: *Yes, I did. What do I do next?*

Federal Government 連邦政府

Legislative Branch
立法機関

1. U.S. Capitol
米国国会議事堂
2. Congress
議会
3. House of Representatives
下院
4. congressperson
下院議員
5. Senate
上院
6. senator
上院議員

Executive Branch
行政機関

7. White House
ホワイトハウス／大統領官邸
8. president
大統領
9. vice president
副大統領
10. Cabinet
閣僚

Judicial Branch
司法機関

11. Supreme Court
最高裁判所
12. justices
判事
13. chief justice
裁判長

The Military 軍隊

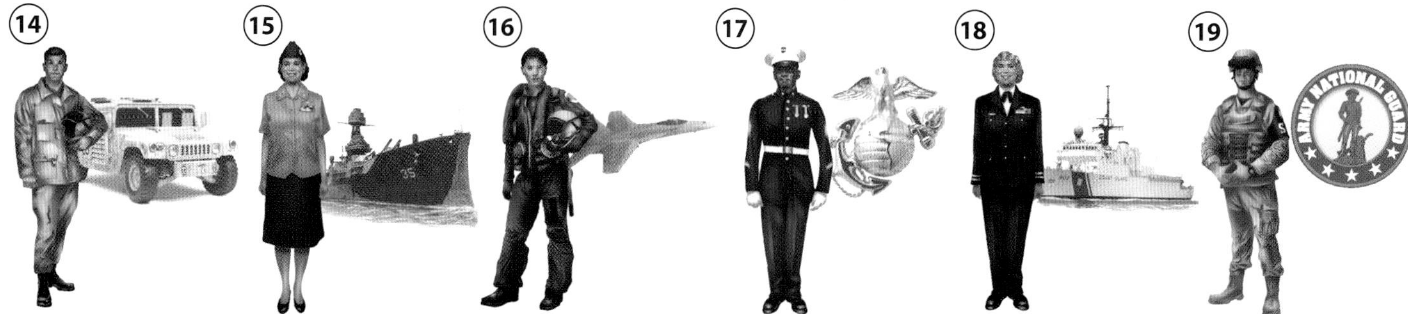

14. Army
陸軍
15. Navy
海軍
16. Air Force
空軍
17. Marines
海兵隊
18. Coast Guard
沿岸警備隊
19. National Guard
州軍

State Government 州政府

20. governor
州知事
21. lieutenant governor
副知事
22. state capital
州都

23. Legislature
州議会
24. assemblyperson
州下院議員
25. state senator
州上院議員

City Government 市政府

26. mayor
市長
27. city council
市議会
28. councilperson
市議会議員

An Election 選挙

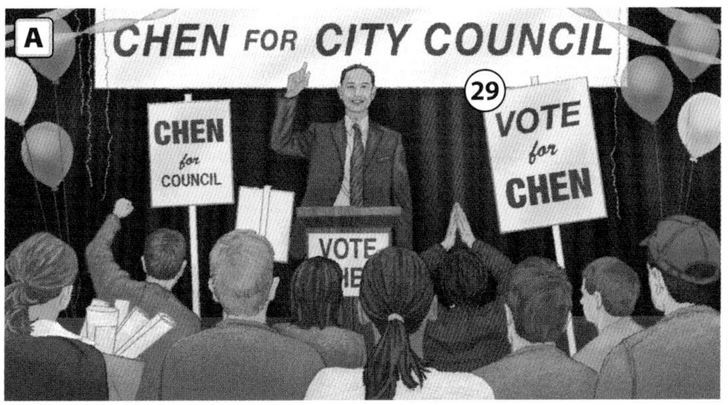

A. **run for** office
立候補する

29. political campaign
選挙運動

B. **debate**
討論する

30. opponent
対立候補

C. **get elected**
選挙で選ばれる

31. election results
投票結果

D. **serve**
任期を務める

32. elected official
当選者

More vocabulary

term: the period of time an elected official serves
political party: a group of people with the same political goals

Think about it. Discuss.

1. Should everyone have to serve in the military? Why or why not?
2. Would you prefer to run for city council or mayor? Why?

Civic Rights and Responsibilities 公民権と義務

Responsibilities 義務

A. **vote**
投票する

B. **pay** taxes
税金を払う

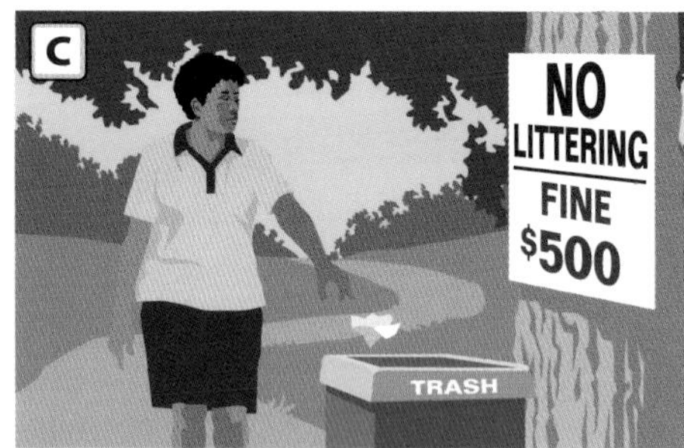

C. **obey** the law
法律を守る

D. **register** with Selective Service*
セレクティブ サービス(義務兵役)に登録する

E. **serve** on a jury
陪審員を務める

F. **be** informed
情報を得る

Citizenship Requirements 市民権獲得条件

G. **be** 18 or older
18歳以上である

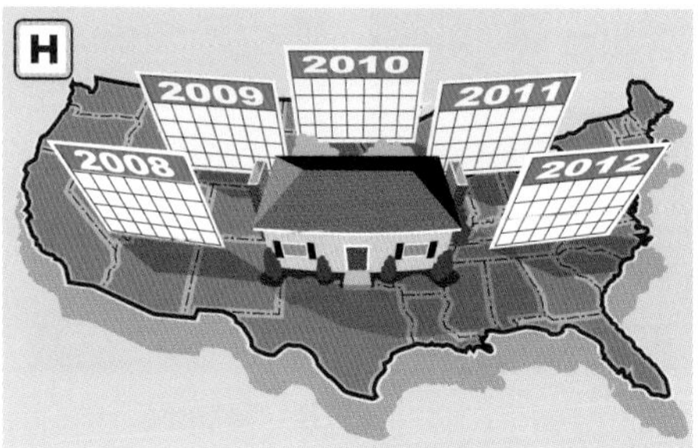

H. **live** in the U.S. for 5 years
米国に5年以上住んでいる

I. **take** a citizenship test
市民権獲得の試験を受ける

Rights 権利

1. peaceful assembly
平和的な集会の自由

2. free speech
言論の自由

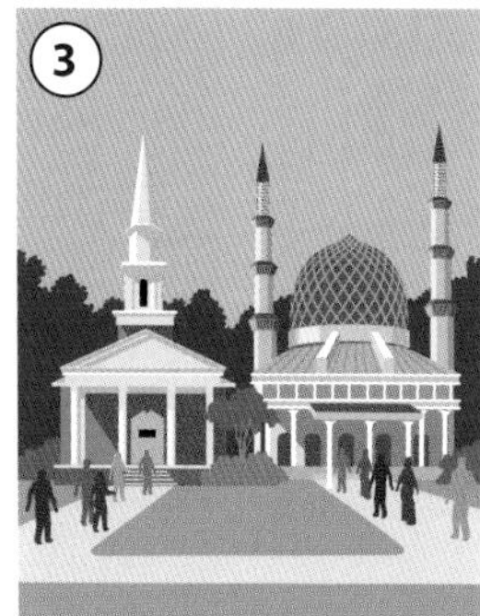

3. freedom of religion
宗教の自由

4. freedom of the press
報道の自由

5. fair trial
公平な裁判

*Note: All males 18 to 26 who live in the U.S. are required to register with Selective Service.

A. **arrest** a suspect
容疑者を**逮捕する**

1. police officer
警察官

2. handcuffs
手錠

B. **hire** a lawyer / **hire** an attorney
弁護士を**雇う**

3. guard
守衛

4. defense attorney
被告側の弁護士

C. **appear** in court
出廷**する**

5. defendant
被告

6. judge
判事

D. **stand** trial
裁判を**受ける**

7. courtroom
法廷

8. jury
陪審員

9. evidence
証拠

10. prosecuting attorney
検察官

11. witness
証人

12. court reporter
法廷速記者

13. bailiff
廷吏

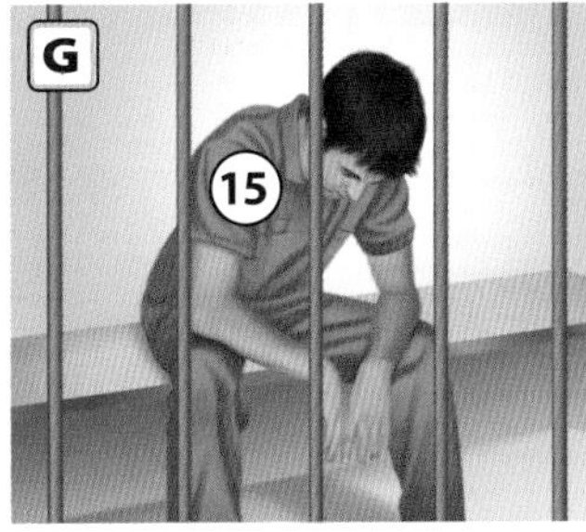

E. **convict** the defendant
被告に**有罪判決を下す**

14. verdict*
評決

F. **sentence** the defendant
被告を**刑に処する**

G. **go** to jail / **go** to prison
刑務所に**入る**

15. convict / prisoner
受刑者

H. **be** released
釈放**される**

*__Note:__ There are two possible verdicts, "guilty" and "not guilty."

Look at the pictures.
Describe what happened.

A: *The police officer arrested a suspect.*
B: *He put handcuffs on him.*

Think about it. Discuss.

1. Would you want to serve on a jury? Why or why not?
2. Look at the crimes on page 142. What sentence would you give for each crime? Why?

Crime

犯罪

1. vandalism
故意の破壊行為
2. burglary
住居侵入／押込み

3. assault
暴行
4. gang violence
集団暴力行為

5. drunk driving
飲酒運転
6. illegal drugs
違法薬物

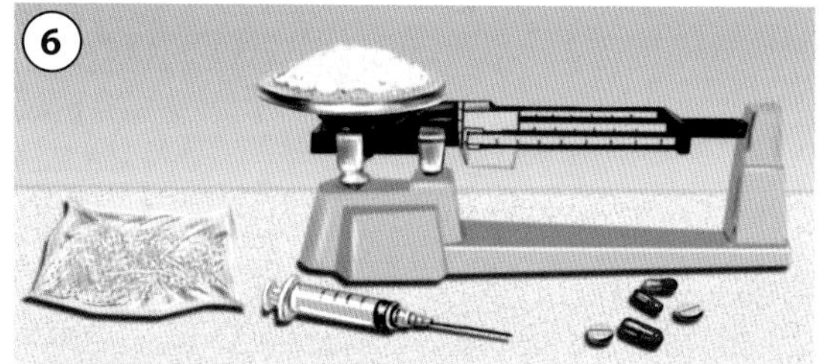

7. arson
放火
8. shoplifting
万引き

9. identity theft
アイデンティティ窃盗
10. victim
被害者

11. mugging
強盗
12. murder
殺人
13. gun
銃

More vocabulary

steal: to take money or things from someone illegally
commit a crime: to do something illegal
criminal: someone who does something illegal

Think about it. Discuss.

1. Is there too much crime on TV or in the movies? Explain.
2. How can communities help stop crime?

Public Safety

A. **Walk** with a friend.
友達と**歩く**

B. **Stay** on well-lit streets.
明るい道を**選ぶ**

C. **Conceal** your PIN number.
暗証番号を**隠す**

D. **Protect** your purse or wallet.
バッグや財布を**守る**

E. **Lock** your doors.
ドアに**鍵をかける**

F. Don't **open** your door to strangers.
知らない人にドアを**開けない**

G. Don't **drink** and **drive**.
飲酒運転をしない

H. **Shop** on secure websites.
安全なウェブサイトで**買い物する**

I. **Be** aware of your surroundings.
周りの様子に**注意する**

J. **Report** suspicious packages.
不審物について**通報する**

K. **Report** crimes to the police.
犯罪を警察に**通報する**

L. **Join** a Neighborhood Watch.
自警団に**参加する**

More vocabulary

sober: not drunk

designated drivers: sober drivers who drive drunk people home safely

Ask your classmates. Share the answers.

1. Do you feel safe in your neighborhood?
2. Look at the pictures. Which of these things do you do?
3. What other things do you do to stay safe?

Emergencies and Natural Disasters

緊急事態と自然災害

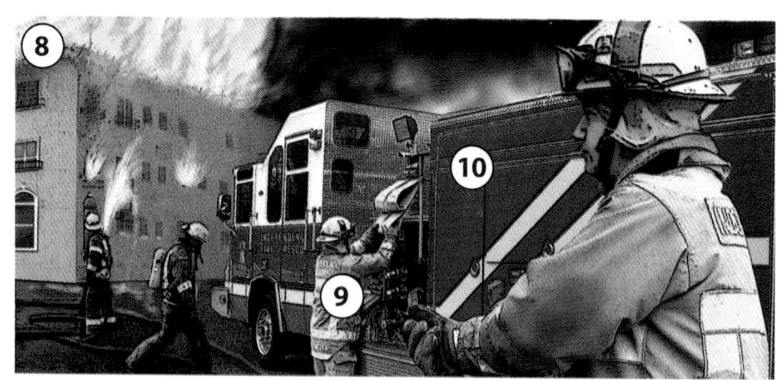

1. lost child
   迷子
2. car accident
   交通事故
3. airplane crash
   飛行機墜落事故
4. explosion
   爆発
5. earthquake
   地震
6. mudslide
   土砂崩れ
7. forest fire
   山火事
8. fire
   火災
9. firefighter
   消防士
10. fire truck
    消防車

Ways to report an emergency

First, give your name. *My name is* *Tim Johnson*.
Then, state the emergency and give the address.
There was *a car accident* *at* *219 Elm Street*.

Role play. Call 911.

A: *911 Emergency Operator.*
B: *My name is* *Lisa Diaz*. *There is* *a fire* *at* *323 Oak Street*. *Please hurry!*

11. drought
干ばつ
12. famine
飢饉
13. blizzard
猛吹雪
14. hurricane
ハリケーン
15. tornado
竜巻
16. volcanic eruption
火山の噴火
17. tidal wave / tsunami
津波
18. avalanche
雪崩（なだれ）
19. flood
洪水
20. search and rescue team
捜査救助隊

Ask your classmates. Share the answers.

1. Which natural disaster worries you the most?
2. Which natural disaster worries you the least?
3. Which disasters are common in your local area?

Think about it. Discuss.

1. What organizations can help you in an emergency?
2. What are some ways to prepare for natural disasters?
3. Where would you go in an emergency?

Before an Emergency 緊急事態が起こる前に

A. Plan for an emergency.
緊急時に備えて**プランを立てる**

1. meeting place
集合場所
2. out-of-state contact
州外への連絡
3. escape route
避難経路
4. gas shut-off valve
ガス遮断バルブ
5. evacuation route
避難路

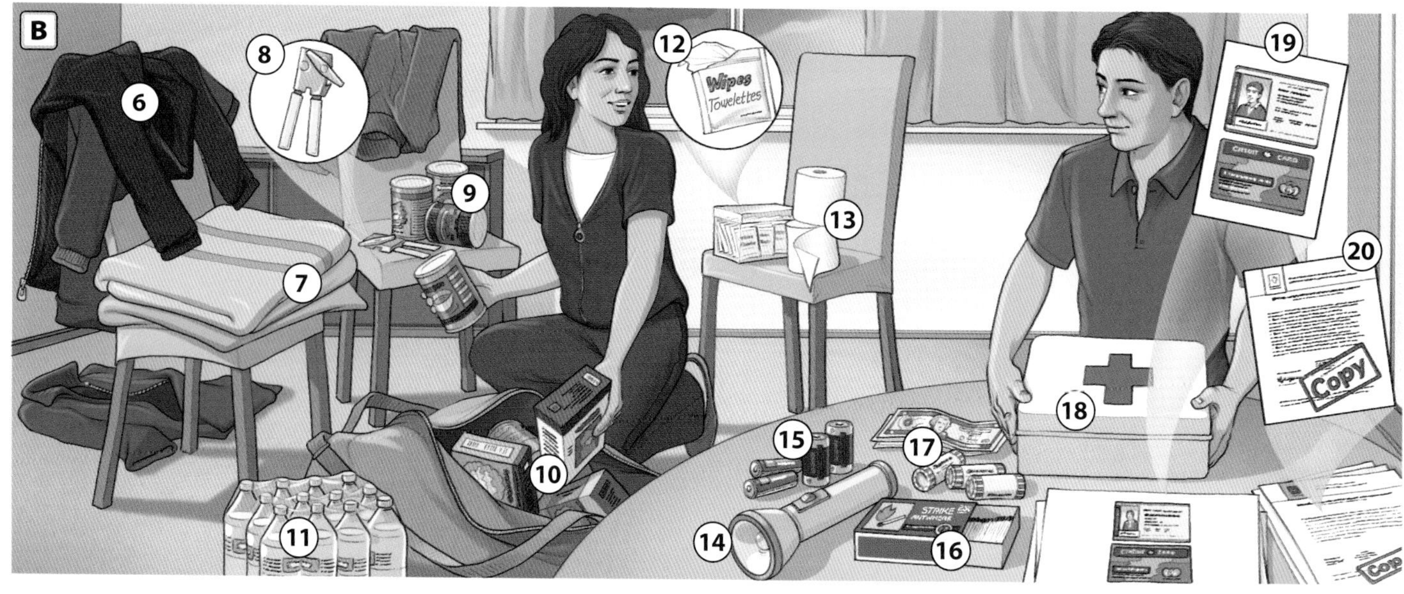

B. Make a disaster kit.
災害キットを**用意する**

6. warm clothes
暖かい服
7. blankets
毛布
8. can opener
缶切り
9. canned food
缶詰
10. packaged food
パッケージ食品
11. bottled water
ボトル入り飲料水
12. moist towelettes
ウエットティッシュ
13. toilet paper
トイレットペーパー
14. flashlight
懐中電灯
15. batteries
電池
16. matches
マッチ
17. cash and coins
現金と小銭
18. first aid kit
救急箱
19. copies of ID and credit cards
身分証明書とクレジットカードのコピー
20. copies of important papers
重要な書類のコピー

Pair practice. Make new conversations.

A: *What do we need for our disaster kit?*
B: *We need blankets and matches.*
A: *I think we also need batteries.*

Ask your classmates. Share the answers.

1. Who would you call first after an emergency?
2. Do you have escape and evacuation routes planned?
3. Are you a calm person in case of an emergency?

During an Emergency 緊急事態が発生したら

C. **Watch** the weather.
天候に**注意する**

D. **Pay attention** to warnings.
警報に**注意を払う**

E. **Remain** calm.
落ち着きを**失わない**

F. **Follow** directions.
指示に**従う**

G. **Help** people with disabilities.
障害者を**助ける**

H. **Seek** shelter.
避難所を**見つける**

I. **Stay away** from windows.
窓から**離れる**

J. **Take** cover.
身を**隠す**

K. **Evacuate** the area.
避難する

After an Emergency 緊急事態発生後

L. **Call** out-of-state contacts.
州外に**連絡する**

M. **Clean up** debris.
瓦れきを**片付ける**

N. **Inspect** utilities.
電気・ガス・水道を**点検する**

Ways to say you're OK

I'm fine.
We're OK here.
Everything's under control.

Ways to say you need help

We need help.
Someone is hurt.
I'm injured. Please get help.

Role play. Prepare for an emergency.

A: *They just issued a hurricane warning.*
B: *OK. We need to stay calm and follow directions.*
A: *What do we need to do first?*

1. graffiti 落書き
2. litter ごみ
3. streetlight 街灯
4. hardware store 金物店
5. petition 嘆願書

A. **give** a speech 演説する
B. **applaud** 喝采する
C. **change** 変える

Look at the pictures.
What do you see?

Answer the questions.

1. What were the problems on Main Street?
2. What was the petition for?
3. Why did the city council applaud?
4. How did the people change the street?

 **Read the story.**

Community Cleanup

Marta Lopez has a donut shop on Main Street. One day she looked at her street and was very upset. She saw graffiti on her donut shop and the other stores. Litter was everywhere. All the streetlights were broken. Marta wanted to fix the lights and clean up the street.

Marta started a petition about the streetlights. Five hundred people signed it. Then she gave a speech to the city council. The council members voted to repair the streetlights. Everyone applauded. Marta was happy, but her work wasn't finished.

Next, Marta asked for volunteers to clean up Main Street. The hardware store manager gave the volunteers free paint. Marta gave them free donuts and coffee. The volunteers painted and cleaned. They changed Main Street. Now Main Street is beautiful and Marta is proud.

Think about it.

1. What are some problems in your community? How can people help?
2. Imagine you are Marta. What do you say in your speech to the city council?

Basic Transportation 基本的な交通機関

1. car
   自動車
2. passenger
   乗客
3. taxi
   タクシー
4. motorcycle
   オートバイ
5. street
   道路
6. truck
   トラック
7. train
   列車
8. (air)plane
   飛行機

Listen and point. Take turns.

A: *Point to the motorcycle.*
B: *Point to the truck.*
A: *Point to the train.*

Dictate to your partner. Take turns.

A: *Write motorcycle.*
B: *Could you repeat that for me?*
A: *Motorcycle. M-o-t-o-r-c-y-c-l-e.*

9. helicopter
ヘリコプター
10. airport
空港
11. subway station
地下鉄の駅
12. subway
地下鉄
13. bus stop
バス停
14. bus
バス
15. bicycle
自転車

Ways to talk about using transportation

Use **take** for buses, trains, subways, taxis, planes, and helicopters. Use **drive** for cars and trucks. Use **ride** for bicycles and motorcycles.

Pair practice. Make new conversations.

A: *How do you get to school?*
B: *I take the bus. How about you?*
A: *I ride a bicycle to school.*

A Bus Stop バス停

BUS 10 Northbound

Main	Elm	Oak
6:00	6:10	6:13
6:30	6:40	6:43
7:00	7:10	7:13
7:30	7:40	7:43

1. bus route
   バス路線
2. fare
   料金
3. rider
   乗客
4. schedule
   時刻表
5. transfer
   乗り換え

A Subway Station 地下鉄の駅

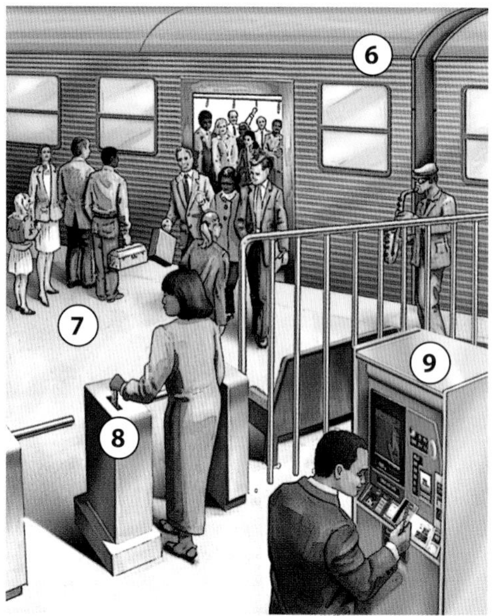

6. subway car
   地下鉄の車両
7. platform
   プラットホーム
8. turnstile
   回転式改札口
9. vending machine
   自動販売機
10. token
    トークン（代用硬貨）
11. fare card
    料金カード

A Train Station 電車の駅

12. ticket window
    切符売場
13. conductor
    車掌
14. track
    線路
15. ticket
    切符
16. one-way trip
    片道
17. round trip
    往復

Airport Transportation 空港の交通

18. taxi stand
    タクシー乗り場
19. shuttle
    シャトルバス
20. town car
    タウンカー
21. taxi driver
    タクシーの運転手
22. taxi license
    タクシー営業許可書
23. meter
    メーター

More vocabulary

hail a taxi: to raise your hand to get a taxi

miss the bus: to get to the bus stop after the bus leaves

Ask your classmates. Share the answers.

1. Is there a subway system in your city?
2. Do you ever take taxis? When?
3. Do you ever take the bus? Where?

Prepositions of Motion

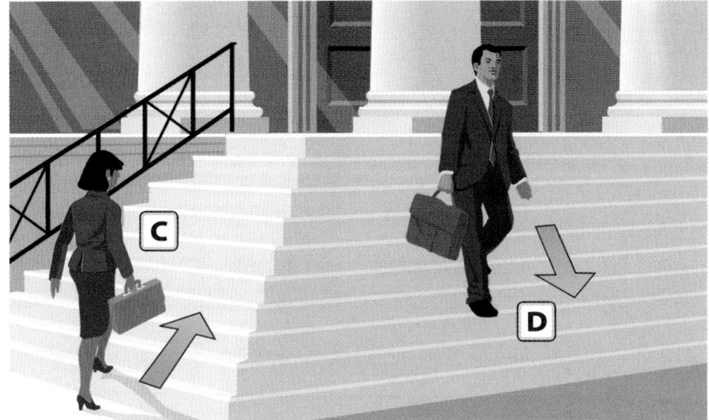

A. **go under** the bridge
橋の**下を行く**

B. **go over** the bridge
橋の**上を行く**

C. **walk up** the steps
階段を**上る**

D. **walk down** the steps
階段を**下りる**

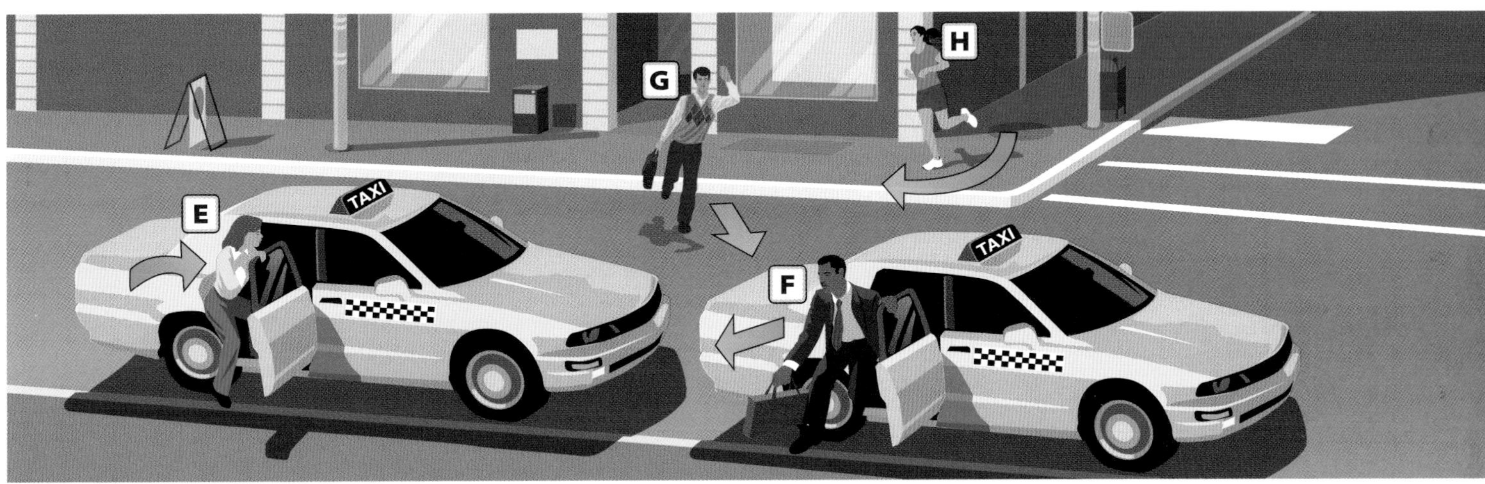

E. **get into** the taxi
タクシーに**乗る**

F. **get out of** the taxi
タクシーから**降りる**

G. **run across** the street
通りを**走って横切る**

H. **run around** the corner
角を**走って曲がる**

I. **get on** the highway
ハイウェイに**乗る**

J. **get off** the highway
ハイウェイから**下りる**

K. **drive through** the tunnel
トンネルの**中を運転する**

Grammar Point: *into, out of, on, off*

Use ***get into*** for taxis and cars.
Use ***get on*** for buses, trains, planes, and highways.

Use ***get out of*** for taxis and cars.
Use ***get off*** for buses, trains, planes, and highways.

1. stop
止まれ

2. do not enter / wrong way
進入禁止

3. one way
一方通行

4. speed limit
制限速度

5. U-turn OK
Uターン可

6. no outlet / dead end
行き止まり

7. right turn only
右折のみ

8. no left turn
左折禁止

9. yield
ゆずれ

10. merge
合流

11. no parking
駐車禁止

12. handicapped parking
身体障害者用駐車スペース

13. pedestrian crossing
横断歩道

14. railroad crossing
踏切

15. school crossing
学童横断路

16. road work
道路工事中

17. U.S. route / highway marker
U.S. 国道／ハイウェイ指標

18. hospital
病院

Pair practice. Make new conversations.

A: *Watch out! The sign says no left turn.*
B: *Sorry, I was looking at the stop sign.*
A: *That's OK. Just be careful!*

Ask your classmates. Share the answers.

1. How many traffic signs are on your street?
2. What's the speed limit on your street?
3. What traffic signs are the same in your native country?

Directions and Maps

Directions 道順

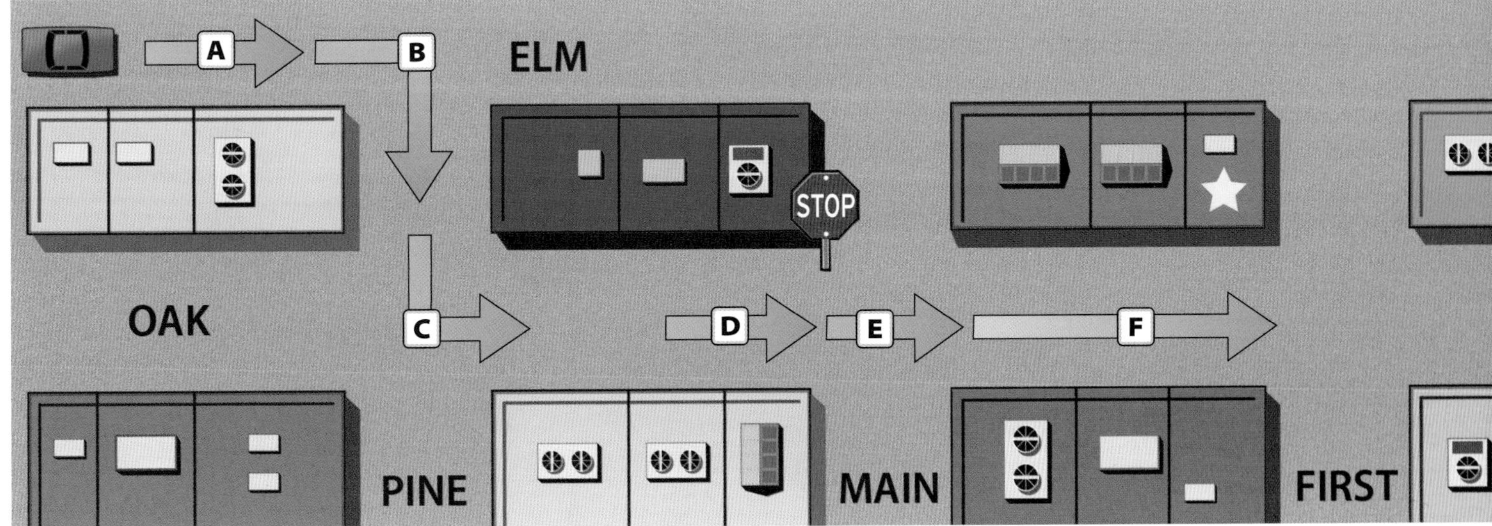

A. **Go straight** on Elm Street.
エルムストリートを**まっすぐ進む**

B. **Turn right** on Pine Street.
パインストリートを**右に曲がる**

C. **Turn left** on Oak Street.
オークストリートを**左に曲がる**

D. **Stop** at the corner.
角で**止まる**

E. **Go** past Main Street.
メインストリートを**通り過ぎる**

F. **Go** one block to First Street.
1ブロック進んでファーストストリートまで**行く**

Maps 地図

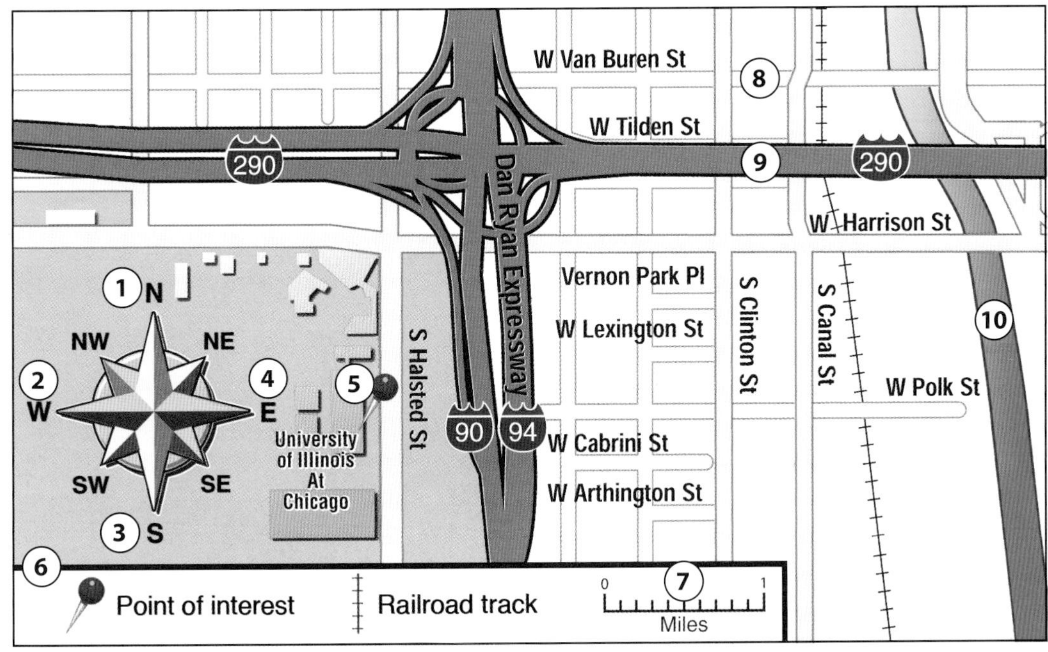

1. north
北
2. west
西
3. south
南
4. east
東
5. symbol
記号
6. key
キー
7. scale
縮尺
8. street
通り
9. highway
ハイウェイ
10. river
川
11. GPS (global positioning system)
GPS (グローバルポジショニングシステム)
12. Internet map
インターネット地図

Role play. Ask for directions.

A: *I'm lost. I need to get to Elm and Pine.*
B: *Go straight on Oak and make a right on Pine.*
A: *Thanks so much.*

Ask your classmates. Share the answers.

1. How often do you use Internet maps? GPS? paper maps?
2. What was the last map you used? Why?

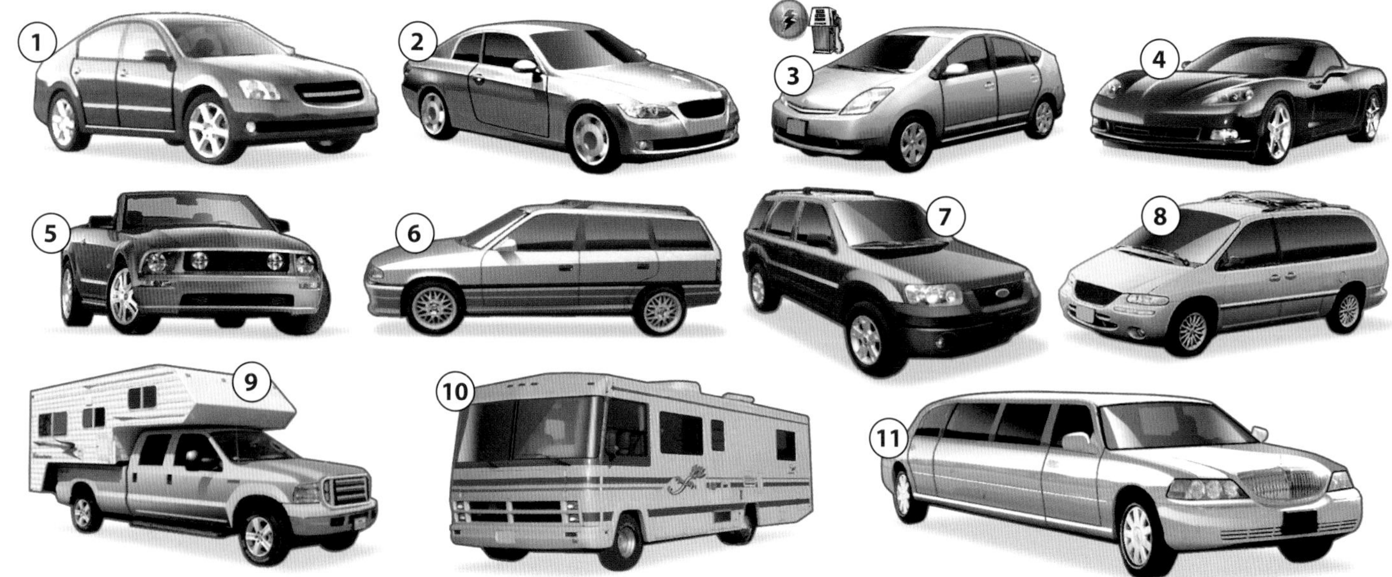

1. 4-door car / sedan
   4ドアセダン
2. 2-door car / coupe
   2ドアクーペ
3. hybrid
   ハイブリッド
4. sports car
   スポーツカー
5. convertible
   オープンカー
6. station wagon
   ステーションワゴン
7. SUV (sport–utility vehicle)
   SUV（スポーツユーティリティ車）
8. minivan
   ミニバン
9. camper
   キャンピングカー
10. RV (recreational vehicle)
    RV（レクリエーションビークル）車
11. limousine / limo
    ハイヤー

12. pickup truck
    小型トラック
13. cargo van
    貨物用バン
14. tow truck
    レッカー車
15. tractor trailer / semi
    トレーラートラック／セミトレーラー
16. cab
    運転台
17. trailer
    トレーラー
18. moving van
    引越しトラック
19. dump truck
    ダンプトラック
20. tank truck
    タンクローリー
21. school bus
    スクールバス

Pair practice. Make new conversations.

A: *I have a new car!*
B: *Did you get a hybrid?*
A: *Yes, but I really wanted a sports car.*

More vocabulary

make: the name of the company that makes the car
model: the style of the car

Buying and Maintaining a Car

Buying a Used Car 中古車を買う

A. **Look at** car ads.
車の広告を**見る**

B. **Ask** the seller about the car.
売り手に車について**尋ねる**

C. **Take** the car to a mechanic.
車を整備会社に**持って行く**

D. **Negotiate** a price.
値段を**交渉する**

E. **Get** the title from the seller.
権利書を売り手から**もらう**

F. **Register** the car.
車を**登録する**

Taking Care of Your Car 車の手入れ

G. **Fill** the tank with gas.
タンクにガソリンを**入れる**

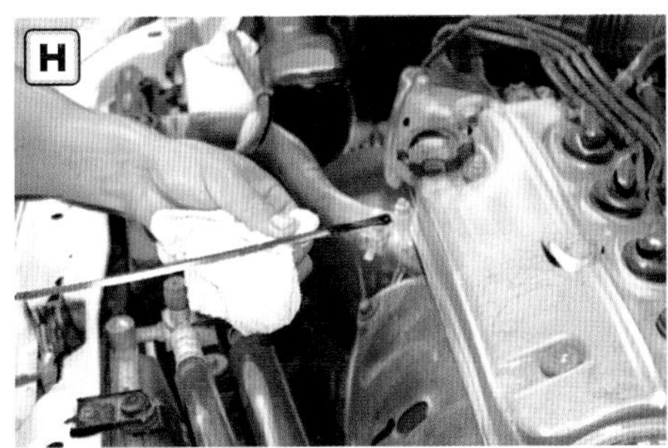

H. **Check** the oil.
オイルを**チェックする**

I. **Put in** coolant.
クーラントを**入れる**

J. **Go** for a smog check.*
排気チェックを**行なう**

*smog check = emissions test

K. **Replace** the windshield wipers.
ワイパーを**交換する**

L. **Fill** the tires with air.
タイヤに空気を**入れる**

Ways to request service

Please check the oil.
Could you fill the tank?
Put in coolant, please.

Think about it. Discuss.

1. What's good and bad about a used car?
2. Do you like to negotiate car prices? Why?
3. Do you know any good mechanics? Why are they good?

At the Dealer
自動車販売店で

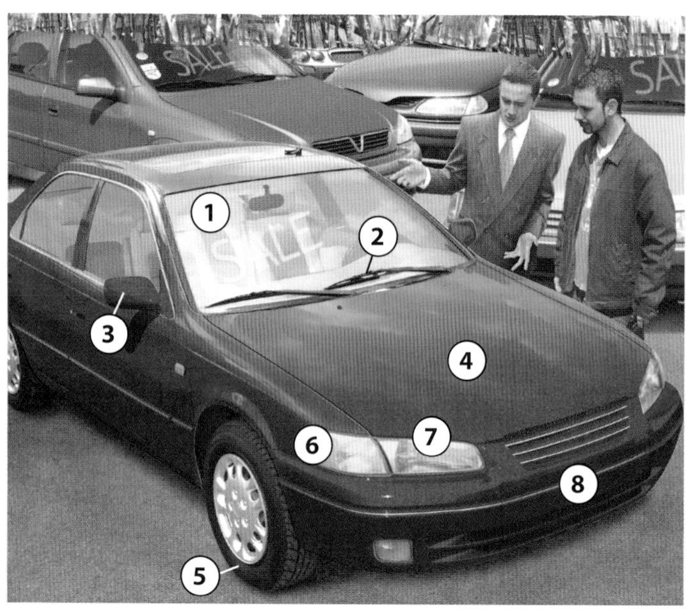

1. windshield
フロントガラス
2. windshield wipers
ワイパー
3. sideview mirror
サイドミラー
4. hood
ボンネット
5. tire
タイヤ
6. turn signal
ウィンカー
7. headlight
ヘッドライト
8. bumper
バンパー

At the Mechanic
整備工場で

9. hubcap / wheel cover
ホイールキャップ
10. gas tank
燃料タンク
11. trunk
トランク
12. license plate
ナンバープレート
13. tail light
テールランプ
14. brake light
ブレーキランプ
15. tail pipe
排気管
16. muffler
マフラー

Under the Hood
ボンネットの中

17. fuel injection system
燃料噴射システム
18. engine
エンジン
19. radiator
ラジエータ
20. battery
バッテリ

Inside the Trunk
トランクの中

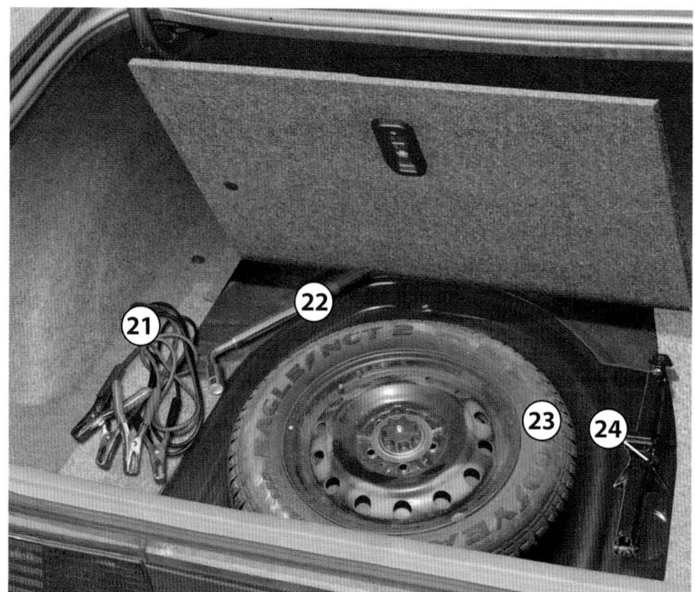

21. jumper cables
ブースターケーブル
22. lug wrench
タイヤ用レンチ
23. spare tire
スペアタイヤ
24. jack
ジャッキ

The Dashboard and Instrument Panel
ダッシュボードと計器パネル

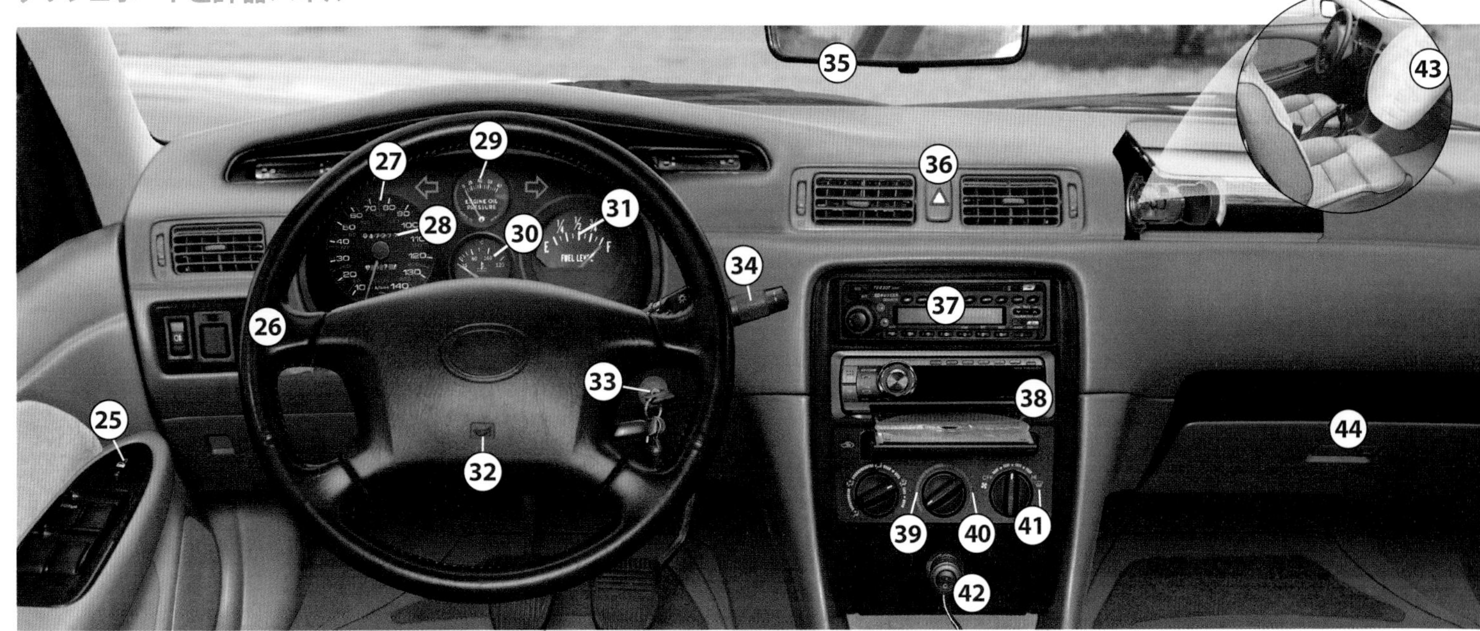

25. door lock
ドアロック

26. steering wheel
ハンドル

27. speedometer
速度計

28. odometer
走行距離計

29. oil gauge
油圧計

30. temperature gauge
水温計

31. gas gauge
燃料計

32. horn
クラクション

33. ignition
イグニッション

34. turn signal
ウィンカー

35. rearview mirror
バックミラー

36. hazard lights
ハザードランプ

37. radio
ラジオ

38. CD player
CDプレーヤー

39. air conditioner
エアコン

40. heater
ヒーター

41. defroster
曇り除去装置

42. power outlet
コンセント

43. air bag
エアバッグ

44. glove compartment
グローブボックス

An Automatic Transmission
オートマチックトランスミッション

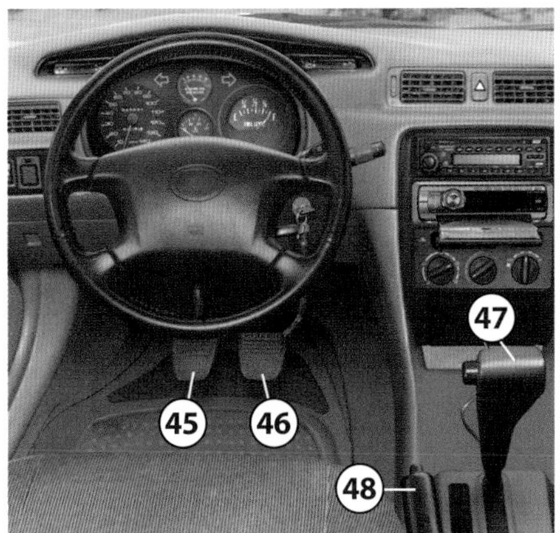

A Manual Transmission
マニュアルトランスミッション

Inside the Car
車内

45. brake pedal
ブレーキペダル

46. gas pedal / accelerator
アクセル

47. gear shift
シフトレバー

48. hand brake
ハンドブレーキ

49. clutch
クラッチ

50. stick shift
シフトレバー

51. front seat
フロントシート

52. seat belt
シートベルト

53. child safety seat
チャイルドシート

54. backseat
後部座席

In the Airline Terminal ターミナルで

At the Security Checkpoint セキュリティチェックポイントで

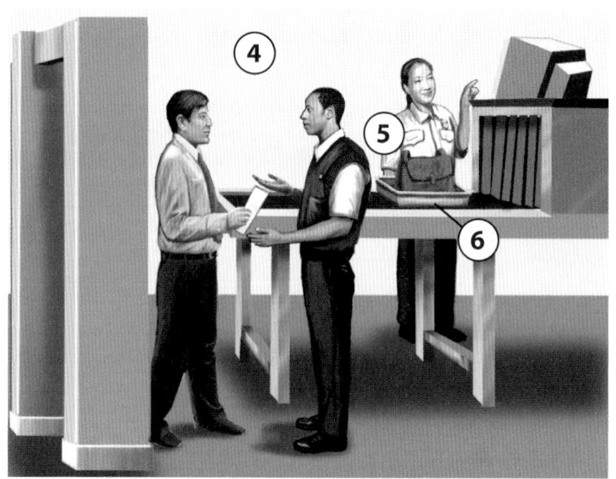

1. skycap
   空港ポーター
2. check-in kiosk
   セルフチェックインコーナー
3. ticket agent
   航空会社の発券担当者
4. screening area
   検査エリア
5. TSA* agent / security screener
   TSA担当員／検査員
6. bin
   トレイ

Taking a Flight 飛行機に乗る

A. **Check in** electronically.
コンピュータで**チェックインする**

B. **Check** your bags.
手荷物を**預ける**

C. **Show** your boarding pass and ID.
搭乗券と身分証明書を**見せる**

D. **Go through** security.
セキュリティチェックを**受ける**

E. **Board** the plane.
搭乗する

F. **Find** your seat.
座席を**見つける**

G. **Stow** your carry-on bag.
手荷物を**収納する**

H. **Fasten** your seat belt.
シートベルトを**締める**

I. **Turn off** your cell phone.
携帯電話の**電源を切る**

J. **Take off**. / **Leave**.
離陸する／**出発する**

K. **Land**. / **Arrive**.
着陸する／**到着する**

L. **Claim** your baggage.
手荷物を**受け取る**

* Transportation Security Administration

At the Gate ゲートで

7. arrival and departure monitors
   到着／出発時刻モニター
8. gate
   ゲート
9. boarding area
   搭乗待合室

On the Airplane 機内で

10. cockpit
    コックピット
11. pilot
    パイロット
12. flight attendant
    客室乗務員
13. overhead compartment
    頭上の荷物入れ
14. emergency exit
    非常口
15. passenger
    乗客

At Customs 税関で

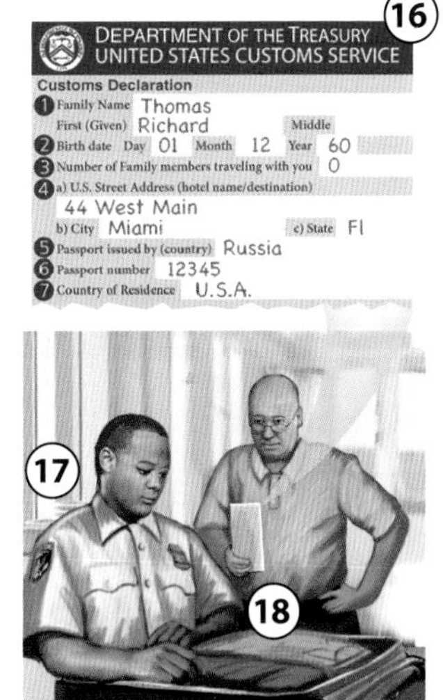

DEPARTMENT OF THE TREASURY
UNITED STATES CUSTOMS SERVICE

Customs Declaration

1 Family Name Thomas
First (Given) Richard Middle
2 Birth date Day 01 Month 12 Year 60
3 Number of Family members traveling with you 0
4 a) U.S. Street Address (hotel name/destination) 44 West Main
b) City Miami c) State Fl
5 Passport issued by (country) Russia
6 Passport number 12345
7 Country of Residence U.S.A.

16. declaration form
    申告書
17. customs officer
    税関係員
18. luggage / bag
    手荷物

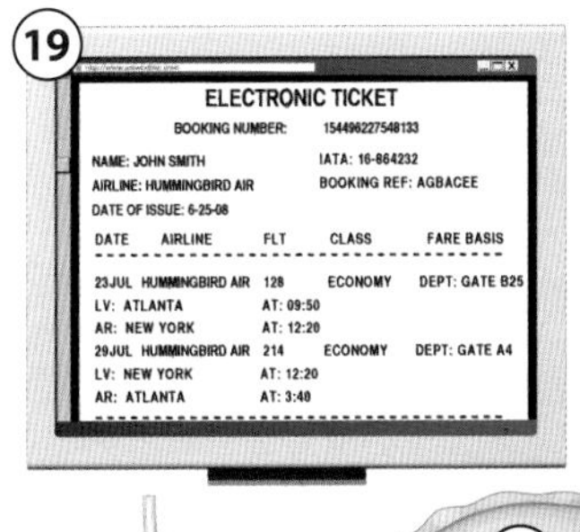

ELECTRONIC TICKET

BOOKING NUMBER: 154496227548133
NAME: JOHN SMITH IATA: 16-864232
AIRLINE: HUMMINGBIRD AIR BOOKING REF: AGBACEE
DATE OF ISSUE: 6-25-08

DATE	AIRLINE	FLT	CLASS	FARE BASIS
23JUL	HUMMINGBIRD AIR	128	ECONOMY	DEPT: GATE B25
LV: ATLANTA		AT: 09:50		
AR: NEW YORK		AT: 12:20		
29JUL	HUMMINGBIRD AIR	214	ECONOMY	DEPT: GATE A4
LV: NEW YORK		AT: 12:20		
AR: ATLANTA		AT: 3:40		

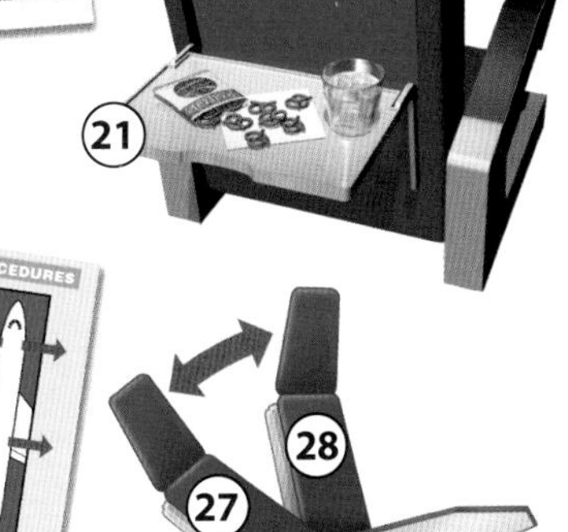

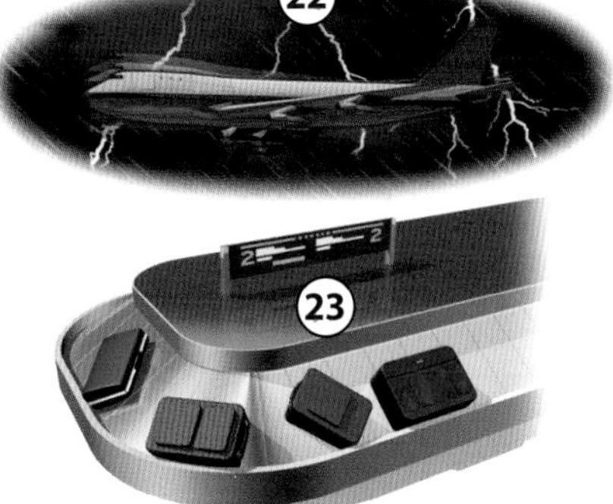

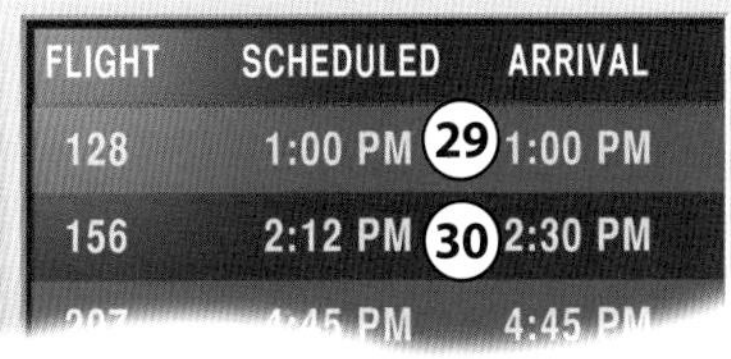

FLIGHT	SCHEDULED	ARRIVAL
128	1:00 PM	1:00 PM
156	2:12 PM	2:30 PM

19. e-ticket
    Eチケット
20. boarding pass
    搭乗券
21. tray table
    トレイテーブル
22. turbulence
    乱気流
23. baggage carousel
    荷物受取所
24. oxygen mask
    酸素マスク
25. life vest
    救命胴衣
26. emergency card
    緊急時のガイド
27. reclined seat
    倒した座席
28. upright seat
    元の位置に戻した座席
29. on-time
    定刻
30. delayed flight
    到着が遅れている便

More vocabulary

departure time: the time the plane takes off
arrival time: the time the plane lands
direct flight: a trip with no stops

Pair practice. Make new conversations.

A: *Excuse me. Where do I check in?*
B: *At the check-in kiosk.*
A: *Thanks.*

Taking a Trip 旅行する

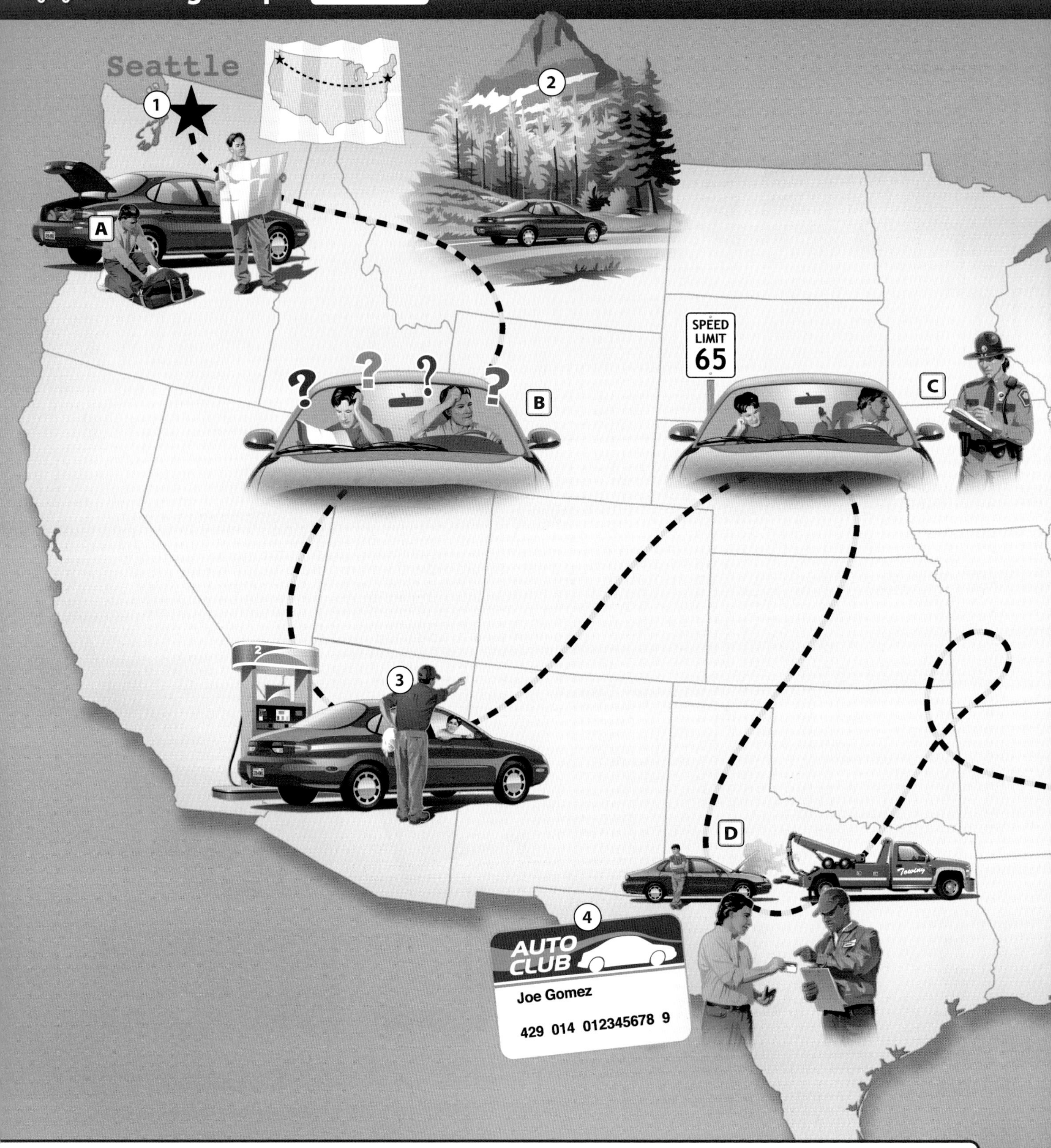

1. starting point
   出発地
2. scenery
   景色
3. gas station attendant
   ガソリンスタンドの係員
4. auto club card
   オートクラブのカード
5. destination
   目的地

A. **pack**
   荷物を詰める

B. **get** lost
   道に**迷う**

C. **get** a speeding ticket
   スピード違反の切符を**切られる**

D. **break down**
   故障する

E. **run out** of gas
   ガソリンが**なくなる**

F. **have** a flat tire
   タイヤが**パンクする**

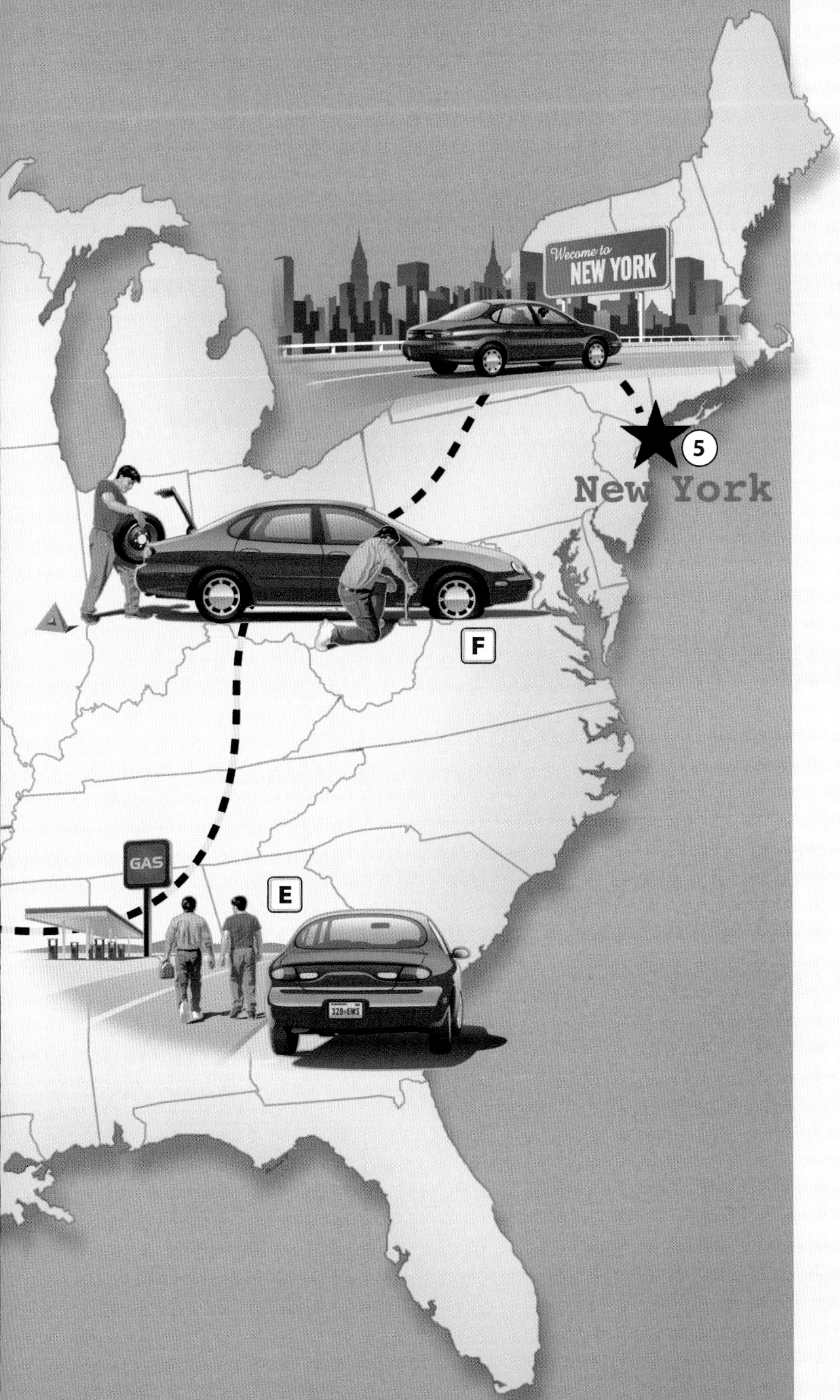

Welcome to NEW YORK

5

New York

F

GAS

E

Look at the pictures.
What do you see?

Answer the questions.

1. What are the young men's starting point and destination?
2. What do they see on their trip?
3. What kinds of problems do they have?

Read the story.

A Road Trip

On July 7th Joe and Rob packed their bags for a road trip. Their starting point was Seattle. Their destination was New York City.

The young men saw beautiful scenery on their trip. But there were also problems. They got lost. Then, a gas station attendant gave them bad directions. Next, they got a speeding ticket. Joe was very upset. After that, their car broke down. Joe called a tow truck and used his auto club card.

The end of their trip was difficult, too. They ran out of gas and then they had a flat tire.

After 7,000 miles of problems, Joe and Rob arrived in New York City. They were happy, but tired. Next time, they're going to take the train.

Think about it.

1. What is the best way to travel across the U.S.? by car? by plane? by train? Why?
2. Imagine your car breaks down on the road. Who can you call? What can you do?

The Workplace 職場

1. entrance
入口
2. customer
顧客
3. office
オフィス
4. employer / boss
雇用者／上司
5. receptionist
受付係
6. safety regulations
安全規則

Listen and point. Take turns.

A: Point to <u>the front entrance</u>.
B: Point to <u>the receptionist</u>.
A: Point to <u>the time clock</u>.

Dictate to your partner. Take turns.

A: *Can you spell <u>employer</u>?*
B: *I'm not sure. Is it <u>e-m-p-l-o-y-e-r</u>?*
A: *Yes, that's right.*

7. time clock
タイムレコーダー
8. supervisor
監督者
9. employee
社員
10. payroll clerk
給与支払い担当者
11. pay stub
給与明細書
12. wages
賃金
13. deductions
天引き
14. paycheck
給料支払小切手

Ways to talk about wages

*I **earn** $250 a week.*
*He **makes** $7 an hour.*
*I'm **paid** $1,000 a month.*

Role play. Talk to an employer.

A: *Is everything correct on your paycheck?*
B: *No, it isn't. I make $250 a week, not $200.*
A: *Let's talk to the payroll clerk. Where is she?*

Jobs and Occupations A–C

仕事と職業 A–C

1. accountant
会計士

2. actor
俳優

3. administrative assistant
経営管理アシスタント

4. appliance repair person
家電製品修理人

5. architect
建築士

6. artist
芸術家

7. assembler
組立工

8. auto mechanic
自動車整備工

9. babysitter
ベビーシッター

10. baker
パン職人

11. business owner
会社経営者

12. businessperson
ビジネスマン

13. butcher
肉屋

14. carpenter
大工

15. cashier
レジ係

16. childcare worker
保育士

Ways to ask about someone's job

What's her job?
What does he do?
What kind of work do they do?

Pair practice. Make new conversations.

A: *What kind of work does she do?*
B: *She's an accountant. What do they do?*
A: *They're actors.*

17. commercial fisher
漁師

18. computer software engineer
コンピュータソフトウェアエンジニア

19. computer technician
コンピュータ技術者

20. customer service representative
カスタマーサービス係員

21. delivery person
配達人

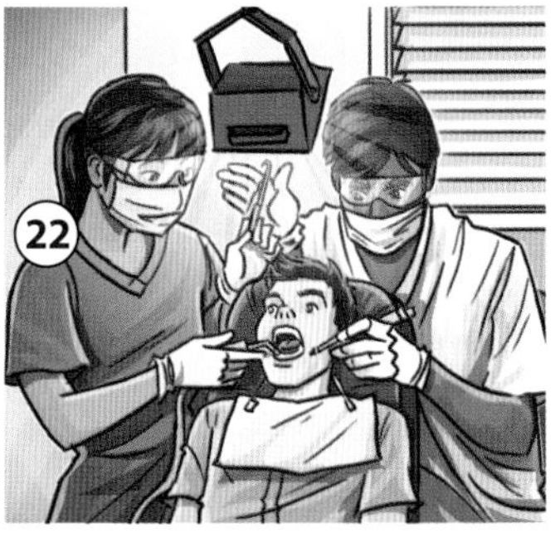

22. dental assistant
歯科助手

23. dockworker
港湾労働者

24. electronics repair person
電子製品修理人

25. engineer
エンジニア

26. firefighter
消防士

27. florist
花屋

28. gardener
庭師

29. garment worker
衣服製作者

30. graphic designer
グラフィックデザイナー

31. hairdresser / hair stylist
美容師／ヘアスタイリスト

32. home health care aide
在宅介護ヘルパー

Ways to talk about jobs and occupations

Sue's a garment worker. She works ***in*** *a factory.*
Tom's an engineer. He works ***for*** *a large company.*
Ann's a dental assistant. She works ***with*** *a dentist.*

Role play. Talk about a friend's new job.

A: *Does your friend like his new job?*
B: *Yes, he does. He's a graphic designer.*
A: *Does he work in an office?*

Jobs and Occupations H–P

仕事と職業 H–P

33. homemaker
主婦／主夫

34. housekeeper
家政婦

35. interpreter / translator
通訳／翻訳者

36. lawyer
弁護士

37. machine operator
機械オペレータ

38. manicurist
ネイリスト

39. medical records technician
医療記録事務員

40. messenger / courier
メッセンジャー／配達者

41. model
モデル

42. mover
引越し業者

43. musician
ミュージシャン／音楽家

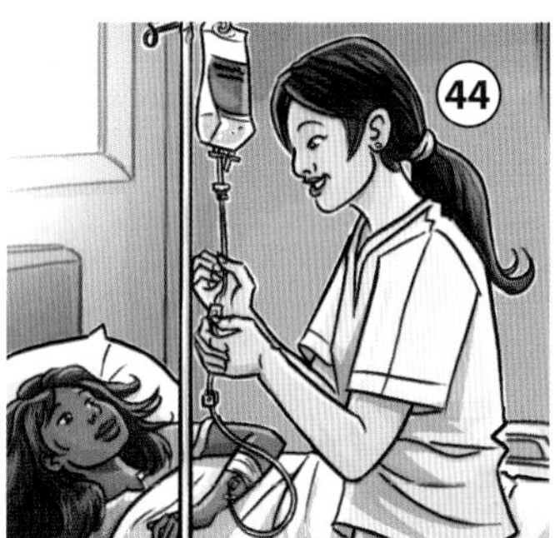

44. nurse
看護師

45. occupational therapist
作業療法士

46. (house) painter
（住宅）塗装屋

47. physician assistant
医師助手

48. police officer
警察官

Grammar Point: past tense of *be*

*I **was** a machine operator for 5 years.*
*She **was** a nurse for a year.*
*They **were** movers from 2003–2007.*

Pair practice. Make new conversations.

A: *What was your first job?*
B: *I was a musician. How about you?*
A: *I was a messenger for a small company.*

49. postal worker
郵便局員

50. printer
印刷工

51. receptionist
受付係

52. reporter
レポーター

53. retail clerk
小売販売店員

54. sanitation worker
清掃作業員

55. security guard
警備員

56. server
給仕人

57. social worker
社会福祉指導員

58. soldier
兵士

59. stock clerk
在庫品係

60. telemarketer
テレマーケッター

61. truck driver
トラック運転手

62. veterinarian
獣医

63. welder
溶接工

64. writer / author
作家／文筆家

Ask your classmates. Share the answers.

1. Which of these jobs could you do now?
2. What is one job you don't want to have?
3. Which jobs do you want to have?

Think about it. Discuss.

1. Which jobs need special training?
2. What kind of person makes a good interpreter? A good nurse? A good reporter? Why?

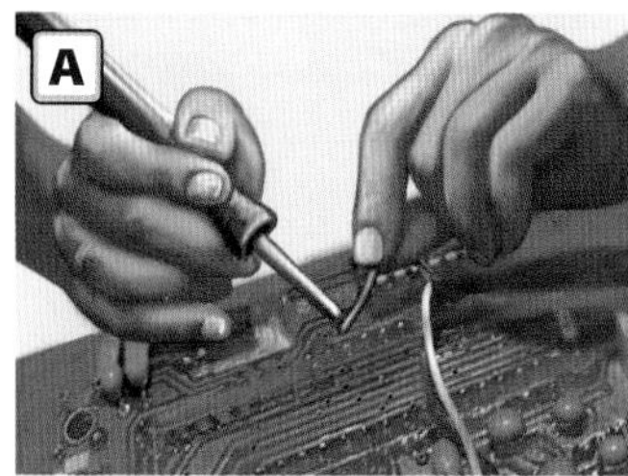

A. **assemble** components
部品を**組み立てる**

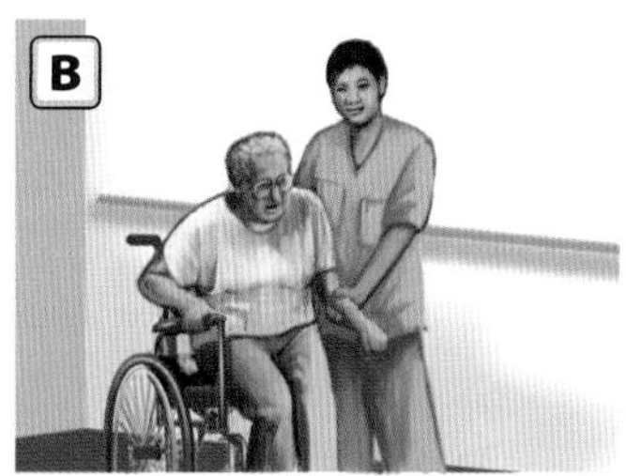

B. **assist** medical patients
患者を**助ける**

C. **cook**
調理する

D. **do** manual labor
肉体労働を**する**

E. **drive** a truck
トラックを**運転する**

F. **fly** a plane
飛行機を**操縦する**

G. **make** furniture
家具を**作る**

H. **operate** heavy machinery
重機を**操作する**

I. **program** computers
コンピュータを**プログラムする**

J. **repair** appliances
家電製品を**修理する**

K. **sell** cars
車を**販売する**

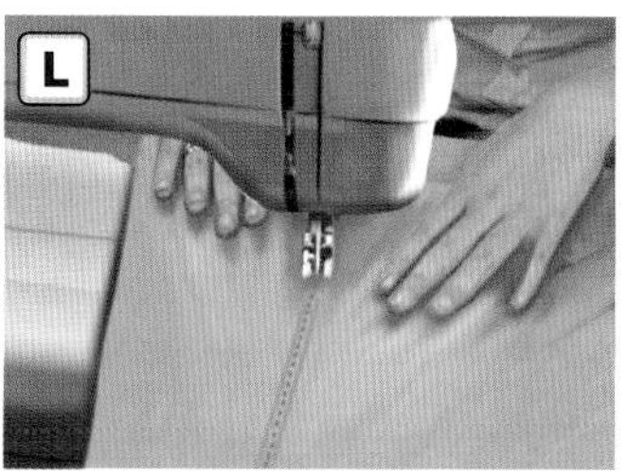

L. **sew** clothes
衣服を**縫う**

M. **solve** math problems
数学の問題を**解く**

N. **speak** another language
外国語を**話す**

O. **supervise** people
人々を**監督する**

P. **take** care of children
子供の**世話をする**

Q. **teach**
教える

R. **type**
タイプする

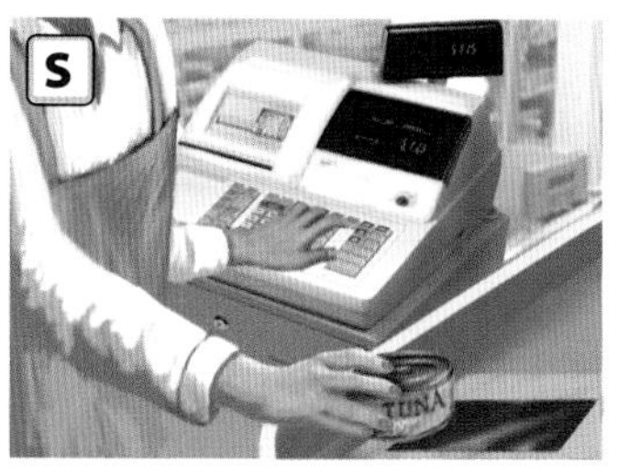

S. **use** a cash register
キャッシュレジスターを**使う**

T. **wait on** customers
接客する

Grammar Point: *can, can't*

I am a chef. I ***can*** *cook.*
I'm not a pilot. I ***can't*** *fly a plane.*
I ***can't*** *speak French, but I* ***can*** *speak Spanish.*

Role play. Talk to a job counselor.

A: *Tell me about your skills. Can you type?*
B: *No, I can't, but I can use a cash register.*
A: *OK. What other skills do you have?*

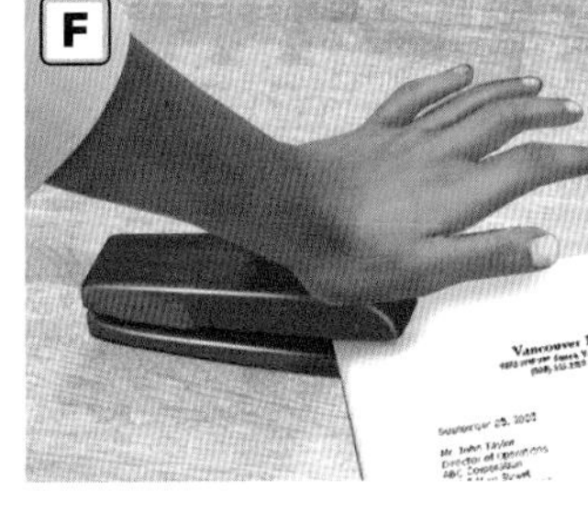

Office Skills
事務能力

A. **type** a letter
手紙をタイプする

B. **enter** data
データを入力する

C. **transcribe** notes
録音を書き取る

D. **make** copies
コピーする

E. **collate** papers
ページ順にそろえる

F. **staple**
ホッチキスで留める

G. **fax** a document
文書をファックスする

H. **scan** a document
文書をスキャンする

I. **print** a document
文書を印刷する

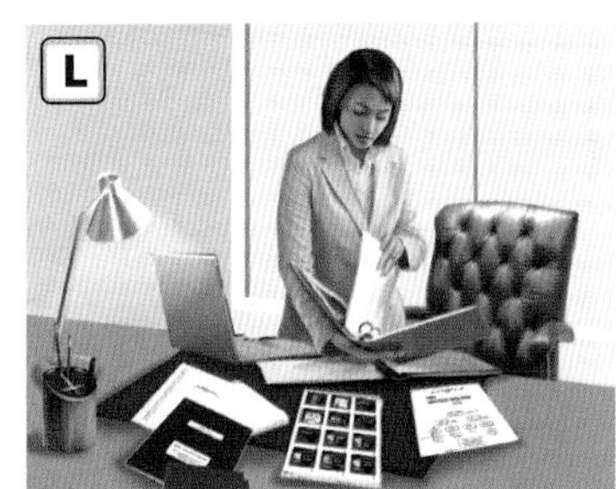

J. **schedule** a meeting
会議の予定を入れる

K. **take** dictation
口述筆記を行う

L. **organize** materials
資料を整理する

Telephone Skills
電話対応能力

M. **greet** the caller
電話の相手に挨拶する

N. **put** the caller on hold
電話を保留にする

O. **transfer** the call
電話を転送する

P. **leave** a message
伝言を残す

Q. **take** a message
伝言を受ける

R. **check** messages
メッセージをチェックする

Career Path キャリアの道

1. entry-level job
初心者レベルの仕事

2. training
トレーニング

3. new job
新しい仕事

4. promotion
昇進

Types of Job Training いろいろな職業訓練

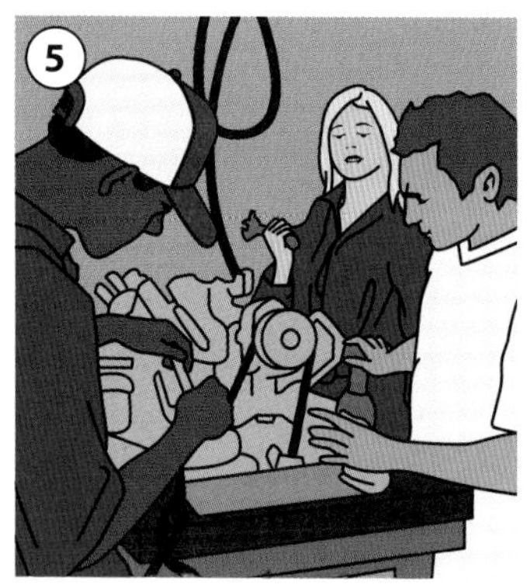

5. vocational training
職業訓練

6. internship
インターンシップ

7. on-the-job training
実地訓練

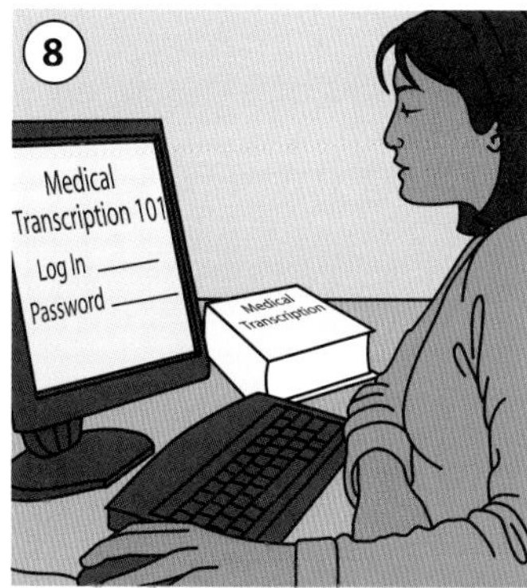

8. online course
オンラインコース

Planning a Career キャリア計画を立てる

9. resource center
リソースセンター

10. career counselor
キャリアカウンセラー

11. interest inventory
職業興味検査

12. skill inventory
技能検査

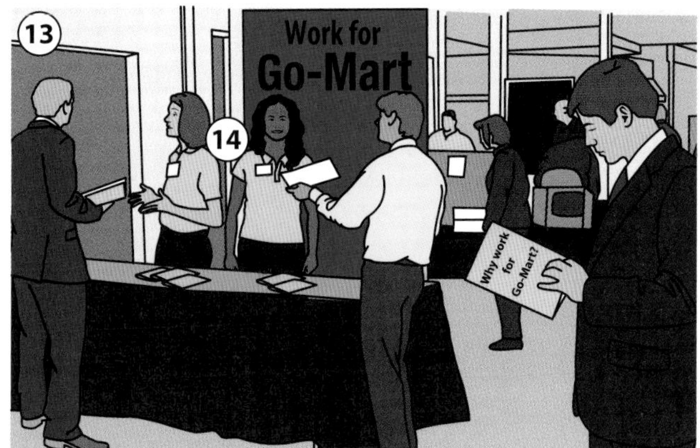

13. job fair
就職説明会

14. recruiter
リクルーター

Ways to talk about job training

I'm looking into an online course.
I'm interested in on-the-job training.
I want to sign up for an internship.

Ask your classmates. Share the answers.

1. What kind of job training are you interested in?
2. Would your rather learn English in an online course or in a classroom?

A. **talk** to friends / **network**
友人と話す／**ネットワークを広げる**

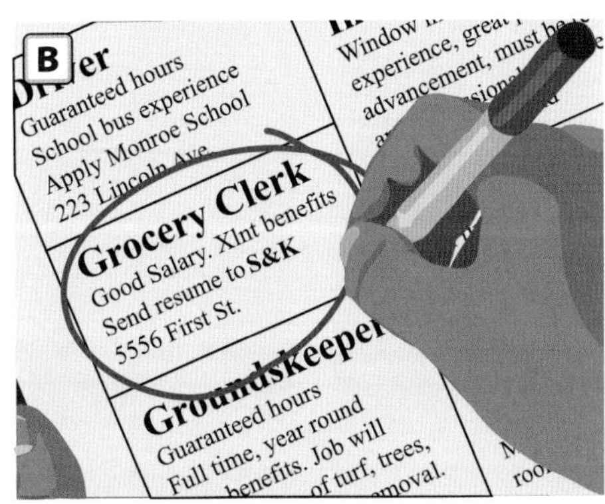

B. **look in** the classifieds
求人募集広告を**見る**

C. **look for** help wanted signs
求人募集の掲示を**探す**

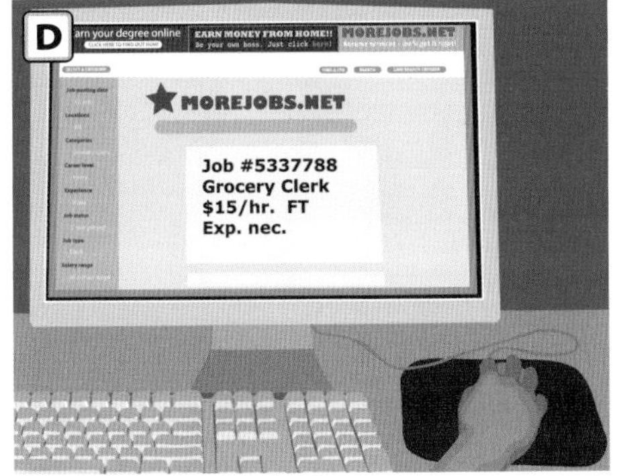

D. **check** Internet job sites
インターネットの求人募集サイトを**チェックする**

E. **go** to an employment agency
職業安定所に**行く**

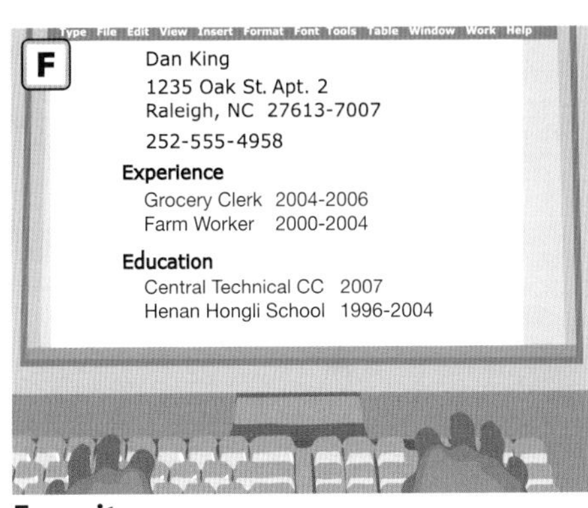

F. **write** a resume
履歴書を**書く**

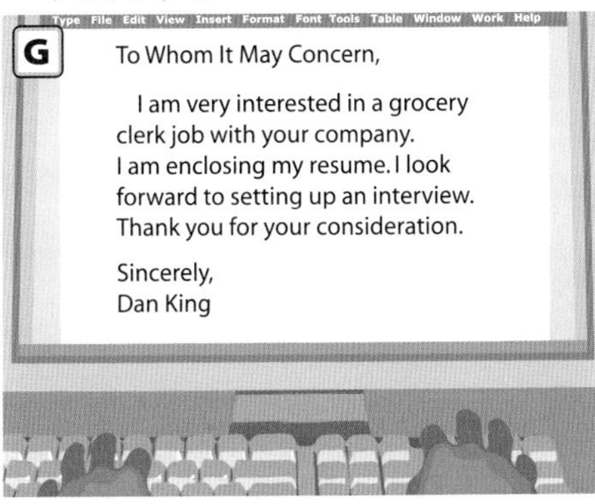

G. **write** a cover letter
カバーレターを**書く**

H. **send in** your resume and cover letter
履歴書とカバーレターを**送る**

I. **set up** an interview
面接を**取り付ける**

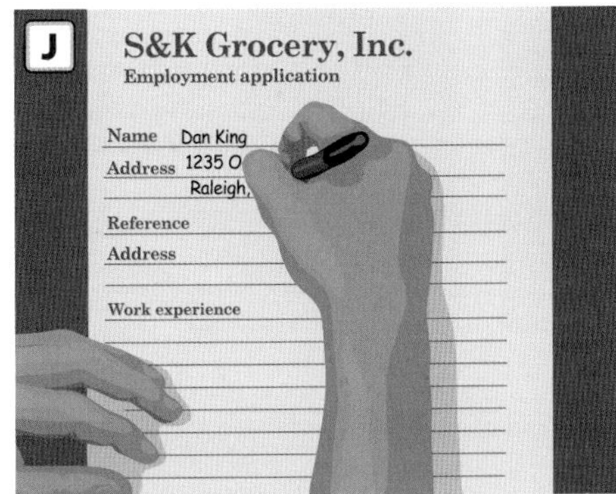

J. **fill out** an application
応募用紙に**記入する**

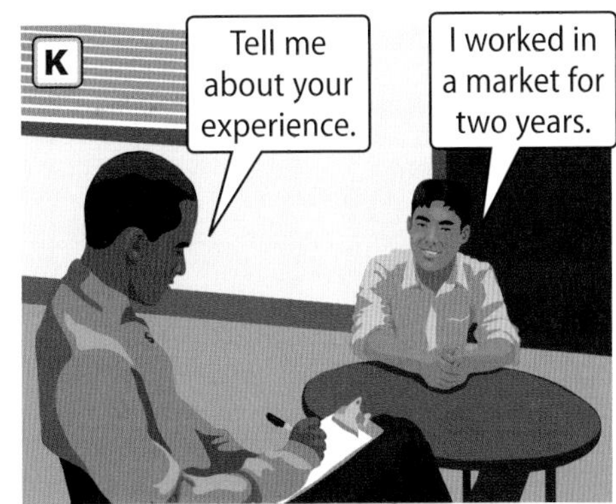

K. **go on** an interview
面接に**行く**

L. **get** hired
採用**される**

Interview Skills

面接技能

A. **Prepare** for the interview.
面接の**準備をする**

B. **Dress** appropriately.
適切な**服を着る**

C. **Be** neat.
身だしなみをきちんと**する**

D. **Bring** your resume and ID.
履歴書と身分証明書を**持参する**

E. **Don't be** late.
遅刻**しない**

F. **Be** on time.
定刻に**着く**

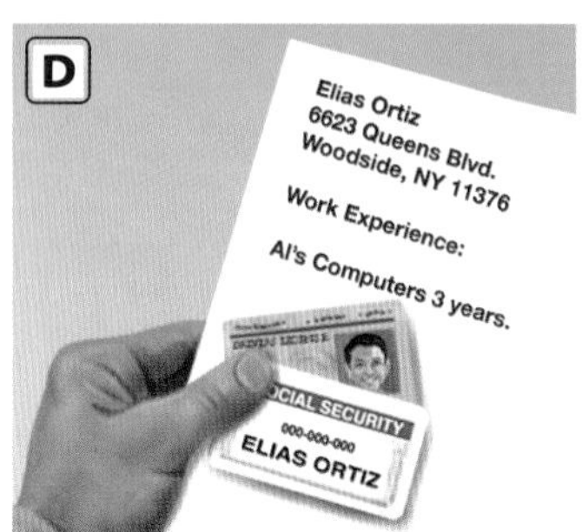

G. **Turn off** your cell phone.
携帯電話の**電源を切る**

H. **Greet** the interviewer.
面接担当者に**挨拶する**

I. **Shake** hands.
握手**する**

J. **Make** eye contact.
相手の目を**見る**

K. **Listen** carefully.
注意して**聞く**

L. **Talk** about your experience.
自分の経験を**話す**

M. **Ask** questions.
質問**する**

N. **Thank** the interviewer.
面接担当者に**お礼を言う**

O. **Write** a thank-you note.
礼状を**書く**

More vocabulary

benefits: health insurance, vacation pay, or other things the employer can offer an employee
inquire about benefits: ask about benefits

Think about it. Discuss.

1. How can you prepare for an interview?
2. Why is it important to make eye contact?
3. What kinds of questions should you ask?

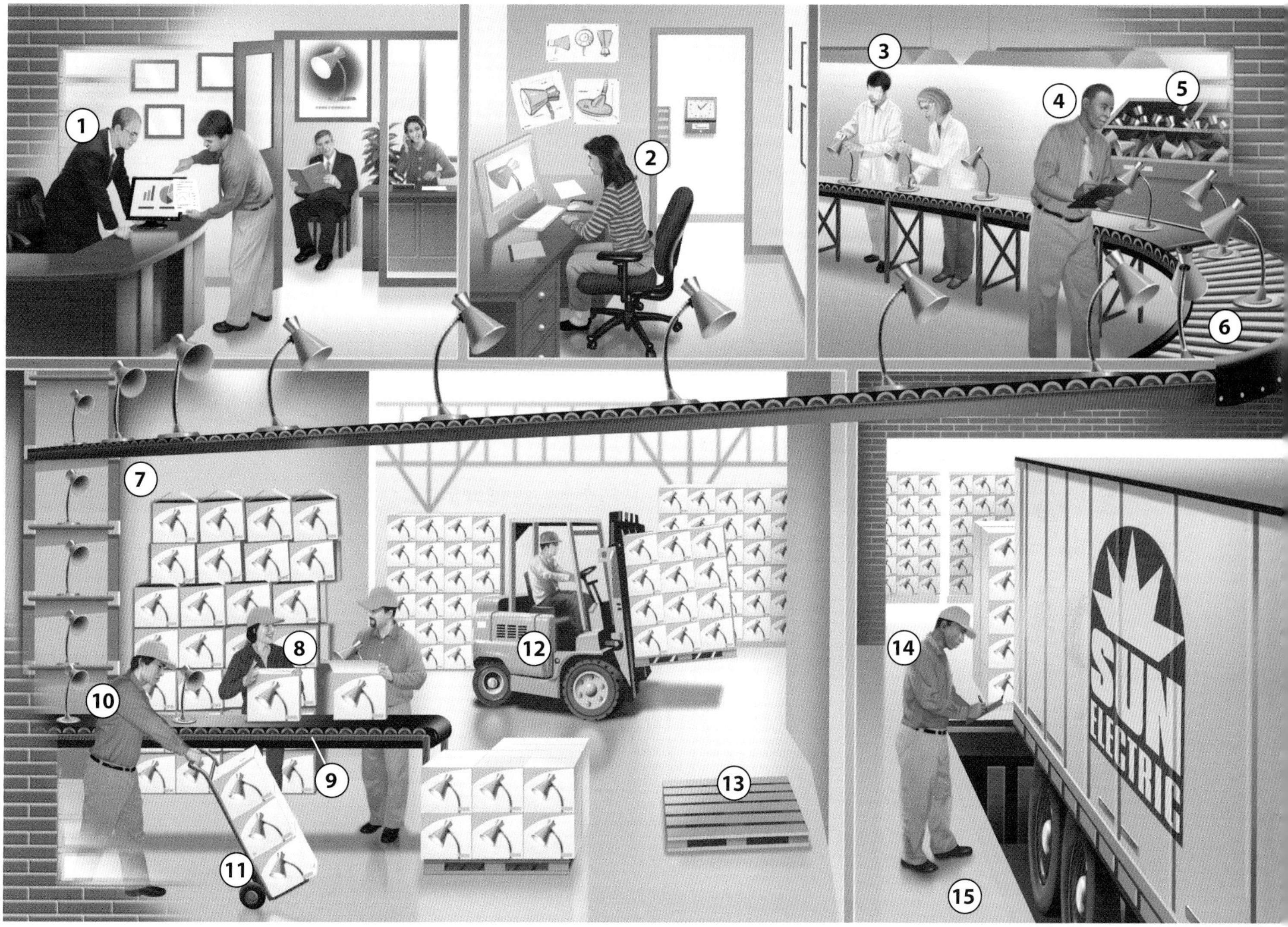

1. factory owner
工場所有者
2. designer
設計者
3. factory worker
工場従業員
4. line supervisor
ライン監督者
5. parts
部品
6. assembly line
組立ライン
7. warehouse
倉庫
8. packer
箱詰め担当者
9. conveyer belt
コンベヤーベルト
10. order puller
注文品取揃え係
11. hand truck
台車
12. forklift
フォークリフト
13. pallet
パレット
14. shipping clerk
出荷係
15. loading dock
荷積みドック

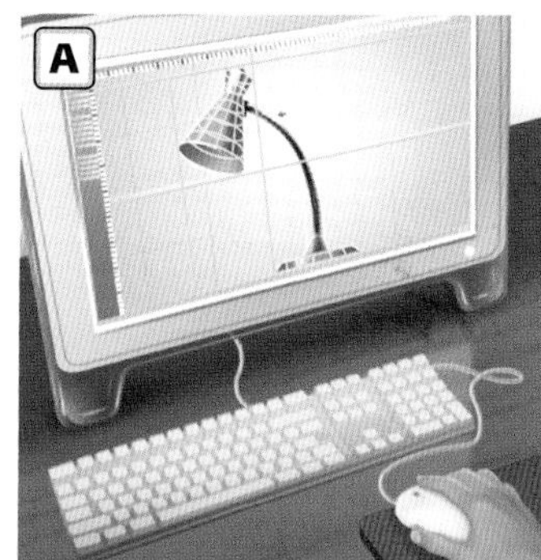

A. **design**
設計する

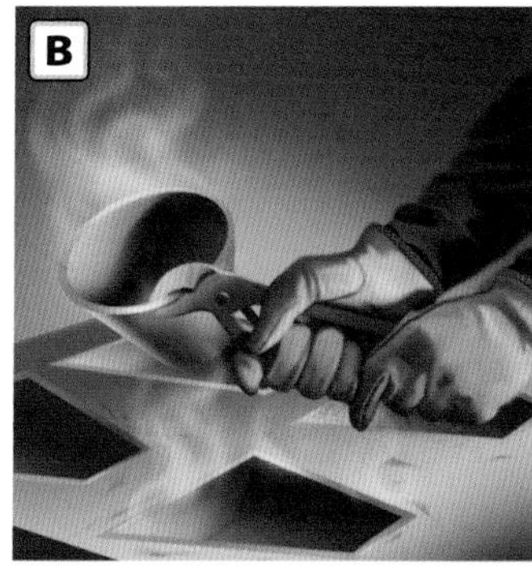

B. **manufacture**
製造する

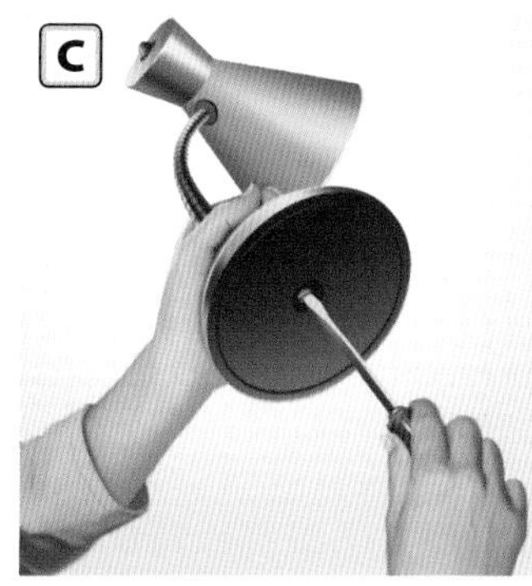

C. **assemble**
組み立てる

D. **ship**
出荷する

Landscaping and Gardening

造園と園芸業

1. gardening crew 造園スタッフ
2. leaf blower リーフブロワー
3. wheelbarrow 手押し車
4. gardening crew leader 造園スタッフのリーダー
5. landscape designer 造園設計家
6. lawn mower 芝刈り機
7. shovel シャベル
8. rake 熊手
9. pruning shears 剪定はさみ
10. trowel スコップ
11. hedge clippers 刈り込みばさみ
12. weed whacker / weed eater 除草器

A. **mow** the lawn 芝生を**刈る**

B. **trim** the hedges 生垣を**刈り込む**

C. **rake** the leaves 枯葉を**かき集める**

D. **fertilize** / **feed** the plants 肥料を**やる**

E. **plant** a tree 木を**植える**

F. **water** the plants 植木に**水をやる**

G. **weed** the flower beds 花壇の**雑草を抜く**

H. **install** a sprinkler system 散水器を**取り付ける**

Use the new words.

Look at page 53. Name what you can do in the yard.

A: *I can mow the lawn.*

B: *I can weed the flower bed.*

Ask your classmates. Share the answers.

1. Do you know someone who does landscaping? Who?
2. Do you enjoy gardening? Why or why not?
3. Which gardening activity is the hardest to do? Why?

Crops 作物

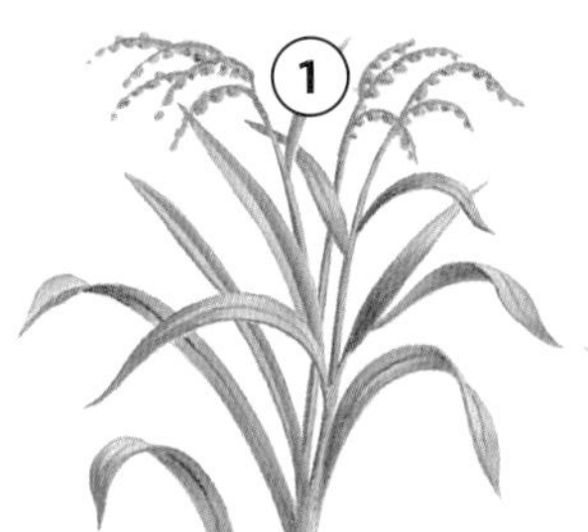

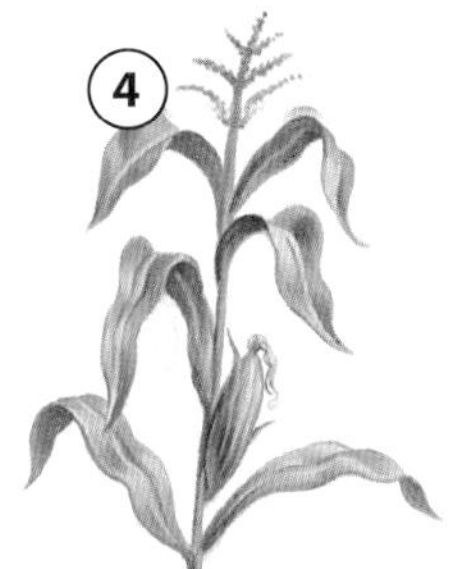

1. rice
米
2. wheat
小麦
3. soybeans
大豆
4. corn
トウモロコシ
5. alfalfa
アルファルファ
6. cotton
綿

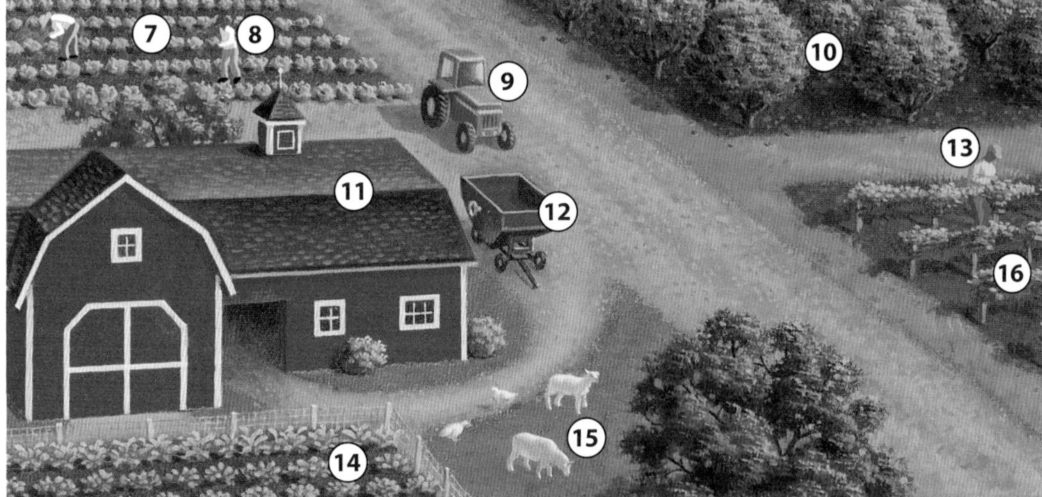

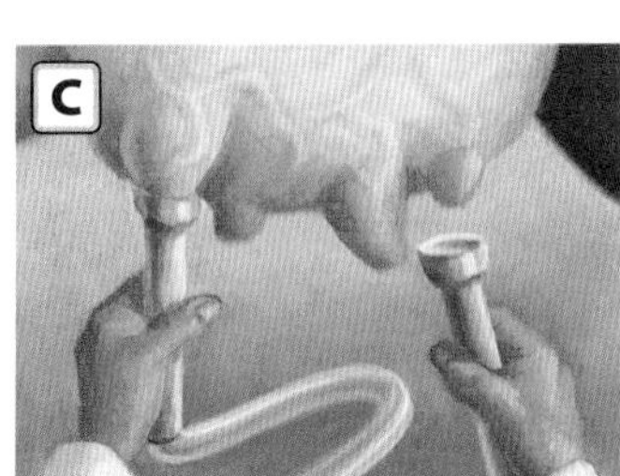

7. field
畑
8. farmworker
農夫
9. tractor
トラクター
10. orchard
果樹園
11. barn
納屋
12. farm equipment
農機具
13. farmer / grower
農業生産者
14. vegetable garden
菜園
15. livestock
家畜
16. vineyard
ブドウ畑
17. corral
家畜を入れる囲い
18. hay
干し草
19. fence
フェンス
20. hired hand
雇い人
21. cattle
畜牛
22. rancher
牧場主

A. **plant**
植える
B. **harvest**
収穫する
C. **milk**
搾乳する
D. **feed**
飼料を与える

Construction

建設業

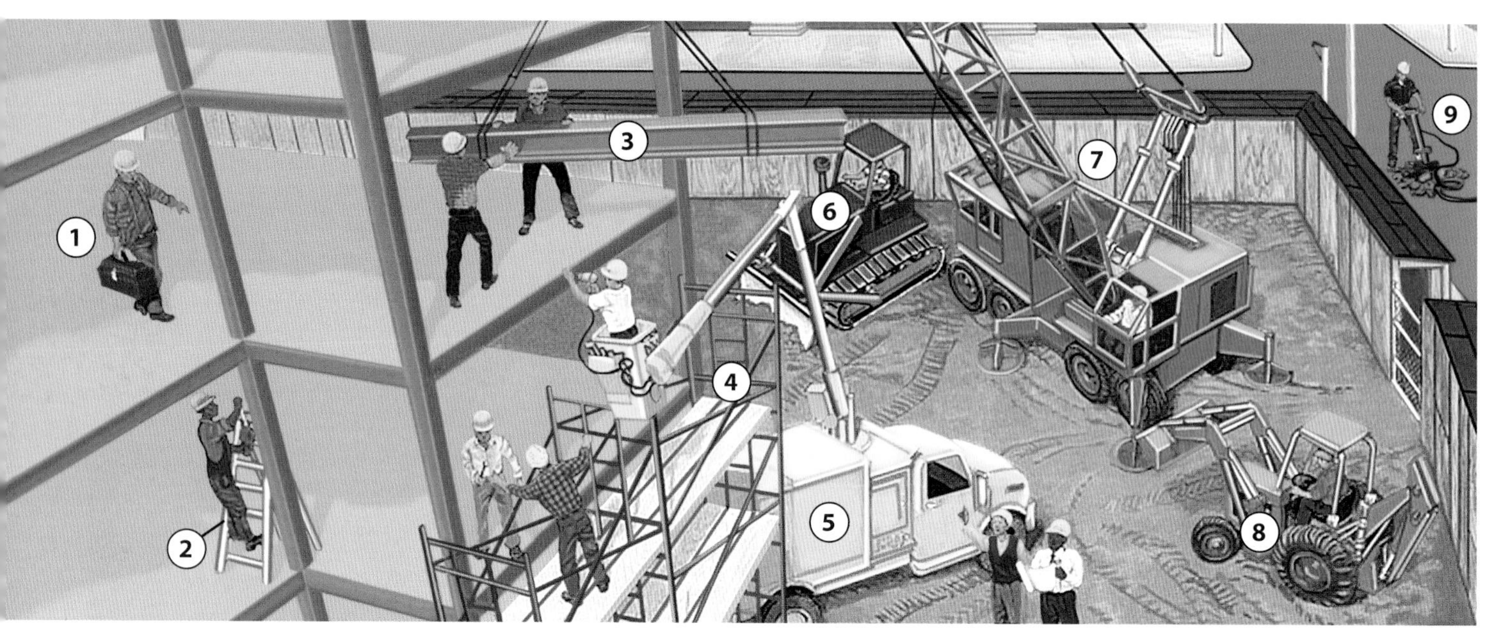

1. construction worker
建設作業員
2. ladder
はしご
3. I beam/girder
I形鋼
4. scaffolding
足場
5. cherry picker
移動クレーン
6. bulldozer
ブルドーザー
7. crane
クレーン
8. backhoe
バックホー
9. jackhammer / pneumatic drill
ジャックハンマー

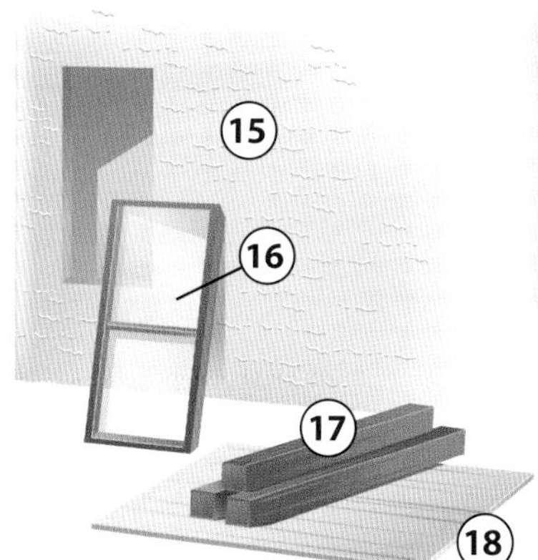
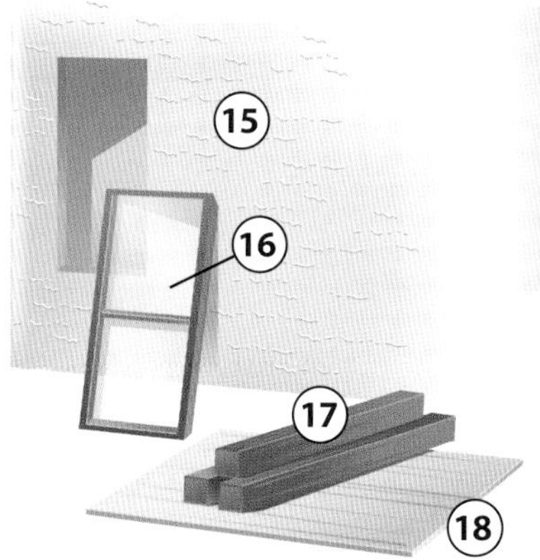
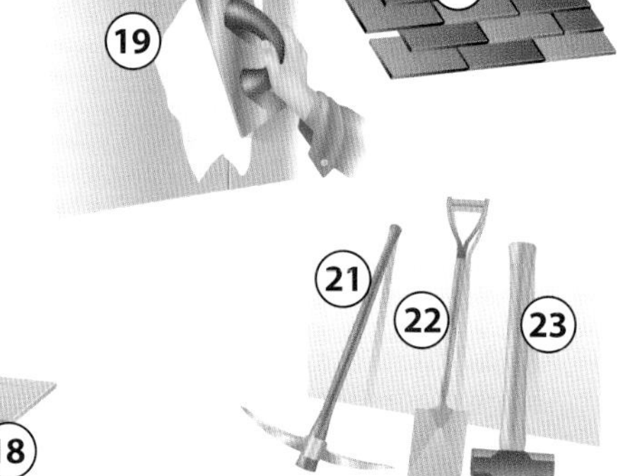
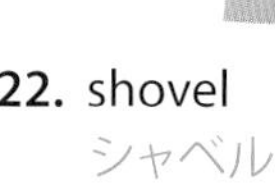

10. concrete
コンクリート
11. tile
タイル
12. bricks
煉瓦
13. trowel
こて
14. insulation
断熱材
15. stucco
しっくい
16. window pane
窓ガラス
17. wood / lumber
材木
18. plywood
合板
19. drywall
ドライウォール
20. shingles
屋根板
21. pickax
つるはし
22. shovel
シャベル
23. sledgehammer
大ハンマー

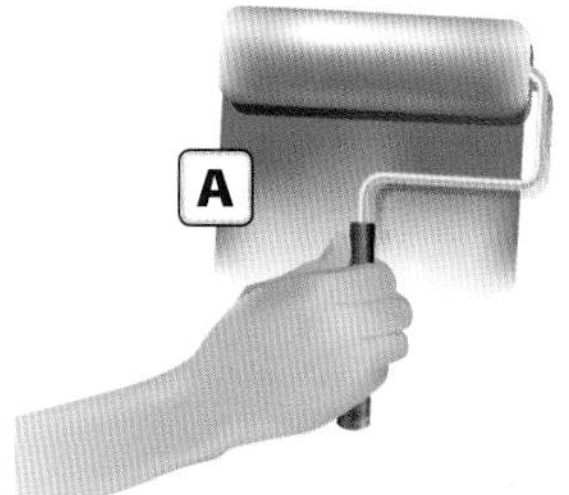
A. **paint**
ペンキを塗る

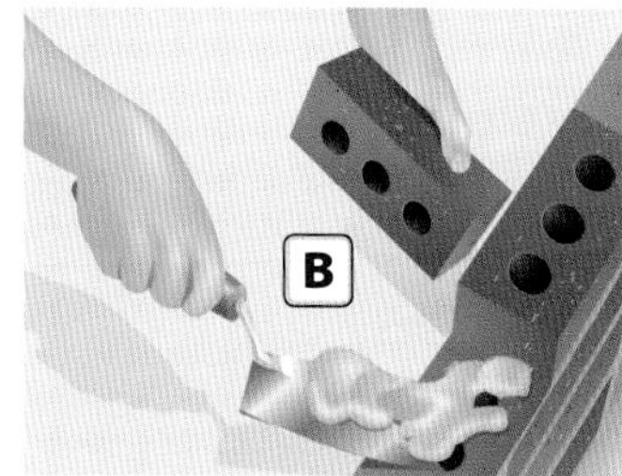
B. **lay** bricks
煉瓦を積む

C. **install** tile
タイルを張る

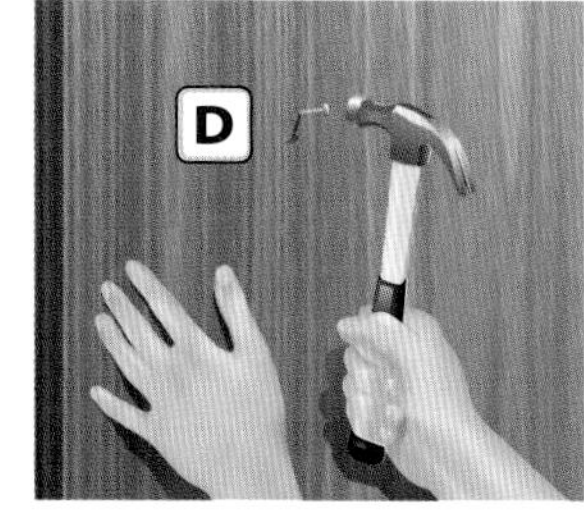
D. **hammer**
ハンマーで打つ

Safety Hazards and Hazardous Materials 安全上の欠陥と危険物質

1. careless worker
不注意な作業者
2. careful worker
注意深い作業者
3. poisonous fumes
有毒ガス
4. broken equipment
壊れた機材
5. frayed cord
擦り切れたコード
6. slippery floor
滑りやすい床
7. radioactive materials
放射性物質
8. flammable liquids
可燃性の液体

Safety Equipment 安全装備

9. hard hat
ヘルメット
10. safety glasses
安全眼鏡
11. safety goggles
安全ゴーグル
12. safety visor
防護バイザー
13. respirator
呼吸マスク
14. particle mask
防塵マスク
15. ear plugs
耳栓
16. earmuffs
耳あて
17. work gloves
作業用手袋
18. back support belt
背中をサポートするベルト
19. knee pads
膝あて
20. safety boots
安全ブーツ
21. fire extinguisher
消火器
22. two-way radio
送受信用無線機

Tools and Building Supplies

工具と建設用品

1. hammer
   ハンマー
2. mallet
   木づち
3. ax
   斧
4. handsaw
   のこぎり
5. hacksaw
   弓のこ
6. C-clamp
   Cクランプ
7. pliers
   ペンチ
8. electric drill
   電気ドリル
9. circular saw
   丸のこ
10. jigsaw
    糸のこ
11. power sander
    電動サンダー
12. router
    溝かんな

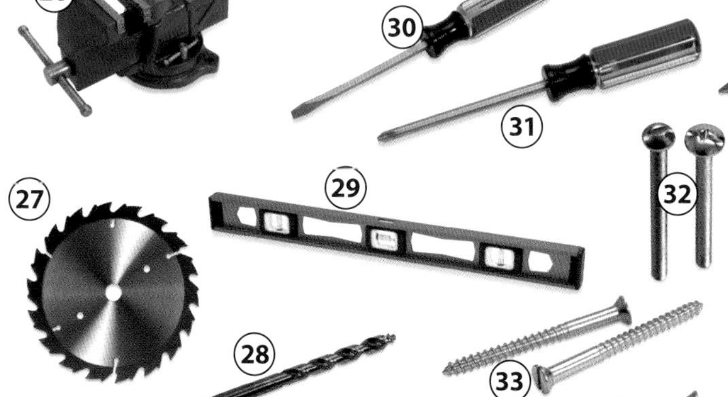

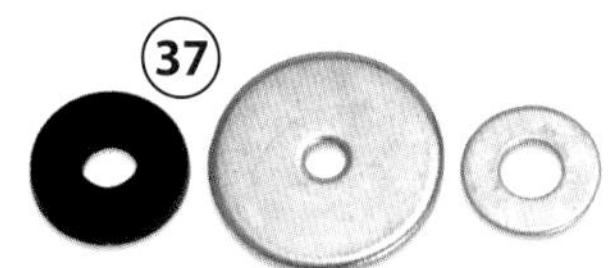

26. vise
    万力
27. blade
    刃
28. drill bit
    ドリルビット
29. level
    水準器
30. screwdriver
    ドライバー
31. Phillips screwdriver
    プラスのドライバー
32. machine screw
    小ネジ
33. wood screw
    木ネジ
34. nail
    釘
35. bolt
    ボルト
36. nut
    ナット
37. washer
    ワッシャ
38. toggle bolt
    トグルボルト
39. hook
    フック
40. eye hook
    アイフック
41. chain
    鎖

Use the new words.

Look at pages 62–63. Name the tools you see.

A: *There's a hammer.*

B: *There's a pipe wrench.*

Ask your classmates. Share the answers.

1. Are you good with tools?
2. Which tools do you have at home?
3. Where can you shop for building supplies?

13. wire
ワイヤ

14. extension cord
延長コード

15. bungee cord
バンジーコード

16. yardstick
ヤード尺

17. pipe
パイプ

18. fittings
継手

19. 2 x 4 (two by four)
2 x 4 (ツー バイ フォー) の木材

20. particle board
パーティクルボード

21. spray gun
スプレーガン

22. paintbrush
塗装用はけ

23. paint roller
ペンキローラー

24. wood stain
ステイン

25. paint
ペンキ

42. wire stripper
ワイヤストリッパ

43. electrical tape
絶縁テープ

44. work light
作業用ライト

45. tape measure
巻尺

46. outlet cover
コンセントカバー

47. pipe wrench
パイプレンチ

48. adjustable wrench
モンキーレンチ

49. duct tape
ダクトテープ

50. plunger
プランジャー

51. paint pan
ペンキ用パン

52. scraper
スクレーパー

53. masking tape
マスキングテープ

54. drop cloth
ペンキ塗り用シート

55. chisel
のみ

56. sandpaper
サンドペーパー

57. plane
かんな

Role play. Find an item in a building supply store.

A: *Where can I find particle board?*
B: *It's on the back wall, in the lumber section.*
A: *Great. And where are the nails?*

Think about it. Discuss.

1. Which tools are the most important to have? Why?
2. Which tools can be dangerous? Why?
3. Do you borrow tools from friends? Why or why not?

An Office

オフィス

1. supply cabinet
備品キャビネット
2. clerk
事務員
3. janitor
清掃員
4. conference room
会議室
5. executive
管理職者
6. presentation
プレゼンテーション
7. cubicle
小部屋／仕切られた空間
8. office manager
オフィスマネージャー
9. desk
机
10. file clerk
ファイル担当者
11. file cabinet
ファイルキャビネット
12. computer technician
コンピュータ技術者
13. PBX
PBX（構内電話交換機）
14. receptionist
受付係
15. reception area
受付エリア
16. waiting area
待合室

Ways to greet a receptionist

I'm here for a job interview.
I have a 9:00 a.m. appointment with Mr. Lee.
I'd like to leave a message for Mr. Lee.

Role play. Talk to a receptionist.

A: *Hello. How can I help you?*
B: *I'm here for a job interview with Mr. Lee.*
A: *OK. What is your name?*

Office Equipment 事務機器

17. computer
コンピュータ
18. inkjet printer
インクジェットプリンタ
19. laser printer
レーザープリンタ
20. scanner
スキャナ
21. fax machine
ファクシミリ機
22. paper cutter
紙裁断機
23. photocopier
コピー機
24. paper shredder
シュレッダー
25. calculator
計算機
26. electric pencil sharpener
電気鉛筆削り
27. postal scale
郵便用はかり

Office Supplies 事務用品

28. stapler
ホッチキス
29. staples
ホッチキスの針
30. clear tape
セロハンテープ
31. paper clip
クリップ
32. packing tape
梱包用テープ
33. glue
糊
34. rubber band
輪ゴム
35. pushpin
押しピン
36. correction fluid
修正液
37. correction tape
修正テープ
38. legal pad
法律用箋
39. sticky notes
付箋紙
40. mailer
郵送用梱包
41. mailing label
宛名ラベル
42. letterhead / stationery
便箋
43. envelope
封筒
44. rotary card file
ロータリーカードファイル
45. ink cartridge
インクカートリッジ
46. ink pad
インクパッド
47. stamp
スタンプ
48. appointment book
スケジュールノート
49. organizer
システム手帳
50. file folder
ファイルフォルダ

A Hotel

ホテル

1. doorman
ドアマン
2. revolving door
回転ドア
3. parking attendant
駐車場係員
4. concierge
コンシェルジェ
5. gift shop
ギフトショップ
6. bell captain
ベルキャプテン
7. bellhop
ベルボーイ
8. luggage cart
ラゲージカート
9. elevator
エレベーター
10. guest
ホテル客
11. desk clerk
フロント係
12. front desk
フロント

13. guest room
客室
14. double bed
ダブルベッド
15. king-size bed
キングサイズベッド
16. suite
スイート
17. room service
ルームサービス
18. hallway
廊下
19. housekeeping cart
清掃カート
20. housekeeper
清掃係

21. pool service
プール清掃
22. pool
プール
23. maintenance
メンテナンス
24. gym
スポーツジム
25. meeting room
会議室
26. ballroom
宴会場

A Restaurant Kitchen レストランの調理室

1. short-order cook
   即席料理担当コック
2. dishwasher
   食器洗い係
3. walk-in freezer
   大型冷凍庫
4. food preparation worker
   食品準備担当者
5. storeroom
   貯蔵室
6. sous chef
   副料理長
7. head chef / executive chef
   料理長

Restaurant Dining レストランのダイニングルーム

8. server
   給仕人
9. diner
   食事客
10. buffet
    ビュッフェ
11. maitre d'
    接客主任
12. headwaiter
    給仕長
13. bus person
    食後のテーブルを片付ける人
14. banquet room
    宴会場
15. runner
    ウェイター
16. caterer
    仕出屋

More vocabulary

line cook: short-order cook
wait staff: servers, headwaiters, and runners

Ask your classmates. Share the answers.

1. Have you ever worked in a hotel? What did you do?
2. What is the hardest job in a hotel?
3. Would you prefer to stay at a hotel in the city or in the country?

A Bad Day at Work 仕事がうまく行かなかった日

LOPEZ CONTRACTING

DRY WALL

BUILDING COSTS

Steel	$1,000,000
Drywall	$200,000
Cement	$300,000
Wiring	$300,000
Plumbing	$200,000
Labor	$1,000,000
TOTAL:	$3,000,000

OUT SICK

JACK OUT

TOM OUT

FLOOR PLAN

SAM LOPEZ

SCHEDULE
Start date: 3/1
Wiring: 7/1
Walls up: 8/1
End date: 9/1

DANGER

1. dangerous
危険
2. clinic
診療所
3. budget
予算
4. floor plan
フロアプラン
5. contractor
請負業者
6. electrical hazard
感電の危険
7. wiring
配線
8. bricklayer
煉瓦職人

A. **call in** sick
病気で休むことを**電話で連絡する**

Look at the picture.
What do you see?

Answer the questions.

1. How many workers are there? How many are working?
2. Why did two workers call in sick?
3. What is dangerous at the construction site?

Read the story.

A Bad Day at Work

Sam Lopez is the contractor for a new building. He makes the schedule and supervises the budget. He also solves problems. Today there are a lot of problems.

Two bricklayers called in sick this morning. Now Sam has only one bricklayer at work. One hour later, a construction worker fell. Now he has to go to the clinic. Sam always tells his workers to be careful. Construction work is dangerous. Sam's also worried because the new wiring is an electrical hazard.

Right now, the building owner is in Sam's office. Her new floor plan has 25 more offices. Sam has a headache. Maybe he needs to call in sick tomorrow.

Think about it.

1. What do you say when you can't come in to work? to school?
2. Imagine you are Sam. What do you tell the building owner? Why?

Schools and Subjects 学校と科目

1. preschool / nursery school
   プリスクール／保育園
2. elementary school
   小学校
3. middle school / junior high school
   中学校
4. high school
   高校
5. vocational school / technical school
   職業訓練校／専門学校
6. community college
   コミュニティカレッジ
7. college / university
   単科大学／総合大学
8. adult school
   成人教育

Listen and point. Take turns.

A: *Point to the preschool.*
B: *Point to the high school.*
A: *Point to the adult school.*

Dictate to your partner. Take turns.

A: *Write preschool.*
B: *Is that p-r-e-s-c-h-o-o-l?*
A: *Yes. That's right.*

13

9. language arts
語学
10. math
数学
11. science
科学
12. history
歴史
13. world languages
外国語
14. ESL / ESOL
ESL／ESOL（第二言語としての英語）
15. arts
美術
16. music
音楽
17. physical education
保健体育

More vocabulary

core course: a subject students have to take. Math is a core course.

elective: a subject students choose to take. Art is an elective.

Pair practice. Make new conversations.

A: *I go to community college.*
B: *What subjects are you taking?*
A: *I'm taking history and science.*

① factory

② I worked in a factory.

③ Little by little, work and success came to me. My first job wasn't good. I worked in a small factory. Now, I help manage two factories.

④

Carlos Lopez
Eng. Comp.
10/21/10

Success in the U.S.

I came to Chicago from Nigeria in 2006. I had no job, no friends and no family here. I was homesick and scared, but I did not go home. I took English classes (always at night) and I studied hard. I believed in my future success!

More than 400,000 new immigrants come to the U.S every year.[1] Most of us need to find work. During my first year here, my routine was the same: get up; look for work; go to class; go to bed. I had to take jobs with long hours and low pay. Often I had two or three jobs.

Little by little, work and success came to me. My first job wasn't good. I worked in a small factory. Now, I help manage two factories.

Hard work makes success possible. Henry David Thoreau said, "Men are born to succeed, not fail." My story shows that he was right.

[1] US Census 2004

1. word 単語
2. sentence 文
3. paragraph 段落
4. essay 小論文

Parts of an Essay 小論文の構成部分

5. title 題名
6. introduction 導入部分
7. body 本文
8. conclusion 結論
9. quotation 引用
10. footnote 脚注

Carlos Lopez
Eng. Comp.
10/21/10

⑤ Success in the U.S.

⑥ I came to Los Angeles from Mexico in 2006. I had no job, no friends, and no family here. I was homesick and scared, but I did not go home. I took English classes (always at night) and I studied hard. I believed in my future success!

⑦ More than 400,000 new immigrants come to the U.S every year.[1] Most of us need to find work. During my first year here, my routine was the same: get up; look for work; go to class; go to bed. I had to take jobs with long hours and low pay. Often I had two or three jobs.

Little by little, work and success came to me. My first job wasn't good. I worked in a small factory. Now, I help manage two factories.

⑧ Hard work makes success possible. Henry David Thoreau said, ⑨ "Men are born to succeed, not fail." My story shows that he was right.

⑩ [1] U.S. Census

Punctuation 句読法

11. . period ピリオド
12. ? question mark クエスチョンマーク
13. ! exclamation mark エクスクラメーションマーク／感嘆符
14. , comma コンマ
15. " " quotation marks クォーテーションマーク
16. ' apostrophe アポストロフィ
17. : colon コロン
18. ; semicolon セミコロン
19. ( ) parentheses カッコ
20. - hyphen ハイフン

Writing Rules 書き方の規則

A
Carlos
Mexico
Los Angeles

B
Hard work makes success possible.

C
I was homesick and scared, but I did not go home.

D
I came to Los Angeles from Mexico in 2006. I had no job, no friends, and no family here. I was homesick and scared, but I did not go home. I took English classes (always at night) and I studied hard. I believed in my future success!

A. **Capitalize** names.
固有名詞は**大文字で始める**

B. **Capitalize** the first letter in a sentence.
文の最初の文字は**大文字**にする

C. **Use** punctuation.
句読法を**用いる**

D. **Indent** the first sentence in a paragraph.
段落の最初の文章は**字下げ**（インデント）する

Ways to ask for suggestions on your compositions

What do you think of this title*?*
Is this paragraph *OK? Is the* punctuation *correct?*
Do you have any suggestions for the conclusion*?*

Pair practice. Make new conversations.

A: What do you think of this *title*?
B: *I think you need to* revise *it.*
A: *Thanks. Do you have any more suggestions?*

The Writing Process 作文の過程

PREWRITING

E. **Think about** the assignment.
課題について考える

F. **Brainstorm** ideas.
アイデアを出す

G. **Organize** your ideas.
考えを整理する

WRITING AND REVISING

H. **Write** a first draft.
最初の草稿を書く

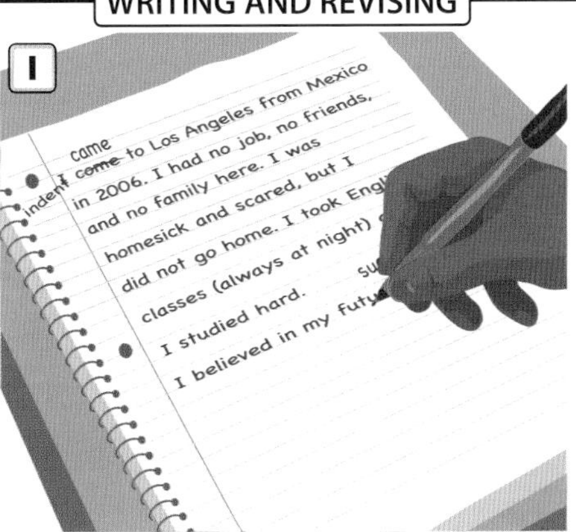

I. **Edit**. / **Proofread**.
編集する／校正する

J. **Revise**. / **Rewrite**.
修正する／書き直す

SHARING AND RESPONDING

K. **Get** feedback.
フィードバックを得る

L. **Write** a final draft.
最終稿を書く

M. **Turn in** your paper.
原稿を提出する

Ask your classmates. Share the answers.

1. Do you like to write essays?
2. Which part of the writing process do you like best? least?

Think about it. Discuss.

1. In which jobs are writing skills important?
2. What tools can help you edit your writing?
3. What are some good subjects for essays?

Mathematics 数学

Integers 整数

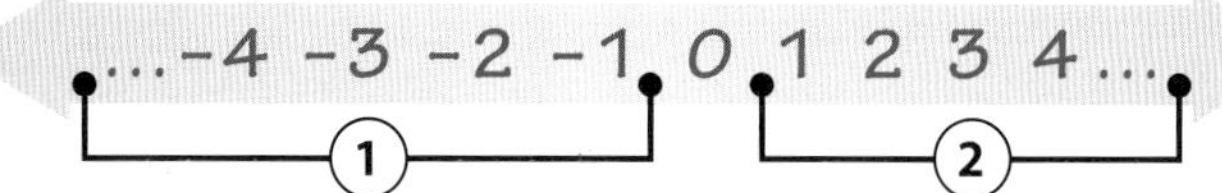

1. negative integers
   負の整数
2. positive integers
   正の整数

(3) 1, 3, 5, 7, 9, 11...

(4) 2, 4, 6, 8, 10...

3. odd numbers
   奇数
4. even numbers
   偶数

Fractions 分数

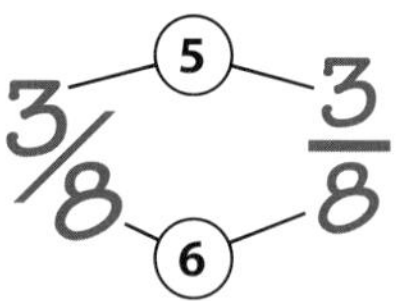

5. numerator
   分子
6. denominator
   分母

Math Operations 演算

A. **add**
足す

B. **subtract**
引く

C. **multiply**
掛ける

D. **divide**
割る

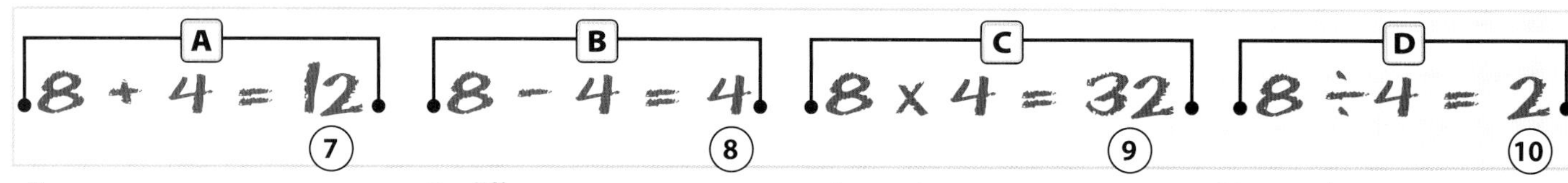

7. sum
   和
8. difference
   差
9. product
   積
10. quotient
    商

A Math Problem 数学の問題

(11) Tom is 10 years older than Kim. Next year he will be twice as old as Kim. How old is Tom this year?

(12) — x = Kim's age now
$x + 10$ = Tom's age now
$x + 1$ = Kim's age next year
$2(x + 1)$ = Tom's age next year

$x + 10 + 1 = 2(x + 1)$
$x + 11 = 2x + 2$ (13)
$11 - 2 = 2x - x$

x = 9, Kim is 9, Tom is 19 (14)

(15) horizontal axis
vertical axis

11. word problem
    文章題
12. variable
    変数
13. equation
    方程式
14. solution
    答え
15. graph
    グラフ

Types of Math 数学の種類

x = the sale price
x = 79.00 - .40 (79.00)
x = $47.40

area of path = 24 square ft.
area of brick = 2 square ft.
24 / 2 = 12 bricks

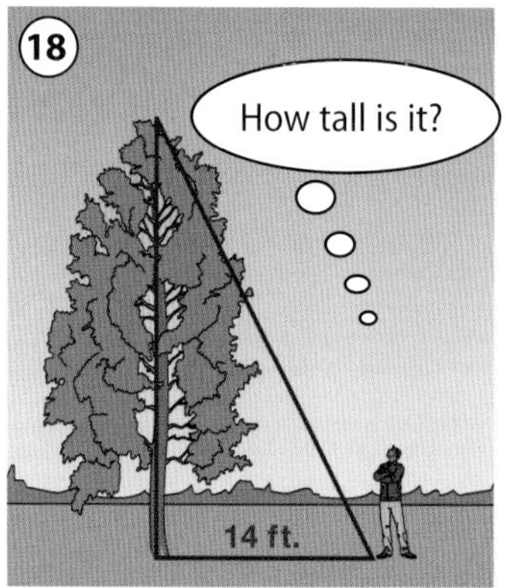

tan 63° = height / 14 feet
height = 14 feet (tan 63°)
height ≃ 27.48 feet

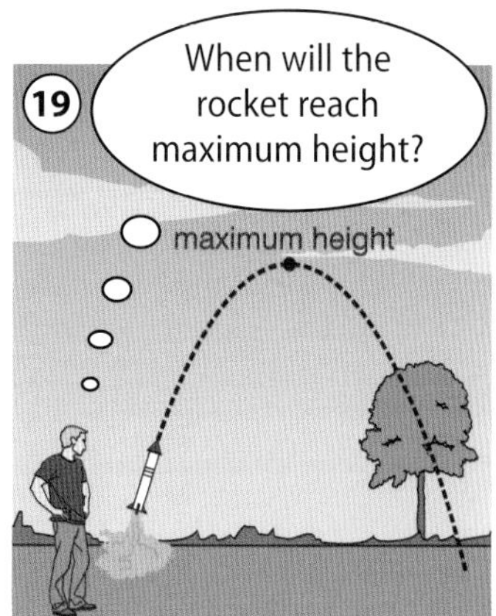

$s(t) = -\frac{1}{2} gt^2 + V_0 t + h$
$s^{I}(t) = -gt + V_0 = 0$
$t = V_0 / g$

16. algebra
    代数
17. geometry
    幾何
18. trigonometry
    三角関数
19. calculus
    微積分

Lines 線

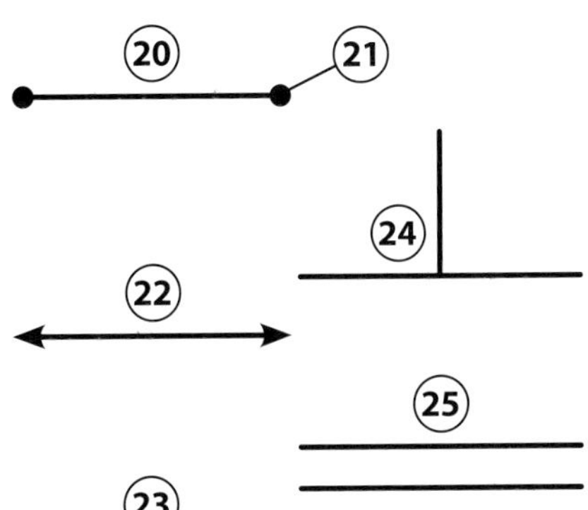

Angles 角度

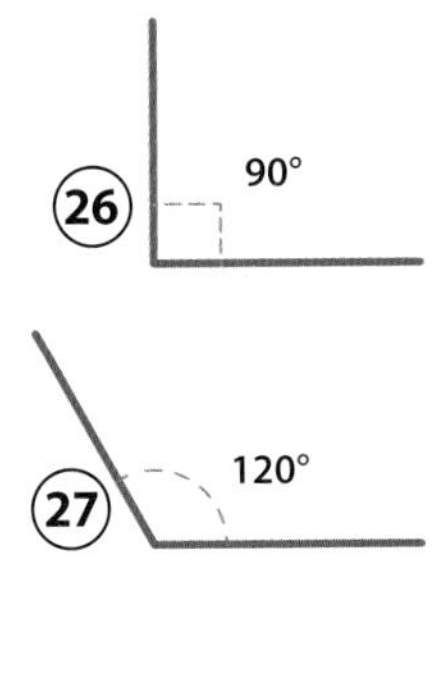

Shapes 図形

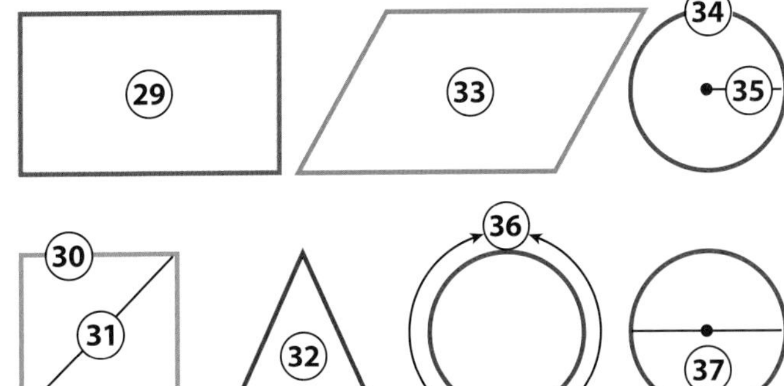

20. line segment
線分

21. endpoint
終点

22. straight line
直線

23. curved line
曲線

24. perpendicular lines
垂線

25. parallel lines
平行線

26. right angle / 90° angle
直角／90°

27. obtuse angle
鈍角

28. acute angle
鋭角

29. rectangle
長方形

30. square
正方形

31. diagonal
対角線

32. triangle
三角形

33. parallelogram
平行四辺形

34. circle
円

35. radius
半径

36. circumference
円周

37. diameter
直径

Geometric Solids 立体

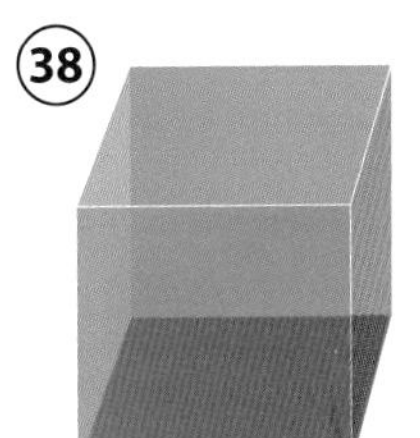

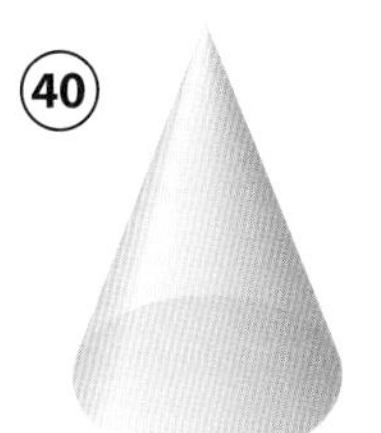

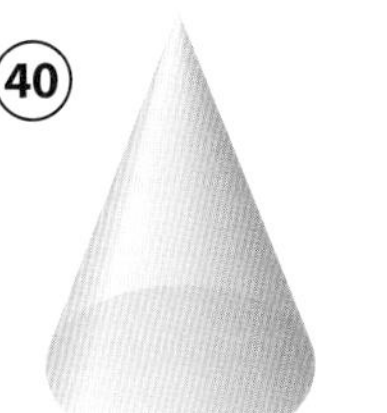

38. cube
立方体

39. pyramid
角錐

40. cone
円錐

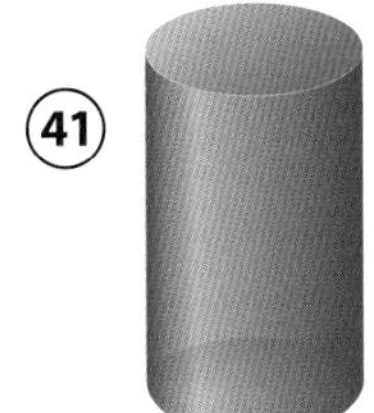

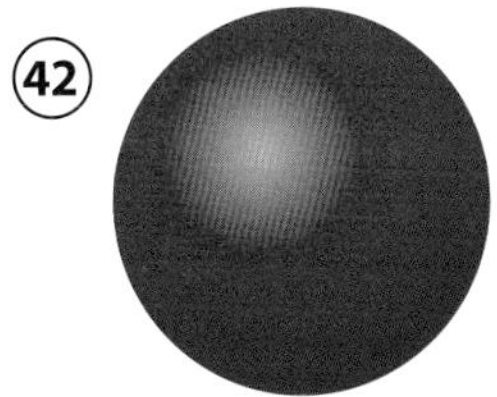

41. cylinder
円柱

42. sphere
球体

Measuring Area and Volume 面積と体積

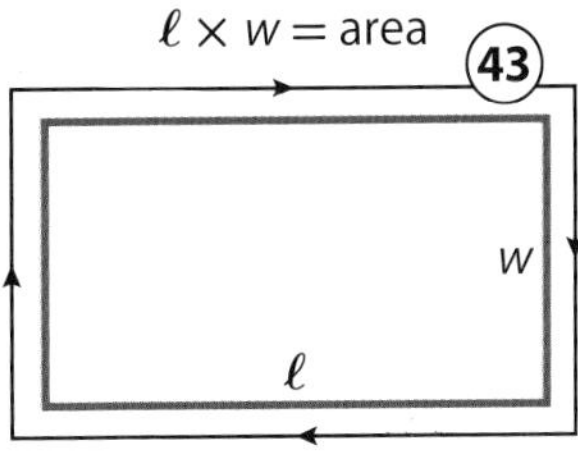

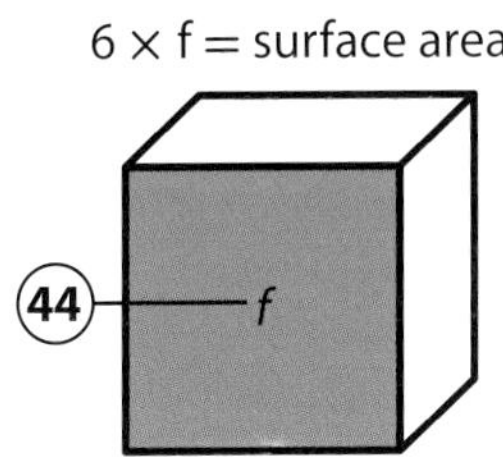

43. perimeter
外周

44. face
表面

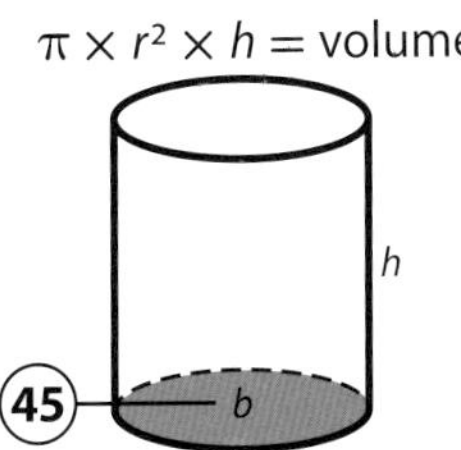

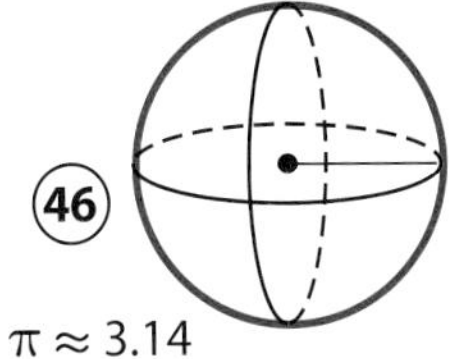

45. base
底面

46. pi
円周率

Ask your classmates. Share the answers.

1. Are you good at math?
2. Which types of math are easy for you?
3. Which types of math are difficult for you?

Think about it. Discuss.

1. What's the best way to learn mathematics?
2. How can you find the area of your classroom?
3. Which jobs use math? Which don't?

Biology 生物学

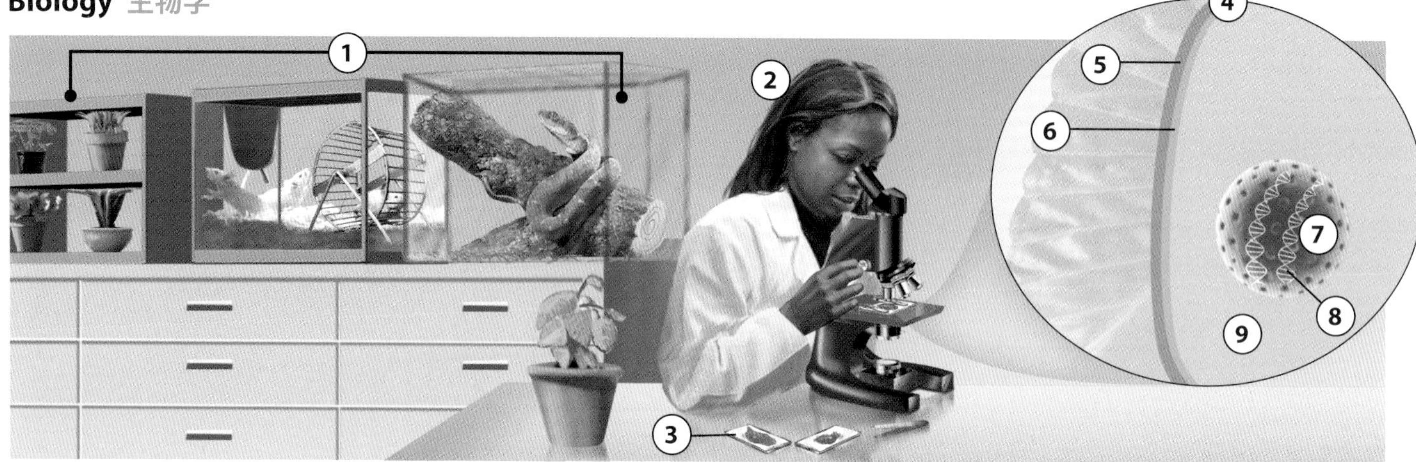

1. organisms 生物
2. biologist 生物学者
3. slide スライドグラス
4. cell 細胞
5. cell wall 細胞壁
6. cell membrane 細胞膜
7. nucleus 核
8. chromosome 染色体
9. cytoplasm 細胞質

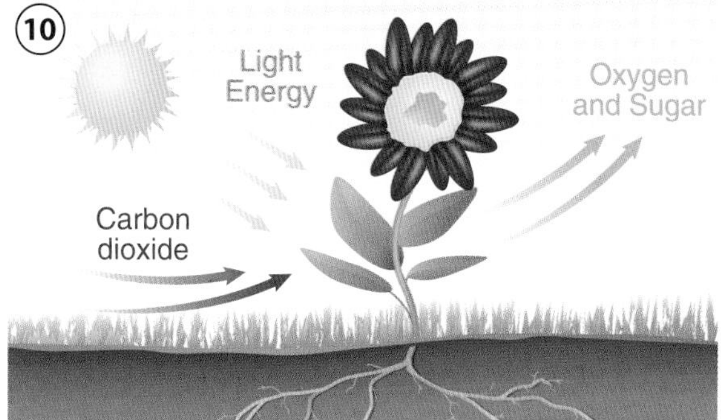

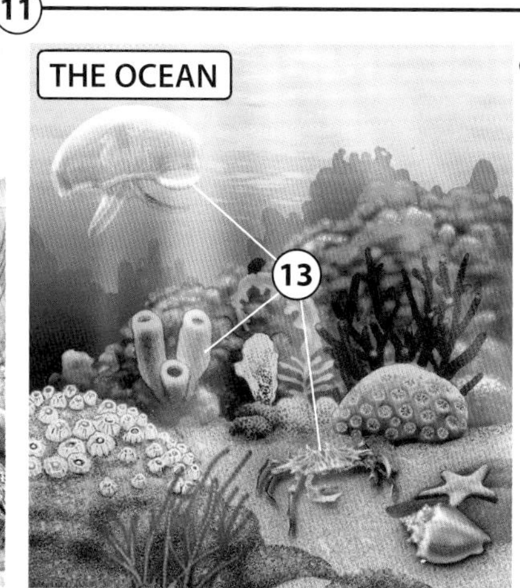

10. photosynthesis 光合成
11. habitat 棲息地
12. vertebrates 脊椎動物
13. invertebrates 無脊椎動物

A Microscope 顕微鏡

14. eyepiece 接眼レンズ
15. revolving nosepiece リボルバー式対物レンズ
16. objective 対物レンズ
17. stage 試料台
18. diaphragm 絞り
19. light source 光源
20. base 基部
21. stage clips 試料台クリップ
22. fine adjustment knob 微調整用ノブ
23. arm アーム
24. coarse adjustment knob 粗調整用ノブ

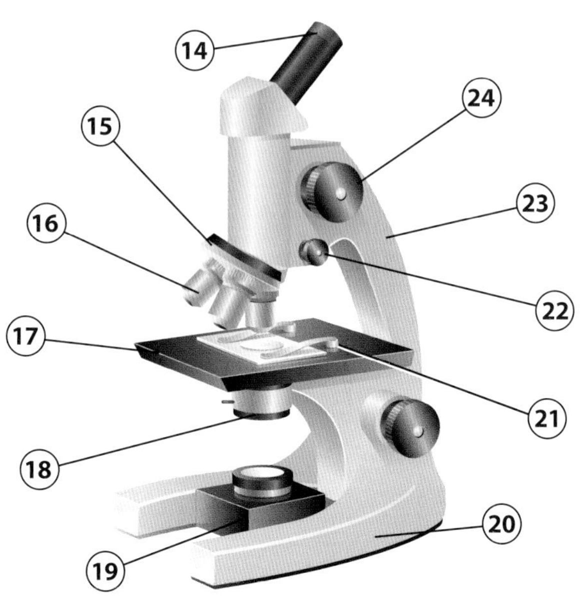

Chemistry 化学

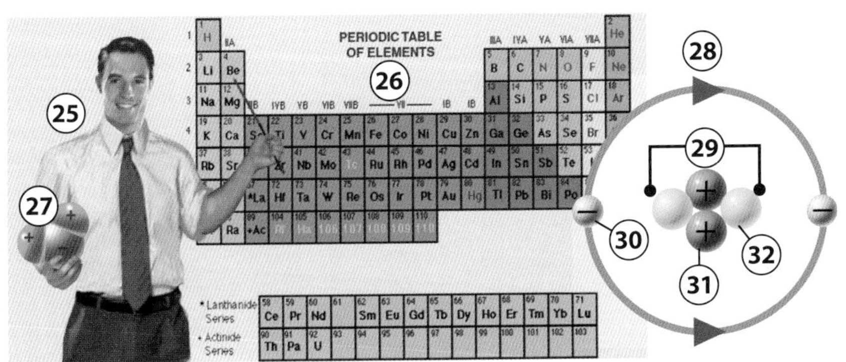

Physics 物理

25. chemist
化学者
26. periodic table
周期表
27. molecule
分子
28. atom
原子
29. nucleus
核
30. electron
電子
31. proton
陽子
32. neutron
中性子
33. physicist
物理学者
34. formula
式
35. prism
プリズム
36. magnet
磁石

A Science Lab 実験室

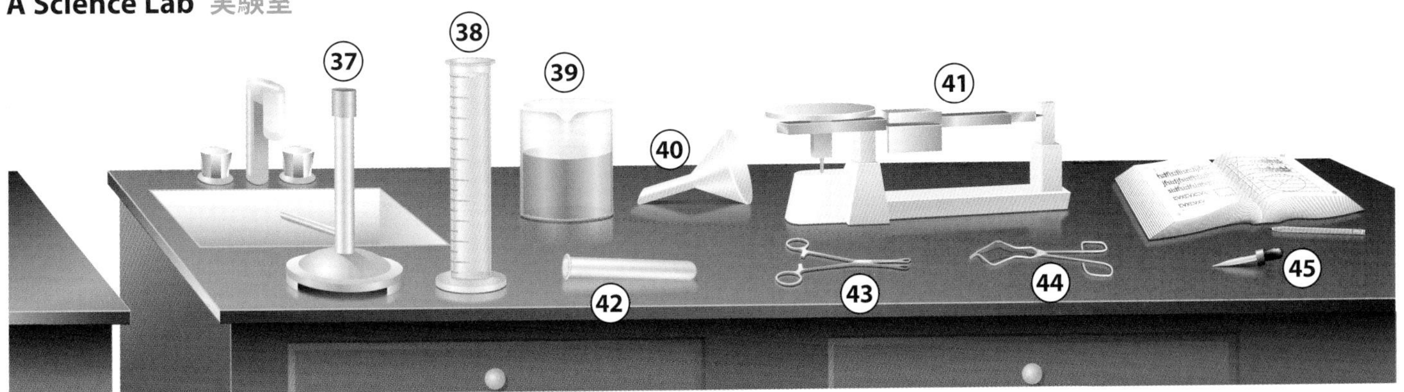

37. Bunsen burner
ブンゼンバーナー
38. graduated cylinder
メスシリンダー
39. beaker
ビーカー
40. funnel
ろうと
41. balance / scale
天秤／はかり
42. test tube
試験管
43. forceps
かんし／ピンセット
44. crucible tongs
るつぼばさみ
45. dropper
スポイト

An Experiment 実験

A. **State** a hypothesis.
仮説を**立てる**

B. **Do** an experiment.
実験を**行う**

C. **Observe.**
観察する

D. **Record** the results.
結果を**記録する**

E. **Draw** a conclusion.
結論を**導き出す**

Computers コンピュータ

Desktop Computer デスクトップコンピュータ

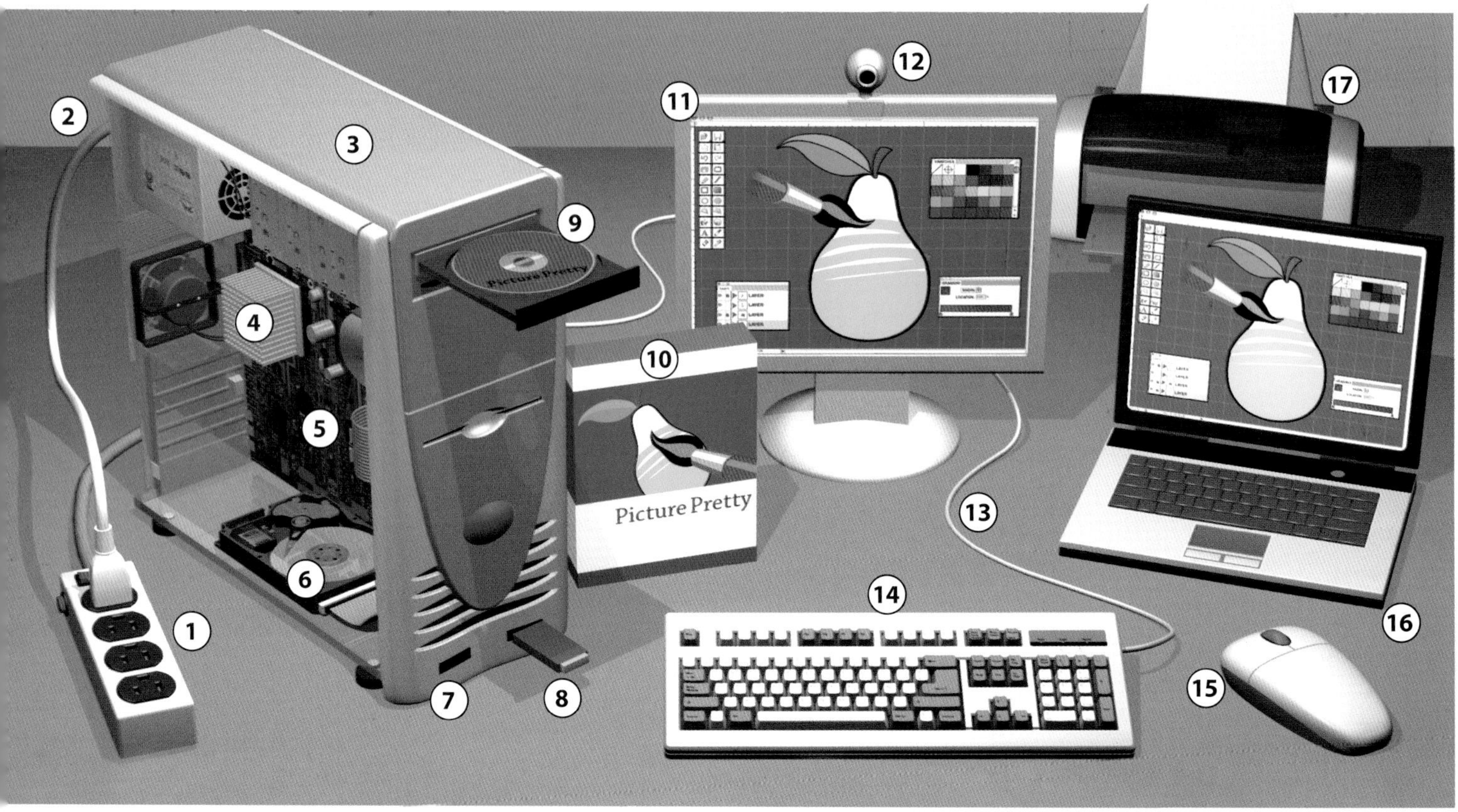

1. surge protector
サージプロテクタ
2. power cord
電源コード
3. tower
タワー
4. microprocessor / CPU
マイクロプロセッサ／CPU
5. motherboard
マザーボード
6. hard drive
ハードドライブ
7. USB port
USBポート
8. flash drive
フラッシュドライブ
9. DVD and CD-ROM drive
DVD と CD-Rom ドライブ
10. software
ソフトウェア
11. monitor /screen
モニタ／画面
12. webcam
ウェブカメラ
13. cable
ケーブル
14. keyboard
キーボード
15. mouse
マウス
16. laptop
ノートブックパソコン
17. printer
プリンタ

Keyboarding キーボードを使う

A. **type**
タイプする

B. **select**
選択する

C. **delete**
削除する

D. **go to** the next line
次の行に進む

Navigating a Webpage ウェブページ内を移動する

1. menu bar
   メニューバー
2. back button
   前に戻るボタン
3. forward button
   次に進むボタン
4. URL / website address
   URL ／ウェブサイトアドレス
5. search box
   検索ボックス
6. search engine
   サーチエンジン
7. tab
   タブ
8. drop-down menu
   ドロップダウンメニュー
9. pop-up ad
   ポップアップ広告
10. links
    リンク
11. video player
    ビデオプレーヤー
12. pointer
    ポインタ
13. text box
    テキストボックス
14. cursor
    カーソル
15. scroll bar
    スクロールバー

Logging on and Sending Email ログオンしてメールを送信する

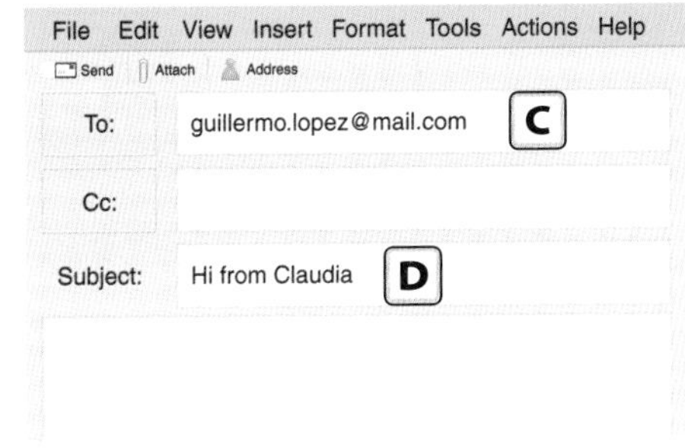

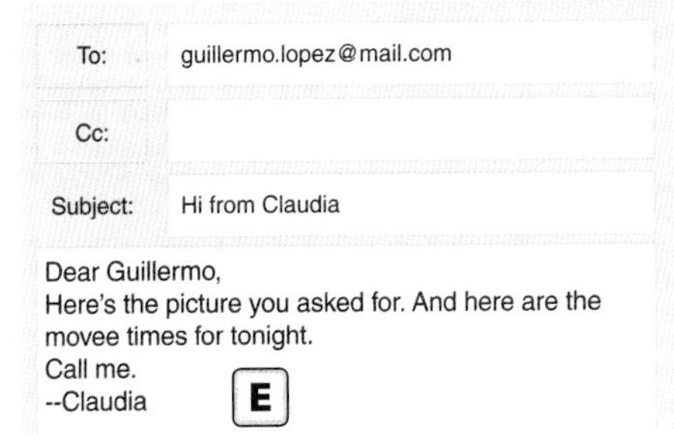

A. **type** your password
   パスワードを**タイプする**

B. **click** "sign in"
   「サインイン」を**クリックする**

C. **address** the email
   宛先の**メールアドレスをタイプする**

D. **type** the subject
   件名を**タイプする**

E. **type** the message
   メッセージを**タイプする**

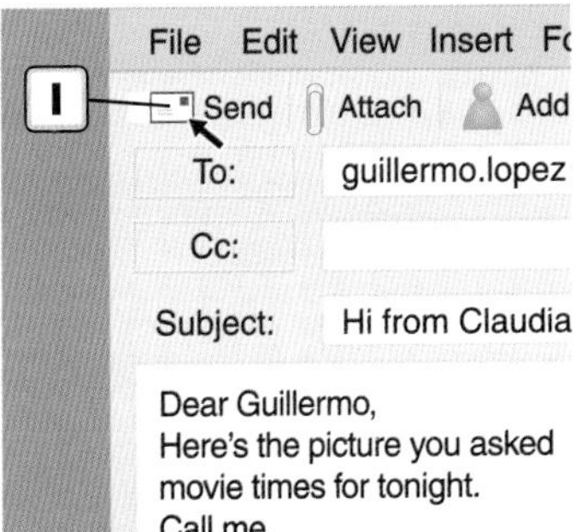

F. **check** your spelling
   スペルを**チェックする**

G. **attach** a picture
   写真を**添付する**

H. **attach** a file
   ファイルを**添付する**

I. **send** the email
   メールを**送信する**

U.S. History

アメリカ史

Colonial Period 植民地時代

1. thirteen colonies
   13の植民地
2. colonists
   入植者
3. Native Americans
   アメリカ先住民
4. slave
   奴隷
5. Declaration of Independence
   独立宣言
6. First Continental Congress
   第一次大陸会議
7. founders
   創設者
8. Revolutionary War
   独立戦争
9. redcoat
   英国兵士
10. minuteman
    民兵
11. first president
    最初の大統領
12. Constitution
    憲法
13. Bill of Rights
    権利章典

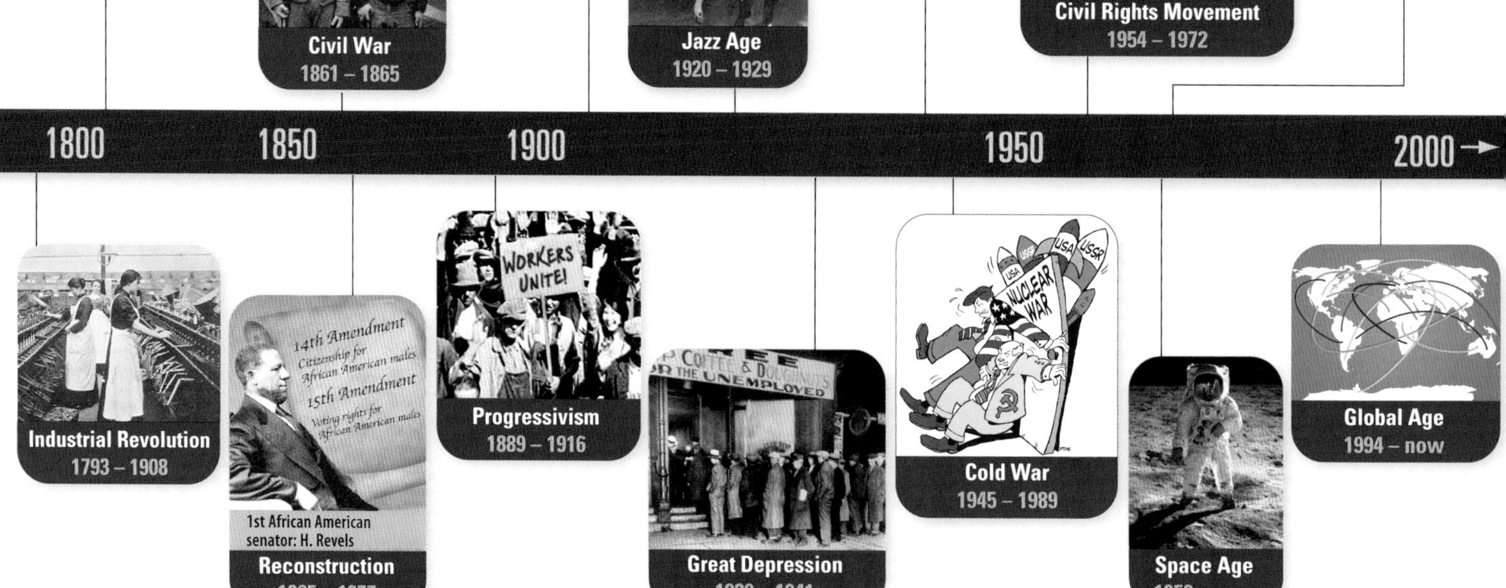

Civilizations 文明

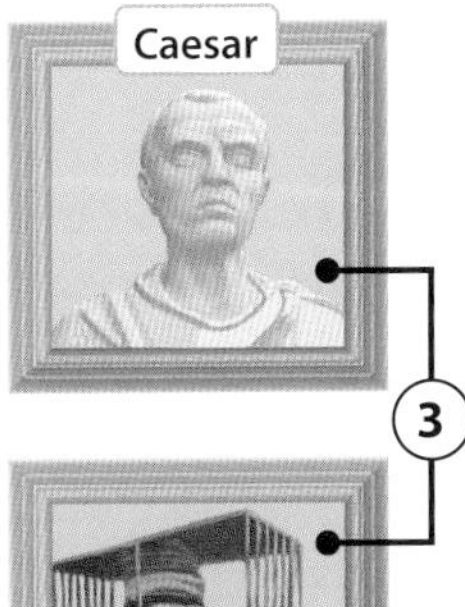

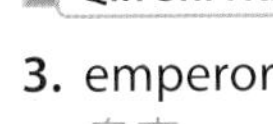

1. ancient
   古代
2. modern
   現代
3. emperor
   皇帝
4. monarch
   君主
5. president
   大統領
6. dictator
   独裁者
7. prime minister
   首相

Historical Terms 歴史用語

8. exploration
   探検
9. explorer
   探検家
10. war
    戦争
11. army
    軍隊
12. immigration
    移住
13. immigrant
    移民

14. composer
    作曲者
15. composition
    作曲
16. political movement
    政治運動
17. activist
    活動家
18. inventor
    発明家
19. invention
    発明

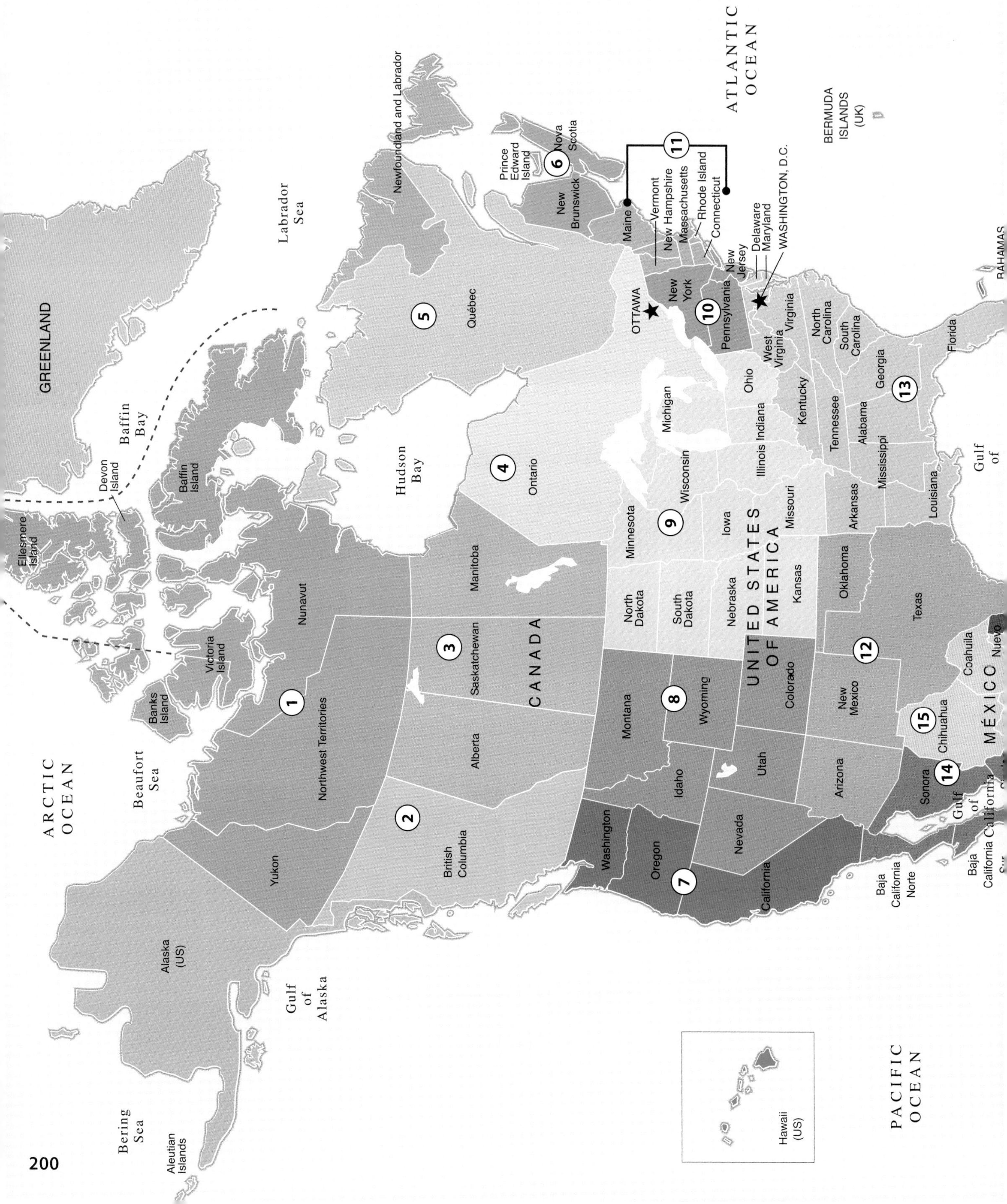

North America and Central America

北アメリカと中央アメリカ

ARCTIC OCEAN
Beaufort Sea
Bering Sea
Aleutian Islands
Gulf of Alaska
Alaska (US)
Yukon
Northwest Territories
1
Banks Island
Victoria Island
Nunavut
Ellesmere Island
Devon Island
Baffin Island
Baffin Bay
GREENLAND
Labrador Sea
British Columbia
2
Alberta
Saskatchewan
3
Manitoba
CANADA
Hudson Bay
Ontario
4
Québec
5
Newfoundland and Labrador
New Brunswick
Prince Edward Island
6
Nova Scotia
OTTAWA
ATLANTIC OCEAN
BERMUDA ISLANDS (UK)
BAHAMAS
Washington
Oregon
California
7
Nevada
Idaho
Montana
Wyoming
8
Utah
Colorado
Arizona
New Mexico
North Dakota
South Dakota
Nebraska
Kansas
Minnesota
Iowa
Wisconsin
9
Michigan
Illinois
Indiana
Ohio
Missouri
UNITED STATES OF AMERICA
New York
Pennsylvania
10
Maine
Vermont
New Hampshire
Massachusetts
Rhode Island
Connecticut
11
New Jersey
Delaware
Maryland
WASHINGTON, D.C.
West Virginia
Virginia
North Carolina
South Carolina
Kentucky
Tennessee
Georgia
Alabama
Mississippi
13
Florida
Arkansas
Louisiana
Oklahoma
Texas
12
Gulf of
Hawaii (US)
PACIFIC OCEAN
Baja California Norte
Baja California Sur
Gulf of California
Sonora
14
Chihuahua
15
Coahuila
Nuevo
MÉXICO

Regions of Canada
カナダの各地方

1. Northern Canada
   カナダ北部
2. British Columbia
   ブリティッシュコロンビア
3. The Prairie Provinces
   プレーリー諸州
4. Ontario
   オンタリオ
5. Québec
   ケベック
6. The Maritime Provinces
   沿海州

Regions of the United States
アメリカ合衆国の各地方

7. The Pacific States / the West Coast
   太平洋岸諸州／西海岸
8. The Rocky Mountain States
   ロッキー山脈諸州
9. The Midwest
   中西部
10. The Mid-Atlantic States
    中部大西洋岸諸州
11. New England
    ニューイングランド地方
12. The Southwest
    南西部
13. The Southeast / the South
    南東部／南部

Regions of Mexico
メキシコの各地方

14. The Pacific Northwest
    太平洋岸北西部
15. The Plateau of Mexico
    メキシコ高原
16. The Gulf Coastal Plain
    湾岸平野
17. The Southern Uplands
    南部台地
18. The Chiapas Highlands
    チアパス高地
19. The Yucatan Peninsula
    ユカタン半島

World Map

世界地図

Continents
大陸

1. North America
   北アメリカ
2. South America
   南アメリカ
3. Europe
   ヨーロッパ
4. Asia
   アジア
5. Africa
   アフリカ
6. Australia
   オーストラリア
7. Antarctica
   南極

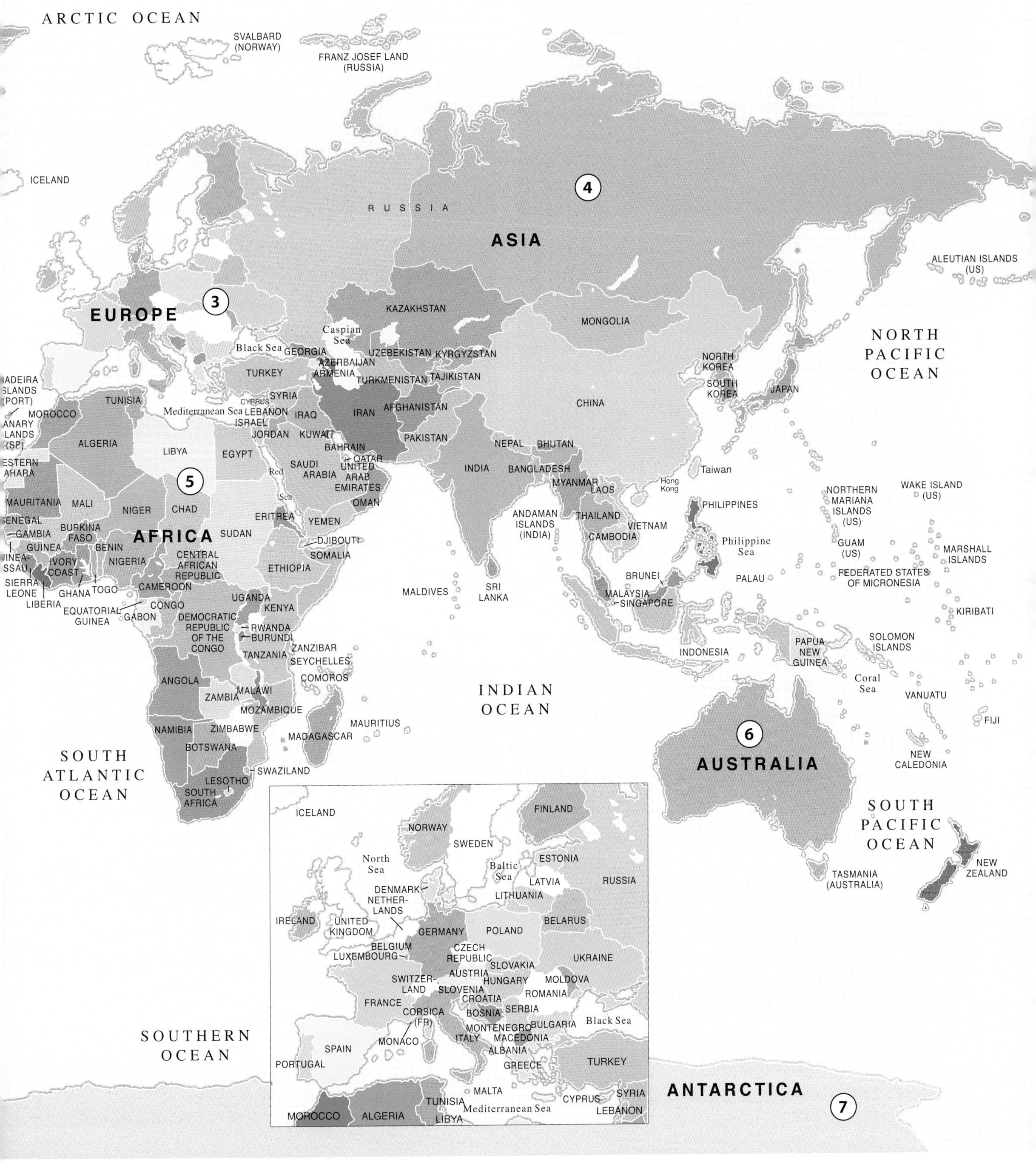

ARCTIC OCEAN
SVALBARD (NORWAY)
FRANZ JOSEF LAND (RUSSIA)
ICELAND
RUSSIA
4
ASIA
ALEUTIAN ISLANDS (US)
3
EUROPE
KAZAKHSTAN
MONGOLIA
Caspian Sea
Black Sea
GEORGIA
UZBEKISTAN
KYRGYZSTAN
AZERBAIJAN
ARMENIA
TURKMENISTAN
TAJIKISTAN
TURKEY
NORTH PACIFIC OCEAN
NORTH KOREA
SOUTH KOREA
JAPAN
CHINA
CYPRUS
SYRIA
TUNISIA
MOROCCO
Mediterranean Sea
LEBANON
ISRAEL
IRAQ
IRAN
AFGHANISTAN
JORDAN
KUWAIT
BAHRAIN
QATAR
PAKISTAN
NEPAL
BHUTAN
ALGERIA
LIBYA
EGYPT
SAUDI ARABIA
UNITED ARAB EMIRATES
Red Sea
INDIA
BANGLADESH
Taiwan
Hong Kong
5
MYANMAR
LAOS
MAURITANIA
MALI
NIGER
CHAD
ERITREA
YEMEN
OMAN
ANDAMAN ISLANDS (INDIA)
THAILAND
VIETNAM
CAMBODIA
PHILIPPINES
NORTHERN MARIANA ISLANDS (US)
WAKE ISLAND (US)
GAMBIA
BURKINA FASO
AFRICA
SUDAN
DJIBOUTI
SOMALIA
Philippine Sea
GUAM (US)
MARSHALL ISLANDS
GUINEA
BENIN
NIGERIA
CENTRAL AFRICAN REPUBLIC
ETHIOPIA
IVORY COAST
SIERRA LEONE
LIBERIA
GHANA
TOGO
CAMEROON
BRUNEI
PALAU
FEDERATED STATES OF MICRONESIA
MALDIVES
SRI LANKA
MALAYSIA
SINGAPORE
EQUATORIAL GUINEA
GABON
CONGO
UGANDA
KENYA
KIRIBATI
DEMOCRATIC REPUBLIC OF THE CONGO
RWANDA
BURUNDI
TANZANIA
ZANZIBAR
SEYCHELLES
INDONESIA
PAPUA NEW GUINEA
SOLOMON ISLANDS
COMOROS
ANGOLA
ZAMBIA
MALAWI
MOZAMBIQUE
INDIAN OCEAN
Coral Sea
VANUATU
NAMIBIA
ZIMBABWE
MAURITIUS
MADAGASCAR
FIJI
BOTSWANA
6
SOUTH ATLANTIC OCEAN
SWAZILAND
AUSTRALIA
NEW CALEDONIA
LESOTHO
SOUTH AFRICA
SOUTH PACIFIC OCEAN
ICELAND
FINLAND
NORWAY
SWEDEN
North Sea
Baltic Sea
ESTONIA
RUSSIA
LATVIA
DENMARK
NETHERLANDS
LITHUANIA
TASMANIA (AUSTRALIA)
NEW ZEALAND
IRELAND
UNITED KINGDOM
BELARUS
GERMANY
POLAND
BELGIUM
LUXEMBOURG
CZECH REPUBLIC
SLOVAKIA
UKRAINE
AUSTRIA
SWITZERLAND
SLOVENIA
HUNGARY
MOLDOVA
CROATIA
ROMANIA
FRANCE
CORSICA (FR)
BOSNIA
SERBIA
MONTENEGRO
BULGARIA
Black Sea
SOUTHERN OCEAN
MONACO
ITALY
MACEDONIA
SPAIN
ALBANIA
PORTUGAL
GREECE
TURKEY
MALTA
ANTARCTICA
CYPRUS
SYRIA
TUNISIA
Mediterranean Sea
LEBANON
7
MOROCCO
ALGERIA
LIBYA

Geography and Habitats

地理と棲息地

1. rain forest 雨林
2. waterfall 滝
3. river 川
4. desert 砂漠
5. sand dune 砂丘
6. ocean 大洋
7. peninsula 半島
8. island 島
9. bay 湾
10. beach 海岸
11. forest 森林
12. shore 岸
13. lake 湖
14. mountain peak 山頂
15. mountain range 山脈
16. hills 丘
17. canyon 峡谷
18. valley 谷間
19. plains 平原
20. meadow 草原
21. pond 池

More vocabulary

a body of water: a river, lake, or ocean
stream / creek: a very small river

Ask your classmates. Share the answers.

1. Would you rather live near a river or a lake?
2. Would you rather travel through a forest or a desert?
3. How often do you go to the beach or the shore?

The Solar System and the Planets 太陽系と惑星

1. Mercury 水星
2. Venus 金星
3. Earth 地球
4. Mars 火星
5. Jupiter 木星
6. Saturn 土星
7. Uranus 天王星
8. Neptune 海王星

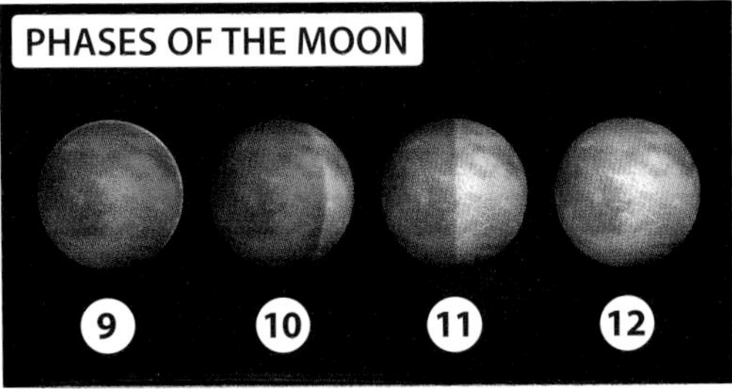

SPACE

9. new moon 新月
10. crescent moon 三日月
11. quarter moon 上弦（下弦）の月
12. full moon 満月
13. star 星
14. constellation 星座
15. galaxy 銀河系
16. solar eclipse 日食

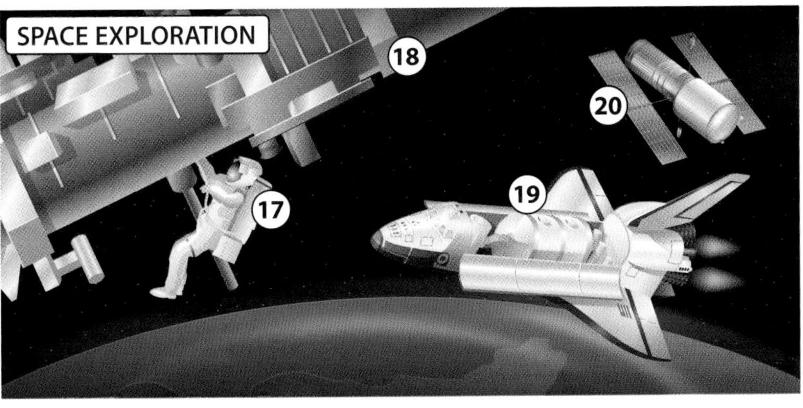

ASTRONOMY

17. astronaut 宇宙飛行士
18. space station 宇宙ステーション
19. space shuttle スペースシャトル
20. satellite 衛星
21. observatory 天文台
22. astronomer 天文学者
23. telescope 望遠鏡
24. comet 彗星

More vocabulary

solar eclipse: when the moon is between the earth and the sun
Big Dipper: a famous part of the constellation Ursa Major
Sirius: the brightest star in the night sky

Ask your classmates. Share the answers.

1. How do you feel when you look at the night sky?
2. Can you name one or more constellations?
3. Do you want to travel in space?

A Graduation 卒業

MySpot.Edu | Help | SignOut

Home | Search | Invite | Mail |

All Adelia's photos

I loved Art History.

My last economics lesson

Marching Band is great!

The photographer was upset.

We look good!

I get my diploma.

Dad and his digital camera

1. photographer 写真家
2. funny photo 面白い写真
3. serious photo まじめな写真
4. guest speaker 来賓講演者
5. podium 演台
6. ceremony 卒業式
7. cap 帽子
8. gown ガウン

A. **take** a picture 写真を撮る
B. **cry** 泣く
C. **celebrate** 祝う

MySpot en Espanol | International

Videos | Music | Classifieds |

People	Comments	
Sara	June 29th 8:19 p.m. Great pictures! What a day!	Delete
Zannie baby	June 30th 10 a.m. Love the funny photo.	Delete

I'm behind the mayor.

We're all very happy.

Look at the pictures. What do you see?

Answer the questions.

1. How many people are wearing caps and gowns?
2. How many people are being funny? How many are being serious?
3. Who is standing at the podium?
4. Why are the graduates throwing their caps in the air?

 **Read the story.**

A Graduation

Look at these great photos on my web page! The first three are from my favorite classes, but the other pictures are from graduation day.

There are two pictures of my classmates in caps and gowns. In the first picture, we're laughing and the photographer is upset. In the second photo, we're serious. I like the serious photo, but I love the funny photo!

There's also a picture of our guest speaker, the mayor. She is standing at the podium. Next, you can see me at the graduation ceremony. My dad wanted to take a picture of me with my diploma. That's my mom next to him. She cries when she's happy.

After the ceremony, everyone was happy, but no one cried. We wanted to celebrate and we did!

Think about it.

1. What kinds of ceremonies are important for children? for teens? for adults?
2. Imagine you are the guest speaker at a graduation. What will you say to the graduates?

Nature Center 自然センター

1. trees
   木
2. soil
   土
3. path
   小道
4. bird
   鳥
5. plants
   植物
6. rock
   岩
7. flowers
   花

Listen and point. Take turns.

A: *Point to the trees.*
B: *Point to a bird.*
A: *Point to the flowers.*

Dictate to your partner. Take turns.

A: *Write it's a tree.*
B: *Let me check that. I-t-'s -a- t-r-e-e?*
A: *Yes, that's right.*

8. sun
太陽
9. sky
空
10. mammals
哺乳類
11. insects
昆虫
12. nest
巣
13. water
水
14. fish
魚

Ways to talk about nature

Look at the sky! Isn't it beautiful?
Did you see the fish / insects?
It's / They're so interesting.

Pair practice. Make new conversations.

A: *Do you know the name of that yellow flower?*
B: *I think it's a sunflower.*
A: *Oh, and what about that blue bird?*

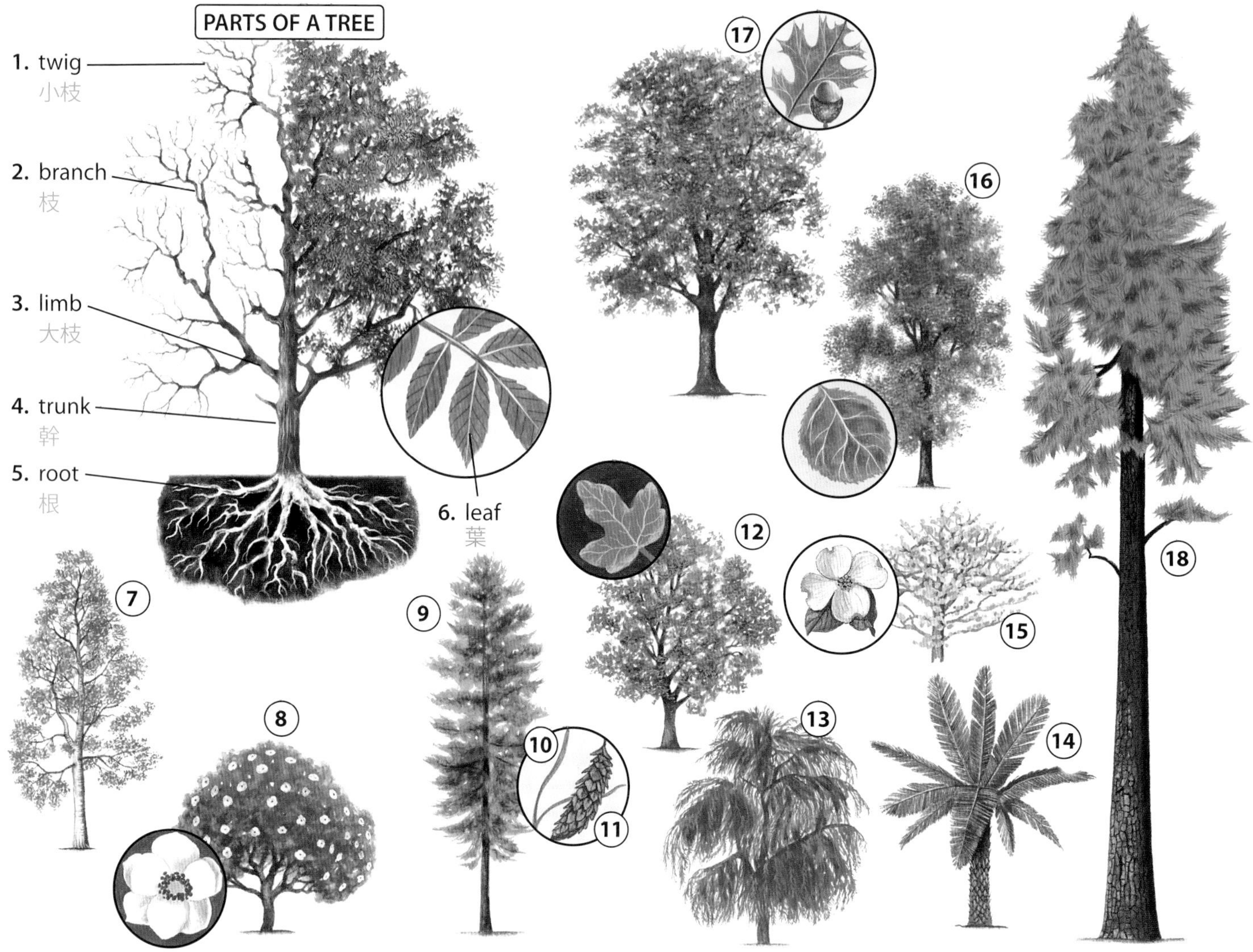

Trees and Plants 木と植物

PARTS OF A TREE

1. twig
小枝
2. branch
枝
3. limb
大枝
4. trunk
幹
5. root
根
6. leaf
葉

7. birch
カバノキ
8. magnolia
タイサンボク
9. pine
マツ
10. needle
針状葉
11. pinecone
松ぼっくり
12. maple
カエデ
13. willow
ヤナギ
14. palm
ヤシ
15. dogwood
ハナミズキ
16. elm
ニレ
17. oak
カシ
18. redwood
アメリカ杉

Plants 植物

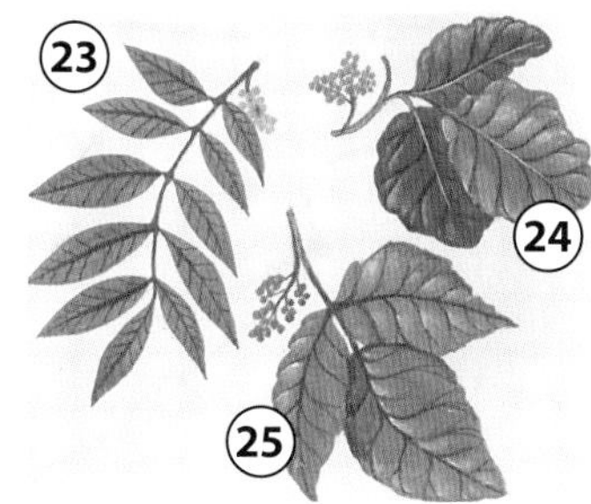

19. holly
ヒイラギ
20. berries
小さな実
21. cactus
サボテン
22. vine
つる植物
23. poison sumac
ドクウルシ
24. poison oak
ウルシ
25. poison ivy
ツタウルシ

Parts of a Flower 花の部分

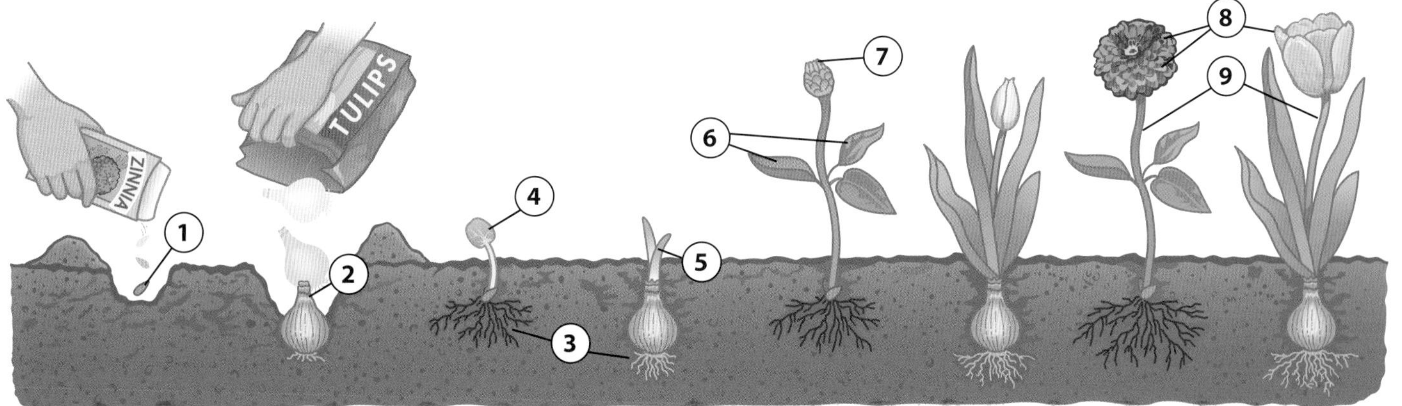

1. seed
種
2. bulb
球根
3. roots
根
4. seedling
種苗
5. shoot
芽
6. leaves
葉
7. bud
つぼみ
8. petals
花びら
9. stems
茎

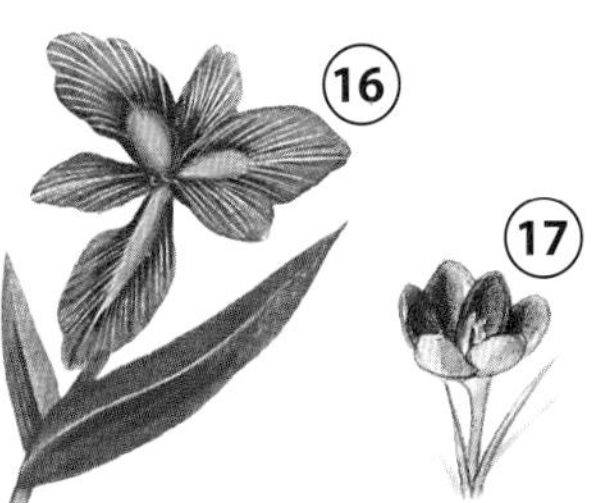

10. sunflower
ヒマワリ
11. tulip
チューリップ
12. hibiscus
ハイビスカス
13. marigold
マリーゴールド
14. daisy
デイジー
15. rose
バラ
16. iris
アイリス
17. crocus
クロッカス
18. gardenia
クチナシ
19. orchid
ラン
20. carnation
カーネーション
21. chrysanthemum
キク
22. jasmine
ジャスミン
23. violet
スミレ
24. poinsettia
ポインセチア
25. daffodil
スイセン
26. lily
ユリ
27. houseplant
室内植物
28. bouquet
花束
29. thorn
とげ

Marine Life, Amphibians, and Reptiles 海洋生物、両生類、爬虫類

Sea Animals 海の生物

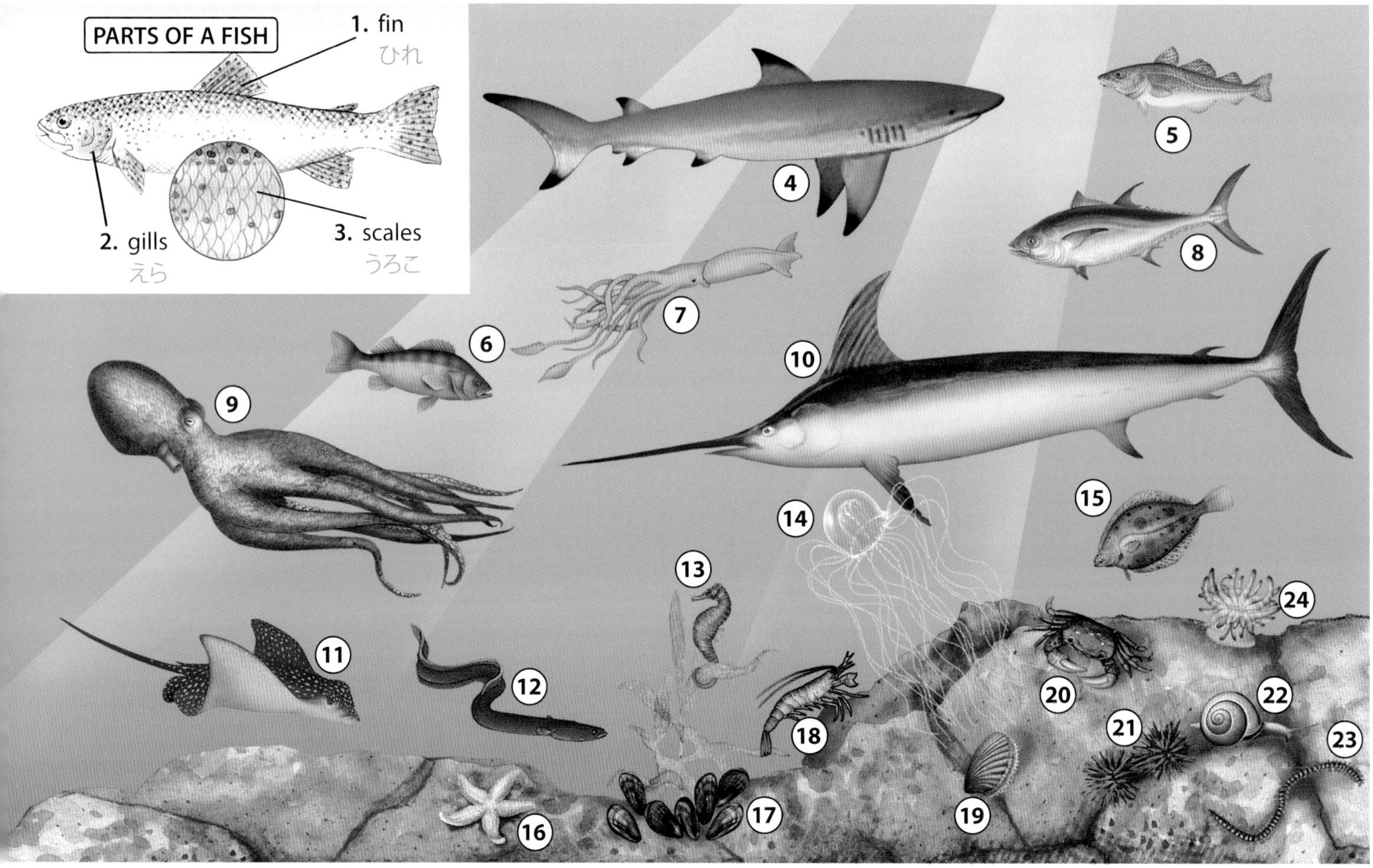

PARTS OF A FISH

1. fin ひれ
2. gills えら
3. scales うろこ

4. shark サメ
5. cod タラ
6. bass スズキ
7. squid イカ
8. tuna マグロ
9. octopus タコ
10. swordfish メカジキ
11. ray エイ
12. eel ウナギ
13. seahorse タツノオトシゴ
14. jellyfish クラゲ
15. flounder ヒラメ／カレイ
16. starfish ヒトデ
17. mussel ムール貝
18. shrimp エビ
19. scallop ホタテ貝
20. crab カニ
21. sea urchin ウニ
22. snail カタツムリ
23. worm ぜん虫
24. sea anemone イソギンチャク

Amphibians 両生類

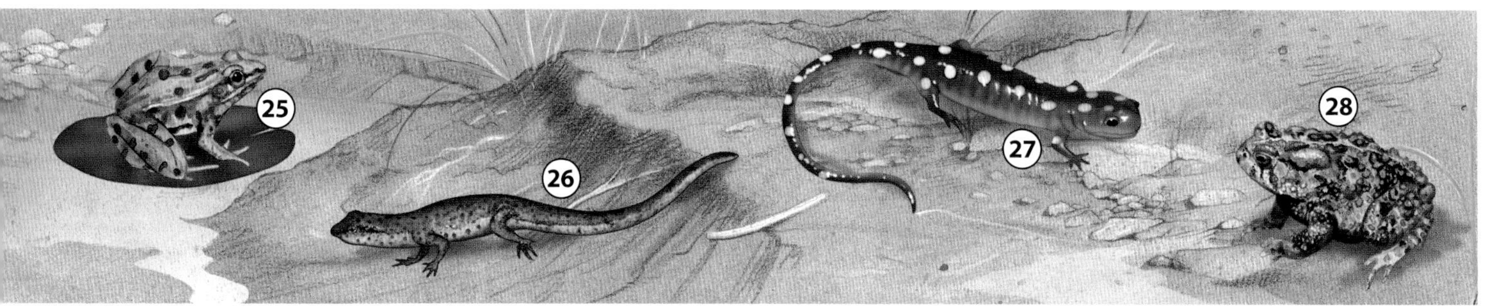

25. frog カエル
26. newt イモリ
27. salamander サンショウウオ
28. toad ヒキガエル

Sea Mammals 海洋哺乳類

29. whale
クジラ
30. porpoise
ネズミイルカ
31. dolphin
イルカ
32. walrus
セイウチ
33. sea lion
アシカ
34. seal
アザラシ
35. sea otter
ラッコ

Reptiles 爬虫類

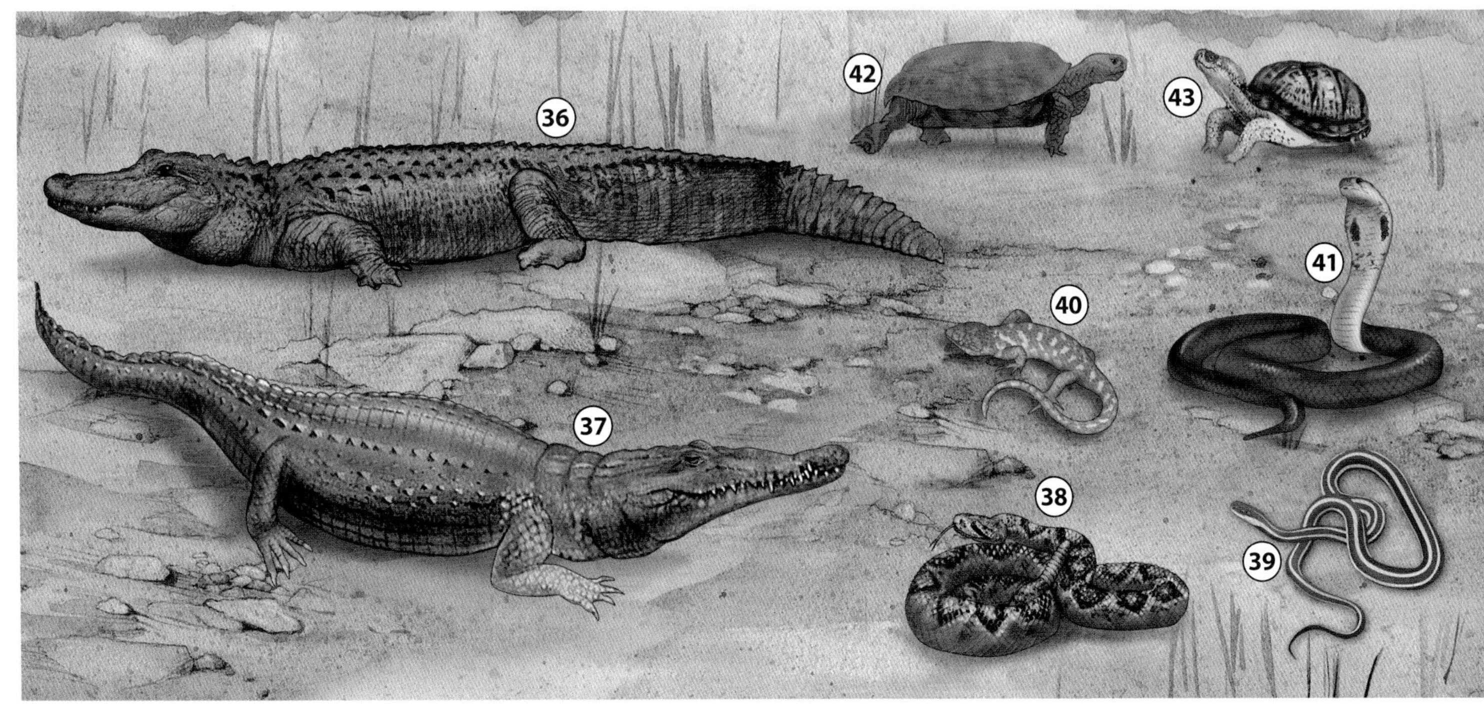

36. alligator
ワニ（アリゲーター）
37. crocodile
ワニ（クロコダイル）
38. rattlesnake
ガラガラヘビ
39. garter snake
ガータースネーク
40. lizard
トカゲ
41. cobra
コブラ
42. tortoise
陸亀
43. turtle
水亀

Birds, Insects, and Arachnids 鳥、昆虫、蜘蛛類

PARTS OF A BIRD

1. wing 翼
2. claw 鉤爪
3. beak / bill くちばし
4. feather 羽

5. owl フクロウ
6. blue jay アオカケス
7. sparrow スズメ
8. woodpecker キツツキ
9. eagle ワシ
10. hummingbird ハチドリ
11. penguin ペンギン
12. duck 鴨
13. goose ガン
14. peacock 孔雀
15. pigeon 鳩
16. robin コマドリ

Insects and Arachnids 昆虫と蜘蛛類

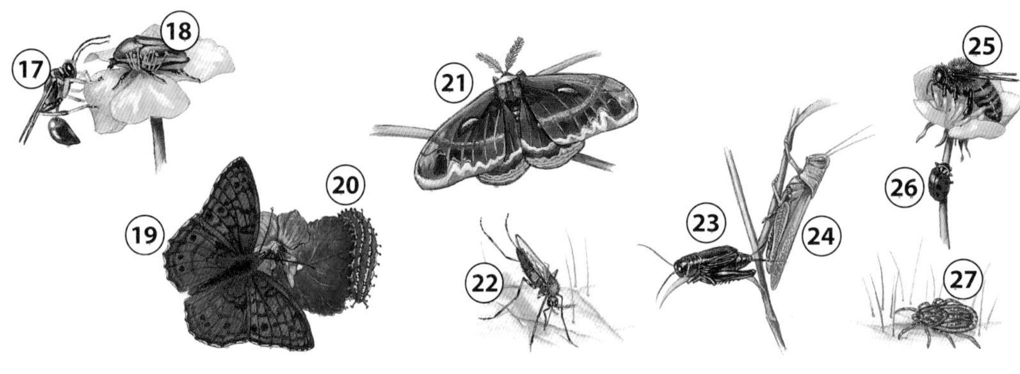

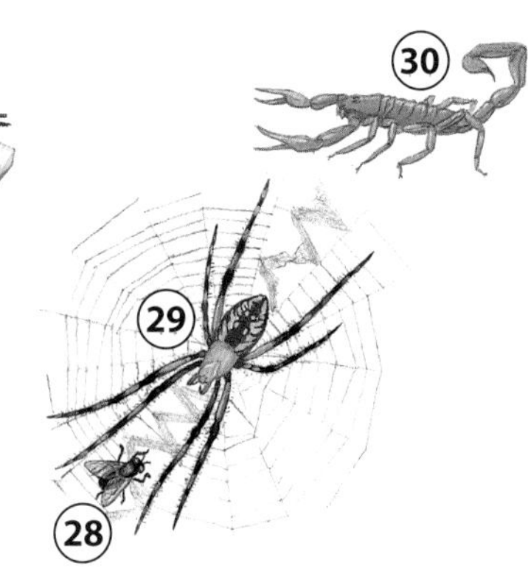

17. wasp スズメバチ
18. beetle カブトムシ
19. butterfly 蝶
20. caterpillar イモムシ
21. moth 蛾
22. mosquito 蚊
23. cricket コオロギ
24. grasshopper バッタ
25. honeybee ミツバチ
26. ladybug テントウムシ
27. tick ダニ
28. fly ハエ
29. spider クモ
30. scorpion サソリ

Domestic Animals and Rodents

Farm Animals 飼育動物

1. cow
牛
2. pig
豚
3. donkey
ロバ
4. horse
馬
5. goat
ヤギ
6. sheep
ヒツジ
7. rooster
雄鶏
8. hen
雌鶏

Pets ペット

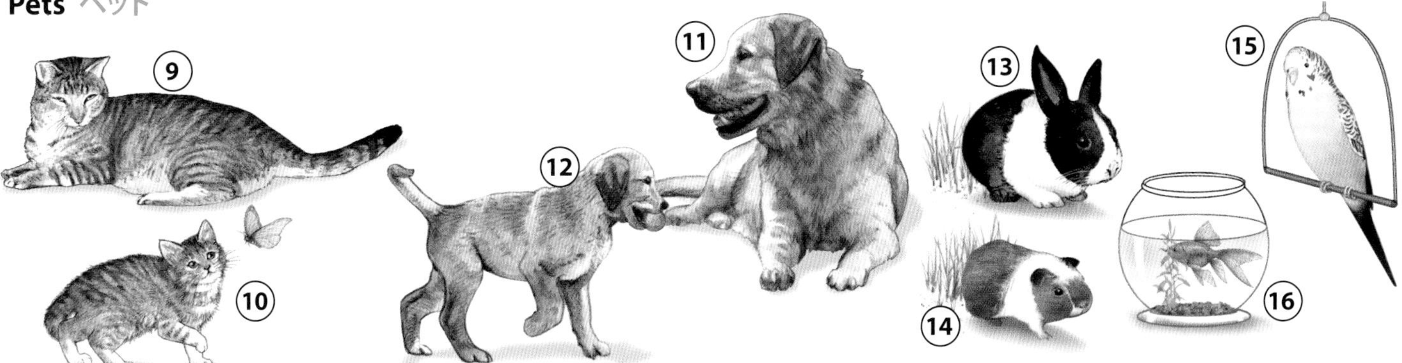

9. cat
猫
10. kitten
子猫
11. dog
犬
12. puppy
仔犬
13. rabbit
ウサギ
14. guinea pig
モルモット
15. parakeet
インコ
16. goldfish
金魚

Rodents げっ歯類

17. rat
ネズミ
18. mouse
ハツカネズミ
19. gopher
ジリス
20. chipmunk
シマリス
21. squirrel
リス
22. prairie dog
プレーリードッグ

More vocabulary

domesticated: animals that work for and / or live with people

wild: animals that live away from people

Ask your classmates. Share the answers.

1. Have you worked with farm animals? Which ones?
2. Are you afraid of rodents? Which ones?
3. Do you have a pet? What kind?

Mammals

哺乳類

1. moose
ヘラジカ
2. mountain lion
ピューマ
3. coyote
コヨーテ
4. opossum
フクロネズミ
5. wolf
オオカミ
6. buffalo / bison
バッファロー
7. bat
コウモリ
8. armadillo
アルマジロ
9. beaver
ビーバー
10. porcupine
ヤマアラシ
11. bear
クマ
12. skunk
スカンク
13. raccoon
アライグマ
14. deer
シカ
15. fox
キツネ

16. antlers
枝角
17. hooves
ひづめ
18. whiskers
ひげ
19. coat / fur
毛皮
20. paw
動物の足
21. horn
角
22. tail
尾
23. quill
（ヤマアラシなどの）針

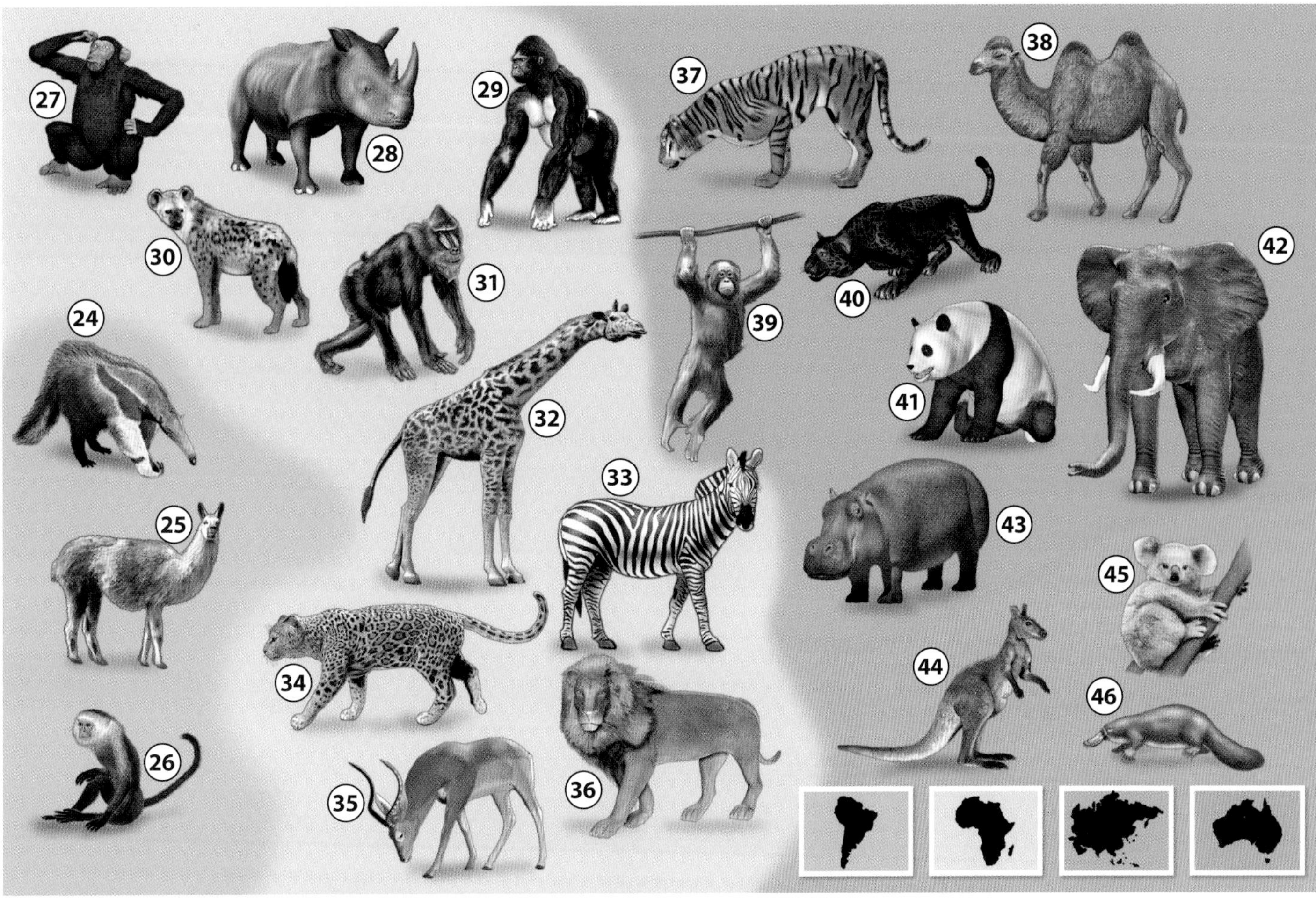

24. anteater
アリクイ
25. llama
ラマ
26. monkey
猿
27. chimpanzee
チンパンジー
28. rhinoceros
サイ
29. gorilla
ゴリラ
30. hyena
ハイエナ
31. baboon
ヒヒ
32. giraffe
キリン
33. zebra
シマウマ
34. leopard
ヒョウ
35. antelope
レイヨウ
36. lion
ライオン
37. tiger
虎
38. camel
ラクダ
39. orangutan
オランウータン
40. panther
パンサー
41. panda
パンダ
42. elephant
象
43. hippopotamus
カバ
44. kangaroo
カンガルー
45. koala
コアラ
46. platypus
カモノハシ

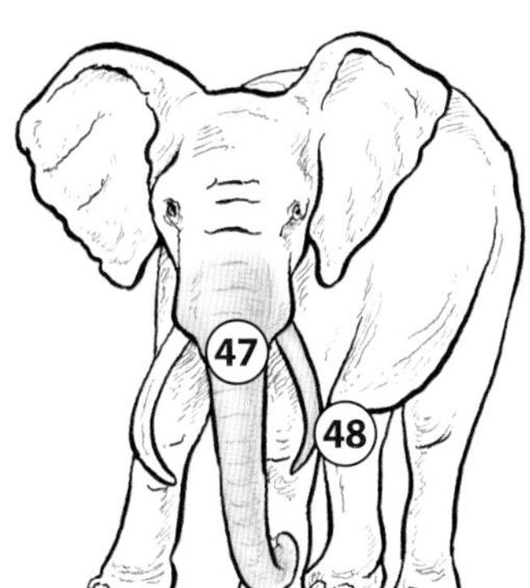

47. trunk
象の鼻
48. tusk
牙
49. mane
たてがみ
50. pouch
カンガルーなどの腹袋
51. hump
ラクダのコブ

Energy and Conservation エネルギーと資源の節約

Energy Sources エネルギー源

1. solar energy
太陽エネルギー

2. wind power
風力

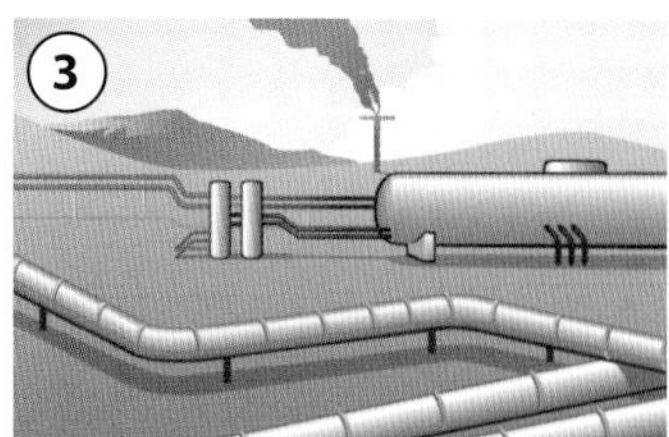

3. natural gas
天然ガス

4. coal
石炭

5. hydroelectric power
水力発電

6. oil / petroleum
石油

7. geothermal energy
地熱エネルギー

8. nuclear energy
原子力エネルギー

9. biomass / bioenergy
バイオマス／バイオエネルギー

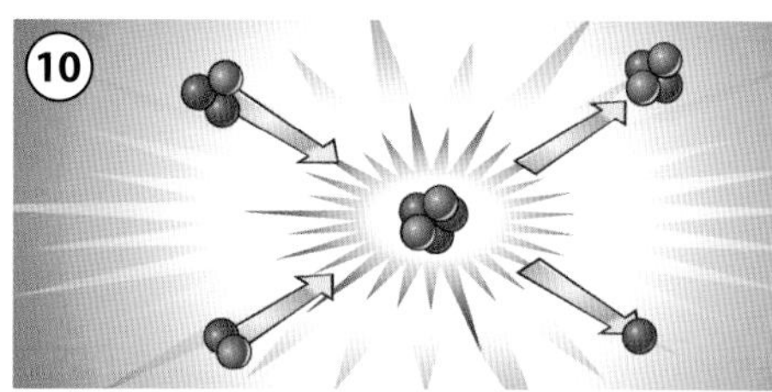

10. fusion
(核) 融合

Pollution 汚染

11. air pollution / smog
大気汚染／スモッグ

12. hazardous waste
危険廃棄物

13. acid rain
酸性雨

14. water pollution
水質汚染

15. radiation
放射線

16. pesticide poisoning
農薬汚染

17. oil spill
重油流出

Ask your classmates. Share the answers.

1. What types of things do you recycle?
2. What types of energy sources are in your area?
3. What types of pollution do you worry about?

Think about it. Discuss.

1. How can you save energy in the summer? winter?
2. What are some other ways that people can conserve energy or prevent pollution?

Ways to Conserve Energy and Resources エネルギーと資源の節約方法

A. **reduce** trash
ごみを減らす

B. **reuse** shopping bags
スーパーの袋を再利用する

C. **recycle**
リサイクルする

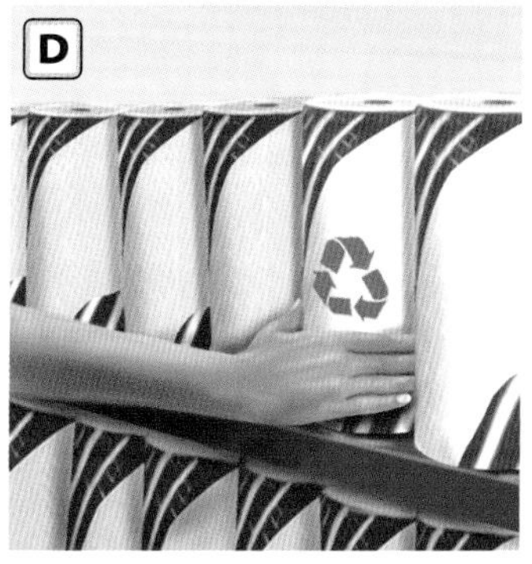

D. **buy** recycled products
リサイクル製品を**購入する**

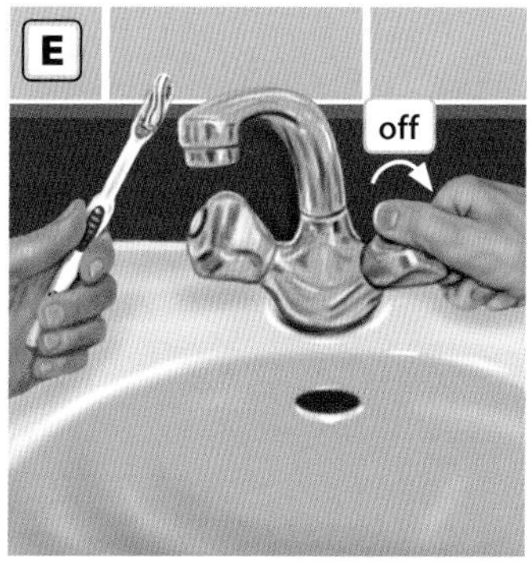

E. **save** water
水を**節約する**

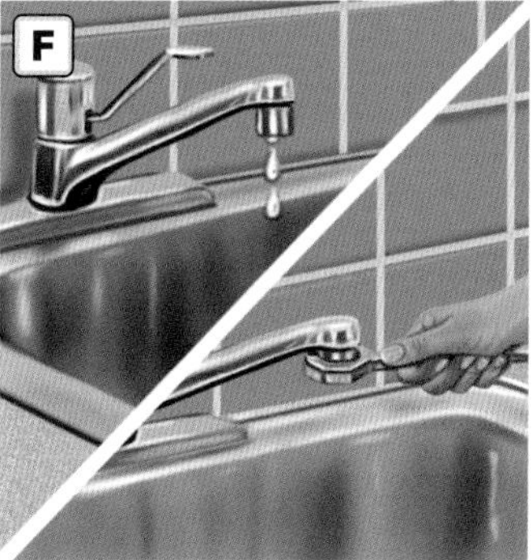

F. **fix** leaky faucets
水漏れする蛇口を**直す**

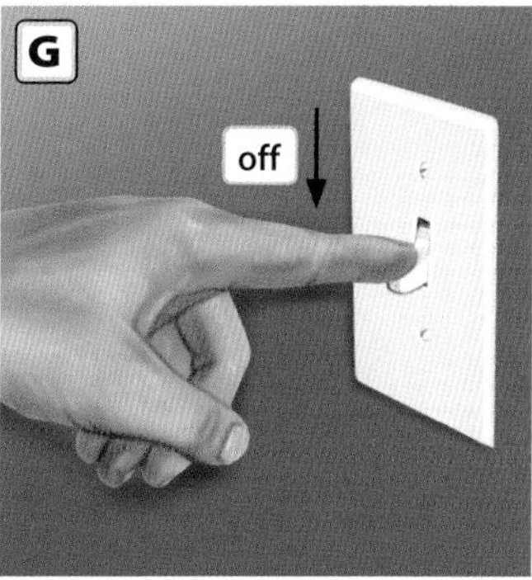

G. **turn off** lights
電気を**消す**

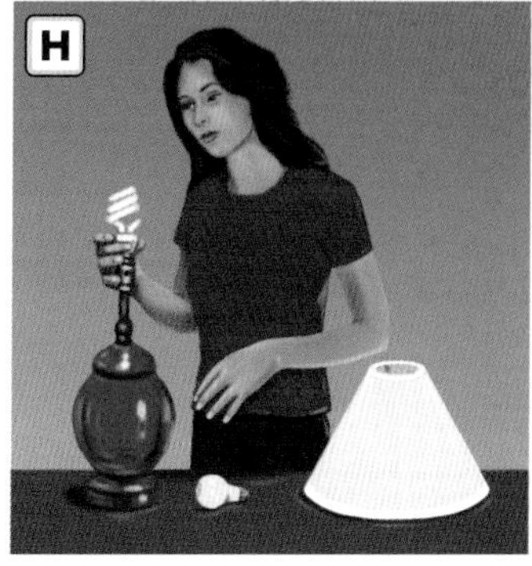

H. **use** energy-efficient bulbs
エネルギー効率の高い電球を**使う**

I. **carpool**
マイカーの相乗りをする

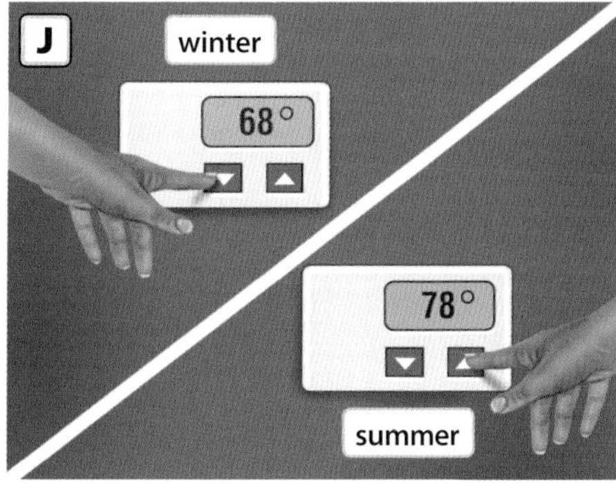

J. **adjust** the thermostat
冷暖房のサーモスタットを**調節する**

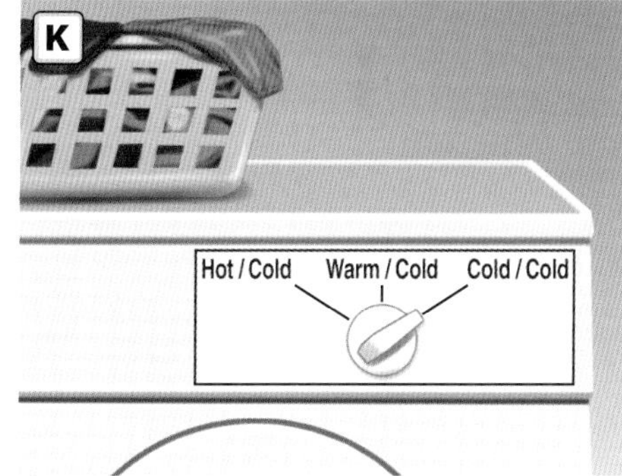

K. **wash** clothes in cold water
冷水で**洗濯する**

L. **don't litter**
ごみを捨てない

M. **compost** food scraps
生ごみを**堆肥にする**

N. **plant** a tree
木を**植える**

Yosemite
NATIONAL PARK

Dry Tortugas
NATIONAL PARK

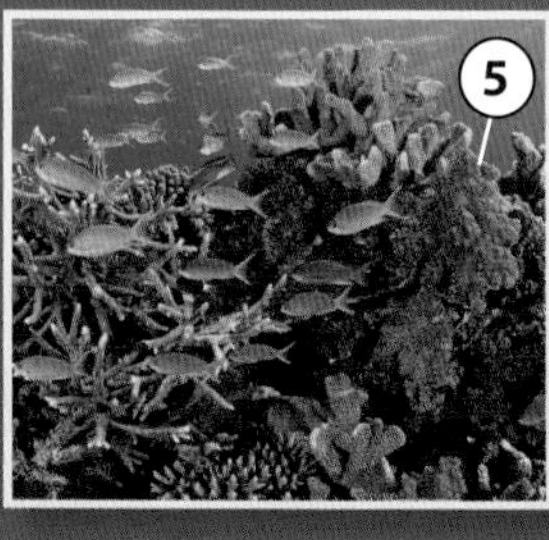

1. landmarks
   名所旧跡
2. park ranger
   パークレンジャー
3. wildlife
   野生生物
4. ferry
   フェリー
5. coral
   サンゴ
6. cave
   洞窟
7. caverns
   大洞窟

A. **take** a tour
   ツアーに参加する

Look at the pictures.
What do you see?

Answer the questions.

1. How many U.S. landmarks are in the pictures?
2. What kinds of wildlife do you see?
3. What can you do at Carlsbad Caverns?

 **Read the story.**

U.S. National Parks

More than 200 million people visit U.S. National Parks every year. These parks protect the wildlife and landmarks of the United States. Each park is different, and each one is beautiful.

At Yosemite, in California, you can take a nature walk with a park ranger. You'll see waterfalls, redwoods, and deer there.

In south Florida, you can take a ferry to Dry Tortugas. It's great to snorkel around the park's coral islands.

There are 113 caves at Carlsbad Caverns in New Mexico. The deepest cave is 830 feet below the desert! You can take a tour of these beautiful caverns.

There are 391 national parks to see. Go online for information about a park near you.

Think about it.

1. Why are national parks important?
2. Imagine you are a park ranger at a national park. Give your classmates a tour of the landmarks and wildlife.

1. zoo
   動物園
2. movies
   映画
3. botanical garden
   植物園
4. bowling alley
   ボウリング場
5. rock concert
   ロックコンサート
6. swap meet / flea market
   のみの市
7. aquarium
   水族館

Places to Go in Our City

Listen and point. Take turns.

A: *Point to the zoo.*
B: *Point to the flea market.*
A: *Point to the rock concert.*

Dictate to your partner. Take turns.

A: *Write these words: zoo, movies, aquarium.*
B: *Zoo, movies, and what?*
A: *Aquarium.*

8. play
   演劇
9. art museum
   美術館
10. amusement park
    遊園地
11. opera
    オペラ
12. nightclub
    ナイトクラブ
13. county fair
    郡の農産物・家畜品評会
14. classical concert
    クラシックコンサート

Ways to make plans using *Let's go*

Let's go *to the amusement park tomorrow.*
Let's go *to the opera on Saturday.*
Let's go *to the movies tonight.*

Pair practice. Make new conversations.

A: *Let's go to the zoo this afternoon.*
B: *OK. And let's go to the movies tonight.*
A: *That sounds like a good plan.*

The Park and Playground

公園と遊び場

1. ball field
   球技場
2. cyclist
   サイクリスト
3. bike path
   自転車道
4. jump rope
   なわとび
5. fountain
   噴水
6. tennis court
   テニスコート
7. skateboard
   スケートボード
8. picnic table
   ピクニックテーブル
9. water fountain
   水飲み場
10. bench
    ベンチ
11. swings
    ブランコ
12. tricycle
    三輪車
13. slide
    すべり台
14. climbing apparatus
    ジャングルジム
15. sandbox
    砂場
16. seesaw
    シーソー

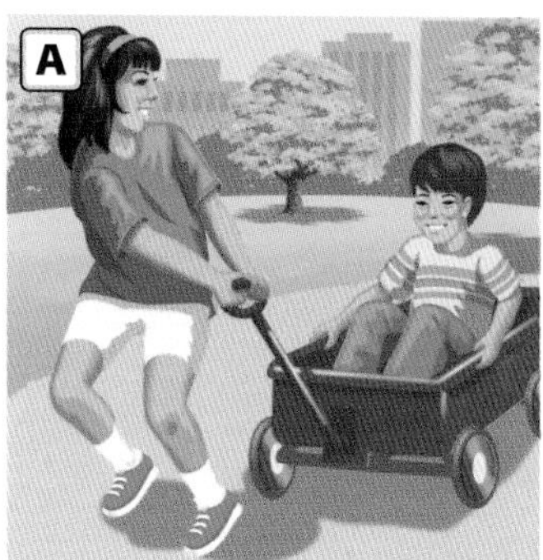

A. **pull** the wagon
ワゴンを引く

B. **push** the swing
ブランコを押す

C. **climb** the bars
棒によじ登る

D. **picnic / have** a picnic
ピクニックをする

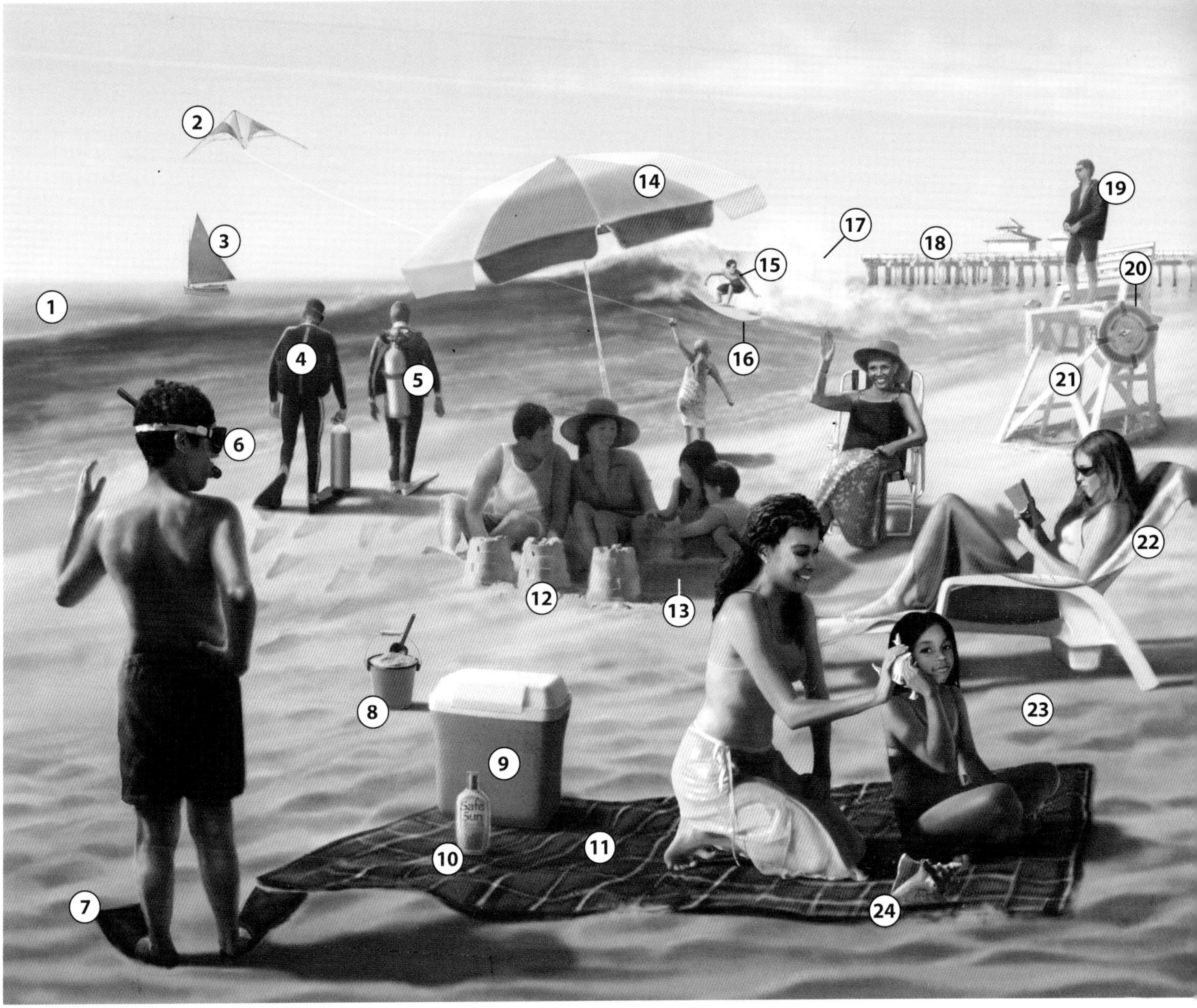

1. ocean / water
   海／水
2. kite
   凧
3. sailboat
   ヨット
4. wet suit
   ウェットスーツ
5. scuba tank
   潜水タンク
6. diving mask
   ダイビングマスク
7. fins
   フィン
8. pail / bucket
   バケツ
9. cooler
   クーラー
10. sunscreen / sunblock
    サンスクリーン／日焼け止め
11. blanket
    毛布
12. sand castle
    砂の城
13. shade
    日陰
14. beach umbrella
    ビーチパラソル
15. surfer
    サーファー
16. surfboard
    サーフボード
17. wave
    波
18. pier
    桟橋
19. lifeguard
    ライフガード
20. lifesaving device
    救命器具
21. lifeguard station
    ライフガード詰め所
22. beach chair
    ビーチチェア
23. sand
    砂
24. seashell
    貝殻

More vocabulary

seaweed: a plant that grows in the ocean

tide: the level of the ocean. The tide goes in and out every 12 hours.

Ask your classmates. Share the answers.

1. Do you like to go to the beach?
2. Are there famous beaches in your native country?
3. Do you prefer to be on the sand or in the water?

1. boating
ボート乗り
2. rafting
いかだ乗り
3. canoeing
カヌー乗り
4. fishing
魚釣り
5. camping
キャンプ
6. backpacking
バックパッキング
7. hiking
ハイキング
8. mountain biking
マウンテンバイキング
9. horseback riding
乗馬

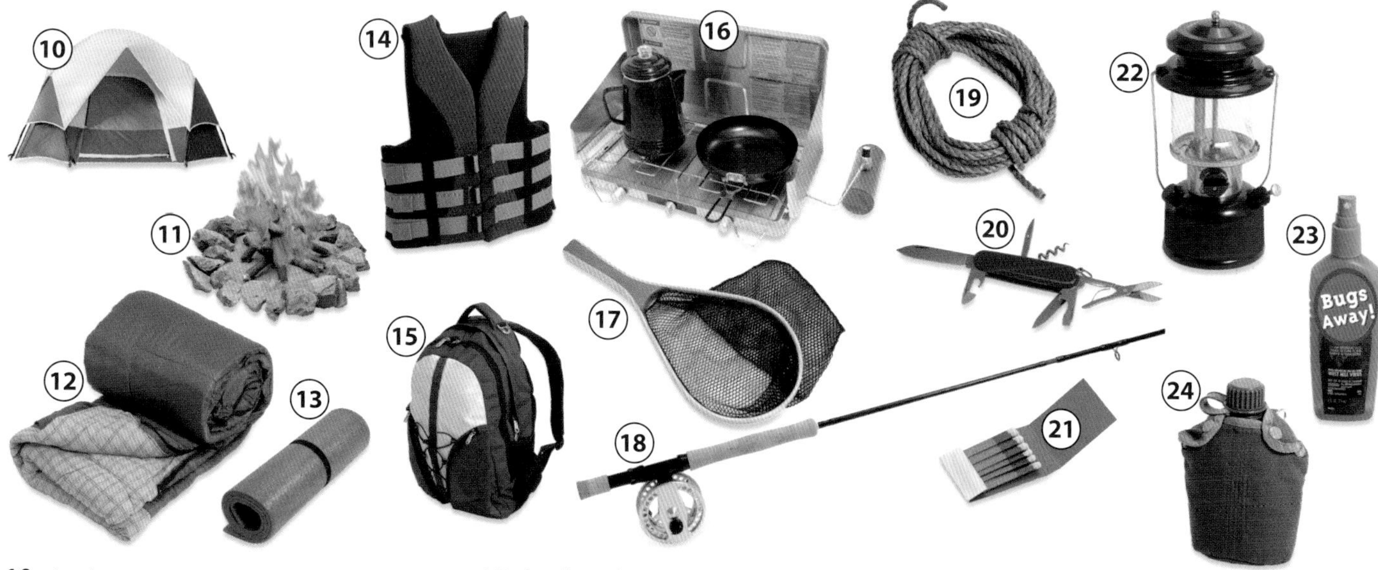

10. tent
テント
11. campfire
キャンプファイヤ
12. sleeping bag
寝袋
13. foam pad
ウレタンフォームパッド
14. life vest
救命胴衣
15. backpack
バックパック
16. camping stove
キャンプ用コンロ
17. fishing net
魚捕り網
18. fishing pole
釣竿
19. rope
ロープ
20. multi-use knife
多目的ナイフ
21. matches
マッチ
22. lantern
手提げランプ
23. insect repellent
虫除けスプレー
24. canteen
水筒

Winter and Water Sports

1. downhill skiing
ダウンヒルスキー

2. snowboarding
スノーボード

3. cross-country skiing
クロスカントリースキー

4. ice skating
アイススケート

5. figure skating
フィギュアスケート

6. sledding
そり遊び

7. waterskiing
水上スキー

8. sailing
セーリング

9. surfing
サーフィン

10. windsurfing
ウィンドサーフィン

11. snorkeling
シュノーケル

12. scuba diving
スキューバダイビング

More vocabulary

speed skating: racing while ice skating
windsurfing: sailboarding

Ask your classmates. Share the answers.

1. Which of these sports do you like?
2. Which of these sports would you like to learn?
3. Which of these sports is the most fun to watch?

Individual Sports

個人競技

1. archery
アーチェリー

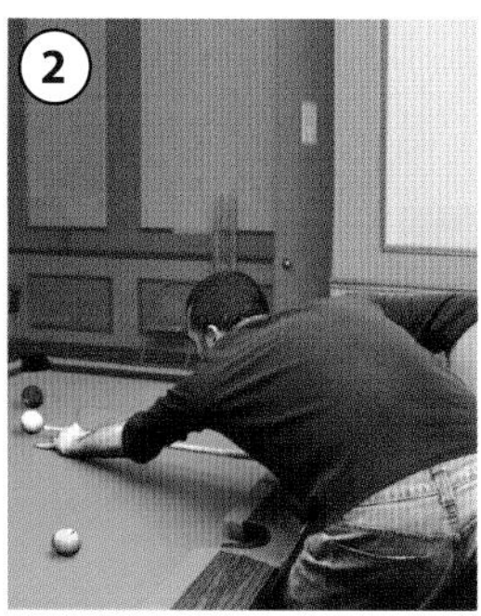

2. billiards / pool
ビリヤード

3. bowling
ボウリング

4. boxing
ボクシング

5. cycling / biking
サイクリング

6. badminton
バドミントン

7. fencing
フェンシング

8. golf
ゴルフ

9. gymnastics
体操

10. inline skating
インラインスケート

11. martial arts
武道

12. racquetball
ラケットボール

13. skateboarding
スケートボード

14. table tennis
卓球

15. tennis
テニス

16. weightlifting
重量上げ

17. wrestling
レスリング

18. track and field
陸上競技

19. horse racing
競馬

Pair practice. Make new conversations.

A: *What sports do you like?*
B: *I like bowling. What do you like?*
A: *I like gymnastics.*

Think about it. Discuss.

1. Why do people like to watch sports?
2. Which sports can be dangerous?
3. Why do people do dangerous sports?

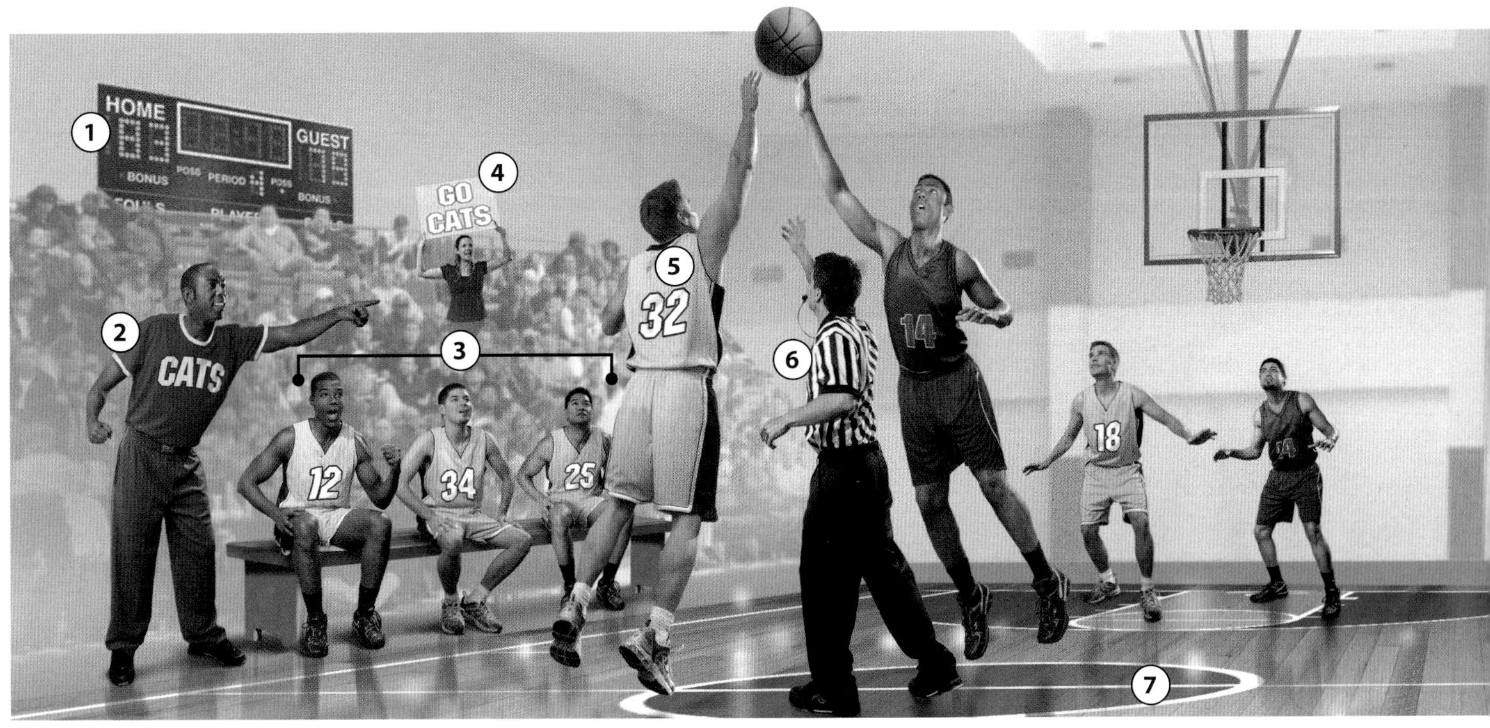

1. score
得点
2. coach
コーチ
3. team
チーム
4. fan
ファン
5. player
選手
6. official / referee
審判員／レフリー
7. basketball court
バスケットボールコート

8. basketball
バスケットボール

9. baseball
野球

10. softball
ソフトボール

11. football
フットボール

12. soccer
サッカー

13. ice hockey
アイスホッケー

14. volleyball
バレーボール

15. water polo
水球

More Vocabulary

win: to have the best score
lose: the opposite of win
tie: to have the same score
captain: the team leader
umpire: the name of the referee in baseball
Little League: a baseball and softball program for children

A. **pitch**
投げる／野球のピッチャーをつとめる

B. **hit**
打つ

C. **throw**
投げる

D. **catch**
キャッチする

E. **kick**
蹴る

F. **tackle**
タックルする

G. **pass**
パスする

H. **shoot**
シュートする

I. **jump**
ジャンプする

J. **dribble**
ドリブルする

K. **dive**
飛び込む

L. **swim**
泳ぐ

M. **stretch**
ストレッチする

N. **exercise / work out**
エクササイズ／運動する

O. **bend**
曲げる

P. **serve**
サーブする

Q. **swing**
(ゴルフクラブで) 打つ

R. **start**
スタートする

S. **race**
競走する

T. **finish**
ゴールインする

U. **skate**
スケートをする

V. **ski**
スキーをする

Use the new words.
Look on page 229. Name the actions you see.

A: *He's throwing.*
B: *She's jumping.*

Ways to talk about your sports skills

I can throw, but I can't catch.
I swim well, but I don't dive well.
I'm good at skating, but I'm terrible at skiing.

Sports Equipment

1. golf club
   ゴルフクラブ
2. tennis racket
   テニスラケット
3. volleyball
   バレーボールのボール
4. basketball
   バスケットボールのボール
5. bowling ball
   ボウリングのボール
6. bow
   弓
7. target
   的
8. arrow
   矢
9. ice skates
   アイススケート靴
10. inline skates
    インラインスケート靴
11. hockey stick
    ホッケースティック
12. soccer ball
    サッカーボール
13. shin guards
    すね当て
14. baseball bat
    野球のバット
15. catcher's mask
    キャッチャーマスク
16. uniform
    ユニフォーム
17. glove
    グローブ
18. baseball
    野球のボール
19. football helmet
    フットボールヘルメット
20. shoulder pads
    ショルダーパッド
21. football
    フットボールのボール
22. weights
    ウエイト／ダンベル
23. snowboard
    スノーボード
24. skis
    スキー板
25. ski poles
    スキーストック
26. ski boots
    スキーブーツ
27. flying disc*
    フリスビー

* **Note:** one brand is Frisbee®, of Wham-O, Inc.

Use the new words.
Look at pages 228–229. Name the sports equipment you see.

A: *Those are* *ice skates.*
B: *That's* *a football.*

Ask your classmates. Share the answers.

1. Do you own any sports equipment? What kind?
2. What do you want to buy at this store?
3. Where is the best place to buy sports equipment?

Hobbies and Games
趣味とゲーム

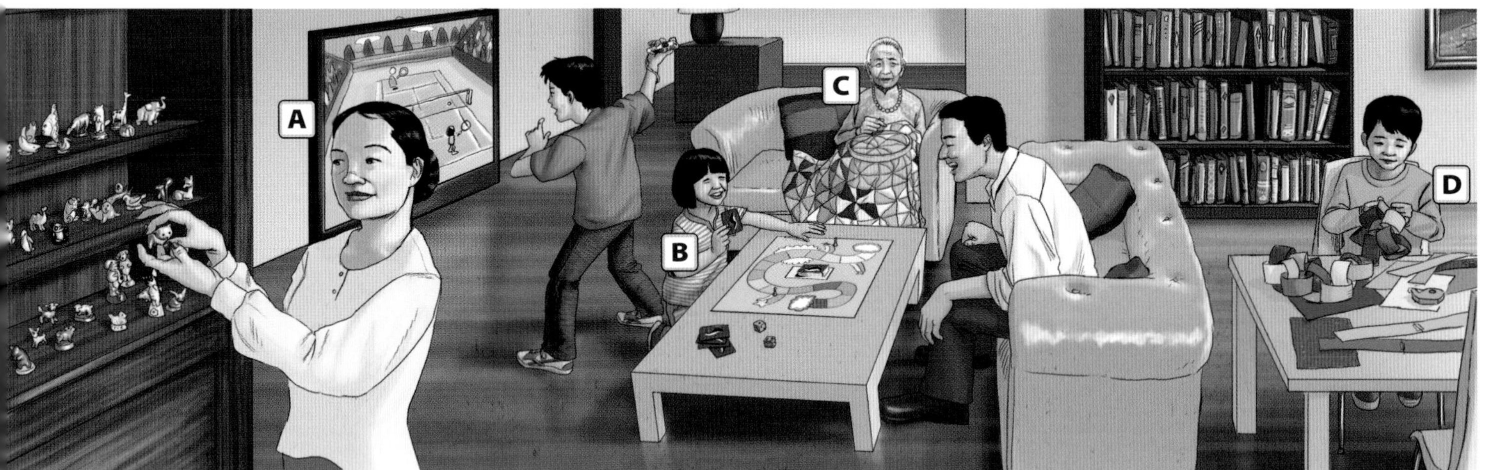

A. **collect** things
物を集める

B. **play** games
ゲームをする

C. **quilt**
キルトを作る

D. **do** crafts
工作をする

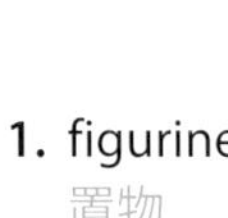

1. figurine
置物
2. baseball cards
野球カード
3. video game console
テレビゲーム機
4. video game control
ゲームコントローラー
5. board game
盤上ゲーム
6. dice
さいころ
7. checkers
チェッカー
8. chess
チェス
9. model kit
プラモデル
10. acrylic paint
アクリル絵具
11. glue stick
スティック糊
12. construction paper
工作用紙
13. doll making kit
人形作りキット
14. woodworking kit
木工キット
15. quilt block
キルトブロック
16. rotary cutter
ロータリーカッター

Grammar Point: *How often do you play cards?*

*I play **all the time**. (every day)*
*I play **sometimes**. (once a month)*
*I **never** play. (0 times)*

Pair practice. Make new conversations.

A: *How often do you do your hobbies?*
B: *I play games all the time. I love chess.*
A: *Really? I never play chess.*

E. **paint**
絵を描く

F. **knit**
編み物をする

G. **pretend**
まねをする

H. **play** cards
トランプをする

17. canvas
キャンバス
18. easel
イーゼル
19. oil paint
油絵具
20. paintbrush
絵筆
21. watercolor
水彩絵具
22. yarn
毛糸
23. knitting needles
編み棒
24. embroidery
刺繍
25. crocheting
かぎ針編み
26. action figure
キャラクター人形
27. model trains
電車の模型
28. paper dolls
紙の着せ替え人形
29. diamonds
ダイヤ
30. spades
スペード
31. hearts
ハート
32. clubs
クラブ

Ways to talk about hobbies and games

*This board game is **interesting**. It makes me think.*
*That video game is **boring**. Nothing happens.*
*I love to play cards. It's **fun** to play with my friends.*

Ask your classmates. Share the answers.

1. Do you collect anything? What?
2. Which games do you like to play?
3. What hobbies did you have as a child?

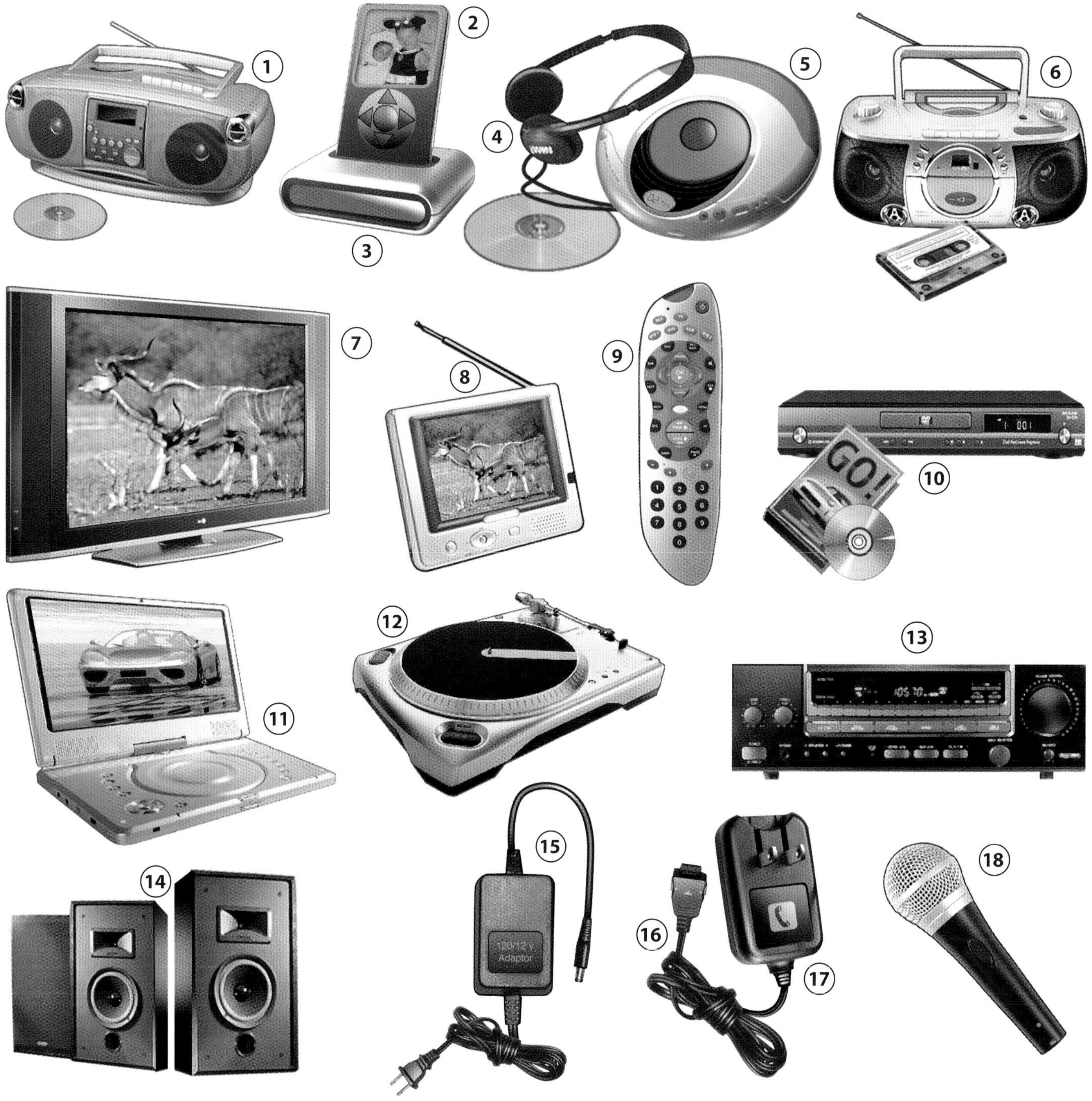

Electronics and Photography 電化製品と写真

1. CD boombox
CDラジカセ
2. MP3 player
MP3プレーヤー
3. dock
ドック
4. headphones
ヘッドホン
5. personal CD player
パーソナルCDプレーヤー
6. portable cassette player
ポータブルカセットプレーヤー
7. flat screen TV / flat panel TV
薄型テレビ
8. portable TV
ポータブルテレビ
9. universal remote
ユニバーサルリモコン
10. DVD player
DVDプレーヤー
11. portable DVD player
ポータブルDVDプレーヤー
12. turntable
ターンテーブル
13. tuner
チューナー
14. speakers
スピーカー
15. adapter
アダプタ
16. plug
プラグ
17. charger
充電器
18. microphone
マイク

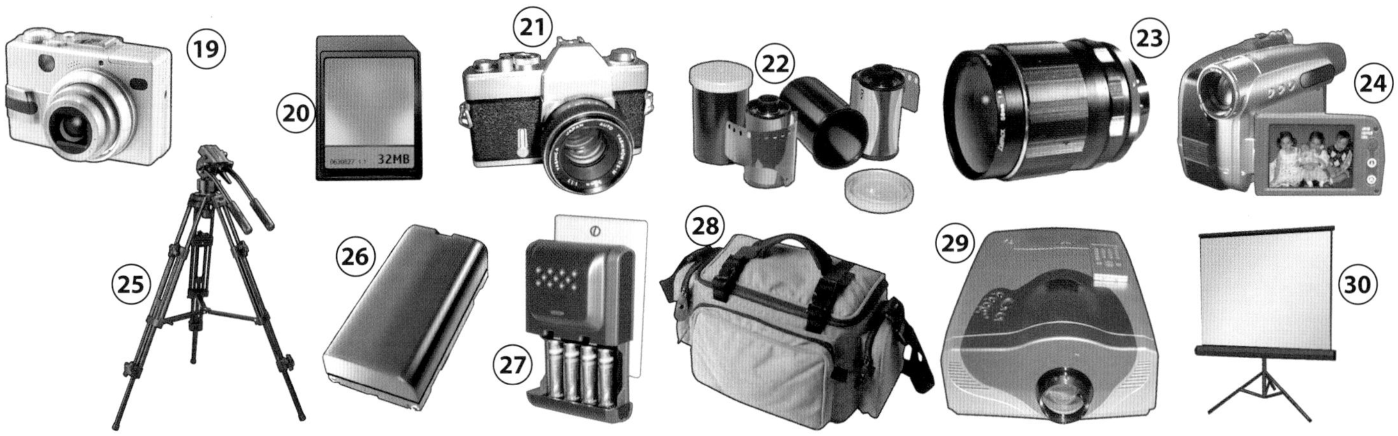

19. digital camera
デジタルカメラ
20. memory card
メモリーカード
21. film camera / 35 mm camera
フィルムカメラ／35mmカメラ
22. film
フィルム
23. zoom lens
望遠レンズ
24. camcorder
ビデオカメラ
25. tripod
三脚
26. battery pack
バッテリーパック
27. battery charger
バッテリーチャージャー
28. camera case
カメラケース
29. LCD projector
LCDプロジェクタ
30. screen
スクリーン

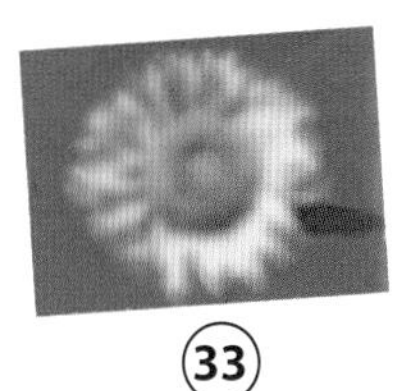

31. photo album
フォトアルバム
32. digital photo album
デジタルフォトアルバム
33. out of focus
ピンぼけ
34. overexposed
露光オーバー
35. underexposed
露光不足

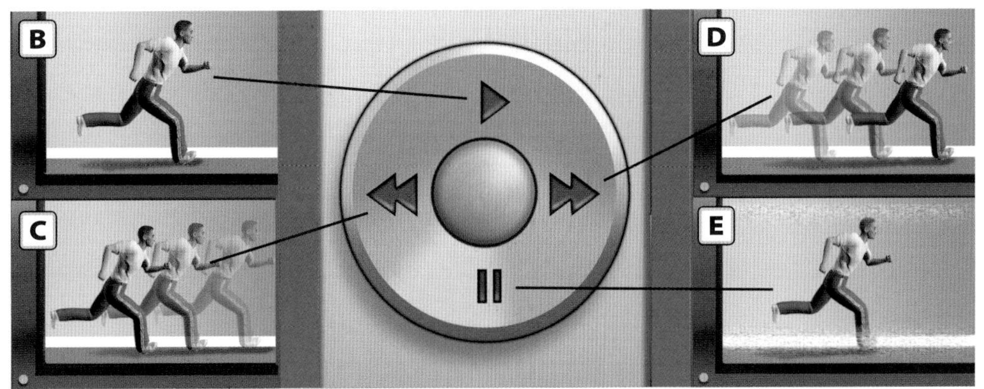

A. **record**
録画する
B. **play**
再生する
C. **rewind**
巻き戻す
D. **fast forward**
早送りする
E. **pause**
一時停止する

Types of TV Programs テレビ番組の種類

1. news program
ニュース

2. sitcom (situation comedy)
連続ホームコメディ

3. cartoon
テレビアニメ

4. talk show
トークショー

5. soap opera
メロドラマ

6. reality show
リアリティショー

7. nature program
自然ドキュメンタリー

8. game show
ゲーム番組／クイズ番組

9. children's program
子供番組

10. shopping program
ショッピング番組

11. sports program
スポーツ番組

12. drama
ドラマ

Types of Movies 映画の種類

13. comedy
コメディ

14. tragedy
悲劇

15. western
西部劇

16. romance
ラブストーリー

17. horror story
ホラー

18. science fiction story
SF

19. action story / adventure story
アクション／アドベンチャー

20. mystery / suspense
ミステリー／サスペンス

Types of Music 音楽の種類

21. classical
クラシック

22. blues
ブルース

23. rock
ロック

24. jazz
ジャズ

25. pop
ポップ

26. hip hop
ヒップホップ

27. country
カントリー

28. R&B / soul
R&B／ソウル

29. folk
フォーク

30. gospel
ゴスペル

31. reggae
レゲエ

32. world music
世界各国の音楽

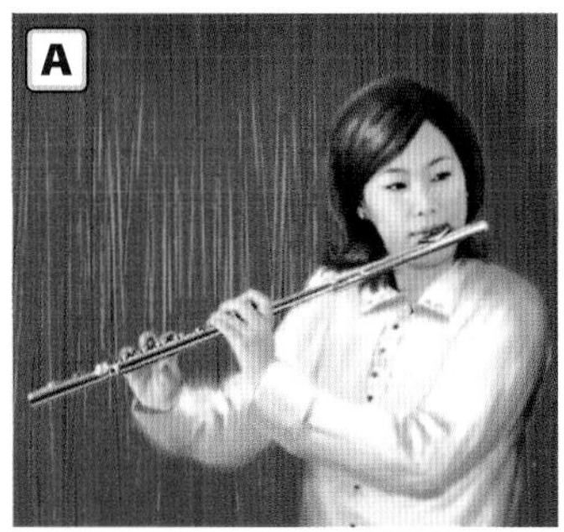

A. **play** an instrument
楽器を**演奏する**

B. **sing** a song
歌を**歌う**

C. **conduct** an orchestra
オーケストラを**指揮する**

D. **be** in a rock band
ロックバンドのメンバー**である**

Woodwinds 木管楽器

1. flute
フルート
2. clarinet
クラリネット
3. oboe
オーボエ
4. bassoon
バスーン
5. saxophone
サクソフォン

Strings 弦楽器

6. violin
バイオリン
7. cello
チェロ
8. bass
コントラバス
9. guitar
ギター

Brass 金管楽器

10. trombone
トロンボーン
11. trumpet / horn
トランペット
12. tuba
チューバ
13. French horn
フレンチホルン

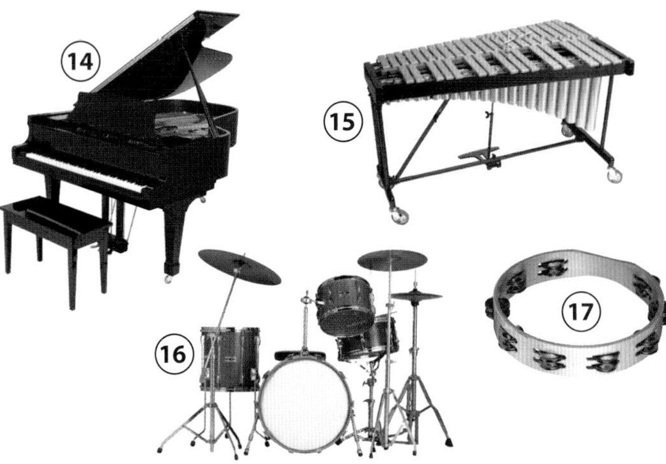

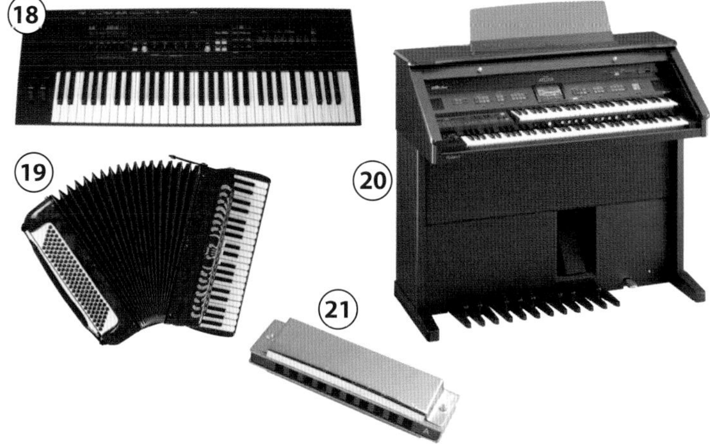

Percussion 打楽器

14. piano
ピアノ
15. xylophone
シロホン
16. drums
ドラム
17. tambourine
タンバリン

Other Instruments その他の楽器

18. electric keyboard
電子キーボード
19. accordion
アコーディオン
20. organ
オルガン
21. harmonica
ハーモニカ

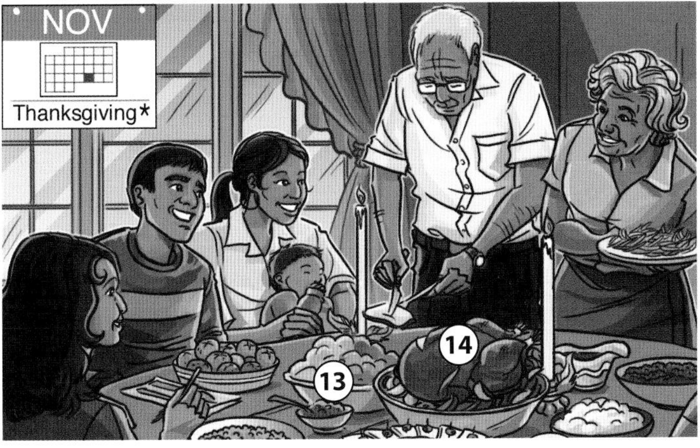

1. parade
   パレード
2. float
   山車
3. confetti
   紙吹雪
4. couple
   カップル
5. card
   カード
6. heart
   ハート
7. fireworks
   花火
8. flag
   旗
9. mask
   お面
10. jack-o'-lantern
    かぼちゃの提灯
11. costume
    衣装
12. candy
    キャンディ
13. feast
    ごちそう
14. turkey
    七面鳥
15. ornament
    飾り
16. Christmas tree
    クリスマスツリー
17. candy cane
    キャンディケーン
18. string lights
    ツリー用の電球

*Thanksgiving is on the fourth Thursday in November.

A Birthday Party バースデーパーティ

1. decorations
   デコレーション
2. deck
   デッキ
3. present / gift
   プレゼント／ギフト

A. **videotape**
   ビデオを撮影する

B. **make** a wish
   願い事をする

C. **blow out**
   ろうそくを吹き消す

D. **hide**
   隠れる

E. **bring**
   持ってくる

F. **wrap**
   プレゼントを包む

Look at the picture.
What do you see?

Answer the questions.

1. What kinds of decorations do you see?
2. What are people doing at this birthday party?
3. What wish did the teenager make?
4. How many presents did people bring?

Read the story.

A Birthday Party

Today is Lou and Gani Bombata's birthday barbecue. There are <u>decorations</u> around the backyard, and food and drinks on the <u>deck</u>. There are also <u>presents</u>. Everyone in the Bombata family likes to <u>bring</u> presents.

Right now, it's time for cake. Gani <u>is blowing out</u> the candles, and Lou <u>is making a wish</u>. Lou's mom wants to <u>videotape</u> everyone, but she can't find Lou's brother, Todd. Todd hates to sing, so he always <u>hides</u> for the birthday song.

Lou's sister, Amaka, has to <u>wrap</u> some <u>gifts</u>. She doesn't want Lou to see. Amaka isn't worried. She knows her family loves to sing. She can put her gifts on the present table before they finish the first song.

Think about it.

1. What wish do you think Gani made?
2. What kinds of presents do you give to relatives? What kinds of presents can you give to friends or co-workers?

Verb Guide

Verbs in English are either regular or irregular in the past tense and past participle forms.

Regular Verbs

The regular verbs below are marked 1, 2, 3, or 4 according to four different spelling patterns. (See page 244 for the irregular verbs which do not follow any of these patterns.)

Spelling Patterns for the Past and the Past Participle	***Example***	
1. Add -ed to the end of the verb.	**ASK**	**ASKED**
2. Add -d to the end of the verb.	**LIVE**	**LIVED**
3. Double the final consonant and add -ed to the end of the verb.	**DROP**	**DROPPED**
4. Drop the final y and add -ied to the end of the verb.	**CRY**	**CRIED**

The Oxford Picture Dictionary List of Regular Verbs

accept (1)
add (1)
address (1)
adjust (1)
agree (2)
answer (1)
apologize (2)
appear (1)
applaud (1)
apply (4)
arrange (2)
arrest (1)
arrive (2)
ask (1)
assemble (2)
assist (1)
attach (1)
bake (2)
bank (1)
bargain (1)
bathe (2)
board (1)
boil (1)
borrow (1)
bow (1)
brainstorm (1)
breathe (2)
browse (2)
brush (1)
bubble (2)
buckle (2)
burn (1)
bus (1)
calculate (2)
call (1)
capitalize (2)
carpool (1)
carry (4)
cash (1)
celebrate (2)
change (2)
check (1)
chill (1)
choke (2)
chop (3)
circle (2)
claim (1)
clean (1)
clear (1)
click (1)
climb (1)
close (2)
collate (2)
collect (1)
color (1)
comb (1)
comfort (1)
commit (3)
compliment (1)
compost (1)
conceal (1)
conduct (1)
convert (1)
convict (1)
cook (1)
copy (4)
correct (1)
cough (1)
count (1)
cross (1)
cry (4)
dance (2)
debate (2)
decline (2)
delete (2)
deliver (1)
design (1)
dial (1)
dice (2)
dictate (2)
die (2)
disagree (2)
discipline (2)
discuss (1)
dive (2)
divide (2)
dress (1)
dribble (2)
drill (1)
drop (3)
drown (1)
dry (4)
dust (1)
dye (2)
edit (1)
empty (4)
enter (1)
erase (2)
evacuate (2)
examine (2)
exchange (2)
exercise (2)
expire (2)
explain (1)
exterminate (2)
fasten (1)
fast forward (1)
fax (1)
fertilize (2)
fill (1)
finish (1)
fix (1)
floss (1)
fold (1)
follow (1)
garden (1)
gargle (2)
graduate (2)
grate (2)
grease (2)
greet (1)
hail (1)
hammer (1)
hand (1)
harvest (1)
help (1)
hire (2)
hug (3)
immigrate (2)
indent (1)
inquire (2)
insert (1)
inspect (1)
install (1)
introduce (2)
invite (2)
iron (1)
jaywalk (1)
join (1)
jump (1)
kick (1)
kiss (1)
knit (3)
label (1)
land (1)
laugh (1)
learn (1)
lengthen (1)

lift (1)
listen (1)
litter (1)
live (2)
load (1)
lock (1)
look (1)
mail (1)
manufacture (2)
match (1)
measure (2)
microwave (2)
milk (1)
misbehave (2)
miss (1)
mix (1)
mop (3)
move (2)
mow (1)
multiply (4)
negotiate (2)
network (1)
numb (1)
nurse (2)
obey (1)
observe (2)
offer (1)
open (1)
operate (2)
order (1)
organize (2)
overdose (2)
pack (1)
paint (1)
park (1)
participate (2)
pass (1)
pause (2)
peel (1)
perm (1)
pick (1)
pitch (1)
plan (3)
plant (1)
play (1)
polish (1)
pour (1)
praise (2)
preheat (1)
prepare (2)
prescribe (2)
press (1)
pretend (1)
print (1)
program (3)
protect (1)
pull (1)
purchase (2)
push (1)
quilt (1)
race (2)
raise (2)
rake (2)
receive (2)
record (1)
recycle (2)
redecorate (2)
reduce (2)
register (1)
relax (1)
remain (1)
remove (2)
renew (1)
repair (1)
replace (2)
report (1)
request (1)
retire (2)
return (1)
reuse (2)
revise (2)
rinse (2)
rock (1)
sauté (1)
save (2)
scan (3)
schedule (2)
scrub (3)
seat (1)
select (1)
sentence (2)
separate (2)
serve (2)
share (2)
shave (2)
ship (3)
shop (3)
shorten (1)
sign (1)
simmer (1)
skate (2)
ski (1)
slice (2)
smell (1)
smile (2)
smoke (2)
sneeze (2)
solve (2)
sort (1)
spell (1)
spoon (1)
staple (2)
start (1)
state (2)
stay (1)
steam (1)
stir (3)
stop (3)
stow (1)
stretch (1)
study (4)
submit (3)
subtract (1)
supervise (2)
swallow (1)
tackle (2)
talk (1)
taste (2)
thank (1)
tie (2)
touch (1)
transcribe (2)
transfer (3)
translate (2)
travel (1)
trim (3)
try (4)
turn (1)
type (2)
underline (2)
undress (1)
unload (1)
unpack (1)
unscramble (2)
use (2)
vacuum (1)
videotape (2)
volunteer (1)
vomit (1)
vote (2)
wait (1)
walk (1)
wash (1)
watch (1)
water (1)
wave (2)
weed (1)
weigh (1)
wipe (2)
work (1)
wrap (3)

Irregular Verbs

These verbs have irregular endings in the past and/or the past participle.

The Oxford Picture Dictionary List of Irregular Verbs

simple	past	past participle
be	was	been
beat	beat	beaten
become	became	become
bend	bent	bent
bleed	bled	bled
blow	blew	blown
break	broke	broken
bring	brought	brought
buy	bought	bought
catch	caught	caught
choose	chose	chosen
come	came	come
cut	cut	cut
do	did	done
draw	drew	drawn
drink	drank	drunk
drive	drove	driven
eat	ate	eaten
fall	fell	fallen
feed	fed	fed
feel	felt	felt
find	found	found
fly	flew	flown
get	got	gotten
give	gave	given
go	went	gone
hang	hung	hung
have	had	had
hear	heard	heard
hide	hid	hidden
hit	hit	hit
hold	held	held
keep	kept	kept
lay	laid	laid
leave	left	left
lend	lent	lent
let	let	let

simple	past	past participle
make	made	made
meet	met	met
pay	paid	paid
picnic	picnicked	picnicked
proofread	proofread	proofread
put	put	put
read	read	read
rewind	rewound	rewound
rewrite	rewrote	rewritten
ride	rode	ridden
run	ran	run
say	said	said
see	saw	seen
seek	sought	sought
sell	sold	sold
send	sent	sent
set	set	set
sew	sewed	sewn
shake	shook	shaken
shoot	shot	shot
show	showed	shown
sing	sang	sung
sit	sat	sat
speak	spoke	spoken
stand	stood	stood
steal	stole	stolen
sweep	swept	swept
swim	swam	swum
swing	swung	swung
take	took	taken
teach	taught	taught
think	thought	thought
throw	threw	thrown
wake	woke	woken
withdraw	withdrew	withdrawn
write	wrote	written

Index

Index Key

Font

bold type = verbs or verb phrases (example: **catch**)
ordinary type = all other parts of speech (example: baseball)
ALL CAPS = unit titles (example: MATHEMATICS)
Initial caps = subunit titles (example: Equivalencies)

Symbols

✦ = word found in exercise band at bottom of page

Numbers/Letters

first number in **bold** type = page on which word appears
second number, or letter, following number in **bold** type = item number on page
(examples: cool [ko͞ol] **13**-5 means that the word *cool* is item number 5 on page 13;
across [ə krösʹ] **153**–G means that the word *across* is item G on page 153).

Pronunciation Guide

The index includes a pronunciation guide for all the words and phrases illustrated in the book. This guide uses symbols commonly found in dictionaries for native speakers. These symbols, unlike those used in pronunciation systems such as the International Phonetic Alphabet, tend to use English spelling patterns and so should help you to become more aware of the connections between written English and spoken English.

Consonants

[b] as in back [băk]
[ch] as in cheek [chēk]
[d] as in date [dāt]
[dh] as in this [dhĭs]
[f] as in face [fās]
[g] as in gas [găs]
[h] as in half [hăf]
[j] as in jam [jăm]
[k] as in key [kē]
[l] as in leaf [lēf]
[m] as in match [măch]
[n] as in neck [nĕk]
[ng] as in ring [rĭng]
[p] as in park [pärk]
[r] as in rice [rīs]
[s] as in sand [sănd]
[sh] as in shoe [sho͞o]
[t] as in tape [tāp]
[th] as in three [thrē]
[v] as in vine [vīn]
[w] as in wait [wāt]
[y] as in yams [yămz]
[z] as in zoo [zo͞o]
[zh] as in measure [mĕzhər]

Vowels

[ā] as in bake [bāk]
[ă] as in back [băk]
[ä] as in car [kär] or box [bäks]
[ē] as in beat [bēt]
[ĕ] as in bed [bĕd]
[ë] as in bear [bër]
[ī] as in line [līn]
[ĭ] as in lip [lĭp]
[ï] as in near [nïr]
[ō] as in cold [kōld]
[ö] as in short [shört] or claw [klö]
[o͞o] as in cool [ko͞ol]
[o͝o] as in cook [ko͝ok]
[ow] as in cow [kow]
[oy] as in boy [boy]
[ŭ] as in cut [kŭt]
[ü] as in curb [kürb]
[ə] as in above [ə bŭvʹ]

All the pronunciation symbols used are alphabetical except for the schwa [ə]. The schwa is the most frequent vowel sound in English. If you use the schwa appropriately in unstressed syllables, your pronunciation will sound more natural.

Vowels before [r] are shown with the symbol [¨] to call attention to the special quality that vowels have before [r]. (Note that the symbols [ä] and [ö] are also used for vowels not followed by [r], as in *box* or *claw*.) You should listen carefully to native speakers to discover how these vowels actually sound.

Stress

This index follows the system for marking stress used in many dictionaries for native speakers.

1. Stress is not marked if a word consisting of a single syllable occurs by itself.

2. Where stress is marked, two levels are distinguished:
a bold accent [**ʹ**] is placed after each syllable with primary (or strong) stress, a light accent [ʹ] is placed after each syllable with secondary (or weaker) stress. In phrases and other combinations of words, stress is indicated for each word as it would be pronounced within the whole phrase.

Syllable Boundaries

Syllable boundaries are indicated by a single space or by a stress mark.

Note: The pronunciations shown in this index are based on patterns of American English. There has been no attempt to represent all of the varieties of American English. Students should listen to native speakers to hear how the language actually sounds in a particular region.

Index

Abbreviations [ə brē/vē ā/shənz] **48**
abdomen [ăb/də mən] **107**–27
about [ə bowt/] **48**–B, **174**–L, **191**–E
above [ə bŭv/] **25**–4
accelerator [ĭk sĕl/ə rā/tər] **159**–46
accept [ĭk sĕpt/] **12**–G, **12**–I, **12** ✦
access number [ăk/sĕs/ nŭm/bər] **14**–16
Accessories [ĭk sĕs/ə rēz] **59, 94–95**
accident [ăk/sə dənt] **144**–2
accordion [ə kör/dē ən] **238**–19
account [ə kownt/] **132**–11, **132**–14
account manager [ə kownt/ măn/ə jər] **132**–9
Account [ə kownt/] **132**
accountant [ə kown/tənt] **166**–1
ache [āk]
backache [băk/āk/] **110**–5
earache [ïr/āk/] **110**–3
headache [hĕd/āk/] **110**–1
stomachache [stŭm/ək/ āk] **110**–4
toothache [to͞oth/āk/] **110**–2
acid rain [ăs/əd rān/] **218**–13
across [ə krös] **153**–G
acrylic paint [ə krĭl/ĭk pānt] **232**–10
action [ăk/shən]
action figure [ăk/shən fĭg/yər] **233**–26
action story [ăk/shən stör/ē] **237**–19
activist [ăk/tə vĭst] **199**–17
actor [ăk/tər] **166**–2
acupuncture [ăk/yə pŭngk/chər] **122**–2
acute angle [ə kyo͞ot/ ăng/gəl] **193**–28
ad [ăd] **48**–2, **197**–9
adapter [ə dăp/tər] **234**–15
add [ăd] **77**–N, **101**–B, **192**–A
address [ə drĕs/, ă/drĕs] **4**–5
mailing address [mā/lĭng ə drĕs/, –ă/drĕs] **134**–22
return address [rĭ türn/ ə drĕs/, –ă/drĕs] **134**–21
website address [wĕb/sit ə drĕs/, –ă/drĕs] **197**–4
address [ə drĕs/] **135**–B, **197**–C
adhesive bandage [əd hē/sĭv băn/dĭj] **117**–5
adjust [ə jŭst/] **219**–J
adjustable wrench [ə jŭs/tə bəl rĕnch/] **181**–48
adjustment [ə jŭst/mənt] **194**–23, **194**–24
administrative assistant
[əd mĭn/ə strā/tĭv ə sĭs/tənt] **166**–3
administrator [əd mĭn/ə strā/tər] **120**–13
Administrators [əd mĭn/ə strā/tərz] **5**
admissions clerk [əd mĭ/shənz klürk/] **120**–14
ADULTS AND CHILDREN [ə dŭlts/ ən chĭl/ drən] **30–31**
adult school [ə dŭlt/ sko͞ol/, ăd/ŭlt–] **188**–8
adventure story [əd vĕn/chər stör/ē] **237**–19
aerobic exercise [ə rō/bĭk ĕk/sər sīz/] **122**–5
afraid [ə frād/] **43**–23
after [ăf/tər]
afternoon [ăf/tər no͞on/] **18**–17
aftershave [ăf/tər shāv/] **109**–30
five after one [fīv/ ăf/tər wŭn/] **18**–7
quarter after one [kwör/tər ăf/tər wŭn/] **18**–9
ten after one [tĕn/ ăf/tər wŭn/] **18**–8
twenty after one [twĕn/tē ăf/tər wŭn/] **18**–10
After an Emergency [ăf/tər ən ĭ mür/jən sē] **147**
Age [āj] **32**
agency [ā/jən sē] **131**–14
agent [ā/jənt] **160**–3, **160**–5
agree [ə grē/] **12**–K
agreement [ə grē/mənt] **51**–28
aid [ād]
first aid kit [fürst/ ād/ kĭt/] **117**–1, **146**–18
first aid manual [fürst/ ād/ măn/yo͞o əl] **117**–2
hearing aid [hïr/ĭng ād/] **115**–10
aide [ād] **167**–32
AIDS (acquired immune deficiency syndrome) [ādz] /
[ə kwī/rd ĭ myo͞on/ də fĭ/shən sē sĭn/drōm] **111** ✦
air [ër]
air bag [ër/ băg/] **159**–43
air conditioner [ër/ kən dĭsh/ə nər] **159**–39
Air Force [ër/ förs/] **138**–16
airmail [ër/māl/] **134**–5
airplane [ër/plān/] **150**–8
airplane crash [ër/plān/ krăsh/] **144**–3
air pollution [ër/ pə lo͞o/shən] **218**–11
airport [ër/pört/] **151**–10
air purifier [ër/ pyo͝or/ə fī ər] **113**–14
Airline Terminal [ër/līn/ tür/mə nəl] **160**
Airplane [ër/plān/] **161**
AIRPORT [ër/pört/] **160–161**
Airport Transportation
[ër/pört/ trăns/pər tā/shən] **152**
aisle [īl] **72**–6
alarm clock [ə lärm/ kläk/] **58**–24
Alaska time [ə lăs/kə tīm/] **19**–28
album [ăl/bəm] **235**–31, **235**–32
alfalfa [ăl făl/fə] **177**–5
algebra [al/jə brə] **192**–16
allergic reaction [ə lür/jĭk rē ăk/shən] **116**–E
allergies [ăl/ər jēz] **111**–8
alley [ăl/ē] **51**–24, **222**–4
alligator [ăl/ə gā/tər] **213**–36
alphabet [ăl/fə bĕt/] **7**–13
Alterations [öl/tə rā/shənz] **100**
ALTERATIONS [öl/tə rā/shənz] **100**
Alteration Shop [öl/tə rā/shən shäp/] **100**
aluminum foil [ə lo͞o/mə nəm foyl/] **72**–23
Alzheimer's disease [älts/hī mərz dĭ zēz/, ălts–] **111** ✦
a.m. [ā/ĕm/] **18**–4
ambulance [ăm/byə ləns] **116**–1, **121**–34
AMERICA [ə mër/ə kə] **200–201**
American cheese [ə mër/ə kən chēz/] **71**–26
Americans [ə mër/ə kənz] **198**–3
Amphibians [ăm fĭb/ē ənz] **212**
AMPHIBIANS [ăm fĭb/ē ənz] **212–213**
amusement park [ə myo͞oz/mənt pärk/] **223**–10
ancient [ān/shənt] **199**–1
anemone [ə nĕ/mə nē] **212**–24
anesthesiologist [ă/nəs thē/zē ä/lə jĭst] **121**–35
angle [ăng/gəl] **193**–26, **193**–27, **193**–28
Angles [ăng/gəlz] **193**
angry [ăng/grē] **43**–29
animals [ăn/ə məlz] **59**–15
Animals [ăn/ə məlz] **212, 215**
ANIMALS [ăn/ə məlz] **215**
ankle [ăng/kəl] **106**–23, **110**–18
ankle socks [ăng/kəl säks/] **91**–7
anklets [ăngk/ləts/] **91**–11
anniversary [ăn/ə vür/sə rē] **22**–3
answer [ăn/sər] **8**–L
answering machine [ăn/sə rĭng mə shēn/] **14**–17
answer sheet [ăn/sər shēt/] **10**–2
antacid [ănt ăs/əd] **113**–28
anteater [ănt/ē/tər] **217**–24
antelope [ăn/tə lōp/] **217**–35
antenna [ăn tĕ/nə] **14**–9
antibacterial ointment
[ăn/tē băk tïr/ē əl oynt/mənt] **117**–10
antihistamine cream [ăn/tĭ hĭs/tə mēn krēm/] **117**–11
antiperspirant [ăn/tē pürs/pə rənt] **108**–5
antlers [ănt/lərz] **216**–16
ants [ănts] **63**–23
apartment [ə pärt/mənt] **48**–3, **48**–4
apartment building [ə pärt/mənt bĭl/dĭng] **50**–1
apartment number [ə pärt/mənt nŭm/bər] **4**–6
Apartment [ə pärt/mənt] **48**
Apartment Complex [ə pärt/mənt käm/plĕx] **51**
Apartment Entryway [ə pärt/mənt ĕn/trē wā/] **51**
APARTMENTS [ə pärt/mənts] **50–51**
APC (automated postal center) [ā/pē/sē/] /
[ö/tə māt ĭd pōs/təl–sĕn/tər] **135**–10
apologize [ə päl/ə jīz/] **12**–F
apostrophe [ə päs/trə fē] **190**–16
apparatus [ăp/ə rā/təs] **224**–14
appear [ə pïr/] **141**–C
Appearance [ə pïr/əns] **32**
applaud [ə plöd/] **148**–B
apples [ăp/əlz] **68**–1
apple juice [ăp/əl jo͞os/] **73**–32
appliance repair person
[ə plī/əns rĭ për/ pür/sən] **166**–4
appliqué [ăp/lə kā/] **99**–31
apply [ə plī/] **109**–P
appointment [ə poynt/mənt] **22**–4, **118**–1
appointment book [ə poynt/mənt bo͝ok/] **183**–48
apricots [ăp/rə käts/] **68**–12
April [ā/prəl] **21**–28
apron [ā/prən] **92**–11, **93**–30
aquarium [ə kwër/ē əm] **222**–7
Arachnids [ə răk/nĭdz/] **214**
ARACHNIDS [ə răk/nĭdz/] **214**
archery [är/chə rē] **228**–1
architect [är/kə tĕkt/] **166**–5
area [ër/ē ə]
area code [ër/ē ə kōd/] **4**–10, **15**–29
boarding area [bör/dĭng ër/ē ə] **161**–9
dining area [dī/nĭng ër/ē ə] **46**–7
play area [plā/ ër/ē ə] **130**–11
reception area [rĭ sĕp/shən ër/ē ə] **182**–5
rural area [ro͝or/əl ër/ē ə] **52**–4
screening area [skrē/nĭng ër/ē ə] **160**–4
testing area [tĕs/tĭng ër/ē ə] **136**–2
urban area [ür/bən ër/ē ə] **52**–1
AREA [ër/ē ə] **55**
Area and Volume [ër/ē ə ən väl/yəm, –yo͞om] **193**
arm [ärm] **105**–14, **194**–15
armchair [ärm/chër/] **56**–22
armadillo [är/mə dĭl/ō] **216**–8
Arm, Hand, and Fingers [ärm/ hănd/ ən fĭng/gərz] **106**
Army [är/mē] **138**–14, **199**–11
around [ə rownd/] **153**–H

Around Campus [ə rownd/ kăm/pəs] **5**
arrange [ə rānj/] **49**–Q
arrest [ə rĕst/] **141**–A
arrival [ə rī/vəl] **161**–7, **161** ✦
arrive [ə rīv/] **160**–K
arrow [ăr/ō] **231**–8
arson [är/sən] **142**–7
artery [är/tə rē] **107**–36
arthritis [är thrī/təs] **111**–16
artichokes [är/tə chōks/] **69**–22
artist [är/tĭst] **166**–6
arts [ärts] **189**–9, **189**–15, **228**–11
art museum [ärt/ myōō zē/əm] **223**–9
ask [ăsk] **2**–B
ask about [ăsk/ ə bowt/] **48**–B, **157**–B
ask for [ăsk/ för/] **10**–F
ask questions [ăsk/ kwĕs/chənz] **8**–K, **174**–M
asparagus [ə spër/ə gəs] **69**–26
assault [ə sölt/] **142**–3
assemble [ə sĕm/bəl] **170**–A, **175**–C
assembler [ə sĕm/blər] **166**–7
assembly [ə sĕm/blē/] **140**–1
assembly line [ə sĕm/blē līn/] **175**–6
assemblyperson [ə sĕm/blē pür/sən] **139**–24
assist [ə sĭst/] **95**–D, **170**–B
assistance [ə sĭs/təns] **14**–22
assistant [ə sĭs/tənt]
administrative assistant
[əd mĭn/ ə strā/ tĭv ə sĭs/tənt] **166**–3
assistant principal [ə sĭs/tənt prĭn/sə pəl] **5**–5
certified nursing assistant (CNA) [sür/tə fīd/
nür/sĭng ə sĭs/tənt] / [sē/ĕn/ā/] **120**–12
dental assistant [dĕn/təl ə sĭs/tənt] **119**–2, **167**–22
physician assistant [fə zĭ/shən ə sĭs/tənt] **168**–47
Assistant [ə sĭs/tənt] **93**
asthma [ăz/mə] **111**–9
astronaut [ăs/trə nöt/] **205**–17
astronomer [ə strä/nə mər] **205**–22
Astronomy [ə strä/nə mē] **205**
At Customs [ăt/ kŭs/təmz] **161**
athletic [ăth lĕt/ĭk]
athletic shoes [ăth lĕt/ĭk shōōz/] **86**–7
athletic supporter [ăth lĕt/ĭk sə pör/tər] **91**–6
Atlantic time [ət lăn/tĭk tīm/] **19**–33
atlas [ăt/ləs] **133**–8
ATM (Automated Teller Machine) [ā/tē/ĕm/] /
[ö/tə māt ĭd tĕ/lər mə shēn/] **132**
ATM card [ā/tē/ĕm/ kärd/] **132**–15
atom [ăt/əm] **195**–28
attach [ə tăch/] **197**–G, **197**–H
attachments [ə tăch/mənts] **61**–11
attack [ə tăk/] **116**–D
attendant [ə tĕn/dənt] **161**–12, **162**–3, **184**–3
At the Dealer [ăt/ dhə dē/lər] **158**
At the Gate [ăt/ dhə gāt/] **161**
At the Mechanic [ăt/ dhə mə kăn/ĭk] **158**
At the Security Checkpoint
[ăt/ dhə sə kyōō/ rə tē/ chĕk/ poynt/] **160**
attic [ăt/ək] **47**–7
attorney [ə tür/nē] **141**–4, **141**–10
attractive [ə trăk/tĭv] **32**–13
audiobook [ö/dē ō bŏŏk/] **133**–17
audiologist [ö dē ä/lə jĭst] **115**–9
auditorium [ö/də tör/ē əm] **5**–18
August [ö/gəst] **21**–32
aunt [ănt] **34**–7
author [ö/thər] **133**–15, **169**–64
auto [ö/tō]
auto club card [ö/tō klŭb/ kärd/] **162**–4
auto mechanic [ö/tō mə kăn/ĭk] **166**–8
automated [ö/tə māt ĭd]
automated phone system
[ö/tə māt ĭd fōn/ sĭs/təm] **14**–23
automated postal center (APC)
[ö/tə māt ĭd pōs/təl sĕn/tər] / [ā/pē/sē/] **135**–10
Automated Teller Machine
[ö/tə māt ĭd tĕl/ər mə shēn/] **132**
Automatic Transmission
[ö tə măt/ĭk trănz mĭ/shən] **159**
Automotive Painter [ö tə mōt/ĭv pān/tər] **92**
autumn [ö/təm] **21**–39
avalanche [ăv/ə lănch/] **145**–18
average [ăv/rĭj]
average height [ăv/rĭj hīt/] **32**–5
average weight [ăv/rĭj wāt/] **32**–8
avocados [ä/və kä/dōz, ăv/ə–] **84**–6
ax [ăks] **180**–3
baboon [bă bōōn/] **217**–31
baby [bā/bē] **31**–7
baby bag [bā/bē băg/] **37**–16
baby carrier [bā/bē kă/rē/ər] **37**–17
baby food [bā/bē fōōd/] **37**–4
baby lotion [bā/bē lō/shən] **37**–13
baby monitor [bā/bē män/ə tər] **59**–7
baby powder [bā/bē pow/dər] **37**–14
babysitter [bā/bē sĭt/ər] **166**–9
baby's room [bā/bēz/ rōōm/] **47**–10
back [băk] **104**–5
backache [băk/āk/] **110**–5
back button [băk/ bŭt/n] **197**–2
backhoe [băk/hō/] **178**–8
backpack [băk/păk/] **94**–18, **226**–15
backpacking [băk/păk/ĭng] **226**–6
backseat [băk/sēt/] **159**–54
back support belt [băk/ sə pört/ bĕlt/] **179**–18
go back [gō/ băk/] **11**–M
horseback riding [hörs/băk/ rī/dĭng] **226**–9
lower back [lō/ər băk/] **107**–29
pay back [pā/ băk/] **26**–D
Backyard [băk/yärd/] **53**
BACK FROM THE MARKET
[băk/ frəm dhə mär/kət] **66–67**
bacon [bā/kən] **70**–11, **80**–1
bad [băd] **23**–18
BAD DAY AT WORK [băd/ dā/ ăt würk/] **186–187**
badge [băj] **93**–21
badminton [băd/mĭn tən] **228**–6
bag [băg] **69**–31, **74**–7, **74**–19, **161**–18
air bag [ër/ băg/] **159**–43
baby bag [bā/bē băg/] **37**–16
clutch bag [klŭch/ băg/] **89**–19
grocery bag [grōs/rē băg/] **67**–13
handbag [hănd/ băg/] **87**–9, **94**–2
plastic storage bags [plăs/tĭk stör/ĭj băgz/] **72**–25
shoulder bag [shōl/dər băg/] **94**–17
sleeping bag [slē/pĭng băg/] **226**–12
totebag [tōt/ băg/] **94**–19
trash bags [trăsh/ băgz/] **61**–24
vacuum cleaner bag
[văk/yōōm klē/nər băg/] **61**–12
bagels [bā/gəlz] **73**–40
baggage [băg/ĭj]
baggage carousel [băg/ĭj kăr/ə sĕl/] **161**–23
bagger [băg/ər] **73**–14
baggy [băg/ē] **97**–30
bailiff [bā/lĭf] **141**–13
bake [bāk] **77**–H
Baked Goods [bākt/ gŏŏdz/] **73**
baked potato [bākt/ pə tā/tō] **81**–25
baker [bā/kər] **166**–10
bakery [bā/kə rē] **127**–19
Baking Products [bā/kĭng präd/ŭkts] **73**
balance [băl/əns] **132**–17, **195**–41
balcony [băl/kə nē] **51**–20
bald [böld] **33**–12
ball [böl] **59**–12, **231**–5, **231**–12
ball field [böl/ fēld/] **224**–1
ballroom [böl/rōōm/] **184**–26
baseball [bās/böl/] **231**–18, **231**–14
basketball [băs/kət böl/] **229**–8, **231**–4
basketball court [băs/kət böl/ kört/] **229**–7
football [fŏŏt/böl/] **229**–11, **231**–21
meatballs [mēt/bölz/] **81**–27
racquetball [răk/ət böl/] **228**–12
softball [söft/böl/] **229**–10
volleyball [väl/ē böl/] **229**–14, **231**–3
balloons [bə lōōnz/] **44**–4
bananas [bə năn/əz] **68**–2
band [bănd] **183**–34
headband [hĕd/bănd/] **90**–3
waistband [wāst/bănd/] **100**–5
bandage [băn/dĭj] **117**–5, **117**–12
bandana [băn dă/nə] **92**–16
bangs [băngz] **33**–8
bank [băngk] **124**–5
bank statement [băngk/ stāt/mənt] **132**–16
bank online [băngk/ än līn/] **132**–C
BANK [băngk] **132**
banner [băn/ər] **44**–1
banquet room [băng/kwət rōōm/] **185**–14
bar [bär]
bar code [bär/ kōd/] **27**–4
candy bar [kăn/dē bär/] **73**–37
grab bar [grăb/ bär/] **57**–9
menu bar [mĕn/yōō bär/] **197**–1
salad bar [săl/əd bär/] **79**–24
scroll bar [skrōl/ bär/] **197**–15
barbecued ribs [bär/bĭ kyōō/d rĭbz/] **76**–2
barbershop [bär/bər shäp/] **129**–19
bargain [bär/gən] **102**–A
barn [bärn] **177**–11
barrette [bə rĕt/] **108**–20
base [bās] **193**–45, **194**–20
baseball [bās/böl/] **229**–9, **231**–18
baseball bat [bās/böl/ băt/] **231**–14
baseball cap [bās/böl/ kăp/] **86**–5

  baseball cards [bās/böl/ kärds/] **232**–2
  baseball game [bās/böl/ gām/] **44**–2
basement [bās/mənt] **47**–13
Basement [bās/mənt] **50**
Basic Colors [bā/sĭk kŭ/lərz] **24**
BASIC TRANSPORTATION
  [bā/sĭk trănz/pər tā/shən] **150–151**
basket [băs/kət] **56**–3
  basketball [băs/kət böl/] **229**–8, **231**–4
  basketball court [băs/kət böl kört/] **229**–7
  bread basket [brĕd/ băs/kət] **83**–11
  laundry basket [lön/drē băs/kət] **101**–2
  shopping basket [shäp/ĭng băs/kət] **73**–9
  wastebasket [wāst/băs/kət] **57**–26
bass [băs] **212**–6, [bās] **238**–8
bassoon [bə so͞on/] **238**–4
bat [băt] **216**–7, **231**–14
bath [băth]
  bath mat [băth/ măt/] **57**–28
  bath powder [băth/ pow/dər] **108**–4
  bathroom [băth/ro͞om/] **46**–4
  bath towel [băth/ tow/əl] **57**–13
  bathtub [băth/tŭb/] **57**–2
  half bath [hăf/ băth/] **57** ✦
bathe [bādh] **36**–F, **108**–B
bathing suit [bā/dhĭng so͞ot/] **90**–26
BATHROOM [băth/ro͞om/] **57**
battery / batteries [băt/ə rē] / [băt/ə rēz]
  146–15, **158**–20
  battery charger [băt/ə rē chär/jər] **235**–27
  battery pack [băt/ə rē păk/] **235**–26
bay [bā] **204**–9
be [bē]
  be aware [bē ə wër/] **143**–I
  be born [bē börn/] **40**–A
  be 18 or older [bē ā/tēn/ ör öld/ər] **140**–G
  be hurt [bē hürt/] **116**–C
  be in a rock band [bē ĭn ə räk/ bănd/] **238**–D
  be informed [bē ĭn förmd/] **140**–F
  be injured [bē ĭn/jərd] **116**–C
  be in shock [bē ĭn shäk/] **116**–B
  be neat [bē nēt/] **174**–C
  be on time [bē ön tīm/] **174**–F
  be released [bē rĭ lēst/] **141**–H
  be unconscious [bē ŭn kän/shəs] **116**–A
  don't be late [dōnt/ bē lāt/] **174**–D
beach [bēch] **204**–10
  beach chair [bēch/ chër/] **225**–22
  beach umbrella [bēch/ ŭm brĕl/ə] **225**–14
BEACH [bēch] **225**
beads [bēdz] **95**–34, **99**–32
beak [bēk] **214**–3
beaker [bē/kər] **195**–39
beam [bēm] **178**–3
beans [bēnz] **69**–8, **72**–17
  soybeans [soy/bēnz/] **177**–3
bear [bër] **37**–23, **216**–11
beard [bërd] **33**–6
beat [bēt] **77**–S
beater [bē/tər]
  eggbeater [ĕg/bē/tər] **78**–20
beautiful [byo͞o/tə fəl] **23**–21
beauty shop [byo͞o/tē shäp/] **130** ✦
beaver [bē/vər] **216**–9
become [bē kŭm/] **40**–G, **41**–N
bed [bĕd] **58**–9
  bedbugs [bĕd/bŭgz/] **63**–24
  bed control [bĕd/ kən trōl/] **121**–27
  bed frame [bĕd/ frām/] **58**–18
  bed pan [bĕd/ păn/] **121**–23
  bedroom [bĕd/ro͞om/] **46**–2
  bedspread [bĕd/sprĕd/] **59**–11
  bed table [bĕd/ tā/bəl] **121**–21
  bunk beds [bŭnk/ bĕdz/] **59**–9
  double bed [dŭb/əl bĕd/] **184**–14
  flower bed [flow/ər bĕd/] **53**–20
  hospital bed [häs/pĭ tl bĕd/] **121**–22
  kids' bedroom [kĭdz/ bĕd/ro͞om/] **47**–9
  king-size bed [kĭng/sīz/ bĕd/] **184**–15
BEDROOM [bĕd/ro͞om/] **58, 59**
bee [bē]
  honeybee [hŭn/ē bē/] **214**–25
beef [bēf]
  beef ribs [bēf/ rĭbz/] **70**–5
  corned beef [körnd/ bēf/] **71**–22
  ground beef [grownd/ bēf/] **70**–4
  roast beef [rōst/ bēf/] **71**–21
  stewing beef [sto͞o/ĭng bēf/] **70**–3
  stir-fried beef [stür/frīd/ bēf/] **76**–6
Beef [bēf] **70**
beetle [bēt/l] **214**–18
beets [bēts] **69**–5
Before an Emergency [bĭ för/ ən ĭ mür/ jən sē] **146**
behind [bĭ hīnd/] **25**–8
beige [bāzh] **24**–18
bell [bĕl]
  bell captain [bĕl/ kăp/tən] **184**–6
  bellhop [bĕl/häp/] **184**–7
  bell peppers [bĕl/pĕp/ərz] **69**–7
  doorbell [dör/bĕl/] **53**–14
below [bĭ lō/] **25**–5
belts [bĕlts] **94**–6
  back support belt [băk/ sə pört/ bĕlt/] **179**–18
  belt buckle [bĕlt/ bŭk/əl] **94**–20
  conveyor belt [kən vā/ər bĕlt/] **175**–9
  garter belt [gär/tər bĕlt/] **91**–16
  seat belt [sēt/ bĕlt/] **159**–52
  tool belt [to͞ol/ bĕlt/] **92**–3
bench [bĕnch] **224**–10
bend [bĕnd] **230**–O
benefits [bĕn/ə fĭts] **174** ✦
berries [bĕr/ēz] **210**–20
  blackberries [blăk/bĕr/ēz] **68**–17
  blueberries [blo͞o/bĕr/ēz] **68**–16
  mixed berries [mĭkst/ bĕr/ēz] **81**–36
  raspberries [răz/bĕr/ēz] **68**–15
  strawberries [strö/bĕr/ēz] **68**–14
between [bĭ twēn/] **25**–12
Beverages [bĕv/rə jəz] **73, 81**
bib [bĭb] **37**–5
bicycle / bike [bī/sĭ kəl] / [bīk] **129**–22, **151**–15
big [bĭg] **23**–2, **97**–38
  Big Dipper [bĭg/ dĭ/pər] **205** ✦
  big-screen TV [bĭg/skrēn/ tē/vē/] **50**–15
bike / bicycle [bīk] / [bī/sĭ kəl] **129**–22, **151**–15
  bike path [bīk/ păth/] **224**–3
biking [bī/kĭng] **226**–8, **228**–5
bikini panties [bə kē/nē păn/tēz] **91**–13
bill [bĭl] **214**–3
Bill [bĭl] **15**
billiards [bĭl/yərdz] **228**–2
Bill of Rights [bĭl/ əv rīts/] **198**–10
Bills [bĭlz] **26**
bin [bĭn] **51**–23, **61**–2, **160**–6
bioenergy [bī/ō ĕn/ər jē] **218**–9
biography [bī ä/grə fē] **133**–15
biologist [bī ä/lə jĭst] **194**–2
Biology [bī ä/lə jē] **194**
biomass [bī/ō măs/] **218**–9
birch [bürch] **210**–7
bird [bürd] **208**–4
Bird [bürd] **214**
BIRDS, INSECTS, AND ARACHNIDS
  [bürdz/ ĭn/sĕkts ən ə răk/nĭdz] **214**
birth [bürth]
  birth certificate [bürth/ sər tĭf/ə kət] **40**–1
  birthday [bürth/dā/] **22**–1
BIRTHDAY PARTY [bürth/dā/ pär/tē] **240–241**
biscuits [bĭs/kəts] **80**–6
bison [bī/sən] **216**–6
bit [bĭt] **180**–28
bite [bīt] **110**–11
black [blăk] **24**–13
  blackberries [blăk/bĕr/ēz] **68**–17
  black hair [blăk/ hër/] **33**–16
bladder [blăd/ər] **107**–46
blade [blād] **107**–28, **109**–28, **180**–27
blankets [blăng/kəts] **58**–15, **146**–7, **225**–11
  blanket sleeper [blăng/kət slē/pər] **91**–27
blazer [blā/zər] **92**–12
bleach [blēch] **101**–7
bleachers [blē/chərz] **5**–3
bleed [blēd] **116**–M
blender [blĕn/dər] **54**–12
blind [blīnd] **32**–11
blister [blĭs/tər] **110**–15
blizzard [blĭz/ərd] **13**–23, **145**–13
blocks [bläks] **59**–19
  quilt block [kwĭlt/ bläk/] **232**–15
  sunblock [sŭn/bläk/] **108**–8, **225**–10
blond hair [bländ/ hër/] **33**–17
blood [blŭd] **111**–14
  blood pressure gauge [blŭd/ prĕsh/ər gāj/] **118**–9
  blood test [blŭd/ tĕst/] **121**–30
  blood work [blŭd/ würk/] **121**–30
  bloody nose [blŭd/ē nōz/] **110**–17
blouse [blows] **87**–8
blow dryer [blō/ drī/ər] **33**–23, **108**–18
blower [blō/ər] **176**–2
blow out [blō/ owt/] **240**–C
blue [blo͞o] **24**–3
  blueberries [blo͞o/bĕr/ēz] **68**–16
  blue jay [blo͞o/ jā/] **214**–6
  bright blue [brīt/ blo͞o/] **24**–12
  dark blue [därk/ blo͞o/] **24**–10
  light blue [līt/ blo͞o/] **24**–11
  navy blue [nā/vē blo͞o/] **28**–5

blues [blo͞oz] **237**–22
blush [blŭsh] **109**–37
board [börd]
board game [börd/ gām/] **232**–5
bulletin board [bo͝ol/ə tn börd/] **7**–14
chalkboard [chök/börd/] **6**–1
cutting board [kŭt/ĭng börd/] **54**–27
emery board [ĕm/ə rē börd/, ĕm/rē–] **109**–32
headboard [hĕd/börd/] **58**–10
ironing board [ī/ər nĭng börd/] **101**–14
motherboard [mŭdh/ər börd/] **196**–5
particle board [pär/tə kəl börd/] **181**–20
skateboard [skāt/börd/] **224**–7
snowboard [snō/börd/] **231**–23
surfboard [sürf/börd/] **225**–16
whiteboard [wīt/börd/] **6**–3
board [börd] **160**–E
boarding [bör/dĭng]
boarding area [bör/dĭng ër/ē ə] **161**–9
boarding pass [bör/dĭng păs/] **161**–20
sailboarding [sāl/bör/dĭng] **227** ✦
skateboarding [skāt/bör/dĭng] **228**–13
snowboarding [snō/bör/dĭng] **227**–2
boat [bōt]
sailboat [sāl/bōt/] **225**–3
boating [bō/tĭng] **226**–1
bobbin [bä/bĭn] **98**–21
bobby pins [bäb/ē pĭnz/] **108**–21
body [bäd/ē] **190**–7
body lotion [bäd/ē lō/shən] **108**–9
body of water [bäd/ē əv wö/tər] **204** ✦
body shaper [bäd/ē/ shā/pər] **91**–15
BODY [bäd/ē] **104–105, 106–107**
boil [boyl] **77**–M
boiled ham [boyld/ hăm/] **76**–5
boiler [boy/lər] **78**–8
bok choy [bäk/ choy/] **69**–15
bolt [bōlt] **51**–34, **180**–35, **180**–38
bolt of fabric [bōlt/ əv făb/rĭk] **98**–15
bone [bōn] **107**–33, **116**–P
boneless [bōn/ləs] **70** ✦
book [bo͝ok]
appointment book [ə poynt/mənt bo͝ok/] **183**–48
audiobook [ö/dē ō bo͝ok/] **133**–17
bookkeeper [bo͝ok/ kē/pər] **175**–2
book of stamps [bo͝ok/ əv stămps/] **134**–18
bookcase [bo͝ok/ kās/] **7**–10
bookstore [bo͝ok/ stör/] **130**–4
check book [chĕk/ bo͝ok/] **132**–12
coloring book [kŭl/ə rĭng bo͝ok/] **59**–13
DMV handbook [dē/ĕm/vē/ hănd/bo͝ok/] **136**–1
notebook [nōt/bo͝ok/] **7**–27
passbook [păs/bo͝ok/] **132**–10
picture book [pĭk/chər bo͝ok/] **133**–12
spiral notebook [spī/rəl nōt/bo͝ok/] **7**–29
test booklet [tĕst/ bo͝ok/lət] **10**–1
textbook [tĕkst/bo͝ok/, tĕks/–] **7**–25
workbook [würk/bo͝ok/] **7**–26
boombox [bo͞om/bäks/] **234**–1
booth [bo͞oth] **82**–4, **122**–3
boots [bo͞ots] **95**–28
hiking boots [hī/kĭng bo͞ots/] **95**–31
rain boots [rān/ bo͞ots/] **90**–20
safety boots [sāf/tē bo͞ots/] **179**–20
ski boots [skē/ bo͞ots/] **231**–26
steel toe boots [stēl/ tō/ bo͞ots/] **92**–6
bored [börd] **43**–25
borrow [bär/ō, bör/ō] **26**–B
boss [bäs] **164**–4
botanical garden [bə tăn/ĭ kəl gär/dn] **222**–3
bottle [bät/l] **37**–1, **74**–1, **74**–13
bottle return [bät/l rĭ türn/] **73**–16
hot water bottle [hät/ wö/tər bät/l] **113**–15
bottled water [bät/ld wö/tər] **146**–11
bouquet [bō kā/, bo͞o–] **211**–28
bow [bō] **231**–6
bow tie [bō/ tī/] **89**–16
bow [bow] **3**–H
bowl [bōl] **55**–2
mixing bowl [mĭks/ĭng bōl/] **54**–28, **78**–31
serving bowl [sürv/ĭng bōl/] **55**–21
soup bowl [so͞op/ bōl/] **83**–21
sugar bowl [sho͝og/ər bōl/] **55**–14
bowling [bō/lĭng] **228**–3
bowling alley [bō/lĭng ăl/ē] **222**–4
bowling ball [bō/lĭng böl/] **231**–5
box / boxes [bäks/, bäks/ĭz] **74**–6, **74**–18
box spring [bäks/ sprĭng/] **58**–19
CD boombox [sē/dē/ bo͞om/bäks/] **234**–1
fuse box [fyo͞oz/ bäks/] **62**–13
mailboxes [māl/bäk/səz] **50**–11, **128**–13
post office box (PO box)
[pōst/ ö/fəs bäks/] / [pē/ō bäks/] **135**–9
safety deposit box [sāf/tē dĭ päz/ət bäks/] **132**–7
sandbox [sănd/bäks/] **224**–15
search box [sürch/ bäks/] **197**–5
text box [tĕkst/ bäks/] **197**–13
to-go box [tə gō/ bäks/] **82**–5
boxer shorts [bäk/sər shörts/] **91**–4
boxing [bäks/ĭng] **228**–4
boy [boy] **31**–9
bra [brä] **91**–20
bracelets [brās/ləts] **95**–9, **117**–3
braces [brā/səz] **119**–6
brain [brān] **107**–34
brainstorm [brān/störm/] **8**–H, **191**–F
brake [brāk] **159**–48
brake light [brāk/ līt/] **158**–14
brake pedal [brāk/ pĕd/l] **159**–45
branch [brănch] **210**–2
Branch [brănch] **138**
Brass [brăs] **238**
bread [brĕd] **67**–11
bread-and-butter plate [brĕd/ n bŭt/ər plāt/] **83**–19
bread basket [brĕd/ băs/kət] **83**–11
garlic bread [gär/lĭk brĕd/] **81**–28
rye bread [rī/ brĕd/] **71**–20
wheat bread [wēt/ brĕd/] **71**–19
white bread [wīt/ brĕd] **71**–18
break [brāk] **77**–Q, **116**–P
break down [brāk/ down/] **162**–D
Breakfast Special [brĕk/fəst spĕ/shəl] **80**
breasts [brĕsts] **70**–19, **107**–26
breathe [brēdh] **116**–N
breathing [brē/dhĭng] **117**–16
bricklayer [brĭk/lā/ər] **186**–8
bricks [brĭks] **178**–12, **178**–B
briefcase [brēf/kās/] **88**–13
briefs [brēfs] **91**–5, **91**–14
bright blue [brīt/ blo͞o/] **24**–12
bring [brĭng] **174**–D, **240**–E
broccoli [bräk/ə lē] **69**–13
broiled steak [broyld/ stāk/] **76**–3
broiler [broy/lər] **54**–21
broken [brō/kən] **62**–5, **62**–6, **62**–7, **63**–15, **97**–39
broken equipment [brō/kən ĭ kwĭp/mənt] **179**–4
broom [bro͞om] **61**–16
brother [brŭdh/ər] **34**–6, **35**–28
brother-in-law [brŭdh/ər ĭn lö/] **34**–17
stepbrother [stĕp/brŭdh/ər] **35**–30
brown [brown] **24**–17
brown hair [brown/ hër/] **33**–18
hash browns [hăsh/ brownz/] **80**–3
browse [browz] **102**–B
bruise [bro͞oz] **110**–12
brush [brŭsh] **33**–22, **108**–14
paintbrush [pānt/brŭsh/] **181**–22, **233**–20
scrub brush [skrŭb/ brŭsh/] **61**–20
toilet brush [toy/lət brŭsh/] **57**–18
toothbrush [to͞oth/brŭsh/] **109**–22
brush [brŭsh] **108**–I, **109**–J
bubble in [bŭ/bəl ĭn/] **10**–K
bucket [bŭk/ət] **61**–7, **225**–8
buckle [bŭk/əl] **94**–20, **99**–28
buckle up [bŭk/əl ŭp/] **36**–L
bud [bŭd] **211**–7
budget [bŭ jĭt/] **186**–3
buffalo [bŭf/ə lō] **216**–6
buffet [bə fā/] **55**–24, **185**–10
bugs [bŭgz]
bedbugs [bĕd/bŭgz/] **63**–24
building [bĭl/dĭng] **50**–1, **124**–2
BUILDING SUPPLIES [bĭl/dĭng sə plīz/] **180–181**
bulb [bŭlb] **56** ✦, **211**–2
bulldozer [bo͝ol/dō/zər] **178**–6
bulletin board [bo͝ol/ə tn börd/] **7**–14
bump cap [bŭmp/ kăp/] **92**–9
bumper [bŭm/pər] **158**–8
bumper pad [bŭm/pər păd/] **59**–4
bunch [bŭnch] **68**–29
bunk beds [bŭngk/ bĕdz/] **59**–9
Bunsen burner [bŭn/sən bür/nər] **195**–37
bureau [byo͝or/ō] **58**–1
burger [bür/gər]
cheeseburger [chēz/bür/gər] **79**–3
hamburger [hăm/bür/gər] **79**–1
burglary [bür/glə rē] **142**–2
burn [bürn]
sunburn [sŭn/bürn/] **110**–14
burn [bürn] **116**–H
burner [bür/nər] **54**–19, **195**–37
burrito [bə rē/tō] **79**–9

bus [bŭs] **128**–9, **151**–14
bus person [bŭs/ pür/sən] **185**–13
bus route [bŭs/ ro͞ot/, –rowt/] **152**–1
bus station [bŭs/ stā/shən] **124**–7
bus stop [bŭs/ stäp/] **129**–16, **151**–13
miss the bus [mĭs/ dhə bŭs/] **152** ✦
bus [bŭs] **82**–G
business [bĭz/nəs]
business owner [bĭz/nəs ō/nər] **166**–11
businessperson [bĭz/nəs pür/sən] **166**–12
business suit [bĭz/nəs so͞ot/] **88**–11
busser [bŭ/sər] **83**–12
Bus Stop [bŭs/ stäp/] **152**
butcher [bo͝och/ər] **166**–13
butter [bŭt/ər] **66**–6, **83**–19
butterfly [bŭt/ər flī/] **214**–19
buttocks [bŭt/əks] **107**–30
button [bŭt/n] **99**–24
back button [băk/ bŭt/n] **197**–2
call button [köl/ bŭt/n] **121**–28
forward button [för/wərd bŭt/n] **197**–3
buy [bī] **27**–G
buy a home [bī/ ə hōm/] **41**–M
buy a snack [bī/ ə snăk/] **11**–K
buy recycled products
[bī/ rē sī/kəld präd/ŭkts] **219**–D
Buying a House [bī/ĭng ə hows/] **49**
BUYING AND MAINTAINING A CAR
[bī/ĭng ən mān tā/nĭng ə kär/] **157**
Buying a Used Car [bī/ĭng ə yo͞ozd/ kär/] **157**
buzzer [bŭz/ər] **51**–31
cab [kăb] **156**–16
cabbage [kăb/ĭj] **69**–2
Cabinet [kăb/ə nət] **138**–10
cabinet [kăb/ə nət] **54**–1
file cabinet [fīl/ kăb/ə nət] **182**–11
medicine cabinet [mĕd/ə sən kăb/ə nət] **57**–20
supply cabinet [sə plī/ kăb/ə nət] **182**–1
cables [kā/bəlz] **158**–21, **196**–13
cactus [kăk/təs] **210**–21
cafeteria [kăf/ə tïr/ē ə] **5**–14
cage [kāj] **107**–48
cake [kāk] **73**–39, **81**–33
cake pan [kāk/ păn/] **78**–26
cheesecake [chēz/kāk/] **81**–34
pancakes [păn/kāks/] **80**–7
Cake [kāk] **77**
calculate [kăl/kyə lāt/] **17**–B
calculator [kăl/kyə lā/tər] **17**–6, **183**–25
calculus [kăl/kyə ləs] **192**–19
CALENDAR [kăl/ən dər] **20–21**
CALENDAR EVENTS [kăl/ən dər ĭ vĕnts/] **22**
calf [kăf] **106**–22
calf-length [kăf/ lĕnth/] **96**–17
call [köl]
call button [köl/ bŭt/n] **121**–28
international call [ĭn/tər năsh/ə nəl köl/] **15**–35
Internet phone call [ĭn/tər nĕt/ fōn/ köl/] **14**–20
local call [lō/kəl köl/] **15**–31
long distance call [löng/ dĭs/təns köl/] **15**–32
call [köl] **48**–A, **147**–L
call in [köl/ ĭn/] **186**–A
calling card [kö/lĭng kärd/] **14**–15
calm [köm] **42**–8
camcorder [kăm/kör dər] **235**–24
camel [kăm/əl] **217**–38
camera [kăm/rə]
camera case [kăm/rə kās/] **235**–28
digital camera [dĭ/jə təl kăm/rə] **235**–19
film camera [fĭlm/ kăm/rə] **235**–21
security camera [sĭ kyo͝or/ə tē kăm/rə] **50**–19
35 mm camera
[thür/tē fīv/ mĭl/ə mē/tər kăm/rə] **235**–21
camisole [kăm/ə sōl/] **91**–21
campaign [kăm pān/] **139**–29
camper [kăm/pər] **156**–9
campfire [kămp/fīr/] **226**–11
camping [kăm/pĭng] **226**–5
camping stove [kăm/pĭng stōv/] **226**–16
Campus [kăm/pəs] **5**
can [kăn] **74**–3, **74**–15
can opener [kăn/ ō/pə nər] **78**–1, **146**–8
electric can opener [ĭ lĕk/trĭk/ kăn/ ō/pə nər] **54**–14
garbage can [gär/bĭj kăn/] **53**–24
cancer [kăn/sər] **111**–10
candle [kăn/dl] **56**–20
candle holder [kăn/dl hōl/dər] **56**–21
candy [kăn/dē] **239**–12
candy bar [kăn/dē bär/] **73**–37
candy cane [kăn/dē kān/] **239**–17
candy store [kăn/dē stör/] **131**–17
cane [kān] **113**–16, **239**–17
canned food [kănd/ fo͞od/] **146**–9
Canned Foods [kănd/ fo͞odz/] **72**
canoeing [kə no͞o/ĭng] **226**–3
can't breathe [kănt/ brēdh/] **116**–N
canteen [kăn tēn/] **226**–24
canvas [kăn/vəs] **233**–17
canyon [kăn/yən] **204**–17
cap [kăp] **88**–1, **206**–7
baseball cap [bās/böl/ kăp/] **86**–5
bump cap [bŭmp/ kăp/] **92**–9
shower cap [show/ər kăp/] **108**–1
surgical cap [sür/jĭ kəl kăp/] **121**–37
surgical scrub cap [sür/jĭ kəl skrŭb/ kăp/] **93**–35
capital [kă/pət əl] **139**–22
capitalize [kă/pət əl īz/] **190**–A, **190**–B
Capitol [kă/pət əl] **138**–1
capris [kə prēz] **88**–8
capsule [kăp/səl] **113**–23
car [kär] **150**–1
car accident [kär/ ăk/sə dənt] **144**–2
car dealership [kär/ dē/lər shĭp/] **126**–4
car safety seat [kär/ sāf/tē sēt/] **37**–19
4-door car [för/dör/ kär/] **156**–1
sports car [spörts/kär/] **156**–4
subway car [sŭb/wā/ kär/] **152**–6
town car [town/ kär/] **152**–20
2-door car [to͞o/dör/ kär/] **156**–2
Car [kär] **157, 159**
CAR [kär] **156, 157, 158–159**
card [kärd] **239**–5
ATM card [ā/tē/ĕm/ kärd/] **132**–15
auto club card [ö tō/ klŭb/ kärd/] **162**–4
baseball cards [bās/böl/ kärdz/] **232**–2
card store [kärd/ stör/] **130**–7
copies of ID and credit cards
[käp/ēz əv ī/dē/ ən krĕd/ət/ kärdz/] **146**–19
emergency card [ĭ mür/jən sē/ kärd/] **161**–23
fare card [fër/ kärd/] **152**–11
folding card table [fōl/dĭng/ kärd/ tā/bəl] **102**–4
green card [grēn/ kärd/] **40**–2
greeting card [grē/tĭng kärd/] **134**–15
health insurance card
[hĕlth/ ĭn sho͝or/əns kärd/] **118**–3
memory card [mĕm/ə rē kärd/] **235**–20
post card [pōst/ kärd/] **134**–16
Resident Alien card [rĕz/ə dənt ā/lē ən kärd/] **40**–2
rotary card file [rō/tə rē kärd/ fīl/] **183**–44
Social Security card
[sō/shəl sĭ kyo͝or/ə tē kärd/] **40**–5
Card [kärd] **135**
cardigan sweater [kär/də gən swĕt/ər] **88**–2
Cardinal Numbers [kärd/nəl nŭm/bərz] **16**
cardiologist [kär/dē äl/ə jĭst] **120**–3
cardiopulmonary resuscitation (CPR)
[kär/dē ō po͝ol mə nër/ē rĭ sŭs/ə tā/shən] /
[sē/pē/är/] **117**–17
care [kër] **167**–32
careful worker [kër/fəl wür/kər] **179**–2
careless worker [kër/ləs wür/kər] **179**–1
childcare worker [chīld/kër wür/kər] **166**–16
CARE [kër] **114–115, 118, 119**
Care of Your Car [kër/ əv yər kär/] **157**
career counselor [kə rēr/ kown/slər] **172**–10
Career Path [kə rēr/ păth/] **172**
CAREER PLANNING [kə rēr/ plăn/ĭng] **172**
cargo van [kär/gō văn/] **156**–13
carnation [kär nā/shən] **211**–20
carousel [kăr/ə sĕl/] **161**–23
carpenter [kär/pən tər] **62**–12, **166**–14
carpet [kär/pət] **56**–24
carpool [kär/po͞ol/] **219**–I
carriage [kăr/ĭj] **37**–20
carrier [kăr/ē ər] **37**–17, **134**–20
carrots [kăr/əts] **69**–3
carry [kăr/ē] **11**–F, **82**–H
CARS AND TRUCKS [kärz/ ən trŭks/] **156**
cart [kärt] **72**–7, **129**–28
housekeeping cart [hows/kē/pĭng kärt/] **184**–19
luggage cart [lŭg/ĭj/ kärt/] **184**–8
carton [kär/tn] **74**–4, **74**–16
cartoon [kär/to͞on] **236**–3
cartridge [kär/trĭj] **183**–45
carving knife [kär/vĭng nīf/] **78**–12
case [kās] **94**–5, **235**–28
cash [kăsh]
cash and coins [kăsh/ ən koynz/] **146**–17
cash register [kăsh/ rĕj/ə stər] **27**–10, **73**–15
cash [kăsh] **27**–F, **132**–A
cashier [kă shïr/] **73**–13, **166**–15
cashmere [kăzh/mïr/] **98**–4
Casserole [kăs/ə rōl] **77**
casserole dish [kăs/ə rōl dĭsh/] **78**–10
cassette [kə sĕt/] **234**–6
videocassette [vĭ/dē ō kə sĕt/] **133**–18

cast [kăst] **113**–20
castle [kă/səl] **225**–12
Casual Clothes [kăzh/o͞o əl klōz/] **88**
CASUAL, WORK, AND FORMAL CLOTHES
[kăzh/o͞o əl würk/ ən för/məl klōz/] **88–89**
cat [kăt] **215**–9
catfish [kăt/fĭsh/] **71**–2
catalog [kăt ə /lög] **133**–11
catch [kăch] **230**–D
catcher's mask [kăch/ərz măsk/] **231**–15
caterer [kā/tər ər] **185**–16
caterpillar [kăt/ə pĭl/ər, kăt/ər–] **214**–20
cattle [kăt/l] **177**–21
cauliflower [kö/lĭ flow/ər, kä/–] **69**–14
cave [kāv] **220**–6
caverns [că/vərnz] **220**–7
cavity [kăv/ə tē] **119**–7
C-clamp [sē/klămp/] **180**–6
CD [sē/dē/] **196**–9, **234**–5
CD boombox [sē/dē/ bo͞om/bäks/] **234**–1
CD player [sē/dē/ plā/ər] **159**–38
celebrate [sĕl/ə brāt] **206**–C
celery [sĕl/ə rē] **69**–9
cell [sĕl] **194**–4
cell membrane [sĕl/ mĕm/brān] **194**–6
cell phone holder [sĕl/ fōn/ hōl/dər] **94**–15
cell phone kiosk [sĕl/ fōn/ kē/ösk] **131**–22
cell phone number [sĕl/ fōn/ nŭm/bər] **4**–12
cell wall [sĕl/ wäl/] **194**–5
cello [chĕl/ō] **238**–7
cellular phone [sĕl/yə lər fōn/] **14**–8
Celsius [sĕl/sē əs] **13**–2
cemetery [sĕ/mə tĕr/ē] **127**–15
cent [sĕnt] **26**–1, **26**–2, **26**–3, **26**–4
center [sĕn/tər]
automated postal center (APC)
[ö/tə māt ĭd pōs/təl sĕn/tər] / [ā/pē/sē/] **135**–10
childcare center [chīld/kër/ sĕn/tər] **129**–30
convention center [kən vĕn/shən sĕn/tər] **127**–24
copy center [käp/ē sĕn/tər] **129**–18
entertainment center
[ĕn/tər tān/mənt sĕn/tər] **56**–5
resource center [rē/sörs sĕn/tər] **172**–9
CENTER [sĕn/tər] **208–209**
centimeter [cm] [sĕn/tə mē/tər] **17**–14
CENTRAL AMERICA [sĕn/trəl ə mĕr/ə kə] **200–201**
Central time [sĕn/trəl tīm/] **19**–31
cereal [sïr/ē əl] **80**–9
ceremony [sĕr/ə mō/nē] **206**–6
certificate [sər tĭf/ə kət] **40**–1, **41**–11
Certificate of Naturalization
[sər tĭf/ə kət əv năch/rə lə zā/shən] **40**–6
certified [sür/tə fīd/]
Certified Mail® [sür/tə fīd/ māl] **134**–4
certified nursing assistant (CNA)
[sür/tə fīd/ nür/sĭng ə sĭs/tənt] / [sē/ĕn/ā/]
120–12
chain [chān] **51**–33, **95**–33, **180**–41
chair [chër] **7**–11
armchair [ärm/chër] **56**–22
beach chair [bēch/ chër/] **225**–22
dining room chair [dī/nĭng ro͞om/chër/] **55**–8
easy chair [ē/zē/ chër] **56**–22
folding chair [fōld/ĭng chër/] **102**–5
high chair [hī/ chër/] **37**–6, **82**–3
rocking chair [räk/ĭng chër/] **37**–21
wheelchair [wēl/chër/] **113**–9
chalk [chök] **7**–18
chalkboard [chök/börd/] **6**–1
challenged [chăl/əngd] **32**–10
change [chānj] **36**–G, **60**–P, **148**–C
change purse [chānj/ pürs/] **94**–14
changing [chān/jĭng]
changing pad [chān/jĭng păd/] **59**–2
changing table [chān/jĭng tā/bəl] **59**–1
charger [chär/jər] **14**–10, **234**–17, **235**–27
chart [chärt] **121**–24
cheap [chēp] **23**–20
check [chĕk] **132**–13
check book [chĕk/ bo͝ok/] **132**–12
check-in kiosk [chĕk/ĭn/ kē/ösk] **160**–2
checkstand [chĕk/stănd/] **73**–12
paycheck [pā/chĕk/] **165**–14
check [chĕk]
check blood pressure [chĕk/ blŭd/ prĕsh/ər] **118**–A
check email [chĕk/ ē/ māl/] **39**–W
check in [chĕk/ ĭn/] **160**–A
check Internet job sites
[chĕk/ ĭn/tər nĕt/ jäb/ sīts/] **173**–D
check messages [chĕk/ mĕs/ə jĭz] **171**–R
check out [chĕk/ owt/] **133**–C
check the correct boxes
[chĕk/ dhə kə rĕkt/ bäk/səz] **9**–U
check the oil [chĕk/ dhə oyl/] **157**–H
check the pronunciation
[chĕk/ dhe prə nən sē ā/ shən] **8**–D
check your bags [chĕk/ yər băgz/] **160**–B
check pulse [chĕk/ pŭls/] **122**–A
check your spelling [chĕk/ yər spĕl/ĭng] **197**–F
check your understanding
[chĕk/ yər ŭn/dər stănd/ĭng] **12**–N
check your work [chĕk/ yər würk/] **10**–L
checked [chĕkt] **96**–24
checkers [chĕk/ərz] **232**–7
checking account number
[chĕk/ĭng ə kownt/ nŭm/bər] **132**–14
checkout [chĕk/owt/] **133**–10
Checkpoint [chĕk/poynt/] **160**
cheddar cheese [chĕd/ər chēz/] **71**–28
cheek [chēk] **106**–3
cheese [chēz] **66**–4
American cheese [ə mĕr/ə kən chēz/] **71**–26
cheddar cheese [chĕd/ər chēz/] **71**–28
cheeseburger [chēz/bür/gər] **79**–3
cheesecake [chēz/kāk/] **81**–34
grilled cheese sandwich
[grĭld/ chēz/ săn/wĭch, –sănd/–] **80**–10
Swiss cheese [swĭs/ chēz/] **71**–27
Cheesy Tofu Vegetable Casserole
[chē/zē tō/fo͞o vĕj/tə bəl kăs/ə rōl] **77**
chef [shĕf] **83**–16
chef's hat [shĕfs/ hăt/] **93**–28
chef's jacket [shĕfs/ jăk/ət] **93**–29
chef's salad [shĕfs/ săl/ əd] **80**–14
executive chef [ĭg zĕk/yə tĭv shĕf/] **185**–7
head chef [hĕd/ shĕf/] **185**–7
sous chef [so͞o/ shĕf/] **185**–6
Chef [shĕf] **93**
chemist [kĕm/ĭst] **195**–25
Chemistry [kĕm/ə strē] **195**
cherries [chĕr/ēz] **68**–11
cherry picker [chĕr/ē pĭk/ər] **178**–5
chess [chĕs] **232**–8
chest [chĕst] **59**–16, **104**–4, **107**–25
chest of drawers [chĕst/ əv drörz/] **59**–6
chicken [chĭk/ən] **66**–3, **70**–16
chicken pox [chĭk/ən päks/] **111**–6
chicken sandwich [chĭk/ən săn/wĭch, –sănd–] **79**–5
fried chicken [frīd/ chĭk/ən] **76**–1
roast chicken [rōst/ chĭk/ən] **81**–22
Chicken [chĭk/ən] **77**
chief justice [chēf/ jŭs/təs] **138**–13
CHILDCARE AND PARENTING
[chīld/kër ən për/ən tĭng] **36–37**
child / children [chīld] / [chĭl/ drən]
childcare center [chīld/kër sĕn/tər] **129**–30
childcare worker [chīld/kër wür/kər] **166**–16
children's program [chĭl/drənz prō/grăm] **236**–9
child safety seat [chīld/ sāf/tē sēt/] **159**–53
grandchild [grăn/chīld/, grănd/–] **34** ✦
lost child [löst/ chīld/] **144**–1
Childhood Diseases [chīld/ho͝od dĭ zē/zəz] **111**
chili peppers [chĭl/ē pĕp/ərz] **69**–29
chill [chĭl] **76**–D
chills [chĭlz] **110**–9
chimney [chĭm/nē] **53**–5
chimpanzee [chĭm/păn zē/] **217**–27
chin [chĭn] **106**–1
chipmunk [chĭp/mŭngk] **215**–20
chips [chĭps] **73**–35
chiropractors [kī/rō präk/tərz] **120**
chisel [chĭz/əl] **181**–55
choke [chōk] **116**–L
choose [cho͞oz] **9**–P
chop [chäp] **77**–L
chops [chäps] **70**–10, **70**–15
Christmas [krĭs/məs] **22**–18
Christmas tree [krĭs/məs trē/] **239**–16
chromosome [krō/mə zōm/] **194**–8
chrysanthemum [krĭ săn/thə məm] **211**–21
church [chürch] **127**–14
chute [sho͞ot] **51**–26
circle [sür/ kəl] **193**–34
circle [sür/ kəl] **9**–Q
circular saw [sür/kyə lər sö/] **180**–9
circulation desk [sür/kyə lā/shən dĕsk/] **133**–2
circumference [sər kŭm/frəns] **193**–36
citizen [sĭt/ə zən] **30**–5
Citizenship Requirements
[sĭt/ə zən shĭp/ rĭ kwīr/mənts] **140**
city [sĭt/ē] **4**–7, **52**–1
city code [sĭt/ē kōd/] **15**–34
city council [sĭt/ē kown/səl] **139**–27
city hall [sĭt/ē häl/] **124**–8
City Government [sĭt/ē gŭ/vərn mənt] **139**
CITY STREETS [sĭt/ē strēts/] **126–127**

Index

CIVIC RIGHTS AND RESPONSIBILITIES
[sĭ/vĭk rīts n rĭ spän/sə bĭl/ə tēz] **140**
Civilizations [sĭ/və lə zā/shenz] **199**
claim [klām] **160**–L
clamp [klămp] **180**–6
clams [klămz] **71**–15
clarinet [klăr/ə nĕt/] **238**–2
classical [kla/sĭ kəl] **237**–21
classical concert [kla/sĭ kəl kän/sərt] **223**–14
classified ad [klăs/e fīd] **48**–2
Classmates [klăs/māts/] **8**
classroom [klăs/ro͞om/] **5**–7
CLASSROOM [klăs/ro͞om/] **6–7**
claw [klö] **214**–2
clean [klēn] **101**–16
clean [klēn] **76**–A
clean teeth [klēn/ tēth/] **119**–A
clean the house [klēn/ dhə hows/] **39**–O
clean the lint trap [klēn/ dhə lĭnt/ trăp/] **101**–D
clean the oven [klēn/ dhə ŭv/ən] **60**–C
clean up [klēn/ ŭp/] **147**–M
cleaner [klēn/ər]
dry cleaners [drī/ klēn/ərz] **128**–2
glass cleaner [glăs/ klēn/ər] **61**–14
oven cleaner [ŭv/ən klēn/ər] **61**–3
vacuum cleaner [văk/yo͞om klēn/ər] **61**–10
vacuum cleaner attachments
[văk/yo͞om klēn/ər ə tăch/mənts] **61**–11
vacuum cleaner bag [văk/yəm klēn/ər băg/] **61**–12
CLEANING SUPPLIES [klē/nĭng sə plīz/] **61**
cleanser [klĕn/zər] **61**–18
CLEANUP [klēn/ŭp/] **148–149**
clear [klïr] **13**–9
clear tape [klïr/tāp/] **183**–30
clear [klïr] **82**–G
clear off [klïr/ äf/] **10**–I
clerk [klürk] **5**–13, **182**–2
admissions clerk [əd mĭsh/ənz klürk/] **120**–14
desk clerk [dĕsk/ klürk/] **184**–11
DMV clerk [dē/ĕm/vē/ klürk/] **136**–3
file clerk [fīl/ klürk/] **182**–10
grocery clerk [grōs/rē klürk/, grōsh/–, grō/sə–] **72**–4
library clerk [lī/brër ē klürk/] **133**–1
payroll clerk [pā/rōl/ klürk/] **165**–10
postal clerk [pō/stəl klürk/] **135**–7
retail clerk [rē/tāl/ klürk/] **169**–53
salesclerk [sālz/klürk/] **94**–3
shipping clerk [shĭp/ĭng klürk/] **175**–16
stock clerk [stäk/ klürk/] **169**–59
click [klĭk] **197**–B
climb [klīm] **224**–C
climbing apparatus [klīm/ĭng ă/pə rā/təs] **224**–14
clinic [klĭn/ĭk] **186**–2
clip-on earrings [klĭp/än ïr/ĭngz, –ön–] **95**–37
clipper [klĭp/ər] **109**–31, **176**–11
clips [klĭps] **108**–19, **183**–31, **194**–24
clock [kläk] **7**–9, **58**–24, **165**–7
clock radio [kläk/ rā/dē ō] **102**–6
close [klōz] **6**–H
closet [kläz/ət] **57** ✦, **58**–5
Closures [klō/zhərz] **99**
cloth [klöth] **181**–54
cloth diaper [klöth/ dī/pərz] **37**–8
tablecloth [tā/bəl klöth/] **55**–12
washcloth [wäsh/klöth/] **57**–4
clothes [klōz] **146**–6
clothesline [klōz/līn/] **101**–9
clothespin [klōz/pĭn/] **101**–10
CLOTHES [klōz] **86–87, 88–89, 96–97, 98–99**
clothing [klō/dhĭng] **102**–2
CLOTHING [klō/dhĭng] **90, 92–93**
Clothing Problems [klō/dhĭng präb/ləmz] **97**
cloudy [klow/dē] **13**–10
club [klŭb] **162**–4, **223**–12, **231**–1
club sandwich [klŭb săn/wĭch/, –sănd–] **80**–12
clubs [klŭbz] **233**–32
clutch [klŭch] **159**–49
clutch bag [klŭch/ băg/] **89**–19
CNA (certified nursing assistant) [sē/ĕn/ā/] /
[sür/tə tə fīd/ nür/sĭng ə sĭs/tənt] **120**–12
coach [kōch] **5**–20, **229**–2
coal [kōl] **218**–4
coarse adjustment knob
[körs/ ə jŭst/mənt näb/] **194**–22
Coast Guard [kōst/ gärd/] **138**–18
coat [kōt] **90**–2, **216**–19
lab coat [lăb/ kōt/] **93**–33
raincoat [rān/ kōt/] **90**–18
sports coat [spörts/ kōt/] **89**–14
trench coat [trĕnch/ kōt/] **90**–21
cobra [kō/brə] **213**–41
cockpit [käk/pĭt/] **161**–10
cockroaches [käk/rō/chəz] **63**–26
cocktail dress [käk/tāl/ drĕs/] **89**–20
coconuts [kō/kə nŭts/] **68**–24
cod [käd] **71**–8, **212**–5
code [kōd]
area code [ër/ē ə kōd/] **15**–29
bar code [bär/ kōd/] **27**–4
city code [sĭt/ē kōd/] **15**–34
country code [kŭn/trē kōd/] **15**–33
coffee [kö/fē] **73**–33, **81**–37, **81**–38
coffeemaker [kö/fē mā/kər] **54**–11
coffee mug [kö/fē mŭg/] **55**–7
coffee shop [kö/fē shäp/] **126**–11
coffee table [kö/fē tā/bəl] **56**–19
COFFEE SHOP MENU [kö/fē shäp/ mĕn/yo͞o] **80–81**
coins [koynz] **146**–17
coin purse [koyn/ pürs/] **94**–14
Coins [koynz] **26**
colander [käl/ən dər] **78**–17
cold [kōld] **13**–6, **42**–4, **111**–1
cold tablets [kōld tăb/ləts] **113**–27
cold water [kōld wö/tər] **57**–7
coleslaw [kōl/slö/] **80**–18
collar [käl/ər] **100**–4
collate [kō/lāt/, kə lāt/] **171**–E
collect [kə lĕkt/] **232**–A
college [käl/ĭj] **127**–17, **188**–6, **188**–7
college degree [käl/ĭj də grē/] **41**–7
college dormitory [käl/ĭj dör/mə tör/ē] **52**–8
cologne [kə lōn/] **108**–6
colon [kō/lən] **190**–17
Colonial Period [kə lō/nē əl pïr/ē əd] **198**
colonies [kä/lə nēz] **198**–1
colonists [kä/lə nĭsts] **198**–2
color [kŭl/ər]
watercolor [wö/tər kŭl/ər] **233**–21
color [kŭl/ər] **33**–D
coloring book [kŭl/ə rĭng bo͝ok/] **59**–13
Colors [kŭl/ərs] **24**
COLORS [kŭl/ərs] **24**
Columbus Day [kə lŭm/bəs dā/] **22**–15
column [käl/ŭm] **107**–49
comb [kōm] **33**–21, **108**–13
comb [kōm] **108**–G
come [kŭm] **39**–R
comedy [käm/ə dē] **236**–2, **237**–13
comet [käm/ət] **205**–24
comfort [kŭm/fərt] **36**–I
comma [käm/ə] **190**–14
commercial fisher [kə mür/shəl fĭsh/ər] **167**–17
commit a crime [kə mĭt/ ə krīm/] **142** ✦
Common Illnesses and Childhood Diseases
[käm/ən ĭl/nə səz ən chīld/ho͝od-dĭ zē/zəz] **111**
COMMUNITY CLEANUP
[kə myo͞o/nə tē klēn/ŭp] **148–149**
community college
[kə myo͞o/nə tē käl/ĭj] **127**–17, **188**–6
Comparing Clothing [kəm për/ĭng klō/dhĭng] **97**
compartment [kəm pärt/mənt] **159**–44, **161**–13
complaint [kəm plānt/] **97** ✦
Complex [käm/plĕks/] **51**
compliment [käm/plə mĕnt/] **12** ✦
compliment [käm/plə mĕnt/] **12**–C
composer [kəm pō/zər] **199**–15
composition [käm/pə zĭsh/ən] **199**–14
compost [käm/pōst/] **219**–M
compost pile [käm/pōst pīl/] **53**–25
computer [kəm pyo͞o/tər] **7**–15, **183**–17
computer lab [kəm pyo͞o/tər lăb/] **5**–15
computer software engineer
[kəm pyo͞o/tər söft/wër/ ĕn/jə nïr/] **167**–18
computer technician [kəm pyo͞o/tər tĕk nĭsh/ən]
167–19, **182**–12
Computer [kəm pyo͞o/tər] **196**
COMPUTERS [kəm pyo͞o/tərz] **196**
conceal [kən sēl/] **143**–C
concert [kän/sərt] **222**–5, **223**–14
concierge [kän/sē ërzh/, kōn/–] **184**–4
conclusion [kən klo͞o/zhən] **190**–8
concrete [käng/krēt, kän krēt/] **178**–10
conditioner [kən dĭsh/ə nər] **108**–11, **159**–39
Conditions [kən dĭsh/ənz] **13, 111**
CONDITIONS [kən dĭsh/ənz] **111**
condominium [kän/də mĭn/ē əm] **52**–5
conduct [kən dŭkt/] **238**–C
conductor [kən dŭk/tər] **152**–13
cone [kōn] **79**–13, **193**–40
pinecone [pīn/kōn] **210**–11
conference room [kän/frəns ro͞om/] **182**–4
confetti [kən fĕt/ē] **239**–3
confused [kən fyo͞ozd/] **43**–26
congestion [kən jĕs/chən] **110**–7
Congress [käng/grəs] **138**–2, **198**–6

congressperson [kän/grəs pür/sən] **138**–4
CONSERVATION [kän/sər vā/shən] **218–219**
Conserve Energy and Resources
[kən sürv/ ĕn/ər jē ən rē/sörs/əz] **219**
console [kän/sōl] **232**–3
constellation [kän/stə lā/shən] **205**–14
Constitution [kän/stə too/shən] **198**–19
construction [kən strŭk/shən]
construction paper [kən strŭk/shən pā/pər] **232**–12
construction site [kən strŭk/shən sīt/] **126**–2
construction worker
[kən strŭk/shən wür/kər] **178**–1
CONSTRUCTION [kən strŭk/shən] **178**
Construction Worker [kən strŭk/shən wür/kər] **92**
contact [kän/tăkt] **146**–2
contact lenses [kän/tăkt lĕn/zəz] **115**–8
container [kən tā/nər] **74**–5, **74**–17, **78**–4
CONTAINERS AND PACKAGING
[kən tā/nərz ən păk/ĭ jĭng] **74**
continental [kän/tə nĕnt/əl] **198**–6
contractor [kän/trăk tər] **186**–5
control [kən trōl/] **121**–27, **232**–4
convenience store [kən vēn/yəns stör/] **128**–3
convention center [kən vĕn/shən sĕn/tər] **127**–24
convert [kən vürt/] **17**–D, **75**–C
convertible [kən vür/tə bəl] **156**–5
conveyer belt [kən vā/ər bĕlt/] **175**–16
convict [kän/vĭkt/] **141**–15
convict [kən vĭkt/] **141**–E
cook [kŏŏk] **185**–1, **185** ✦
cook [kŏŏk] **39**–Q, **76**–C, **170**–C
cooked [kŏŏkt] **70**–25
cookies [kŏŏk/ēz] **73**–38
cookie sheet [kŏŏk/ē shēt/] **78**–27
cool [kool] **13**–5
cooler [koo/lər] **225**–19
co-op [kō/äp/] **52** ✦
copier [kä/pē ər]
photocopier [fō/tō kä/pē ər]**183**–23
copies / copy [kä/pēz] / [kä/pē]
copies of ID and credit cards
[käp/ēz əv ī/dē ən krĕd/ət kärdz/] **146**–19
copies of important papers
[käp/ēz əv ĭm pört/ənt pā/pərz] **146**–20
copy center [käp/ē sĕn/tər] **129**–18
copy [käp/ē] **8**–E
coral [kör/əl] **220**–5
cord [körd] **14**–2
bungee cord [bŭn/jē körd/] **181**–15
cordless phone [körd/ləs fōn/] **15**–24
extension cord [ĭk stĕn/shən körd/] **181**–14
frayed cord [frād/ körd/] **179**–5
power cord [pow/ər körd/] **196**–2
corduroy [kör/də roy/] **99**–11
core course [kör/ körs/] **189** ✦
corn [körn] **69**–12, **177**–4
corn rows [körn/ rōz/] **33**–14
corned beef [körnd/ bēf/] **71**–22
corner [kör/nər] **128**–7
coronary disease [kör/ə nĕ/rē dĭ zēz/] **111** ✦
corral [kə răl/] **177**–17
correct [kə rĕkt/] **10**–N
correction [kə rĕk/shən]
correction fluid [kə rĕk/shən floo/əd] **183**–36
correction tape [kə rĕk/shən tāp/] **183**–37
cost [köst] **27**–7, **122**–1
costume [käs/toom] **239**–11
cotton [kät/n] **98**–1, **177**–6
couch [kowch] **56**–18
cough [köf] **110**–A
cough syrup [köf/ sĭr/əp, –sür/–] **113**–29
council [kown/səl] **139**–27
councilperson [kown/səl pür/sən] **139**–28
counselor [kown/slər] **5**–6, **172**–10
count [kownt] **84**–A
counter [kown/tər] **54**–22, **113**–18
counterperson [kown/tər pür/sən] **79**–17
Counterperson [kown/tər pür/sən] **93**
country [kŭn/trē] **52**–4, **227**–3, **237**–27
country code [kŭn/trē kōd/] **15**–33
county fair [kown/tē fër/] **223**–13
coupe [koop] **156**–2
couple [kŭ/pəl] **35**–20, **35**–21, **239**–4
coupons [koo/pönz/] **67**–15
courier [kür/ē ər, kŏŏr/–] **168**–40
course [körs] **172**–8, **189** ✦
court [kört]
basketball court [băs/kət böl/ kört/] **229**–7
courthouse [kört/hows/] **125**–13
courtroom [kört/room/] **141**–7
court reporter [kört/ rĭ pör/tər] **141**–12
courtyard [kört/yärd/] **51**–21
food court [food/ kört/] **131**–15
Supreme Court [sə prēm/ kört/] **138**–11
tennis court [tĕ/nəs kört/] **224**–6
cousin [kŭz/ən] **34**–9
cover [kŭv/ər] **158**–9, **181**–46
coveralls [kŭv/ər ölz/] **92**–8
cover-up [kŭv/ər ŭp/] **90**–25
cow [kow] **215**–1
cowboy hat [kow/boy/ hăt/] **92**–18
coyote [kī ō/tē, kī/ōt/] **216**–3
CPR (cardiopulmonary resuscitation) [sē/pē/är/] /
[kär/dē ō pŏŏl/mə nër/ē-rē sŭs/ə tā/shən] **117**–17
CPU [sē/pē/yoo/] **196**–4
crab [krăb] **71**–9, **212**–20
cracked [krăkt] **62**–4
cradle [krād/l] **59**–20
crane [krān] **178**–7
crash [krăsh] **144**–3
crayons [krā/änz] **59**–14
cream [krēm] **24**–16, **81**–41, **113**–25
antihistamine cream
[ăn/tĭ hĭs/tə mēn krēm/] **117**–11
ice-cream [īs/ krēm/] **72**–26
ice-cream cone [īs/ krēm kōn/] **79**–13
ice cream shop [īs/ krēm shäp/] **131**–16
shaving cream [shā/vĭng krēm/] **109**–29
sour cream [sow/ər krēm/] **72**–21
creamer [krē/mər] **55**–15
credit [krĕd/ət] **146**–19
creek [krēk, krĭk] **204** ✦
crescent moon [krĕs/ənt moon/] **205**–10
crew [kroo] **176**–1, **176**–4
crewneck [kroo/nĕk] **96**–7
crew socks [kroo/säks/] **91**–8
crib [krĭb] **59**–3
cricket [krĭk/ət] **214**–23
crime [krīm] **142** ✦
CRIME [krīm] **142**
criminal [krĭm/ə nəl] **142** ✦
crocheting [krō shā/ĭng] **233**–25
crocodile [kräk/ə dīl/] **213**–37
crocus [krō/kəs] **211**–17
Crops [kräps] **177**
cross [krös]
cross-country skiing [krös/kŭn/trē skē/ĭng] **227**–3
crosswalk [krös/wök/] **128**–15
cross [krös] **128**–A
cross out [krös/ owt/] **9**–R
crossing [krö/sĭng] **154**–13, **154**–14, **154**–15
crown [krown] **119**–9
crucible tongs [kroo/sə bəl tängz/, –töngz/] **195**–44
crutches [krŭch/əz] **113**–10
cry [krī] **206**–B
cube [kyoob] **193**–38
cubicle [kyoob/ə kəl] **182**–7
cucumbers [kyoo/kŭm bərz] **69**–10
cuff [kŭf] **100**–9
cup [kŭp] **75**–2, **75**–10, **83**–24
1/2 cup [hăf/ kŭp/] **75**–9
1/4 cup [kwör/tər kŭp/] **75**–8
teacup [tē/kŭp/] **55**–6
curb [kürb] **129**–21
curling iron [kür/lĭng ī/ərn] **108**–17
curly hair [kür/lē hër/] **33**–11
cursor [kür/sər] **197**–14
curtains [kür/tnz] **57**–12, **58**–7
curved line [kürvd/ līn/] **193**–23
cushion [kŏŏ/shən] **56** ✦, **100**–13
customer [kŭs/tə mər] **72**–1, **94**–4, **132**–2, **164**–2
customer service [kŭs/tə mər sür/vəs] **97** ✦
customer service representative
[kŭs/tə mər-sür/vəs rĕ/prə zĕn/tə tĭv] **167**–20
Customs [kŭs/təmz] **161**
customs officer [kŭs/təmz ö/fə sər] **161**–17
cut [kŭt] **91**–10, **110**–13
cut [kŭt] **33**–A, **109**–N
cut up [kŭt/ ŭp/] **77**–I
cute [kyoot] **32**–14
cutlets [kŭt/ləts] **70**–6
cutter [kut/ər] **183**–22, **232**–16
cutting board [kŭt/ĭng börd/] **54**–27
cycling [sī/klĭng] **228**–5
cyclist [sī/klĭst] **224**–2
cylinder [sĭl/ən dər] **193**–41, **195**–38
cytoplasm [sī/tə plăzm] **194**–9
daffodil [dăf/ə dĭl/] **211**–25
daily [dā/lē] **20**–21
DAILY ROUTINES [dā/lē roo tēnz/] **38–39**
Dairy [dër/ē] **72**
daisy [dā/zē] **211**–14
dance [dăns] **64**–A
dangerous [dān/jər əs] **186**–1
dark blue [därk/ bloo/] **24**–10

Dashboard and Instrument Panel
[dăsh/börd/ ən ĭn/strə mənt păn/əl] **159**
dates [dāts] **20**–1, **68**–28
date of birth [dāt əv bürth/] **4**–13
expiration date
[ĕk/spə rā/shən dāt/] **112**–7, **136**–10
daughter [dö/tər] **34**–14
daughter-in-law [dö/tər ĭn lö/] **34** ✦
granddaughters [grăn/dö/tərz] **34** ✦
stepdaughter [stĕp/dö/tər] **35** ✦
day [dā] **20**–2
birthday [bürth/dā/] **22**–1
Columbus Day [kə lŭm/bəs dā] **22**–15
daylight saving time [dā/līt/ sā/vĭng tīm/] **19**–25
every day [ĕv/rē dā/] **20**–21
Independence Day [ĭn/də pĕn/dəns dā/] **22**–13
Labor Day [lā/bər dā/] **22**–14
Martin Luther King Jr. Day
[mär/tən lo͞o/thər kĭng/ jo͞on/yər-dā/] **22**–10
Memorial Day [mə mör/ē əl dā/] **22**–12
New Year's Day [no͞o/ yïrz/ dā/] **22**–9
Presidents' Day [prĕz/ə dənts dā/] **22**–11
Veterans Day [vĕt/ər ənz dā/] **22**–16
Day [dā] **18**
DAY AT SCHOOL [dā/ ăt sko͞ol/] **11**
DAY AT WORK [dā/ ăt würk/] **186–187**
Days of the Week [dāz/ əv dhə wēk/] **20**
dead [dĕd]
dead-bolt lock [dĕd/bōlt/ läk/] **51**–34
dead end [dĕd/ĕnd/] **154**–6
deaf [dĕf] **32**–12
Dealer [dē/lər] **158**
dealership [dē/lər shĭp/] **126**–4
death certificate [dĕth/ sər tĭf/ə kət] **41**–11
debate [də bāt/] **139**–B
decaf coffee [dē/kăf/ kö/fē] **81**–38
decay [də kā/] **119**–7
December [dĭ sĕm/bər] **21**–36
decimal point [dĕ/sə məl poynt/] **17**–7
Decimals [dĕ/sə məlz] **17**
deck [dĕk] **240**–2
declaration [dĕk/lə rā/shən]
declaration form [dĕk/lə rā/shən förm/] **161**–16
Declaration of Independence
[dĕk/lə rā/shən əv ĭn/də pĕn/dəns] **198**–5
decline [də klīn/] **12**–J
decorations [dĕk/ə rā/shənz] **240**–1
deductions [də dŭk/shənz] **165**–13
deed [dēd] **41**–9
deer [dïr] **216**–14
defendant [dĭ fĕn/dənt] **141**–5
defense attorney [dĭ fĕns/ ə tür/nē] **141**–4
defroster [də frö/stər] **159**–41
degrees [də grēz/] **13**–8, **193**–26
delayed flight [də lād/ flīt/] **161**–30
delete [də lēt/] **196**–C
DELI [dĕl/ē] **71**
deliver [də lĭv/ər] **11**–G, **135**–E
delivery person [də lĭv/ə rē pür/sən] **167**–21
dementia [də mĕn/shə] **111**–18
demonstration [dĕ/mən strā/shən] **122**–6
denim [dĕ/nəm] **99**–7
denominator [də nömə nā/tər] **192**–6
dental [dĕn/təl]
dental assistant [dĕn/təl ə sĭs/tənt] **119**–2, **167**–22
dental floss [dĕn/təl flös/, –fläs/] **109**–24
dental hygienist [dĕn/təl hī jē/nĭst, –jĕ/nĭst] **119**–3
dental instruments [dĕn/təl ĭn/strə mənts] **119**–4
DENTAL CARE [dĕn/təl kër/] **119**
Dental Problems [dĕn/təl präb/ləmz] **119**
dentist [dĕn/tĭst] **119**–1
Dentistry [dĕn/təs trē/] **119**
dentures [dĕn/chərz] **119**–10
deodorant [dē ō/dər ənt] **108**–5
department [dĭ pärt/mənt] **95**–7, **95**–8
Department of Motor Vehicles
[dĭ pärt/mənt əv mō/tər vē/ĭ kəlz] **124**–4
department store [dĭ pärt/mənt stör/] **131**–13
DEPARTMENT OF MOTOR VEHICLES (DMV)
[dĭ pärt/mənt əv mō/tər vē/ĭ kəlz] / [dē/ĕm/vē/]
136–137
departure [dĭ pär/chər] **161**–5, **161**–7
deposit [dĭ päz/ət] **132**–3, **132**–7
deposit slip [dĭ päz/ət slĭp/] **132**–4
depression [də prĕ/shən] **115**–5
depth [dĕpth] **17**–18
DESCRIBING CLOTHES [dĭ skrī/bĭng klōz/] **96–97**
DESCRIBING HAIR [dĭ skrī/bĭng hër/] **33**
DESCRIBING PEOPLE [dĭ skrī/bĭng pē/pəl] **32**
DESCRIBING THINGS [dĭ skrī/bĭng thĭngz/] **23**
desert [dĕz/ərt] **204**–4
design [dĭ zīn/] **175**–A
designated drivers [dĕz/ĭg nā/təd drī/vərz] **143** ✦
designer [dĭ zī/nər] **98** ✦, **167**–30, **175**–2, **176**–5
desk [dĕsk] **6**–7, **182**–9
circulation desk [sür/kyə lā/shən dĕsk/] **133**–2
desk clerk [dĕsk klürk/] **184**–11
front desk [frŭnt/ dĕsk/] **184**–12
Desktop Computer [dĕsk/täp/ kəm pyo͞o/tər] **196**
Desserts [dĭ zürts] **81**
dessert tray [dĭ zürt/ trā/] **83**–10
destination [dĕs/tə nā/shən] **161** ✦
detector [dĭ tĕk/tər] **51**–29
detergent [dĭ tür/jənt] **101**–8
device [də vīs/] **225**–20
diabetes [dī/ə bē/tēz, –təs] **111**–12
diagonal [dī ăg/ə nəl, –ăg/nəl] **193**–31
dial [dī/əl] **15**–A, **15**–E
diameter [dī ăm/ə tər] **193**–37
diamonds [dī/məndz] **233**–29
diaper [dī/pər] **37**–8, **37**–10
diaper pail [dī/pər pāl/] **37**–7
diaphragm [dī/ə frăm] **194**–19
dice [dīs] **232**–6
dice [dīs] **77**–J
dictate [dĭk/tāt] **8**–N
dictator [dĭk/tā/tər] **199**–6
dictionary [dĭk/shə nër/ē] **7**–30, **7**–31
die [dī] **41**–R
dietician [dī/ə tĭsh/ən] **120**–15
difference [dĭf/rəns] **192**–8
different [dĭ/frənt, dĭ/fə rənt] **23**–16
DIFFERENT [dĭ/frənt, dĭ/fə rənt] **28–29**
DIFFERENT PLACES TO LIVE
[dĭ/frənt plā/səz tə lĭv/, dĭ/fə rənt] **52**
difficult [dĭf/ĭ kŭlt/] **23**–24
digital [dĭ/jə təl]
digital camera [dĭ/jə təl kăm/rə] **235**–19
digital photo album [dĭ/jə təl fō/tō ăl/bəm] **235**–32
dime [dīm] **26**–3
Dimensions [də mĕn/shənz] **17**
diner [dī/nər] **82**–6, **185**–9
dining [dī/nĭng]
dining area [dī/nĭng ër/ē ə] **46**–7
dining room [dī/nĭng ro͞om/] **82**–1
dining room chair [dī/nĭng ro͞om/ chër/] **55**–8
dining room table [dī/nĭng ro͞om/tā/bəl] **55**–9
Dining [dī/nĭng] **185**
DINING AREA [dī/nĭng ër/ē ə] **55**
dinner [dĭn/ər] **72**–28
dinner fork [dĭn/ər förk/] **83**–28
dinner plate [dĭn/ər plāt/] **83**–18
dinner salad [dĭn/ər săl/əd] **80**–15
Dinner [dĭn/ər] **81**
diploma [də plō/mə] **40**–3
direct flight [də rĕkt/ flīt/, dī–] **161** ✦
Directions [də rĕk/shənz] **9, 155**
DIRECTIONS AND MAPS
[də rĕk/shənz ən măps/, dī–] **155**
directory [də rĕk/tə rē, dī–] **131**–24
directory assistance
[də rĕk/tə rē ə sĭs/təns, dī–] **14**–22
dirty [dür/tē] **101**–15
Disabilities [dĭ/sə bĭ/lə tēz] **32**
disagree [dĭ/sə grē/] **12**–L
disappointed [dĭ/sə poyn/təd] **28**–4
DISASTERS [dĭ/zăs tərz] **144–145**
disc [dĭsk] **231**–27
discipline [dĭs/ə plən] **36**–K
discuss [dĭ skŭs/] **8**–G
disease [dĭ zēz/] **111**–11, **111** ✦, **119**–11
Diseases [dĭ zē/zəz] **111**
disgusted [dĭ skŭs/təd] **42**–7
dish [dĭsh] **55**–1
casserole dish [kăs/ə rōl dĭsh/] **78**–10
dish rack [dĭsh/ răk/] **54**–5
dish room [dĭsh/ ro͞om/] **83**–13
dish towel [dĭsh/ tow/əl] **61**–22
dishwasher [dĭsh/wä/shər, –wö/–]
54–8, **83**–14, **185**–2
dishwashing liquid [dĭsh/wä/shĭng lĭk/wəd] **61**–21
satellite dish [săt/ə lit dĭsh/] **53**–6
soap dish [sōp/ dĭsh/] **57**–25
disinfectant wipes [dĭs/ən fĕk/tənt wīps/] **61**–23
display case [dĭ splā/ kās/] **94**–5
disposable [dĭ spō/zə bəl]
disposable diaper [dĭ spō/zə bəl dī/pər] **37**–10
disposable gloves [dĭ spō/zə bəl glŭvz/] **93**–27
disposal [dĭ spō/zəl] **54**–7, **121**–31
dive [dīv] **230**–K
divide [də vīd/] **17**–A, **192**–D
diving [dī/vĭng] **227**–12
diving mask [dī/vĭng măsk/] **225**–6
divorced couple [də vörst/ kŭ/pəl] **35**–21
DJ [dē/jā/] **64**–4

DMV [dē/ĕm/vē/]
  DMV clerk [dē/ĕm/vē/ klürk/] **136**–3
  DMV handbook [dē/ĕm/vē/ hănd/bo͝ok/] **136**–1
do [do͞o] **39**–T
  do an experiment [do͞o ən ĭk spĕr/ə mənt] **195**–B
  do crafts [do͞o krăfts/] **232**–D
  do errands [do͞o ĕr/əndz] **128** ✦
  do manual labor [do͞o măn/yo͞o əl lā/bər] **170**–D
  do not drink [do͞o nät drĭnk/] **112**–F
  do not enter [do͞o nät/ ĕn/tər] **154**–2
  do not operate [do͞o nät/ äp/ə rāt/] **112**–E
  do not take [do͞o nät/ tāk/] **112**–F
  don't be late [dōnt/ bē/ lāt/] **174**–E
  don't litter [dōnt/ lĭ/tər] **219**–L
  don't smoke [dōnt/ smōk/] **114**–G
dock [däk] **175**–15, **234**–3
  dockworker [däk/wür/kər] **167**–23
doctor [däk/tər] **118**–5
DOCUMENTS [dä/kyə mənts] **40–41**
dog [dög] **79**–6, **215**–11, **215**–22
dogwood [dög/wo͝od/] **210**–15
DOING THE LAUNDRY [do͞o/ĭng dhə lön/drē] **101**
doll [däl] **59**–21, **233**–28
  dollhouse [däl/hows/] **59**–16
  doll making kit [däl/ mā/kĭng kĭt/] **232**–13
dollar [däl/ər] **26**–7
  dollar coin [däl/ər koyn/] **26**–6
  fifty dollars [fĭf/tē däl/ərz] **26**–11
  five dollars [fīv/ däl/ərz] **26**–8
  half dollar [hăf/ däl/ər] **26**–5
  one hundred dollars
    [wŭn/ hŭn/drəd däl/ərz] **26**–12
  ten dollars [tĕn/ däl/ərz] **26**–9
  twenty dollars [twĕn/tē däl/ərz] **26**–10
dolphin [däl/fən, döl/–] **213**–31
domesticated [də mĕs/tə kā/təd] **215** ✦
DOMESTIC ANIMALS AND RODENTS
  [də mĕs/tĭk ăn/ə məlz ən rōd/nts] **215**
donkey [däng/kē, dŭng/–, döng/–] **215**–3
donut [dō/nŭt] **79**–15
  donut shop [dō/nŭt shäp/] **129**–17
door [dör] **46**–3
  doorbell [dör/bĕl/] **53**–14
  door chain [dör/ chān/] **51**–33
  doorknob [dör/näb/] **53**–12
  door lock [dör/ läk] **159**–25
  doorman [dör/măn/] **184**–1
  4-door car [för/dör kär/] **156**–1
  front door [frŭnt/ dör/] **53**–11
  garage door [gə räj/ dör/] **53**–7
  revolving door [rĭ väl/vĭng dör/] **184**–2
  screen door [skrēn/ dör/] **53**–15
  sliding glass door [slī/dĭng glăs/dör] **53**–18
  storm door [störm/ dör/] **53**–10
  2-door car [to͞o/dör kär/] **156**–2
dorm / dormitory [dörm] / [dör/mə tör/ē] **52**–8
dosage [dō/sĭj] **112**–6
double [dŭb/əl]
  double bed [dŭb/əl bĕd/] **184**–14
  double boiler [dŭb/əl boy/lər] **78**–8
down [down]
  break down [brāk/ down/] **162**–D
  downhill skiing [down/hĭl/ skē/ĭng] **227**–1
  down jacket [down jăk/ət] **90**–16
  down vest [down vĕst/] **90**–14
  drop-down menu [dräp/ down/ mĕn/yo͞o/] **197**–8
  put down [po͝ot/ down/] **6**–J
  sit down [sĭt down/] **6**–F
  walk down [wäk down/] **153**–D
downstairs [down/stërz/] **51** ✦
DOWNTOWN [down/town/] **124–125**
drain [drān] **57**–5
drama [drä/mə] **236**–12
drapes [drāps] **56**–16
draw [drö] **8**–F, **118**–F, **195**–E
drawer [drör] **54**–23, **58**–2, **59**–6
dress [drĕs] **86**–3, **88**–5, **89**–20
  dressmaker [drĕs/mā/kər] **100**–1
  dressmaker's dummy [drĕs/mā/kərz dŭ/mē] **100**–2
  dress socks [drĕs/ säks/] **91**–9
dress [drĕs] **36**–H, **174**–B
dressed [drĕst] **38**–D
dresser [drĕs/ər] **58**–1
Dressings [drĕs/ĭngz] **80**
dribble [drĭb/əl] **230**–J
drill [drĭl] **178**–9, **180**–8
  drill bit [drĭl bĭt] **180**–28
drill [drĭl] **119**–D
drink [drĭnk] **11**–J
  do not drink alcohol
    [do͞o/ nät/ drĭnk/ ăl/kə höl/] **112**–F
  don't drink and **drive** [dōnt/ drĭnk ən drīv/] **143**–G
  drink fluids [drĭnk flo͞o/ədz] **114**–C
drip [drĭp] **121**–25
dripping [drĭp/ĭng] **63**–17
drive [drīv] **196**–6, **196**–8, **196**–9
  drive-thru window [drīv/thro͞o/ wĭn/dō] **128**–11
  driveway [drīv/wā/] **53**–8
drive [drīv]
  don't drink and **drive** [dōnt/drĭnk ən drīv/] **143**–G
  drive a truck [drīv ə trŭk] **170**–E
  drive through [drīv/ thro͞o] **153**–K
  drive to work [drīv/ tə würk/] **38**–I
driver [drī/vər] **152**–21, **169**–61
  designated drivers [dĕz/ĭg nā/təd drī/vərz] **143** ✦
  driver's license [drī/vərz lī/səns] **40**–4, **136**–9
  driver's license number
    [drī/vərz lī/səns nŭm/bər] **136**–11
  Phillips screwdriver [fĭl/ĭps skro͞o/drī/vər] **180**–31
  screwdriver [skro͞o/drī/vər] **180**–30
driving [drī/vĭng] **142**–5
drop [dräp]
  drop cloth [dräp/ klöth/] **181**–54
  drop-down menu [dräp/ down/ mĕn/yo͞o/] **197**–8
drop off [dräp/ öf/] **38**–G
dropper [dräp/ər] **195**–45
drops [dräps] **113**–31
drought [drowt] **145**–11
drown [drown] **116**–I
drugs [drŭgz] **116**–K, **142**–6
drums [drŭmz] **238**–16
drumsticks [drŭm/stĭks/] **70**–23
drunk driving [drŭngk/ drī/vĭng] **142**–5
dry [drī] **101**–18
  dry cleaners [drī/ klē/nərz] **128**–2
  dry erase marker [drī/ ĭ rās/ mär/kər] **7**–17
  drywall [drī/wöl/] **178**–19
dry [drī] **60**–N, **108**–H
dryer [drī/ər] **50**–13, **101**–4
  blow dryer [blō/ drī/ər] **33**–23, **108**–18
  dryer sheets [drī/ər shēts/] **101**–5
Dry Measures [drī/ mĕzh/ərz] **75**
duck [dŭk] **70**–18, **214**–12
duct tape [dŭkt/ tāp/] **181**–49
dummy [dŭ/mē] **100**–2
dump truck [dŭmp/ trŭk/] **156**–19
dune [do͞on] **204**–5
duplex [do͞o/plĕks/] **52** ✦
During an Emergency [do͞o/rĭng ən ĭ mür/jən sē] **147**
dust [dŭst]
  dustpan [dŭst/păn/] **61**–17
  dust ruffle [dŭst/ rŭf/əl] **58**–17
  dust storm [dŭst/ störm/] **13**–19
dust [dŭst] **60**–A
duster [dŭs/tər] **61**–1
DVD [dē/vē/dē/] **133**–19, **234**–11
  DVD and CD-ROM drive
    [dē/vē/dē/ ən sē/dē/räm/ drīv/] **196**–9
  DVD player [dē/vē/dē/ plā/ ər] **56**–7, **234**–10
dye [dī] **33**–D
eagle [ē/gəl] **214**–9
ear [ïr] **32**–17, **105**–11
  earache [ïr/āk/] **110**–3
  ear infection [ïr/ ĭn fĕk/shən] **111**–3
  earmuffs [ïr/mŭfs/] **90**–13, **179**–16
  ear plugs [ïr/ plŭgz/] **179**–15
  pierced earrings [pïrst/ ïr/ĭngz] **95**–36
early [ür/lē] **19**–22
Earth [ürth] **205**–3
earthquake [ürth/kwāk/] **144**–5
easel [ē/zəl] **233**–18
east [ēst] **155**–4
Eastern time [ē/stərn tīm/] **19**–32
easy [ē/zē] **23**–23, **76**–11
  easy chair [ē/zē chër/] **56**–22
Easy Chicken Soup [ē/zē chĭk/ən so͞op/] **77**
eat [ēt] **11**–1
  eat a healthy diet [ēt ə hĕl/thē dī/ət] **114**–F
  eat breakfast [ēt brĕk/fəst] **38**–E
  eat dinner [ēt dĭn/ər] **39**–S
  eat out [ēt/ owt/] **82** ✦
eater [ē/tər] **176**–12
eclipse [ĭ klĭps/] **205**–16, **205** ✦
edit [ĕd/ət] **191**–I
education [ĕ jyo͞o/ kā/shən] **189**–17
eel [ēl] **212**–12
eggplants [ĕg/plănts/] **69**–23
eggs [ĕgz] **66**–7
  eggbeater [ĕg/bē/tər] **78**–20
  eggs over easy [ĕgz ō/vər ē/zē] **76**–11
  eggs sunny-side up [ĕgz sŭn/ē sīd/ ŭp/] **76**–10
  hardboiled eggs [härd/ boyld/ ĕgz/] **76**–8
  poached eggs [pōcht/ ĕgz/] **76**–9
  scrambled eggs [skrăm/bəld ĕgz/] **76**–7
Eggs [ĕgz] **76**

eight [āt] **16**
eighteen [ā/tēn/] **16**
eighteenth [ā/tēnth/] **16**
eighth [ātth, āth] **16**
eightieth [ā/tē/əth] **16**
eighty [ā/tē] **16**
elastic bandage [ĭ lăs/tĭk băn/dĭj] **117**–12
elbow [ĕl/bō] **106**–12
elderly [ĕl/dər lē] **32**–3
elected [ĭ lĕk/təd] **139**–C
elected official [ĭ lĕk/təd ə fĭ/shəl] **139**–32
Election [ĭ lĕk/shən] **139**
election results [ĭ lĕk/shən rĭ zŭltz/] **139**–31
elective [ĭ lĕk/tĭv] **189** ✦
electric [ĭ lĕk/trĭk] **116**–F
electric can opener [ĭ lĕk/trĭk kăn/ ō/pə nər] **54**–14
electric drill [ĭ lĕk/trĭk drĭl/] **180**–8
electric keyboard [ĭ lĕk/trĭk kē/bōrd/] **238**–18
electric mixer [ĭ lĕk/trĭk mĭk/sər] **54**–25
electric pencil sharpener
[ĭ lĕk/trĭk pĕn/səl shär/pə nər] **183**–26
electric shaver [ĭ lĕk/trĭk shā/vər] **109**–26
electrical [ĭ lĕk/trĭ kəl]
electrical hazard [ĭ lĕk/trĭ kəl hăz/ərd] **186**–6
electrical tape [ĭ lĕk/trĭ kəl tāp/] **181**–43
electrician [ĭ lĕk trĭsh/ən] **62**–9
electron [ĭ lĕk/trän] **195**–30
electronics [ĭ lĕk trän/ĭks]
electronics repair person
[ĭ lĕk trän/ĭks rĭ pĕr/ pür/sən] **167**–24
electronics store [ĭ lĕk trän/ĭks stör/] **131**–20
ELECTRONICS AND PHOTOGRAPHY
[ĭ lĕk trän/ĭks ən fə täg/rə fē] **234–235**
elementary school [ĕl/ə mĕn/trē skōōl/] **188**–2
elephant [ĕl/ə fənt] **217**–42
elevator [ĕl/ə vā/tər] **50**–9, **131**–21, **184**–9
eleven [ĭ lĕv/ən] **16**
eleventh [ĭ lĕv/ənth] **16**
elm [ĕlm] **210**–16
Email [ē/māl/] **197**
embarrassed [ĭm băr/əst] **43**–24
embroidery [ĭm broy/də rē] **233**–24
EMERGENCIES [ĭ mür/jən sēz] **116**
EMERGENCIES AND NATURAL DISASTERS
[ĭ mür/jən sēz ən năch/rəl dĭ zăs/tərz,–năch/ə rəl–]
144–145
emergency [ĭ mür/jən sē] **117**–3
emergency card [ĭ mür/jən sē kärd/] **161**–26
emergency exit
[ĭ mür/jən sē ĕg/zət,–ĕk/sət] **51**–25, **161**–14
emergency medical technician (EMT) [ĭ mür/jən sē
mĕd/ĭ kəl tĕk nĭsh/ən] / [ē/ĕm/tē/] **121**–32
Emergency [ĭ mür/jən sē] **146–147**
Emergency Call [ĭ mür/jən sē köl/] **15**
EMERGENCY PROCEDURES
[ĭ mür/jən sē prə sē/jərz] **146–147**
Emergency Room Entrance
[ĭ mür/jən sē rōōm/ ĕn/trəns] **121**
Emergency Worker [ĭ mür/jən sē wür/kər] **93**
emery board [ĕm/ə rē bōrd/, ĕm/rē-] **109**–32
emperor [ĕm/pər ər] **199**–3
employee [ĕm ploy/ē] **165**–9
employer [ĕm ploy/ər] **164**–4
empty [ĕmp/tē] **23**–10
empty [ĕmp/tē] **60**–L
EMT (emergency medical technician) [ē/ĕm/tē/] /
[ĭ mür/jən sē mĕd/ĭ kəl tĕk nish/ən] **121**–32
end [ĕnd] **154**–6
endpoint [ĕnd/poynt/] **193**–21
end table [ĕnd/ tā/bəl] **56**–14
energy [ĕn/ər jē] **218**–1, **218**–7, **218**–8
bioenergy [bī/ō ĕn/ər jē] **218**–9
ENERGY AND CONSERVATION
[ĕn/ər jē ən kän/sər vā/shən] **218–219**
Energy and Resources [ĕn/ər jē ən rē/sör/səz] **219**
Energy Sources [ĕn/ər jē sör/səz] **218**
engine [ĕn/jən] **158**–18, **197**–6
engineer [ĕn/jə nïr/] **167**–18, **167**–25
ENGLISH COMPOSITION
[ĭng/glĭsh käm/pə zĭsh/ən] **190–191**
English muffin [ĭng/glĭsh mŭf/ən] **80**–5
enter [ĕn/tər]
do not enter [dōō/ nät/ ĕn/tər] **154**–2
enter data [ĕn/tər dā/tə] **171**–B
enter the room [ĕn/tər dhe rōōm/] **11**–A
enter your PIN [ĕn/tər yər pĭn/] **132**–E
ENTERTAINMENT [ĕn/tər tān/mənt] **236–237**
entertainment center [ĕn/tər tān/mənt sĕn/tər] **56**–5
entrance [ĕn/trəns] **164**–1
Entrance [ĕn/trəns] **50, 121**
entry-level job [ĕn/trē lĕv/əl jäb/] **172**–1
Entryway [ĕn/trē wā/] **51**
envelope [ĕn/və lōp/] **134**–14, **183**–43
equation [ĭ kwā/zhən] **192**–13
equipment [ĭ kwĭp/mənt] **177**–12, **179**–4
Equipment [ĭ kwĭp/mənt] **179, 183**
EQUIPMENT [ĭ kwĭp/mənt] **231**
Equivalencies [ĭ kwĭ/və lən sēz/] **17, 75**
erase [ĭ rās/] **10**–M
eraser [ĭ rā/sər] **7**–19, **7**–21
errands [ĕr/əndz] **128** ✦
eruption [ĭ rŭp/shən] **145**–16
escalator [ĕs/kə lā/tər] **131**–23
escape [ĭs kāp/] **50**–2
escape route [ĭs kāp/ rōōt/, rowt/] **146**–3
ESL [ē/ĕs/ĕl/] **189**–14
ESOL [ē/ĕs/ō/ĕl/] **189**–14
essay [ĕs/ā] **190**–4
Essay [ĕs/ā] **190**
e-ticket [ē/tĭ kət] **161**–19
evacuate [ĭ văk/yōō/ āt] **147**–K
evacuation route [ĭ văk/yōō/ā shən rōōt/, rowt/] **146**–5
evening [ēv/nĭng] **18**–19
evening gown [ēv/nĭng gown/] **89**–18
even numbers [ē/vən nŭm/bərz] **192**–4
EVENTS [ĭ vĕnts/] **22, 40–41**
every day [ĕv/rē dā/] **20**–21
EVERYDAY CLOTHES [ĕv/rē dā/ klōz] **86–87**
EVERDAY CONVERSATION
[ĕv/rē dā/ kän/vər sā/shən] **12**
evidence [ĕv/ĭ dəns/] **141**–9
exam [ĭg zăm/] **122**–1, **136**–6
examination table [ĭg zăm/ə nā/shən tā/bəl] **118**–7
examine [ĭg zăm/ən] **118**–D, **118**–E
Examining Room [ĭg zăm/ə nĭng rōōm/] **118**
exchange [ĭks chānj/] **27**–I
excited [ĭk sī/təd] **43**–22
exclamation mark [ĕk/sklə mā/shən märk/] **190**–13
executive [ĭg zĕk/yə tĭv] **182**–5
executive chef [ĭg zĕk/yə tĭv shĕf/] **185**–7
Executive Branch [ĭg zĕk/yə tĭv brănch/] **138**
exercise [ĕk/sər sīz/] **122**–4
exercise [ĕk/sər sīz/] **39**–P, **230**–N
Exercise Wear [ĕk/sər sīz/wër] **89**
exhausted [ĭg zö/stəd] **43** ✦
ex-husband [ĕks/ hŭz/bənd] **35** ✦
exit [ĕg/zət, ĕk/sət] **51**–25, **51** ✦, **161**–14
expensive [ĭk spĕn/sĭv] **23**–19, **97**–44
Experiment [ĭk spër/ə mənt] **195**
expiration date [ĕk/spə rā/shən dāt/] **112**–7, **136**–10
expire [ĕk/spīr/] **136** ✦
explain [ĭk splān/] **12**–M
exploration [ĕk/splə rā/shən] **199**–8
explorer [ĭk splör/ər] **199**–9
explosion [ĭk splō/zhən] **144**–4
exposed [ĭk spōzd/]
overexposed [ō/vər ĭk spōzd/] **235**–34
underexposed [ŭn/dər ĭk spōzd/] **235**–35
Express Mail® [ĭk sprĕs/ māl/] **134**–2
Extended Family [ĭk stĕn/dəd făm/lē, făm/ə lē] **34**
extension cord [ĭk stĕn/shən körd/] **181**–14
exterminate [ĭk stür/mə nāt/] **62** ✦
exterminator [ĭk stür/mə nā/tər] **63**–21
extinguisher [ĭk stĭn/gwə shər] **179**–21
extra [ĕk/strə]
extra large [ĕk/strə lärj/] **96**–5
extra small [ĕk/strə smöl/] **96**–1
ex-wife [ĕks/ wīf/] **35** ✦
eye [ī] **99**–27, **105**–11
eyebrow [ī/brow/] **106**–9
eyebrow pencil [ī/brow/ pĕn/səl] **109**–34
eye drops [ī/dräps/] **113**–31
eye hook [ī/hŏŏk/] **180**–40
eyelashes [ī/lăsh/əz] **106**–11
eyelid [ī/lĭd/] **106**–10
eyeliner [ī/lī/nər] **109**–36
eyepiece [ī/pēs/] **194**–14
eye shadow [ī/shă/dō] **109**–35
Eye [ī] **106**
fabric [făb/rĭk] **98**–15
fabric softener [făb/rĭk sö/fə nər] **101**–6
Fabric Store [făb/rĭk stör/] **99**
face [fās] **193**–44
face mask [fās măsk/] **93**–32
face powder [fās/ pow/dər] **109**–41
Face [fās] **106**
factory [făk/tə rē, –trē] **126**–3
factory owner [făk/tə rē ō/nər] **175**–1
factory worker [făk/tə rē wür/kər] **175**–3
Factory [făk/tə rē] **98**
FACTORY [făk/tə rē] **175**
Fahrenheit [făr/ən hīt/] **13**–1
fair [fër] **172**–13, **223**–13
fair trial [fër/ trī/əl] **140**–5
FAIR [fër] **122–123**
fall [föl] **21**–39

fall [föl] **40**–H, **116**–O
FAMILIES [făm/lēz, făm/ə lēz] **34–35**
Family [făm/lē, făm/ə lē] **34**
FAMILY REUNION
[făm/lē rē yo͞on/yən, făm/ə lē] **44–45**
famine [fă/mĭn] **145**–12
fan [făn] **55**–19, **229**–4
fancy [făn/sē] **97**–34
far from [fär/ frŭm/, –frəm/] **25** ✦
fare [fër] **152**–2
fare card [fër kärd/] **152**–11
farm [färm] **52**–9
farm equipment [färm ĭ kwĭp/mənt] **177**–12
farmworker [färm/ wür/kər] **177**–8
Farm Animals [färm/ ăn/ə məlz] **215**
farmer [fär/mər] **177**–13
FARMERS' MARKET [fär/mərz mär/kət] **84–85**
FARMING AND RANCHING
[fär/mĭng ən răn/chĭng] **177**
Farmworker [färm/ wür/kər] **92**
fashion [făsh/ən] **88** ✦
fashion designer [făsh/ən dĭ zī/nər] **98** ✦
fast [făst] **23**–3
fast food restaurant [făst/ fo͞od/ rĕs/tə rənt, –ränt]
128–10
fasten [făs/ən] **160**–H
fastener [făs/nər] **99**–29
FAST FOOD RESTAURANT
[făst/ fo͞od/ rĕs/tə rənt, –ränt] **79**
fast forward [făst/ för/wərd] **235**–D
fat [făt] **32**–7
father [fä/dhər] **34**–4, **35**–23
father-in-law [fä/dhər ĭn lö/] **34**–11
grandfather [grăn/fä/dhər, grănd/–] **34**–2
stepfather [stĕp/fädhər] **35**–25
faucet [fö/sət] **57**–6
fax [făks] **171**–G
fax machine [făks/ mə shēn/] **183**–21
feast [fēst] **239**–13
feather [fĕdh/ər] **214**–4
feather duster [fĕdh/ər dŭs/tər] **61**–1
February [fĕb/yo͞o ër/ē, fĕb/ro͞o–] **21**–26
Federal Government
[fĕ/də rəl gŭ/vərn mənt, fĕ/drəl] **138**
feed [fēd] **36**–C, **176**–D, **177**–D
feed dog / feed bar [fēd/dög/ / fēd/ bär/] **98**–20
feel [fēl] **110**–C, **110**–D
FEELINGS [fē/lĭngz] **42–43**
female [fē/māl/] **4**–18
fence [fĕns] **177**–19
fencing [fĕn/sĭng] **228**–7
ferry [fër/ē] **220**–4
fertilize [fürt/ əl īz/] **176**–D
fever [fē/vər] **110**–8
fiction [fĭk/shən] **237**–18
field [fēld] **5**–2, **177**–7
ball field [böl/ fēld/] **224**–1
track and field [trăk/ ən fēld/] **228**–18
fifteen [fĭf/tēn/] **16**
fifteenth [fĭf/tēnth/] **16**
fifth [fĭfth] **16**
fiftieth [fĭf/tē əth] **16**
fifty [fĭf/tē] **16**
fifty dollars [fĭf/tē däl/ərz] **26**–11
50 percent [fĭf/tē pər sĕnt/] **17**–10
fighter [fī/tər]
firefighter [fīr/fī/tər] **144**–9, **167**–26
figs [fĭgz] **68**–27
figure [fĭg/yər] **233**–26
figure skating [fĭg/yər skā/tĭng] **227**–5
figurine [fĭg/yə rēn/] **232**–1
file [fīl] **183**–44
file cabinet [fīl kăb/ə nət] **182**–11
file clerk [fīl klürk/] **182**–10
file folder [fīl fōl/dər] **183**–50
fill [fĭl]
fill a cavity [fĭl/ ə kăv/ə tē] **119**–E
fill prescriptions [fĭl/ prĭ skrĭp/shənz] **112** ✦
fill in [fĭl/ ĭn] **9**–O
fill out [fĭl/ owt/] **173**–J
fill the tank [fĭl/ dhe tănk/] **157**–G
fill the tires [fĭl/ dhe tīrz/] **157**–L
filling [fĭl/ĭng] **119**–8
Filling Out a Form [fĭl/ĭng owt ə förm/] **4**
film [fĭlm] **235**–22
film camera [fĭlm kăm/rə] **235**–21
find [fīnd] **160**–F
FINDING A HOME [fīn/dĭng ə hōm/] **48–49**
fine adjustment knob [fīn/ ə jŭst/mənt näb/] **194**–23
fingers [fĭng/gərz] **105**–16, **110**–16
fingernail [fĭng/gər nāl/] **106**–18
fingerprint [fĭng/gər prĭnt/] **136**–5
Fingers [fĭng/gərz] **106**
finish [fĭn/ĭsh] **112**–C, **230**–T
fins [fĭnz] **212**–1, **225**–7
fire [fīr] **144**–7, **144**–8
campfire [kămp/fīr/] **226**–11
fire escape [fīr ĭ skāp/] **50**–2
fire exit [fīr/ ĕg/zət, –ĕk/sət] **51** ✦
fire extinguisher [fīr ĭk stĭng/gwĭ shər] **179**–21
firefighter [fīr/fī/tər] **144**–9, **167**–26
fire hydrant [fīr hī/drənt] **129**–27
fireplace [fīr/plās/] **56**–13
fire screen [fīr skrēn/] **56**–12
fire station [fīr stā/shən] **125**–12
fire truck [fīr trŭk/] **144**–10
fireworks [fīr/würks/] **239**–7
first [fürst] **16**
first aid kit [fürst/ ād/ kĭt/] **117**–1, **146**–18
first aid manual [fürst/ ād/ măn/yo͞o əl] **117**–2
First Continental Congress
[fürst/ kän/tə nĕnt/ əl käng/grəs] **198**–6
first name [fürst/ nām/] **4**–2
first president [fürst/ prĕz/ə dənt] **198**–11
First Aid [fürst/ ād/] **117**
FIRST AID [fürst/ ād/] **117**
First Aid Procedures [fürst/ ād/ prə sē/ jərz] **117**
First Floor [fürst/ flör/] **50**
First License [fürst/ lī/səns] **137**
fish [fĭsh] **66**–1, **81**–29, **209**–14
catfish [kăt/fĭsh/] **71**–2
goldfish [gōld/fĭsh/] **215**–16
jellyfish [jĕ/lē fĭsh/] **212**–14
starfish [stär/fĭsh/] **212**–16
swordfish [sörd/fĭsh/] **71**–5
Fish [fĭsh] **71, 212**
fisher [fĭsh/ər] **167**–17
fishing [fĭsh/ĭng] **226**–4
fishing net [fĭsh/ĭng nĕt/] **226**–17
fishing pole [fĭsh/ĭng pōl/] **226**–18
fitted sheet [fĭt/əd shēt/] **58**–12
fittings [fĭt/ĭngz] **181**–18
five [fīv] **16**
five after one [fīv ăf/tər wŭn/] **18**–7
five dollars [fīv däl/ərz] **26**–8
fix [fĭks] **62** ✦, **219**–F
fixture [fĭks/chər] **55**–18
flag [flăg] **239**–8
flammable liquids [flăm/ə bəl lĭk/wədz] **179**–8
flashlight [flăsh/līt/] **146**–14
flat [flăt]
flat panel TV [flăt/ păn/əl tē/vē/] **234**–7
flat screen TV [flăt/ skrēn/ tē/vē/] **234**–7
flat sheet [flăt/ shēt] **58**–13
have a flat tire [hăv/ ə flăt/ tīr/] **162**–F
flats [flăts] **95**–27
fleas [flēz] **63**–25
flea market [flē/ mär/kət] **222**–6
flight [flīt] **161**–30, **161** ✦
flight attendant [flīt/ ə tĕn/dənt] **161**–12
Flight [flīt] **160**
float [flōt/] **239**–2
flood [flŭd] **145**–19
floor [flör] **46**–6, **58**–21, **179**–6
floor lamp [flör lămp/] **56**–15
floor plan [flör plăn/] **186**–4
Floor [flör] **50**
floral [flör/əl] **96**–25
florist [flör/ĭst] **130**–8, **167**–27
floss [flös, fläs] **109**–24
floss [flös, fläs] **109**–K
flounder [flown/dər] **212**–15
flour [flow/ər] **73**–29
Flower [flow/ər] **211**
flowers [flow/ərz] **208**–7
flower bed [flow/ər bĕd/] **53**–20
FLOWERS [flow/ərz] **211**
flu [flo͞o] **111**–2
fluid [flo͞o/əd] **183**–36
fluid ounce [flo͞o/əd owns/] **75**–1
flute [flo͞ot] **238**–1
fly [flī] **214**–28
fly [flī] **170**–F
flyer [flī/ər] **102**–1
flying disc [flī/ĭng dĭsk/] **231**–27
foam pad [fōm/ păd/] **226**–13
focus [fō/kəs] **235**–33
foggy [fö/gē, fäg/ē] **13**–20
foil [foyl] **72**–23
fold [fōld] **101**–F
folder [fōl/dər] **183**–50
folding [fōl/dĭng]
folding card table [fōl/dĭng kärd/ tā/bəl] **102**–4
folding chair [fōl/dĭng chër/] **102**–5
folk [fōk] **237**–29
follow [fäl/ō] **114**–J, **147**–F
Following Directions [fäl/ō də rek/shənz, –dī–] **9**

food [fo͞od]
baby food [bā′bē fo͞od′] **37**–4
canned food [kănd′ fo͞od] **146**–9
fast food restaurant [făst′ fo͞od′ rĕs′tə ränt] **128**–10
food court [fo͞od′kört] **131**–15
food preparation worker
[fo͞od′ prĕ′pə rā′shən wür′kər] **185**–4
food processor [fo͞od′ prä′sĕ sər] **54**–26
packaged food [păk′ĭjd fo͞od′] **146**–10
pet food [pĕt′ fo͞od′] **72**–5
FOOD [fo͞od] **79**
FOOD PREPARATION AND SAFETY
[fo͞od′ prĕ′pə rā′shən ən sāf′tē] **76–77**
Food Processor [fo͞od′ prä′sĕ sər] **92**
Foods [fo͞odz] **72, 73**
Food Safety [fo͞od′ sāf′tē] **76**
FOOD SERVICE [fo͞od′sür′vəs] **185**
foot [fo͝ot] **104**–8
football [fo͝ot′böl′] **229**–11, **231**–21
football helmet [fo͝ot′böl′ hĕl′mət] **231**–19
footnote [fo͝ot′nōt′] **190**–10
Foot [fo͝ot] **106**
for [för] **128**–B, **173**–C
forceps [för′səps, –sĕps] **195**–43
forearm [för′ärm′] **106**–13
forehead [för′əd′, –hĕd′, fär′–] **106**–2
forest [för′əst, fär′–] **204**–1, **204**–11
forest fire [för′əst fīr′] **144**–7
fork [förk] **55**–3, **83**–27, **83**–28
forklift [förk′lĭft′] **175**–12
Form [förm] **4**
Formal Clothes [förm′əl klōz′] **89**
former husband [för′mər hŭz′bənd] **35** ✦
former wife [för′mər wīf′] **35** ✦
forms [förmz] **118**–4, **134**–19, **161**–16
formula [för′myə lə] **37**–3, **195**–34
fortieth [för′tē əth] **16**
forty [för′tē] **16**
forward [för′wərd] **235**–D
forward button [för′wərd bŭt′n] **197**–3
foundation [fown dā′shən] **109**–40
founders [fown′dərz] **198**–7
fountain [fown′tn] **224**–5, **224**–9
four [för] **16**
4-door car [för′dör kär′] **156**–1
2 x 4 (two by four) [to͞o′ bī för′] **181**–19
fourteen [för′tēn′] **16**
fourteenth [för′tēnth′] **16**
fourth [förth] **16**
Fourth Floor [förth flör′] **50**
Fourth of July [förth əv jo͞o lī′] **22**–13
fox [fäks] **216**–15
Fractions [frăk′shənz] **192**
Fractions and Decimals [frăk′shənz ən dĕ′sə məlz] **17**
frame [frām] **58**–4, **58**–18
frayed cord [frād′ körd′] **179**–5
free [frē] **122**–7
free speech [frē′ spēch′] **140**–2
freedom [frē′dəm]
freedom of religion [frē′dəm əv rĭ lĭ′jən] **140**–3
freedom of the press [frē′dəm əv dhə prĕs′] **140**–4
freezer [frē′zər] **54**–10, **185**–3
freezing [frē′zĭng] **13**–7
French [frĕnch]
french fries [frĕnch′ frīz′] **79**–2
French horn [frĕnch′ hörn′] **238**–13
Frequency [frē′kwən sē′] **20**
fresh [frĕsh] **71**–16
Friday [frī′dā, –dē] **20**–13
fried [frīd] **76**–6
fried chicken [frīd′ chĭk′ən] **76**–1
fringe [frĭnj] **99**–34
frog [frög, fräg] **212**–25
front [frŭnt] **25**–7
front desk [frŭnt′ dĕsk′] **184**–12
front door [frŭnt′ dör′] **53**–11
front seat [frŭnt′ sēt′] **159**–51
front walk [frŭnt′ wök′] **53**–2
Front Porch [frŭnt′ pörch′] **53**
Font Yard and House [frŭnt′ yärd′ en hows′] **53**
frostbite [fräst′bīt′] **116**–G
frozen [frō′zən] **63**–16, **71**–17
frozen dinner [frō′zən dĭn′ər] **72**–28
frozen vegetables [frō′zən vĕj′tə bəlz] **72**–27
Frozen Foods [frō′zən fo͞odz′] **72**
fruit [fro͞ot] **67**–9
fruit salad [fro͞ot săl′əd] **80**–21
FRUIT [fro͞ot] **68**
frustrated [frŭs′trā′təd] **43**–27
frying pan [frī′ĭng păn′] **78**–5
fuel injection system
[fyo͞o′əl ĭn jĕk′shən sĭs′təm] **158**–17
full [fo͝ol] **23**–9, **42**–6
full-length mirror [fo͝ol′lĕnth′ mïr′ər] **58**–6
full moon [fo͝ol′ mo͞on′] **205**–12
full slip [fo͝ol′ slĭp′] **91**–22
fumes [fyo͞omz] **179**–3
funnel [fŭn′əl] **195**–40
funny photo [fŭn′ē fō′tō] **206**–2
fur [für] **216**–19
furious [fyo͝or′ē əs] **43** ✦
furnished apartment [für′nĭsht ə pärt′mənt] **48**–3
furniture [für′nĭ chər] **53**–19
furniture polish [für′nĭ chər päl′ĭsh] **61**–8
furniture store [für′nĭ chər stör′] **126**–8
Furniture and Accessories
[für′nĭ chər ən ĭk sĕs′ə rēz] **59**
fuse box [fyo͞oz′ bäks′] **62**–13
fusion [fyo͞o′zhən] **218**–10
galaxy [găl′ək sē] **205**–15
gallbladder [göl′blăd′ər] **107**–44
gallon [găl′ən] **75**–5
game [gām]
baseball game [bās′böl gām′] **44**–2
board game [börd′ gām′] **232**–5
game show [gām′ shō′] **236**–8
video game console [vĭd′ē ō gām′ kän′sōl] **232**–3
video game control [vĭd′ē ō gām kən trōl′] **232**–4
Games [gāmz] **59**
GAMES [gāmz] **232–233**
gang violence [găng′ vī′ə ləns] **142**–4
garage [gə räzh′, –räj′] **47**–14, **124**–1
garage door [gə räzh′ dör′] **53**–7
Garage [gə räzh′, –räj′] **50**
GARAGE SALE [gə räzh′ sāl′] **102–103**
garbage [gär′bĭj]
garbage can [gär′bĭj kăn′] **53**–24
garbage disposal [gär′bĭj dĭ spō′zəl] **54**–7
garbage truck [gär′bĭj trŭk′] **127**–22
garden [gär′dn]
botanical garden [bə tăn′ə kəl gär′dn] **222**–3
roof garden [ro͞of′gär′dn] **50**–4
vegetable garden [vĕj′tə bəl gär′dn] **53**–27, **177**–14
garden [gär′dn] **53**–B
gardener [gär′dn er, gärd′nər] **167**–28
gardenia [gär dēn′yə] **211**–18
gardening [gärd′nĭng]
gardening crew [gärd′nĭng kro͞o′] **176**–1
gardening crew leader
[gärd′nĭng kro͞o lēd′ər] **176**–4
GARDENING [gärd′nĭng] **176**
gargle [gär′gəl] **109**–L
garlic [gär′lĭk] **69**–30
garlic bread [gär′lĭk brĕd′] **81**–28
garlic press [gär′lĭk prĕs′] **78**–11
Garment Factory [gär′mənt făk′tə rē, făk′trē] **98**
garment worker [gär′mənt wür′kər] **167**–29
garter [gär′tər]
garter belt [gär′tər bĕlt′] **91**–16
garter snake [gär′tər snāk′] **213**–39
gas [găs] **218**–3
gas gauge [găs′gāj′] **159**–31
gas meter [găs mē′tər] **62**–14
gas pedal [găs pĕd′l] **159**–46
gas shut-off valve [găs′ shŭt′öf vălv′] **146**–4
gas station [găs stā′shən] **125**–10
gas station attendant
[găs stā′shən ə tĕn′dənt] **162**–3
gas tank [găs tăngk′] **158**–10
gate [gāt] **50**–16, **53**–9, **161**–8
Gate [gāt] **161**
gauge [gāj]
blood pressure gauge [blŭd′ prĕsh′ər gāj′] **118**–9
gas gauge [găs′gāj′] **159**–31
oil gauge [oyl′gāj′] **159**–29
temperature gauge [tĕm′prə chər gāj′] **159**–30
gauze [göz] **117**–8
gear shift [gïr′ shĭft′] **159**–47
gel [jĕl] **108**–2, **108**–16
GEOGRAPHY AND HABITATS
[jē äg′rə fē ən hă′bə tăts′] **204**
Geometric Solids [jē′ə mĕ′trĭk săl′ədz] **193**
geometry [jē äm′ə trē] **192**–17
geothermal energy [jē′ō thür′məl ĕn′ər jē] **218**–7
get [gĕt]
get a job [gĕt′ ə jäb′] **40**–F
get a learner's permit
[gĕt′ ə lürn′ərz pür′mĭt] **137**–F
get a library card [gĕt′ ə lī′brër ē kärd′] **133**–A
get a loan [gĕt′ ə lōn′] **49**–J
get an electric shock [gĕt′ ən ĭ lĕk′trĭk shäk′] **116**–F
get a speeding ticket [gĕt′ ə spē′dĭng tĭk′ət] **162**–C
get bed rest [gĕt′ bĕd′ rĕst′] **114**–B
get change [gĕt′ chānj′] **26**–A
get dressed [gĕt′ drĕst′] **38**–D
get elected [gĕt′ ĭ lĕk′təd] **139**–C

get engaged [gĕt/ ĭn gājd/] **41**–J
get feedback [gĕt/ fēd/băk/] **191**–K
get frostbite [gĕt/ frŏst/bīt/] **116**–G
get good grades [gĕt/ gŏŏd/ grādz/] **10**–H
get hired [gĕt/ hīrd/] **173**–L
get home [gĕt/ hōm/] **39**–R
get immunized [gĕt/ ĭm/yə nīzd] **114**–I
get into [gĕt/ ĭn/tōō] **153**–E
get lost [gĕt/ lŏst/] **162**–B
get married [gĕt/ măr/ēd] **41**–K
get off [gĕt/ ŏf/] **153**–J
get on [gĕt/ än/, ŏn/] **153**–I
get out of [gĕt/ owt/ əv] **153**–F
get the title [gĕt/ dhə tīt/l] **157**–E
get up [gĕt/ ŭp/] **38**–B
get your license [gĕt/ yər lī/səns] **137**–I
Getting Your First License
[gĕt/ĭng yər fürst/ lī/səns] **137**
Get Well [gĕt/ wĕl/] **114**
gift [gĭft] **94** ✦, **240**–3
gift shop [gĭft/ shäp/] **130** ✦, **184**–5
gills [gĭlz] **212**–2
giraffe [jə răf/] **217**–32
girder [gür/dər] **178**–3
girdle [gür/dl] **91**–15
girl [gürl] **31**–10
give [gĭv] **15**–F, **122**–B, **148**–A,
glad [glăd] **44**–5
glass [glăs] **53**–18, **83**–22, **83**–23
glass cleaner [glăs klē/nər] **61**–14
glasses [glăs/əz] **92**–10, **115**–7, **179**–10
sunglasses [sŭn/glăs/əz] **90**–27
global positioning system (GPS) [glō/bəl
pə zĭ/shə nĭng sĭs/təm] / [jē/pē/ĕs/] **155**–11
gloves [glŭvz] **90**–6, **231**–17
disposable gloves [dĭ spō/ zə bəl glŭvz/] **93**–27
glove compartment [glŭv/ kəm pärt/mənt] **159**–44
latex gloves [lā/tĕks glŭvz/] **93**–34
rubber gloves [rŭb/ər glŭvz/] **61**–4
surgical gloves [sür/jĭ kəl glŭvz/] **121**–39
work gloves [würk/ glŭvz/] **92**–17, **179**–17
glue [glōō] **183**–33
glue stick [glōō/ stĭk] **232**–11
go [gō]
go back [gō/ băk/] **11**–M
go for [gō/ fər] **157**–J
go on [gō/ än] **173**–K
go over [gō/ ō/vər] **153**–B
go past [gō/ păst/] **155**–E
go straight [gō/ strāt/] **155**–A
go through [gō/ thrōō/] **160**–D
go to an employment agency
[gō/ tə ən ĭm ploy/mənt ā/jən sē] **173**–E
go to bed [gō/ tə bĕd/] **39**–Y
go to college [gō/ tə käl/ĭj] **41**–I
go to jail [gō/ tə jāl/] **141**–G
go to prison [gō/ tə prĭz/ən] **141**–G
go to school [gō/ tə skōōl] **38**–J
go to sleep [gō/ tə slēp/] **39**–Z
go to the grocery store
[gō/ tə dhə grōs/rē stör/, grōsh/rē] **38**–L
go to the next line [gō/ tə dhə nĕkst/ līn] **196**–D
go to work [gō/ tə würk/] **38**–I
go under [gō/ ŭn/dər] **153**–A
to-go box [tə gō/ bäks/] **82**–5
GO [gō] **222–223**
goat [gōt] **215**–5
goggles [gäg/əlz] **179**–11
goldfish [gōld/fĭsh/] **215**–16
golf [gälf, gölf] **228**–8
golf club [gälf/ klŭb/] **231**–1
good [gŏŏd] **23**–17
Goods [gŏŏdz] **73**
goose [gōōs] **214**–13
gopher [gō/fər] **215**–19
gorilla [gə rĭl/ə] **217**–29
gospel [gäs/pəl] **237**–30
Government [gŭ/ vərn mənt] **138–139**
GOVERNMENT AND MILITARY SERVICE
[gŭ/ vərn mənt ən mĭ/ lə tër ē sür/vəs]**138–139**
governor [gŭ/ vər nər] **139**–20, **139**–21
gown [gown] **206**–8
evening gown [ēv/nĭng gown/] **89**–18
hospital gown [häs/pĭ tl gown/] **121**–19
nightgown [nīt/gown/] **91**–25
surgical gown [sür/jə kəl gown/] **93**–37, **121**–38
GPS (global positioning system) [jē/pē/ĕs/] /
[glō/bəl pə zĭ/shə nĭng sĭs/təm] **155**–11
grab bar [grăb/ bär/] **57**–9
grades [grādz] **10**–4
graduate [grăj/ōō āt/] **40**–D
graduated cylinder [grăj/ōō ā/təd sĭl/ən dər] **195**–38
GRADUATION [grăj/ōō ā/shən] **206–207**
graffiti [grə fē/tē] **148**–1
grandchild [grăn/chīld/, grănd/–] **34** ✦
granddaughters [grăn/dö/tərz] **34** ✦
grandfather [grăn/fä/dhər, grănd/–] **34**–2
grandmother [grăn/mŭdh/ər, grănd/–] **34**–1
Grandparents [grăn/pĕr/ənts, grănd/–] **34**
grandson [grăn/sŭn/, grănd/–] **34** ✦
grapefruit [grāp/frōōt/] **68**–6
grapes [grāps] **68**–3
graph [grăf] **192**–15
graphic designer [grăf/ĭk dĭ zī/nər] **167**–30
grasshopper [grăs/häp/ər] **214**–24
grate [grāt] **77**–G
grater [grā/tər] **78**–2
gray [grā] **24**–15
gray hair [grā hër/] **33**–13
grease [grēs] **77**–B
green [grēn] **24**–5
green card [grēn/ kärd/] **40**–2
green onions [grēn/ ŭn/yənz] **69**–20
greet [grēt] **3**–G, **171**–M, **174**–H
GREETING [grē/tĭng] **2–3**
greeting card [grē/tĭng kärd/] **134**–15
grill [grĭl] **53**–17
grilled [grĭld/]
grilled cheese sandwich
[grĭld/ chēz/ săn/wĭch, –sănd/–] **80**–10
grilled fish [grĭld/ fĭsh/] **81**–29
grilled ribs [grĭld/ rĭbz/] **76**–2
grocery [grōs/rē, grōsh/rē]
grocery bag [grōs/rē băg/] **67**–13
grocery clerk [grōs/rē klürk/] **72**–4
Grocery Products [grōs/rē präd/ŭkts] **72**
GROCERY STORE [grōs/ rē stör/] **72–73**
ground [grownd]
ground beef [grownd/ bēf/] **70**–4
ground post [grownd/ pōst/] **134**–6
playground [plā/grownd/] **50**–3
group [grōōp] **115**–15
grower [grō/ər] **177**–13
guard [gärd] **141**–3
Coast Guard [kōst/ gärd/] **138**–18
lifeguard [līf/gärd/] **225**–19
lifeguard station [līf/gärd/ stā/shən] **225**–21
National Guard [nă/shə nəl gärd/] **138**–19
security guard [sĭ kyōōr/ə tē gärd/] **132**–5, **169**–55
shin guards [shĭn/ gärdz/] **231**–13
guest [gĕst] **184**–10
guest room [gĕst/ rōōm] **184**–13
guest services [gĕst/ sür/vəs əs] **130**–12
guest speaker [gĕst/ spē/kər] **206**–4
guinea pig [gĭn/ē pĭg/] **215**–14
guitar [gĭ tär/] **238**–9
gums [gŭmz] **106**–6
gum disease [gŭm/ dĭ zēz/] **119**–11
gun [gŭn] **142**–13, **181**–21
gurney [gür/nē] **121**–33
gutter [gŭt/ər] **53**–4
gym [jĭm] **5**–19, **126**–10, **184**–24
gymnastics [jĭm năs/tĭks] **228**–9
gynecologists [gī/nə käl/ə jĭsts] **120** ✦
habitat [hă/bə tăt/] **194**–12
HABITATS [hă/bə tăts/] **204**
hacksaw [hăk/sö/] **180**–5
hail a taxi [hāl/ ə tăx/ē/]] **152** ✦
hailstorm [hāl/störm/] **13**–21
hair [hër] **104**–2
black hair [blăk/ hër/] **33**–16
blond hair [blănd/ hër/] **33**–17
brown hair [brown/ hër/] **33**–18
curly hair [kür/lē hër/] **33**–11
gray hair [grā/ hër] **33**–13
hair clip [hër klĭp/] **108**–19
hairdresser [hër/drĕs/ər] **167**–31
hair gel [hër jĕl/] **108**–16
hairnet [hër nĕt/] **93**–25
hair salon [hër sə län/] **131**–18
hair spray [hër sprā/] **108**–12
hair stylist [hër stī/lĭst] **167**–31
long hair [lŏng/ hër/] **33**–3
red hair [rĕd/ hër/] **33**–15
short hair [shört/hër/] **33**–1
shoulder-length hair [shōl/dər lĕnth/ hër/] **33**–2
straight hair [strāt/ hër/] **33**–9
wavy hair [wā/vē hër/] **33**–10
HAIR [hër] **33**

half [hăf]
half bath [hăf/ băth/] **57** ✦
half brother [hăf/ brŭdh/ər] **35**–28
1/2 cup [hăf/ kŭp/] **75**–9
half dollar [hăf/ däl/ər] **26**–5
half past one [hăf/ păst/ wŭn/] **18**–11
half sister [hăf/ sĭs/tər] **35**–27
half slip [hăf/ slĭp/] **91**–23
halibut steak [hăl/ə bət stāk/] **71**–6
hall [höl] **124**–8
hallway [höl/wā/] **5**–10, **184**–18
Hallway [höl/wā/] **51**
ham [hăm] **70**–9, **76**–5
hamburger [hăm/bür/gər] **79**–1
hammer [hăm/ər] **180**–1
jackhammer [jăk/hăm/ər] **178**–9
sledgehammer [slĕj/ hăm/ər] **178**–23
hammer [hăm/ər] **178**–D
hammock [hăm/ək] **53**–23
hamper [hăm/pər] **57**–1
hand [hănd] **105**–15, **177**–20
DMV handbook [dē/ĕm/vē/ hănd/bo͝ok] **136**–1
handbag [hănd/băg/] **87**–9, **94**–2
handbrake [hănd/ brāk/] **59**–48
handcuffs [hănd/kŭfs/] **141**–2
handsaw [hănd/sö/] **180**–4
handset [hănd/sĕt] **14**–1
hand towel [hănd tow/əl] **57**–15
hand truck [hănd trŭk/] **175**–11
Hand [hănd] **106**
handicapped parking [hăn/dē kăpt pär/kĭng]
128–6, **154**–12
hand in [hănd/ ĭn/] **10**–O
hanger [hăng/gər] **101**–11
hang up [hăng/ ŭp/] **15**–D, **101**–H
happy [hăp/ē] **28**–6, **43**–31
hard [härd] **23**–5, **23**–24
hardboiled eggs [härd/boyld/ ĕgz/] **76**–8
hard drive [härd/ drīv/] **196**–6
hard hat [härd/ hăt/] **92**–1, **179**–9
hardware store [härd/wër/stör/] **148**–4
harmonica [här mä/ nĭ kə] **238**–21
harvest [här/vəst] **177**–B
hash browns [hăsh/ brownz/] **80**–3
hats [hăts] **90**–1, **95**–11
chef's hat [shĕfs/ hăt/] **93**–28
cowboy hat [kow/boy/ hăt/] **92**–18
hard hat [härd/ hăt/] **92**–1, **179**–9
ski hat [skē/ hăt/] **90**–11
straw hat [strö/ hăt/] **90**–23
have [hăv]
have a baby [hăv/ ə bā/bē] **41**–L
have a conversation [hăv/ ə kän/vər sā/shən] **11**–L
have a heart attack [hăv/ ə härt/ ə tăk/] **116**–D
have an allergic reaction
[hăv/ ən ə lür/jĭk rē ăk/shən] **116**–E
have a picnic [hăv/ ə pĭk/nĭk] **224**–D
have dinner [hăv/ dĭn/ər] **39**–S
have regular checkups
[hăv/ rĕg/yə lər chĕk/ups] **114**–H
Hawaii-Aleutian time [hə wī/ē ə lo͞o/shən tīm/] **19**–27
hay [hā] **177**–18
hazard [hăz/ ərd] **186**–6
hazard lights [hăz/ərd līts/] **159**–36
Hazardous Materials [hăz/ər dəs mə tïr/ē əlz] **179**
hazardous waste [hăz/ər dəs wāst/] **218**–12
Hazards [hăz/ərdz] **179**
head [hĕd] **69**–32, **104**–1
headache [hĕd/āk/] **110**–1
headband [hĕd/bănd/] **90**–3
headboard [hĕd/börd/] **58**–10
head chef [hĕd/ shĕf/] **185**–7
headlight [hĕd/līt/] **158**–7
headline [hĕd/līn] **133**–7
headphones [hĕd/fōnz/] **6**–8, **234**–4
headset [hĕd/sĕt] **14**–13
headwaiter [hĕd/wā/tər] **185**–12
headwrap [hĕd/răp/] **90**–7
letterhead [lĕt/ər hĕd] **183**–42
overhead compartment
[ō/vər hĕd/ kəm pärt/mənt] **161**–13
overhead projector [ō/vər hĕd/prə jĕk/tər] **7**–16
wireless headset [wīr/ləs hĕd/sĕt] **14**–14
health [hĕlth] **167**–32
health history form [hĕlth/ hĭs/tə rē förm/] **118**–4
health insurance card
[hĕlth/ ĭn sho͝or/əns kärd/] **118**–3
HEALTH [hĕlth] **114–115**
HEALTH FAIR [hĕlth/ fër/] **122–123**
Health Problems [hĕlth/ präb/ləmz] **115**
hear [hïr] **106**–B
hearing [hïr/ĭng]
hearing aid [hïr/ĭng ăd/] **115**–10
hearing impaired [hïr/ĭng ĭm përd/] **32**–12
hearing loss [hïr/ĭng lös/] **115**–2
heart [härt] **107**–38, **116**–D, **239**–6
heart disease [härt/ dĭ zēz/] **111**–11
hearts [härts] **233**–31
heater [hē/tər] **159**–40
heating pad [hē/tĭng păd/] **113**–13
heat wave [hēt/ wāv/] **13**–13
heavy [hĕv/ē] **23**–13, **32**–7, **97**–27
hedge clippers [hĕj/ klĭp/ərz] **176**–11
heel [hēl] **94**–22, **106**–24
high heels [hī/ hēlz/] **89**–21, **95**–25
height [hīt] **17**–16, **32**–5
Height [hīt] **32**
Heimlich maneuver [hīm/lĭk mə no͞o/vər] **117**–18
helicopter [hĕl/ə käp/tər] **151**–9
helmet [hĕl/mət] **93**–23, **231**–19
help [hĕlp] **8**–J, **147**–G
Help with Health Problems
[hĕlp/ wĭth/ hĕlth/ präb/ləmz] **115**
hem [hĕm] **100**–8
hen [hĕn] **215**–8
herbal tea [ür/bəl tē/, hür/bəl–] **81**–40
herbs [ürbz, hürbz] **84**–9
hibiscus [hī bĭs/kəs, hĭ–] **211**–12
hide [hīd] **240**–D
high [hī] **91**–12, **97**–32, **188**–3
high blood pressure [hī/ blŭd/ prĕsh/ər] **111**–14
high chair [hī/ chër/] **37**–6, **82**–3
high heels [hī/ hēlz/] **89**–21, **95**–25
high-rise [hī/ rīz/] **127**–13
high school [hī/ sko͞ol] **188**–4
highway [hī/wā] **155**–9
highway marker [hī/wā mär/kər] **154**–17
hiking [hī/kĭng] **226**–7
hiking boots [hī/kĭng bo͞ots/] **95**–31
hills [hĭlz] **204**–16
downhill skiing [down/hĭl/ skē/ĭng] **227**–1
hip hop [hĭp/häp] **237**–26
hippopotamus [hĭp/ə pät/ə məs] **217**–43
hire [hīr] **141**–B
hired hand [hīrd/ hănd/] **177**–20
Historical Terms [hĭs/tör/ə kəl türmz/] **199**
history [hĭs/tə rē] **118**–4, **189**–12
HISTORY [hĭs/tə rē] **198–199**
hit [hĭt] **230**–B
HIV (human immunodeficiency virus)
[āch/ī/vē/] / [hyo͞o/mən ĭm/yə nō
dĭ fĭsh/ən sē vī/rəs] **111**–17
Hi-Visibility safety vest [hī/vĭ/zə bĭl/ə tē vĕst/] **92**–4
HOBBIES AND GAMES [häb/ēz ən gāmz/] **232–233**
hockey [häk/ē] **229**–13
hockey stick [häk/ē stĭk/] **231**–11
hold [hōld] **36**–A
holder [hōl/dər]
candle holder [kăn/dl hōl/dər] **56**–21
cell phone holder [sĕl/ fōn/ hōld/ər] **94**–15
magazine holder [măg/ə zēn/ hōld/ər] **56**–23
pot holders [pät/ hōl/dərz] **78**–29
toothbrush holder [to͞oth/brŭsh/ hōld/ər] **57**–22
holiday [häl/ə dā/] **22**–7, **22**–8
Holidays [häl/ə dāz/] **22**
HOLIDAYS [häl/ə dāz/] **239**
holly [häl/ē] **210**–19
home [hōm] **52**–7, **52**–12
home health care aide [hōm/ hĕlth/ kër ăd] **167**–32
home improvement store
[hōm/ ĭm pro͞ov/mənt stör/] **127**–20
homemaker [hōm/mā/kər] **168**–33
homesick [hōm/sĭk/] **43**–20
HOME [hōm] **46–47, 48–49**
honeybee [hŭn/ē bē/] **214**–25
hood [ho͝od] **158**–4
Hood [ho͝od] **158**
hoof / hooves [ho͝of] / [ho͝ovz] **216**–17
hook [ho͝ok] **180**–39, **180**–40
hook and eye [ho͝ok/ ən ī/] **99**–27
hook and loop fastener
[ho͝ok/ ən lo͞op/ fă/sən ər] **99**–29
horn [hörn] **159**–32, **216**–21, **238**–11
French horn [frĕnch/ hörn] **238**–13
horror story [hör/ər stör/ē, här/–] **237**–17
horse [hörs] **215**–4
horseback riding [hörs/băk rī/dĭng] **226**–9
horse racing [hörs/ rā/sĭng] **228**–19
seahorse [sē/hörs/] **212**–13
hose [hōz] **53**–21, **91**–18
hospital [häs/pĭ tl] **125**–9, **154**–18
hospital bed [häs/pĭ tl bĕd/] **121**–22
hospital gown [häs/pĭ tl gown/] **121**–19
HOSPITAL [häs/pĭ tl] **120–121**
Hospital Room [häs/pĭ tl ro͞om/] **121**

Hospital Staff [häs/pĭ tl stăf/] **120**
hostess [hō/stəs] **82**–2
hot [hät] **13**–3, **42**–1
hot cereal [hät sïr/ē əl] **80**–9
hot dog [hät/ dög/] **79**–6
hot water [hät/ wö/tər] **57**–8
hot water bottle [hät/ wö/tər bät/l] **113**–15
hotel [hō tĕl/] **124**–3
A HOTEL [hō tĕl/] **184**
hour [ow/ər] **18**–1
house [hows]
courthouse [kört/hows/] **125**–13
dollhouse [däl/hows/] **59**–18
housekeeper [hows/kē/pər] **168**–34, **184**–20
housekeeping cart [hows/kē/pĭng kärt/] **184**–19
House of Representatives
[hows/ əv rĕp/rĭ zĕn/tə tĭvz] **138**–3
house painter [hows/ pān/tər] **168**–46
houseplant [hows/plănt/] **56**–4, **211**–27
townhouse [town/hows/] **52**–6
two-story house [too͞/stör/ē hows/] **52** ✦
warehouse [wër/hows/] **175**–7
White House [wīt/ hows/] **138**–7
House [hows] **49, 53**
A HOUSE AND YARD [hows/ən yärd/] **53**
HOUSEHOLD PROBLEMS AND REPAIRS
[hows/hōld/ präb/ləmz ən rĭ përz/] **62**–**63**
HOUSEWORK [hows/würk/] **60**
housing [how/zĭng] **52**–11
hubcap [hŭb/kăp/] **158**–9
hug [hŭg] **2**–E
human immunodeficiency virus (HIV)
[hyo͞o/mən ĭm/yə nō dĭ fĭsh/ən sē vī/rəs] /
[āch/ī/vē/] **111**–17
humid [hyo͞o/məd] **13**–15
humidifier [hyo͞o mĭd/ə fī/ər] **113**–11
humiliated [hyo͞o mĭl/ē ā/təd] **43** ✦
hummingbird [hŭm/ĭng bürd/] **214**–10
hump [hŭmp] **217**–51
hungry [hŭng/grē] **42**–5
hurricane [hür/ə kān/] **145**–14
hurt [hürt] **42**–16, **116**–C
husband [hŭz/bənd] **34**–13
ex-husband [ĕks/ hŭz/bənd] **35** ✦
former husband [för/mər hŭz/bənd] **35** ✦
hutch [hŭch] **55**–22
hybrid [hy/brĭd] **156**–3
hydrant [hī/drənt] **129**–27
hydroelectric power [hī/drō ĭ lĕk/trĭk pow/ər] **218**–5
hydrogen peroxide [hī/drə jən pə räk/sīd] **117**–9
hyena [hī ē/nə] **217**–30
HYGIENE [hy/jēn] **108**–**109**
hygienist [hī jē/nĭst, –jĕn/ĭst] **119**–3
hypertension [hī/pər tĕn/shən] **111**–14
hyphen [hy/fən] **190**–20
hypoallergenic [hī/pō ăl/ər jĕn/ĭk] **108** ✦
I beam [ī/ bēm/] **178**–3
ice [īs]
ice cream [īs/ krēm/] **72**–26
ice-cream cone [īs/ krēm/ kōn] **79**–13
ice cream shop [īs/ krēm/ shäp] **131**–16
ice hockey [īs/ häk/ē] **229**–13
ice pack [īs/ păk/] **117**–13
ice skates [īs/ skāts/] **231**–9
ice skating [īs/ skā/tĭng] **227**–4
iced tea [īst/ tē/] **79**–12
icy [ī/sē] **13**–22
ID [ī/dē/] **146**–19
identity theft [ī dĕn/tə tē thĕft/] **142**–9
ignition [ĭg nĭsh/ən] **159**–33
illegal drugs [ĭ lē/gəl drŭgz/] **142**–6
Illnesses and Childhood Diseases
[ĭl/nə səz ən chīld/ho͝od dĭ zēz/ əz] **111**
ILLNESSES AND MEDICAL CONDITIONS
[ĭl/nə səz ən mĕd/ĭ kəl kən dĭsh/ənz] **111**
Immediate Family
[ĭ mē/ dē ət făm/lē, –fă/məlē] **34**
immigrant [ĭm/ə grənt] **199**–19
immigrate [ĭm/ə grāt/] **40**–C
immigration [ĭm/ə grā/shən] **199**–18
immunization [ĭm/yə nə zā/shən] **114** ✦
immunodeficiency [ĭm/yə nō dĭ fĭsh/ən sē] **111**–17
impaired [ĭm përd/] **32**–11, **32**–12
important [ĭm pört/ənt] **146**–19
improvement [ĭm pro͞ov/mənt] **127**–20
in [ĭn] **25**–6
be in shock [bē/ ĭn shäk/] **116**–B
bubble in [bŭb/l ĭn/] **10**–K
call in [käl/ ĭn/] **186**–A
check in [chĕk/ ĭn/] **160**–A
check-in kiosk [chĕk/ĭn kē/äsk/] **160**–2
fall in love [fäl/ ĭn lŭv/] **40**–H
fill in [fĭl/ ĭn/] **9**–O
hand in [hănd/ĭn/] **10**–O
in fashion [ĭn făsh/ən] **88** ✦
in front of [ĭn frŭnt/ əv] **24**–7
in love [ĭn lŭv/] **42**–18
in pain [ĭn pān/] **42**–11
in style [ĭn stīl/] **88** ✦
in the middle [ĭn dhə mĭd/l] **24**–2
look in [lo͝ok/ ĭn] **173**–B
move in [mo͞ov/ ĭn/] **48**–F
send in [sĕnd/ ĭn/] **173**–H
take in [tāk/ ĭn/] **100**–D
turn in [türn/ ĭn/] **191**–M
walk-in freezer [wäk/ĭn frē/zər] **185**–3
inch [ĭnch] **17**–15
indent [ĭn dĕnt/] **190**–D
independence [ĭn/də pĕn/dəns]
Declaration of Independence
[dĕk/lə rā/shən əv ĭn/də pĕn/dəns] **198**–5
Independence Day [ĭn/də pĕn/dəns dā/] **22**–13
INDIVIDUAL SPORTS [ĭn/də vĭj/o͞o əl spörts/] **228**
infant [ĭn/fənt] **31**–6
infection [ĭn fĕk/shən] **111**–3
infectious disease [ĭn fĕk/shəs dĭ zēz/] **111** ✦
influenza [ĭn/flo͞o ĕn/zə] **111** ✦
INFORMATION [ĭn/fər mā/shən] **4**
inhaler [ĭn hā/lər] **113**–33
injection [ĭn jək/shən] **114** ✦, **158**–17
injured [ĭn/ jərd] **116**–C
INJURIES [ĭn/jə rēz] **110**
ink [ĭnk]
ink cartridge [ĭnk/ kär/trĭj] **183**–45
inkjet printer [ĭnk/jĕt prin/tər] **183**–18
ink pad [ĭnk/ păd/] **183**–46
inline [ĭn/līn/]
inline skates [ĭn/līn/ skāts/] **231**–10
inline skating [ĭn/līn/ skā/tĭng] **228**–10
inquire about benefits
[ĭn kwīr/ ə bowt/bĕn/ə fĭts] **174** ✦
insects [ĭn/sĕkts] **209**–11
insect bite [ĭn/sĕkt bīt/] **110**–11
insect repellent [ĭn/sĕkt rĭ pĕl/ənt] **226**–23
Insects [ĭn/sĕkts] **214**
INSECTS [ĭn/sĕkts] **214**
insert [ĭn sürt/] **132**–D
INSIDE AND OUTSIDE THE BODY
[ĭn/sīd/ ən owt/sīd/ dhə bäd/ē] **106**–**107**
Inside the Car [ĭn/sīd/ dhə kär/] **159**
Inside the Kit [ĭn/sīd/ dhə kĭt/] **117**
Inside the Trunk [ĭn/sīd/ dhə trŭnk/] **158**
inspect [ĭn spĕkt/] **147**–N
install [ĭn stäl/] **176**–H, **178**–C
instructor [ĭn strŭk/tər] **6**–4
Instrument Panel [ĭn/strə mənt păn/əl] **159**
instruments [ĭn/strə mənts] **119**–4, **238**
insulation [ĭn/sə lā/shən] **178**–14
insurance [ĭn sho͝or/əns] **118**–3, **136**–8
integers [ĭn/tə jərz] **192**–1, **192**–2
Integers [ĭn/tə jərz] **192**
intercom [ĭn/tər käm/] **50**–5
interest inventory [ĭn/trəst ĭn/vən tör/ ē] **172**–11
international call [ĭn/tər năsh/ə nəl köl/] **15**–35
Internet [ĭn/tər nĕt/]
Internet listing [ĭn/tər nĕt/ lĭst/ĭng] **48**–1
Internet map [ĭn/tər nĕt/ măp] **155**–12
Internet phone call [ĭn/tər nĕt/ fōn/ käl] **14**–20
INTERNET [ĭn/tər nĕt/] **197**
internist [ĭn/tür/nĭst] **120**–1
internship [ĭn/türn shĭp/] **172**–6
interpreter [ĭn tür/prə tər] **168**–35
INTERSECTION [ĭn/tər sĕk/shən] **128**–**129**
INTERVIEW SKILLS [ĭn/tər vyo͞o/ skĭlz/] **174**
intestinal parasites [ĭn tĕs/tə nəl păr/ə sīts/] **111**–13
intestines [ĭn tĕs/tənz] **107**–42
In the Airline Terminal [ĭn dhə ër/līn tür/mə nəl] **160**
In the Examining Room
[ĭn dhə ĭg zăm/ə nĭng ro͞om/] **118**
In the Waiting Room [ĭn dhə wā/tĭng ro͞om/] **118**
into [ĭn/to͞o, –tə] **153**–E
intravenous drip (IV)
[ĭn/trə vē/nəs drĭp/] / [ī/vē/] **121**–25
introduce [ĭn/trə do͞os/] **2**–C, **3**–I
introduction [ĭn/trə dŭk/shən] **190**–6
invention [ĭn vĕn/shən] **199**–12
inventor [ĭn vĕn/tər] **199**–13
inventory [ĭn/vən tör/ ē] **172**–11, **172**–12
invertebrates [ĭn vür/ tə brəts/] **194**–13
invitation [ĭn və tā/shən] **12**–I, **12**–J, **64**–9
invite [ĭn vīt/] **12**–H
iris [ī/rəs] **211**–16
iron [ī/ərn] **101**–13, **108**–17
iron [ī/ərn] **101**–G

ironed [ī/ərnd] **101**–20
ironing board [ī/ər nĭng börd/] **101**–14
irritated [ïr/ə tā/təd] **64**–6
island [ī/lənd] **204**–8
IV (intravenous drip)
[ī/vē/] / [ĭn/trə vē/nəs drĭp/] **121**–25
ivory [ī/vər ē] **24**–16
ivy [ī/vē] **210**–25
jack [jăk] **158**–24
jacket [jăk/ət] **90**–8
chef's jacket [shĕfs/ jăk/ət] **93**–29
down jacket [down/ jăk/ət] **90**–16
leather jacket [lĕdh/ər jăk/ət] **90**–4
sports jacket [spörts/ jăk/ət] **89**–14
jackhammer [jăk/ hăm/ər] **178**–9
jack-o'-lantern [jăk/ə lăn/tərn] **239**–10
janitor [jăn/ĭ tər] **182**–3
January [jăn/yōō ër/ē] **21**–25
jar [jär] **74**–2, **74**–14
jasmine [jăz/mən] **211**–22
jaw [jö] **106**–4
jay [jā] **214**–6
jaywalk [jā/wäk] **128**–C
jazz [jăz] **237**–24
jeans [jēnz] **86**–2, **92**–19
jellyfish [jĕl/ē fĭsh/] **212**–14
jewelry [jōō/əl rē]
jewelry department [jōō/əl rē dĭ pärt/mənt] **95**–8
jewelry store [jōō/əl rē stör/] **130**–2
jigsaw [jĭg/sö/] **180**–10
job [jäb] **172**–1, **172**–3, **172**–7
job fair [jäb/ fër] **172**–13
JOB SAFETY [jäb/ sāf/tē] **179**
JOBS AND OCCUPATIONS
[jäbz/ ən äk/yə pā/shənz] **166–169**
JOB SEARCH [jäb/ sürch/] **173**
JOB SKILLS [jäb/ skĭlz/] **170**
Job Training [jäb/ trān/ĭng] **172**
jockstrap [jäk/străp/] **91**–6
join [joyn] **143**–L
judge [jŭj] **141**–6
Judicial Branch [jōō dĭ/shəl brănch/] **138**
juice [jōōs] **73**–32
July [jōō lī/] **21**–31
jump [jŭmp] **230**–I
jumper cables [jŭm/pər kā/bəlz] **158**–21
jump rope [jŭmp/ rōp/] **224**–4
jumpsuit [jŭmp/sōōt/] **93**–24
June [jōōn] **21**–30
junior high school [jōōn/yər hī/ skōōl] **188**–3
junk mail [jŭnk/ māl/] **135** ✦
Jupiter [jōō/pə tər] **205**–5
jury [jür/ē] **141**–8
justices [jŭs/tə səz] **138**–12, **138**–13
kangaroo [kăng/gə rōō/] **217**–44
keep [kēp] **28**–B
ketchup [kĕch/əp, kăch/–] **79**–21
kettle [kĕt/l] **54**–21
key [kē] **51**–30, **155**–9
key pad [kē/ păd/] **14**–5
pound key [pownd/ kē/] **14**–7
star key [stär/ kē/] **14**–6
keyboard [kē/börd/] **196**–14, **238**–18
Keyboarding [kē/börd/ĭng] **196**
kick [kĭk] **230**–E
kidney [kĭd/nē] **107**–43
kids' bedroom [kĭdz/ bĕd/rōōm/] **47**–9
KIDS' BEDROOM [kĭdz/ bĕd/rōōm/] **59**
king-size bed [kĭng/sīz/ bĕd/] **184**–15
kiosk [kē/äsk/] **131**–22, **160**–2
kiss [kĭs] **3**–K, **36**–P
kit [kĭt]
doll making kit [däl/ mā/kĭng kĭt/] **232**–13
first aid kit [fürst/ ād/ kĭt/] **117**–1, **146**–18
model kit [mäd/l kĭt/] **232**–9
woodworking kit [wŏŏd/wür/kĭng kĭt/] **232**–14
Kit [kĭt] **117**
kitchen [kĭch/ən] **46**–5, **83**–15
kitchen timer [kĭch/ən tī/mər] **78**–18
A KITCHEN [ə kĭch/ən] **54**
Kitchen [kĭch/ən] **185**
KITCHEN UTENSILS [kĭch/ən yōō tĕn/səlz] **78**
kite [kīt] **225**–2
kitten [kĭt/n] **215**–10
kiwi [kē/wē] **68**–22
knee [nē] **106**–20
knee highs [nē/hīz/] **91**–12
knee pads [nē/pădz/] **179**–19
knife [nīf] **55**–4, **83**–30
carving knife [kär/vĭng nīf/] **78**–12
multi-use knife [mŭl/tē yōōs/nīf/, mŭl/tī–] **226**–20
paring knife [për/ĭng nīf/] **78**–16
steak knife [stāk/ nīf/] **83**–29
knit [nĭt] **233**–F
knitting needles [nĭt/ĭng nēd/lz] **233**–23
knit top [nĭt/ täp/] **88**–7
knob [näb] **194**–22, **194**–23
doorknob [dör/näb/] **53**–12
knuckle [nŭk/l] **106**–17
koala [kō ä/lə] **217**–45
lab [lăb] **5**–15
lab coat [lăb/ kōt/] **93**–33
Lab [lăb] **195**
label [lā/bəl]
mailing label [mā/lĭng lā/bəl] **183**–41
nutrition label [nōō trĭ/shən lā/bəl] **122**–8
prescription label [prĭ skrĭp/shən lā/bəl] **112**–4
warning label [wär/nĭng lā/bəl] **112**–8
label [lā/bəl] **9**–V
Labor Day [lā/bər dā/] **22**–14
lace [lās] **99**–9
shoelaces [shōō/lā səz] **94**–24
ladder [lăd/ər] **178**–2
ladle [lā/dl] **78**–7
ladybug [lā/dē bŭg/] **214**–26
lake [lāk] **204**–13
lamb [lăm] **70**–14
lamb chops [lăm/ chäps/] **70**–15
lamb shanks [lăm/ shăngks/] **70**–13
Lamb [lăm] **70**
lamp [lămp] **56**–15, **58**–25
lampshade [lămp/shād/] **56** ✦, **58**–26
land [lănd] **160**–K
landlord [lănd/lörd/] **51**–27
landmarks [lănd/märks/] **220**–1
landscape designer [lănd/skāp/ dĭ zī/nər] **176**–5
LANDSCAPING AND GARDENING
[lănd/skā/pĭng ən gärd/nĭng] **176**
languages [lăng/gwĭ jəz] **189**–13
language arts [lăng/gwĭj ärts/] **189**–9
lantern [lăn/tərn] **226**–22, **239**–10
laptop [lăp/täp/] **196**–16
large [lärj] **96**–4, **96**–5
laser printer [lā/zər prĭn/tər] **183**–19
lashes [lăsh/əz]
eyelashes [ī/lăsh/əz] **106**–11
last [lăst]
last name [lăst/ nām/] **4**–4
last week [lăst/wēk/] **20**–18
late [lāt] **19**–24
latex gloves [lā/tĕks glŭvz/] **93**–34
laugh [lăf] **44**–A
laundromat [lön/drə măt/] **128**–1
laundry [lön/drē] **101**–1
laundry basket [lön/drē băs/kət] **101**–2
laundry detergent [lön/drē dĭ tür/jənt] **101**–8
LAUNDRY [lön/drē] **101**
Laundry Room [lön/drē rōōm/] **50**
lawn [lön] **53**–26
lawn mower [lön/ mō/ər] **176**–6
lawyer [lö/yər] **168**–36
lay [lā] **178**–B
layer cake [lā/ər kāk] **81**–33
LCD projector [ĕl/sē/dē/ prə jĕk/tər] **6**–6, **235**–29
leader [lē/dər] **176**–4
leaf / leaves [lēf] / [lēvz] **210**–6, **211**–6
leaf blower [lēf/ blō/ər] **176**–2
leaking [lē/kĭng] **62**–3
learn [lürn] **40**–E
Learning New Words [lür/nĭng nōō/ würdz/] **8**
lease [lēs] **48** ✦, **51**–28
leather [lĕdh/ər] **98**–6
leather jacket [lĕdh/ər jăk/ət] **90**–4
leave [lēv] **11**–O, **38**–N, **82**–J, **160**–J, **171**–P
leaves / leaf [lēvz] / [lēf] **210**–6, **211**–6
leaf blower [lēf/ blō/ər] **176**–2
lecture [lĕk/chər] **122**–9
left [lĕft] **25**–1, **154**–8, **155**–C
legal [lē/gəl]
legal holiday [lē/gəl häl/ə dā/] **22**–8
legal pad [lē/gəl păd/] **183**–38
Legal Holidays [lē/gəl häl/ə dāz/] **22**
LEGAL SYSTEM [lē/gəl sĭs/təm] **141**
Leg and Foot [lĕg/ ən fŏŏt/] **106**
leggings [lĕg/ĭngz] **90**–12
Legislature [lĕ/jəs lā/chər] **139**–23
legs [lĕgz] **70**–21, **105**–9
leg of lamb [lĕg/ əv lăm/] **70**–14
lemonade [lĕm/ə nād/] **84**–2
lemons [lĕm/ənz] **68**–7
lend [lĕnd] **26**–C
length [lĕngkth] **17**–17, **96**–17
lengthen [lĕngk/thən] **100**–A
lens / lenses [lĕnz] / [lĕnz/əz] **115**–8, **235**–23
leopard [lĕp/ərd] **217**–34
let out [lĕt/ owt/] **100**–C

letter [lĕt/ər] **134**–13
letter carrier [lĕt/ər kär/ē ər] **134**–20
letterhead [lĕt/ər hĕd/] **183**–42
lettuce [lĕt/əs] **69**–1
level [lĕv/əl] **172**–1, **180**–29
librarian [lī brër/ē ən] **133**–9
library [lī/brër ē] **5**–17, **125**–15
library clerk [lī/brër ē klürk/] **133**–1
library patron [lī/brër ē pā/trən] **133**–3
LIBRARY [lī/brër ē] **133**
license [lī/səns]
driver's license [drī/vərz lī/səns] **40**–4, **136**–9
driver's license number [drī/vərz lī/səns nŭm/bər] **136**–11
license plate [lī/səns plāt/] **136**–12, **158**–12
marriage license [măr/ĭj lī/səns] **41**–8
renew a license [rĭ noo/ ə lī/səns, –nyoo/–] **136** ✦
taxi license [tăk/sē lī/səns] **152**–22
License [lī/səns] **137**
licensed practical nurse (LPN) [lī/sənst prăk/tə kəl nürs/] / [ĕl/pē/ĕn/] **120**–11
lid [lĭd] **78**–24
lieutenant governor [loo tĕ/nənt gŭ/ vər nər] **139**–21
life [līf]
lifeguard [līf/gärd/] **225**–19
lifeguard station [līf/gärd/ stā/shən] **225**–21
lifesaving device [līf/sā/vĭng dĭ vīs/] **225**–20
life vest [līf/ vĕst/] **161**–25, **226**–14
wildlife [wīld/ līf/] **220**–3
LIFE [līf] **212–213**
LIFE EVENTS AND DOCUMENTS [līf/ ĭ vĕnts/ ən dä/kyə mənts] **40–41**
lift [lĭft] **11**–E
light [līt] **23**–14, **97**–28
brake light [brāk/ līt/] **158**–14
daylight saving time [dā/līt/ sā/vĭng tīm/] **19**–25
flashlight [flăsh/līt/] **146**–14
hazard lights [hăz/ərd līts/] **159**–36
headlight [hĕd/ līt/] **158**–7
light blue [līt/ bloo/] **24**–11
light bulb [līt/ bŭlb/] **56** ✦
light fixture [līt/ fĭks/chər] **55**–18
light source [līt/ sörs/] **194**–21
light switch [līt/ swĭch/] **58**–27
night light [nīt/ līt/] **37**–27
porch light [pörch/ līt/] **53**–13
streetlight [strēt/līt/] **148**–3
string lights [strĭng/ lītz/] **239**–18
tail light [tāl/ līt/] **158**–13
traffic light [trăf/ĭk līt/] **128**–8
work light [würk/ līt/] **181**–44
lightning [līt/nĭng] **13**–17
lily [lĭl/ē] **211**–26
limbs [lĭmz] **106** ✦, **210**–3
limes [līmz] **68**–8
limit [lĭ/mət] **154**–4
limo / limousine [lĭ/mō] / [lĭ/mə zēn] **156**–11
line [līn] **73**–11
assembly line [ə sĕm/blē līn] **175**–6
clothesline [klōz/līn/] **101**–9
curved line [kürvd/ līn/] **193**–23
headline [hĕd/līn/] **133**–7
line cook [līn/ kook/] **93, 185** ✦
line segment [līn/ sĕg/mənt] **193**–20
line supervisor [līn/ soo/pər vī zər] **175**–4
parallel lines [pă/rə lĕl līnz/] **193**–25
perpendicular lines [pür/pən dĭk/yə lər līnz/] **193**–24
straight line [strāt/ līn/] **193**–22
linen [lĭn/ən] **98**–2
linen closet [lĭn/ən kläz/ət] **57** ✦
liner [lī/nər]
eyeliner [ī/lī/nər] **109**–36
Lines [līnz] **193**
lingerie [län/zhə rā/, –jə–] **91** ✦
links [lĭnkz] **197**–10
lion [lī/ən] **213**–33, **216**–2, **217**–36
lip [lĭp] **106**–5
lipstick [lĭp/stĭk/] **109**–38
Liquid Measures [lĭk/wəd mĕzh/ərz] **75**
liquids [lĭk/wədz] **61**–21, **179**–8
list [lĭst] **67**–14
listen [lĭs/ən] **6**–C, **118**–C, **174**–K
listing [lĭst/ĭng] **48**–1
litter [lĭ/tər] **148**–2
litter [lĭ/tər] **219**–L
little [lĭt/l] **23**–1
Little League [lĭt/l lēg/] **229** ✦
live [lĭv] **140**–H
LIVE [lĭv] **52**
live music [līv/ myoo/zĭk] **84**–1
liver [lĭv/ər] **70**–7, **107**–40
livestock [līv/stäk/] **177**–15
living room [lĭv/ĭng room/] **47**–12
LIVING ROOM [lĭv/ĭng room/] **56**
lizard [lĭz/ərd] **213**–40
llama [lä/mə] **217**–25
load [lōd] **101**–C
loading dock [lō/dĭng däk/] **175**–15
loaf [lōf] **74**–10, **74**–22
meatloaf [mēt/lōf/] **81**–31
loafers [lō/fərz] **95**–30
Lobby [läb/ē] **50**
lobster [läb/stər] **71**–10
local call [lō/kəl köl/] **15**–31
lock [läk] **51**–34, **159**–25
locksmith [läk/smĭth/] **62**–11
lock [läk] **143**–E
locker [lä/kər] **5**–11, **50**–17
locket [läk/ət] **95**–35
Logging on and Sending Email [lög/ĭng än/ ən sĕnd/ĭng ē/māl, –ön–] **197**
lonely [lōn/lē] **42**–17
long [löng] **96**–18
long distance call [löng/dĭs/təns köl/] **15**–32
long hair [löng/ hër/] **33**–3
long-sleeved [löng/slēvd/] **96**–14
long underwear [löng/ ŭn/dər wër/] **91**–3
look [look]
look at [look/ ăt/, –ət] **49**–H, **157**–A
look for [look/ för/] / [look/ fər] **133**–B, **173**–C
look in [look/ ĭn] **173**–B
look up [look/ ŭp] **8**–A
loop [loop] **99**–29
loose [loos] **97**–30
lose [looz] **229** ✦
loss [lös] **115**–2
lost child [löst/ chīld/] **144**–1
lotion [lō/shən] **37**–13, **108**–9
loud [lowd] **23**–11
loungewear [lownj/wër/] **91** ✦
love [lŭv] **40**–H, **42**–18
love seat [lŭv sēt/] **56**–1
low [lō] **97**–31
low-cost exam [lō/köst ĭg zăm/] **122**–1
low-cut socks [lō/kŭt/ säks/] **91**–10
low-fat milk [lō/făt/ mĭlk/] **81**–42
lower back [lō/ər băk/] **107**–29
lozenges [läz/ən jəz] **113**–30
LPN (licensed practical nurse) [ĕl/pē/ĕn/] / [lī/sənst prăk/tə kəl nürs/] **120**–11
luggage [lŭg/ĭj] **161**–18
luggage cart [lŭg/ĭj kärt/] **184**–8
lug wrench [lŭg/ rĕnch/] **158**–22
lumber [lŭm/bər] **178**–17
Lunch [lŭnch] **80**
lung [lŭng] **107**–39
machine [mə shēn/]
answering machine [ăn/sər ĭng mə shēn/] **14**–17
ATM (Automated Teller Machine) [ā/tē/ĕm/] / [ö/tə māt ĭd tĕ/lər mə shēn/] **132**
fax machine [făks/ mə shēn/] **183**–21
machine operator [mə shēn/ äp/ə rā tər] **168**–37
machine screw [mə shēn/ skroo/] **180**–32
sewing machine [sō/ĭng mə shēn/] **98**–13
sewing machine operator [sō/ĭng mə shēn/ äp/ə rā/tər] **98**–14
stamp machine [stămp/ mə shēn/] **135**–11
vending machine [vĕnd/ĭng mə shēn/] **152**–9
Machine [mə shēn/] **98, 132**
magazine [măg/ə zēn/, măg/ə zēn/] **133**–5
magazine holder [măg/ə zēn/ hōl/dər] **56**–23
magnet [măg/nət] **195**–36
magnolia [măg nōl/yə] **210**–8
mail
airmail [ër/māl/] **134**–5
Certified Mail® [sür/tə fīd māl/] **134**–4
Express Mail® [ĭk sprĕs/ māl/] **134**–2
junk mail [jŭnk/ māl/] **135** ✦
mailboxes [māl/bäk/səz] **50**–11, **53**–1, **128**–13, **135**–12
media mail [mē/dē ə māl/] **134**–3
overnight / next day mail [ō/vər nīt/ / nĕkst/ dā/ māl/] **135** ✦
Priority Mail® [prī/ör ə tē māl/] **134**–1
mail [māl/] **135**–D
mailer [mā/lər] **183**–40
mailing [mā/lĭng]
mailing address [mā/lĭng ə drĕs/, ă/drĕs] **134**–22
mailing label [mā/lĭng la/bəl] **183**–41
main office [mān/ ö/fəs] **5**–12
MAINTAINING A CAR [mān/tā nĭng ə kär/] **157**
maintenance [mān/tn əns] **184**–23
maitre d' [mā/trə dē/] **185**–11
make [māk] **156** ✦

make [māk]
make a deposit [māk/ ə dĭ päz/ət] **132**–B
make a disaster kit [māk/ ə dĭ zăs tər kĭt/] **146**–B
make a mortgage payment
[māk/ ə mör/gəj pā/mənt] **49**–L
make an offer [māk/ ən ö/fər] **49**–I
make a wish [māk/ ə wĭsh/] **240**–B
make copies [māk/ käp/ēz] **171**–D
make dinner [māk/ dĭn/ər] **39**–Q
make eye contact [māk/ ī/ kän/tăkt] **174**–J
make furniture [māk/ für/nĭ chər] **170**–G
make lunch [māk/ lŭnch/] **38**–F
make progress [māk/ prä/grəs] **10**–G
make small talk [māk/ smöl/tök] **12**–B
make the bed [māk/dhə bĕd/] **60**–F
maker [mā/kər]
dressmaker [drĕs/mā/kər] **100**–1
dressmaker's dummy [drĕs/mā/kərz dŭ/mē] **100**–2
homemaker [hōm/mā/kər] **168**–33
Makeup [māk/ŭp] **109**
makeup remover [māk/ŭp rĭ mōōv/ər] **109**–42
making [mā/kĭng] **232**–13
MAKING ALTERATIONS [māk/ĭng öl/tə rā/shənz] **100**
MAKING CLOTHES [māk/ĭng klōz/] **98–99**
Making an Emergency Call
[mā/kĭng ən ĭ mür/jən sē köl/] **15**
Making a Phone Call [mā/kĭng ə fōn/ köl/] **15**
male [māl] **4**–17
mall [möl] **126**–7
MALL [möl] **130–131**
mallet [măl/ət] **180**–2
mammals [măm/əlz] **209**–10
Mammals [măm/əlz] **213**
MAMMALS [măm/əlz] **216–217**
manager [măn/ĭ jər] **50**–8, **72**–8
account manager [ə kownt/ măn/ĭ jər] **132**–9
office manager [ö/fəs măn/ĭ jər] **182**–8
Manager [măn/ĭ jər] **92**
mane [mān] **217**–49
maneuver [mə nōō/vər] **117**–18
mangoes [măng/gōz] **68**–21
manicurist [mă/nə kyōō/rĭst] **168**–38
man / men [măn] / [mĕn] **30**–1, **30**–4
doorman [dör/măn/] **184**–1
mantle [măn/təl] **56**–11
manual [măn/yōō əl] **117**–2
Manual Transmission [măn/yōō əl trănz mĭsh/ən] **159**
manufacture [măn/yə făk/chər] **175**–B
map [măp] **7**–12, **155**–12
Map [măp] **13**
maple [mā/pəl] **210**–12
Maps [măps] **155**
MAPS [măps]**155**
March [märch] **21**–27
margarine [mär/jər ən] **72**–20
marigold [măr/ə gōld/] **211**–13
MARINE LIFE, AMPHIBIANS, AND REPTILES
[mə rēn/ līf/ ăm fĭb/ē ənz ən rĕp/tīlz] **212–213**
Marines [mə rēnz/] **138**–17
mark [märk] **190**–12, **190**–13, **190**–15
postmark [pōst/märk/] **134**–24
markers [mär/kərz] **7**–17, **7**–24, **154**–17
market [mär/kət] **222**–6
supermarket [sōō/pər mar/kət] **127**–18
MARKET [mär/kət] **66–67**
marriage license [măr/ĭj lī/səns] **41**–8
married couple [măr/ēd kŭ/pəl] **35**–20
Mars [märz] **205**–4
martial arts [mär/shəl ärts/] **228**–11
Martin Luther King Jr. Day
[mär/tən lōō/thər-kĭng/ jōōn/yər dā/] **22**–10
mascara [mă skăr/ə] **109**–39
mashed potatoes [măsht/ pə tā/tōz] **81**–23
mask [măsk] **239**–9
catcher's mask [kăch/ərz măsk/] **231**–15
diving mask [dī/vĭng măsk/] **225**–6
face mask [fās/ măsk/] **93**–32
oxygen mask [äk/sĭ jən măsk/] **161**–24
particle mask [pär/tĭ kəl măsk/] **179**–14
ski mask [skē/ măsk/] **90**–15
surgical mask [sür/jĭ kəl măsk/] **93**–36
ventilation mask [vĕnt/əl ā/shən măsk/] **92**–7
masking tape [măs/kĭng tāp/] **181**–53
mat [măt] **57**–3, **57**–28
placemat [plās/măt] **55**–11
match [măch] **9**–T
matches [măch/əz] **146**–16, **226**–21
matching [mă/chĭng] **28**–3
Material [mə tïr/ē əl] **98**
materials [mə tïr/ē əlz] **98** ✦, **179**–7
Materials [mə tïr/ē əlz] **179**
maternity [mə tür/nə tē]
maternity dress [mə tür/nə tē drĕs/] **88**–5
maternity store [mə tür/nə tē stör/] **131**–19
math [măth] **189**–10
MATHEMATICS [măth/ə măt/ĭks] **192–193**
Math Operations [măth/ äp/ə rā/shənz] **192**
Math Problem [măth/ präb/ləmz] **192**
mattress [mă/trəs] **58**–20
May [mā] **21**–29
mayonnaise [mā/ə nāz/, mā/ə nāz/] **79**–23
mayor [mā/ər] **139**–26
meadow [mĕd/ō] **204**–20
measles [mē/zəlz] **111**–5
measure [mĕzh/ər] **100**–17, **181**–45
measure [mĕzh/ər] **17**–C
Measurement [mĕzh/ər mənt] **17**
MEASUREMENTS [mĕzh/ər mənts] **17, 75**
Measures [mĕzh/ərz] **75**
Measuring Area and Volume
[mĕ/zhər ĭng ër/ē ə ən väl/yəm, –yōōm] **193**
meat [mēt] **66**–2
meatballs [mēt/bölz] **81**–27
meatloaf [mēt/lōf/] **81**–31
Meat [mēt] **70, 76**
MEAT AND POULTRY [mēt/ n pōl/trē] **70**
mechanic [mə kăn/ĭk] **166**–8
Mechanic [mə kăn/ĭk] **158**
media mail [mē/dē ə māl/] **134**–3
medical [mĕd/ĭ kəl] **121**–32
medical chart [mĕd/ĭ kəl chärt/] **121**–24
medical emergency bracelet
[mĕd/ĭ kəl ĭ mür/jən sē brās/lət] **117**–3
medical records technician
[mĕd/ĭ kəl rĕkərdz tĕk nĭsh/ən] **168**–39
medical waste disposal
[mĕd/ĭ kəl wāst/ dĭ spō/zəl] **121**–31
MEDICAL CARE [mĕd/ĭ kəl kër/] **118**
MEDICAL CONDITIONS [mĕd/ĭ kəl kən dĭsh/ənz] **111**
MEDICAL EMERGENCIES [mĕd/ĭ kəl ĭ mür/jən sēz] **116**
Medical Procedures [mĕd/ĭ kəl prə se/jərz] **118**
Medical Specialists [mĕd/ĭ kəl spĕ/shə lĭsts] **120**
Medical Technician [mĕd/ĭ kəl tĕk nĭsh/ən] **93**
Medical Warnings [mĕd/ĭ kəl wör/nĭngz] **112**
medication [mĕd/ə kā/shən] **112**–3, **112** ✦,
113–18, **121**–20
Medication [mĕd/ə kā/shən] **113**
medicine cabinet [mĕd/ə sən kăb/ə nət] **57**–20
medium [mē/dē əm] **96**–3
meet [mēt] **222**–6
meet [mēt] **49**–G, **49**–R
meeting [mē/tĭng]
meeting place [mē/tĭng plās/] **146**–1
meeting room [mē/tĭng rōōm/] **184**–25
MEETING AND GREETING [mē/tĭng ən grē/tĭng] **2–3**
melons [mĕl/ənz] **68**–19
watermelons [wö/tər mĕl/ənz] **68**–18
membrane [mĕm/brān] **194**–6
Memorial Day [mə mör/ē əl dā/] **22**–12
memory card [mĕm/ə rē kärd/] **235**–20
men / man [mĕn] / [măn] **30**–1, **30**–4
doorman [dör/măn/] **184**–1
men's store [mĕnz/ stör/] **130** ✦
Men's Underwear [mĕnz/ un/dər wër/] **91**
menu [mĕn/yōō] **82**–7, **197**–8
menu bar [mĕn/yōō bär/] **197**–1
MENU [mĕn/yōō] **80–81**
Mercury [mür/kyə rē] **205**–1
merge [mürj] **154**–10
mess [mĕs] **64**–8
message [mĕs/ĭj] **14**–18, **14**–19
messenger [mĕs/ən jər] **168**–40
meter [mē/tər] **62**–14, **129**–25, **152**–23
mice / mouse [mīs] / [mows] **63**–28, **196**–15, **215**–18
microphone [mī/krə fōn/] **234**–18
microprocessor [mī/krō prä/sĕ sər] **196**–4
Microscope [mī/krə skōp/] **194**
microwave [mī/krə wāv/] **77**–T
microwave oven [mī/krə wāv/ ŭv/ən] **54**–13
middle [mĭd/l] **25**–2
middle-aged [mĭd/l ājd/] **32**–2
middle initial [mĭd/l ĭ nĭsh/əl] **4**–3
middle school [mĭd/l skōōl/] **188**–3
mid-length [mĭd/lĕnth] **96**–17
midnight [mĭd/nīt/] **18**–21
Military [mĭ/lə tër ē] **138**
MILITARY SERVICE [mĭ/lə tër ē sür/vəs] **138–139**
milk [mĭlk] **66**–5, **81**–42
milkshake [mĭlk shāk/] **79**–14
milk [mĭlk] **177**–C
mini [mĭn/ē] **96**–15
mini-blinds [mĭn/ē blīndz/] **58**–8
minivan [mĭn/ē văn/] **156**–8
minister [mĭ/nə stər] **199**–7

minutes [mĭn/əts] **18**–2
mirror [mïr/ər] **57**–16
full-length mirror [fo͝ol/lĕnth mïr/ər] **58**–6
rearview mirror [rïr/vyo͞o/ mïr/ər] **159**–35
sideview mirror [sīd/vyo͞o/ mïr/ər] **158**–3
misbehave [mĭs/bĭ hāv/] **44**–B
miss the bus [mĭs dhə bŭs/] **152** ✦
missing [mĭs/ĭng] **97**–40
mittens [mĭt/nz] **90**–10
mix [mĭks] **77**–R
mixed berries [mĭkst/ bĕr/ēz] **81**–36
mixer [mĭk/sər] **54**–25
mixing bowl [mĭk/sĭng bōl/] **54**–28, **78**–31
mobile [mō/bēl] **59**–5
mobile home [mō/bəl hōm/] **52**–7
model [mäd/l] **156** ✦, **168**–41
model kit [mäd/l kĭt/] **232**–9
model trains [mäd/l trānz/] **233**–27
modern [mä/dərn] **199**–2
moist towelettes [moyst/ tow/əl ĕts] **146**–12
moisturizer [moys/chə rī/zər] **108**–9
mole [mōl] **32**–16
molecule [mäl/ĭ kyo͞ol/] **195**–27
monarch [mä/nərk, mä/närk/] **199**–4
Monday [mŭn/dā, –dē] **20**–9
MONEY [mŭn/ē] **26**
monitor [män/ə tər] **196**–11
arrival and departure monitors
[ə rī/vəl ən dĭ pär/chər män/ə tərz] **161**–7
baby monitor [bā/bē män/ə tər] **59**–7
vital signs monitor [vī/təl sīnz män/ə tər] **121**–26
monkey [mŭng/kē] **217**–26
month [mŭnth] **20**–3
Months of the Year [mŭnths/ əv dhə yïr/] **21**
moon [mo͞on]
crescent moon [krĕs/ənt mo͞on/] **205**–10
full moon [fo͝ol/ mo͞on/] **205**–12
new moon [no͞o/ mo͞on/] **205**–9
quarter moon [kwör/tər mo͞on/] **205**–11
Moon [mo͞on] **205**
moose [mo͞os] **216**–1
mop [mäp] **61**–6
mop [mäp] **60**–D
morning [mör/nĭng] **18**–15
mosque [mäsk] **126**–5
mosquito [mə skē/tō] **214**–22
motel [mō tĕl/] **126**–12
moth [möth] **214**–21
mother [mŭdh/ər] **34**–3, **35**–22
grandmother [grăn/mŭdh/ər, grănd/–] **34**–1
motherboard [mŭdh/ər börd/] **196**–5
mother-in-law [mŭdh/ər ĭn lö/] **34**–10
stepmother [stĕp/mŭdh/ər] **35**–26
MOTION [mō/shən] **153**
motor [mō/tər] **124**–4
motorcycle [mō/tər sī/kəl] **150**–4
mountain [mown/tn]
mountain biking [mown/tn bī/kĭng] **226**–8
mountain lion [mown/tn lī/ən] **216**–2
mountain peak [mown/tn pēk/] **204**–14
mountain range [mown/tn rānj/] **204**–15
Mountain time [mown/tn tīm/] **19**–30
mouse / mice [mows] / [mīs] **63**–28, **196**–15, **215**–18
mouth [mowth] **104**–7
mouthwash [mowth/wäsh/, –wösh/] **109**–25
Mouth [mowth] **106**
move in [mo͞ov/ ĭn/] **48**–F
move out [mo͞ov/ owt/] **48** ✦
movement [mo͞ov/mənt] **199**–16
mover [mo͞o/vər] **168**–42
movies [mo͞o/vēz] **222**–2
movie theater [mo͞o/vē thē/ə tər] **126**–6
Movies [mo͞o/vēz] **237**
Moving In [mo͞o/vĭng ĭn] **49**
moving van [mo͞o/vĭng văn/] **156**–18
mow [mō] **176**–A
mower [mō/ər] **176**–6
mozzarella cheese [möts/ə rĕ lə chēz/] **71**–29
MP3 player [ĕm/pē/thrē/ plā/ər] **234**–2
mudslide [mŭd/slīd/] **144**–6
muffin [mŭf/ən] **79**–16, **80**–5
muffler [mŭf/lər] **158**–16
muffs [mŭfs] **179**–16
mug [mŭg] **55**–7
mugging [mŭg/ĭng] **142**–11
multiply [mŭl/tə plī] **192**–C
multi-use knife [mŭl/tē yo͞os/ nīf/, mŭl/tī–] **226**–20
mumps [mŭmps] **111**–7
murder [mür/dər] **142**–12
muscle [mŭs/əl] **107**–32
mushrooms [mŭsh/ro͞omz/] **69**–27
music [myo͞o/zĭk] **64**–3, **189**–15
live music [līv/ myo͞o/zĭk] **84**–1
music store [myo͞o/zĭk stör/] **130**–1
world music [würld/ myo͞o/zĭk] **237**–32
Music [myo͞o/zĭk] **237**
MUSIC [myo͞o/zĭk] **238**
musician [myo͞o zĭsh/ən] **168**–43
mussels [mŭs/əlz] **71**–13, **212**–17
mustache [mŭs/tăsh] **33**–5
mustard [mŭs/tərd] **79**–22
mystery [mĭs/tə rē] **237**–20
nachos [nä/chōz] **79**–7
nail [nāl] **180**–34
fingernail [fĭng/gər nāl/] **106**–18
nail clipper [nāl klĭp/ər] **109**–31
nail polish [nāl päl/ĭsh] **109**–33
nail salon [nāl sə län/] **130**–3
toenail [tō/nāl/] **106** ✦
name [nām] **4**–1, **4**–2, **4**–4
name tag [nām/ tăg/] **92**–15
napkin [năp/kĭn] **55**–10, **83**–26
narrow [năr/ō] **97**–35
nasal [nā/zəl]
nasal congestion [nā/zəl kən jĕs/chən] **110**–7
nasal spray [nā/zəl sprā/] **113**–32
National Guard [nă/shə nəl gärd/] **138**–19
NATIONAL PARKS [nă/shə nəl pärks/] **220–221**
Native Americans [nā/tĭv ə mĕr/ə kənz] **198**–3
natural [năch/rəl/, năch/ər əl/]
natural gas [năch/rəl găs/] **218**–3
natural materials [năch/rəl mə tïr/ē əlz] **98** ✦
NATURE CENTER [nā/chər sĕn/tər] **208–209**
nature program [nā/chər prō/grăm] **236**–7
Navigating a Webpage [nă/və gā/tĭng ə wĕb/pāj] **197**
Navy [nā/vē] **138**–15
navy blue [nā/vē blo͞o/] **28**–5
near [nïr] **25** ✦
neck [nĕk] **96**–8, **96**–10, **104**–3
crewneck [kro͞o/nĕk] **96**–7
necklaces [nĕk/lə sĕz] **95**–10
turtleneck [tür/tl nĕk/] **96**–9
needle [nēd/l] **98**–17, **100**–10, **210**–10, **233**–23
needle plate [nēd/l plāt/] **98**–18
negative integers [nĕ/gə tĭv ĭn/tə jərz] **192**–1
negotiate [nĭ gō/shē āt/] **157**–D
neighborhood [nā/bər ho͝od/] **128** ✦
nephew [nĕf/yo͞o] **34**–19
Neptune [nĕp/to͞on] **205**–8
nervous [nür/vəs] **42**–10
nest [nĕst] **209**–12
net [nĕt] **226**–17
hairnet [hër/nĕt/] **93**–25
network [nĕt/würk/] **173**–A
Neutral Colors [no͞o/trəl kŭl/ərz] **24**
neutron [no͞o/trän] **195**–32
new [no͞o]
new job [no͞o/ jäb/] **172**–3
new moon [no͞o/ mo͞on/] **205**–9
New Year's Day [no͞o/ yïrz/ dā/] **22**–9
Newfoundland time [no͞o/fən lənd tīm/, –fənd–] **19**–34
news [no͞oz]
newspaper [no͞oz/pā/pər] **133**–6
news program [no͞oz prō/grăm] **236**–1
newsstand [no͞oz/stănd/] **128**–12
newt [no͞ot] **212**–26
New Words [no͞o/ würdz/] **8**
next [nĕkst]
next day mail [nĕkst/ dā/ māl/] **135** ✦
next to [nĕkst/ to͞o, –tə] **24**–9
next week [nĕkst/ wēk/] **20**–20
nickel [nĭk/əl] **26**–2
niece [nēs] **34**–18
night [nīt] **18**–20
nightclub [nīt/klŭb/] **223**–12
nightgown [nīt/gown/] **91**–25
night light [nīt/līt/] **37**–27
nightshirt [nīt/shürt/] **91**–28
nightstand [nīt/stănd/] **58**–23
night table [nīt/ tā/bəl] **58**–23
nine [nīn] **16**
nineteen [nīn/tēn/] **16**
nineteenth [nīn/tēnth/] **16**
ninetieth [nīn/tē əth] **16**
ninety [nīn/tē] **16**
90° angle [nīn/tē də grē/ ăng/gəl] **193**–26
ninth [nīnth] **16**
nipple [nĭp/əl] **37**–2
no [nō]
no left turn [nō/ lĕft/ türn] **154**–8
no outlet [nō/ owt/lĕt, –lət] **154**–6
no parking [nō/ pär/kĭng] **154**–11
noise [noyz] **64**–5
noisy [noy/zē] **23**–11
noon [no͞on] **18**–16
afternoon [ăf/tər no͞on/] **18**–17

north [nörth] **155**–1
NORTH AMERICA AND CENTRAL AMERICA
  [nörth/ ə mĕr/ə kə ən sĕn/trəl ə mĕr/ə kə] **200–201**
nose [nōz] **104**–6, **110**–17
  revolving nosepiece [rə väl/vĭng nōz/pēs] **194**–17
not [nät]
  can't breathe [kănt/ brēdh/] **116**–N
  do not drink [do͞o/ nät/ drĭnk] **112**–F
  do not enter [do͞o/ nät/ ĕn/tər] **154**–2
  do not operate [do͞o/ nät/ äp/ər āt/] **112**–E
  do not take [do͞o nät/ tāk/] **112**–D
  don't be late [dōnt/ bē/ lāt/] **174**–E
  don't litter [dōnt/ lĭt/ər] **219**–L
  don't smoke [dōnt/ smōk/] **114**–G
  not working [nät/ wür/kĭng] **62**–1
note [nōt] **183**–39
  footnote [fo͝ot/nōt/] **190**–10
  notebook [nōt/bo͝ok/] **7**–27
  notebook paper [nōt/bo͝ok/ pā/pər] **7**–28
  spiral notebook [spī/rəl nōt/bo͝ok/] **7**–29
novel [nä/vəl] **133**–16
November [nō vĕm/bər] **21**–35
nuclear energy [no͞o/klē ər ĕn/ər jē] **218**–8
nucleus [no͞o/klē əs] **194**–7, **195**–29
numb [nŭm] **119**–C
number [nŭm/bər]
  access number [ăk/sĕs/ nŭm/bər] **14**–16
  apartment number [ə pärt/mənt nŭm/bər] **4**–6
  cell phone number [sĕl/ fōn/ nŭm/bər] **4**–12
  checking account number
    [chĕk/ĭng ə kownt/ nŭm/bər] **132**–14
  driver's license number
    [drī/vərz lī/səns nŭm/bər] **136**–11
  even numbers [ē/vən nŭm/bərz] **192**–4
  odd numbers [öd/ nŭm/bərz] **192**–3
  phone number [fōn/ nŭm/bər] **4**–11, **15**–30
  prescription number
    [prĭ skrĭp/shən nŭm/bər] **112**–5
  savings account number
    [sā/vĭngz ə kownt/ nŭm/bər] **132**–11
  SKU number [ĕs/kā/yo͞o/ nŭm/bər] **27**–5
  Social Security number
    [sō/shəl sĭ kyo͝or/ə tē nŭm/bər] **4**–15
Numbers [nŭm/bərz] **16**
NUMBERS [nŭm/bərz] **16**
Numerals [no͞o/mər əlz] **16**
numerator [no͞o/mər ā/ tər] **192**–5
nurse [nürs] **118**–8, **168**–44
  licensed practical nurse (LPN) [lī/sənst
    prăk/tə kəl nürs/] / [ĕl/pē/ĕn/] **120**–11
  nurse midwives [nürs/ mĭd/wīvz] **120** ✦
  nurse practitioners [nürs/ prăk tĭ/shən ərz] **120** ✦
  registered nurse (RN) [rĕj/ə stərd nürs/] / [är/ĕn/]
    120–10
  surgical nurse [sür/jĭ kəl nürs/] **120**–9
nurse [nürs] **36**–B
Nurse [nürs] **93**
nursery [nür/sə rē]
  nursery rhymes [nür/sə rē rīmz/] **37**–22
  nursery school [nür/sə rē sko͞ol/] **188**–1
nursing [nür/sĭng] **120**–12
  nursing home [nür/sĭng hōm/] **52**–12
Nursing Staff [nür/sĭng stăf/] **120**
nutrition label [no͞o trĭ/shən lā/bəl] **122**–8
nuts [nŭts] **73**–36, **180**–36
nylon [nī/län] **99**–12
oak [ōk] **210**–17, **210**–24
obey [ō bā/] **140**–C
objective [əb jĕk/tĭv] **194**–18
oboe [ō/bō] **238**–3
observatory [əb zür/və tör/ē] **205**–21
observe [əb zürv/] **195**–C
obstetrician [äb/stə trĭsh/ən] **120**–2
obtuse angle [äb/to͞os ăng/gəl] **193**–27
occupational therapist
  [äk/yə pā/shən əl thĕr/ə pĭst] **168**–45
OCCUPATIONS [äk/yə pā/shənz] **166–169**
ocean [ō/shən] **204**–6, **225**–1
o'clock [ə kläk/] **18**–6
October [äk tō/bər] **21**–34
octopus [äk/tə pəs] **212**–9
odd numbers [öd/ nŭm/bərz] **192**–3
odometer [ō däm/ə tər] **159**–28
off [öf]
  clear off [klïr/ öf/] **10**–I
  drop off [dräp/ öf/] **38**–G
  gas shut-off valve [găs/ shŭt/öf vălv/] **146**–4
  get off [gĕt/ öf/] **153**–J
  take off [tāk/ öf/] **109**–Q
  turn off [türn/ öf/] **11**–P, **160**–I, **174**–G, **219**–G
offer [ö/fər] **12**–D
office [ö/fəs] **164**–3
  main office [mān/ ö/fəs] **5**–12
  office building [ö/fəs bĭld/ĭng] **124**–2
  office manager [ö/fəs măn/ĭ jər] **182**–8
  office supply store [ö/fəs sə plī/ stör/] **127**–21
  post office [pōst/ ö/fəs] **125**–11
  post office box (PO box) [pōst/ ö/fəs bäks/] /
    [pē/ō bäks/] **135**–9
  run for office [rŭn/ fər ö/fəs] **139**–A
Office [ö/fəs] **51**
OFFICE [ö/fəs] **134–135, 182–183**
Office Equipment [ö/fəs ĭ kwĭp/mənt] **183**
officer [ö/fə sər] **161**–17, **168**–48
Office Skills [ö/fəs skĭlz/] **171**
OFFICE SKILLS [ö/fəs skĭlz/] **171**
Office Supplies [ö/fəs sə plīz/] **183**
Office Visit [ö/fəs vĭ/zət] **119**
official [ə fĭsh/əl] **139**–32, **229**–6
oil [oyl] **73**–31, **218**–6
  oil gauge [oyl/ gāj/] **159**–29
  oil paint [oyl/ pānt/] **233**–19
  oil spill [oyl/ spĭl/] **218**–17
ointment [oynt/mənt] **113**–24, **117**–10
OK [ō kā/] **154**–5
old [ōld] **31**–9, **31**–10
omelet [äm/lət, ä/mə lət] **76**–12
on [än, ön] **25**–11
  get on [gĕt/ än, –ön] **153**–I
  go on [gō/ än, –ön] **173**–K
  on-the-job training [än dhə jäb/ trā/nĭng, –ön]
    172–7
  on the left [än dhə lĕft/, –ön] **25**–1
  on the right [än dhə rīt/, –ön] **25**–3
  on time [än tīm/, –ön] **19**–23, **16**–29
  overdose on drugs [ō/vər dōs/ än drŭgz/] **116**–K
  put on [po͝ot/ än/, –ön/] **87**–B, **108**–D, **109**–P
  try on [trī/ än/, –ön/] **95**–C
  turn on [türn/ än/, –ön/] **11**–B
once a week [wŭns/ə wēk/] **20**–22
oncologist [ön/kö lə jĭst/] **120**–5
one [wŭn] **16**
  five after one [fīv/ ăf/ tər wŭn/] **18**–7
  one billion [wŭn/ bĭl/yən] **16**
  one eighth [wŭn/ ātth/, –āth/] **17**–5
  one-fifteen [wŭn/fĭf/tēn/] **18**–9
  one-forty [wŭn/för/tē] **18**–12
  one-forty-five [wŭn/för/tē fīv/] **18**–13
  one fourth [wŭn/ förth/] **17**–4
  one half [wŭn/ hăf/] **17**–2
  one hundred [wŭn/ hŭn/drəd] **16**
  one hundred dollars
    [wŭn/ hŭn/drəd däl/ərz] **26**–12
  one hundred one [wŭn/ hŭn/drəd wŭn/] **16**
  100 percent [wŭn/ hŭn/drəd pər sĕnt/] **17**–8
  one hundredth [wŭn/ hŭn/drəth] **16**
  one hundred thousand
    [wŭn/ hŭn/drəd thow/zənd] **16**
  one million [wŭn/ mĭl/yən] **16**
  one o'clock [wŭn/ ə kläk/] **18**–6
  one-oh-five [wŭn/ō fīv/] **18**–7
  one-size-fits-all [wŭn/sīz fĭts/äl] **96**–6
  one-ten [wŭn/tĕn/] **18**–8
  one third [wŭn/ thürd/] **17**–3
  one-thirty [wŭn/thür/tē] **18**–11
  one thousand [wŭn/ thow/zənd] **16**
  one thousandth [wŭn/ thow/zənth] **16**
  one-twenty [wŭn/twĕn/tē] **18**–10
  one way [wŭn/ wā/] **154**–3
  one-way trip [wŭn/wā/ trĭp/] **152**–16
  one whole [wŭn/hōl/] **17**–1
  quarter after one [kwör/tər ăf/tər wŭn/] **18**–9
  ten after one [tĕn/ ăf/tər wŭn/] **18**–8
  twenty after one [twĕn/tē ăf/tər wŭn/] **18**–10
onions [ŭn/yənz] **69**–19, **69**–20
  onion rings [ŭn/yən rĭngz/] **79**–4
online [än/līn/, ön–]
  online catalog [än/līn/ kă/tə lög, ön–] **133**–11
  online course [än/līn/ körs/, ön–] **172**–8
only [ōn/lē] **154**–7
On the Airplane [än/ dhe ër/plān/] **161**
open [ō/pən] **6**–G, **143**–F
opener [ō/pən ər] **54**–8, **78**–1, **146**–8
Opening an Account [ō/pə nĭng ən ə kownt/] **132**
opera [äp/rə] **223**–11, **236**–5
operate [äp/ə rāt/] **112**–E, **170**–H
Operating Room [äp/ə rā/tĭng ro͞om/] **121**
operating table [äp/ə rā/tĭng tā/bəl] **121**–40
Operations [äp/ə rā/shənz] **192**
operator [äp/ə rā/tər] **14**–21, **98**–14, **168**–37
ophthalmologist
  [äf/thəl mäl/ə jĭst, –thə mäl/–, äp/–] **120**–7
opinion [ə pĭn/yən] **44**–3
opossum [ə päs/əm, päs/əm] **216**–4
opponent [ə pō/nənt] **139**–30
optician [äp tĭsh/ən] **130**–9

optometrist [äp täm/ə trĭst] **115**–6
orange [ör/ənj, är/–] **24**–4
oranges [ör/ən jəz, är/–] **68**–5
orangutan [ə răng/ə tăng/, –tăn/] **217**–39
orchard [ör/chərd] **177**–10
orchid [ör/kĭd] **211**–19
order [ör/dər] **185**–1
  order puller [ör/dər po͝ol/ər] **175**–10
order [ör/dər] **82**–D
orderly [ör/dər lē] **120**–16
Ordinal Numbers [ör/dn əl nŭm/bərz] **16**
organ [ör/gən] **238**–20
organic [ör gă/nĭk] **84**–2
organisms [ör/gə nĭzmz] **194**–1
organize [ör/gə nīz/] **171**–L, **191**–G
organizer [ör/gə nī/zər] **183**–49
ornament [ör/nə mənt] **239**–15
Orthodontics [ör/thə dän/tĭks] **119**
orthodontist [ör/thə dän/tĭst] **119**–5
orthopedists [ör/thə pē/dĭsts] **120** ✦
Other Instruments [ŭdh/ər ĭn/strə mənts] **238**
otter [ät/ər] **213**–35
ounce [owns] **75**–1, **75**–11
out [owt] **62**–2
  blow out [blō/ owt/] **240**–C
  check out [chĕk/ owt/] **133**–C
  cross out [krös/ owt/] **9**–R
  eat out [ēt/ owt/] **82** ✦
  fill out [fĭl/ owt/] **173**–J
  get out of [gĕt/ owt/ əv] **153**–F
  let out [lĕt/ owt/] **100**–C
  move out [mo͞ov/ owt/] **48** ✦
  outfit [owt/fĭt] **88** ✦
  out of focus [owt/ əv fō/kəs] **235**–33
  out-of-state contact [owt/əv stāt/ kän/tăkt] **146**–2
  run out of gas [rŭn/ owt/ əv găs/] **162**–E
  take out [tāk/ owt/] **9**–Y, **60**–Q, **82** ✦
  work out [würk/ owt/] **230**–N
OUTDOOR RECREATION [owt/dör rĕk/rē ā/shən] **226**
outlet [owt/lĕt, –lət] **58**–28, **154**–6, **159**–42
  outlet cover [owt/lĕt kŭv/ər] **181**–46
OUTSIDE THE BODY [owt/sīd/ dhe bä/dē] **106**–**107**
oven [ŭv/ən] **54**–15, **54**–20
  oven cleaner [ŭv/ən klē/nər] **61**–3
over [ō/vər] **76**–11, **153**–B
  overalls [ō/vər ölz/] **88**–6
  overcoat [ō/vər kōt/] **90**–2
  overexposed [ō/vər ĭk spōzd/] **235**–34
  overflowing [ō/vər flō/ĭng] **63**–17
  overhead compartment
    [ō/vər hĕd/ kəm pärt/mənt] **161**–13
  overhead projector [ō/vər hĕd/ prə jĕk/tər] **7**–16
  overjoyed [ō/vər joyd/] **43** ✦
  overnight mail [ō/vər nīt/ māl/] **135** ✦
  over-the-counter medication
    [ō/vər dhə -kown/tər mĕd/ə kā/shən] **113**–18
overdose [ō/vər dōs/, ō/vər dōs/] **116**–K
Over-the-Counter Medication
  [ō/vər dhə kown/tər mĕd/ə kā/shən] **113**
owl [owl] **214**–5
owner [ō/nər] **166**–11, **175**–1
oxfords [äks/fərdz] **95**–29
oxygen mask [äk/sĭ jən măsk/] **161**–24
oysters [oy/stərz] **71**–14
Pacific time [pə sĭf/ĭk tīm/] **19**–29
pacifier [păs/ə fī/ər] **37**–24
pack [păk] **74**–9, **117**–13, **235**–26
  backpack [băk/păk/] **94**–18, **226**–15
pack [păk] **49**–M, **162**–A
package [păk/ĭj] **74**–8, **74**–20, **134**–17
packaged food [păk/ĭjd fo͞od/] **146**–10
PACKAGING [păk/ə jĭng] **74**
packer [păk/ər] **175**–18
packing tape [păk/ĭng tāp/] **183**–32
pad [păd]
  bumper pad [bŭm/pər păd/] **59**–4
  changing pad [chānj/ĭng păd/] **59**–2
  foam pad [fōm/ păd/] **226**–13
  heating pad [hē/tĭng păd/] **113**–13
  ink pad [ĭnk/ păd/] **183**–46
  knee pads [nē/ pădz/] **179**–19
  legal pad [lē/gəl păd/] **183**–38
  shoulder pads [shōl/dər pădz/] **231**–20
  steel-wool soap pads [stēl/wo͝ol/sōp/ pădz/] **61**–5
  sterile pad [stĕr/əl păd/] **117**–6
pail [pāl] **37**–7, **61**–7, **225**–8
pain [pān] **42**–11, **115**–3
  pain reliever [pān rĭ lē/vər] **113**–26
paint [pānt] **181**–25, **232**–10, **233**–19
  paintbrush [pānt/brŭsh/] **181**–22, **233**–20
  paint pan [pānt/ păn/] **181**–51
  paint roller [pānt/ rō/lər] **181**–23
paint [pānt] **49**–P, **178**–A, **233**–E
painter [pān/tər] **168**–46
Painter [pān/tər] **92**
painting [pān/tĭng] **56**–9
pair of scissors [pĕr/ əv sĭz/ərz] **100**–16
paisley [pāz/lē] **96**–26
pajamas [pə jä/məz, –jă/–] **91**–24
pallet [pă/lət] **175**–13
palm [päm] **106**–15, **210**–14
pan [păn] **54**–24
  bed pan [bĕd/ păn/] **121**–28
  cake pan [kāk/ păn/] **78**–26
  dustpan [dŭst/ păn/] **61**–17
  frying pan [frī/ĭng păn/] **78**–5
  paint pan [pānt/ păn/] **181**–51
  pancakes [păn/kāks/] **80**–7
  pie pan [pī/ păn/] **78**–28
  roasting pan [rō/stĭng păn/] **78**–13
  saucepan [sös/păn/] **78**–25
pancreas [păng/krē əs] **107**–45
panda [păn/də] **217**–41
pane [pān] **178**–16
panel [păn/əl] **234**–7
Panel [păn/əl] **159**
panther [păn/thər] **217**–40
panties [păn/tēz] **91**–13
pants [pănts] **87**–12
  security pants [sĭ kyo͝or/ə tē pănts/] **93**–22
  training pants [trā/nĭng pănts/] **37**–11
  work pants [würk/ pănts/] **92**–5
panty hose [păn/tē hōz/] **91**–18
papayas [pə pī/əz] **68**–20
paper [pā/pər]
  construction paper [kən strŭk/shən pā/pər] **232**–12
  copies of important papers
    [kä/pēz əv ĭm pört/ənt pā/pərz] **146**–20
  newspaper [no͞oz/pā/pər] **133**–6
  notebook paper [nōt/bo͝ok/ pā/pər] **7**–28
  paper clip [pā/pər klĭp/] **183**–31
  paper cutter [pā/pər kŭt/ər] **183**–22
  paper dolls [pā/pər dälz/] **233**–28
  paper shredder [pā/pər shrĕd/ər] **183**–24
  paper towels [pā/pər tow/əlz] **54**–3
  sandpaper [sănd/ pā/pər] **181**–56
  toilet paper [toy/lət pā/pər] **57**–17, **146**–13
  wallpaper [wäl/ pā/pər] **59**–8
parade [pə rād/] **239**–1
paragraph [păr/ə grăf/] **190**–3
parakeet [păr/ə kēt/] **215**–15
parallel lines [păr/ə lĕl/ līnz/] **193**–25
parallelogram [păr/ə lĕl/ə grăm/] **193**–33
paramedic [păr/ə mĕ/dĭk] **116**–2
parasites [păr/ə sīts/] **111**–13
parcel post [pär/səl pōst/] **134**–6
parentheses [pə rĕn/thə sēz/] **190**–19
PARENTING [păr/ən tĭng, pĕr/–] **36**–**37**
Parents [păr/ənts, pĕr/–] **34**
parent-teacher conference
  [păr/ənt tē/chər kän/frəns, pĕr/–] **22**–5
paring knife [pĕr/ĭng nīf/] **78**–16
park [pärk] **223**–10
  park ranger [pärk/ rāng/jər] **220**–2
park [pärk] **129**–E
parka [pär/kə] **90**–9
PARK AND PLAYGROUND [pärk/ ən plā/grownd/] **224**
parking [pär/kĭng] **128**–6, **154**–11, **154**–12
  parking attendant [pär/kĭng ə tĕn/dənt] **184**–3
  parking garage [pär/kĭng gə räzh/, –räj/] **124**–1
  parking meter [pär/kĭng mē/tər] **129**–25
  parking space [pär/kĭng spās/] **50**–18, **128**–5
PARKS [pärks] **220**–**221**
parochial school [pə rō/kē əl sko͞ol/] **5** ✦
parsley [pär/slē] **69**–28
part [pärt] **33**–4
participate [pär tĭ/sə pāt/] **10**–B
particle [pär/tĭ kəl]
  particle board [pär/tĭ kəl börd/] **181**–20
  particle mask [pär/tĭ kəl măsk/] **179**–14
Partner [pärt/nər] **8**
parts [pärts] **175**–5
Parts of a Bird [pärts/ əv ə bürd/] **214**
PARTS OF A CAR [pärts/ əv ə kär/] **158**–**159**
Parts of a Fish [pärts/ əv ə fĭsh/] **212**
Parts of a Flower [pärts/ əv ə flow/ər] **211**
Parts of an Essay [pärts/ əv ən ĕs/ā] **190**
Parts of a Phone [pärts/ əv ə fōn/] **14**
Parts of a Sewing Machine
  [pärts/ əv ə sō/ĭng mə shēn/] **98**
Parts of a Tree [pärts/ əv ə trē/] **210**
party [pär/tē] **64**–2
pass [păs] **161**–20
  passbook [păs/bo͝ok/] **132**–10
  passport [păs/pört/] **41**–10
pass [păs] **10**–E, **137**–H, **230**–G

passenger [păs/ən jər] **150**–2, **161**–15
past [păst] **155**–E
pasta [päs/tə] **67**–12
pasta salad [päs/tə săl/əd] **80**–20
paste [pāst]
toothpaste [to͞oth/pāst/] **109**–23
pastrami [pə strä/mē] **71**–23
path [păth] **208**–3, **224**–3
Path [păth] **172**
patient [pā/shənt] **118**–6, **121**–18
patio [păt/ē ō] **53**–16
patio furniture [păt/ē ō für/nĭ chər] **53**–19
patron [pā/trən] **82**–6, **133**–3
pattern [păt/ərn] **99**–22
PATTERNS [păt/ərnz] **96**
pause [pöz] **235**–E
paw [pö] **216**–20
pay [pā]
paycheck [pā/chĕk/] **165**–14
payroll clerk [pā/rōl klürk/] **165**–10
pay stub [pā/ stŭb/] **165**–11
pay [pā]
pay a late fine [pā/ ə lāt/ fīn/] **133**–E
pay attention [pā/ ə tĕn/shən] **147**–D
pay back [pā/ băk/] **26**–D
pay cash [pā/ kăsh/] **27**–A
pay for [pā/ för/, –fər] **27**–G
pay phone [pā/ fōn] **15**–25, **129**–23
pay taxes [pā/ tăks/əz] **140**–B
pay the application fee
[pā/ dhe ăp/lə kā/shən fē/] **137**–D
pay the check [pā/ dhe chĕk/] **82**–I
pay the rent [pā/ dhe rĕnt/] **48**–E
Pay [pā] **27**
PBX [pē/ bē/ ĕks/] **182**–13
peaceful assembly [pēs/fəl ə sĕm/blē] **140**–1
peaches [pē/chəz] **68**–10
peacock [pē/käk/] **214**–14
peak [pēk] **204**–14
pearls [pürlz] **95**–39
pears [pērz] **68**–4
peas [pēz] **69**–21
pedal [pĕd/əl] **159**–45, **159**–46
pedestrian [pə dĕs/trē ən] **128**–14
pedestrian crossing [pə dĕs/trē ən krö/sĭng] **154**–13
pediatrician [pē/dē ə trĭsh/ən] **120**–4
peel [pēl] **77**–K
peeler [pē/lər] **78**–15
peephole [pēp/hōl/] **51**–32
pelvis [pĕl/vəs] **107**–50
pen [pĕn] **7**–22
pencil [pĕn/səl] **7**–20, **109**–34
pencil eraser [pĕn/səl ĭ rā/sər] **7**–21
pencil sharpener [pĕn/səl shär/pə nər] **7**–23, **183**–26
penguin [pĕng/wĭn] **214**–11
peninsula [pə nĭn/sə lə] **204**–7
penny [pĕn/ē] **26**–1
PEOPLE [pē/pəl] **32**
pepper [pĕp/ər] **55**–13, **69**–7, **69**–29
percent [pər sĕnt/]
50 percent [fĭf/tē pər sĕnt/] **17**–10
100 percent [wŭn/ hŭn/drəd pər sĕnt/] **17**–8
75 percent [sĕv/ən tē fīv/ pər sĕnt/] **17**–9
10 percent [tĕn/ pər sĕnt/] **17**–12
25 percent [twĕn/tē fīv/ pər sĕnt/] **17**–11
Percents [pər sĕnts/] **17**
Percussion [pər kŭsh/ən] **238**
perfume [pür/fyo͞om/, pər fyo͞om/] **108**–6
perimeter [pə rĭ/mə tər] **193**–43
period [pïr/ē əd] **190**–11
Period [pïr/ē əd] **198**
periodicals [pïr/ē äd/ĭ kəlz] **133**–4
periodic table [pïr/ē äd/ĭk tā/bəl] **195**–26
perm [pürm] **33**–B
peroxide [pə räk/ sīd] **117**–9
perpendicular lines [pür/pən dĭk/yə lər līnz/] **193**–24
person [pür/sən]
appliance repair person
[ə plī/əns rĭ pĕr/ pür/sən] **166**–4
assemblyperson [ə sĕm/blē pür/sən] **139**–24
businessperson [bĭz/nəs pür/sən] **166**–12
bus person [bŭs/ pür/sən] **185**–13
congressperson [kän/grəs pür/sən] **138**–4
councilperson [kown/səl pür/sən] **139**–28
counterperson [kown/tər pür/sən] **79**–17
delivery person [də lĭv/ə rē pür/sən] **167**–21
electronics repair person
[ĭ lĕk trän/ĭks rĭ pĕr/ pür/sən] **167**–24
repair person [rĭ pĕr/ pür/sən] **62**–10
personal CD player [pür/sə nəl sē/dē/ plā/ər] **234**–5
PERSONAL HYGIENE [pür/sə nəl hī/jēn] **108–109**
PERSONAL INFORMATION
[pür/sə nəl ĭn/fər mā/shən] **4**
pesticide poisoning [pĕs/tə sīd/ poy/zə nĭng] **218**–16
pests [pĕsts] **62** ✦
pet [pĕt]
pet food [pĕt fo͞od/] **72**–5
pet store [pĕt stör/] **130**–6
petals [pĕt/lz] **211**–8
petition [pə tĭ/shən] **148**–5
petroleum [pə trō/lē əm] **218**–6
Pets [pĕts] **215**
pharmacist [fär/mə sĭst] **112**–1
pharmacy [fär/mə sē] **128**–4
PHARMACY [fär/mə sē] **112–113**
Phase of the Moon [fāz/ əf dhə mo͞on/] **205**
Phillips screwdriver [fĭl/ĭps skro͞o/drī/vər] **180**–31
phlebotomist [flĭ bä/tə mĭst] **121**–29
phone [fōn]
automated phone system
[ö/tə māt ĭd fōn/ sĭs/təm] **14**–23
cell phone holder [sĕl/ fōn/ hōl/dər] **94**–15
cell phone kiosk [sĕl/ fōn/ kē/ösk] **131**–22
cell phone number [sĕl/ fōn/ nŭm/bər] **4**–12
cellular phone [sĕl/yə lər fōn/] **14**–8
cordless phone [körd/ləs fōn/] **15**–24
headphones [hĕd/ fōnz/] **6**–8, **234**–4
Internet phone call [ĭn/tər nĕt/ fōn/ käl/] **14**–20
microphone [mī/krə fōn/] **234**–18
pay phone [pā/ fōn/] **15**–25, **129**–23
phone bill [fōn/ bĭl/] **15**–28
phone jack [fōn/ jăk/] **14**–3
phone line [fōn/ līn/] **14**–4
phone number [fōn/ nŭm/bər] **4**–11, **15**–30
smart phone [smärt/ fōn/] **15**–27
Phone [fōn] **14**
Phone Bill [fōn/ bĭl/] **15**
Phone Call [fōn/ köl/] **15**
photo [fō/tō] **58**–3, **136**–4
digital photo album [dĭ/jə təl fō/tō ăl/bəm] **235**–32
funny photo [fŭn/ē fō/tō] **206**–2
photo album [fō/tō ăl/bəm] **235**–31
photocopier [fō/tə käp/ē ər] **183**–23
serious photo [sïr/ē əs fō/tō] **206**–3
photographer [fə täg/rə fər] **206**–1
PHOTOGRAPHY [fə täg/rə fē] **234–235**
photosynthesis [fō/tō sĭn/thə səs] **194**–10
physical [fĭz/ĭ kəl]
physical education [fĭz/ĭ kəl ĕ jə kā/shən] **189**–17
physical therapist [fĭz/ĭ kəl thĕr/ə pĭst] **115**–12
physical therapy [fĭz/ĭ kəl thĕr/ə pē] **115**–11
physically challenged [fĭz/ĭ klē chăl/əndj] **32**–10
physician assistant [fĭ zĭ shən ə sĭs/tənt] **168**–47
physicist [fĭz/ĭ sĭst/] **195**–33
Physics [fĭz/ĭks] **195**
pi (π) [pī] **193**–46
piano [pē ăn/ō] **238**–14
pick [pĭk] **108**–15
pickax [pĭk/ăks/] **178**–21
picker [pĭ/kər] **178**–5
pickle [pĭk/l] **80**–11
pick up [pĭk/ ŭp/] **6**–I, **11**–E, **38**–M, **112** ✦
pickup truck [pĭk/ŭp trŭk/] **156**–12
picnic [pĭk/nĭk] **224**–D
picnic table [pĭk/nĭk tā/bəl] **224**–8
picture [pĭk/chər]
picture book [pĭk/chər bo͝ok/] **133**–12
picture dictionary [pĭk/chər dĭk/shə nër ē] **7**–31
picture frame [pĭk/chər frām/] **58**–4
pie [pī] **81**–35
pie pan [pī/ păn/] **78**–28
pier [pïr] **225**–18
pierced [pïrst]
pierced ear [pïrst/ ïr/] **32**–17
pierced earrings [pïrst/ ïr/ĭngz] **95**–36
pig [pĭg] **215**–2, **215**–14
pigeon [pĭj/ən] **214**–15
pile [pīl] **53**–25
pill [pĭl] **113**–21
pillow [pĭl/ō] **56**–2, **58**–11
pillowcase [pĭl/ō kās/] **58**–14
pilot [pī/lət] **161**–11
pin [pĭn] **95**–38
bobby pins [bäb/ē pĭnz/] **108**–21
clothespin [klōz/ pĭn/] **101**–10
pin cushion [pĭn/ ko͝osh/ən] **100**–13
pushpin [po͝osh/pĭn/] **183**–35
rolling pin [rō/lĭng pĭn] **78**–30
safety pin [sāf/tē pĭn/] **37**–9, **100**–14
straight pin [strāt pĭn/] **100**–12
pine [pīn] **210**–9
pinecone [pīn/kōn/] **210**–11
pineapples [pī/năp/əlz] **68**–23
pink [pĭnk] **24**–7
pint [pīnt] **75**–3
pipe [pīp] **158**–15, **181**–17
pipe wrench [pīp rĕnch/] **181**–47

pitch [pĭch] **230**–A
pizza [pēt/sə] **79**–10
place [plās] **146**–1
fireplace [fïr/plās/] **56**–13
placemat [plās măt/] **55**–11
place of birth [plās/ əv bürth/] **4**–14
place setting [plās/ sĕt/ĭng] **83**–17
PLACES TO GO [plā/səz tə gō/] **222–223**
PLACES TO LIVE [plā/səz tə lĭv/] **52**
plaid [plăd] **96**–22
plain [plān] **97**–33
plains [plānz] **204**–19
plan [plăn] **186**–4
plan [plăn] **146**–A
plane [plān] **144**–3, **150**–8, **181**–57
Planets [plăn/əts] **205**
Planning a Career [plă/nĭng ə kə rēr/] **172**
plant [plănt] **176**–E, **177**–A, **219**–N
plants [plănts] **208**–5
houseplant [hows/plănt/] **56**–4, **211**–27
Plants [plănts] **210**
PLANTS [plănts] **210**
plaque [plăk] **119**–12
plastic [plăs/tĭk]
plastic storage bags [plăs/tĭk stör/ĭj băgz] **72**–25
plastic storage container
[plăs/tĭk stör/ĭj kən tā/nər] **78**–4
plastic utensils [plăs/tĭk yōō tĕn/ səlz] **79**–19
plastic wrap [plăs/tĭk răp/] **72**–24
plate [plāt] **55**–1
bread-and-butter plate [brĕd/n bŭt/ər plāt/] **83**–19
dinner plate [dĭn/ər plāt/] **83**–18
license plate [lī/səns plāt/] **136**–12, **158**–12
salad plate [săl/əd plāt/] **83**–20
vanity plate [vă/nə tē plāt/]**136** ✦
platform [plăt/förm/] **152**–7
platter [plăt/ər] **55**–20
platypus [plăt/ĭ pəs, –pŏŏs/] **217**–46
play [plā] **223**–8
play area [plā/ ër/ē ə] **130**–11
playground [plā/grownd/] **50**–3
play [plā] **235**–B
play an instrument [plā/ ən ĭn/strə mənt] **238**–A
play cards [plā/ kärdz/] **233**–H
play games [plā/ gāmz/] **232**–B
play with [plā/ wĭth/] **36**–M
player [plā/ər] **229**–5
CD player [sē/dē plā/ər] **159**–38
DVD player [dē/vē/dē/ plā/ər] **56**–7, **234**–10
MP3 player [ĕm/pē/thrē/ plā/ər] **234**–2
personal CD player [pür/sə nəl sē/dē plā/ər] **234**–5
portable cassette player
[pör/tə bəl kə sĕt/ plā/ər] **234**–6
portable DVD player
[pör/tə bəl dē/vē/dē/ plā/ər] **234**–11
video player [vĭd/ē ō plā/ər] **197**–11
PLAYGROUND [plā/grownd/] **224**
pliers [plī/ərz] **180**–7
plugs [plŭgz] **179**–15, **234**–16
plumber [plŭm/ər] **63**–20
plums [plŭmz] **68**–13
plunger [plŭn/jər] **181**–50
plywood [plī/wŏŏd/] **178**–18
p.m. [pē/ĕm/] **18**–5
pneumatic drill [nōō măt/ĭk drĭl/] **178**–9
poached eggs [pōcht/ ĕgz/] **76**–9
PO box (post office box) [pē/ō bäks/] /
[pōst/ ö/fəs bäks/] **135**–9
pocket [päk/ət] **100**–7
podium [pō/dē əm] **206**–5
poinsettia [poyn sĕt/ē ə, –sĕt/ə] **211**–24
point [poynt] **17**–7,
endpoint [ĕnd/poynt/] **193**–21
pointer [poyn/tər] **197**–12
poison [poy/zən] **116**–J
poison ivy [poy/zən ī/vē] **210**–25
poison oak [poy/zən ōk/] **210**–24
poison sumac [poy/zən sōō/măk, –shōō/–] **210**–23
poisoning [poy/zən ĭng] **218**–16
poisonous fumes [poy/zən əs fyōōmz/] **179**–3
poles [pōlz] **226**–18, **231**–25
police [pə lēs/]
police officer [pə lēs/ ö/fə sər] **141**–1, **168**–48
police station [pə lēs/ stā/shən] **124**–6
polish [päl/ĭsh] **61**–8, **109**–33
polish [päl/ĭsh] **60**–E, **109**–O
political [pə lĭ/tĭ kəl]
political campaign [pə lĭ/tĭ kəl kăm pān/] **139**–29
political movement [pə lĭ/tĭ kəl mōōv/mənt] **199**–16
political party [pə lĭ/tĭ kəl pär/tē] **139** ✦
polka-dotted [pō/kə dät/əd] **96**–21
pollution [pə lōō/shən] **218**–11, **218**–14
Pollution [pə lōō/shən] **218**
polo [pō/lō] **229**–15
polo shirt [pō/lō shĭrt/] **92**–14
poncho [păn/chō] **90**–19
pond [pănd] **204**–21
pool [pōōl] **51**–22, **184**–22, **228**–2
pool service [pōōl/ sür/vəs] **184**–21
pool table [pōōl/ tā/bəl] **50**–14
pop [päp] **73**–34, **237**–25
pop-up ad [päp/ŭp] **197**–9
porch light [pörch/ līt/] **53**–13
porcupine [pör/kyə pīn/] **216**–10
Pork [pörk] **70**
pork chops [pörk/ chäps/] **70**–10
porpoise [pör/pəs] **213**–30
port [pört] **196**–7
airport [ër/pört/] **151**–10
portable [pör/tə bəl]
portable cassette player
[pör/tə bəl kə sĕt/ plā/ər] **234**–6
portable DVD player
[pör/tə bəl dē/vē/dē/ plā/ər] **234**–11
portable TV [pör/tə bəl tē/ vē/] **234**–8
positive integers [pö/zə tĭv ĭn/tə jərz] **192**–2
post [pōst] **134**–6
post card [pōst/kärd/] **134**–16
postmark [pōst/märk/] **134**–24
post office [pōst/ ö/fəs] **125**–11
post office box (PO box) [pōst/ ö/fəs bäks/] /
[pē/ō bäks/] **135**–9
postage [pō/stĭj] **135** ✦
postal [pō/stəl] **135**–10
postal clerk [pō/stəl klürk/] **135**–7
postal forms [pō/stəl förmz/] **134**–19
postal scale [pō/stəl skāl/] **183**–27
postal worker [pō/stəl wür/kər] **169**–49
POST OFFICE [pōst/ ö/fəs] **134–135**
pot [păt] **54**–16, **78**–6
pot holders [păt hōl/dərz] **78**–29
teapot [tē/păt/] **55**–16
potatoes [pə tā/tōz] **69**–17
baked potato [bākt/ pə tā/tō] **81**–25
mashed potatoes [măsht/ pə tā/tōz] **81**–23
potato chips [pə tā/tō chĭps/] **73**–35
potato salad [pə tā/tō săl/əd] **80**–19
sweet potatoes [swēt/ pə tā/tōz] **69**–18
potty seat [păt/ē sēt/] **37**–12
pouch [powch] **217**–50
Poultry [pōl/trē] **70, 76**
POULTRY [pōl/trē] **70**
pound [pownd] **75**–12
pound key [pownd/ kē/] **14**–7
pour [pör] **82**–C
powder [pow/dər] **37**–14, **108**–4, **109**–41
power [pow/ər] **218**–2, **218**–5
power cord [pow/ər körd/] **196**–2
power outlet [pow/ər owt/lĕt] **159**–42
power sander [pow/ər săn/dər] **180**–11
pox [pöks] **111**–6
practical [prăk/tə kəl] **120**–11
prairie dog [prër/ē dög/] **215**–22
praise [prāz] **36**–J
pregnant [prĕg/nənt] **32**–15
preheat [prē/hēt/] **77**–A
preparation [prĕ/pə rā/shən] **185**–4
PREPARATION [prĕ/pə rā/shən] **76–77**
prepare [prĭ/për] **174**–A
PREPOSITIONS [prĕp/ə zĭsh/ənz] **25**
PREPOSITIONS OF MOTION
[prĕp/ə zĭsh/ənz əv mō/shən] **153**
preschool [prē/skōōl/] **188**–1
prescribe medication [prĭ skrīb/mĕd/ə kā/shən] **112** ✦
prescription [prĭ skrĭp/shən] **112**–2
pick up a prescription
[pĭk/ ŭp/ə prĭ skrĭp/shən] **112** ✦
prescription label [prĭ skrĭp/shən lā/bəl] **112**–4
prescription medication
[prĭ skrĭp/shən mĕd/ə kā/shən] **112**–3
prescription number [prĭ skrĭp/shən nŭm/bər]
112–5
present [prĕz/ənt] **94** ✦, **240**–3
presentation [prĕ/zən tā/shən] **182**–6
president [prĕz/ə dənt] **138**–8, **199**–5
first president [fürst/ prĕz/ə dənt] **198**–11
Presidents' Day [prĕz/ə dənts dā/] **22**–11
vice president [vīs/ prĕz/ə dənt] **138**–9
press [prĕs] **78**–11, **140**–4
press [prĕs] **15**–B, **15**–D
presser foot [prĕs/ər fŏŏt/] **98**–19
pressure [prĕsh/ər] **111**–14, **118**–9
pretend [prĭ tĕnd/] **233**–G
Prewriting [prē/rī/tĭng] **191**

price [prīs] **27**–2, **27**–3, **27**–7
price tag [prīs tăg/] **27**–1
prime minister [prīm/ mĭn/ə stər] **199**–7
principal [prĭn/sə pəl] **5**–4
print [prĭnt] **96**–23
fingerprint [fĭng/gər prĭnt/] **136**–5
print [prĭnt] **4**–C, **171**–I
printer [prĭn/tər] **169**–50, **196**–17
inkjet printer [ĭnk/jĕt prĭn/tər] **183**–18
laser printer [lā/zər prĭn/tər] **183**–19
Priority Mail® [prī ör/ə tē māl/, –är/–] **134**–1
prism [prĭz/əm] **195**–35
prisoner [prĭz/nər] **141**–15
private school [prī/vət skōōl/] **5** ✦
Problem [präb/ləm] **192**
problems [präb/ləmz] **115**–1, **192**–11
Problems [präb/ləmz] **115, 119**
PROBLEMS [präb/ləmz] **62–63**
Procedures [prə sē/jərz] **117, 118**
PROCEDURES [prə sē/jərz] **146–147**
Process [prä/sĕs] **191**
processor [prä/sĕ sər] **54**–26
Processor [prä/sĕ sər] **92**
produce section [prō/dōōs sĕk/shən] **72**–2
product [präd/ŭkt] **192**–9
Products [präd/ŭkts] **72, 73**
program [prō/grăm]
children's program [chĭl/drənz prō/grăm] **236**–9
nature program [nā/chər prō/grăm] **236**–7
news program [nōōz/ prō/grăm] **236**–1
shopping program [shäp/ĭng prō/grăm] **236**–10
sports program [spörtz/ prō/grăm] **236**–11
program [prō/grăm] **170**–I
Programs [prō/grămz] **236**
projector [prə jĕk/tər] **6**–6, **7**–16, **235**–29
promotion [prə mō/shən] **172**–4
proof of insurance [prōōf/ əv/ĭn shŏŏr/əns] **136**–8
proofread [prōōf/rēd/] **191**–I
prosecuting attorney
[präs/ĭ kyōō/tĭng ə tür/nē] **141**–10
protect [prə tĕkt/] **143**–D
protector [prə tĕk/tər] **196**–1
proton [prō/tön] **195**–31
proud [prowd] **43**–21
prunes [prōōnz] **68**–26
pruning shears [prōō/nĭng shïrz/] **176**–11
psychiatrist [sī kī/ə trĭst, sə–] **120**–8
PUBLIC SAFETY [pŭb/lĭk sāf/tē] **143**
public school [pŭb/lĭk skōōl/] **5** ✦
PUBLIC TRANSPORTATION
[pŭb/lĭk trăns/pər tā/shən] **152**
pull [pŏŏl] **119**–F, **224**–A
puller [pŏŏl/ər] **175**–10
pullover sweater [pŏŏl/ō/vər swĕt/ər] **88**–3
pulse [pŭls] **122**–A
pumps [pŭmps] **95**–26
Punctuation [pŭngk/chōō ā/shən] **190**
puppy [pŭp/ē] **215**–12
purchase [pür/chəs] **94**–A
purifier [pyōō/rə fī/ ər] **113**–13
purple [pür/pəl] **24**–6
purses [pür/səz] **94**–2, **94**–14
push [pŏŏsh] **224**–B
pushpin [pŏŏsh/pĭn/] **183**–35
put [pŏŏt] **9**–X
put away
[pŏŏt/ə wā/] **9**–Z, **60**–G
put down [pŏŏt/ down/] **6**–J
put in coolant [pŏŏt/ ĭn kōō/lənt] **157**–I
put on [pŏŏt/ än/, –ön/] **87**–B, **108**–D, **109**–P, **135**–C
put on hold [pŏŏt/ än hōld/, –ön] **171**–N
put the utilities in your name
[pŏŏt/ dhe yōō tĭl/ə tēz ĭn yər nām/] **49**–O
puzzle [pŭz/əl] **59**–17
pyramid [pïr/ə mĭd] **193**–39
quad [kwäd] **5**–1
quart [kwört] **75**–4
quarter [kwör/tər] **26**–4
quarter after one [kwör/tər ăf/tər wŭn/] **18**–9
1/4 cup [kwör/tər kŭp/] **75**–8
quarter moon [kwör/tər mōōn/] **205**–11
quarter to two [kwör/tər tə tōō/] **18**–13
3/4 sleeved [thrē/ kwör/tər slēvd/] **96**–13
question mark [kwĕs/chən märk/] **190**–12
Quick and Easy Cake [kwĭk/ ən ē/zē kāk/] **77**
quiet [kwī/ət] **23**–12
quill [kwĭl] **216**–23
quilt [kwĭlt] **58**–16
quilt block [kwĭlt/ bläk/] **232**–15
quilt [kwĭlt] **232**–C
quotation [kwō tā/shən] **190**–9
quotation marks [kwō tā/shən märks/] **190**–15
quotient [kwō /shənt] **192**–10
rabbit [răb/ət] **215**–13
raccoon [ră kōōn/] **216**–13
race [rās] **230**–S
racing [rā/sĭng] **228**–19
rack [răk] **98**–16
dish rack [dĭsh/ răk/] **54**–5
roasting rack [rō/stĭng răk/] **78**–14
towel rack [tow/əl răk/] **57**–13
racket [răk/ət] **231**–2
racquetball [răk/ət böl/] **228**–12
radiation [rā/dē ā/shən] **218**–15
radiator [rā/dē ā/tər] **158**–19
radio [rā/dē ō] **102**–6, **159**–37, **179**–22
radioactive materials
[rā/dē ō ăk/tĭv mə tïr/ē əlz] **179**–7
radiologist [rā/dē äl/ə jĭst] **120**–6
radishes [răd/ĭ shəz] **69**–4
radius [rā/dē əs] **193**–35
rafting [răf/tĭng] **226**–2
rags [răgz] **61**–9
rail [rāl] **59**–10
railroad crossing [rāl/rōd krö/sĭng] **154**–14
rain [rān] **218**–13
rain boots [rān/ bōōts/] **90**–20
raincoat [rān/kōt/] **90**–18
rain forest [rān/ för/əst, fär/–] **204**–1
raining [rā/nĭng] **13**–11
raise [rāz] **6**–A
raisins [rā/zənz] **68**–25
rake [rāk] **176**–8
rake [rāk] **176**–C
ranch [rănch] **52**–10
rancher [răn/chər] **177**–22
Ranch Hand [rănch hănd/] **92**
RANCHING [răn/chĭng] **177**
R&B [är/n bē/] **237**–28
range [rānj] **204**–15
ranger [rān/jər] **220**–2
rash [răsh] **110**–10
raspberries [răz/bĕr/ēz] **68**–15
rats [răts] **63**–27, **215**–17
rattle [răt/l] **37**–26
rattlesnake [răt/l snāk/] **213**–38
raw [rö] **70**–24
ray [rā] **212**–11
razor [rā/zər] **109**–27
razorblade [rā/zər blād/] **109**–28
reaction [rē/ăk shən] **116**–E
read [rēd]
proofread [prōōf/rēd/] **191**–I
read the card [rēd/ dhe kärd/] **135**–G
read the definition [rēd/ dhe dĕ/fə nĭ/shən] **8**–B
read the paper [rēd/ dhe pā/pər] **39**–V
read to [rēd/ tōō] **36**–N
Reading a Phone Bill [rē/dĭng ə fōn/ bĭl/] **15**
reality show [rē ă lə tē shō/] **236**–6
rearview mirror [rïr/vyōō/ mïr/ər] **159**–35
receipt [rĭ sēt/] **27**–6
receive [rĭ sēv/] **135**–F
receiver [rĭ sē/vər] **14**–1
reception area [rĭ sĕp/shən ër/ē ə] **182**–15
receptionist [rĭ sĕp/shə nĭst] **118**–2, **164**–5, **169**–51, **182**–14
reclined seat [rĭ klīnd/ sēt/] **161**–27
record [rĭ körd/] **195**–D, **235**–A
records [rĕk/ərdz] **168**–39
RECREATION [rĕk/rē ā/shən] **226**
recreational vehicle (RV)
[rĕk/rē ā/shən əl vē/ə kəl] / [är/vē/] **156**–10
Recreation Room [rĕk/rē ā/shən rōōm/] **50**
recruiter [rə krōō/tər] **172**–14
rectangle [rĕk/tăng/gəl] **193**–29
recycle [rē sī/kəl] **60**–B, **219**–C
recycling bin [rē sī/klĭng bĭn/] **61**–2
red [rĕd] **24**–1
red hair [rĕd/ hër/] **33**–15
redwood [rĕd/wŏŏd/] **210**–18
redecorate [rē dĕk/ə rāt/] **48** ✦
reduce [rĭ dōōs/] **219**–A
referee [rĕf/ə rē/] **229**–6
reference librarian [rĕf/rəns lī brër/ē ən] **133**–9
refrigerator [rĭ frĭj/ə rā/tər] **54**–9
refund [rē/fŭnd] **97** ✦
reggae [rĕ gā/] **237**–31
register [rĕj/ə stər] **73**–15
register [rĕj/ə stər] **140**–D, **157**–F
registered nurse (RN)
[rĕj/ə stərd nürs/] / [är/ĕn/] **120**–10
registration [rĕj/ə strā/shən]
registration sticker
[rĕj/ə strā/shən stĭk/ər] **136**–13
registration tag [rĕj/ə strā/shən tăg/] **136**–13
regular price [rĕg/yə lər prīs/] **27**–2

regulations [rĕ gyə lā/shənz] **164**–6
relatives [rĕ lə tĭvz] **44**–6
relax [rĭ lăks/] **39**–U
relieved [rĭ lēvd/] **42**–15
reliever [rĭ lēv/ər] **113**–26
religious holiday [rĭ lĭj/əs häl/ə dā/] **22**–7
remain [rē/mān] **147**–E
remarried [rē măr/ēd] **35**–24
remote [rĭ mōt/] **234**–9
remove [rĭ mōōv/] **109**–Q, **132**–G
remover [rĭ mōō/vər] **109**–42
renew a license [rĭ nōō/ ə lī/səns, –nyōō/–] **136** ✦
rental agreement [rĕn/təl ə grē/mənt] **51**–28
Rental Office [rĕn/təl ö/fəs] **51**
Renting an Apartment [rĕn/tĭng ən ə pärt/mənt] **48**
repair [rĭ për/] **166**–4, **167**–24
repair person [rĭ për/ pür/sən] **62**–10
repair [rĭ për/] **170**–J
REPAIRS [rĭ përz/] **62–63**
repellent [rĭ pĕl/ənt] **226**–23
replace [rĭ plās/] **157**–K
report [rĭ pört/] **143**–J, **143**–K
reporter [rĭ pör/tər] **169**–52
representative [rĕ/prĭ zĕn/tə tĭv] **138**–3, **167**–20
Reptiles [rĕp/tīlz] **213**
REPTILES [rĕp/tīlz] **212–213**
request [rĭ kwĕst/] **12** ✦
Requirements [rĭ kwīr/mənts] **140**
rescue [rĕs/kyōō] **145**–20
rescue breathing [rĕs/kyōō brē/dhĭng] **117**–16
Resident Alien card [rĕz/ə dənt ā/lē ən kärd/] **40**–2
resource center [rē/sörs sĕn/tər] **172**–9
Resources [rē/sörs/səz, rĭ sör/səz] **219**
respirator [rĕs/pə rā/tər] **179**–13
Responding [rĭ spän/dĭng] **191**
Responsibilities [rĭ spän/sə bĭl/ə tēz] **140**
RESPONSIBILITIES [rĭ spän/sə bĭl/ə tēz] **140**
restaurant [rĕs/tə rənt, –ränt/] **125**–14, **128**–10
RESTAURANT [rĕs/tə rənt, –ränt/] **79, 82–83**
Restaurant Dining [rĕs/tə rənt dī/nĭng, –ränt/] **185**
Restaurant Kitchen [rĕs/tə rənt kĭ/chən, –ränt/] **185**
restrooms [rĕst/ rōōmz/] **5**–10
results [rĭ zŭltz/] **139**–31
resuscitation [rĭ sə sə tā/shən] **117**–17
retail clerk [rē/tāl/ klürk/] **169**–53
retire [rĭ tïr/] **41**–O
return [rĭtürn/] **73**–16
return address [rĭ türn/ ə drĕs/, –ă/drĕs] **134**–21
return [rĭ türn/] **27**–H, **133**–D
REUNION [rē yōōn/yən] **44–45**
reuse [rē yōōz/] **219**–B
revise [rĭ vīz/] **191**–J
Revising [rĭ vī/zĭng] **191**
Revolutionary War [rĕ/və lōō/shə nër ē wör/] **198**–8
revolving [rĭ väl/vĭng]
revolving door [rĭ väl/vĭng dör/] **184**–2
revolving nosepiece [rĭ väl/vĭng nōz/pēs/] **194**–17
rewind [rē wīnd/] **235**–C
rewrite [rē rīt/] **191**–J
rhinoceros [rī näs/ər əs] **217**–28
ribbon [rĭ/bən] **99**–30
ribs [rĭbz] **70**–5, **76**–2
rib cage [rĭb/ kāj/] **107**–48
rice [rīs] **67**–10, **81**–30, **177**–1
ride [rīd] **129**–D
rider [rī/dər] **152**–3
riding [rī/dĭng] **226**–9
right [rīt] **25**–3, **155**–B, **198**–10
right angle [rīt/ ăng/gəl] **193**–26
right turn only [rīt/ türn/ ōn/lē] **154**–7
Rights [rīts] **140**
RIGHTS AND RESPONSIBILITIES
[rīts/ ən rĭ spän/sə bĭl/ə tēz] **140**
ring [rĭng] **37**–25, **79**–4, **95**–40
clip-on earrings [klĭp/än ïr/ĭngz, –ön–] **95**–37
pierced earrings [pïrst/ ïr/ĭngz] **95**–36
rinse [rĭns] **108**–F
ripe [rīp] **68**–30
ripped [rĭpt] **97**–41
ripper [rĭ/pər] **100**–18
rise [rīz] **127**–13
sunrise [sŭn/rīz/] **18**–14
river [rĭv/ər] **155**–10, **204**–3
RN (registered nurse) [är/ĕn/] / [rĕj/ə stərd nürs/]
120–10
road work [rōd/ würk/] **154**–16
Road Worker [rōd/ wür/kər] **92**
roast [rōst] **70**–1
roast beef [rōst bēf/] **71**–21
roast chicken [rōst chĭk/ən] **81**–22
roasted turkey [rō/stəd tür/kē] **76**–4
roasting pan [rō/stĭng păn/] **78**–13
roasting rack [rō/stĭng răk/] **78**–14
robe [rōb] **91**–29
robin [räb/ən] **214**–16
rock [räk] **36**–D
rock concert [räk/ kän/sərt] **222**–5
rocking chair [räk/ĭng chër/] **37**–21
rocks [räks] **208**–6, **237**–23
Rodents [rōd/nts] **215**
RODENTS [rōd/nts] **215**
rollers [rō/lərz] **33**–19, **181**–23
rolling pin [rō/lĭng pĭn/] **78**–30
rolls [rōlz] **74**–11, **74**–23, **80**–17
romance [rō măns/, rō/măns] **237**–16
Roman Numerals [rō/mən nōō/mər əlz] **16**
roof [rōōf] **46**–1
roof garden [rōōf/ gär/dn] **50**–4
roofer [rōō/fər] **62**–8
room [rōōm]
baby's room [bā/bēz rōōm/] **47**–10
ballroom [böl/ rōōm/] **184**–26
banquet room [băn/kwət rōōm/] **185**–14
bathroom [băth/rōōm/] **46**–4
bedroom [bĕd/rōōm/] **46**–2
conference room [kän/frəns rōōm/] **182**–4
dining room [dī/nĭng rōōm/] **82**–1
dining room chair [dī/nĭng rōōm/ chër/] **55**–8
dining room table [dī/nĭng rōōm/ tā/bəl] **55**–9
dish room [dĭsh/ rōōm/] **83**–13
guest room [gĕst/ rōōm/] **184**–13
kids' bedroom [kĭdz/ bĕd/rōōm/] **47**–9
living room [lĭv/ĭng rōōm/] **47**–12
meeting room [mē/tĭng rōōm/] **184**–25
roommates [rōōm/māts/] **64**–1
room service [rōōm/ sür/vəs] **184**–17
storeroom [stör/rōōm/] **185**–5
Room [rōōm] **50, 118, 121**
ROOM [rōōm] **56**
rooster [rōō/stər] **215**–7
roots [rōōts] **210**–5, **211**–3
rope [rōp] **224**–4, **226**–19
rose [rōz] **211**–15
rotary [rō/tə rē]
rotary card file [rō/tə rē kärd/ fīl/] **183**–44
rotary cutter [rō/tə rē kŭt/ər] **232**–16
rotten [rät/n] **68**–32
round trip [rownd/ trĭp/] **152**–17
route [rōōt] / [rowt]
bus route [bŭs/ rōōt, –rowt] **152**–1
escape route [ĕs/kāp rōōt, –rowt] **146**–3
evacuation route
[ĭ văk/yōō/ā shən rōōt, –rowt] **146**–5
U.S. route [yōō/ĕs/ rōōt, –rowt] **154**–17
router [row/tər] **180**–12
ROUTINES [rōō tēnz/] **38–39**
rubber [rŭb/ər]
rubber band [rŭb/ər bănd/] **183**–34
rubber gloves [rŭb/ər glŭvz/] **61**–4
rubber mat [rŭb/ər măt/] **57**–3
ruffle [rŭ/fəl] **58**–17
rug [rŭg] **58**–22
ruler [rōō/lər] **17**–13
rules [rōōlz] **64**–8
Rules [rōōlz] **190**
run [rŭn] **11**–D
run across [rŭn/ə krös/] **153**–G
run around [rŭn/ə rownd/] **153**–H
run for office [rŭn/ fər ö/fəs] **139**–A
run out [rŭn/owt/] **162**–E
runner [rŭ/nər] **185**–15
rural area [rōōr/əl ër/ē ə] **52**–4
RV (recreational vehicle)
[är/vē/] / [rĕk/rē ā/shən əl vē/ə kəl] **156**–10
rye bread [rī/ brĕd/] **71**–20
sad [săd] **43**–19
safety [sāf/tē] **37**–19, **92**–4, **159**–53
safety boots [sāf/tē bōōts/] **179**–20
safety deposit box [sāf/tē dĭ päz/ət bäks/] **132**–7
safety glasses [sāf/tē glăs/əz] **92**–10, **179**–10
safety goggles [sāf/tē gäg/əlz] **179**–11
safety pin [sāf/tē pĭn/] **37**–9, **100**–14
safety rail [sāf/tē rāl/] **59**–10
safety regulations [sāf/tē rĕ/gyə lā/shənz] **164**–6
safety visor [sāf/tē vī/zər] **179**–12
Safety [sāf/tē] **76**
SAFETY [sāf/tē] **76–77, 143, 179**
Safety Equipment [sāf/tē ĭ kwĭp/mənt] **179**
Safety Hazards and Hazardous Materials
[sāf/tē hăz/ərdz ən hăz/ər dəs-mə tïr/ē əlz] **179**
sailboat [sāl/bōt/] **225**–3
sailing [sā/lĭng] **227**–8

salad [săl/əd]
chef's salad [shĕfs/ săl/əd] **80**–14
dinner salad [dĭn/ər săl/əd] **80**–15
fruit salad [fro͞ot/ săl/əd] **80**–21
pasta salad [päs/tə săl/əd] **80**–20
potato salad [pə tā/tō săl/əd] **80**–19
salad bar [săl/əd bär/] **79**–24
salad fork [săl/əd förk/] **83**–27
salad plate [săl/əd plāt/] **83**–20
spinach salad [spĭ/nĭch săl/əd] **80**–13
Salad Dressings [săl/əd drĕ/sĭngz] **80**
Salads [săl/ədz] **80**
salamander [săl/ə măn/dər] **212**–27
salami [sə lä/mē] **71**–24
SALE [sāl] **102–103**
sales [sālz]
sale price [sāl/ prīs/] **27**–3
salesclerk [sālz/klürk/] **94**–3
sales tax [sālz/ tăks/] **27**–8
Salesperson [sālz/pür/sən] **92**
salmon [săm/ən] **71**–3
salmon steak [săm/ən stāk/] **71**–4
salon [sə lŏn/] **130**–3, **131**–18
salt and pepper shakers
[sölt/ n pĕp/ər shā/kərz] **55**–13
same [sām] **23**–15
SAME AND DIFFERENT
[sām/ ən dĭ/frənt, –dĭ fə rənt] **28–29**
samples [săm/pəlz] **84**–5
sand [sănd] **225**–23
sandbox [sănd/bäks/] **224**–15
sand castle [sănd kăs/əl] **225**–12
sand dune [sănd do͞on/] **204**–5
sandpaper [sănd/pā/pər] **181**–56
sandals [săn/dlz] **88**–9
sander [săn/dər] **180**–11
sandwich [săn/wĭch, –sănd/–] **79**–5, **80**–10, **80**–12
sanitation worker [săn/ə tā/shən wür/kər] **169**–54
satellite [săt/əl īt/] **205**–20
satellite dish [săt/əl līt/ dĭsh/] **53**–6
satisfied [săt/ĭs fīd/] **42**–6
Saturday [săt/ər dā/, –dē] **20**–14
Saturn [săt/ərn] **205**–6
saucepan [sös/păn/] **78**–25
saucer [sö/sər] **83**–25
sausage [sö/sĭj] **70**–12, **80**–2
sauté [sö tā/, sō –] **77**–E
save [sāv] **219**–E
saving [sā/vĭng] **19**–25, **225**–20
savings account number
[sā/vĭngz ə kownt/ nŭm/bər] **132**–11
saw [sö] **180**–9
hacksaw [hăk/sö/] **180**–5
jigsaw [jĭg/sö/] **180**–10
saxophone [săk/sə fōn/] **238**–5
say [sā] **2**–A, **3**–L, **4**–A
scaffolding [skăf/əl dĭng] **178**–4
scales [skālz] **57**–27, **72**–3, **135**–8, **155**–7, **195**–41, **212**–3
postal scale [pō/stəl skāl/] **183**–27
scallions [skăl/yənz] **69**–20
scallops [skăl/əps, skäl/–] **71**–12, **212**–19
scan [skăn] **171**–H
scanner [skăn/ər] **183**–20
scared [skërd] **43**–23
scarf / scarves [skärf] / [skärvz] **95**–12
winter scarf [wĭn/tər skärf/] **90**–5
scenery [sē/ nə rē] / [sēn/rē] **162**–3
schedule [skĕj/o͞ol, –o͞o əl] **152**–4
schedule [skĕj/o͞ol, –o͞o əl] **171**–J
school [sko͞ol] **126**–9
adult school [[ə dŭlt/–, ăd/ŭlt sko͞ol/] **188**–8
elementary school [ĕl/ə mĕn/trē sko͞ol/] **188**–2
high school [hī/ sko͞ol/] **188**–4
junior high school [jo͞on/yər hī/ sko͞ol/] **188**–3
middle school [mĭd/l sko͞ol/] **188**–3
nursery school [nür/sə rē sko͞ol/] **188**–1
parochial school [pə rō/kē əl sko͞ol/] **5** ✦
preschool [prē/sko͞ol] **188**–1
private school [prī/vət sko͞ol/] **5** ✦
public school [pŭb/lĭk sko͞ol/] **5** ✦
school bus [sko͞ol/ bŭs/] **156**–21
school crossing [sko͞ol/ krö/sĭng] **154**–15
technical school [tĕk/nĭ kəl sko͞ol/] **188**–5
vocational school [vō kā/shə nəl sko͞ol/] **188**–5
SCHOOL [sko͞ol] **5, 10, 11**
School Registration Form
[sko͞ol/ rĕj/ə strā/shən förm/] **4**
SCHOOLS AND SUBJECTS
[sklo͞oz ən sŭb/jĭkts] **188–189**
science [sī/əns] **189**–11
SCIENCE [sī/əns] **194–195**
Science Lab [sī/əns lăb/] **195**
scissors [sĭz/ərz] **33**–20, **100**–16
scoop neck [sko͞op/ nĕk/] **96**–10
score [skör] **10**–3, **229**–1
scorpion [skör/pē ən] **214**–30
scrambled eggs [skrăm/bəld ĕgz/] **76**–7
scraper [skrā/pər] **181**–52
screen [skrēn] **6**–2, **196**–11, **235**–30
big-screen TV [bĭg/skrēn/ tē/ vē/] **50**–15
fire screen [fīr/ skrēn/] **56**–12
flat screen TV [flăt/ skrēn/ tē/vē/] **234**–7
screen door [skrēn/ dör/] **53**–15
sunscreen [sŭn/skrēn/] **108**–7, **225**–10
screener [skrēn/ər] **160**–5
screening area [skrē/nĭng ër/ē ə] **160**–4
screw [skro͞o] **180**–32, **180**–33
Phillips screwdriver [fĭl/ĭps skro͞o/drī/vər] **180**–31
screwdriver [skro͞o/drī/vər] **180**–30
scroll bar [skrōl/bär/] **197**–15
scrub [skrŭb] **60**–K
scrubs [skrŭbz] **93**–31
scrub brush [skrŭb/ brŭsh/] **61**–20
surgical scrub cap [sür/jĭ kəl skrŭb/ kăp/] **93**–35
surgical scrubs [sür/jĭ kəl skrŭbz/] **93**–38
scuba [sko͞o/bə]
scuba diving [sko͞o/bə dī/vĭng] **227**–12
scuba tank [sko͞o/bə tăngk/] **225**–5
sea [sē]
sea anemone [sē/ ə nĕm/ə nē] **212**–24
seahorse [sē/ hörs/] **212**–13
sea lion [sē/ lī/ən] **213**–33
sea otter [sē/ ät/ər] **213**–35
seashell [sē/shĕl/] **225**–24
sea urchin [sē/ ür/chən] **212**–21
seaweed [sē/ wēd/] **225** ✦
Sea Animals [sē/ ăn/ə məlz] **212**
SEAFOOD AND DELI [sē/fo͞od/ ən dĕ/lī] **71**
seal [sēl] **213**–34
Sea Mammals [sē/ măm/əlz] **213**
seam ripper [sēm/ rĭp/ər] **100**–18
search [sürch]
search and rescue team
[sürch/ ən rĕs/kyo͞o tēm/] **145**–20
search box [sürch/ bäks/] **197**–5
search engine [sürch/ ĕn/jən] **197**–6
SEARCH [sürch] **173**
SEASONAL CLOTHING [sē/zə nəl klō/dhĭng] **90**
Seasons [sē/zənz] **21**
seat [sēt]
backseat [băk/ sēt/] **159**–54
car safety seat [kär/ sāf/tē sēt/] **37**–19
child safety seat [chīld/ sāf/tē sēt/] **159**–53
front seat [frŭnt/ sēt/] **159**–51
love seat [lŭv/ sēt/] **56**–1
potty seat [pät/ē sēt/] **37**–12
reclined seat [rĭ klīnd/ sēt/] **161**–27
seat belt [sēt/ bĕlt/] **159**–52
upright seat [ŭp/rīt/ sēt/] **161**–28
seat [sēt] **82**–B
second [sĕk/ənd] **16**
Second Floor [sĕk/ənd flör/] **50**
seconds [sĕk/əndz] **18**–3
section [sĕk/shən] **72**–2
security [sĭ kyo͝or/ə tē]
security camera [sĭ kyo͝or/ə tē kăm/rə] **50**–19
security gate [sĭ kyo͝or/ə tē gāt/] **50**–16
security guard [sĭ kyo͝or/ə tē gärd/] **132**–5, **169**–55
security pants [sĭ kyo͝or/ə tē pănts/] **93**–22
security screener [sĭ kyo͝or/ə tē skrē/nər] **160**–5
security shirt [sĭ kyo͝or/ə tē shürt] **93**–20
Security Checkpoint [sĭ kyo͝or/ə tē chĕk/poynt/] **160**
Security Guard [sĭ kyo͝or/ə tē gärd/] **93**
sedan [sə dăn/] **156**–1
see [sē] **106**–A
seed [sēd] **211**–1
seedling [sēd/lĭng] **211**–4
seek [sēk] **114**–A, **147**–H
seesaw [sē/sö/] **224**–16
select [sə lĕkt/] **196**–B
self-checkout [sĕlf/ chĕk/owt] **73**–10, **133**–10
sell [sĕl] **170**–K
semi [sĕm/ī] **156**–15
semicolon [sĕm/ē kō/lən] **190**–18
Senate [sĕn/ət] **138**–5
senator [sĕn/ə tər] **138**–6
state senator [stāt/ sĕn/ə tər] **139**–25
send [sĕnd] **197**–I
send in [sĕnd/ ĭn] **173**–H
Sending a Card [sĕn/dĭng ə kärd/] **135**
Sending Email [sĕn/dĭng ē/māl/] **197**
senior [sēn/yər]
senior citizen [sēn/yər sĭt/ə zən] **30**–5
senior housing [sēn/yər howz/ĭng] **52**–11
Senses [sĕn/səz] **106**

sentence [sĕn/tns] **190**–2
sentence [sĕn/tns] **141**–E
separate [sĕ/pə rāt/] **76**–B
September [sĕp tĕm/bər] **21**–33
sequins [sē/kwĭnz/] **99**–33
Serious Medical Conditions
[sïr/ē əs mĕd/ĭ kəl kən dĭsh/ənz] **111**
serious photo [sïr/ē əs fō/tō] **206**–3
serve [sürv] **139**–D, **230**–P
serve on a jury [sürv/ ăn ə jŏŏr/ē, –ön–] **140**–E
serve the meal [sürv/ dhə mēl/] **82**–F
Serve [sürv] **76**
server [sür/vər] **82**–8, **83**–9, **169**–56, **185**–8
service [sür/vəs]
customer service [kŭs/tə mər sür/vəs] **97** ✦
customer service representative
[kŭs/tə mər-sür/vəs rĕ/prə zĕn/tə tĭv] **167**–20
guest services [gĕst/ sür/vəs əz] **130**–12
pool service [pōōl/ sür/vəs] **184**–21
room service [rōōm/ sür/vəs] **184**–17
SERVICE [sür/vəs] **138–139**, **185**
serving bowl [sür/vĭng bōl/] **55**–21
set [sĕt] **10**–A, **33**–C, **82**–A
set up [sĕt/ ŭp/] **173**–I
sunset [sŭn/sĕt/] **18**–18
setting [sĕ/tĭng] **83**–17
seven [sĕv/ən] **16**
seventeen [sĕv/ən tēn/] **16**
seventeenth [sĕv/ən tēnth/] **16**
seventh [sĕv/ənth] **16**
seventieth [sĕv/ən tē əth] **16**
seventy [sĕv/ən tē] **16**
75 percent [sĕv/ən tē fīv/ pər sĕnt/] **17**–9
sew [sō] **98**–A, **98**–B, **170**–L
sewing [sō/ĭng]
sewing machine [sō/ĭng mə shēn/] **98**–13
sewing machine operator
[sō/ĭng mə shēn/ äp/ə rā/ tər] **98**–14
Sewing Machine [sō/ĭng mə shēn/] **98**
Sewing Supplies [sō/ĭng sə plīz/] **100**
sex [sĕks] **4**–16
shade [shād] **225**–13
lampshade [lămp/shād/] **56** ✦, **58**–26
shadow [shă/dō/] **109**–35
shake [shāk]
milkshake [mĭlk/shāk/] **79**–14
shake [shāk] **3**–J, **174**–I
shakers [shā/kərz] **55**–13
shampoo [shăm pōō/] **108**–10
shanks [shănks] **70**–13
shaper [shā/pər] **91**–15
Shapes [shāps] **193**
share [shër] **8**–M
Sharing and Responding
[shër/ĭng ən rĭ spän/dĭng] **191**
shark [shärk] **212**–4
sharpener [shär/pən ər] **183**–26
shave [shāv]
aftershave [ăf/tər shāv/] **109**–30
shave [shāv] **109**–M
shaver [shā/vər] **109**–26
shaving cream [shā/vĭng krēm/] **109**–29
shears [shïrz] **176**–9
sheep [shēp] **215**–6
sheet [shēt]
cookie sheet [kŏŏk/ē shēt/] **78**–27
dryer sheets [drī/ər shēts/] **101**–5
fitted sheet [fĭt/əd shēt/] **58**–12
flat sheet [flăt/ shēt/] **58**–13
shelf [shĕlf] **54**–2
shell [shĕl]
seashell [sē/shĕl/] **225**–24
Shellfish [shĕl/fĭsh/] **71**
shelter [shĕl/tər] **52**–13
shield [shēld]
windshield [wĭnd/shēld/] **158**–1
windshield wipers [wĭnd/shēld wī/pərz] **158**–2
shift [shĭft] **159**–49, **159**–50
shin [shĭn] **106**–21
shin guards [shĭn/ gärdz/] **231**–13
shingles [shĭng/gəlz] **178**–20
ship [shĭp] **175**–D
shipping clerk [shĭp/ĭng klürk/] **175**–14
shirt [shürt] **86**–1
nightshirt [nīt/shürt/] **91**–28
polo shirt [pō/lō shürt/] **92**–14
security shirt [sĭ kyŏŏr/ə tē shürt/] **93**–20
sports shirt [spörts/ shürt/] **88**–4
T-shirt [tē/shürt/] **86**–4
work shirt [würk/ shürt/] **92**–2
shock [shäk] **116**–B, **116**–F
shoes [shōōz] **86**–7, **87**–13, **95**–32
shoe department [shōō/ dĭ pärt/mənt] **95**–7
shoelaces [shōō/lās əz] **94**–24
shoe store [shōō/ stör/] **130**–10
SHOES AND ACCESSORIES
[shōōz/ ən ĭk sĕs/ə rēz] **94–95**
shoot [shōōt] **211**–5
shoot [shōōt] **230**–H
shop [shäp]
barbershop [bär/bər shäp/] **129**–19
beauty shop [byōō/tē shäp/] **130** ✦
coffee shop [kö/fē shäp/] **126**–11
donut shop [dō/nŭt shäp/] **129**–17
gift shop [gĭft/ shäp/] **130** ✦, **184**–5
ice cream shop [īs/ krēm shäp] **131**–16
shop [shäp] **28**–A, **143**–H
Shop [shäp] **100**
SHOP [shäp] **80–81**
shoplifting [shäp/lĭf/tĭng] **142**–8
shopping [shäp/ĭng]
shopping basket [shäp/ĭng băs/kət] **73**–9
shopping list [shäp/ĭng lĭst/] **67**–14
shopping mall [shäp/ĭng mäl/] **126**–7
shopping program [shäp/ĭng mäl/] **236**–10
SHOPPING [shäp/ĭng] **27**
shore [shör] **204**–12
short [shört] **32**–6, **96**–16
short hair [shört/ hër/] **33**–1
short-order cook [shört/ör/dər kŏŏk/] **185**–1
short-sleeved [shört/slēvd/] **96**–12
shorten [shört/ən] **100**–B
shorts [shörts] **89**–25, **91**–4
shoulder [shōl/dər] **105**–13
shoulder bag [shōl/dər băg/] **94**–17
shoulder blade [shōl/dər blād/] **107**–28
shoulder-length hair [shōl/dər lĕngkth/ hër/] **33**–2
shoulder pads [shōl/dər pădz/] **231**–20
shovel [shŭv/əl] **176**–7, **178**–22
show [shō] **236**–4, **236**–6, **236**–8
show [shō] **137**–C, **160**–C
shower [show/ər]
shower cap [show/ər kăp/] **108**–1
shower curtain [show/ər kür/tn] **57**–12
shower gel [show/ər jĕl/] **108**–2
showerhead [show/ər hĕd/] **57**–11
stall shower [stöl/ show/ər] **57** ✦
shredder [shrĕ/dər] **183**–24
shrimp [shrĭmp] **71**–11, **212**–18
shut [shŭt] **146**–4
shuttle [shŭt/l] **152**–19, **205**–19
sick [sĭk] **42**–12
homesick [hōm/sĭk/] **43**–20
side [sīd] **76**–10
sideburns [sīd/bürnz/] **33**–7
sideview mirror [sīd/vyōō/ mïr/ər] **158**–3
Side Salads [sīd/ săl/ədz] **80**
sidewalk [sīd/wök/] **129**–24
sight impaired [sīt/ ĭm përd/] **32**–11
sign [sīn] **4**–D
street sign [strēt/ sīn/] **129**–26
vacancy sign [vā/kən sē sīn/] **50**–7
vital signs monitor [vīt/l sīnz/ män/ə tər] **121**–26
sign [sīn] **48**–D
signal [sĭg/nəl]
strong signal [ströng/ sĭg/nəl] **14**–11
turn signal [türn/ sĭg/nəl] **158**–6, **159**–34
weak signal [wēk/ sĭg/nəl] **14**–12
signature [sĭg/nə chər] **4**–19
SIGNS [sīnz] **154**
silk [sĭlk] **98**–5
simmer [sĭm/ər] **77**–P
sing [sĭng] **36**–O, **238**–B
single [sĭng/gəl]
single father [sĭng/gəl fä/dhər] **35**–23
single mother [sĭng/gəl mŭdh/ər] **35**–22
sink [sĭnk] **54**–4, **57**–23
Sirius [sïr/ē əs] **205** ✦
sister [sĭs/tər] **34**–5, **35**–27
sister-in-law [sĭs/tər ĭn lö/] **34**–16
stepsister [stĕp/sĭs/tər] **35**–29
sitcom (situation comedy)
[sĭt/käm/] / [sĭch/ōō ā/shən käm/ə dē] **236**–2
sit down [sĭt/ down/] **6**–F
site [sīt] **126**–2
sitter [sĭt/ər] **166**–9
situation comedy (sitcom)
[sĭch/ōō ā/shən-käm/ə dē] / [sĭt/käm/] **236**–2
six [sĭks] **16**
six-pack [sĭks/păk/] **74**–9, **74**–21
6-year-old boy [sĭks/yïr öld/boy/] **31**–9
sixteen [sĭks/tēn/] **16**
sixteenth [sĭks/tēnth/] **16**
sixth [sĭksth] **16**
sixtieth [sĭks/tē əth] **16**

sixty [sĭks/tē] **16**
Sizes [sī/zəz] **96**
skate [skāt] **230**–U
skates [skāts] **231**–9, **231**–10
skateboard [skāt/börd/] **224**–7
skateboarding [skāt/bör/dĭng] **228**–13
skating [skā/tĭng] **227**–4, **227**–5, **227** ✦, **228**–10
ski [skē] **230**–V
skiing [skē/ĭng] **227**–1, **227**–3
waterskiing [wö/tər skē/ĭng] **227**–7
skill inventory [skĭl/ ĭn/vən tör/ē] **172**–12
Skills [skĭlz] **171**
SKILLS [skĭlz] **170, 171, 174**
skin [skĭn] **107**–31
skinless [skĭn/ləs] **70** ✦
skirt [skürt] **87**–10
skis [skēz] **231**–24
ski boots [skē/ bo͞ots] **231**–26
ski hat [skē/ hăt/] **90**–11
ski mask [skē/ măsk/] **90**–15
ski poles [skē/ pōlz/] **231**–25
skull [skŭl] **107**–47
skunk [skŭngk] **216**–12
SKU number [ĕs/kā/yo͞o/ nŭm/bər, skyo͞o/] **27**–5
sky [skī] **209**–9
skycap [skē/kăp/] **160**–1
skyscraper [skī/skrā/pər] **127**–13
slacks [slăks] **87** 12
slaves [slāvz] **198**–4
sledding [slĕd/ĭng] **227**–6
sledgehammer [slĕj/hăm/ər] **178**–23
sleeper [slē/pər] **91**–27
sleeping bag [slē/pĭng băg/] **226**–12
Sleepwear [slēp/wër] **91**
SLEEPWEAR [slēp/wër] **91**
sleepy [slē/pē] **42**–3
sleeve [slēv] **100**–6
long-sleeved [lŏng/slēvd/] **96**–14
short-sleeved [shört/slēvd] **96**–12
sleeveless [slēv/ləs] **96**–11
3/4 sleeved [thrē/kwör/tər slēvd/] **96**–13
slender [slĕn/dər] **32**–9
slice [slīs] **77**–C
slide [slīd] **194**–3, **224**–13
mudslide [mŭd/slīd/] **144**–6
sliding glass door [slī/dĭng glăs/ dör/] **53**–18
sling [slĭng] **113**–19
slip [slĭp] **91**–22, **91**–23, **132**–4
slippers [slĭp/ərz] **91**–26
slippery floor [slĭ/pər ē flör/] **179**–6
slow [slō] **23**–4
small [smöl] **96**–1, **96**–2, **97**–37
small town [smöl/ town/] **52**–3
smart phone [smärt/ fōn/] **15**–27
smell [smĕl] **106**–C
smile [smīl] **2**–D
smock [smŏk] **93**–26
smog [smäg, smög] **218**–11
smoggy [smä/gē, smö/–] **13**–14
smoke [smōk] **114**–G
smoke detector [smōk/ dĭ tĕk/tər] **51**–29
smoked turkey [smōkt/ tür/kē] **71**–25
Snack Foods [snăk/ fo͞odz/] **73**
snail [snāl] **212**–22
snake [snāk] **213**–39
rattlesnake [ră/təl snāk] **213**–38
snap [snăp] **99**–26
sneeze [snēz] **110**–B
snorkeling [snör/kə lĭng] **227**–11
snow [snō]
snowboard [snō/börd/] **231**–23
snowboarding [snō/bör/dĭng] **227**–2
snowstorm [snō/störm/] **13**–23
snowing [snō/ĭng] **13**–12
soap [sōp] **57**–24, **61**–5, **108**–3
soap dish [sōp/ dĭsh/] **57**–25
soap opera [sōp/ äp/rə] **236**–5
sober [sō/ bər] **143** ✦
soccer [säk/ər] **229**–12
soccer ball [säk/ər böl/] **231**–12
social [sō/shəl]
Social Security card
[sō/shəl sĭ kyo͝or/ə tē kärd/] **40**–5
Social Security number
[sō/shəl sĭ kyo͝or/ə tē nŭm/bər] **4**–15
social worker [sō/shəl wür/kər] **169**–57
socks [säks] **86**–6
ankle socks [ang/kəl säks/] **91**–7
crew socks [kro͞o/ säks/] **91**–8
dress socks [drĕs/ säks] **91**–9
low-cut socks [lō/kŭt säks/] **91**–10
Socks [säks] **91**
soda [sō/də] **73**–34, **79**–11
sofa [sō/fə] **56**–18
sofa cushions [sō/fə ko͝o/shənz] **56** ✦
soft [söft] **23**–6
softball [söft/böl/] **229**–10
softener [sö/fən ər] **101**–6
software [söft/wër/] **167**–18, **196**–10
soil [soyl] **208**–2
solar [sō/lər]
solar eclipse [so/lər ĭ klĭps/] **205**–16, **205** ✦
solar energy [sō/lər ĕn/ər jē] **218**–1
Solar System and the Planets
[sō/lər sĭs/təm ən dhə plăn/əts] **205**
soldier [sōl/jər] **169**–58
sole [sōl] **94**–21
solid [säl/əd] **96**–19
Solids [säl/ədz] **193**
solution [sə lo͞o/ shən] **192**–14
solve [sölv] **170**–M
son [sŭn] **34**–15
grandson [grăn/sŭn/, grănd/–] **34** ✦
son-in-law [sŭn/ĭn lö/] **34** ✦
sore throat [sör/ thrōt/] **110**–6
sort [sört] **101**–A
soul [sōl] **237**–28
soup [so͞op] **72**–18, **80**–16
soup bowl [so͞op/ bōl/] **83**–21
soupspoon [so͞op/spo͞on/] **83**–32
Soup [so͞op] **77**
sour [söw/ər] **84**–4
sour cream [sow/ər krēm/] **72**–21
Sources [sör/səz] **218**
sous chef [so͞o/ shĕf/] **185**–6
south [sowth] **155**–3
soybeans [soy/bēnz/] **177**–3
space [spās] **50**–18, **128**–5
space shuttle [spās/ shŭt/əl] **205**–19
space station [spās/ stā/shən] **205**–18
Space [spās] **205**
Space Exploration [spās/ ĕk/splə rā/shən] **205**
spades [spādz] **233**–30
spaghetti [spə gĕt/ē] **81**–26
spare tire [spër/ tīr/] **158**–23
sparrow [spăr/ō] **214**–7
spatula [spăch/ə lə] **78**–19
speak [spēk] **170**–N
speakers [spē/kərz] **50**–5, **206**–4, **234**–14
Special [spē/shəl] **80**
Specialists [spĕsh/ə lĭsts/] **120**
speech [spēch] **140**–2
speed limit [spēd/ lĭm/ət] **154**–4
speedometer [spĭ däm/ə tər] **159**–27
speed skating [spēd/skā/tĭng] **227** ✦
spell [spĕl] **4**–B
sphere [sfïr] **193**–42
spider [spī/dər] **214**–29
spill [spĭl] **218**–17
spinach [spĭn/ĭch] **69**–11
spinach salad [spĭn/ĭch săl/əd] **80**–13
spinal column [spī/nəl käl/əm] **107**–49
spiral notebook [spī/rəl nōt/bo͝ok/] **7**–29
splint [splĭnt] **117**–14
sponge [spŭnj] **61**–19
sponge mop [spŭnj/ mäp/] **61**–6
spoon [spo͞on] **55**–5, **78**–9
soupspoon [so͞op/spo͞on/] **83**–32
tablespoon [tā/bəl spo͞on/] **75**–7
teaspoon [tē/spo͞on/] **75**–6, **83**–31
spoon [spo͞on] **77**–F
sports [spörts]
sports car [spörts/ kär/] **156**–4
sports coat [spörts/ kōt/] **89**–14
sports jacket [spörts/ jăk/ət] **89**–14
sports program [spörts/ prō/grăm] **236**–11
sports shirt [spörts/ shürt/] **88**–4
sport-utility vehicle (SUV) [spört/
yo͞o tĭl/ə tē vē/ĭ kəl] / [ĕs/yo͞o/vē/] **156**–7
SPORTS [spörts] **228, 229, 230, 231**
SPORTS EQUIPMENT [spörts/ ĭ kwĭp/mənt] **231**
SPORTS VERBS [spörts/ vürbz/] **230**
sprained ankle [sprānd/ ăng/kəl] **110**–18
spray [sprā] **108**–12, **113**–32
spray gun [sprā/ gŭn/] **181**–21
spray starch [sprā/ stärch/] **101**–12
spread [sprĕd]
bedspread [bĕd/sprĕd] **59**–11
spring [sprĭng] **21**–37, **58**–19
sprinkler [sprĭng/klər] **53**–22
square [skwër] **193**–30
squash [skwäsh, skwösh] **69**–24
squeegee [skwē/jē] **61**–15
squid [skwĭd] **212**–7
squirrel [skwür/əl] **215**–21
stadium [stā/dē əm] **126**–1

staff [stăf] **185** ✦
Staff [stăf] **120**
stage [stāj] **194**–16
  stage clips [stāj/ klĭps/] **194**–24
stain [stān] **181**–24
stained [stānd] **97**–42
stairs [stërz] **50**–10
stairway [stër/wā/] **50**–10
stall shower [stöl/ show/ər] **57** ✦
stamps [stămps] **134**–18, **134**–23, **183**–47
  stamp machine [stămp/ mə shēn/] **135**–11
stand [stănd] **152**–18
  checkstand [chĕk/stănd/] **73**–12
  newsstand [no͞oz/stănd/] **128**–12
  nightstand [nīt/stănd/] **58**–23
stand [stănd] **141**–D
  stand up [stănd/ ŭp/] **6**–D
standard time [stăn/dərd tīm/] **19**–26
staple [stā/pəl] **171**–F
stapler [stā/plər] **183**–28
staples [stā/pəlz] **183**–29
star [stär] **205**–13
  starfish [stär/fĭsh/] **212**–16
  star key [stär/ kē/] **14**–6
starch [stärch] **101**–12
start [stärt] **12**–A, **40**–B, **230**–R
starting point [stär/tĭng poynt/] **162**–1
starving [stär/vĭng] **43** ✦
state [stāt] **4**–8, **146**–2
  state capital [stāt kă/pət əl] **139**–22
  state senator [stāt sĕn/ə tər] **139**–25
state [stāt] **15**–G, **195**–A
State Government [stāt gŭ/ vərn mənt] **139**
statement [stāt/mənt] **132**–16
station [stā/shən]
  bus station [bŭs/ stā/shən] **124**–7
  fire station [fīr/ stā/shən] **125**–12
  gas station [găs/ stā/shən] **125**–10
  gas station attendant
    [găs/ stā/shən ə tĕn/dənt] **162**–3
  lifeguard station [līf/gärd/ stā/shən] **225**–21
  police station [pə lēs/ stā/shən] **124**–6
  space station [spās/ stā/shən] **205**–18
  station wagon [stā/shən wăg/ən] **156**–6
  subway station [sŭb/wā/ stā/shən] **151**–11
Station [stā/shən] **152**
stationery [stā/shə nër/ ē] **183**–42
stay [stā]
  stay away [stā ə wā/] **147**–I
  stay fit [stā fĭt/] **114**–E
  stay on the line [stā ön dhə līn/] **15**–H
  stay on well-lit streets [stā ön wĕl lĭt/ strēts/] **143**–B
Stay Well [stā wĕl/] **114**
steak [stāk] **70**–2, **81**–24
  broiled steak [broyld/ stāk/] **76**–3
  halibut steak [hăl/ə bŭt stāk] **71**–6
  salmon steak [săm/ən stāk/] **71**–4
  steak knife [stāk/ nīf/] **83**–29
steal [stēl] **142** ✦
steam [stēm] **77**–D
steamed vegetables [stēmd/ vĕj/tə bəlz] **81**–32
steamer [stē/mər] **78**–3
steel [stēl]
  steel toe boots [stēl/ tō/ bo͞ots/] **92**–6
  steel-wool soap pads [stēl/wo͝ol/ sōp/ pădz/] **61**–5
steering wheel [stïr/ĭng wēl/] **159**–26
stems [stĕmz] **211**–9
step [stĕp]
  stepbrother [stĕp/brŭdh/ər] **35**–30
  stepdaughter [stĕp/dö/tər] **35** ✦
  stepfather [stĕp/fä/dhər] **35**–25
  stepladder [stĕp/lăd/ər] **61**–13
  stepmother [stĕp/mŭdh/ər] **35**–26
  steps [stĕps] **53**–3
  stepsister [stĕp/sĭs/tər] **35**–29
stereo system [stër/ē ō sĭs/təm] **56**–8
sterile [stër/əl]
  sterile pad [stër/əl păd/] **117**–6
  sterile tape [stër/əl tāp/] **117**–7
stethoscope [stĕth/ə skōp/] **118**–10
stewing beef [sto͞o/ĭng bēf/] **70**–3
stick [stĭk] **231**–11, **232**–11
  drumsticks [drŭm/stĭks/] **70**–23
  lipstick [lĭp/stĭk/] **109**–38
  stick shift [stĭk/ shĭft/] **159**–50
  yardstick [yärd/stĭk/] **181**–16
sticker [stĭk/ər] **102**–3, **136**–13
sticky notes [stĭk/ē nōts/] **183**–39
stir [stür] **77**–O
  stir-fried beef [stür/frīd/ bēf/] **76**–6
stitches [stĭch/əz] **117**–15
stock clerk [stäk/ klürk/] **169**–59
stockings [stäk/ĭngz] **91**–17
stomach [stŭm/ək] **107**–41
  stomachache [stŭm/ək āk/] **110**–4
stop [stäp] **129**–16, **151**–13, **154**–1
  stopover [stäp/ō/vər] **161** ✦
stop [stäp] **155**–D
Stop [stäp] **152**
stopped up [stäpt/ ŭp/] **63**–19
storage [stör/ĭj] **72**–25, **78**–4
  storage locker [stör/ĭj läk/ər] **50**–17
store [stör]
  bookstore [bo͝ok/stör/] **130**–4
  candy store [kăn/dē stör/] **131**–17
  card store [kärd/stör/] **130**–7
  convenience store [kən vēn/yəns stör/] **128**–3
  department store [dĭ pärt/mənt stör/] **131**–13
  electronics store [ē lĕk trän/ĭks stör/] **131**–20
  furniture store [für/nĭ chər stör/] **126**–8
  hardware store [härd/wër/ stör/] **148**–4
  home improvement store
    [hōm/ ĭm pro͞ov/mənt stör/] **127**–20
  jewelry store [jo͞o/əl rē stör/] **130**–2
  maternity store [mə tür/nə tē stör/] **131**–19
  men's store [mĕnz/ stör/] **130** ✦
  music store [myo͞o/zĭk stör/] **130**–1
  office supply store [ö/fəs sə plī/ stör/] **127**–21
  pet store [pĕt/ stör/] **130**–6
  shoe store [sho͞o/ stör/] **130**–10
  toy store [toy/ stör/] **130**–5
  video store [vĭd/ē ō stör/] **129**–20
Store [stör] **99**
STORE [stör] **72–73**
storeroom [stör/ro͞om/] **185**–3
storm [störm] **13**–19
  hailstorm [hāl/störm/] **13**–21
  snowstorm [snō/störm/] **13**–23
  storm door [störm/ dör/] **53**–10
  thunderstorm [thŭn/dər störm/] **13**–16
story [stör/ē]
  action story [ăk/shən stör/ē] **237**–19
  adventure story [ăd vĕn/chər stör/ē] **237**–19
  horror story [hör/ər stör/ē, här/–] **237**–17
  science fiction story [sī/əns fĭk/shən stör/ē] **237**–18
  two-story house [to͞o/stör/ē hows/] **52** ✦
stove [stōv] **54**–18, **226**–16
stow [stō] **160**–G
straight [strāt] **155**–A
  straight hair [strāt/ hër/] **33**–9
  straight line [strāt/ līn/] **193**–22
  straight pin [strāt/ pĭn/] **100**–12
strainer [strā/nər] **78**–22
straw [strö] **79**–18
  strawberries [strö/bër/ēz] **68**–14
  straw hat [strö/ hăt/] **90**–23
stream [strēm] **204** ✦
street [strēt] **150**–5, **155**–8
  streetlight [strēt/līt/] **148**–3
  street sign [strēt/ sīn] **129**–26
  street vender [strēt/ vĕn/dər] **129**–29
STREETS [strēts] **126–127**
strep throat [strĕp/ thrōt/] **111**–4
stress [strĕs] **115**–4
stretch [strĕch] **230**–M
stretcher [strĕch/ər] **121**–33
string [strĭng]
  string beans [strĭng/ bēnz/] **69**–8
  string lights [strĭng/ līts/] **239**–18
  string of pearls [strĭng/ əv pürlz/] **95**–39
Strings [strĭngz] **238**
striped [strīpt] **96**–20
stripper [strĭ/pər] **181**–42
stroller [strō/lər] **37**–18
strong signal [ströng/ sĭg/nəl] **14**–11
stub [stŭb] **165**–11
stucco [stŭk/ō] **178**–15
student [sto͞od/nt] **6**–5
study [stŭ/dē] **10**–D, **137**–A
STUDYING [stŭ/dē ĭng] **8–9**
stuffed animals [stŭft/ ăn/ə məlz] **59**–15
style [stīl/] **88** ✦
Styles [stīlz] **96**
STYLES [stīlz] **96**
stylist [stī/lĭst] **167**–31
SUBJECTS [sŭb/jĭkts/] **188–189**
submit [səb mĭt/] **48**–C
substitute [sŭb/stə to͞ot/] **79**–20
subtract [səb trăkt/] **192**–B
suburbs [sŭb/ürbz] **52**–2
subway [sŭb/wā/] **151**–12
  subway car [sŭb/wā/ kär/] **152**–6
  subway station [sŭb/wā/ stā/shən] **151**–11
Subway Station [sŭb/wā/ stā/shən] **152**
Succeed [sək sēd/] **10**
SUCCEEDING IN SCHOOL [sək sē/dĭng ən sko͞ol/] **10**

suede [swād] **99**–8
sugar [shŏŏg/ər] **73**–30
sugar bowl [shŏŏg/ər bōl/] **55**–14
sugar-free [shŏŏg/ər frē/] **122**–7
sugar substitute [shŏŏg/ər sŭb/stə tōōt/] **79**–20
suit [sōōt] **87**–11
bathing suit [bā/dhĭng sōōt/] **90**–26
business suit [bĭz/nəs sōōt/] **88**–11
jumpsuit [jŭmp/sōōt/] **93**–24
three piece suit [thrē/pēs/ sōōt/] **88** ✦
wet suit [wĕt/ sōōt/] **225**–4
suite [swēt] **184**–16
sum [sŭm] **192**–7
sumac [sōō/măk] **210**–23
summer [sŭm/ər] **21**–38
sun [sŭn] **209**–8
sunblock [sŭn/bläk/] **108**–8, **225**–0
sunburn [sŭn/bürn/] **110**–14
sunflower [sŭn/flow/ər] **211**–10
sunglasses [sŭn/glăs/əz] **90**–27
sunrise [sŭn/ rīz] **18**–14
sunscreen [sŭn/skrēn/] **108**–7, **225**–10
sunset [sŭn/ sĕt] **18**–19
Sunday [sŭn/dā, –dē] **20**–8
sunny [sŭn/ē] **13**–9, **76**–10
superintendent [sōō/prĭn tĕn/dənt, sōō/pər ĭn–] **50**–8
supermarket [sōō/pər/ mär/kət] **127**–18
supervise [sōō/pər vīz/] **170**–O
supervisor [sōō/pər vī/zər] **165**–8, **175**–4
Supplies [sə plīz/] **100, 183**
SUPPLIES [sə plīz/] **61, 180–181**
supply [sə plī/] **127**–21
supply cabinet [sə plī/ kăb/ə nət] **182**–1
support [sə pört/] **179**–18
support group [sə pört/ grōōp/] **115**–15
supporter [sə pör/tər] **91**–6
Supreme Court [sə prēm/ kört/] **138**–11
surfboard [sürf/börd/] **225**–16
surfer [sür/fər] **225**–15
surfing [sür/fĭng] **227**–9, **227**–10, **227** ✦
surgeon [sür/jən] **121**–36
Surgeon [sür/jən] **93**
surge protector [sürj/ prə tĕk/tər] **196**–1
surgical [sür/jĭ kəl]
surgical cap [sür/jĭ kəl kăp/] **121**–37
surgical gloves [sür/jĭ kəl glŭvz/] **121**–39
surgical gown [sür/jĭ kəl gown/] **93**–37, **121**–38
surgical mask [sür/jĭ kəl măsk/] **93**–36
surgical nurse [sür/jĭ kəl nürs/] **120**–9
surgical scrub cap [sür/jĭ kəl skrŭb/ kăp/] **93**–35
surgical scrubs [sür/jĭ kəl skrŭbz/] **93**–38
Surgical Assistant [sür/jĭ kəl ə sĭs/tənt] **93**
surprised [sər prīzd/, sə–] **43**–30
suspenders [sə spĕn/dərz] **94**–1
suspense [sŭs/pĕns] **237**–20
SUV (sport-utility vehicle) [ĕs/yōō/vē/] /
[spört/ yōō tĭl/ə tē vē/ĭ kəl] **156**–7
swallow [swäl/ō] **116**–J
swap meet [swäp/ mēt/] **222**–6
sweat [swĕt]
sweatpants [swĕt/pănts/] **89**–23
sweatshirt [swĕt/shürt/] **89**–22
sweater [swĕt/ər] **28**–2, **87**–14
cardigan sweater [kär/də gən swĕt/ər] **88**–2
pullover sweater [pŏŏl/ō/vər swĕt/ər] **88**–3
sweep [swēp] **60**–J
sweet potatoes [swēt pə tā/tōz] **69**–18
sweets [swēts] **84**–9
swim [swĭm] **230**–L
swimsuit [swĭm/sōōt/] **90**–26
swimming [swĭm/ĭng]
swimming pool [swĭm/ĭng pōōl/] **51**–22
swimming trunks [swĭm/ĭng trŭngks/] **90**–22
swing [swĭng] **230**–Q
swings [swĭngz] **224**–11
Swiss cheese [swĭs/ chēz/] **71**–27
switch [swĭch] **58**–27
swollen finger [swō/lən fĭng/gər] **110**–16
swordfish [sörd/fĭsh/] **71**–5, **212**–10
symbol [sĭm/bəl] **155**–8
SYMPTOMS AND INJURIES
[sĭmp/təmz ən ĭn/jə rēz] **110**
synagogue [sĭn/ə gäg/] **127**–16
synthetic materials [sĭn thĕ/tĭk mə tïr/ē əlz] **98** ✦
syringe [sə rĭnj/] **118**–12
syrup [sĭr/əp, sür/–] **113**–29
system [sĭs/təm]
fuel injection system
[fyōō/əl ĭn jĕk/shən sĭs/təm] **158**–17
stereo system [stĕr/ē ō sĭs/təm] **56**–8
SYSTEM [sĭs/təm] **141**
tab [tăb] **197**–7
table [tā/bəl]
bed table [bĕd/ tā/bəl] **121**–21
changing table [chān/jĭng tā/bəl] **59**–1
coffee table [kö/fē tā/bəl] **56**–19
dining room table [dī/nĭng rōōm/ tā/bəl] **55**–9
end table [ĕnd/ tā/bəl] **56**–14
examination table [ĭg zăm/ə nā/shən tā/bəl] **118**–7
folding card table [fōl/dĭng kärd/ tā/bəl] **102**–4
night table [nīt/ tā/bəl] **58**–23
operating table [äp/ə rā/tĭng tā/bəl] **121**–40
periodic table [pïr/ē äd/ĭk tā/bəl] **195**–26
picnic table [pĭk/nĭk tā/bəl] **224**–8
pool table [pōōl/ tā/bəl] **50**–15
tablecloth [tā/bəl klöth/] **55**–12
tablespoon [tā/bəl spōōn/] **75**–7
table tennis [tā/bəl tĕn/əs] **228**–14
tray table [trā/ tā/bəl] **161**–21
turntable [türn/tā/bəl] **234**–12
tablet [tăb/lət] **113**–22, **113**–27
tackle [tăk/əl] **230**–F
taco [tä/kō] **79**–8
tags [tăgz] **92**–15, **136**–13
tail [tāl] **216**–22
tail light [tāl/ līt/] **158**–13
tail pipe [tāl/ pīp/] **158**–15
tailor [tā/lər] **100**–3
take [tāk]
do not take with dairy products
[dōō nät/ tāk/ wĭth dër/ē präd/ŭkts] **112**–A
take a bath [tāk/ ə băth/] **108**–B
take a break [tāk/ ə brāk/] **11**–H
take a citizenship test
[tāk/ ə sĭt/ə zən shĭp tĕst/] **140**–I
take a driver education course
[tāk/ ə drī/vərz ĕj/ə kā/shən körs/] **137**–B
take a driver's training course
[tāk/ ə drī/vərz trā/nĭng körs/] **137**–G
take a message [tāk/ ə mĕs/ĭj] **171**–Q
take a nap [tāk/ ə năp/] **53**–A
take a picture [tāk/ ə pĭk/chər] **206**–B
take a seat [tāk/ ə sēt/] **6**–F
take a shower [tāk/ ə show/ər] **38**–C, **108**–A
take a tour [tāk/ ə tōōr/] **220**–A
take a written test [tāk/ ə rĭt/ən tĕst] **137**–E
take care of children [tāk/ kër/ əv chĭl/drən] **170**–P
take cover [tāk/ kŭv/ər] **147**–J
take dictation [tāk/ dĭk/tā shən] **171**–K
take in [tāk/ ĭn] **100**–D
take medicine [tāk/ mĕd/ə sən] **114**–D
take notes [tāk/ nōts/] **10**–C
take off [tāk/ öf/] **109**–Q, **160**–J
take one hour before eating
[tāk/ wŭn/ ow/ər bĭ för/ ē/tĭng] **112**–B
take out [tāk/ owt/] **9**–Y, **60**–Q, **82** ✦
take ownership [tāk/ ō/nər shĭp/] **49**–K
take temperature [tāk/ tĕm/prə chər] **118**–B
take the bus to school
[tāk/ dhə bŭs/ tə skōōl/] **38**–H
take the car to a mechanic
[tāk/ dhə kär/ tə dhə mə kăn/ĭk] **157**–C
take the children to school
[tāk/ dhə chĭl/drən tə skōōl/] **38**–G
take the order [tāk/ dhē ör/dər] **82**–E
take with food [tāk/ wĭth fōōd/] **112**–A
take x-rays [tāk/ ĕks/rāz/] **119**–B
Taking a Flight [tā/kĭng ə flīt/] **160**
Taking a Test [tā/kĭng ə tĕst/] **10**
TAKING A TRIP [tā/kĭng ə trĭp/] **162–163**
Taking Care of Your Car [tā/kĭng kër/ əv yər kär/] **157**
TAKING CARE OF YOUR HEALTH
[tā/kĭng kër əv yər hĕlth/] **114–115**
talk [tök]
talk show [tök/ shō/] **236**–4
talk therapy [tök/ thër/ ə pē] **115**–13
talk [tök]
talk about [tök ə bowt/] **174**–L
talk on the phone [tök/ ön dhə fōn/] **15**–C
talk to friends [tök/ tə frĕndz/] **173**–A
talk to the teacher [tök/ tə dhə tē/chər] **6**–B
tall [töl] **32**–4
tambourine [tăm/bə rēn/] **238**–17
tan [tăn] **24**–18
tangerines [tăn/jə rēnz/] **68**–9
tank [tăngk] **158**–10, **225**–5
tank top [tăngk/ täp/] **89**–24
tank truck [tăngk/ trŭk] **156**–20
tape [tāp]
clear tape [klēr/ tāp/] **183**–30
correction tape [kə rĕk/shən tāp/] **183**–37
duct tape [dŭkt/ tāp/] **181**–49
electrical tape [ĭ lek/trĭ kəl tāp/] **181**–43
masking tape [măs/kĭng tāp/] **181**–53
packing tape [păk/ĭng tāp/] **183**–32
sterile tape [stĕr/ əl tāp/] **117**–7
tape measure [tāp mĕzh/ər] **100**–17, **181**–45

target [tär/gət] **231**–7
taste [tāst] **106**–D
tattoo [tă to͞o/] **32**–18
tax / taxes [tăks] / [tăks/əz] **27**–8
taxi [tăk/sē] **150**–3
  hail a taxi [hāl/ ə tăk/sē] **152** ✦
  taxi driver [tăk/sē drī/vər] **152**–21
  taxi license [tăk/sē lī/səns] **152**–22
  taxi stand [tăk/sē stănd/] **152**–18
TB (tuberculosis) [tē/bē/] / [to͞o bür/kyə lō/səs] **111**–15
TDD [tē/dē/dē/] **15**–26
tea [tē] **79**–12, **81**–39, **81**–40
  teacup [tē/kŭp] **55**–6
  tea kettle [tē/ kĕt/l] **54**–21
  teapot [tē/pät/] **55**–16
  teaspoon [tē/spo͞on/] **75**–6, **83**–31
teach [tēch] **170**–Q
teacher [tē/chər] **5**–8, **6**–4, **22**–5
  teacher's aide [tē/chərz ād/] **5**–16
team [tēm] **145**–20, **229**–3
TEAM SPORTS [tēm/ spörts/] **229**
technical school [tĕk/nĭ kəl sko͞ol/] **188**–5
technician [tĕk nĭsh/ən]
  computer technician
    [kəm pyo͞o/tər tĕk nĭsh/ən] **167**–19, **182**–12
  emergency medical technician (EMT)
    [ĭ mür/jən sē mĕd/ĭ kəl tĕk nish/ən] / [ē/ĕm/tē]
      121–32
  medical records technician
    [mĕd/ĭ kəl rĕk/ərdz tĕk nish/ən] **168**–39
Technician [tĕk nĭsh/ən] **93**
teddy bear [tĕd/ē bër/] **37**–23
teen / teenager [tēn] / [tē/nā/jər] **31**–11
teething ring [tē/dhĭng rĭng/] **37**–25
teeth / tooth [tēth] / [to͞oth] **106**–7
  toothache [to͞oth/āk/] **110**–2
  toothbrush [to͞oth/brŭsh/] **57**–21, **109**–22
  toothbrush holder [to͞oth/brŭsh/ hōl/dər] **57**–22
  toothpaste [to͞oth/pāst/] **109**–23
telemarketer [tĕl/ə mär/kə tər] **169**–60
TELEPHONE [tĕl/ə fōn/] **14**–**15**
Telephone Skills [tĕl/ə fōn/ skĭlz/] **171**
telescope [tĕl/ə skōp/] **205**–23
television / TV [tĕl/ə vĭzh/ən] / [tē/vē/] **56**–6
  big-screen TV [bĭg/skrēn/ tē/vē/] **50**–14
  flat panel TV [flăt/ păn/əl tē/vē/] **234**–7
  flat screen TV [flăt/ skrēn/ tē/vē/] **234**–7
  portable TV [pör/tə bəl tē/vē/] **234**–8
teller [tĕl/ər] **132**–1
Teller [tĕl/ər] **132**
Telling Time [tĕ/lĭng tīm/] **18**
temperature [tĕm/prə chər] **110**–8
  temperature gauge [tĕm/prə chər gāj/] **159**–30
Temperature [tĕm/prə chər] **13**
ten [tĕn] **16**
  ten after one [tĕn/ ăf/tər wŭn/] **18**–8
  ten dollars [tĕn/ däl/ərz] **26**–9
  10 percent [tĕn/ pər sĕnt/] **17**–12
  ten thousand [tĕn/ thow/zənd] **16**
  10-year-old girl [tĕn/yïr ōld/ gürl/] **31**–10
tenant [tĕn/ənt] **50**–6
TENANT MEETING [tĕn/ənt mē/tĭng] **64**–**65**
tennis [tĕn/əs] **228**–15
  table tennis [tā/bəl tĕn/əs] **228**–14
  tennis court [tĕn/əs kört/] **224**–6
  tennis racket [tĕn/əs răk/ət] **231**–2
  tennis shoes [tĕn/əs sho͞oz/] **95**–32
tent [tĕnt] **226**–10
tenth [tĕnth] **16**
Terminal [tür/mə nəl] **160**
termites [tür/mīts] **63**–22
term [türm] **139** ✦
Terms [türmz] **199**
terrified [tĕr/ə fīd/] **43** ✦
test [tĕst] **121**–30
  test booklet [tĕst/ bo͝ok/lət] **10**–1
  testing area [tĕs/tĭng ër/ē ə] **136**–2
  test tube [tĕst/ to͞ob/] **195**–42
Test [tĕst] **10**
text [tĕkst]
  textbook [tĕkst/bo͝ok/, tĕks/-] **7**–25
  text box [tĕkst/ bäks/, tĕks/-] **197**–13
  text message [tĕkst/ mĕs/ĭj, tĕks/-] **14**–19
thank [thăngk] **12**–E, **174**–N
Thanksgiving [thăngks gĭv/ĭng] **22**–17
theater [thē/ə tər] **126**–6, **127**–23
theft [thĕft] **142**–9
therapist [thĕr/ ə pĭst] **115**–12, **115**–14, **168**–45
therapy [thĕr/ ə pē] **115**–11, **115**–13
thermal undershirt [thür/məl ŭn/dər shürt/] **91**–2
thermometer [thər mäm/ə tər] **118**–11
thick [thĭk] **23**–7
thighs [thīz] **70**–22, **106**–19
thimble [thĭm/bəl] **100**–15
thin [thĭn] **23**–8, **32**–9
THINGS [thĭngz] **23**
think [thĭnk] **191**–E
third [thürd] **16**
Third Floor [thürd/ flör/] **50**
thirsty [thür/stē] **42**–2
thirteen [thür/tēn/] **16**
  thirteen colonies [thür/tēn/ kä/lə nēz] **198**–1
thirteenth [thür/tēnth/] **16**
thirtieth [thür/tē əth] **16**
thirty [thür/tē] **16**
  35 mm camera
    [thür/tē fīv/ mĭl/ə mē/tər kăm/rə] **235**–21
this week [dhĭs/ wēk/] **20**–19
thorn [thörn] **211**–29
thread [thrĕd] **99**–23, **100**–11
three [thrē] **16**
  three piece suit [thrē/pēs/ so͞ot/] **88** ✦
  3-ring binder [thrē/ rĭng/ bīn/dər] **7**–27
  3/4 sleeved [thrē/kwör/tər slēv/] **96**–13
  three times a week [thrē/ tīmz/ ə wēk/] **20**–24
throat [thrōt] **107**–35, **110**–6, **111**–4
  throat lozenges [thrōt/ läz/ən jəz] **113**–30
through [thro͞o] **153**–K
throw [thrō] **230**–C
  throw away [thrō/ ə wā/] **11**–N
  throw up [thrō/ ŭp/] **110**–E
throw pillow [thrō/ pĭl/ō] **56**–2
thumb [thŭm] **106**–16
thunderstorm [thŭn/dər störm/] **13**–16
Thursday [thürz/dā, –dē] **20**–12
tick [tĭk] **214**–27
ticket [tĭk/ət] **152**–15, **161**–19
  ticket agent [tĭk/ət ā/jənt] **160**–3
  ticket window [tĭk/ət wĭn/dō/] **152**–12
tidal wave [tīd/l wāv/] **145**–17
tide [tīd] **225** ✦
tie [tī] **88**–12, **89**–16, **92**–13, **229** ✦
tie [tī] **86**–A
tiger [tī/gər] **217**–37
tight [tīt] **97**–29
tights [tīts] **91**–19
tile [tīl] **57**–10, **178**–11, **178**–D
time [tīm]
  Alaska time [ə lăs/kə tīm/] **19**–28
  arrival time [ə rī/vəl tīm/] **161** ✦
  Atlantic time [ət lăn/tĭk tīm/] **19**–33
  Central time [sĕn/trəl tīm/] **19**–31
  daylight saving time [dā/līt/ sā/vĭng tīm/] **19**–25
  departure time [dĭ pär/chər tīm/] **161** ✦
  Eastern time [ē/stərn tīm/] **19**–32
  Hawaii-Aleutian time
    [hə wī/ē ə lo͞o/shən tīm/] **19**–27
  Mountain time [mown/tn tīm/] **19**–30
  Newfoundland time
    [no͞o/fən lənd tīm/, –fənd–] **19**–34
  on time [än/ tīm/, ön/ tīm/] **19**–23, **161**–29
  Pacific time [pə sĭf/ĭk tīm/] **19**–29
  standard time [stăn/dərd tīm/] **19**–26
  three times a week [thrē tīmz/ ə wēk/] **20**–24
  time clock [tīm/ kläk/] **165**–7
Time [tīm] **18**
TIME [tīm] **18**–**19**
timer [tī/mər] **78**–18
Times of Day [tīmz/ əv dā/] **18**
Time Zones [tīm/ zōnz/] **19**
tire [tīr] **158**–5, **158**–23, **162**–F
tired [tīrd] **43**–32
title [tīt/l] **133**–14, **190**–5
toad [tōd] **212**–28
toast [tōst] **80**–4
toaster [tō/stər] **54**–6
  toaster oven [tō/stər ŭv/ən] **54**–15
today [tə dā/] **20**–5
toddler [täd/lər] **31**–8
toe [tō] **92**–6, **94**–23, **105**–10
  toenail [tō/nāl/] **106** ✦
Tofu [tō/fo͞o/] **77**
toggle bolt [täg/əl bōlt/] **180**–38
to-go box [tə gō/ bäks/] **82**–5
toilet [toy/lət] **57**–19
  toilet brush [toy/lət brŭsh/] **57**–18
  toilet paper [toy/lət pā/pər] **57**–17, **146**–13
token [tō/kən] **152**–10
tomatoes [tə mā/tōz] **69**–6
tomorrow [tə mär/ō, –mör/ō] **20**–6
tongs [tängz, töngz] **78**–23, **195**–44
tongue [tŭng] **106**–8
too [to͞o]
  too big [to͞o/ bĭg/] **97**–38
  too expensive [to͞o/ ĭk spĕn/sĭv] **97**–44
  too small [to͞o/ smöl/] **97**–37

tool belt [to͞ol/ bělt/] **92**–3
TOOLS AND BUILDING SUPPLIES
[to͞olz/ ən bĭl/dĭng sə plīz/] **180–181**
tooth / teeth [to͞oth] / [tēth] **106**–7
toothache [to͞oth/āk/] **110**–2
toothbrush [to͞oth/brŭsh/] **57**–21, **109**–22
toothbrush holder [to͞oth/brŭsh/ hōl/dər] **57**–22
toothpaste [to͞oth/pāst/] **109**–23
top [täp] **88**–7, **89**–24
torn [törn] **97**–41
tornado [tör nā/dō] **145**–15
torso [tör/sō/] **106** ✦
tortoise [tör/təs] **213**–42
total [tōt/l] **27**–9
totebag [tōt/ băg/] **94**–19
touch [tŭch] **106**–E
towel [tow/əl]
bath towel [băth/ tow/əl] **57**–14
dish towel [dĭsh/ tow/əl] **61**–22
hand towel [hănd/ tow/əl] **57**–15
paper towels [pā/pər tow/əlz] **54**–3
towel rack [tow/əl răk/] **57**–13
towelettes [tow/əl ěts] **146**–12
tower [tow/ər] **196**–3
town [town] **52**–3
town car [town/ kär/] **152**–20
townhouse [town/hows/] **52**–6
tow truck [tō/ trŭk/] **156**–14
toy [toy]
toy chest [toy/ chěst/] **59**–16
toy store [toy/ stör/] **130**–5
Toys and Games [toyz/ ən gāmz/] **59**
track [trăk] **5**–21, **152**–14
track and field [trăk/ ən fēld/] **228**–18
tractor [trăk/tər] **177**–9
tractor trailer [trăk/tər trā/lər] **156**–15
traffic light [trăf/ĭk līt/] **128**–8
TRAFFIC SIGNS [trăf/ĭk sīnz/] **154**
tragedy [trăj/ə dē] **237**–14
trailer [trā/lər] **156**–15, **156**–17
train [trān] **150**–7, **233**–27
training [trā/nĭng] **172**–2, **172**–5, **172**–7
training pants [trā/nĭng pănts/] **37**–11
Training [trā/nĭng] **172**
Train Station [trān/ stā/shən] **152**
transcribe [trăn skrīb/] **171**–C
transfer [trăns für/, trăns/fər] **152**–5
transfer [trăns für/, trăns/fər] **171**–O
translate [trănz/lāt] **8**–C
translator [trănz/lā/tər, trăns/–] **168**–35
Transmission [trănz mĭsh/ən, trăns–] **159**
Transportation [trăns/pər tā/shən] **152**
TRANSPORTATION [trăns/pər tā/shən] **150–151, 152**
trash [trăsh]
trash bags [trăsh/ băgz/] **61**–24
trash bin [trăsh/ bĭn/] **51**–23
trash chute [trăsh/ sho͞ot/] **51**–26
travel [trăv/əl] **41**–P
travel agency [trăv/əl ā/jən sē] **131**–14
tray [trā] **55**–17, **83**–10
tray table [trā tā/bəl] **161**–21
Tree [trē] **210**
trees [trēz] **208**–1, **239**–16
TREES AND PLANTS [trēz/ ən plănts/] **210**
trench coat [trěnch/ kōt/] **90**–21
trial [trī/əl] **140**–5
triangle [trī/ăng/gəl] **193**–32
tricycle [trī/sĭ kəl] **224**–12
trigonometry [trĭg/ə näm/ə trē] **192**–18
trim [trĭm] **176**–B
trip [trĭp] **152**–16, **152**–17
tripe [trīp] **70**–8
tripod [trī/päd] **235**–25
trombone [träm bōn/] **238**–10
trout [trowt] **71**–1
trowel [trow/əl] **176**–10, **178**–13
truck [trŭk] **150**–5
dump truck [dŭmp/trŭk/] **156**–19
fire truck [fīr/ trŭk/] **144**–10
garbage truck [gär/bĭj trŭk/] **127**–22
hand truck [hănd/ trŭk/] **175**–11
pickup truck [pĭk/ŭp trŭk/] **156**–12
tank truck [tăngk/ trŭk/] **156**–20
tow truck [tō/ trŭk/] **156**–14
truck driver [trŭk/ drī/vər] **169**–61
TRUCKS [trŭks] **156**
trumpet [trŭm/pət] **238**–11
Trunk [trŭngk] **158**
trunks [trŭngks] **158**–11, **210**–4, **217**–47
swimming trunks [swĭm/ĭng trŭngks/] **90**–22
try on [trī/ön] **95**–C
TSA agent [tē/ěs/ā/ ā/jənt] **160**–5
T-shirt [tē/shürt/] **86**–4
tsunami [so͞o nä/ mē/, tso͞o–] **145**–17
tub [tŭb]
bathtub [băth/tŭb/] **57**–2
tuba [to͞o/bə] **238**–12
tube [to͞ob] **74**–12, **74**–24, **195**–42
tuberculosis (TB)
[to͞o bür/kyə lō/səs] / [tē/bē/] **111**–15
Tuesday [to͞oz/dā, –dē] **20**–10
tulip [to͞o/ləp] **211**–11
tuna [to͞o/nə] **71**–7, **72**–19, **212**–8
tuner [to͞o/nər] **234**–13
turbulence [tür/byə ləns] **161**–22
turkey [tür/kē] **70**–17, **239**–14
roasted turkey [rōs/təd tür/kē] **76**–4
smoked turkey [smōkt/ tür/kē] **71**–25
turn [türn] **154**–5, **154**–7, **154**–8
turn signal [türn/ sĭg/nəl] **158**–6, **159**–34
turnstile [türn/stīl/] **152**–8
turntable [türn/tā/bəl] **234**–12
turn [türn]
turn in [türn/ ĭn/] **191**–M
turn left [türn/ lěft/] **155**–C
turn off [türn/ öf/] **11**–P, **160**–I, **174**–G, **219**–G
turn on [türn/ ön/, –än/] **11**–B
turn right [türn/ rīt/] **155**–B
turnips [tür/nəps] **69**–16
turquoise [tür/koyz, –kwoyz] **24**–9
turtle [tür/tl] **213**–43
turtleneck [tür/tl něk/] **96**–9
tusk [tŭsk] **217**–48
tuxedo [tŭk sē/dō] **89**–17
TV Programs [tē/vē/ prō/grămz] **236**
TV / television [tē/vē/] / [těl/ə vĭzh/ən] **56**–6
big-screen TV [bĭg/skrēn/ tē/vē/] **50**–14
flat panel TV [flăt/ păn/əl tē/vē] **234**–7
flat screen TV [flăt/ skrēn/ tē/ vē/] **234**–7
portable TV [pör/tə bəl tē/vē/] **234**–8
tweezers [twē/zərz] **117**–4
twelfth [twělfth] **16**
twelve [twělv] **16**
twentieth [twěn/tē əth] **16**
twenty [twěn/tē] **16**
twenty after one [twěn/tē ăf/tər wŭn/] **18**–10
twenty dollars [twěn/tē däl/ərz] **26**–10
twenty-first [twěn/tē fürst/] **16**
twenty-five [twěn/tē fīv/] **16**
25 percent [twěn/fīv/ pər sěnt/] **17**–11
twenty-four [twěn/tē för] **16**
twenty-one [twěn/tē wŭn/] **16**
twenty-three [twěn/tē thrē/] **16**
twenty to two [twěn/tē tə to͞o/] **18**–12
twenty-two [twěn/tē to͞o/] **16**
twice a week [twīs/ ə wēk/] **20**–23
twig [twĭg] **210**–1
twins [twĭnz] **28**–1
two [to͞o]**16**
2-door car [to͞o/dör kär/] **156**–2
two-story house [to͞o/stör/ē hows/] **52** ✦
two-way radio [to͞o/wā rā/dē ō] **179**–22
2 x 4 (two by four) [to͞o/ bī/ för/] **181**–19
type [tīp] **170**–R, **196**–A
type a letter [tīp/ə lět/ər] **171**–A
type the message [tīp/ dhə měs/ĭj] **197**–E
type the subject [tīp/ dhə sŭb/jĭkt] **197**–D
type your password [tīp/ yər păs/würd/] **197**–A
Types of Health Problems
[tīps/ əv hělth/ präb/ləmz] **115**
Types of Job Training [tīps/ əv jäb/ trā/nĭng] **172**
Types of Material [tīps/ əv mə tïr/ē əl] **99**
Types of Math [tīps/ əv măth/] **192**
Types of Medication [tīps/ əv měd/ə kā/shən] **113**
Types of Movies [tīps/ əv mo͞o/vēz] **237**
Types of Music [tīps/ əv myo͞o/zĭk] **237**
Types of TV Programs [tīps/ əv tē/vē/ prō/grămz] **236**
ugly [ŭg/lē] **23**–22
umbrella [ŭm brěl/ə] **90**–17, **225**–14
umpire [ŭm/pīr] **229** ✦
uncle [ŭng/kəl] **34**–8
uncomfortable [ŭn kŭmf/tə bəl, –tər–] **42**–9
unconscious [ŭn/kän/shəs] **116**–A
under [ŭn/dər] **25**–10, **153**–A
long underwear [löng/ ŭn/dər wër] **91**–3
thermal undershirt [thür/məl ŭn/dər shürt] **91**–2
underexposed [ŭn/dər ĭk spōzd/] **235**–35
underpants [ŭn/dər pănts/] **91**–14
undershirt [ŭn/dər shürt/] **91**–1
underline [ŭn/dər līn/] **9**–S
Under the Hood [ŭn/dər dhə ho͝od/] **158**
Underwear [ŭn/dər wër/] **91**
UNDERWEAR AND SLEEPWEAR
[ŭn/dər wër/ ən slēp/wër/] **91**
undress [ən drěs/] **36**–E

unfurnished apartment
[ŭn/für nĭsht ə pärt/ mənt] **48**–4
uniform [yo͞o/nə förm/] **88**–10, **231**–16
Unisex Socks [yo͞o/nə sĕks/ säks/] **91**
Unisex Underwear [yo͞o/nə sĕks/ ŭn/dər wër] **91**
universal remote [yo͞o/nə vür/səl rĭ mōt/] **234**–9
UNIVERSE [yo͞o/nə vürs/] **205**
university [yo͞o/nə vür/sə tē] **188**–7
unload [ŭn lōd/] **101**–E
unpack [ŭn păk/] **49**–N
unraveling [ŭn răv/əl ĭng] **97**–43
unripe [ŭn rīp/] **68**–31
unscented [ŭn sĕn/təd] **108** ✦
unscramble [ŭn skrăm/bəl] **9**–W
up [ŭp]
buckle up [bŭk/əl ŭp/] **36**–L
clean up [klēn/ ŭp/] **147**–M
cut up [kŭt/ ŭp/] **77**–I
eggs sunny-side up [ĕgz/ sŭn/ē sīd/ ŭp/] **76**–10
get up [gĕt/ ŭp/] **38**–B
hang up [hăng/ ŭp/] **15**–D, **101**–H
look up [lo͝ok/ ŭp/] **8**–A
pick up [pĭk/ ŭp/] **6**–I, **11**–E, **38**–M
pop-up ad [päp/ ŭp ăd/] **197**–9
set up [sĕt/ ŭp/] **173**–I
stand up [stănd/ ŭp/] **6**–D
stopped up [stäpt/ ŭp/] **63**–19
throw up [thrō/ ŭp/] **110**–E
wake up [wāk/ ŭp/] **38**–A
walk up [wök/ ŭp/] **153**–C
upright seat [ŭp/rīt/ sēt/] **161**–28
upset [ŭp sĕt/] **43**–28
upstairs [ŭp/stërz/] **51** ✦
Uranus [yo͝or/ə nəs, yo͝o rā/nəs] **205**–7
urban area [ür/bən ër/ē ə] **52**–1
urchin [ür/chən] **212**–21
URL [yo͞o/är/ĕl/] **197**–4
U.S. [yo͞o/ĕs/]
U.S. Capitol [yo͞o/ĕs/ kă/pət əl] **138**–1
U.S. route [yo͞o/ĕs/ ro͞ot/, –rowt/] **154**–17
USB port [yo͞o/ĕs/ bē/ pört/] **196**–7
use [yo͞oz]
use a cash register [yo͞oz/ə kăsh/ rĕj/ə stər] **170**–S
use a credit card [yo͞oz/ə krĕ/dət kärd/] **27**–B
use a debit card [yo͞oz/ə dĕ/bət kärd/] **27**–C
use a gift card [yo͞oz/ ə gĭft/ kärd/] **27**–E
use deodorant [yo͞oz/dē ō/dər ənt] **108**–C
use energy-efficient bulbs
[yo͞oz/ ĕn/ər jē ĭ fĭ/shənt bŭlbz] **219**–H
use punctuation [yo͞oz/ pŭngk/cho͞o ā/shən] **190**–C
Used Car [yo͞ozd/ kär/] **157**
used clothing [yo͞ozd/ klō/dhĭng] **102**–2
U.S. HISTORY [yo͞o/ĕs/ hĭs/tə rē] **198**
U.S. NATIONAL PARKS
[yo͞o/ĕs năsh/ə nəl pärks/] **220–221**
utensils [yo͞o tĕn/səlz] **79**–19
utility / utilities [yo͞o tĭl/ə tē] / [yo͞o tĭl/ə tēz]
48–5, **156**–7
U-turn [yo͞o/türn/] **154**–5
vacancy sign [vā/kən sē sīn/] **50**–7
vacation [vā kā/shən] **22**–6
vaccination [văk/sə nā/shən] **114** ✦
vacuum [văk/yo͞om]
vacuum cleaner [văk/yo͞om klē/nər] **61**–10
vacuum cleaner attachments
[văk/yo͞om klē/nər ə tăch/mənts] **61**–11
vacuum cleaner bag
[văk/yo͞om klē/nər băg/] **61**–12
vacuum [văk/yo͞om] **60**–H
valley [văl/ē] **204**–17
valuables [văl/yə bəlz, –yə wə–] **132**–8
valve [vălv] **146**–4
van [văn] **156**–13, **156**–18
vandalism [văn/də lĭz/əm] **142**–1
vanity plate [vă/nə tē plāt/]**136** ✦
variable [vër/ē ə bəl] **192**–12
vase [vās, vāz, väz] **55**–23
vault [völt] **132**–6
VCR [vē/sē/är/] **102**–7
veal cutlets [vēl/ kŭt/ləts] **70**–6
Vegetable [vĕj/tə bəl] **77**
vegetables [vĕj/tə bəlz] **66**–8, **72**–27, **81**–32
vegetable garden [vĕj/tə bəl gär/dn] **53**–27, **177**–14
vegetable peeler [vĕj/tə bəl pē/lər] **78**–15
VEGETABLES [vĕj/tə bəlz] **69**
vegetarian [vĕj/ə tër/ē ən] **70** ✦
vehicles [vē/ĭ kəlz] **124**–4, **156**–7, **156**–10
vein [vān] **107**–37
velvet [vĕl/vət] **99**–10
vending machine [vĕn/dĭng mə shēn/] **152**–9
vendors [vĕn/dərz] **84**–7, **129**–29
ventilation mask [vĕnt/əl ā/shən măsk/] **92**–7
Venus [vē/nəs] **205**–2
verdict [vür/dĭkt] **141**–14
vertebrates [vür/ tə brəts] **194**–13
vest [vĕst] **89**–15
down vest [down/ vĕst] **90**–14
Hi-Visibility safety vest
[hī/vĭz/ə bĭl/ə tē sāf/tē vĕst] **92**–6
life vest [līf/ vĕst/] **161**–25, **226**–14
Veterans Day [vĕt/ər ənz dā/] **22**–16
veterinarian [vĕt/ər ə nër/ē ən] **169**–62
vice president [vīs/ prĕz/ə dənt] **138**–9
victim [vĭk/təm] **142**–10
video [vĭd/ē ō]
videocassette [vĭd/ē ō kə sĕt/] **133**–18
video game console [vĭd/ē ō gām/ kän/sōl/] **232**–3
video game control [vĭd/ē ō gām/ kän trōl/] **232**–4
video player [vĭd/ē ō plā ər] **197**–11
video store [vĭd/ē ō stör/] **129**–20
videotape [vĭd/ē ō tāp/] **240**–A
view [vyo͞o]
rearview mirror [rïr/vyo͞o/ mïr/ər] **159**–35
sideview mirror [sīd/vyo͞o/ mïr/ər] **158**–3
village [vĭ/lĭj] **52**–3
vine [vīn] **210**–22
vineyard [vĭn/yərd] **177**–16
violence [vī/ləns, vī/ə–] **142**–4
violet [vī/ə lət, vī/lət] **24**–8, **211**–23
violin [vī/ə lĭn/] **238**–6
virus [vī/rəs] **111**–17
vise [vīs] **180**–26
vision [vĭ/zhən]
vision exam [vĭ/zhən ĭg zăm/] **136**–6
vision problems [vĭ/zhən präb/ləmz] **115**–1
Visit [vĭ/zət] **119**
visor [vī zər] **179**–12
vital signs monitor [vīt/l sīnz/ män/ə tər] **121**–26
vitamins [vī/tə mənz] **113**–17
v-neck [vē/nĕk/] **96**–8
vocational [vō kā/shə nəl]
vocational school [vō kā/shə nəl sko͞ol/] **188**–5
vocational training [vō kā/shə nəl trā/nĭng] **172**–5
voice message [voys mĕs/ĭj] **14**–18
volcanic eruption [väl kăn/ĭk ĭ rŭp/shən] **145**–16
volleyball [väl/ē böl/] **229**–14, **231**–3
Volume [väl/yəm, –yo͞om] **75, 193**
volunteer [väl/ən tïr/] **121**–17
volunteer [väl/ən tïr/] **41**–Q
vomit [väm/ət] **110**–E
vote [vōt] **140**–A
waffles [wä/fəlz, wö/–] **80**–8
wages [wā/jĭz] **165**–12
wagon [wă/gən] **156**–6
waist [wāst]
waist apron [wāst/ ā/prən] **93**–30
waistband [wāst/bănd/] **100**–5
wait [wāt] **94**–B, **128**–B, **170**–T
waiter [wā/tər] **82**–8
headwaiter [hĕd/wā/tər] **185**–12
waiting area [wā/tĭng ër/ē ə] **182**–16
Waiting Room [wā/tĭng ro͞om/] **118**
waitress [wā/trəs] **83**–9
wait staff [wāt/ stăf/] **185** ✦
wake up [wāk/ ŭp/] **38**–A
walk [wök] **53**–2
crosswalk [krös/wök/] **128**–15
walk-in freezer [wök/ĭn frē/zər] **185**–3
walk [wök]
walk a dog [wök ə dög/] **129**–F
walk down [wök/ down/] **153**–D
walk to class [wök/ tə klăs/] **11**–C
walk up [wök/ ŭp/] **153**–C
walk with a friend [wök/ wĭth ə frĕnd/] **143**–A
walker [wö/kər] **113**–11
wall [wöl] **56**–10, **194**–5
drywall [drī/wöl/] **178**–19
wallpaper [wöl/pā/pər] **59**–8
wallet [wä/lət, wö/–] **94**–13
walrus [wöl/rəs] **213**–32
war [wör] **199**–10
Revolutionary War [rĕ/və lo͞o/shə nër/ē wör/] **198**–8
warehouse [wër/hows/] **175**–7
warm [wörm] **13**–4
warm clothes [wörm/ klōz/] **146**–6
warning label [wör/nĭng lā/bəl] **112**–8
Warnings [wör/nĭngz] **112**
wash [wäsh, wösh]
mouthwash [mowth/wäsh/, –wösh/–] **109**–25
washcloth [wäsh/klöth/, wösh/–] **57**–4
wash [wäsh, wösh]
wash clothes [wäsh/ klōz/, wösh/–] **219**–K
wash hair [wäsh/ hër/, wösh/–] **108**–E
wash the dishes [wäsh/ dhə dĭsh/əz, wösh/–] **60**–M
wash the windows
[wäsh/ dhə wĭn/dōz, wösh/–] **60**–I
washer [wä/shər, wö/–] **50**–12, **101**–3, **180**–37
dishwasher [dĭsh/wäsh/ər, –wö–] **54**–8, **185**–2

washing [wä/shĭng, wö/–] **61**–21
wasp [wäsp, wösp] **214**–17
waste [wāst] **121**–31, **218**–12
  wastebasket [wāst/bās/kət] **57**–26
watch [wäch, wöch] **94**–16
watch [wäch, wöch] **39**–X, **147**–C
water [wö/tər] **209**–3, **225**–1
  body of water [bäd/ē əv wö/tər] **204** ✦
  bottled water [bät/ld wö/tər] **146**–11
  cold water [kōld/ wö/tər] **57**–7
  hot water [hät/ wö/tər] **57**–8
  hot water bottle [hät/ wö/tər bät/l] **113**–15
  watercolor [wö/tər kŭl/ər] **233**–21
  waterfall [wä/tər föl/] **204**–2
  water fountain [wö/tər fown/tn] **224**–9
  water glass [wö/tər glăs/] **83**–22
  watermelons [wö/tər mĕl/ənz] **68**–18
  water pollution [wö/tər pə lo͞o/shən] **218**–14
  water polo [wö/tər pō/lō] **229**–15
  waterskiing [wö/tər skē/ĭng] **227**–7
water [wö/tər] **176**–F
WATER SPORTS [wö/tər spörts/] **227**
wave [wāv] **145**–17, **225**–17
wave [wāv] **2**–F
wavy hair [wā/vē hër/] **33**–10
way [wā]
  hallway [häl/wā/] **184**–18
  one way [wŭn/ wā/] **154**–3
  one-way trip [wŭn/wā/ trĭp/] **152**–16
  two-way radio [to͞o/wā/ rā/dē ō] **179**–22
  wrong way [röng/ wā/] **154**–2
Ways to Conserve Energy and Resources
  [wāz/ tə kən sürv/ ĕn/ər jē n rē/sör/səz,
  –rĭ sör/səz] **219**
Ways to Get Well [wāz/ tə gĕt/ wĕl/] **114**
Ways to Pay [wāz/ tə pā/] **27**
Ways to Serve Eggs [wāz/ tə sürv/ ĕgz/] **76**
Ways to Serve Meat and Poultry
  [wāz/ tə sürv/ mēt/ n pōl/trē/] **76**
Ways to Stay Well [wāz/ tə stā/ wĕl/] **114**
Ways to Succeed [wāz/tə sək sēd/] **10**
weak signal [wēk/ sĭg/nəl] **14**–12
WEATHER [wĕdh/ər] **13**
Weather Conditions [wĕdh/ər kən dĭsh/ənz] **13**
Weather Map [wĕdh/ər măp/] **13**
webcam [wĕb/kăm/] **196**–12
Webpage [wĕb/pāg/] **197**
website address [wĕb/sīt ə drĕs/] **197**–4
wedding [wĕ/dĭng] **22**–2
Wednesday [wĕnz/dā, –dē] **20**–11
weed [wēd]
  seaweed [sē/ wēd/] **225** ✦
  weed eater [wēd/ ē/tər] **176**–12
  weed whacker [wēd/ wăk/ər] **176**–12
weed [wēd] **176**–G
week [wēk] **20**–15
  last week [lăst/ wēk/] **20**–18
  next week [nĕkst/ wēk/] **20**–20
  once a week [wŭns/ ə wēk/] **20**–22
  this week [dhĭs/ wēk/] **20**–19
  three times a week [thrē/ tīmz/ ə wēk/] **20**–24
  twice a week [twīs/ ə wēk/] **20**–23
  weekdays [wēk/dāz/] **20**–16
  weekend [wēk/ĕnd/] **20**–17
Week [wēk] **20**
weigh [wā] **75**–B
weight [wāt] **32**–8
Weight [wāt] **32, 75**
weightlifting [wāt/lĭf/tĭng] **228**–16
weights [wāts] **231**–22
WEIGHTS AND MEASUREMENTS
  [wāts/ ən mĕzh/ər mənts] **75**
welder [wĕl/dər] **169**–63
well [wĕl] **42**–14
Well [wĕl] **114**
west [wĕst] **155**–2
western [wĕs/tərn] **237**–15
wet [wĕt] **101**–17
  wet suit [wĕt/ so͞ot/] **225**–4
whacker [wăk/ər] **176**–12
whale [wāl] **213**–29
wheat [wēt] **177**–2
wheat bread [wēt/ brĕd/] **71**–19
wheel [wēl] **159**–26
  wheelbarrow [wēl/băr/ō] **176**–3
  wheelchair [wēl/chër/] **113**–9
  wheel cover [wēl/ kŭv/ər] **158**–9
whisk [wĭsk] **78**–21
whiskers [wĭs/kərz] **216**–18
white [wīt] **24**–14
  whiteboard [wīt/börd/] **6**–3
  white bread [wīt/ brĕd/] **71**–18
  White House [wīt/ hows/] **138**–7
whole salmon [hōl/ săm/ən] **71**–3
wide [wīd] **97**–36
widow [wĭd/ō] **41** ✦
widower [wĭd/ō ər] **41** ✦
width [wĭdth, wĭtth] **17**–19
wife [wīf] **34**–12
  ex-wife [ĕks/ wīf/] **35** ✦
  former wife [för/mər wīf/] **35** ✦
wild [wīld] **215** ✦
wildlife [wīld/līf] **220**–3
willow [wĭl/ō] **210**–13
win [wĭn] **229** ✦
wind [wĭnd]
  windbreaker [wĭnd/brā/kər] **90**–24
  wind power [wĭnd/ pow/ər] **218**–2
  windshield [wĭnd/ shēld/] **158**–1
  windshield wipers [wĭnd/shēld/wī/pərz] **158**–2
  windsurfing [wĭnd/sür/fĭng] **227**–10, **227** ✦
window [wĭn/dō] **47**–11, **56**–17, **136**–7
  drive-thru window [drīv/thro͞o/ wĭn/dō] **128**–11
  ticket window [tĭk/ət wĭn/dō] **152**–12
  window pane [wĭn/dō pān/] **178**–16
windy [wĭn/dē] **13**–18
wine glass [wīn/ glăs/] **83**–23
wing [wĭng] **70**–20, **214**–1
winter [wĭn/tər] **21**–40
  winter scarf [wĭn/tər/skärf/] **90**–5
WINTER AND WATER SPORTS
  [wĭn/tər ən wö/tər spörts/] **227**
wipe [wīp] **60**–O
wipers [wī/pərz] **158**–2
wipes [wīps] **37**–15, **61**–23
wire [wīr] **181**–13
  wire stripper [wīr/ strĭp/ər] **181**–42
wireless headset [wīr/ləs hĕd/sĕt] **14**–14
wiring [wīr/ĭng] **186**–7
withdraw [wĭdh drö/, wĭth–] **132**–F
witness [wĭt/nəs] **141**–11
wolf [wo͝olf] **216**–5
woman [wo͝om/ən] **30**–2
women [wĭ/mən] **30**–3
Women's Socks [wĭ/mənz säks/] **91**
Women's Underwear [wĭ/mənz ŭn/dər wër/] **91**
wood [wo͝od] **178**–18
  plywood [plī/wo͝od] **178**–17
  redwood [rĕd/wo͝od] **210**–18
  wood floor [wo͝od/ flör/] **58**–21
  woodpecker [wo͝od/pĕk/ər] **214**–8
  wood screw [wo͝od/ skro͞o/] **180**–33
  wood stain [wo͝od/ stān/] **181**–24
  woodworking kit [wo͝od/wür/kĭng kĭt/] **232**–14
wooden spoon [wo͝od/n spo͞on/] **78**–9
Woodwinds [wo͝od/wĭndz/] **238**
wool [wo͝ol] **61**–5, **98**–3
word [würd] **190**–1
word problem [würd/ prä/bləm] **192**–11
Words [wördz] **8**
work [würk/] **121**–30, **154**–16
  workbook [würk/bo͝ok/] **7**–26
  work gloves [würk/ glŭvz/] **92**–17, **179**–17
  work light [würk/ līt/] **181**–44
  work pants [würk/ pănts/] **92**–5
  work shirt [würk/ shürt/] **92**–2
work [würk] **8**–I, **10**–J, **38**–K
WORK [würk] **186–187**
Work Clothes [würk/ klōz/] **88**
worker [wür/kər]
  careful worker [kër/fəl wür/kər] **179**–2
  careless worker [kër/ləs wür/kər] **179**–1
  childcare worker [chīld/kër wür/kər] **166**–16
  construction worker
    [kən strŭk/shən wür/kər] **178**–1
  dockworker [däk/wür/kər] **167**–23
  factory worker [făk/tə rē wür/kər, –trē] **175**–3
  farmworker [färm/wür/kər] **177**–8
  food preparation worker
    [fo͞od/ prĕp ə rā/shən wür/kər] **185**–4
  garment worker [gär/mənt wür/kər] **167**–29
  postal worker [pō/stəl wür/kər] **169**–49
  sanitation worker [săn/ə tā/shən wür/kər] **169**–54
  social worker [sō/shəl wür/kər] **169**–57
Worker [wür/kər] **92, 93**
working [wür/kĭng]
  not working [nät/ wür/kĭng] **62**–1
  woodworking kit [wo͝od/wür/kĭng kĭt] **232**–14
Working with a Partner [wür/kĭng wĭth ə pärt/nər] **8**
Working with Your Classmates
  [wür/kĭng wĭth yər klăs/māts/] **8**
work out [würk/ owt/] **230**–N
WORKPLACE [würk/ plās/] **164–165**
WORKPLACE CLOTHING
  [würk/ plās/ klō/dhĭng] **92–93**

world [würld]
world languages [würld/ lăng/gwĭ jəz] **189**–13
world music [würld/ myōō/zĭk] **237**–32
WORLD MAP [würld/măp/] **202–203**
WORLD HISTORY [würld hĭs/tə rē] **199**
worm [würm] **212**–23
worried [wür/ēd] **42**–13
wrap [răp] **72**–24
wrap [răp] **240**–F
wrench [rĕnch] **158**–22, **181**–47, **181**–48
wrestling [rĕs/lĭng] **228**–17
wrinkled [rĭng/kəld] **101**–19
wrist [rĭst] **106**–14
wristwatch [rĭst/wäch/, –wöch/] **94**–16
write [rīt]
write a check [rīt/ ə chĕk/] **27**–D
write a cover letter [rīt/ ə kŭv/ər lĕt/ər] **173**–G
write a final draft [rīt/ ə fī/nəl drăft/] **191**–L
write a first draft [rīt/ ə fürst/ drăft/] **191**–H
write a note [rīt/ ə nōt/] **135**–A
write a resume [rīt/ ə rĕ/zə mā/] **173**–F
write a thank-you note
[rīt/ ə thăngk/ yōō nōt/] **174**–O
write back [rīt/ băk/] **135**–H
write on the board [rīt/ ön dhə börd/] **6**–E
writer [rī/tər] **169**–64
Writing and Revising [rī/tĭng ən rĭ vī/ zĭng] **191**
Writing Process [rī/tĭng prä/sĕs] **191**
Writing Rules [rī/tĭng rōōlz] **190**
wrong way [röng/ wā/] **154**–2
xylophone [zī/lə fōn/] **238**–15
yard [yärd]
courtyard [kört/ yärd/] **51**–21
yardstick [yärd/stĭk/] **181**–16
YARD [yärd] **53**
yarn [yärn] **233**–22
year [yïr] **20**–4, **31**–9, **31**–10
Year [yïr] **21**
yellow [yĕl/ō] **24**–2
yesterday [yĕs/tər dā/, –dē] **20**–7
yield [yēld] **154**–9
yoga [yō/gə] **122**–4
yogurt [yō/gərt] **72**–22
young [yŭng] **32**–1
Your First License [yər fürst/ lī/səns] **137**
YOUR HEALTH [yər hĕlth/] **114–115**
zebra [zē/brə] **217**–33
zero [zïr/ō] **16**
ZIP code [zĭp/ kōd/] **4**–9
zipper [zĭp/ər] **99**–25
Zones [zōnz] **19**
zoo [zōō] **222**–1
zoom lens [zōōm/ lĕnz/] **235**–23
zucchini [zōō kē/nē] **69**–25

Geographical Index

Continents

Africa [ăf′rĭ kə] **202–5**
Antarctica [ănt ärk′tĭ kə, –är′tĭ–] **202–7**
Asia [ā′zhə] **202–4**
Australia [ö strāl′yə] **202–6**
Europe [yŏŏr′əp] **202–3**
North America [nörth′ ə mĕr′ə kə] **200–201, 202–1**
South America [sowth′ ə mĕr′ə kə] **202–2**

Countries and other locations

Afghanistan [ăf găn′ə stăn′] **203**
Albania [ăl bā′nē ə] **203**
Aleutian Islands [ə lōō′shən ī′ləndz] **200, 203**
Algeria [ăl jïr′ē ə] **203**
American Samoa [ə mĕr′ə kən sə mō′ə] **202**
Andaman Islands [ăn′də mən ī′ləndz] **203**
Angola [ăng gō′lə] **203**
Argentina [är′jən tē′nə] **202**
Armenia [är mē′nē ə] **203**
Austria [ö′strē ə] **203**
Azerbaijan [ăz′ər bī jän′] **203**
Azores [ā′zörz] **202**
Baffin Island [băf′ən ī′lənd] **200**
Bahamas [bə hä′məz] **200, 202**
Bahrain [bä rān′] **203**
Bangladesh [bäng′glə dĕsh′, băng′–] **203**
Banks Island [bănks′ ī′lənd] **200**
Belarus [bē′lə rōōs′, byĕl′ə–] **203**
Belgium [bĕl′jəm] **203**
Belize [bə lēz′] **201, 202**
Benin [bə nĭn′, –nēn′] **203**
Bermuda Islands [bər myōō′də ī′ ləndz] **200, 202**
Bhutan [bōō tän′] **203**
Bolivia [bə lĭv′ē ə] **202**
Bosnia [bäz′nē ə] **203**
Botswana [bät swä′nə] **203**
Brazil [brə zĭl′] **202**
Brunei [brōō nī′] **203**
Bulgaria [bŭl gër′ē ə] **203**
Burkina Faso [bər kē′nə fä′sō] **203**
Burma [bür′mə] **203**
Burundi [bōō rōōn′dē] **203**
Cambodia [kăm bō′dē ə] **203**
Cameroon [kăm′ə rōōn′] **203**
Canada [kăn′ə də] **200, 202**
Canary Islands [kə nër′ē ī′ ləndz] **203**
Cape Verde [kăp′ vürd′] **202**
Central African Republic [sĕn′trəl ăf′rĭ kən rĭ pŭb′lĭk] **203**
Chad [chăd] **203**
Chile [chĭl′ē] **202**
China [chī′nə] **203**
Colombia [kə lŭm′bē ə] **202**
Comoros [kăm′ə rōz] **203**
Congo [käng′gō] **203**
Cook Islands [kŏŏk′ ī′ləndz] **202**
Corsica [kör′sĭ kə] **203**
Costa Rica [kōs′tə rē′kə, käs′–] **201, 202**
Croatia [krō ā′shə] **203**
Cuba [kyōō′bə] **201, 202**
Cyprus [sī′prəs] **203**
Czech Republic [chĕk′ rĭ pŭb′lĭk] **203**
Democratic Republic of the Congo [dĕm′ə krăt′ĭk rĭ pŭb′lĭk əv dhə käng′gō] **203**
Denmark [dĕn′märk] **203**
Devon Island [dĕv′ən ī′lənd] **200**
Djibouti [jĭ bōō′tē] **203**
Dominican Republic [də mĭn′ĭ kən rĭ pŭb′lĭk] **201, 202**
Ecuador [ĕk′wə dör′] **202**
Egypt [ē′jĭpt] **203**
Ellesmere Island [ĕl′əs mïr′ ī′lənd] **200**
El Salvador [ĕl săl′və dör′] **201, 202**
Equatorial Guinea [ē′kwə tör′ē əl gĭn′ē, ĕk′wə–] **203**
Eritrea [ĕr′ə trē′ə] **203**
Estonia [ĕ stō′nē ə] **203**
Ethiopia [ē′thē ō′pē ə] **203**
Federated States of Micronesia [fĕ′də rā′təd stāts′ əv mī′krə nē′zhə] **203**
Fiji [fē′jē] **203**
Finland [fĭn′lənd] **203**
France [frăns] **203**
Franz Josef Land [fränz′ yō′səf lănd′] **203**
French Guiana [frĕnch′ gē ăn′ə, –ä′nə] **202**
French Polynesia [frĕnch′ päl′ə nē′zhə] **202**
Gabon [gă bōn′] **203**
Galápagos Islands [gə lä pə gōs ī′ləndz] **202**
Gambia [găm′bē ə] **203**
Georgia [jör′jə] **203**
Germany [jür′mə nē] **203**
Ghana [gä′nə] **203**
Greater Antilles [grā′tər ăn tĭl′ēz] **201**
Greece [grēs] **203**
Greenland [grēn′lənd, –lănd′] **200, 202**
Guam [gwäm] **203**
Guatemala [gwä′tə mä′lə] **201, 202**
Guinea [gĭn′ē] **203**
Guinea-Bissau [gĭn′ē bĭ sow′] **203**
Guyana [gī ăn′ə] **202**
Haiti [hā′tē] **201, 202**
Hawaiian Islands [hə wī′ən ī′lənds] **200, 202**
Hispaniola [hĭs′pən yō′lə] **201**
Honduras [hän dŏŏr′əs] **201, 202**
Hong Kong [häng′ käng′] **203**
Hungary [hŭng′gə rē] **203**
Iceland [īs′lənd] **203**
India [ĭn′dē ə] **203**
Indonesia [ĭn′də nē′zhə] **203**
Iran [ĭ rän′, ī răn′] **203**
Iraq [ĭ räk′, ī răk′] **203**
Ireland [īr′lənd] **203**
Israel [ĭz′rē əl, –rā–] **203**
Italy [ĭt′l ē] **203**
Ivory Coast [īv′rē kōst′] **203**
Jamaica [jə mā′kə] **201, 202**
Japan [jə păn′] **203**
Jordan [jör′dn] **203**
Kazakhstan [kä′zäk stän′] **203**
Kenya [kĕn′yə, kēn′–] **203**
Kiribati [kïr′ə băs′] **203**
Kuwait [kōō wāt′] **203**
Kyrgyzstan [kïr′gĭ stän′, –stăn′] **203**
Laos [lows, lä′ōs] **203**
Latvia [lăt′vē ə] **203**
Lebanon [lĕb′ə nən, –năn′] **203**
Lesotho [lə sō′tō, –sōō′tōō] **203**
Lesser Antilles [lĕ′sər ăn tĭl′ēz] **201, 202**
Liberia [lī bïr′ē ə] **203**
Libya [lĭb′ē ə] **203**
Lithuania [lĭth′ōō ā′nē ə] **203**
Luxembourg [lŭk′səm bürg′] **203**
Macedonia [măs′ə dō′nē ə] **203**
Madagascar [măd′ə găs′kər] **203**
Madeira Islands [mə dïr′ə ī′ləndz] **203**
Malawi [mə lä′wē] **203**
Malaysia [mə lā′zhə] **203**
Maldives [möl′dēvz, mäl′–] **203**
Mali [mä′lē] **203**
Malta [möl′tə] **203**
Marshall Islands [mär′shəl ī′ləndz] **203**
Mauritania [mör′ə tā′nē ə] **203**
Mauritius [mö rĭsh′əs] **203**
Mexico [mĕk′sĭ kō′] **200, 201, 202**
Moldova [möl dō′və, mäl–] **203**
Monaco [män′ə kō′] **203**
Mongolia [mäng gō′lē ə] **203**
Montenegro [män′tə nē′grō, –nĕ′–] **203**
Morocco [mə räk′ō] **203**
Mozambique [mō′zəm bēk′] **203**
Namibia [nə mĭb′ē ə] **203**
Nepal [nə pöl′, –päl′] **203**
Netherlands [nĕdh′ər ləndz] **203**
New Caledonia [nōō′ kăl′ə dō′nē ə] **203**
New Zealand [nōō′ zē′lənd] **203**
Nicaragua [nĭk′ə rä′gwə] **201, 202**
Niger [nī′jər, nē zhër′] **203**
Nigeria [nī jïr′ē ə] **203**
Northern Mariana Islands [nördh′ərn mä′rē ä′nə ī′ləndz] **203**
North Korea [nörth′ kə rē′ə] **203**
Norway [nör′wā] **203**
Oman [ō män′] **203**
Pakistan [păk′ə stăn′] **203**
Palau [pə low′] **203**
Panama [păn′ə mä′] **201, 202**
Papua New Guinea [păp′yōō ə nōō′ gĭn′ē] **203**
Paraguay [păr′ə gwī′, –gwā′] **202**
Peru [pə rōō′] **202**
Philippines [fĭl′ə pēnz′, fĭl′ə pēnz′] **203**
Poland [pō′lənd] **203**
Portugal [pör′chə gəl] **203**
Puerto Rico [pwĕr′tə rē′kō, pör′tə–] **201, 202**
Qatar [kä′tär, kə tär′] **203**
Romania [rō mā′nē ə, rōō–] **203**
Russia [rŭsh′ə] **203**
Rwanda [rōō än′də] **203**
Samoa [sə mō′ə] **202**
Saudi Arabia [sow′dē ə rā′bē ə, sö′dē–] **203**
Senegal [sĕn′ə göl′, –gäl′] **203**
Serbia [sür′bē ə] **203**
Seychelles [sā shĕlz′, –shĕl′] **203**
Sierra Leone [sē ër′ə lē ōn′, –lē ō′nē] **203**
Singapore [sĭng′ə pör′] **203**
Slovakia [slō vä′kē ə] **203**
Slovenia [slō vē′nē ə] **203**
Society Islands [sə sī′ə tē ī′ləndz] **202**
Solomon Islands [säl′ə mən ī′ləndz] **203**

Somalia [sə mä′lē ə] **203**
South Africa [sowth′ ăf′rĭ kə] **203**
South Georgia [sowth′ jör′jə] **202**
South Korea [sowth′ kə rē′ə] **203**
Spain [spān] **203**
Sri Lanka [srē′ läng′kə, shrē′–] **203**
Sudan [so͞o dăn′] **203**
Suriname [so͝or′ə nä′mə] **202**
Svalbard [sväl′bärd] **203**
Swaziland [swä′zē lănd′] **203**
Sweden [swēd′n] **203**
Switzerland [swĭt′sər lənd] **203**
Syria [sĭr′ē ə] **203**
Tahiti [tə hē′tē] **202**
Taiwan [tī′wän′] **203**
Tajikistan [tä jĭk′ə stăn′, –stän′] **203**
Tanzania [tăn′zə nē′ə] **203**
Tasmania [tăz mā′nē ə] **203**
Thailand [tī′lănd′, –lənd] **203**
Togo [tō′gō] **203**
Tonga [täng′gə] **202**
Tunisia [to͞o nē′zhə] **203**
Turkey [tür′kē] **203**
Turkmenistan [türk mĕn′ə stăn′, –stän′] **203**
Uganda [yo͞o găn′də] **203**
Ukraine [yo͞o′krān, yo͞o krān′] **203**
United Arab Emirates [yo͞o nī′təd ăr′əb ĕm′ər əts] **203**
United Kingdom [yo͞o nī′təd kĭng′dəm] **203**
United States of America
[yo͞o nī′təd stāts′ əv ə mĕr′ə kə] **200, 202**
Uruguay [yo͝or′ə gwī′, –gwā′] **202**
Uzbekistan [o͝oz bĕk′ə stăn′, –stän′] **203**
Vanuatu [vä′no͞o ä′to͞o] **203**
Venezuela [vĕn′ə zwā′lə] **202**
Victoria Island [vĭk′tör ē ə ī′lənd] **200**
Vietnam [vē′ĕt näm′, –năm′] **203**
Wake Island [wāk′ ī′lənd] **203**
Western Sahara [wĕs′tərn sə hăr′ə] **203**
Yemen [yĕm′ən] **203**
Zambia [zăm′bē ə] **203**
Zanzibar [zăn′zə bär] **203**
Zimbabwe [zĭm bäb′wā] **203**

Bodies of water
Arctic Ocean [ärk′tĭk ō′shən] **200, 203**
Atlantic Ocean [ət lăn′ tĭk ō′shən] **200, 202–203**
Baffin Bay [băf′ən bā′] **200, 202**
Baltic Sea [böl′tĭk sē′] **203**
Beaufort Sea [bō′fərt sē′] **200**
Bering Sea [bër′ĭng sē′, bïr′–] **200**
Black Sea [blăk′ sē′] **203**
Caribbean Sea [kăr′ə bē′ən sē′, kə rĭb′ē ən–] **201**
Caspian Sea [kăs′pē ən sē′] **203**
Coral Sea [kör′əl sē′] **203**
Gulf of Alaska [gŭlf′ əv ə lăs′kə] **200, 202**
Gulf of California [gŭlf′ əv kăl′ə förn′yə] **200**
Gulf of Mexico [gŭlf′ əv mĕk′sĭ kō′] **200, 202**
Hudson Bay [hŭd′sən bā′] **200, 202**
Indian Ocean [ĭn′dē ən ō′shən] **203**
Labrador Sea [lăb′rə dör′ sē′] **200**
Mediterranean Sea [mĕd′ə tə rā′nē ən sē′] **203**
North Atlantic Ocean [nörth′ ət lăn′tĭk ō′shən] **202**
North Pacific Ocean [nörth′ pə sĭf′ĭk ō′shən] **202, 203**
North Sea [nörth′ sē′] **203**
Pacific Ocean [pə sĭf′ĭk ō′shən] **200, 202, 203**
Philippine Sea [fĭl′ə pēn′ sē′] **203**
Red Sea [rĕd′ sē′] **203**
South Atlantic Ocean [sowth′ ət lăn′tĭk ō′shən] **203**
Southern Ocean [sŭdh′ərn ō′shən] **203**
South Pacific Ocean [sowth′ pə sĭf′ĭk ō′shən] **202, 203**

The United States of America
Capital: Washington, D.C. (District of Columbia)
[wä′shĭng tən dē′sē′, wö′–] **200**

Regions of the United States
Mid–Atlantic States [mĭd′ət lăn′tĭk stāts′] **201**–10
Midwest [mĭd′wĕst′] **201**–9
New England [no͞o′ ĭng′glənd] **201**–11
Pacific States [pə sĭf′ĭk stāts′] **201**–7
Rocky Mountain States [räk′ē mown′tn stāts′] **201**–8
South [sowth] **201**–13
Southeast [sowth′ēst′] **201**–13
Southwest [sowth′wĕst′] **201**–12
West Coast [wĕst′ kōst′] **201**–7

States of the United States
Alabama [ăl′ə băm′ə] **200**
Alaska [ə lăs′kə] **200, 202**
Arizona [ăr′ə zō′nə] **200**
Arkansas [är′kən sö′] **200**
California [kăl′ə förn′yə] **200**
Colorado [käl′ə răd′ō, –ra′dō] **200**
Connecticut [kə nĕt′ĭ kət] **200**
Delaware [dĕl′ə wër′] **200**
Florida [flör′ə də, flär′–] **200**
Georgia [jör′jə] **200**
Hawaii [hə wī′ē] **200**
Idaho [ī′də hō′] **200**
Illinois [ĭl′ə noy′] **200**
Indiana [ĭn′dē ăn′ə] **200**
Iowa [ī′ə wə] **200**
Kansas [kăn′zəs] **200**
Kentucky [kən tŭk′ē] **200**
Louisiana [lo͞o ē′zē ăn′ə] **200**
Maine [mān] **200**
Maryland [mër′ə lənd] **200**
Massachusetts [măs′ə cho͞o′səts] **200**
Michigan [mĭsh′ĭ gən] **200**
Minnesota [mĭn′ə sō′tə] **200**
Mississippi [mĭs′ə sĭp′ē] **200**
Missouri [mə zo͝or′ē, –zo͝or′ə] **200**
Montana [män tăn′ə] **200**
Nebraska [nə brăs′kə] **200**
Nevada [nə văd′ə, –vä′də] **200**
New Hampshire [no͞o′ hămp′shər] **200**
New Jersey [no͞o′ jür′zē] **200**
New Mexico [no͞o′ mĕk′sĭ kō′] **200**
New York [no͞o′ yörk′] **200**
North Carolina [nörth′ kăr′ə lī′nə] **200**
North Dakota [nörth′ də kō′tə] **200**
Ohio [ō hī′ō] **200**
Oklahoma [ō′klə hō′mə] **200**
Oregon [ör′ĭ gən, –gän′, är′–] **200**
Pennsylvania [pĕn′səl vān′yə] **200**
Rhode Island [rōd′ ī′lənd] **200**
South Carolina [sowth′ kăr′ə lī′nə] **200**
South Dakota [sowth′ də kō′tə] **200**
Tennessee [tĕn′ə sē′] **200**
Texas [tĕk′səs] **200**
Utah [yo͞o′tö, –tä] **200**
Vermont [vər mänt′] **200**
Virginia [vər jĭn′yə] **200**
Washington [wä′shĭng tən, wö′–] **200**
West Virginia [wĕst′ vər jĭn′yə] **200**
Wisconsin [wĭs kän′sən] **200**
Wyoming [wī ō′mĭng] **200**

Canada
Capital: Ottawa [ät′ə wə] **201**

Regions of Canada
British Columbia [brĭt′ĭsh kə lŭm′bē ə] **201**–2
Maritime Provinces [mër′ə tīm präv′ən səz] **201**–6
Northern Canada [nör′dhərn kăn′ə də] **201**–1
Ontario [än tër′ē ō′] **201**–4
Prairie Provinces [prër′ē präv′ən səz] **201**–3
Québec [kwĭ bĕk′] **201**–5

Provinces of Canada
Alberta [ăl bür′tə] **200**
British Columbia [brĭt′ĭsh kə lŭm′bē ə] **200**
Manitoba [măn′ə tō′bə] **200**
New Brunswick [no͞o′ brŭnz′wĭk] **200**
Newfoundland and Labrador
[no͞o′fən lənd ən lă′brə dör′] **200**
Northwest Territories [nörth′wĕst′ tër′ə tör′ēz] **200**
Nova Scotia [nō′və skō′shə] **200**
Nunavut [no͞o′nə vo͝ot′] **200**
Ontario [än tër′ē ō′] **200**
Prince Edward Island [prĭns′ ĕd′wərd ī′lənd] **200**
Québec [kwĭ bĕk′] **200**
Saskatchewan [să skăch′ə wən, –wän′] **200**
Yukon [yo͞o′kän] **200**

Mexico
Capital: Mexico (City) [mĕk′sĭ kō′ (sĭt′ē)] **201**

Regions of Mexico
Chiapas Highlands [chē ä′pəs hī′ləndz] **201**–18
Gulf Coastal Plain [gŭlf′ kō′stəl plān′] **201**–16
Pacific Northwest [pə sĭf′ĭk nörth′wĕst] **201**–14
Plateau of Mexico [plă tō′ əv mĕk′sĭ kō′] **201**–15
Southern Uplands [sŭdh′ərn ŭp′ləndz] **201**–17
Yucatan Peninsula
[yo͞o′kə tăn′ pə nĭn′sə lə, yo͞o′kə tăn′–] **201**–19

States of Mexico
Aguascalientes [ä′gwəs käl yĕn′tās] **201**
Baja California Norte [bä′hä kăl′ə förn′yə nör′tā] **200**
Baja California Sur [bä′hä kăl′ə förn′yə so͝or′] **200**
Campeche [kăm pā′chā, kăm pē′chē] **201**
Chiapas [chē ä′pəs] **201**
Chihuahua [chĭ wä′wä, –wə] **200**
Coahuila [kō′ə wē′lə] **200**
Colima Michoacán [kə lē′mə mē′chō ə kän′] **201**
Distrito Federal [dĭ strē′tō fĕd′ə räl′] **201**
Durango [do͞o răng′gō, –räng′–] **201**

Geographical Index

Guanajuato [gwä/nə hwä/tō] **201**
Guerrero [gə rĕr/ō] **201**
Hidalgo [hĭ dăl/gō, ē dhäl/gō] **201**
Jalisco [hə lĭs/kō, –lēs/–] **201**
México [mĕk/sĭ kō/, mĕ/hē kō] **201**
Morelos [mö rĕl/ōs] **201**
Nayarit [nä/yə rēt/] **201**
Nuevo León [nwā/vō lā ōn/] **200**
Oaxaca [wə hä/kə, wä–] **201**
Puebla [pwĕb/lä] **201**
Querétaro [kə rĕt/ə rō/] **201**
Quintana Roo [kēn tä/nə rō/] **201**
San Luis Potosí [sän/ lo͞o ēs/ pō/tə sē/] **201**
Sinaloa [sē/nə lō/ə] **200**
Sonora [sə nör/ə] **200**
Tabasco [tə băs/kō] **201**
Tamaulipas [tä/mow lē/pəs] **201**
Tlaxcala [tlä skä/lə] **201**
Veracruz [vĕr/ə kro͞oz/, –kro͞os/] **201**
Yucatán [yo͞o/kə tăn/, –tän/] **201**
Zacatecas [zä/kə tā/kəs, sä/–] **201**

Index 索引

アーチェリー **228**–1
アーティチョーク **69**–22
アーム **194**–23
R&B／ソウル **237**–28
RV（レクリエーションビークル）車 **156**–10
I形鋼 **178**–3
あいさつする **3**–G
アイシャドー **109**–35
アイスクリーム **72**–26
アイスクリームコーン **79**–13
アイスクリーム屋 **131**–16
アイススケート **227**–4
アイススケート靴 **231**–9
アイスティー **79**–12
アイスパック **117**–13
アイスホッケー **229**–13
アイデアを出す **191**–F
相手の目を見る **174**–J
アイデンティティ窃盗 **142**–9
アイフック **180**–40
アイライナー **109**–36
アイリス **211**–16
アイロン **101**–13
アイロンのかかったシャツ **101**–20
アイロン台 **101**–14
合う項目を選ぶ **9**–T
青色のセーターは赤色のセーターの下にあります **25**–5
青色 **24**–3
アオカスケ **214**–6
青緑色 **24**–9
青緑色のセーターは箱の中にあります **25**–6
青物市（ファーマーズマーケット） **84–85**
赤色 **24**–1
赤色のセーターは青色のセーターの上にあります **25**–4
赤毛 **33**–15
赤ちゃん **31**–7
赤ちゃんの部屋 **47**–10
明るい道を選ぶ **143**–B
秋 **21**–39
空部屋の表示 **50**–7
握手する **3**–J, **174**–I
アクション／アドベンチャー **237**–19
アクセス番号 **14**–16
アクセル **159**–46
アクリル絵具 **232**–10
あご **106**–1
アコーディオン **238**–19
あごひげ **33**–6
朝 **18**–15
麻 **98**–2
アザラシ **213**–34
脚 **105**–9
足（くるぶしから下） **104**–8
アジア **202**–4
アシカ **213**–33
足首 **106**–23
足首の捻挫 **110**–18
明日 **20**–6
脚と足 **106**
足場 **178**–4
味わう **106**–D
アスパラガス **69**–26
遊びに行く場所 **222–223**
遊び場 **50**–3
暖かい **13**–4
温かいシリアル **80**–9
暖かい服 **146**–6
アダプタ **234**–15
頭 **104**–1
新しい仕事 **172**–3
新しい単語を学ぶ **8**
暑い **13**–3, **42**–1
厚い本 **23**–7
厚手のジャケット **97**–27
アップリケ **99**–31
宛先の住所 **134**–22
宛先のメールアドレスをタイプする **197**–C
宛名ラベル **183**–41
兄 **34**–6
姉 **34**–5
アパート **50–51**
アパートの入り口 **51**
アパートの建物 **50**–1
アパートを借りる **48**
アパート番号 **4**–6
アフターシェーブローション **109**–30
油 **73**–31
油1カップ **75**–2
油絵具 **233**–19
アフリカ **202**–5
アフロヘア用コーム **108**–15
アボカド **84**–6
アポストロフィ **190**–16
甘いもの **84**–8
雨靴 **90**–20
雨どい **53**–4
網戸 **53**–15
編み棒 **233**–23
編み物をする **233**–F
雨 **13**–11
アメリカンチーズ **71**–26
アメリカ先住民 **198**–3
アメリカ史 **198**
アメリカ合衆国の各地方 **201**
アメリカ杉 **210**–18
あやまる **12**–F
アライグマ **216**–13
アラスカ時間 **19**–28
あり **63**–23
アリクイ **217**–24
アルコール類は飲まないでください **112**–F
アルファベット **7**–13
アルファルファ **177**–5
アルマジロ **216**–8
アルミホイル **72**–23
アレルギー **111**–8
アレルギー反応を起こす **116**–E
泡立て器 **78**–21
アンクルソックス **91**–7
アンクレットソックス **91**–11
暗唱番号を隠す **143**–C
暗証番号を入力する **132**–E
安心して **42**–15
アンズ **68**–12
安全規則 **164**–6
安全ゴーグル **179**–11
安全上の欠陥と危険物質 **179**
安全装備 **179**
安全なウェブサイトで買い物する **143**–H
安全パッド **59**–4
安全ピン **37**–9, **100**–14
安全ブーツ **179**–20
安全眼鏡 **92**–10, **179**–10
アンダーシャツ **91**–1
アンテナ **14**–9
案内係 **82**–2
案内広告 **48**–2
案内板 **131**–24
胃 **107**–41
ESL／ESOL（第二言語としての英語） **189**–14
イーゼル **233**–18
Eチケット **161**–19
家で学習する **10**–D
家と庭 **53**
家に帰る **39**–R
家の掃除をする **39**–O
家の問題と修理 **62**–63
家を買う **41**–M, **49**
家を見つける **48–49**
家を見る **49**–H
イカ **212**–7
いかだ乗り **226**–2
行き止まり **154**–6
イグニション **159**–33
池 **204**–21
生垣を刈り込む **176**–B
意見 **44**–3
医師 **118**–5
意識を失う **116**–A
医師助手 **168**–47
医師のアドバイスに従う **114**–J
医師の診察を受ける **114**–A
移住 **199**–12
移住する **40**–C
衣装 **239**–11
椅子 **7**–11
イソギンチャク **212**–24
痛い **42**–11
板チョコ **73**–37
痛み **115**–3
炒めた牛肉 **76**–6
一 **16**
1カートンの卵 **74**–16
1月 **21**–25
イチゴ **68**–14
1時 **18**–6
イチジク **68**–27
1時5分 **18**–7
1時5分すぎ **18**–7
1時30分 **18**–11
1時30分すぎ **18**–11
1時15分 **18**–9
1時15分過ぎ **18**–9
1時10分 **18**–8
1時10分すぎ **18**–8
一時停止する **235**–E
1時20分 **18**–10
1時20分すぎ **18**–10
1時45分 **18**–13
1時40分 **18**–12
1ドル **26**–7
1ドル硬貨 **26**–6
1日の時間 **18**
1パックのカッテージチーズ **74**–17
一番 **16**
1ブロック進んでファーストストリートまで行く **155**–F
一万 **16**
胃痛 **110**–4
1巻のペーパータオル **74**–23
1斤のパン **74**–22
1個のレタス **69**–32
一緒に遊ぶ **36**–M
1セント **26**–1
1反の布 **98**–15
いっぱいに入ったコップ **23**–9
一般的な疾患と子供がよくかかる病気 **111**
一方通行 **154**–3
1本の練り歯みがき **74**–24
1本の水 **74**–13
糸 **100**–11
糸 **99**–23
移動クレーン **178**–5
糸切り **100**–18
糸くずを取り除く **101**–D
いとこ **34**–9
糸のこ **180**–10
稲光り **13**–17
犬 **215**–11
犬を散歩させる **129**–F
胃の食用部分 **70**–8
衣服製作者 **167**–29

衣服の説明 **96–97**
衣服の比較 **97**
衣服の問題 **97**
衣服を縫う **170**–L
イブニングドレス **89**–18
違法薬物 **142**–6
異母(異父)兄弟 **35**–28
異母(異父)姉妹 **35**–27
移民 **199**–13
妹 **34**–5
イモムシ **214**–20
イモリ **212**–26
いやな **42**–7
イライラする **64**–6
入口 **50**, **164**–1
医療 **118**
医療衣 **93**–31
医療記録事務員 **168**–39
医療廃棄物用ごみ箱 **121**–31
イルカ **213**–31
刺青 **32**–18
入れ歯 **119**–10
色 **24**
いろいろな職業訓練 **172**
岩 **208**–6
祝う **206**–C
インクカートリッジ **183**–45
インクジェットプリンタ **183**–18
インクパッド **183**–46
イングリッシュマフィン **80**–5
インゲン **69**–8
インコ **215**–15
印刷工 **169**–50
飲酒運転 **142**–5
飲酒運転をしない **143**–G
インターネット **197**
インターネット地図 **155**–12
インターネット電話 **14**–20
インターネットの求人募集サイトをチェックする **173**–D
インターネット物件リスト **48**–1
インターホン **50**–5
インターンシップ **172**–6
引退する **41**–O
インチ [in.] **17**–15
インフルエンザ **111**–2
引用 **190**–9
インラインスケート **228**–10
インラインスケート靴 **231**–10
ウィンカー **158**–6, **159**–34
ウィンタースポーツとウォータースポーツ **227**
ウィンドサーフィン **227**–10
ウィンドブレーカー **90**–24
ウール **98**–3
ウエイター **82**–8, **185**–15
ウェイト **231**–22
ウエイトレス **83**–9
ウェーブした髪 **33**–10
植木に水をやる **176**–F
ウエストバンド **100**–5
ウェットスーツ **225**–4
ウェットティッシュ **146**–12
ウェブカメラ **196**–12
ウェブページ内を移動する **197**
植える **177**–A
うがいする **109**–L
請負業者 **186**–5
受け皿 **83**–25
受付エリア **182**–15
受付係 **118**–2, **164**–5, **169**–51, **182**–14
ウサギ **215**–13
牛 **215**–1
薄い本 **23**–8
薄型テレビ **234**–7
薄手のジャケット **97**–28
右折のみ **154**–7
歌を歌う **238**–B
打ち身 **110**–12
宇宙 **205**
宇宙ステーション **205**–18
宇宙飛行士 **205**–17
打つ **230**–B
美しい眺め **23**–21
打つ(ゴルフクラブで) **230**–Q
うつ病 **115**–5
腕 **105**–14
腕、手、指 **106**
腕時計 **94**–16
ウナギ **212**–12
ウニ **212**–21
乳母車 **37**–20
馬 **215**–4
生まれる **40**–A
海／水 **225**–1
海の生物 **212**
裏庭 **53**
売上税 **27**–8
売り子 **84**–7
売り手に車について尋ねる **157**–B
雨林 **204**–1
ウルシ **210**–24
うれしい **43**–31, **44**–5
ウレタンフォームパッド **226**–13
うろこ **212**–3
運営管理者 **120**–13
運転教習を受ける **137**–G
運転試験に合格する **137**–H
運転台 **156**–16
運転免許証 **40**–4, **136**–9
運転免許証番号 **136**–11
運動靴 **86**–7
運動する **39**–P
エアコン **159**–39
エアバッグ **159**–43
エアロビクスエクササイズ **122**–5
エイ **212**–11
映画 **222**–2
映画館 **126**–6
鋭角 **193**–28
映画の種類 **237**
英国兵士 **198**–9
英作文 **190–191**
永住権カード **40**–2
衛星 **205**–20
衛星放送受信アンテナ **53**–6
HIV(ヒト免疫不全ウイルス) **111**–17
ATM(現金自動預入支払機) **132**
ATMカード **132**–15
ATMカードを挿入する **132**–D
栄養士 **120**–15
液体の計量 **75**
エクササイズ／運動する **230**–N
エクササイズして健康を維持する **114**–E
エクスクラメーションマーク **190**–13
エクスプレスメール(速達) **134**–2
絵辞典 **7**–31
SF **237**–18
エスカレーター **131**–23
SKU(在庫)番号 **27**–5
SUV(スポーツユーティリティ車) **156**–7
枝 **210**–2
枝角 **216**–16
エネルギー源 **218**
エネルギー効率の高い電球を使う **219**–H
エネルギーと資源の節約方法 **219**
エネルギーと資源の節約 **218–219**
絵の表す意味を示す **9**–V
エビ **212**–18
絵筆 **233**–20
エプロン **92**–11
絵本 **133**–12
MP3プレーヤー **234**–2
えら **212**–2
襟 **100**–4
襟ぐりの大きいセーター **96**–10
LCDプロジェクタ **6**–6, **235**–29
エルムストリートをまっすぐ進む **155**–A
エレベーター **50**–9, **131**–21, **184**–9
絵を描く **8**–F, **233**–E
円 **193**–34
沿海州 **201**–6
宴会場 **184**–26, **185**–14
沿岸警備隊 **138**–18
演劇 **223**–8
演算 **192**
エンジニア **167**–25
円周 **193**–36
円周率 **193**–46
援助を求める **10**–F
エンジン **158**–18
円錐 **193**–40
縁石 **129**–21
演説する **148**–A
演台 **206**–5
延滞料を支払う **133**–E
円柱 **193**–41
延長コード **181**–14
煙突 **53**–5
鉛筆 **7**–20
鉛筆削り **7**–23
鉛筆を置く **6**–J
鉛筆を手に取る **6**–I
尾 **216**–22
甥 **34**–19
オイルをチェックする **157**–H
応急処置 **117**
応急処置の手引書 **117**–2
応急手当 **117**
横断歩道 **128**–15, **154**–13
横断幕 **44**–1
往復 **152**–17
応募用紙に記入する **173**–J
OHP **7**–16
大枝 **210**–3
大型冷凍庫 **185**–3
オオカミ **216**–5
大きい手 **23**–2
大きすぎる **97**–38
オークストリートを左に曲がる **155**–C
オーケストラを指揮する **238**–C
大皿 **55**–20
オーストラリア **202**–6
オーディオブック **133**–17
オートクラブのカード **162**–4
オートバイ **150**–4
オートマチックトランスミッション **159**
オーバーイージー(両面を焼いた目玉焼きで、黄身は半熟のもの) **76**–11
オーバーオール **88**–6
オーブン **54**–20
オープンカー **156**–5
オーブンクリーナー **61**–3
オーブンで焼く **77**–H
オーブントースター **54**–15
オーブンを掃除する **60**–C
オーブンを予熱する **77**–A
オーボエ **238**–3
丘 **204**–16
お金を返す **26**–D
お金を貸す **26**–C
お金を借りる **26**–B
オキシドール **117**–9
置物 **232**–1
起きる **38**–B
屋上 **50**–4
奥行き **17**–18

送り部分 **98**–20
「お元気ですか」と尋ねる **2**–B
怒って **43**–29
押さえ金 **98**–19
伯父 **34**–8
叔父 **34**–8
数える **84**–A, **170**–Q
おじぎする **3**–H
押込み **142**–2
押しピン **183**–35
おしゃぶり **37**–24
おしり拭き **37**–15
おしろい **109**–41
汚染 **218**
遅い **19**–24
恐れて **43**–23
おそろい **28**–3
おたふく風邪 **111**–7
おたま **78**–7
落ち着いた **42**–8
落ち着きを失わない **147**–E
オックスフォードシューズ **95**–29
夫 **34**–13
弟 **34**–6
弦楽器 **238**
男 **4**–17
落とす **109**–Q
おとなしい子供 **23**–12
大人と子供 **30**–31
踊る **64**–A
驚いて **43**–30
お腹がいっぱいの **42**–6
お腹がすいた **42**–5
同じ色 **23**–15
オニオンリング **79**–4
斧 **180**–3
伯母 **34**–7
叔母 **34**–7
おびえて **43**–23
オヒョウのステーキ **71**–6
オフィス **164**–3, **182**–183
オフィスビル **124**–2
オフィスマネージャー **182**–8
オペラ **223**–11
オペレータ **14**–21
お弁当を作る **38**–F
お盆 **55**–17
お盆を運ぶ **82**–H
おまる **37**–12, **121**–23
おむつ交換台 **59**–1
おむつ交換用のパッド **59**–2
おむつ外しトレーニング用パンツ **37**–11
おむつを替える **36**–G
オムレツ **76**–12
お面 **239**–9
重い症状と病気 **111**
重い箱 **23**–13
重さ **75**
重さと計量 **75**
面白い写真 **206**–2
おもちゃやゲーム **59**
おもちゃをしまう **60**–G
おもちゃ屋 **130**–5
おもちゃ箱 **59**–16
おやすみのキスをする **36**–P
親指 **106**–16
お湯 **57**–9
泳ぐ **230**–L
オランウータン **217**–39
折りたたみ椅子 **102**–5
折りたたみ式テーブル **102**–4
オルガン **238**–20
オレンジ **68**–5
オレンジ色 **24**–4
オレンジ色のセーターは灰色のセーターの上にあります **25**–9
おろしがね **78**–2
音楽 **64**–3, **189**–16, **238**
音楽家 **168**–43
音楽の種類 **237**
温水器が故障している **62**–1
オンタリオ **201**–4
温度 **13**–8
雄鶏 **215**–7
女 **4**–18
オンラインカタログ **133**–11
オンラインコース **172**–8
オンラインで銀行取引を行う **132**–C
蚊 **214**–22
蛾 **214**–21
ガーゼ **117**–8
カーソル **197**–14
ガータースネーク **213**–39
ガーターベルト **91**–16
カーディガン **88**–2
ガーデニングをする **53**–B
カーテン **56**–16, **58**–7
カート **129**–28
カード **239**–5
カードショップ **130**–7
カードに文章を書く **135**–A
ガードル **91**–15
カードを受け取る **135**–F
カードを送る **135**
カードを取り出す **132**–G
カードを配達する **135**–E
カードを郵送する **135**–D
カードを読む **135**–G
カートン **74**–4
カーネーション **211**–20
カーペット **56**–24
カーペットに掃除機をかける **60**–H
カーラー **33**–19
ガーリックプレス **78**–11
ガーリックブレッド **81**–28
カーリングアイロン **108**–17
海王星 **205**–8
絵画 **56**–9
貝殻 **225**–24
海岸 **204**–10, **225**
会議室 **182**–4, **184**–25
会議の予定を入れる **171**–J
海軍 **138**–15
会計士 **166**–1
解決方法/回答についてアイデアを出し合う **8**–H
外見 **32**
外国語 **189**–13
外国語を話す **170**–N
会社経営者 **166**–11
会社を出る **38**–N
外周 **193**–43
海水パンツ **90**–22
階段 **50**–10, **53**–3
階段が壊れている **62**–7
階段を下りる **153**–D
階段を上る **153**–C
害虫駆除業者 **63**–21
懐中電灯 **146**–14
回転式改札口 **152**–8
回転ドア **184**–2
街灯 **148**–3
解答用紙 **10**–2
解答欄を塗りつぶす **10**–K
解答を確かめる **10**–L
買値を伝える **49**–I
海兵隊 **138**–17
買い物 **27**
買い物かご **73**–9
買い物リスト **67**–14
買い物をする **28**–A
海洋生物、両生類、爬虫類 **212–213**
海洋哺乳類 **213**
会話をする **11**–L
会話を始める **12**–A
下院 **138**–3
下院議員 **138**–4
買う **27**–G
カウボーイハット **92**–18
ガウン **91**–29, **206**–8
カウンセラー **5**–6
カエデ **210**–12
変える **148**–C
カエル **212**–25
顔 **106**
家屋 **46**–47
化学 **195**
科学 **189**–11, **194**–195
化学者 **195**–25
かかと **94**–22, **106**–24
鏡 **57**–18
鍵 **51**–30
カキ **71**–14
鍵が壊れている **62**–6
書き方の規則 **190**
鉤爪 **214**–2
かぎ針編み **233**–25
カギホック **99**–27
家禽 **70**
核 **194**–7, **195**–29
学習 **8**–9
角錐 **193**–39
学生 **6**–5
学生寮 **52**–8
家具付きアパート **48**–3
カクテルドレス **89**–20
角度 **193**
学童横断路 **154**–15
家具なしのアパート **48**–4
家具のつやだし **61**–8
家具のほこりをはらう **60**–A
家具屋 **126**–8
家具や備品 **59**
閣僚 **138**–10
隠れる **240**–D
家具を作る **170**–G
家具を配置する **49**–Q
家具を磨く **60**–E
掛ける **192**–C
傘 **90**–17
火災 **144**–8
飾り **99**, **239**–15
火山の噴火 **145**–16
華氏 **13**–1
家事 **60**
カシ **210**–17
貸金庫 **132**–7
加湿器 **113**–12
カシミア **98**–4
カジュアルな服装 **88**
カジュアルな服装、仕事着、フォーマルな服装 **88–89**
果樹園 **177**–10
ガス遮断バルブ **146**–4
カスタマーサービス係員 **167**–20
ガスメーター **62**–14
ガスレンジ **54**–18
風邪 **111**–1
火星 **205**–4
家政婦 **168**–34
風が強い **13**–18
風邪薬 **113**–27
仮説を立てる **195**–A
家族 **34**–35
ガソリンがなくなる **162**–E
ガソリンスタンド **125**–10
ガソリンスタンドの係員 **162**–3
肩 **105**–13

Index 索引

固い椅子 **23**–5
課題について考える **191**–E
型紙 **99**–22
カタツムリ **212**–22
片手鍋 **78**–25
肩までの髪 **33**–2
片道 **152**–16
花壇 **53**–20
花壇の雑草を抜く **176**–G
家畜 **177**–15
家畜とげっ歯類 **215**
家畜を入れる囲い **177**–17
月 **20**–3
がっかりする **28**–4
楽器を演奏する **238**–A
カッコ **190**–19
学校 **5**, **126**–9
学校での1日 **11**
学校で良い成績を収める **10**
学校登録用の用紙 **4**
学校と科目 **188–189**
学校まで車で連れていく **38**–G
喝采する **148**–B
活動家 **199**–17
カップル **239**–4
カツレツ用子牛肉 **70**–6
家庭菜園 **53**–27
家電製品修理人 **166**–4
家電製品を修理する **170**–J
角 **128**–7
角で止まる **155**–D
角を走って曲がる **153**–H
悲しい **43**–19
カナダの各地方 **201**
カナダ北部 **201**–1
金物店 **148**–4
カニ **71**–9, **212**–20
カヌー乗り **226**–3
可燃性の液体 **179**–8
カバ **217**–43
カバーオール **92**–8
カバーオール寝巻き **91**–27
カバーレターを書く **173**–G
カバノキ **210**–7
花びん **55**–23
カブ **69**–16
カフェインレスコーヒー **81**–37
カフェテリア **5**–14
カプセル **113**–23
カブトムシ **214**–18
カプリパンツ **88**–8
壁 **56**–10
壁紙 **59**–8
かぼちゃの提灯 **239**–10
髪 **104**–2
紙おむつ **37**–10
髪型の特徴 **33**
紙裁断機 **183**–22
かみそり **109**–27
かみそりの刃 **109**–28
髪にブラシをかける **108**–I
紙の着せ替え人形 **233**–28
髪のスタイリング **33**
紙吹雪 **239**–3
髪を洗う **108**–E
紙を1枚取り出す **9**–Y
髪を乾かす **108**–H
髪を切る **33**–A
髪をすすぐ **108**–F
髪をセットする **33**–C
髪を染める **33**–D
髪をとかす **108**–G
髪を分ける **33**–4
カメラケース **235**–28
鴨 **214**–12
貨物用バン **156**–13
カモ肉 **70**–18
カモノハシ **217**–46
火曜日 **20**–10
がらがら **37**–26
ガラガラヘビ **213**–38
ガラスクリーナー **61**–14
ガラスの引き戸 **53**–18
ガラスワイパー **61**–15
体 **104–105**
体の内側と外側 **106–107**
体を洗うタオル **57**–6
空のコップ **23**–10
刈込みばさみ **176**–11
カリフラワー **69**–14
仮免許を取る **137**–F
軽い箱 **23**–14
カルテ **121**–24
カレイ **212**–15
ガレージ **47**–14
ガレージセール **102–103**
ガレージドア **53**–7
瓦れきを片付ける **147**–M
枯葉をかき集める **176**–C
カレンダー **20**–21
川 **155**–10, **204**–3
革 **98**–6
かわいい **32**–14
乾いたシャツ **101**–18
革のジャケット **90**–4
缶 **74**–3
がん **111**–10
ガン **214**–13
眼科医 **120**–7
考えを整理する **191**–G
感覚 **106**
カンガルー **217**–44
カンガルーなどの腹袋 **217**–50
寒気 **110**–9
換気用マスク **92**–7
缶切り **78**–1, **146**–8
看護師 **118**–8, **168**–44
看護スタッフ **120**
観察する **195**–C
換算する **17**–D
かんし **195**–43
患者 **118**–6, **121**–18
感謝祭 **22**–17
疾患と症状 **111**
患者を助ける **170**–B
感情 **42–43**
勘定を払う **82**–I
関節炎 **111**–16
がん専門医 **120**–5
肝臓 **107**–40
乾燥機 **50**–13, **101**–4
乾燥機から洗濯物を取り出す **101**–E
乾燥機用柔軟剤シート **101**–5
元旦 **22**–9
簡単なチキンスープ **77**
簡単な問題 **23**–23
感嘆符 **190**–13
缶詰 **72**, **146**–9
感電の危険 **186**–6
感電する **116**–F
監督者 **165**–8
カントリー **237**–27
かんな **181**–57
干ばつ **145**–11
丸薬 **113**–21
観葉植物 **56**–4
観覧席 **5**–3
管理者 **5**
管理職者 **182**–5
管理人 **50**–8
管理人室 **51**
管理人に電話する **48**–A
木 **208**–1
キー **155**–6
キーウィ **68**–22
聞いたことを確認する **12**–N
キーパッド **14**–5
キーボード **196**–14
キーボードを使う **196**
黄色 **24**–2
黄色のセーターは左側にあります **25**–1
気温 **13**
幾何 **192**–17
議会 **138**–2
機械オペレータ **168**–37
気が転倒して **43**–28
飢饉 **145**–12
聞く **106**–B
キク **211**–21
危険 **186**–1
危険廃棄物 **218**–12
記号 **155**–5
岸 **204**–12
気象条件 **13**
奇数 **192**–3
傷口の縫合 **117**–15
キスする **3**–K
傷ついた **42**–16
季節 **21**
季節の衣服 **90**
規則 **64**–7
北 **155**–1
ギター **238**–9
北アメリカ **202**–1
北アメリカと中央アメリカ **200–201**
貴重品 **132**–8
きついズボン **97**–29
喫茶店 **126**–11
喫茶店のメニュー **80–81**
木づち **180**–2
キッチン **46**–5, **54**
キッチンタイマー **78**–18
キツツキ **214**–8
切手 **134**–23
切手販売機 **135**–11
切手ブックレット **134**–18
切手を貼る **135**–C
キツネ **216**–15
切符 **152**–15
切符売場 **152**–12
木と植物 **210**
機内で **161**
木ネジ **180**–33
記念日 **22**–3
昨日 **20**–7
技能検査 **172**–12
キノコ類 **69**–27
木のスプーン **78**–9
木の床 **58**–21
牙 **217**–48
基部 **194**–20
義父 **34**–11
ギプス **113**–20
ギフトカードを使う **27**–E
ギフトショップ **184**–5
気分が良い **42**–14
気分が悪い **42**–12
義母 **34**–10
基本色 **24**
基本的な交通機関 **150–151**
義務 **140**
客室 **184**–13
客室乗務員 **161**–12
脚注 **190**–10
キャセロール皿 **78**–10
脚立 **61**–13
薬局 **112–113**
キャッシュレジスターを使う **170**–S

キャッチする **230**–D
キャッチャーマスク **231**–15
キャベツ **69**–2
キャミソール **91**–21
キャラクター人形 **233**–26
キャリアカウンセラー **172**–10
キャリア計画 **172**
キャリア計画を立てる **172**
キャリアの道 **172**
キャンディ **239**–12
キャンディケーン **239**–17
キャンデーショップ **131**–17
キャンドル **56**–20
キャンドル立て **56**–21
キャンバス **233**–17
キャンパス **5**
キャンパス周辺 **5**
キャンピングカー **156**–9
キャンプ **226**–5
キャンプファイヤ **226**–11
キャンプ用コンロ **226**–16
九 **16**
911をダイヤルする **15**–E
休暇 **22**–6
球技場 **224**–1
救急医療士 **121**–32
救急救命士 **116**–2
救急車 **116**–1, **121**–34
救急の病状 **116**
救急箱 **117**–1, **146**–18
救急箱の中身 **117**
救急病院入口 **121**
救急用の医療腕輪 **117**–3
球根 **211**–2
給仕長 **185**–12
給仕人 **82**–9, **83**–9, **169**–56, **185**–8
九十 **16**
九十番 **16**
求人募集広告を見る **173**–B
求人募集の掲示を探す **173**–C
休憩を取る **11**–H
球体 **193**–42
牛肉 **70**
牛乳 **66**–5
牛乳1オンス **75**–1
牛乳1クォート **75**–4
九番 **16**
救命器具 **225**–20
救命胴衣 **161**–25, **226**–14
給与支払い担当者 **165**–10
給与明細書 **165**–11
キュウリ **69**–10
給料支払小切手 **165**–14
今日 **20**–5
教員助手 **5**–16
教会 **127**–14
教科書 **7**–25
競技場 **5**–2
峡谷 **204**–17
教師 **5**–8, **6**–4
教室 **5**–7, **6–7**
教室から出る **11**–O
教室に入る **11**–A
教室に戻る **11**–M
教室まで歩く **11**–C
教室まで走る **11**–D
教習を受ける **137**–B
矯正器 **119**–6
行政機関 **138**
競走する **230**–S
魚介類とお惣菜 **71**
曲線 **193**–23
霧が出ている **13**–20
切り傷 **110**–13
義理の兄弟 **34**–17
義理の姉妹 **34**–16
キリン **217**–32
着る **87**–B
キルト **58**–16
キルトブロック **232**–15
キルトを作る **232**–C
きれいなTシャツ **101**–16
きれいにする **76**–A
木を植える **176**–E, **219**–N
斤 **74**–10
銀河系 **205**–15
金管楽器 **238**
緊急事態が起こる前に **146**
緊急事態が発生したら **147**
緊急事態と自然災害 **144–145**
緊急事態発生後 **147**
緊急事態を説明する **15**–G
緊急時に備えてプランを立てる **146**–A
緊急時のガイド **161**–26
緊急対策 **146–147**
緊急電話をかける **15**
金魚 **215**–16
キングサイズベッド **184**–15
キング牧師誕生日 **22**–10
銀行 **124**–5, **132**
銀行取引明細書 **132**–16
銀行の窓口係 **132**–1
金庫室 **132**–6
近所の人にあいさつする **49**–R
金星 **205**–2
緊張して **42**–10
筋肉 **107**–32
金髪 **33**–17
金曜日 **20**–13
クイズ番組 **236**–8
空気清浄機 **113**–14
空軍 **138**–16
空港 **151**–10, **160–161**
空港の交通 **152**
空港ポーター **160**–1
偶数 **192**–4
クーラー **225**–9
クーラントを入れる **157**–I
空欄を埋める **9**–O
クエスチョンマーク **190**–12
クォーター **26**–4
クォーテーションマーク **190**–15
９月 **21**–33
茎 **211**–9
釘 **180**–34
腐ったバナナ **68**–32
鎖 **180**–41
口座を開く **132**
クシ **108**–13
くし **33**–21
孔雀 **214**–14
くしゃみをする **110**–B
クジラ **213**–29
くずかご **57**–26
くずかごを空にする **60**–L
薬 **121**–20
薬の種類 **113**
薬を過量にとる **116**–K
薬を飲む **114**–D
果物 **67**–9, **68**
果物ナイフ **78**–16
口 **104**–7, **106**
クチナシ **211**–18
くちばし **214**–3
口ひげ **33**–5
唇 **106**–5
口紅 **109**–38
靴 **87**–13
靴売場 **95**–7
クッキー **73**–38
クッキーシート **78**–27
クッション **56**–2
靴底 **94**–21
靴とアクセサリー **94–95**
靴ひも **94**–24
靴屋 **130**–10
くつろぐ **39**–U
靴をはいてみる **95**–C
句読法 **190**
句読法を使う **190**–C
国番号 **15**–33
首 **104**–3
クマ **216**–11
熊手 **176**–8
組立工 **166**–7
組立ライン **175**–6
組み立てる **175**–C
クモ **214**–29
曇り **13**–10
曇り除去装置 **159**–41
クラウン **119**–9
クラクション **159**–32
クラゲ **212**–14
クラシック **237**–21
クラシックコンサート **223**–14
クラスメートと学習する **8**
クラスメートを手伝う **8**–J
クラッチ **159**–49
クラッチバッグ **89**–19
グラフ **192**–15
クラブ **233**–32
グラフィックデザイナー **167**–30
クラブサンドイッチ **80**–12
クラリネット **238**–2
グリーティングカード **134**–15
クリーム **81**–41, **113**–25
クリーム入れ **55**–15
クリーム色 **24**–16
グリーンカード **40**–2
クリスマス **22**–18
クリスマスツリー **239**–16
クリップ **183**–31
クリップイヤリング **95**–37
グリル **53**–17
グリルしたリブ **76**–2
グリルチーズサンドイッチ **80**–10
グリンピース **69**–21
クルーソックス **91**–8
グループで学習する **8**–I
車椅子 **113**–9
車で通勤する **38**–I
車とトラック **156**
車の運転や大型機械の操作はしないでください **112**–E
車の運転を習う **40**–E
車の広告を見る **157**–A
車の購入とメンテナンス **157**
車の手入れ **157**
車の部品 **158–159**
車を整備会社に持って行く **157**–C
車を駐車する **129**–E
車を登録する **157**–F
車を販売する **170**–K
グレープフルーツ **68**–6
クレーン **178**–7
クレジットカードを使う **27**–B
クレヨン **59**–14
クレンザー **61**–18
クレンジングクリーム **109**–42
黒色 **24**–13
黒色のセーターは白色のセーターの後ろにあります **25**–8
クローゼット **58**–5
グローブ **231**–17
グローブボックス **159**–44
黒髪 **33**–16
クロスカントリースキー **227**–3
クロッカス **211**–17

君主 **199**–4
軍隊 **138**, **199**–11
郡の農産物・家畜品評会 **223**–13
経営管理アシスタント **166**–3
継兄弟 **35**–30
警告ラベル **112**–8
警察官 **141**–1, **168**–48
警察署 **124**–6
計算機 **17**–6, **183**–25
計算する **17**–B
掲示板 **7**–14
継姉妹 **35**–29
芸術家 **166**–6
軽食を買う **11**–K
携帯電話 **14**–8
携帯電話ケース **94**–15
携帯電話の電源を切る **160**–I, **174**–G
携帯電話番号 **4**–12
携帯電話販売所 **131**–22
毛糸 **233**–22
競馬 **228**–19
警備員のシャツ **93**–20
警備員 **132**–5, **165**–55
警備員のズボン **93**–22
継父 **35**–25
継母 **35**–26
警報に注意を払う **147**–D
刑務所に入る **141**–G
計量値を換算する **75**–C
ケーキ **73**–39
ケーキ型 **78**–26
ゲート **161**–8
ゲートで **161**
ケーブル **196**–13
ゲームコントローラー **232**–4
ゲーム番組 **236**–8
ゲームをする **232**–B
外科医 **121**–36
外科専門の看護師 **120**–9
毛皮 **216**–19
けがをする **116**–C
劇場 **127**–23
消印 **134**–24
景色 **162**–2
黒板消し **7**–19
消しゴム **7**–21
ゲストサービス(案内所) **130**–12
ケチャップ **79**–21
血圧計 **118**–9
血圧を測る **118**–A
血液を採る **118**–F
結核 **111**–15
結果を記録する **195**–D
血液検査 **121**–30
結婚式 **22**–2
結婚する **41**–K
結婚証明書 **41**–8
げっ歯類 **215**
月曜日 **20**–9
結論 **190**–8
結論を導き出す **195**–E
毛抜き **117**–4
ケベック **201**–5
煙探知機 **51**–29
蹴る **230**–E
弱い信号 **14**–12
検眼 **136**–6
検眼医 **115**–6
玄関のドア **53**–11
現金で払う **27**–A
現金と小銭 **146**–17
現金を引き出す **132**–F
肩甲骨 **107**–28
健康上のいろいろな問題 **115**
健康的な食事をとる **114**–F
健康に気をつける **114–115**
健康保険証 **118**–3
健康問題の改善 **115**
健康を維持する方法 **114**
原稿を提出する **191**–M
検査員 **160**–5
検査エリア **160**–4
検索ボックス **197**–5
検査室 **121**
検察官 **141**–10
原子 **195**–28
原子力エネルギー **218**–8
建設業 **178**
建設作業員 **178**–1
現代 **199**–2
建築士 **166**–5
顕微鏡 **194**
憲法 **198**–12
件名をタイプする **197**–D
権利 **140**
権利書 **41**–9
権利章典 **198**–13
権利書を売り手からもらう **157**–E
言論の自由 **140**–2
五 **16**
コアラ **217**–45
仔犬 **215**–12
故意の破壊行為 **142**–1
恋をして **42**–18
恋をする **40**–H
コインランドリー **128**–1
公園と遊び場 **224**
硬貨 **26**
郊外 **52**–2
甲殻類 **71**
講義する **122**–B
公共の安全 **143**
公共の交通機関 **152**
抗菌性軟膏 **117**–11
航空会社の発券担当者 **160**–3
航空便 **134**–5
工具と建設用品 **180–181**
工具ベルト **92**–3
合計 **27**–9
高血圧 **111**–14
光源 **194**–19
高校 **188**–4
光合成 **194**–10
広告 **102**–1
工作用紙 **232**–12
工作をする **232**–D
口座担当者 **132**–9
交差点 **128–129**
講師 **6**–4
格子柄 **96**–22
工事現場 **126**–2
公衆電話 **15**–25, **129**–23
口述筆記を行う **171**–K
工場 **126**–3, **175**
工場従業員 **175**–3
工場所有者 **175**–1
香水 **108**–6
洪水 **145**–19
校正する **191**–I
高層ビル **127**–13
高速で運転する人 **23**–3
紅茶 **81**–38
校長 **5**–4
交通規則を無視して通りを渡る **128**–C
交通局(DMV) **124**–4, **136–137**
交通事故 **144**–2
交通信号 **128**–8
交通標識 **154**
皇帝 **199**–3
講堂 **5**–18
強盗 **142**–11
口内に麻酔をかける **119**–C
購入する **94**–A
光熱費 **48**–5
合板 **178**–18
抗ヒスタミンクリーム **117**–10
後部座席 **159**–54
興奮して **43**–22
公平な裁判 **140**–5
公民権と義務 **140**
コウモリ **216**–7
小売販売店員 **169**–53
合流 **154**–10
高齢者 **30**–5
高齢者向け住宅 **52**–11
高齢の **32**–3
港湾労働者 **167**–23
小枝 **210**–1
小エビ **71**–11
コーチ **5**–20, **229**–2
コーデュロイ **99**–11
コード **14**–2
コート **90**–2
コードレス電話 **15**–24
コーヒー **73**–33, **81**–37
コーヒー(紅茶)カップ **83**–24
コーヒーテーブル **56**–19
コーヒーマグ **55**–7
コーヒーメーカー **54**–11
氷が張っている **13**–22
ゴールインする **230**–T
コールスロー **80**–18
凍るように寒い **13**–7
コオロギ **214**–23
コーンロウ(細く編み上げた髪型) **33**–14
語学 **189**–9
小型トラック **156**–12
5月 **21**–29
小切手 **132**–13
小切手帳 **132**–12
小切手を換金する **132**–A
ゴキブリ **63**–26
顧客 **72**–1, **82**–6, **94**–4, **132**–2, **164**–2
顧客の品選びを手伝う **95**–D
呼吸数・脈拍などを示すモニター **121**–26
呼吸できない **116**–N
呼吸マスク **179**–13
国際電話 **15**–35
黒板 **6**–1
黒板に書く **6**–E
午後 **18**–5, **18**–17
ココナッツ **68**–24
腰 **107**–29
五十 **16**
50ドル **26**–11
五十番 **16**
50セント **26**–5
50パーセント **17**–10
故障する **162**–D
個人競技 **228**
(個人用)小切手を書く **27**–D
コスト **27**–7
ゴスペル **237**–30
小銭入れ **94**–14
午前 **18**–4
5セント **26**–2
午前零時 **18**–21
古代 **199**–1
答え **192**–14
答えを丸で囲む **9**–Q
ごちそう **239**–13
コックコート **93**–29
コックピット **161**–10
コック帽 **93**–28
骨折する **116**–P
小包 **134**–17
小包郵便 **134**–6

骨盤 **107**–50
お釣りをもらう **26**–A
こて **178**–13
子どもが生まれる **41**–L
子供の世話をする **170**–P
子供番組 **236**–9
子供部屋 **47**–9, **59**
子供を学校に連れていく **38**–G
子供を学校に迎えにいく **38**–M
５ドル **26**–8
子猫 **215**–10
小ネジ **180**–32
五番 **16**
コピー機 **183**–23
コピーする **171**–D
コピーセンター **129**–18
コブラ **213**–41
５分間電子レンジで加熱する **77**–T
小部屋 **182**–7
コマドリ **214**–16
ごみ **148**–2
ごみ置き場 **51**–23
ごみ収集車 **127**–22
小道 **208**–3
ごみバケツ **53**–24
ごみ袋 **61**–24
コミュニティカレッジ **127**–17, **188**–6
ごみを捨てない **219**–L
ごみを捨てる **11**–N
ごみを出す **60**–Q
ごみを減らす **219**–A
小麦 **177**–2
小麦粉 **73**–29
小麦粉1カップ **75**–10
ゴムマット **57**–5
ゴム手袋 **61**–4
米 **67**–10, **177**–1
コメディ **237**–13
子守唄を歌う **36**–O
固有名詞は大文字で始める **190**–A
雇用者 **164**–4
コヨーテ **216**–3
娯楽 **236–237**
ゴリラ **217**–29
ゴルフ **228**–8
ゴルフクラブ **231**–1
ころぶ **116**–O
コロン **108**–6, **190**–17
コロンブス記念日 **22**–15
壊れた機材 **179**–4
紺色 **24**–10, **28**–5
コンクリート **178**–10
コンシェルジェ **184**–4
今週 **20**–19
コンセント **58**–28, **159**–42
コンセントカバー **181**–46
コンタクトレンズ **115**–8
昆虫 **209**–11
昆虫と蜘蛛類 **214**
コンディショナー **108**–11
コンドミニアム **52**–5
コントラバス **238**–8
「こんにちは」と言う **2**–A
コンビーフ **71**–22
コンビニエンスストア **128**–3
コンピュータ **7**–15, **183**–17, **196**
コンピュータ技術者 **167**–19, **182**–12
コンピュータ室 **5**–15
コンピュータソフトウェアエンジニア **167**–18
コンピュータでチェックインする **160**–A
コンピュータをプログラムする **170**–I
コンベイヤーベルト **175**–9
コンベンションセンター **127**–24
梱包用テープ **183**–32
コンポスト **53**–25
コンマ **190**–14
婚約する **41**–J
混乱して **43**–26
コンロ **54**–19
差 **192**–8
サージプロテクタ **196**–1
サーチエンジン **197**–6
サーティファイドメール（配達証明付き郵便） **134**–4
サービングボウル **55**–21
サーファー **225**–15
サーフィン **227**–9
サーブする **230**–P
サーフボード **225**–16
サーマルアンダーシャツ **91**–2
サイ **217**–28
「サインイン」をクリックする **197**–B
菜園 **177**–14
災害キットを用意する **146**–B
サイクリスト **224**–2
サイクリング **228**–5
採血専門家 **121**–29
最高裁判所 **138**–11
在庫品係 **169**–59
最後まで服用してください **112**–C
さいころ **232**–6
再婚 **35**–24
最終稿を書く **191**–L
最初の草稿を書く **191**–H
最初の大統領 **198**–11
最初の月と最後の月の家賃を払う **48**–E
サイズ **96**
サイズ直し **100**
サイズ直しの専門店 **100**
再生する **235**–B
サイドテーブル **56**–14
サイドボード **55**–24
サイドミラー **158**–3
裁判所 **125**–13
裁判長 **138**–13
裁判を受ける **141**–D
財布 **94**–13
細胞 **194**–4
細胞質 **194**–9
裁縫道具 **100**
細胞壁 **194**–5
細胞膜 **194**–6
材木 **178**–17
採用される **173**–L
材料を計る **75**–A
材料を混ぜる **77**–R
魚 **66**–1, **71**, **209**–14
魚釣り **226**–4
魚捕り網 **226**–17
魚のグリル **81**–29
砂丘 **204**–5
作業着 **92**–93
作業ズボン **92**–5
作業用シャツ **92**–2
作業用手袋 **92**–17, **179**–17
作業用ライト **181**–44
作業療法士 **168**–45
削除する **196**–C
サクソフォン **238**–5
搾乳する **177**–C
作文の過程 **191**
作物 **177**
サクランボ **68**–11
サケのステーキカット **71**–4
サケまるごと１匹 **71**–3
差出人の住所 **134**–21
砂塵（さじん）嵐 **13**–19
サスペンダー **94**–1
座席を見つける **160**–F
左折禁止 **154**–8
サソリ **214**–30
作家 **169**–64
サッカー **229**–12
サッカーボール **231**–12
作曲 **199**–15
作曲家 **199**–14
殺菌ワイプ **61**–23
雑誌 **133**–5
殺人 **142**–12
雑談する **12**–B
サツマイモ **69**–18
砂糖 **73**–30
砂糖入れ **55**–14
砂糖大さじ1杯 **75**–7
砂漠 **204**–4
寂しい **42**–17
サポートグループ **115**–15
サボテン **210**–21
さまざまな住宅環境 **52**
寒い **13**–6, **42**–4
サメ **212**–4
「さようなら」と言う **3**–L
皿 **55**–1
皿洗い機 **54**–8
サラダバー **79**–24
サラダフォーク **83**–27
サラダ用の皿 **83**–20
サラミ **71**–23
皿を洗う **60**–M
皿を片付ける **82**–G
皿を拭く **60**–N
猿 **217**–26
ざる **78**–22
サワークリーム **72**–21
騒がしい子供 **23**–11
三 **16**
三温糖1/4カップ **75**–8
産科医 **120**–2
三角関数 **192**–18
三角巾 **113**–19
三角形 **193**–32
山岳時間 **19**–30
3月 **21**–27
三脚 **235**–25
サングラス **90**–27
サンゴ **220**–5
参考文献担当司書 **133**–9
三十 **16**
三十番 **16**
サンショウウオ **212**–27
散水器を取り付ける **176**–H
サンスクリーン **108**–7
サンスクリーン／日焼け止め **225**–10
サンスクリーンを塗る **108**–D
酸性雨 **218**–13
酸素マスク **161**–24
残高 **132**–17
サンダル **88**–9
山頂 **204**–14
サンドペーパー **181**–56
桟橋 **225**–18
三番 **16**
3分の１ **17**–3
山脈 **204**–15
3リングバインダー／ノート **7**–27
三輪車 **224**–12
市 **4**–7
幸せな **28**–6, **43**–31
飼育動物 **215**
Cクランプ **180**–6
シーソー **224**–16
シーツを換える **60**–P
CD店 **130**–1
CDプレーヤー **159**–38
CDラジカセ **234**–1
CDを聞く **6**–C
シートベルト **159**–52

シートベルトを締める **36**–L, **160**–H
GPS（グローバルポジショニングシステム）**155**–11
シール **102**–3
ジーンズ **86**–2, **92**–19
シェービングクリーム **109**–29
シェフ **83**–16
シェフサラダ **80**–14
耳炎 **111**–3
塩入れとコショウ入れ **55**–13
塩小さじ1杯 **75**–6
歯科 **119**
シカ **216**–14
歯科医 **119**–1
市外局番 **4**–10, **15**–29
歯科医に行く **119**
歯科衛生士 **119**–3
歯科器具 **119**–4
歯科矯正 **119**
歯科助手 **119**–2, **167**–22
4月 **21**–28
時間 **18**–1, **18**–19
指関節 **106**–17
時間通り **19**–23
時間を告げる **18**
式 **195**–34
市議会 **139**–27
市議会議員 **139**–28
敷物 **58**–22
仕切られた空間 **182**–7
自警団に参加する **143**–L
試験管 **195**–42
歯垢 **119**–12
時刻表 **152**–4
自己紹介 **4**
自己紹介する **2**–C
仕事がうまく行かなかった日 **186**–187
仕事着 **88**
仕事と職業 **166**–169
指示に従う **9**, **147**–F
磁石 **195**–36
刺繍 **233**–24
辞書 **7**–30
試食用サンプル **84**–5
私書箱 **135**–9
地震 **144**–5
システム手帳 **183**–49
市政府 **139**
自然センター **208**–209
自然ドキュメンタリー **236**–7
歯槽膿漏（のうろう）**119**–11
舌 **106**–8
下あご **106**–4
下着とスリープウェア **91**
仕出屋 **185**–16
仕立て屋 **100**–3
仕立て用のマネキン **100**–2
7月 **21**–31
七分袖シャツ **96**–13
七面鳥 **239**–14
七面鳥の肉 **70**–17
シチュー用肉 **70**–3
市長 **139**–26
歯痛 **110**–2
実演 **122**–6
しっくい **178**–15
しつける **36**–K
実験 **195**
実験室 **195**
実験を行う **195**–B
湿疹 **110**–10
実地訓練 **172**–7
湿度が高い **13**–15
室内植物 **211**–27
質問する **8**–K, **174**–M
質問に答える **8**–L
自転車 **129**–22, **151**–15
自転車道 **224**–3
自転車に乗る **129**–D
自動車 **150**–1
自動車整備工 **166**–8
自動車販売店 **126**–4
自動車販売店で **158**
自動車保険の証明書 **136**–8
自動電話応答システム **14**–23
自動販売機 **152**–9
自動郵便業務センター（APC）**135**–10
市内通話 **15**–31
死ぬ **41**–R
地熱エネルギー **218**–7
芝刈り機 **176**–6
芝生 **53**–26
芝生を刈る **176**–A
支払方法 **27**
市販薬 **113**, **113**–18
シフトレバー **159**–47, **159**–50
自分で解答する **10**–J
自分の経験を話す **174**–L
紙幣 **26**
司法機関 **138**
死亡証明書 **41**–11
絞り **194**–18
島 **204**–8
シマウマ **217**–33
縞模様 **96**–20
シマリス **215**–20
染みがついている **97**–42
市民権獲得条件 **140**
市民権獲得証明書 **40**–6
市民権獲得の試験を受ける **140**–I
事務員 **5**–13, **182**–2
事務機器 **183**
事務所 **5**–12
事務能力 **171**
事務用品 **183**
氏名 **4**–1
指紋 **136**–5
シャープボタン **14**–7
社員 **136**–4, **165**–9
社会福祉指導員 **169**–57
社会保障番号 **4**–15
社会保障番号証 **40**–5
ジャガイモ **69**–17
市役所 **124**–8
蛇口 **57**–8
蛇口が水漏れする **63**–17
釈放される **141**–H
借家人 **50**–6
借家人と話し合う **64–65**
ジャケット **90**–8
謝罪を受け入れる **12**–G
車掌 **152**–13
写真 **58**–3
写真家 **206**–1
写真立て **58**–4
写真を添付する **197**–G
写真を撮る **206**–A
ジャズ **237**–24
ジャスミン **211**–22
シャツ **86**–1
ジャッキ **158**–24
ジャックハンマー **178**–9
シャトルバス **152**–19
車内 **159**
シャベル **176**–7, **178**–22
車輪つき担架 **121**–33
シャワーカーテン **57**–14
シャワーキャップ **108**–1
シャワーヘッド **57**–13
シャワー用ジェル状石けん **108**–2
シャワーを浴びる **38**–C, **108**–A
ジャングルジム **224**–14
シャンプー **108**–10
ジャンプスーツ **93**–24
ジャンプする **230**–I
州 **4**–8
週 **20**–15
十 **16**
銃 **142**–14
週１度 **20**–22
週２度 **20**–23
週３度 **20**–24
獣医 **169**–62
十一 **16**
11月 **21**–35
十一番 **16**
十億 **16**
州外に連絡する **147**–L
州外への連絡 **146**–2
州下院議員 **139**–24
収穫する **177**–B
10月 **21**–34
州上院議員 **139**–25
州議会 **139**–23
周期表 **195**–26
十九 **16**
十九番 **16**
宗教上の祭日 **22**–7
宗教の自由 **140**–3
住居侵入 **142**–2
重機を操作する **170**–H
州軍 **138**–19
十五 **16**
集合場所 **146**–1
十五番 **16**
十三 **16**
13の植民地 **198**–1
十三番 **16**
住所 **4**–5
就職する **40**–F
就職説明会 **172**–13
修正液 **183**–36
修正する／書き直す **191**–J
修正テープ **183**–37
州政府 **139**
在宅介護ヘルパー **167**–32
住宅ローンを払う **49**–L
集団暴力行為 **142**–4
州知事 **139**–20
終点 **193**–21
充電器 **14**–10, **234**–17
州都 **139**–22
シュートする **230**–H
10ドル **26**–9
十七 **16**
十七番 **16**
柔軟仕上げ剤 **101**–6
十二 **16**
12月 **21**–36
十二番 **16**
十八 **16**
十八番 **16**
18歳以上である **140**–G
十番 **16**
週末 **20**–17
十万 **16**
重油流出 **218**–17
収容施設 **52**–13
重要な書類のコピー **146**–20
十四 **16**
十四番 **16**
修理人 **62**–10
重量上げ **228**–16
十六 **16**
十六番 **16**
守衛 **141**–3
シュガーレス **122**–7
授業中のやりとりに参加する **10**–B

授業に行く **38**–J
祝祭日 **239**
熟したバナナ **68**–30
熟していないバナナ **68**–31
縮尺 **155**–7
宿題をする **39**–T
受刑者 **141**–15
手術衣 **93**–37, **121**–38
手術着 **93**–38
手術室 **121**
手術台 **121**–40
手術用手袋 **121**–39
手術用帽子 **93**–35
手術用マスク **93**–36
首相 **199**–7
手術帽 **121**–37
出荷係 **175**–14
出荷する **175**–D
出血する **116**–M
10歳の少女 **31**–10
出生証明書 **40**–1
出生地 **4**–14
10セント **26**–3
出廷する **141**–C
10パーセント **17**–12
出発する **160**–J
出発地 **162**–1
授乳する **36**–B
授乳用ミルク **37**–3
シュノーケル **227**–11
種苗 **211**–4
主婦／主夫 **168**–33
趣味とゲーム **232–233**
シュレッダー **183**–24
受話器 **14**–1
准看護師（LPN） **120**–11
順番 **16**
商 **192**–10
小 **96**–2
上院 **138**–5
上院議員 **138**–6
障害 **32**
障害者を助ける **147**–G
消火器 **179**–21
消火栓 **129**–27
小学校 **188**–2
定規 **17**–13
使用期限 **112**–7
乗客 **150**–2, **152**–3, **161**–15
上弦（下弦）の月 **205**–11
証拠 **141**–9
正午 **18**–16
錠剤 **113**–22
上司 **164**–4
昇進 **172**–4
小数点 **17**–7
使用済みおむつ入れ **37**–7
小説 **133**–16
招待 **64**–9
招待を受け入れる **12**–I
招待を断る **12**–J
小児科医 **120**–4
証人 **141**–11
乗馬 **226**–9
消防士 **144**–9, **167**–26
消防車 **144**–10
消防署 **125**–12
情報を得る **140**–F
錠前師 **62**–11
照明器具 **55**–18
静脈 **107**–37
常夜灯 **37**–27
小論文 **190**–4
小論文の構成部分 **190**
ショーケース **94**–5
ショートスカート **96**–16
ショートパンツ **89**–25
職業安定所に行く **173**–E
職業技能 **170**
職業興味検査 **172**–11
職業訓練 **172**–5
職業訓練校／専門学校 **188**–5
食後のテーブルを片付ける人 **83**–12, **185**–13
職探し **173**
食事客 **185**–9
食事客 **82**–6
食事客を席に案内する **82**–B
食事の1時間前に服用してください **112**–B
食事または牛乳とともに服用してください **112**–A
食事を与える **36**–C
食卓 **55**–9
食堂 **5**–14
職場 **164**–165
職場の安全 **179**
食品サービス **185**
食品準備担当者 **185**–4
食品成分ラベル **122**–8
食品の安全 **76**
食品の重さを量る **75**–B
食品保存用のビニール袋 **72**–25
食品用ラップ **72**–24
植物 **208**–5, **210**
植物園 **222**–3
植民地時代 **198**
食料雑貨 **72**
初心者レベルの仕事 **172**–1
女性 **30**–2
女性用下着 **91**
女性用ソックス **91**
除草器 **176**–12
食器洗い係 **185**–2
食器だな **55**–22
食器用洗剤 **61**–21
食器用の部屋 **83**–13
食器を洗う人 **83**–14
ショック状態になる **116**–B
ショッピングカート **72**–7
ショッピング番組 **236**–10
ショッピングモール **126**–7
ショッピングモール **130–131**
書店 **130**–4
処方箋 **112**–2
処方番号 **112**–5
処方薬 **112**–3
処方ラベル **112**–4
署名 **4**–19
ショルダーバッグ **94**–17
ショルダーパッド **231**–20
知らない人にドアを開けない **143**–F
尻 **107**–30
ジリス **215**–19
試料台 **194**–17
試料台クリップ **194**–21
飼料を与える **177**–D
資料を整理する **171**–L
視力障害 **32**–11
視力の問題 **115**–1
シルク **98**–5
歯列矯正医 **119**–5
シロアリ **63**–22
白色 **24**–14
白色のセーターは黒色のセーターの前にあります **25**–7
シロホン **238**–15
しわだらけのシャツ **101**–19
心音を聞く **118**–C
シングルファーザー **35**–23
シングルマザー **35**–22
新月 **205**–9
信号が変わるのを待つ **128**–B
人工甘味料 **79**–20
人工呼吸 **117**–16
申告書 **161**–17
診察室で **118**
診察台 **118**–7
診察用ガウン **121**–19
寝室 **46**–2, **58**
伸縮性のある包帯 **117**–12
人生の出来事と各種証明書 **40–41**
申請料を払う **137**–D
親戚 **44**–6
心臓 **107**–38
腎臓 **107**–43
心臓専門医 **120**–3
心臓発作を起こす **116**–D
親族会 **44**–45
身体障害者用駐車スペース **128**–6, **154**–12
身体障害の **32**–10
身長 **32**
進入禁止 **154**–2
心配して **42**–13
心肺蘇生法 **117**–17
審判員／レフリー **229**–6
新聞 **133**–6
新聞雑誌売店 **128**–12
新聞紙をリサイクルする **60**–B
新聞を読む **39**–V
進歩する **10**–G
診療所 **186**–2
森林 **204**–11
心臓病 **111**–11
巣 **209**–12
スイート **184**–16
水温計 **159**–30
スイカ **68**–18
水球 **229**–15
水彩絵具 **233**–21
水質汚染 **218**–14
水準器 **180**–29
水上スキー **227**–7
スイスチーズ **71**–27
彗星 **205**–24
水星 **205**–1
垂線 **193**–24
スイセン **211**–25
すい臓 **107**–45
水族館 **222**–7
スイッチ **58**–27
水筒 **226**–24
水道管が凍結している **63**–16
水分をとる **114**–C
水曜日 **20**–11
水力発電 **218**–5
スーツ **87**–11
スウェットパンツ **89**–23
数学 **189**–10
数学 **192**–193
数学の種類 **192**
数学の問題 **192**
数学の問題を解く **170**–M
数字 **16**
スーパーから戻る **66–67**
スーパーに行く **38**–L
スーパーの袋 **67**–13
スーパーの袋を再利用する **219**–B
スーパーマーケット **72**, **127**–18
スーパーマーケット **72–73**
スープ **72**–18, **80**–16
スープ皿 **83**–21
スープスプーン **83**–32
スエード **99**–8
スカート **87**–10
スカーフ **95**–12
頭蓋骨 **107**–47
姿見 **58**–6
スカンク **216**–12

スキー板 **231**–24
スキーストック **231**–25
スキーブーツ **231**–26
スキー帽 **90**–11
スキーマスク **90**–15
スキーをする **230**–V
スキャナ **183**–20
スキューバダイビング **227**–12
スクールバス **156**–21
スクランブルエッグ **76**–7
スクリーン **6**–2, **235**–30
スクレーパー **181**–52
スクロールバー **197**–15
スクワッシュ **69**–24
図形 **193**
スケートボード **224**–7, **228**–13
スケートをする **230**–U
スケジュールノート **183**–48
スコップ **176**–10
頭上の荷物入れ **161**–13
スズキ **212**–6
涼しい **13**–5
スズメ **214**–7
スズメバチ **214**–17
裾 **100**–8
裾の折り返し **100**–9
スタートする **230**–R
スタイル **96**
スタジアム **126**–1
スタンプ **183**–47
頭痛 **110**–1
ズッキーニ **69**–25
酸っぱい **84**–4
スティック糊 **232**–11
ステイン **181**–24
ステーキ **81**–24
ステーキナイフ **83**–29
ステーキ用肉 **70**–2
ステーションワゴン **156**–6
すてきな **32**–13
ステレオ **56**–8
ストッキング **91**–17
ストレス **115**–4
ストレッチする **230**–M
ストロー **79**–18
砂 **225**–23
スナックフード **73**
スナップボタン **99**–26
砂の城 **225**–12
砂場 **224**–15
すね **106**–21
すね当て **231**–13
スノーボード **227**–2, **231**–23
スパゲッティ **81**–26
スパッツ **90**–12
素早く簡単にできるケーキ **77**
スパンコール **99**–33
スピーカー **234**–14
スピード違反の切符を切られる **162**–C
スプーン **55**–5
スプリンクラー **53**–22
スプレーガン **181**–21
スプレー糊 **101**–12
スペアタイヤ **158**–23
スペースシャトル **205**–19
スペード **233**–30
すべり台 **224**–13
滑りやすい床 **179**–6
スペルをチェックする **197**–F
スポイト **195**–45
スポーツウェア **89**
スポーツカー **156**–4
スポーツ関連の動詞 **230**
スポーツコート **89**–14
スポーツジム **5**–19, **126**–10, **184**–24
スポーツジャケット **89**–14
スポーツシャツ **88**–4
スポーツ番組 **236**–11
スポーツ用品 **231**
ズボン **87**–12
スポンジ **61**–19
ズボン下 **91**–3
スポンジモップ **61**–6
ズボンの裾を出す **100**–C
ズボンの裾を詰める **100**–D
ズボンを長くする **100**–A
ズボンを短くする **100**–B
スマートフォン **15**–27
スミレ **211**–23
スミレ色 **24**–8
スモークターキー **71**–25
スモック **93**–26
スモッグが出ている **13**–14
スライドグラス **194**–3
スラックス **87**–12
スリープウェア **91**
擦り切れたコード **179**–5
スリッパ **91**–26
スリップ **91**–22
座る **6**–F
寸法 **17**
姓 **4**–4
セイウチ **213**–32
税関係員 **161**–17
正看護師(RN) **120**–10
制汗剤 **108**–5
税関で **161**
税金を払う **140**–B
制限速度 **154**–4
星座 **205**–14
制酸剤 **113**–28
政治運動 **199**–16
精神科医 **120**–8
成人教育 **188**–8
整数 **192**
成績 **10**–4
生鮮食品売場 **72**–2
清掃員 **182**–3
清掃カート **184**–19
清掃係 **184**–20
清掃作業員 **169**–54
製造する **175**–B
棲息地 **194**–11
生年月日 **4**–13
正の整数 **192**–2
精白パン **71**–18
整備工場で **158**
西部劇 **237**–15
生物 **194**–1
生物学 **194**
生物学者 **194**–2
政府と軍隊 **138–139**
性別 **4**–16
正方形 **193**–30
整理だんす **58**–1
セーター **28**–2, **88**–3, **87**–14
セーフティレール **59**–10
セーリング **227**–8
セール価格 **27**–3
世界各国の音楽 **237**–32
世界史 **199**
世界地図 **202–203**
背が高い **32**–4
背が低い **32**–6
積 **192**–9
石炭 **218**–4
脊柱 **107**–49
脊椎動物 **194**–12
せき止めシロップ **113**–29
席につく **6**–F
石油 **218**–6
セキュリティチェックポイントで **160**
セキュリティチェックを受ける **160**–D
せきをする **110**–A
摂氏 **13**–2
絶縁テープ **181**–43
接眼レンズ **194**–14
接客主任 **185**–11
接客する **170**–T
設計者 **175**–2
設計する **175**–A
石けん **57**–4, **108**–3
石けん入れ **57**–3
石けん付きスチールウール **61**–5
説明する **12**–M
背中 **104**–5
背中をサポートするベルト **179**–18
セミコロン **190**–18
セミトラック **156**–15
セルフチェックアウト **73**–10, **133**–10
セルフチェックインコーナー **160**–2
セレクティブサービス(義務兵役)に登録する **140**–D
ゼロ **16**
セロハンテープ **183**–30
セロリ **69**–9
セロリをさいの目に切る **77**–J
千 **16**
線 **193**
選挙 **139**
選挙運動 **139**–29
選挙で選ばれる **139**–C
洗剤を加える **101**–B
選手 **229**–5
先週 **20**–18
染色体 **194**–8
潜水タンク **225**–5
先生と話す **6**–B
戦争 **199**–10
喘息 **111**–9
喘息用の吸入剤 **113**–33
洗濯かご **101**–2
洗濯機 **50**–12, **101**–3
洗濯機に入れる **101**–C
洗濯ばさみ **101**–10
洗濯物 **101**–1
洗濯物かご **57**–1
洗濯物を仕分ける **101**–A
洗濯物をたたむ **101**–F
洗濯用洗剤 **101**–8
洗濯をする **101**
前置詞 **25**
センチメートル [cm] **17**–14
ぜん虫 **212**–23
剪定はさみ **176**–9
前道 **53**–2
千番 **16**
全部 **17**–1
扇風機 **55**–19
線分 **193**–20
戦没将兵記念日 **22**–12
洗面台 **57**–25
専門医 **120**
全粒パン **71**–19
線路 **152**–14
前腕 **106**–13
象 **217**–42
造園スタッフ **176**–1
造園スタッフのリーダー **176**–4
造園設計者 **176**–5
造園と園芸業 **176**
騒音 **64**–5
ぞうきん **61**–9
草原 **204**–20
倉庫 **175**–7
走行距離計 **159**–28
捜査救助隊 **145**–20
掃除機 **61**–10

掃除機のごみパック **61**–12
掃除機の付属品 **61**–11
掃除・洗濯の用具 **61**
相似と相違 **28–29**
送受信用無線機 **179**–22
装飾の多いブラウス **97**–34
創設者 **198**–7
象の鼻 **217**–47
添え木 **117**–14
ソースをスプーンでかける **77**–F
ソーセージ **70**–12, **80**–2
即席料理担当コック **185**–1
測定 **17**
測定する **17**–C
速度計 **159**–27
粗調整用ノブ **194**–24
卒業 **206–207**
卒業式 **206**–6
卒業証書 **40**–3
卒業する **40**–D
ソックス **86**–6
袖 **100**–6
その他の楽器 **238**
祖父 **34**–2
ソファー **56**–18
ソフトウェア **196**–10
ソフトボール **229**–10
祖母 **34**–1
空 **209**–9
空色 **24**–12
そり遊び **227**–6
タートルネックのセーター **96**–9
ターミナルで **160**
ターンテーブル **234**–12
大 **96**–4
第一次大陸会議 **198**–6
体温計 **118**–11
体温を測る **118**–B
対角線 **193**–31
大学卒業証書 **41**–7
大学に進学する **41**–I
大学の寮 **52**–8
大画面テレビ **50**–14
抱き合う **2**–E
大気汚染／スモッグ **218**–11
大工 **62**–12, **166**–14
退屈して **43**–25
タイサンボク **210**–8
台車 **175**–11
体重 **32**
体重計 **57**–27
大豆 **177**–3
代数 **192**–16
大西洋時間 **19**–33
体操 **228**–9
タイツ **91**–19
大洞窟 **220**–7
大統領 **138**–8, **199**–5
大統領官邸 **138**–7
大統領の日 **22**–11
台所用品 **78**
ダイニング **46**–7, **55**
ダイニングルーム **82**–1
ダイニングルームの椅子 **55**–8
ダイニングルームのテーブル **55**–9
大ハンマー **178**–23
ダイビングマスク **225**–6
タイプする **170**–R, **196**–A
対物レンズ **194**–16
太平洋岸諸州／西海岸 **201**–7
太平洋岸北西部 **201**–14
太平洋時間 **19**–29
ダイム **26**–3
タイムゾーン **19**
タイムレコーダー **165**–7
題名 **133**–14, **190**–5
タイヤ **158**–5
ダイヤ **233**–29
タイヤがパンクする **162**–F
タイヤに空気を入れる **157**–L
タイヤ用レンチ **158**–22
太陽 **209**–8
大洋 **204**–6
太陽エネルギー **218**–1
太陽系と惑星 **205**
大陸 **202**
対立候補 **139**–30
タイル **57**–12, **178**–11
タイルにひびが入っている **62**–4
タイルを張る **178**–C
タウンカー **152**–20
ダウンジャケット **90**–16
ダウンタウン **124–125**
タウンハウス **52**–6
ダウンヒルスキー **227**–1
ダウンベスト **90**–14
倒した座席 **161**–27
タオルかけ **57**–15
高いかかと **97**–32
高い指輪 **23**–19
高さ **17**–16
高すぎる **97**–44
打楽器 **238**
滝 **204**–2
タキシード **89**–17
抱く **36**–A
タクシー **150**–3
タクシー営業許可書 **152**–22
タクシーから降りる **153**–F
タクシーに乗る **153**–E
タクシーの運転手 **152**–21
タクシー乗り場 **152**–18
ダクトテープ **181**–49
凧 **225**–2
タコ **79**–8, **212**–9
山車 **239**–2
足す **192**–A
ダストシュート **51**–26
正しい解答を選ぶ **9**–P
正しい欄に印を付ける **9**–U
立つ **6**–D
卓球 **228**–14
タックルする **230**–F
ダッシュボードと計器パネル **159**
タツノオトシゴ **212**–13
竜巻 **145**–5
たてがみ **217**–49
たな **54**–2
ダニ **214**–27
谷間 **204**–18
種 **211**–1
タバコを吸わない **114**–G
タブ **197**–7
ダブルベッド **184**–14
食べる **11**–I
卵 **66**–7
卵２個を耐熱ボウルに割りいれる **77**–Q
卵の泡立て器 **78**–20
卵の調理方法 **76**
タマネギ **69**–19
タマネギを刻む **77**–L
多目的ナイフ **226**–20
タラ **71**–8, **212**–5
タルカムパウダー **108**–4
誰かにお礼を言う **12**–E
誰かを招待する **12**–H
誰かをほめる **12**–C
タワー **196**–3
たわし **61**–20
単科大学／総合大学 **188**–7
嘆願書 **148**–5
タンクトップ **89**–24
タンクにガソリンを入れる **157**–G
タンクローリー **156**–20
探検 **199**–8
探検家 **199**–9
単語 **190**–1
単語に下線を引く **9**–S
単語を書き写す **8**–E
単語を調べる **8**–A
単語を線で消す **9**–R
単語を訳す **8**–C
炭酸飲料 **73**–34, **79**–11
誕生日 **22**–1
男女兼用ソックス **91**
男女兼用の下着 **91**
たんす **59**–6
男性 **30**–1
男性用下着 **91**
男性用スポーツサポーター **91**–6
団体競技 **229**
断熱材 **178**–14
胆のう **107**–44
短髪 **33**–1
タンバリン **238**–17
ダンプトラック **156**–19
ダンベル **231**–22
暖房炉が故障している **63**–15
段落 **190**–3
段落の最初の文章は字下げ
（インデント）する **190**–D
暖炉 **56**–13
暖炉だな **56**–11
暖炉のついたて **56**–12
チアパス高地 **201**–18
地域の清掃 **148**–149
小さい手 **23**–1
小さすぎる **97**–37
小さな町 **52**–3
小さな実 **210**–20
チーズ **66**–4
チーズ1オンス **75**–11
チーズ入り豆腐と野菜のキャセロ
ール **77**
チーズケーキ **81**–34
チーズバーガー **79**–3
チーズをおろす **77**–G
チーム **229**–3
チェーン **95**–33
チェス **232**–8
チェダーチーズ **71**–28
チェッカー **232**–7
チェック柄 **96**–24
チェロ **238**–7
違う色 **23**–16
地下室 **47**–13, **50**
地下鉄 **151**–12
地下鉄の駅 **151**–11, **152**
地下鉄の車両 **152**–6
地球 **205**–3
チキンバーガー **79**–5
畜牛 **177**–21
遅刻しない **174**–E
地図 **7**–12, **155**
地図帳 **133**–8
父親 **34**–4
チップを置く **82**–J
地方 **52**–4
チャイルドシート **37**–19, **159**–53
茶色 **24**–17
着陸する **160**–K
茶色のセーターは右側にあります **25**–3
茶髪 **33**–18
中 **96**–3
注意して聞く **174**–K
注意深い作業者 **179**–2
中間色 **24**
中古車を買う **157**

注射器 **118**–12
駐車禁止 **154**–11
駐車場 **50**–18, **124**–1
駐車場係員 **184**–3
駐車スペース **128**–5
中性子 **195**–32
中西部 **201**–9
チューナー **234**–13
中年の **32**–2
チューバ **238**–12
チューブ **74**–12
中部時間 **19**–31
中部大西洋岸諸州 **201**–10
注文品取揃え係 **175**–10
注文を受ける **82**–E
チューリップ **211**–11
中学校 **188**–3
腸 **107**–42
蝶 **214**–19
蝶ネクタイ **89**–16
聴覚検査士 **115**–9
長距離電話 **15**–32
朝食を食べる **38**–E
聴診器 **118**–10
腸の寄生虫 **111**–13
長髪 **33**–3
長方形 **193**–29
調味料・乾物類の計量 **75**
調理済みの鶏肉 **70**–25
調理する **76**–C, **170**–C
調理台 **54**–22
調理台を拭く **60**–O
調理場 **83**–15
調理用ヘラ **78**–19
聴力障害 **32**–12
聴力障害者用の文字電話 **15**–26
聴力低下 **115**–2
チョーク **7**–18
直線 **193**–22
直毛 **33**–9
著者 **133**–15
貯蔵室 **185**–5
直角／90° **193**–26
直径 **193**–37
散らかし **64**–8
地理と棲息地 **204**
ちりとり **61**–17
治療 **118**
賃金 **165**–12
賃貸契約者 **51**–28
賃貸契約書に署名する **48**–D
鎮痛剤 **113**–26
チンパンジー **217**–27
ツアーに参加する **220**–A
通貨 **26**
通勤する **38**–I
２ドアクーペ **156**–2
２x４（ツーバイフォー）の木材 **181**–19
通訳／翻訳者 **168**–35
通路 **72**–6
通話料請求書 **15**–28
通話料請求書の読み方 **15**
「通話」を押す **15**–B
つえ **113**–16
使い捨て手袋 **93**–27
疲れた **43**–32
月 **21**
継手 **181**–18
次に進むボタン **197**–3
次の行に進む **196**–D
机 **6**–7, **182**–9
机の上を片付ける **10**–I
つける **109**–P
ツタウルシ **210**–25
土 **208**–2
ツナ **72**–19
津波 **145**–17
角 **216**–21
翼 **214**–1
つぼみ **211**–7
妻 **34**–12
つま先 **94**–23, **105**–10
つま先がスチールで保護された作業用ブーツ **92**–6
積み木 **59**–19
爪 **106**–18
爪きり **109**–31
爪にマニキュアを塗る **109**–O
詰め物 **119**–8
爪やすり **109**–32
爪を切る **109**–N
ツリー用の電球 **239**–18
釣竿 **226**–18
つり包帯 **113**–19
つる植物 **210**–22
つるはし **178**–21
手 **105**–15
TSA担当員 **160**–5
DMV係員 **136**–3
DMVハンドブック **136**–1
ティーカップ **55**–6
DJ **64**–4
Tシャツ **86**–4
ティースプーン **83**–31
DVD **133**–19
DVDとCD-Romドライブ **196**–9
DVDプレーヤー **56**–7, **234**–10
ティーポット **55**–16
ティーンエージャー **31**–11
定価 **27**–2
定期刊行物 **133**–4
定期健診を受ける **114**–H
定義を読む **8**–B
テイクアウトボックス **82**–5
定刻 **161**–29
定刻に着く **174**–F
デイジー **211**–14
低脂肪ミルク **81**–42
ディスポーザー **54**–7
停電している **62**–2
ディナー皿 **83**–18
ディナーサラダ **80**–15
ディナーフォーク **83**–28
ディナーロール **80**–17
底面 **193**–45
廷吏 **141**–13
低料金の健康診断 **122**–1
データを入力する **171**–B
デーツ **68**–28
テーブルクロス **55**–12
テーブルセッティング **83**–17
テーブルを整える **82**–A
テールランプ **158**–13
手押し車 **176**–3
デオドラント **108**–5
デオドラントを使う **108**–C
手紙 **134**–13
手紙をタイプする **171**–A
テキスト（メール）メッセージ **14**–19
テキストボックス **197**–13
テキストメッセージ **14**–19
適切な服を着る **174**–B
手首 **106**–14
デコレーション **240**–1
デザートトレー **83**–10
手提げランプ **226**–22
デジタルカメラ **235**–19
デジタルフォトアルバム **235**–32
手錠 **141**–2
デスクトップコンピュータ **196**
テストエリア **136**–2
テストに合格する **10**–E
テストの問題用紙 **10**–1
テストを受ける **10**
テストを提出する **10**–O
手すり **57**–11
デッキ **240**–2
デッドボルト錠 **51**–34
テディベア **37**–23
手で縫う **98**–B
テニス **228**–15
テニスコート **224**–6
テニスシューズ **95**–32
テニスラケット **231**–2
デニム **99**–7
手荷物 **161**–18
手荷物を預ける **160**–B
手荷物を受け取る **160**–L
手荷物を収納する **160**–G
手のひら **106**–15
手羽 **70**–20
デパート **131**–13
デビットカードを使う **27**–C
手袋 **90**–6
デモ **122**–6
テラス **53**–16
テラス用家具 **53**–19
テレビ **56**–6
テレビアニメ **236**–3
テレビゲーム機 **232**–3
テレビ番組の種類 **236**
テレビ用キャビネット **56**–5
テレビを見る **39**–X
テレホンカード **14**–15
テレマーケッター **169**–60
手をあげる **6**–A
手を振る **2**–F
天板ラック **78**–14
店員 **72**–4, **79**–17
田園地帯 **52**–4
天王星 **205**–7
電化製品と写真 **234–235**
天気 **13**
伝記 **133**–13
電気鉛筆削り **183**–26
電気かみそり **109**–26
電気工 **62**–9
天気図 **13**
電気・ガス・水道を点検する **147**–N
電気・水道・ガス会社に連絡し、名義変更する **49**–O
電気店 **131**–20
電気ドリル **180**–8
電気を消す **11**–P, **219**–G
電気をつける **11**–B
電源コード **196**–2
天候に注意する **147**–C
伝言を受ける **171**–Q
伝言を残す **171**–P
電子 **195**–30
電子キーボード **238**–18
電子製品修理人 **167**–24
電車の模型 **233**–27
電車の駅 **152**
電子レンジ **54**–13
選択する **196**–B
デンタルフロス **109**–24
電池 **146**–15
店長 **72**–8
点滴 **121**–25
テント **226**–10
電動缶切り **54**–14
電動サンダー **180**–11
電動ミキサー **54**–25
テントウムシ **214**–26
天然ガス **218**–3
天引き **165**–13
天秤／はかり **195**–41

天文学者 **205**–22
天文台 **205**–21
電話 **14**–15
電話回線コード **14**–4
電話対応能力 **171**
電話で話す **15**–C
電話の相手に挨拶する **171**–M
電話のかけ方 **15**
電話番号 **4**–11, **15**–30
電話番号をダイヤルする **15**–A
電話用ジャック **14**–3
電話を切らずに待機する **15**–H
電話を切る／「切」を押す **15**–D
電話を転送する **171**–O
電話を保留にする **171**–N
ドア **46**–3
ドアに鍵をかける **143**–E
ドアのチェーン **51**–33
ドアノブ **53**–12
ドアベル **53**–14
ドアマン **184**–1
ドアロック **159**–25
トイレ **5**–9
トイレットペーパー **57**–19, **146**–13
トイレブラシ **57**–20
同意する **12**–K
唐辛子 **69**–29
洞窟 **220**–6
動作の前置詞 **153**
当座預金口座番号 **132**–14
搭乗券 **161**–20
搭乗券と身分証明書を見せる **160**–C
搭乗する **160**–E
凍傷になる **116**–G
搭乗待合室 **161**–9
当選者 **139**–32
到着／出発時刻モニター **161**–7
到着が遅れている便 **161**–30
到着する **160**–K
導入部分 **190**–6
糖尿病 **111**–12
投票結果 **139**–31
投票する **140**–A
東部時間 **19**–32
動物園 **222**–1
動物の足 **216**–20
豆腐を切る **77**–C
動脈 **107**–36
トウモロコシ **69**–12, **177**–4
童謡 **37**–22
道路 **150**–5
登録シール **136**–13
道路工事中 **154**–16
討論する **139**–B
トークショー **236**–4
トークセラピー **115**–13
トークン（代用硬貨） **152**–10
トースター **54**–6
トースト **80**–4
トートバッグ **94**–19
ドーナッツ **79**–15
ドーナッツ屋 **129**–17
通り **155**–8
通りを走って横切る **153**–G
通りを渡る **128**–A
都会 **52**–1
戸外のレクリエーション **226**
トカゲ **213**–40
ドクウルシ **210**–23
独裁者 **199**–6
特小 **96**–1
特大 **96**–5
特徴について尋ねる **48**–B
得点 **10**–3, **229**–1
毒物を飲む **116**–J
独立記念日 **22**–13
独立宣言 **198**–5
独立戦争 **198**–8
トグルボルト **180**–38
とげ **211**–29
時計 **7**–9
都市 **52**–1
都市コード **15**–34
土砂崩れ **144**–6
図書館 **125**–15, **133**
図書館 **5**–17
図書館員 **133**–1
図書館カードを作る **133**–A
図書館の貸し出し返却受付デスク **133**–2
図書館利用者 **133**–3
土星 **205**–6
塗装屋（住宅） **168**–46
塗装用はけ **181**–22
戸だな **54**–1, **57**–22
ドック **234**–3
とっておく **28**–B
飛び込む **230**–K
トマト **69**–6
止まれ **154**–1
友達と歩く **143**–A
友達を紹介する **3**–I
土曜日 **20**–14
虎 **217**–37
ドライウォール **178**–19
ドライクリーニング店 **128**–2
ドライバー **180**–30
ドライブウェイ **53**–8
ドライブスルー用の窓口 **128**–11
ドライヤー **108**–18
トラクター **177**–9
トラック **150**–6
トラック運転手 **169**–61
トラックを運転する **170**–E
トラベラーズチェックを換金する **27**–F
ドラマ **236**–12
ドラム **238**–16
ドラムスティック **70**–23
トランク **158**–11
トランクの中 **158**
トランプをする **233**–H
トランペット **238**–11
鳥 **208**–4
取り替える **27**–I
鳥、昆虫、蜘蛛類 **214**
鶏肉 **66**–3, **70**–16
鶏肉を切る **77**–I
鶏肉をゆでる **77**–M
ドリブルする **230**–J
度量衡 **17**
ドリルビット **180**–28
取る **109**–Q
奴隷 **198**–4
トレイ **160**–6
トレイテーブル **161**–21
トレーナー **89**–22
トレーニング **172**–2
トレーラー **156**–17
トレーラートラック **156**–15
トレーラーハウス **52**–7
ドレスソックス **91**–9
トレンチコート **90**–21
ドロップダウンメニュー **197**–8
トロンボーン **238**–10
鈍角 **193**–27
トング **78**–23
トンネルの中を運転する **153**–K
名 **4**–2
内科医 **120**–1
ナイトクラブ **223**–12
ナイトテーブル **58**–23
ナイフ **55**–4, **83**–30
ナイロン **99**–12
長さ **17**–17
流しから水があふれている **63**–18
流し台 **54**–4
流しを洗う **60**–K
長袖シャツ **96**–14
中庭 **5**–1, **51**–21
長ネギ **69**–20
泣く **206**–B
投げる **230**–A, **230**–C
なし **68**–4
ナス **69**–23
なだめる **36**–I
雪崩（なだれ） **145**–18
ナチョス **79**–7
夏 **21**–38
夏時間 **19**–25
ナッツ **73**–36
ナット **180**–36
七 **16**
七十 **16**
七十番 **16**
七番 **16**
75パーセント **17**–9
何かを勧める **12**–D
ナプキン **55**–10, **83**–26
名札 **92**–15
鍋 **54**–16, **78**–6
鍋つかみ **78**–29
名前を言う **4**–A
名前を活字体で書く **4**–C
名前をサインする **4**–D
名前をつづる **4**–B
名前を名乗る **15**–F
ナマズ **71**–2
生の魚 **71**–16
生の鶏肉 **70**–24
波 **225**–17
納屋 **177**–11
なわとび **224**–4
南極 **202**–7
南京虫 **63**–24
軟膏 **113**–24
南西部 **201**–12
南東部／南部 **201**–13
ナンバープレート **136**–12, **158**–12
南部台地 **201**–17
二 **16**
匂いを嗅ぐ **106**–C
2月 **21**–26
肉 **66**–2
肉切り用ナイフ **78**–12
肉体労働をする **170**–D
肉屋 **166**–13
肉類 **70**
肉類と家禽類の調理方法 **76**
煮込む **77**–P
西 **155**–2
2時15分前 **18**–13
2時20分前 **18**–12
二十 **16**
二十一 **16**
二十五 **16**
25セント **26**–4
25パーセント **17**–11
二十三 **16**
20ドル **26**–10
二重鍋 **78**–8
二十二 **16**
二十一番 **16**
二十番 **16**
二十四 **16**
２段ベッド **59**–9
日常会話 **12**
日常生活 **38**–39
日没 **18**–18
日曜日 **20**–8

荷造りする **49**–M
ニッケル **26**–2
日食 **205**–16
ニットトップ **88**–7
荷積みドック **175**–15
荷解きする **49**–N
二番 **16**
荷物受取所 **161**–23
荷物を詰める **162**–A
入院受付係 **120**–14
ニューイングランド地方 **201**–11
入学する **40**–B
乳児 **31**–6
入植者 **198**–2
ニュース **236**–1
乳製品 **72**
乳製品とともに服用しないでください **112**–D
ニューファンドランド時間 **19**–34
入浴させる **36**–F
入浴する **108**–B
ニレ **210**–16
庭師 **167**–28
人形 **59**–21
人形作りキット **232**–13
人形の家 **59**–18
任期を務める **139**–D
ニンジン **69**–3
妊娠している **32**–15
ニンジンの皮をむく **77**–K
認知症 **111**–18
認定看護助手(CAN) **120**–12
ニンニク **69**–30
妊婦服 **88**–5
ぬいぐるみ **59**–15
布おむつ **37**–8
布地の種類 **98–99**
布地屋 **99**
ぬりえ **59**–13
塗る **109**–P
濡れたシャツ **101**–17
根 **210**–5, **211**–3
ネイリスト **168**–38
ネイルサロン **130**–3
願い事をする **240**–B
ネクタイ **86**–A, **88**–12, **92**–13
ネグリジェ **91**–25
猫 **215**–9
ネズミ **63**–27, **215**–17
ネズミイルカ **213**–30
値段 **27**–7
値段を交渉する **102**–A, **157**–D
熱 **110**–8
ネックレス **95**–10
ネットワークを広げる **173**–A
熱波 **13**–13
寝袋 **226**–12
値札 **27**–1
寝巻き **91**–28
眠い **42**–3
眠る **39**–Z
練り歯みがき **109**–23
寝る **39**–Y
年 **20**–4
年間の行事 **22**
燃料計 **159**–31
燃料タンク **158**–10
燃料噴射システム **158**–17
年齢 **32**
脳 **107**–34
農家 **52**–9
農機具 **177**–12
農業生産者 **177**–13
農業と牧畜業 **177**
農夫 **177**–8
農薬汚染 **218**–16
ノースリーブシャツ **96**–11
ノートブックパソコン **196**–16
ノートを取る **10**–C
のこぎり **180**–4
のぞき穴 **51**–32
〜の代金を払う **27**–G
のど **107**–35
のどが渇いた **42**–2
のどがつまる **116**–L
のどの痛み **110**–6
喉の痛みを和らげる薬用ドロップ **113**–30
のどを診察する **118**–E
ノミ **63**–25
のみ **181**–55
のみの市 **222**–6
飲み物 **73**
飲む **11**–J
糊 **183**–33
乗り換え **152**–5
刃 **180**–27
歯 **106**–7
葉 **210**–6, **211**–6
パーカー **90**–9
パーキングメーター **129**–25
パークレンジャー **220**–2
バーコード **27**–4
バースデーパーティ **240–241**
パーセント **17**
パーソナルCDプレーヤー **234**–5
パーティ **64**–2
パーティクルボード **181**–20
ハート **233**–31, **239**–6
ハードドライブ **196**–6
ハーブ **84**–9
ハーブティー **81**–40
バーベキューした **76**–2
パーマをかける **33**–B
ハーモニカ **238**–21
パールのネックレス **95**–39
肺 **107**–39
パイ **81**–35
灰色 **24**–15
灰色のセーターはオレンジ色のセーターの下にあります **25**–11
ハイウェイ **155**–9
ハイウェイから下りる **153**–J
ハイウェイ指標 **154**–17
ハイウェイに乗る **153**–I
ハイエナ **217**–30
バイオマス／バイオエネルギー **218**–9
バイオリン **238**–6
バイオレットのセーターは灰色のセーターの隣にあります **25**–10
配管工 **63**–20
排気管 **158**–15
排水口 **57**–7
排気チェックを行う **157**–J
ハイキング **226**–7
ハイキングブーツ **95**–31
パイ皿 **78**–28
陪審員 **141**–8
陪審員を務める **140**–E
配線 **186**–7
ハイソックス **91**–12
配達者 **168**–40
配達人 **167**–21
ハイヒール **89**–21, **95**–25
ハイビスカス **211**–12
パイプ **181**–17
ハイブリッド **156**–3
パイプレンチ **181**–47
ハイフン **190**–20
ハイムリック法(異物を吐き出させる応急処置) **117**–18
ハイヤー **156**–11
俳優 **166**–2
パイロット **161**–11
パインストリートを右に曲がる **155**–B
パインナップル **68**–23
ハエ **214**–28
葉書 **134**–16
歯固めリング **37**–25
はかり **72**–3, **135**–8
吐き気がする **110**–D
吐く **110**–E
白衣 **93**–33
歯茎 **106**–6
パクチョイ **69**–15
白髪 **33**–13
爆発 **144**–4
はげ **33**–12
バケツ **61**–7, **225**–8
箱 **74**–6
箱詰め担当者 **175**–8
ハザードランプ **159**–36
はさみ **33**–20, **100**–16
はしか **111**–5
はしご **178**–2
橋の上を行く **153**–B
橋の下を行く **153**–A
始めて運転免許を取る **137**
パジャマ **91**–24
バス **128**–9, **151**–14
バスーン **238**–4
恥ずかしい **43**–24
バスケット **56**–3
バスケットボール **229**–8
バスケットボールのボール **231**–4
バスケットボールコート **229**–7
パスする **230**–G
パスタ **67**–12
バスタオル **57**–16
パスタサラダ **80**–20
バス停 **124**–7, **129**–16, **151**–13, **152**
パストラミ **71**–23
バスに乗って学校に行く **38**–H
パスポート **41**–10
バスマット **57**–28
パズル **59**–17
バスルーム **46**–4
バス路線 **152**–1
パスワードをタイプする **197**–A
パセリ **69**–28
旗 **239**–8
バター **66**–6
はたき **61**–1
畑 **177**–7
働く **38**–K
八 **16**
８月 **21**–32
八十 **16**
八十番 **16**
ハチドリ **214**–10
八番 **16**
８分の１ **17**–5
爬虫類 **213**
発音をチェックする **8**–D
ハツカネズミ **63**–28, **215**–18
バックパック **94**–18, **226**–15
バックパッキング **226**–6
バックホー **178**–8
バックミラー **159**–35
バッグや財布を守る **143**–D
バックル **94**–20, **99**–28
パッケージ **74**–8
パッケージ食品 **146**–10
バッジ **93**–21
ハッシュブラウン **80**–3
バッタ **214**–24
バッテリ **158**–20
バッテリーチャージャー **235**–27
バッテリーパック **235**–26

バッファロー **216**–6
発明 **199**–19
発明家 **199**–18
鳩 **214**–15
バドミントン **228**–6
花 **208**–7, **211**
鼻 **104**–6
花柄 **96**–25
鼻血 **110**–17
話し合い療法 **115**–13
花束 **211**–28
鼻づまり **110**–7
バナナ **68**–2
鼻のスプレー **113**–32
花の部分 **211**
花火 **239**–7
花びら **211**–8
ハナミズキ **210**–15
花屋 **130**–8, **167**–27
歯にデンタルフロスをかける **109**–K
羽 **214**–4
歯のクリーニングを行う **119**–A
歯の治療 **119**
歯の問題 **119**
幅 **17**–19
パパイヤ **68**–20
母親 **34**–3
歯ブラシ **57**–23, **109**–22
歯ブラシ立て **57**–24
ハマグリ **71**–15
ハム **70**–9
早い **19**–22
早送りする **235**–D
バラ **211**–15
針 **98**–17, **100**–10
鍼 **122**–2
針板 **98**–18
ハリケーン **145**–14
針刺し **100**–13
針状葉 **210**–10
針（ヤマアラシなどの） **216**–23
春 **21**–37
バルコニー **51**–20
晴れ **13**–9
パレード **239**–1
バレーボール **229**–14
バレーボールのボール **231**–3
腫れた指 **110**–16
バレッタ **108**–20
パレット **175**–13
ハワイ・アリューシャン時間 **19**–27
歯を削る **119**–D
歯を抜く **119**–F
歯を磨く **109**–J
パン **67**–11
ハンガー **101**–11
半径 **193**–35
番号案内 **14**–22
パンサー **217**–40
犯罪 **142**
犯罪を警察に通報する **143**–K
判事 **138**–12, **141**–6
バンジーコード **181**–15
反射安全ベルト **92**–4
盤上ゲーム **232**–5
パン職人 **166**–10
ばんそうこう **117**–5
半袖シャツ **96**–12
パンダ **217**–41
反対する **12**–L
バンダナ **92**–16
パンツ **91**–14
パンティストッキング **91**–18
半島 **204**–7
ハンドセット **14**–1
ハンドタオル **57**–17
パンとバター用の皿 **83**–19
ハンドバッグ **87**–9, **94**–2
ハンドブックを学習する **137**–A
ハンドブレーキ **159**–48
ハンドル **159**–26
バンパー **158**–8
ハンバーガー **79**–1
販売員 **94**–3
パンプス **95**–26
半分 **17**–2
ハンマー **180**–1
ハンマーで打つ **178**–D
ハンモック **53**–23
パン屋 **127**–19
ピアス **95**–36
ピアスをした耳 **32**–17
ピアノ **238**–14
ビーカー **195**–39
ビーズ **95**–34, **99**–32
ヒーター **159**–40
ビーチガウン **90**–25
ビーチチェア **225**–22
ビーチパラソル **225**–14
ヒーティングパッド **113**–13
ビート **69**–5
ビーバー **216**–9
PBX（構内電話交換機） **182**–13
ピーマン **69**–7
ヒイラギ **210**–19
被害者 **142**–10
日陰 **225**–13
東 **155**–4
ヒキガエル **212**–28
引き出し **54**–23, **58**–2
（ビキニ型）パンティ **91**–13
挽肉 **70**–4
引く **192**–B
低いかかと **97**–31
ピクニックテーブル **224**–8
ピクニックをする **224**–D
ピクルス **80**–11
ひげ **216**–18
悲劇 **237**–14
ひげを剃る **109**–M
飛行機 **150**–8
飛行機墜落事故 **144**–3
飛行機に乗る **160**
飛行機を操縦する **170**–F
被告 **141**–5
被告側の弁護士 **141**–4
被告に有罪判決を下す **141**–E
被告を刑に処する **141**–F
膝 **106**–20
ピザ **79**–10
膝あて **179**–19
ひじ **106**–12
ひじかけ椅子 **56**–22
ビジネススーツ **88**–11
ビジネスマン **166**–12
美術 **189**–15
美術館 **223**–9
非常口 **50**–2, **51**–25, **161**–14
ビスケット **80**–6
微積分 **192**–19
ひたい **106**–2
ビタミン **113**–17
微調整用ノブ **194**–22
筆記試験を受ける **137**–E
日付 **20**–1
引越し **49**
引越し業者 **168**–42
引越しトラック **156**–18
引っ越す **48**–F
ヒツジ **215**–6
ヒップホップ **237**–26
ひづめ **216**–17
ビデオカセット **133**–18
ビデオカメラ **235**–24
ビデオテープレコーダー **102**–7
ビデオ店 **129**–20
ビデオプレーヤー **197**–11
ビデオを撮影する **240**–A
ひとかたまり **74**–10
1缶の豆 **74**–15
ヒトデ **212**–16
人と会ってあいさつする **2–3**
人の特徴 **32**
1箱のクッキー **74**–20
1箱のシリアル **74**–18
人々を監督する **170**–O
1瓶のジャム **74**–14
1袋のレタス **69**–31
1袋の小麦粉 **74**–19
1房のバナナ **68**–29
避難経路 **146**–3
避難所を見つける **147**–H
非難する **147**–K
避難路 **146**–5
日の出 **18**–14
ヒヒ **217**–31
備品キャビネット **182**–1
皮膚 **107**–31
ヒマワリ **211**–10
百 **16**
百一 **16**
100ドル **26**–12
100パーセント **17**–8
百番 **16**
百万 **16**
日焼け **110**–14
日焼け止め **108**–8
冷やす **76**–D
ヒューズボックス **62**–13
ピューマ **216**–2
ビュッフェ **185**–10
秒 **18**–3
ヒョウ **217**–34
病院 **120–121**
病院 **125**–9, **154**–18
病院の職員 **120**
病院のベッド **121**–22
病気で休むことを電話で連絡する **186**–A
病気の症状とけが **110**
病気を治す方法 **114**
美容師 **167**–31
評決 **141**–14
標識 **129**–26
病室 **121**
標準時 **19**–26
病棟勤務員 **120**–16
氷のう **117**–13
漂白剤 **101**–7
表面 **193**–44
雹（ひょう）をともなった嵐 **13**–21
平鍋 **54**–24
ヒラメ **212**–15
ピリオド **190**–11
ビリヤード **228**–2
ビリヤード台 **50**–15
肥料をやる **176**–D
昼寝する **53**–A
ひれ **212**–1
びん **74**–2
ピンク色 **24**–7
ピンセット **195**–43
便箋 **183**–42
頻度 **20**
びんの返却口 **73**–16
ピンぼけ **235**–33
ファイルキャビネット **182**–11
ファイル担当者 **182**–10
ファイルフォルダ **183**–50

ファイルを添付する **197**–H
ファクシミリ機 **183**–21
ファーストフード店 **128**–10
ファーストフードの店 **79**
ファスナー **99**–25
ファスナーが壊れている **97**–39
ファン **229**–4
ファンデーション **109**–40
フィードバックを得る **191**–K
フィールド **5**–2
フィギュアスケート **227**–5
VCR **102**–7
フィットシーツ **58**–12
Vネックのセーター **96**–8
フィリング **119**–8
フィルム **235**–22
フィルムカメラ／35mmカメラ **235**–21
フィン **225**–7
ブース **122**–3
ブースターケーブル **158**–21
風船 **44**–4
ブーツ **95**–28
封筒 **134**–14, **183**–43
封筒に住所を書く **135**–B
フードコート **131**–15
フードプロセッサー **54**–56
フード付きトレーナー **89**–22
夫婦 **35**–20
風力 **218**–2
プール **51**–22, **184**–22
プール清掃 **184**–21
フェースマスク **93**–32
フェリー **220**–4
フェンシング **228**–7
フェンス **177**–19
フォーク **55**–3, **237**–29
フォークリフト **175**–12
４ドアセダン **156**–1
フォーマルな服装 **89**
フォトアルバム **235**–31
不快な **42**–9
不快な眺め **23**–22
深さ **17**–18
服用量 **112**–6
布巾 **61**–22
復員軍人の日 **22**–16
副校長 **5**–5
複数の女性 **30**–3
複数の男性 **30**–4
副大統領 **138**–9
副知事 **139**–21
腹痛 **110**–4
服にアイロンをかける **101**–G
腹部 **107**–27
服用にあたっての注意 **112**
ふくらはぎ **106**–22
副料理長 **185**–6
袋 **74**–7
フクロウ **214**–5
袋詰め係 **73**–14
フクロネズミ **216**–4
服を着せる **36**–H
服を着る **38**–D
服を作る **98–99**
服を脱がせる **36**–E
服をハンガーにかける **101**–H
ブザー **51**–31
無作法にふるまう **44**–B
婦人服の仕立て屋 **100**–1
不審物について通報する **143**–J
付箋紙 **183**–39
ふた **78**–24
豚 **215**–2
双子 **28**–1
豚肉 **70**
２人で学習する **8**
普段着 **86–87**
不注意な作業者 **179**–1
普通預金口座番号 **132**–11
フック **180**–39
フットボール **229**–11
フットボールのボール **231**–21
フットボールヘルメット **231**–19
物理 **195**
物理学者 **195**–33
太いネクタイ **97**–36
武道 **228**–11
ブドウ **68**–3
ブドウ園 **177**–16
不動産業者と会う **49**–G
太っている **32**–7
負の整数 **192**–1
部品 **175**–5
部品を組み立てる **170**–A
吹雪 **13**–23
不満な **43**–27
踏切 **154**–14
冬 **21**–40
プライオリティメール
（優先扱い郵便） **134**–1
フライドチキン **76**–1
フライドポテト **79**–2
フライパン **78**–5
ブラインド **58**–8
ブラウス **87**–8
プラグ **234**–16
ブラシ **33**–22, **108**–14
ブラジャー **91**–20
プラスチックのフォークやナイフ **79**–19
プラスチックの保存容器 **78**–4
プラスのドライバー **180**–31
ブラックベリー **68**–17
フラッシュドライブ **196**–8
フラットシーツ **58**–13
フラットシューズ **95**–27
プラットホーム **152**–7
プラム **68**–13
プラモデル **232**–9
ブランコ **224**–11
ブランコを押す **224**–B
プランジャー **181**–50
フリーサイズ **96**–6
ブリーフ **91**–5
ブリーフケース **88**–13
プリスクール **188**–1
フリスビー **231**–27
プリズム **195**–35
ブリティッシュコロンビア **201**–2
ブリトー **79**–9
フリンジ **99**–34
プリンタ **196**–17
プリント柄 **96**–23
ブルース **237**–22
フルーツサラダ **80**–21
フルート **238**–1
ブルーベリー **68**–16
プルーン **68**–26
古着 **102**–2
ブルドーザー **178**–6
プレイエリア **130**–11
ブレーキペダル **159**–45
ブレーキランプ **158**–14
プレーリー諸州 **201**–3
プレーリードッグ **215**–22
ブレザー **92**–12
ブレスレット **95**–9
プレゼンテーション **182**–6
プレゼント／ギフト **240**–3
プレゼントを包む **240**–F
ブレッドバスケット **83**–11
触れる **106**–E
フレンチホルン **238**–13
フロアプラン **186**–4
フロアランプ **56**–15
ブロイラー **54**–21
ブロイルしたステーキ **76**–3
フローズンヨーグルト１パイント **75**–3
ブローチ **95**–38
ブロッコリ **69**–13
ブロッコリーを蒸す **77**–D
風呂に入る **108**–B
風呂場 **57**
フロント係 **184**–11
フロントガラス **158**–1
フロントシート **159**–51
フロントデスク **184**–12
フロントポーチ **53**
分 **18**–2
文 **190**–2
分割する **17**–A
分子 **192**–5, **195**–27
文章題 **192**–11
文章を書き取り用に口述する **8**–N
文章を正しい順に並べる **9**–X
文書を印刷する **171**–I
文書をスキャンする **171**–H
文書をファックスする **171**–G
噴水 **224**–5
分数 **192**
分数と小数 **17**
ブンゼンバーナー **195**–37
文の最初の文字は大文字にする **190**–B
文筆家 **169**–64
分母 **192**–6
文房具店 **127**–21
文明 **199**
ヘアクリップ **108**–19
ヘアサロン **131**–18
ヘアジェル **108**–16
ヘアスタイリスト **167**–31
ヘアスプレー **108**–12
ヘアドライヤー **33**–23
ヘアネット **93**–25
平均的な身長 **32**–5
平均的な体重 **32**–8
平原 **204**–19
平行四辺形 **193**–33
平行線 **193**–25
米国国会議事堂 **138**–1
米国市民になる **40**–G
米国に5年以上住んでいる **140**–H
米国の国立公園 **220–221**
兵士 **169**–58
平日 **20**–16
平和的な集会の自由 **140**–1
ベーカリー製品 **73**
ベーキング用製品 **73**
ベークドポテト **81**–25
ベーグル **73**–40
ベーコン **70**–11, **80**–1
ページ順にそろえる **171**–E
ベージュ色 **24**–18
ペーズリー柄 **96**–26
ペーパータオル **54**–3
ベスト **89**–15
ペチコート **91**–23
ペット **215**
ベッド **58**–9
ベッドカバー **59**–11
ペットショップ **130**–6
ベッドスカート **58**–17
ヘッドセット **14**–13
ベッド調整 **121**–27
ベッドテーブル **121**–21
ヘッドバンド **90**–3
ペットフード **72**–5
ベッドフレーム **58**–18
ヘッドボード **58**–10

ヘッドホン **6**–8, **234**–4
ヘッドライト **158**–7
ヘッドラップ **90**–7
ベッドを整える **60**–F
ペニー **26**–1
ベビーカー **37**–18
ベビーキャリア **37**–17
ベビーシッター **166**–9
ベビーチェア／ハイチェア **37**–6, **82**–3
ベビーパウダー **37**–14
ベビーバッグ **37**–16
ベビーフード **37**–4
ベビーベッド **59**–3
ベビーモニター **59**–7
ベビーローション **37**–13
ヘラジカ **216**–1
ヘリコプター **151**–9
ベルキャプテン **184**–6
ヘルスフェア **122–123**
ベルト **94**–6
ベルベット **99**–10
ベルボーイ **184**–7
ヘルメット **92**–1, **93**–23, **179**–9
ペン **7**–22
便器 **57**–21, **121**–23
ペンキ **181**–25
便器が詰っている **63**–19
ペンキ塗り用シート **181**–54
ペンキ用パン **181**–51
ペンキローラー **181**–23
ペンキを塗る **49**–P, **178**–A
ペンギン **214**–11
弁護士 **168**–36
弁護士を雇う **141**–B
編集する **191**–I
返事を書く **135**–H
変数 **192**–12
ペンチ **180**–7
ベンチ **224**–10
返品する **27**–H
ホイールキャップ **158**–9
保育園 **129**–30, **188**–1
保育士 **166**–16
保育と育児 **36–37**
ボイスメッセージ **14**–18
ポインセチア **211**–24
ポインタ **197**–12
望遠鏡 **205**–23
望遠レンズ **235**–23
放火 **142**–7
防寒用耳あて **90**–13
ほうき **61**–16
暴行 **142**–3
膀胱 **107**–46
防護バイザー **179**–12
帽子 **88**–1, **90**–1, **95**–11, **206**–7
放射性物質 **179**–7
放射線 **218**–15
放射線医 **120**–6
防塵マスク **179**–14
縫製工場 **98**
宝石売場 **95**–8
宝石店 **130**–2
法廷 **141**–7
法廷速記者 **141**–12
法定休日 **22**, **22**–8
方程式 **192**–13
報道の自由 **140**–4
棒によじ登る **224**–C
防犯カメラ **50**–19
防犯ゲート **50**–16
防風ドア **53**–10
法律制度 **141**
法律用箋 **183**–38
法律を守る **140**–C
ボウリング **228**–3
ボウリング場 **222**–4
ボウリングのボール **231**–5
ボウル **55**–2
ホウレンソウ **69**–11
ホウレンソウサラダ **80**–13
頬 **106**–3
ポークチョップ **70**–10
ホース **53**–21
ポータブルDVDプレーヤー **234**–11
ポータブルカセットプレーヤー **234**–6
ポータブルテレビ **234**–8
ポーチドエッグ **76**–9
ポーチの電灯 **53**–13
ボート乗り **226**–1
頬紅 **109**–37
ホームシックにかかった **43**–20
ホームセンター **127**–20
ボール **59**–12
ボクサーショーツ **91**–4
牧場 **52**–10
牧場主 **177**–22
ボクシング **228**–4
ほくろ **32**–16
ポケット **100**–7
保健体育 **189**–17
歩行器 **113**–11
歩行者 **128**–14
保護者面談 **22**–5
保護用帽子 **92**–9
誇りに思って **43**–21
星 **205**–13
干し草 **177**–18
星印ボタン **14**–6
細いネクタイ **97**–35
ホタテ貝 **71**–12, **212**–19
ボタン **99**–24
ボタンが取れている **97**–40
ボタン類 **99**
墓地 **127**–15
ホッチキスで留める **171**–F
ホッチキスの針 **183**–29
補聴器 **115**–10
ボックススプリング **58**–19
ボックス席 **82**–4
ホッケースティック **231**–11
ホッチキス **183**–28
ホットケーキ **80**–7
ホットドック **79**–6
ポップ **237**–25
ポップアップ広告 **197**–9
ほつれている **97**–43
ホテル客 **184**–10
ボディースーツ **91**–15
ボディローション **108**–9
ポテトサラダ **80**–19
ポテトチップ **73**–35
ホテル **124**–3, **184**
歩道 **129**–24
ボトル **74**–1
ボトル入り飲料水 **146**–11
哺乳びん **37**–1
（哺乳びんの）乳首 **37**–2
哺乳類 **209**–10
哺乳類 **216–217**
骨 **107**–33
骨付きのあばら肉 **70**–5
ボビーピン **108**–21
ボビン **98**–21
ほめる **36**–J
ホラー **237**–17
ボランティア **121**–17
ボランティア活動をする **41**–Q
ボルト **180**–35
ポロシャツ **92**–14
ホワイトハウス **138**–7
ホワイトボード **6**–3
ホワイトボード用マーカー **7**–17
本だな **7**–10
ポンチョ **90**–19
ボンネット **158**–4
ボンネットの中 **158**
本文 **190**–7
本を一緒に使う **8**–M
本を返す **133**–D
本を借り出す **133**–C
本を探す **133**–B
本をしまう **9**–Z
本を閉じる **6**–H
本を届ける **11**–G
本を運ぶ **11**–F
本を開く **6**–G
本を持ち上げる **11**–E
本を読み聞かせる **36**–N
マーガリン **72**–20
マイカーの相乗りをする **219**–I
マイク **234**–18
マイクロプロセッサ／CPU **196**–4
迷子 **144**–1
毎日 **20**–21
マウス **196**–15
マウスウォッシュ **109**–25
マウンテンバイキング **226**–8
前掛け **93**–30
前髪 **33**–8
前に戻るボタン **197**–2
前庭と家 **53**
マガジンラック **56**–23
巻 **74**–11
巻毛 **33**–11
巻尺 **100**–17, **181**–45
巻き戻す **235**–C
枕 **58**–11
枕カバー **58**–14
マグロ **71**–7, **212**–8
曲げる **230**–O
孫が生まれる **41**–N
マザーボード **196**–5
マジックペン **7**–24
まじめな写真 **206**–3
マス **71**–1
麻酔医 **121**–35
マスカラ **109**–39
マスキングテープ **181**–53
マスタード **79**–22
混ぜた材料を泡立てる **77**–S
混ぜる **77**–O
マタニティストア **131**–19
街 **126–127**
待合室で **118**
間違いを消す **10**–M
間違いを直す **10**–N
まち針 **100**–12
マツ **210**–9
まつげ **106**–11
マッシュポテト **81**–23
マッシュルームを炒める **77**–E
マッチ **146**–16, **226**–21
マットレス **58**–20
松葉杖 **113**–10
松ぼっくり **210**–11
的 **231**–7
窓 **47**–11, **56**–17
窓ガラス **178**–16
窓から離れる **147**–I
窓が割れている **62**–5
窓口 **136**–7
窓を拭く **60**–I
まな板 **54**–27
生ごみを堆肥にする **219**–M
マニキュア液 **109**–33
マニュアルトランスミッション **159**
まねをする **233**–G

マフィン **79**–16
まぶた **106**–10
マフラー **90**–5, **158**–16
豆類 **72**–17
眉毛 **106**–9
眉墨 **109**–34
真夜中 **18**–21
マヨネーズ **79**–23
マリーゴールド **211**–13
丸首のセーター **96**–7
丸のこ **180**–9
周りの様子に注意する **143**–I
満月 **205**–12
マンゴー **68**–21
万引き **142**–8
満腹の **42**–6
万力 **180**–26
ミートボール **81**–27
ミートローフ **81**–32
三日月 **205**–10
ミカン **68**–9
幹 **210**–4
ミキサー **54**–12
ミキシングボウル **54**–28, **78**–31
ミシン **98**–13
ミシンで縫う **98**–A
ミシンの部品 **98**
ミシンを使う人 **98**–14
水 **57**–10, **209**–13
水1ガロン **75**–5
水色 **24**–11
湖 **204**–13
水亀 **213**–43
水着 **90**–26
水切りかご **54**–5
水きり器 **78**–17
水玉模様 **96**–21
ミステリー／サスペンス **237**–20
水飲み場 **224**–9
水ぶくれ **110**–15
水ぼうそう **111**–6
水漏れする蛇口を直す **219**–F
水を入れるコップ **83**–22
水を節約する **219**–E
水を注ぐ **82**–C
溝かんな **180**–12
見出し **133**–7
身だしなみをきちんとする **174**–C
みだしなみ **108–109**
道順 **155**
道順と地図 **155**
道に迷う **162**–B
ミックスベリー **81**–36
ミツバチ **214**–25
ミディ丈のスカート **96**–17
見て回る **102**–B
緑色 **24**–5
緑色のセーターはピンク色のセーターの間にあります **25**–12
ミドルネームのイニシャル **4**–3
ミトン **90**–10
南 **155**–3
南アメリカ **202**–2
ミニスカート **96**–15
ミニバン **156**–8
身分証明書とクレジットカードのコピー **146**–19
身分証明書を見せる **137**–C
耳 **105**–12
耳あて **179**–16
耳が聞こえない **32**–12
耳栓 **179**–15
耳の痛み **110**–3
脈を計る **122**–A
ミュージシャン **168**–43
見る **106**–A
ミルクシェイク **79**–14
身を隠す **147**–J
民兵 **198**–10
ムール貝 **71**–13, **212**–17
麦わら帽子 **90**–23
無菌ガーゼ **117**–6
無菌テープ **117** 7
無地 **96**–19
蒸し器 **78**–3
虫さされ **110**–11
蒸した野菜 **81**–32
無地のブラウス **97**–33
虫歯 **119**–7
虫歯を埋める **119**–E
虫除けスプレー **226**–23
難しい問題 **23**–24
息子 **34**–15
娘 **34**–14
無脊椎動物 **194**–13
胸 **104**–4, **107**–25
胸(乳房) **107**–26
胸肉 **70**–19
村 **52**–3
紫色 **24**–6
紫色のセーターは真ん中にあります **25**–2
目 **105**–11, **106**
芽 **211**–5
姪 **34**–18
名所旧跡 **220**–1
メインストリートを通り過ぎる **155**–E
メークアップ **109**
メーター **152**–23
メールを送信する **197**–I
メールをチェックする **39**–W
メカジキ **71**–5, **212**–10
眼鏡 **115**–7
眼鏡店 **130**–9
目が見えない **32**–11
メキシコ高原 **201**–15
メキシコの各地方 **201**
目薬 **113**–31
目覚まし時計 **58**–24
目覚まし時計付きラジオ **102**–6
メスシリンダー **195**–38
目玉焼き **76**–10
メッセージをタイプする **197**–E
メッセージをチェックする **171**–R
メッセンジャー **168**–40
メディアメール **134**–3
メニュー **82**–7
メニューバー **197**–1
メニューを見て注文する **82**–D
めまいがする **110**–C
メモリカード **235**–20
メロドラマ **236**–5
メロン **68**–19
目を覚ます **38**–A
目を診察する **118**–D
綿 **98**–1, **177**–6
免許を取る **137**–I
面積と体積 **193**
面接技能 **174**
面接担当者に挨拶する **174**–H
面接担当者にお礼を言う **174**–N
面接に行く **173**–K
面接の準備をする **174**–A
面接を取り付ける **173**–I
メンテナンス **184**–23
雌鶏 **215**–8
面ファスナー **99**–29
麺棒 **78**–30
モイスチャライザー **108**–9
申込書を提出する **48**–C
毛布 **58**–15, **146**–7, **225**–11
猛吹雪 **13**–23, **145**–13
モーテル **126**–12
木星 **205**–5
目的地 **162**–5
目標を立てる **10**–A
木曜日 **20**–12
文字を並べ替える **9**–W
モスク **126**–5
持ち主となる **49**–K
木管楽器 **238**
木工キット **232**–14
モッツァレラチーズ **71**–29
持ってくる **240**–E
モデル **168**–41
元の位置に戻した座席 **161**–28
モニタ／画面 **196**–11
物置 **50**–17
物の描写 **23**
物干しロープ **101**–9
物を集める **232**–A
モビール **59**–5
もみあげ **33**–7
腿 **106**–19
モモ **68**–10
もも肉 **70**–22
模様 **96**
モルモット **215**–14
溺れる **116**–I
門 **53**–9
モンキーレンチ **181**–48
問診票 **118**–4
問題について話し合う **8**–G
矢 **231**–8
ヤード尺 **181**–16
やかん **54**–17
ヤギ **215**–5
焼き皿に油を塗る **77**–B
野球 **229**–9
野球カード **232**–2
野球の試合 **44**–2
野球のバット **231**–14
野球のピッチャーをつとめる **230**–A
野球のボール **231**–18
野球帽 **86**–5
薬剤師 **112**–1
火傷をする **116**–H
野菜 **66**–8, **69**
野菜の皮むき器 **78**–15
野菜を加える **77**–N
ヤシ **210**–14
安い指輪 **23**–20
野生生物 **220**–3
やせている **32**–9
屋台 **129**–29
薬局 **128**–4
雇い人 **177**–20
ヤナギ **210**–13
家主 **51**–27
屋根 **46**–1
屋根板 **178**–20
屋根裏 **47**–8
屋根が雨漏りしている **62**–3
屋根職人 **62**–8
破れている **97**–41
ヤマアラシ **216**–10
山火事 **144**–7
柔らかい椅子 **23**–6
油圧計 **159**–29
URL ／ウェブサイトアドレス **197**–4
U.S. 国道 **154**–17
USBポート **196**–7
遊園地 **223**–10
夕方 **18**–19
有機食品 **84**–2
融合(核) **218**–10
有効期限 **136**–10
夕食を食べる **39**–S

友人と話す **173**–A
郵送用梱包 **183**–40
Uターン可 **154**–5
有毒ガス **179**–3
夕飯を作る **39**–Q
郵便受け **50**–11, **53**–1
郵便関係の書類 **134**–19
郵便局 **125**–11
郵便局 **134–135**
郵便局員 **169**–49
郵便局の係員 **135**–7
郵便集配人 **134**–20
郵便番号 **4**–9
郵便ポスト **128**–13, **135**–12
郵便用はかり **183**–27
床 **46**–6
ユカタン半島 **201**–19
床屋 **129**–19
床を掃く **60**–J
床をモップで拭く **60**–D
雪 **13**–12
揺する **36**–D
ゆずれ **154**–9
ユダヤ教会 **127**–16
湯たんぽ **113**–15
ゆっくり運転する人 **23**–4
ゆでたハム **76**–5
ゆで卵 **76**–8
ユニバーサルリモコン **234**–9
ユニフォーム **88**–10, **231**–16
指 **105**–16
指ぬき **100**–15
指輪 **95**–40
弓 **231**–6
弓のこ **180**–5
ユリ **211**–26
揺り椅子 **37**–21
ゆりかご **59**–20
ゆるいズボン **97**–30
良い犬 **23**–17
良い成績を収める方法 **10**
良い成績を取る **10**–H
容器 **74**–5
容疑者を逮捕する **141**–A
容器とパッケージ **74**
陽子 **195**–31
幼児 **31**–8
用紙の記入 **4**
溶接工 **169**–63
腰痛 **110**–5
曜日 **20**, **20**–2
溶連菌感染による咽頭炎 **111**–4
ヨーグルト **72**–22
ヨーロッパ **202**–3
ヨガ **122**–4
預金 **132**–3
預金する **132**–B
預金通帳 **132**–10
預金伝票 **132**–4
浴槽 **57**–2
横になって休む **114**–B
汚れたTシャツ **101**–15
予算 **186**–3
よだれかけ **37**–5
ヨット **225**–3
呼び出しボタン **121**–28
予防注射を受ける **114**–I
予約（医師などの） **22**–4
予約（医師や検査の） **118**–1
夜 **18**–20
強い信号 **14**–11
四 **16**
四十 **16**
四十番 **16**
四番 **16**
４分の１ **17**–4
雷雨 **13**–16
ライオン **217**–36
来週 **20**–20
ライス **81**–30
来賓講演者 **206**–4
ライフガード **225**–19
ライフガード詰め所 **225**–21
ライブミュージック **84**–1
ライム **68**–8
ライ麦パン **71**–20
ライン監督者 **175**–4
落書き **148**–1
ラクダ **217**–38
ラクダのコブ **217**–51
ラゲージカート **184**–8
ラケットボール **228**–12
ラジエータ **158**–19
ラジオ **159**–37
ラズベリー **68**–15
ラック **98**–16
ラッコ **213**–35
ラディッシュ **69**–4
ラテックス製手袋 **93**–34
ラブシート／２人用ソファー **56**–1
ラブストーリー **237**–16
ラマ **217**–25
ラムチョップ **70**–15
ラム肉 **70**
ラムのすね肉 **70**–13
ラムレッグ **70**–14
ラン **211**–19
乱気流 **161**–22
ランチョンマット **55**–11
ランプ **58**–25
ランプシェード **58**–26
リアリティショー **236**–6
リース契約書 **51**–28
リーフブロワー **176**–2
理学療法 **115**–11
理学療法士 **115**–12
陸亀 **213**–42
陸軍 **138**–14
陸上競技 **228**–18
陸上競技のトラック **5**–21
リクルーター **172**–14
離婚した夫婦 **35**–21
リサイクルする **219**–C
リサイクル製品を購入する **219**–D
リサイクル品入れ **61**–2
リス **215**–21
リソースセンター **172**–9
立候補する **139**–A
立体 **193**
立法機関 **138**
立方体 **193**–38
リビング **47**–12, **56**
リボルバー式対物レンズ **194**–15
リボン **99**–30
料金 **152**–2
料金カード **152**–11
漁師 **167**–17
領収書 **27**–6
両生類 **212**
療法士 **115**–14
料理長 **185**–7
料理と安全 **76**–77
料理を出す **82**–F
旅行する **162–163**
旅行する **41**–P
旅行代理店 **131**–14
離陸する **160**–J
履歴書とカバーレターを送る **173**–H
履歴書と身分証明書を持参する **174**–D
履歴書を書く **173**–F
リンク **197**–10
リングノート **7**–29
リンゴ **68**–1
リンゴジュース **73**–32
ルーズリーフ **7**–28
ルームサービス **184**–17
ルームメート **64**–1
留守番電話 **14**–17
るつぼばさみ **195**–44
礼状を書く **174**–O
冷水で洗濯する **219**–K
冷蔵庫 **54**–9
冷暖房のサーモスタットを調節する **219**–J
冷凍庫 **54**–10
冷凍食品 **72**
冷凍ディナー **72**–28
冷凍の魚 **71**–17
冷凍野菜 **72**–27
レイヤーケーキ **81**–33
レイヨウ **217**–35
レインコート **90**–18
レーザープリンタ **183**–19
レース **99**–9
レーズン **68**–25
レーズン1/2カップ **75**–9
歴史 **189**–12
歴史用語 **199**
レゲエ **237**–32
レジ **27**–10, **73**–15
レシート **27**–6
レジ係 **73**–13, **166**–15
レジ台 **73**–12
レストラン **125**–14
レストラン **82–83**
レストランのダイニングルーム **185**
レストランの調理室 **185**
レスリング **228**–17
レタス **69**–1
列 **73**–11
レッカー車 **156**–14
レッグ **70**–21
列車 **150**–7
列に並んで待つ **94**–B
レバー **70**–7
レポーター **169**–52
レモネード **84**–3
レモン **68**–7
煉瓦 **178**–12
煉瓦職人 **186**–8
煉瓦を積む **178**–B
連続ホームコメディ **236**–2
レントゲンを撮る **119**–B
連邦政府 **138**
廊下 **5**–10, **51**, **184**–18
老人ホーム **52**–12
ろうそくを吹き消す **240**–C
ろうと **195**–40
労働者の日 **22**–14
ローカットソックス **91**–10
ロース **70**–1
ロースとした七面鳥 **76**–4
ローストチキン **81**–22
ローストビーフ **71**–21
ローストビーフ1ポンド **75**–12
ロースト用天板 **78**–13
ロータリーカードファイル **183**–44
ロータリーカッター **232**–16
ロープ **226**–19
ローファー **95**–30
ローマ数字 **16**
ローンを組む **49**–J
六 **16**
ログオンしてメールを送信する **197**
録音を書き取る **171**–C
録画する **235**–A
6月 **21**–30
6歳の少年 **31**–9
六十 **16**

Index 索引

六十番 **16**
六番 **16**
ロケット **95**–35
露光オーバー **235**–34
露光不足 **235**–35
路地 **51**–24
ロッカー **5**–11
ロッキー山脈諸州 **201**–8
ロック **237**–23
ロックコンサート **222**–5
ロックバンドのメンバーである **238**–D
肋骨 **107**–48
6本入りのソーダ1パック **74**–21
6本入りのパック **74**–9
ロバ **215**–3
ロビー **50**
ロブスター **71**–10
ロングスカート **96**–18
和 **192**–7
ワークブック **7**–26
ワイパー **158**–2
ワイパーを交換する **157**–K
ワイヤ **181**–13
ワイヤストリッパ **181**–42
ワイヤレスヘッドセット **14**–14
ワイングラス **83**–23
若い **32**–1
ワケギ **69**–20
分ける **76**–B
輪ゴム **183**–34
ワゴンを引く **224**–A
ワシ **214**–9
ワッシャ **180**–37
ワッフル **80**–8
ワニ（アリゲーター） **213**–36
ワニ（クロコダイル） **213**–37
笑いかける **2**–D
笑う **44**–A
割引クーポン **67**–15
割る **192**–D
悪い犬 **23**–18
湾 **204**–9
湾岸平野 **201**–16
ワンピース **86**–3

Research Bibliography

The authors and publisher wish to acknowledge the contribution of the following educators for their research on vocabulary development, which has helped inform the principals underlying OPD.

Burt, M., J. K. Peyton, and R. Adams. *Reading and Adult English Language Learners: A Review of the Research.* Washington, D.C.: Center for Applied Linguistics, 2003.

Coady, J. "Research on ESL/EFL Vocabulary Acquisition: Putting it in Context." In *Second Language Reading and Vocabulary Learning*, edited by T. Huckin, M. Haynes, and J. Coady. Norwood, NJ: Ablex, 1993.

de la Fuente, M. J. "Negotiation and Oral Acquisition of L2 Vocabulary: The Roles of Input and Output in the Receptive and Productive Acquisition of Words." *Studies in Second Language Acquisition* 24 (2002): 81–112.

DeCarrico, J. "Vocabulary learning and teaching." In *Teaching English as a Second or Foreign Language,* edited by M. Celcia-Murcia. 3rd ed. Boston: Heinle & Heinle, 2001.

Ellis, R. *The Study of Second Language Acquisition.* Oxford: Oxford University Press, 1994.

Folse, K. *Vocabulary Myths: Applying Second Language Research to Classroom Teaching.* Ann Arbor, MI: University of Michigan Press, 2004.

Gairns, R. and S. Redman. *Working with Words: A Guide to Teaching and Learning Vocabulary*. Cambridge: Cambridge University Press, 1986.

Gass, S. M. and M.J.A. Torres. "Attention When?: An Investigation Of The Ordering Effect Of Input And Interaction." *Studies in Second Language Acquisition* 27 (Mar 2005): 1–31.

Henriksen, Birgit. "Three Dimensions of Vocabulary Development." *Studies in Second Language Acquisition* 21 (1999): 303–317.

Koprowski, Mark. "Investigating the Usefulness of Lexical Phrases in Contemporary Coursebooks." *Oxford ELT Journal* 59(4) (2005): 322–32.

McCrostie, James. "Examining Learner Vocabulary Notebooks." *Oxford ELT Journal* 61 (July 2007): 246–55.

Nation, P. *Learning Vocabulary in Another Language*. Cambridge: Cambridge University Press, 2001.

National Center for ESL Literacy Education Staff. *Adult English Language Instruction in the 21st Century*. Washington, D.C.: Center for Applied Linguistics, 2003.

National Reading Panel. *Teaching Children to Read: An Evidenced-Based Assessment of the Scientific Research Literature on Reading and its Implications on Reading Instruction.* 2000. http://www.nationalreadingpanel.org/Publications/summary.htm/.

Newton, J. "Options for Vocabulary Learning Through Communication Tasks." *Oxford ELT Journal* 55(1) (2001): 30–37.

Prince, P. "Second Language Vocabulary Learning: The Role of Context Versus Translations as a Function of Proficiency." *Modern Language Journal* 80(4) (1996): 478-93.

Savage, K. L., ed. *Teacher Training Through Video - ESL Techniques: Early Production.* White Plains, NY: Longman Publishing Group, 1992.

Schmitt, N. *Vocabulary in Language Teaching.* Cambridge: Cambridge University Press, 2000.

Smith, C. B. *Vocabulary Instruction and Reading Comprehension*. Bloomington, IN: ERIC Clearinghouse on Reading English and Communication, 1997.

Wood, K. and J. Josefina Tinajero. "Using Pictures to Teach Content to Second Language Learners." *Middle School Journal* 33 (2002): 47–51.